GOLDEN GATE
GARDENING

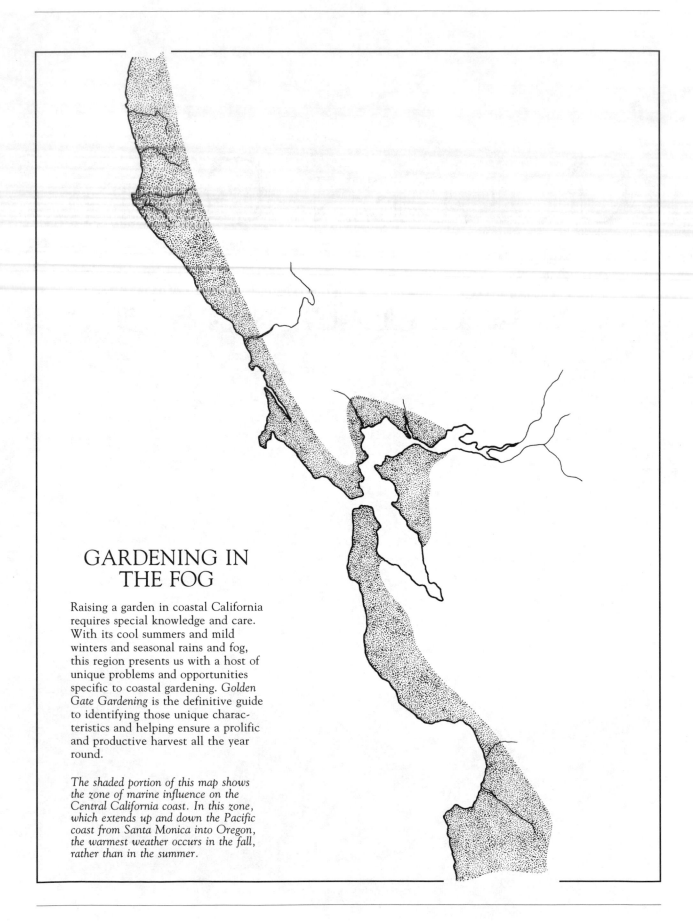

GARDENING IN
THE FOG

Raising a garden in coastal California
requires special knowledge and care.
With its cool summers and mild
winters and seasonal rains and fog,
this region presents us with a host of
unique problems and opportunities
specific to coastal gardening. *Golden
Gate Gardening* is the definitive guide
to identifying those unique characteristics and helping ensure a prolific
and productive harvest all the year
round.

*The shaded portion of this map shows
the zone of marine influence on the
Central California coast. In this zone,
which extends up and down the Pacific
coast from Santa Monica into Oregon,
the warmest weather occurs in the fall,
rather than in the summer.*

GOLDEN GATE GARDENING

The complete guide to
year-round
food gardening
in the San Francisco Bay Area
& Coastal California

Pam Peirce

SASQUATCH BOOKS
SEATTLE

Originally published in 1993 by agAccess, Davis, California,
in cooperation with Riverhouse Nursery, Sacramento, California.

Printed in the United States of America.
Distributed in Canada by Raincoast Books Ltd.
02   5 4 3

Cover art: Jennie Oppenheimer
Interior illustrations: Mimi Osborne
Interior composition: Patrick David Barber

Library of Congress Cataloging-in-Publication Data
Peirce, Pam.
      Golden Gate gardening : the complete guide to year-round food gardening in the
      San Francisco Bay area & coastal California / by Pam Peirce.
            p.   cm.
      Originally published: Davis, Calif. : agAccess, 1993
      Includes bibliographical references (p.   ) and index.
      ISBN 1-57061-136-X (pbk.)
      1. Vegetable gardening—California—San Francisco Bay Area.
2. Vegetable gardening—California—Pacific Coast. 3. Gardening—California—
San Francisco Bay Area 4. Gardening—California—Pacific Coast. I. Title.
      SB321.5.C2P45   1998
      635'.09794'6—dc21   97-52716

Sasquatch Books
615 Second Avenue
Seattle, Washington 98104
(206) 467–4300
books@SasquatchBooks.com
www.SasquatchBooks.com

For my parents,

Sheldon James Peirce and Lynton Wicks Peirce,
who taught me to think, to garden, and to dream big dreams.

TABLE OF CONTENTS

ACKNOWLEDGMENTS   *xi*
INTRODUCTION   *xiii*
A NOTE TO READERS   *xiv*

—ONE—

YEAR-ROUND BOUNTY   *1*

Our region's seasonal changes and the opportunities
they provide for gardeners.

—TWO—

ON LEARNING TO GARDEN   *7*

Thoughts on garden planning, experimenting
& management.

—THREE—

WHAT CAN YOU GROW?   *11*

Specific information about what is possible in our region:

- Microclimates   11
- Crops that will grow in coastal California   12
- When to plant (tables for foggy and sunny microclimates)   18
- Winter gardening   26

—FOUR—

PLANNING YOUR GARDEN   *29*

Advice on arranging the garden to take advantage of our climate and minimize its drawbacks:

- Getting enough sunlight   29
- Sheltering plants from the wind   30
- Using microclimates within the garden   31
- Salt spray   32
- Planting food among the flowers   34
- Raised beds   35
- Sloping yards   35
- Container planting & rooftop gardens   38

—FIVE—

OBTAINING SEEDS & OTHER STARTS   *39*

Increase your chances of success by using the best plant material you can find:

- Choosing and buying seeds and transplants   39
- Storing and testing seeds   40
- Saving seeds   41
- Gardening with hybrid and open-pollinated plants   43

—SIX—

GETTING PLANTS STARTED   *45*

Guidelines to help ensure your plants will grow:

- Sowing seeds   45
- Protecting seedlings   49
- Use of floating row covers   50
- Starting and growing transplants   51
- Preparing soil   54
- Providing adequate light for seedlings   55
- Cold frames   58
- Minigreenhouses   59
- Propagating plants by division, layering or cuttings   61

—SEVEN—

HOW TO WATER   *63*

Advice on watering, specifically oriented to this region:

- Different kinds of equipment   64
- Checking soil moisture   65
- How seasonal changes affect watering needs   67
- Water conservation   69
- Dealing with drought conditions   69

—EIGHT—

DOWN TO EARTH   71

Detailed information on garden soil:

- Evaluating soil   71
- Adding organic matter   72
- Local soil types   73
- Polluted soil   75
- Green manures   76
- Mulching   77
- Earthworms   79
- Fertilizing   80
- Digging   83
- Crop rotation   84
- Compost   86

—NINE—

GROWING LIKE WEEDS   91

Contending with the uninvited plants which inhabit our gardens:

- Uses and management of weeds   92
- Eradication versus tolerance   93
- Herbicides   96
- Reclaiming neglected land   98
- Soil solarization   99
- A detailed chart of local weeds, with suggestions
  for their use and control   101
- Compendium of weeds   104

—TEN—

MANAGING BUGS & BLIGHT   121

A compendium of information on insects, animals and plant diseases that may cause problems in the garden:

- When and how to act against pests   121
- The problems with pesticides   122
- Least toxic pest management, beneficial insects & ornamentals   123
- Recognizing and controlling damage   125
- Encouraging your natural allies   131
- Using pesticides safely   133
- A comprehensive list of local pests with specifics on how to deal with them   136

—ELEVEN—

VEGETABLES FROM A TO Z   161

The heart of the book, this is an illustrated compendium of vegetables that can be grown in this region:

- Ample growing and harvesting information with advice on pest control and sources
- Easy and delicious ways to use these familiar and unfamiliar vegetables

—TWELVE—

HERBS FOR ALL SEASONS 269

An illustrated compendium of herbs, with advice
on how to grow and use them.

—THIRTEEN—

EATING THE FLOWERS 307

Recommendations for growing and using
edible flowers, including safety precautions.

—FOURTEEN—

THE BACKYARD FLORIST 313

Suggestions on growing and arranging the
multitude of cutting flowers which thrive in our region.

—FIFTEEN—

FRUIT FROM THE FOG 323

The limitations and advantages of the coastal regions
for growing fruit, along with a compendium of advice
on choosing and growing specific varieties.

—SIXTEEN—

A GARDEN-BASED CUISINE 343

How to take advantage of our region's year-round
array of fresh food from the garden.

APPENDICES

I.   The Climate of Our Region   357
II. Using Scientific Plant Names   361
III. Pesticide Toxicity:
     A List of Common Active Ingredients   362
IV. Mail Order Seed Companies   368
V.   Resources for Gardeners   371
VI. Suggested Reading   380

INDEX 389

ACKNOWLEDGMENTS

The idea for this book took root after I saw Binda Colebrook's book *Winter Garden ing in the Maritime Northwest* (Sasquatch Books). I was able to adapt her planting dates to my winter garden, and doing so made me see how useful a local book could be.

Since that time, many people have inspired and helped me to get this book from idea to paper and print.

Early on, I told Sue Reid, who coordinated the city-sponsored Community Garden ing Program in San Francisco, of my plans to write a local book, and her close questioning helped me see what I needed to know and to form a plan of both garden and library research.

Kathy Van Velsor, past Director of the San Francisco Ecology Center, first suggested that I teach vegetable gardening. The material I developed for those first four-week classes lies at the core of this book.

Jane Radcliffe and the members of her Community College writing workshop listened to my first attempts to put the words for this book on paper, and their advice and encouragement nurtured the seedling.

Leonard Rifas drafted more accessible versions of the climate maps that appeared in *Publications in Geography* and redrew some of my planting charts. This material helped in the drawing of the final versions as they appear in this book.

Doug Brentlinger and Mark Zielenski offered both emergency and (in calmer times) ongoing computer support, ranging from rescuing files being devoured by computer bugs to helping me keep my hard disk organized.

Many experts kindly accepted my requests for information and/or read portions of the manuscript for accuracy. Following are their names and the subjects in which they provided expertise:

Laura Brainin-Rodriguez, Nutritionist, Stanford University Student Health Center, (nutrition); Larry Costello, Cooperative Extension, San Mateo County, (soils); Jeff Cox, writer for *Organic Gardening* magazine, (various subjects); Barbara Emerson, Weed Specialist, (weeds); Denise Erickson, Pier 39, (cutting flowers); Nancy Garrison, Cooperative Extension, Santa Clara County, (various subjects); Dr. Ken Hagen, Division of Biological Control, U. C. Berkeley, (beneficial insects); Dr. Ann King, Cooperative Extension, San Mateo County, (various subjects); Gordon Lane, Pest Control Advisor, (pesticides and pest control); Dr. Rex Marsh, Department of Wildlife and Fisheries Biology, U. C. Davis, (vertebrate pests); Doria Mueller, Pesticide Education and Action Project, (pesticides); E. Jan Null, Meteorologist, National Weather Service, (weather and climate); Chester Prince, U.C. Cooperative Extension, San Francisco, (various topics); Dr. Robert Raabe, Department of Plant Pathology, U.C. Berkeley, (pest chapter); Dr. Charles Turner, weed specialist, (weed list); Dr. Jim Vlamis, U.C. Berkeley, (soils); Ron Voss, Deptartment of Vegetable Crops, U.C. Davis, (onions); Norm Welch, U.C. Cooperative Extension, Watsonville, (strawberries); and Dr. Becky Westerdahl, Department of Nematology, U.C. Davis, (nematodes). I am most grateful for the time and information provided by all of the above experts, although I, of course, take final responsibility for the accuracy of all of the information in this book.

In addition, I would like to thank Barbara Pitchel, Head Librarian of the Helen Crocker Russell Library of the Strybing Arboretum Society of San Francisco for her cheerful support and thorough reference work during my years of research.

Many people, gardening in different microclimates within the fog-affected coastal California area, contributed to this book by sharing their experiences with me either through long conversations or by returning questionnaires. They include: Jeff Brown, The Farm; Pat Casio, Dogpatch Community Garden; Diana Colby, Alice Street Garden; Robert Conover; Rosalind Creasy; Ed Dierauf, Argonne Community Garden; Kristina

Elmstrom; David Gilden; Bill Grimes, California Rare Fruit Growers; John Hooper, Sonoma Antique Apple Nursery; Wendy Johnson and Peter Rudnick, Green Gulch Farm; Caroline Morrison, Hooker Alley Community Garden; Liz Milazzo, Dearborn Community Garden; Robin Parer, Hooker Alley Community Garden; Mimi Osborne, Fort Mason Community Garden; Jean Scherr, Argonne Community Garden; Jake Sigg, California Native Plant Society; and Tree, Kaliflower Garden. Thanks also to the community gardeners of Dearborn Garden, to all of my gardening class students, and to everyone who asked so many great gardening questions.

In addition, I would like to thank the many volunteers who helped me carry out the San Francisco tomato trials of 1986-88. These include Anthony Del Nuovocared, Eric Engles, Megan Evart, Eleanor Ewing, Richard Fashbinder, Lotta Garrity, Tanya Harjan, Bernadette McAnulty, Pilar Mejia, Eileen Neustadt, Richard Peltier, Dannette Peltier, Michael Peltier, Amy Peltier, Rosanna Scott, Maya Slocum, John Sanroma, Mary Sullivan, and Pat Wynne.

There are also many people who are unaware of how much they helped with this book, because I learned by watching their gardens grow. Many thanks to all of the community gardeners of San Francisco whose gardens, the unsuccessful as well as the successful ones, taught me more about what doesn't work, and what does, than I could ever learn from my garden alone.

Thanks to Maria-Marta Herrara for many evenings of delightful conversation over the tasting of garden foods. Also thanks for letting me start unruly crops that would take over her tiny backyard, and then for being able to laugh.

Thanks to Iris Goldman for her moral and material support during the too-long process of getting this book published.

Thanks to Mimi Osborne, for patience and precision in translating my requests into the drawings that illustrate this book.

I would like to thank the following people for help in editing the book:

Jo Brownold, who read the first finished chapters and called them excellent; David Goldberg, who read it all and gave good advice; Susan Lang, who edited the first eleven chapters with a gardener's eye; and Karen Van Epen of agAccess, who pulled the whole book together. For proofreading the manuscript, thanks to Ellen Zagory. For turning the manuscript into the finished book: Timothy Rice, Clara Maria Okrongly, and Dave Reagan.

Special thanks to Morrie Camhi, who helped the book out of publishing limbo, and to Daniel Reidy, who helped to negotiate its rescue. And thanks to AgAccess, for producing the first edition.

And I want to thank my husband, David Goldberg, for listening to my thoughts and plans, for offering good advice, for buying me a decent office chair, and for being extraordinarily patient throughout the long process of writing and publishing this book.

As I conclude the first revision of *Golden Gate Gardening*, I would like to add thanks to people who helped with this second edition. I consulted the following experts about the subjects that follow their names: Barri Bonapart, Attorney (tree law), Doug Heath of Seminis Seeds (tomatoes), Carolyn Harrison of Sonoma Antique Apple Nursery (fruit), Adam Kushner of Pesticide Action Network of North America (pesticides), Steve Temple of the Cooperative Extension (beans), Mary Risely of Tante Marie's Cooking School in San Francisco, and Matt Sartwell of the bookstore Kitchen Arts and Letters in New York City (choosing recent cookbooks for the Suggested Reading list).

I would also like to thank Christina Faulkenburg for checking all of the websites to make sure the addresses were correct.

Finally, thanks to Gary Luke and Sasquatch Books for publishing the second edition of *Golden Gate Gardening*, to Joan Gregory, who ably saw it through production, and Patrick Barber, typesetter and gardener, for his skill and enthusiasm.

INTRODUCTION

Food gardening is relatively new to our area. The coastal California land is so bountiful that Native Americans in the area ate well without planting. But food gardening is the earth's oldest and most common kind of gardening. As such, it has much to teach about being human.

Eating what you have grown completes a cycle, from seed to table, that humans have been fulfilling for thousands of years. In our busy and alienated existence, we rarely have opportunities to meet our physical needs so directly. Any subsistence skill will give us this pleasure—weaving, carpentry, fishing with a pole and line, navigating by the stars. I chose gardening. I offer it to you, and hope it brings you pleasure also.

May your garden give you a wonderful sense of accomplishment, many delicious meals, and a strong and flexible body. May it add to your stock of patience, persistence, thrift, and to your understanding of our dependence upon the earth and upon each other.

A NOTE TO READERS

Golden Gate Gardening was intended to be a pathfinding example of a regional gardening book, and it has fulfilled that promise. It has helped thousands of California gardeners—beginners to experienced, newcomers to California natives—learn to grow more crops, more of the year, in our ocean-influenced microclimates.

The volume you are now holding is the 1998 Revised Edition of this book, which has been carefully amended and updated. While preserving the original detail and organization, it includes up-to-the-minute information on gardening and pest management, as well as current sources for seeds and other garden necessities. Those who have read the first edition will notice that information on several more vegetables has been slipped into this one. In addition, the resource appendices now include websites. Those who plow the web as well as the garden will enjoy digging into the many online resources that are becoming available for gardeners.

A number of changes in this edition were prompted by good suggestions from readers. As in the first edition, I encourage comments and gardening reports. If you live in a California microclimate represented in this book, I welcome any gardening information you wish to share and will consider it for inclusion in future editions of *Golden Gate Gardening*.

ONE

Year-Round Bounty

YES, WE CAN GARDEN ALL YEAR long in San Francisco and the nearby coastal regions. Whereas most other parts of the country have a single growing season from spring to fall, we can enjoy twelve full months of productive and rewarding gardening. There are crops to plant and harvests to enjoy every month of the year.

In much of the continental United States, winter is a time to shovel snow and read seed catalogs while dreaming of the next summer's bounty. But here, winter days are likely to find us out in our gardens, maybe even in shirtsleeves, picking tender salad greens, cutting stately artichoke buds, and making sure our pea vines are finding the trellis. And because our winter chill is so brief, we can begin our "spring" gardens long before the calendar tells us that spring has begun. By April or May, when gardeners in colder climates are just beginning to dig and plant, we are already harvesting crops planted in February—pulling sweet spring carrots and cutting succulent stems of broccoli. As we move into summer, we have another advantage. Crops that are impossible to grow in hot summers in most of the nation produce harvests for us throughout our cool summers. We can pick mild-flavored salad greens and cut creamy heads of cauliflower all summer long. In the areas closest to the coast, summer gardens may even include peas, a crop that must be relegated to early spring and fall in hot-summer regions.

But, of course, our climate is not a perfect one for gardening. Our biggest challenge is growing crops that require more sunshine and heat than our cool, often foggy summers provide. Unfortunately, these crops include some that most gardeners yearn to grow. Every year seed catalogs entice us with photographs of large plump tomatoes, eggplants, melons, and peppers—but when we try to grow these crops, we are often disappointed. Not only is the harvest smaller than promised, but each fruit is often smaller as well. We become aware that, for these crops, our summers do not measure up.

Gardening in the San Francisco Bay Area and along the coastal regions from Mendocino to Monterey Bay is largely rewarding, even though some aspects of it may be frustrating. This book will help you to take advantage of the region's opportunities and minimize its drawbacks. Here, season by season, is what you should expect.

Summer and Early Fall

What gardeners in this region notice most about summer is the fog. The amount varies from neighborhood to neighborhood and from one side of a hill to another. During much of the summer, cottony fog banks billow over the hills, fog fingers slide down the valleys, high fogs blot out the sun, and low fogs shroud our gardens.

Even when there is no fog, summers are chilly. June, July, and August are known for blustery days and brisk nights, with a cold sea breeze blowing even on days when the sun is shining. A typical summer weather report announces temperatures in the nineties or hundreds in the Central Valley, whereas the highs in the coastal area are only in

Two tomatoes growing by the back fence, the one on the right warmed by a "Wall o' Water™"

the sixties or seventies. It is the chilly, often foggy nature of our summers that defines the area covered by this book.

The combination of chill and fog-reduced light plays havoc with warm-season crops, such as tomatoes, corn, peppers, eggplants, and melons, which would thrive in a Midwestern summer. Nothing contributes more to the reputation of our region as a difficult place to garden than the poor performance of tomatoes. Actually, among the warm-season crops, tomatoes do rather well here, ripening at least some crop in all but the most severe microclimates. However, the plants often form fruit late and ripen it late. Tomatoes that do ripen tend to be smaller and of poorer quality than those grown in warmer climates. Corn and peppers are a little more limited in range, refusing to bear a crop at all in the foggiest, coolest areas. Two other warm-season crops, eggplants and melons, require even more heat to bear well and thus are risky in much of the region.

That's the bad news.

The good news is that you can considerably improve your chances with tomatoes, peppers, and corn by choosing varieties developed to cope with cool summers and planting them in protected areas of your garden. Although these plants may not reach their full glory here, the harvested crop will be fresher, and will often taste better than the average produce available at supermarkets.

The best news is that there are many vegetables that do not just tolerate our cool summers but actually thrive in them. These include all of the cool-season crops, such as beets, broccoli, carrots, lettuce, peas, and potatoes. In most other parts of the country gardeners have to squeeze these crops in during the early spring, before the summer heat hits, or just before the first autumn frost. In our region, these crops will gladly, even enthusiastically, grow throughout the summer.

If you live in one of the foggier neighborhoods, make cool-season crops the backbone of your summer garden. But even here you won't be limited entirely to cool-season crops. Some warm-season vegetables, such as scarlet runner beans and zucchini, brave the fog. Pumpkins, winter squash, bush and pole beans, cucumbers, and sunflowers tolerate almost as much fog. If you have any success growing bush beans, zucchini, or short-season corn, you can probably plant these crops more than once during a summer. In one of San Francisco's warmer neighborhoods, I plant successive crops of corn every month from the middle of April to the middle of

July and harvest sweet corn on the cob from the middle of July to the middle of October.

In July or August, as you are sowing your last successive plantings of warm-season crops, you can also plant some of the best crops for fall and winter harvests. Carrots, beets, and kohlrabi should be seeded, and broccoli and celery seedlings transplanted. All of these crops will grow quickly in late summer, then more slowly as the days shorten. In very foggy neighborhoods, midsummer plantings should be in the ground by July 15; in sunnier parts of the region, crops planted in August or even September may still mature before winter.

Even during the foggiest of summers, the sun will occasionally peek through. Fog often spreads and retreats in roughly weekly cycles, separated by one or more days of sunshine. Once in a while, these sunny days heat up as warmer air from the Central Valley temporarily replaces the cold sea breeze. The temperature reaches the high eighties or beyond, and everyone who can do so heads for the coolness of the beach. When this happens our gardens, accustomed to foggy days, may wilt temporarily in the unusual heat. The whole garden, and especially midsummer seedbeds, will need extra water.

At the very end of summer and into early fall, the fog usually relents. September and early October often mark the longest stretch of warm, sunny days. Summer and early fall harvests can be spectacularly large and varied, and the combination of warm- and cool-season crops lets you work wonders in the kitchen. Every time I venture into my garden, I return with a huge basket filled with ripe, richly colored, fragrant vegetables and herbs. I whirl bright green, satiny basil leaves and plump, piquant garlic cloves into a savory pesto sauce or make a creamy primavera sauce with tender green beans and yellow summer squash. I make coleslaw and green salads with all manner of fresh salad vegetables. From my small corn patch, I harvest ears that are sweeter than any in the grocery stores, and I make memorable shortcakes from sweet everbearing strawberries. In late summer I simmer a hearty minestrone made with flavorful homegrown green beans, zucchini, potatoes, carrots, and herbs, adding fresh homemade tomato sauce if I have enough tomatoes.

And, if the bounty of vegetables and herbs were not enough, there are the flowers. Summer and early fall offer a profusion of flowers for bouquets. There are blossoms of every hue—yellow, orange, white, and purple cosmos; pink, peach, and red godetias; pink, blue, and purple cornflowers—to decorate the harvest table. Flowers become part of the menu as well. I fry delicate squash blossoms, serve nasturtium hors d'oeuvres, and use violas to accent a fruit salad.

The bounty continues well into fall. One day, as I harvest, I notice that the garden looks unkempt and overgrown, with flowers and vegetables reaching over each other in a lanky tangle. Summer vegetables either look ragged or have begun to die back. The summer garden has given its all, but fortunately the gardening year does not stop then.

Fall and Winter

If the first heavy rains of fall are late, you could be harvesting your last summer flowers and vegetables in the middle of November or even later. Sooner or later, however, cold days with heavy rains will kill cucumbers, squash, tomatoes, and other summer sojourners. Now is the time to pull out the decaying plants. Relish the last cucumber of summer; harvest the remaining tomatoes from their blackened vines and let them ripen indoors or use them green. Pick over flowers for the last bouquet of summer, and cover any unused garden areas with a winter mulch.

As early fall turns into a typically wet and chilly winter, your garden will be far from barren. Those beets and carrots you planted in July or August will be nearly mature, and they will wait in the ground until you are ready for them. Summer-planted kohlrabi and radicchio will add interest to your winter meals. As the weather turns cool, brussels sprout plants begin to bear their knobby sprouts. Broccoli may form heads in fall or, in the case of some varieties, in February or March. Your winter harvest can also include leeks, Swiss chard, and sunchokes planted as long ago as the previous January.

Some crops can be planted into late fall. You need only plant on a couple of days in October or November to collect great harvest dividends later. Now is the best time to plant two of the crops best suited to the area: garlic and artichoke. November is also a good time to plant peas and a less familiar winter legume, the fava bean. Onion sets (planted for harvest as green onions) and seedling lettuce plants are also worth growing through the winter months.

Rainfall, like fog, varies from place to place and from one year to the next. Kentfield in Marin County receives 46 inches of rain in a season, whereas nearby San Francisco averages only 23 inches. Within San Francisco, rainfall is heaviest nearest the ocean and on the south and west sides of hills. The entire region experiences many winters of continuously waterlogged soil as well as periodic bouts with drought. But, generally, we rarely need to water our gardens between late October and the end of March.

Although we get our share of soggy winters, heavy frosts are rare. Many San Francisco winters pass with no recorded freezing temperatures at all; other winters may bring one or two light frosts, usually in December or January. Areas farther from the ocean or where high hills stand between your garden and the ocean are more likely to experience frosty nights from November through March. Gardens in low-lying areas and on the shady, north side of hills and mountains are also more likely to receive frost.

Still, these tend to be frosts, not freezes, meaning that the soil is not frozen and tender roots are not killed. Many cool-season vegetables can withstand considerable frost. A few, such as peas, potatoes, and artichoke, may need protection on the coldest nights, but most will survive in style.

During most years, my fall harvest includes the last of summer's treats. I savor the last crisp cucumber in a spicy Indian cucumber salad and the last green beans and zucchini in a cheesy omelet, and I pick the remaining green tomatoes to slice and fry. Soon my attention turns to the gifts of winter. I steam fresh, sweet brussels sprouts to dip in mayonnaise mixed with soy sauce, stir-fry pungent mustard greens with tofu and noodles, and warm up December evenings with steaming potato leek soup. My winter salads combine lettuce with spinach, chicory, sorrel, grated carrots, and gleanings of wild greens. Sunchokes may add crunch to salads or, seasoned with garden herbs, make a salad by themselves.

There are even flowers for bouquets—not many, but a few—that bloom into the colder months. Sweet-scented stock, colorful pansies, and sunny calendulas are winter standbys; calla lilies and forget-me-nots number among the flowers blooming by January. Often, a few plants of some summer flower will survive and bloom through the winter chill. I take particular joy in culling a small bouquet from the flowers that do appear in winter, often finding enough of them only after a careful search and valuing them more for their rarity.

Spring

By February, the days become noticeably longer and warmer. Delicate, pink plum blossoms and bright yellow daffodils assure us that winter is ending. The air smells sweet. We are rooting about for the last of winter's sweet carrots and beets. Overwintering broccoli varieties are forming their dark green or vibrant chartreuse heads. Artichokes are responding to the warmth and lengthening days by forming promising buds, nestled deep in pale, lacy leaves. Fall-planted peas are so sweet that they beg to be eaten right from the vine. Greens, from celery to lettuce, are more tender and crisp than at any other time of year. In cold-winter climates, the period from February to April is sometimes called the "hunger gap." Our year-round gardens close that gap, and close it deliciously.

February marks the start of the early spring planting season. Carrots, radishes, onions, broccoli, cabbage, lettuce, Swiss chard, potatoes, and other cool-season vegetables thrive in the cool temperatures, high humidity, and increasing sunlight. The climate will vary from year to year, during dry years allowing you to get a crop or two planted in January and during exceptionally wet years forcing you to delay planting until the end of March. But, generally, you can plant all kinds of cool-season spring crops after the middle of February, whenever the soil is dry enough.

During very warm springs, or with careful protection, tomatoes and zucchini can be planted as early as February. Early plantings of these summer crops are not without risk. If late rains are heavy, darkening the days and keeping the soil from warming, early growth will be slow.

All February plantings are vulnerable to late winter storms, which are especially likely to bring hail. Icy pellets may damage seedlings, and they will leave their mark on older plants. Look for small white dots on the tops of leaves, indicating where hailstones have killed the surface cells.

Gradually you will see more rainbows than rain, with spectacular cloud displays at the edges of passing storms. It is a time to begin noticing how long it has been since your garden received its last good soaking. Your plants will probably need their first deep watering by March or April, although seedbeds will certainly have demanded water earlier. Until next fall, you are your garden's only effective water source. Any rainfall during that period is usually too brief to penetrate very far into the soil.

Late spring is often warmer and sunnier than midsummer. Local gardeners often get a tan while planting squash and beans in May, but they lose the tan to summer fog long before the crops are ready to pick.

My spring harvests combine the last of winter's crops with the first crops of the new year. I bake the last of winter's cabbage into savory stuffed cabbage leaves for Saturday supper, or serve an elegant leek and shrimp quiche at a spring brunch. I shred the last of the beet harvest and pickle it to add a vermilion accent to spring salads. As the days warm in April and May, I pull the first tender spring carrots and pick the season's first strawberries. Soon there are new potatoes to steam for a delicate potato salad and young cactus pads to serve in a peppery Mexican sauce.

Spring bouquets are colorful and varied, from fragrant sweet peas and freesias to brightly colored ranunculus and elegantly formed columbine. As I pick spring flowers, I admire my garden. The freshly planted seedlings of spring always fill my heart with hope and joy, even in a climate that allows gardeners a never-ending cycle of fresh starts.

TWO

ON LEARNING TO GARDEN

S YOU SURVEY YOUR BACKYARD you probably have a vision of a beautiful garden—green and thriving all year, either neat and orderly or wild and profuse. You can just see those lettuce leaves sparkling with dew, strawberries glowing like jewels, and lush tomato plants sagging with ripe fruit. In your vision, flowers bloom profusely in every imaginable color, and herbs offer their pungent or sweet flavors from tidy hedges. The branches of fruiting trees and shrubs droop under the weight of their bounty. But there are precious few gardeners, no matter how expert, who haven't experienced failed visions: seeds that never came up, plants that were eaten by pests, even gardens that ended up looking like wastelands. Your goal as a gardener is to bring your gardening reality closer to your gardening vision.

Many of the most difficult tasks facing a gardener come at the beginning: understanding the climate, grasping the basics of what to grow and when to plant, reclaiming the land from rampant pests and weeds, building the soil, and learning to water properly. Once you've mastered these tasks, gardening successes will follow one another quickly. Soon you can begin the fun of fine tuning—growing more and better vegetables, herbs, fruits, and flowers. I can provide part of what you need to succeed: a knowledge of the problems you are most likely to encounter in this region and how to solve them. I can give you specific advice on the following aspects of gardening in our area.

- Choosing planting times that will produce the strongest plants and the best crops.
- Getting your seeds or seedlings off to a good start.
- Watering successfully, in harmony with our seasons.
- Turning your shifting sand or reluctant clay into a fertile, easy-to-work soil that will let plants thrive.
- Rescuing your garden from the clutches of tenacious weeds, such as fennel, oxalis, bindweed, and blackberry.
- Controlling those consummate garden consumers: snails and slugs.
- Preventing predation by local pest insects.
- Preventing damage by plant diseases.
- Harvesting in ways that will stimulate the plants to bear more food or flowers.

You must provide the rest of the solution, which consists of a can-do attitude and some roll-up-your-sleeves effort!

The Importance of Starting Small

It is vital not to take on too much garden too fast. If this is your first experience gardening, start with a few crops and a small plot of land. This approach is especially important if you are a beginner dealing with an overgrown garden and uncooperative soil. Once you get one small area under control, you will be carried along by the sweet feeling of success.

Even if you plan to use your whole yard as a garden, divide it into sections and plant only one section at first. With our year-round climate, you can start another section every couple of months if the first ones are going along nicely, or you can reseed them if they are not faring well. This will help keep your garden from getting away from you. If the garden begins to be too much, make your next section smaller and simpler.

If you start with too much variety or too large an area, you may find that you are missing harvests, overlooking serious pests until too late, or feeling overwhelmed because too many tasks need doing all at once. A garden requires a special kind of attention and patience. Although a plant may require very little care for most of its life cycle, it cannot be ignored when it does need your attention. A more modest beginning will give you time to adjust to the rhythms of just a few crops at first, before adding others.

Harvesting is often a large part of the work of food gardening. What a pity to miss out on the rewards of your efforts! It can happen all too easily. Although harvesting is usually fun, it can take up to two-thirds of your gardening time. Some crops must be picked as often as every couple of days, and they will not always be ready on a schedule that is convenient for you.

The worst consequence of taking on too much at once is that, if your garden is not running smoothly, it becomes a source of bad feelings rather than the positive ones you hoped it would bring. If you are a beginner or a very busy person, rest assured that you can reap the same satisfying feeling from a few square feet of productive, well-maintained space as from a much larger garden.

Looking, Recording, and Thinking

Make a conscious effort to look at your garden. Look at plants for the pleasure of watching them unfold. Look to spot problems in time to solve them. Look to decide the best time to harvest. And look to develop a feel for the plants—how they grow and how they react to stress.

Take your morning coffee or tea to the garden, or maybe an apple when you get home from work. Walk around and see how things are going. Turn leaves over. Notice what is flying or crawling about. Sit down. If there is no place to sit, get a little watching stool. Study a plant or a square foot of ground until you've learned something new.

Look at other people's gardens and compare your plants with theirs. Try to find out how their microcli-

Think of your garden as a tapestry - the more you study it, the more details you discover.

mate differs from yours. Ask when they planted, what varieties they chose, and what they added to their soil. This information will help you decide what your plants need and how best to provide it.

No one learns to garden all at once. Often things go right the very first time, but it may take two or more years of adjustments to get some crops right. Sometimes problems pop up after years of success. Talking to other gardeners, reading about gardening, trying new things—these are all ways to increase your successes.

Keeping a record will help you learn faster, as it allows you to repeat successes and encourages you to learn from failures. Record keeping can be as simple or as complex as you want it to be. The simplest method is to record on a calendar or in a date book when you put in seeds and what varieties you planted. You can also record the beginning and end of the harvest. Some gardeners keep a file card on each plant variety, recording planting times, harvest dates, whether it tasted good, problems encountered, and how they might grow it differently in the future.

You may want to map your garden. A drawing of the plots marking the different crops you planted will help you identify seedlings when they come up. A new map each season will help you plan crop rotation, a practice that helps control pests and maintain good soil health. (See page 85 for more on rotating crops.) These seasonal maps are a good place to record what you added to the soil in different parts of your garden.

You can also keep a gardening diary, in which you record the weather, how the plants are growing, what you did that day, and so on. Keep in mind that you must organize the information so that you can find it later. I begin by recording the date on a separate line. In the left-hand margin where it will be obvious, I put the most important information: a bed or plot number and the name of the crop and the variety. Underneath I describe the condition of the plant, the amount harvested, and any problems encountered and treatments applied. I leave a little room on the right-hand side for notes, such as identification of pests or the results of treatments I tried.

Learning From Experiments

As you watch your garden grow, read this and other books, review your gardening diary, and talk to your neighbors, questions will come to mind. Will September-planted carrots mature before winter in my garden? Will the pepper variety that the seed catalog lists as "the earliest ever" produce better than the one I grew last year? What if I planted by the moon?

Whenever you aren't sure if something will work, it is a good idea to set up an experiment. This is not hard to do if you remember four principles: (1) test only one factor at a time; (2) have a control so that you will have something to which you can compare your experimental results; (3) use a large enough sample (more than one plant, more than one trial) to be sure that your results aren't a fluke; and (4) make a

record of your results, so that you will have a clearer idea of what happened and will be able to compare later tests more precisely.

If you experiment by planting carrots at a later time than usual, create a control by planting some of the same carrot variety at your usual earlier planting time. Plant ten or more carrots in each planting. Give both plantings similar soil conditions and sun exposure; water and fertilize them in the same way. Then measure and record the growth of each planting when the plants are one, two, and three months old.

To test a new variety of any crop, seed it on the same day that you sow a familiar variety. At least four plants of each variety are necessary for the experiment; in that way, you won't accidentally compare individual plants that are atypical of the varieties. Grow both the test and control varieties randomly intermixed (but, of course, carefully labeled) in an area with similar soil, light, and other conditions. Then measure and compare their height, amount of foliage or fruit, or other important information on the same day several times during their growing season.

To test a technique, such as planting by the moon, plant several specimens of the same crop variety under similar conditions. Only vary the factor you are testing, in this case the time you plant in relation to the phase of the moon. Use information in a current-year almanac to pick planting times that are considered exactly right for the moon phases and others that are thought to be exactly wrong. Then record the height or productivity of the plants, at the same age, several times during the season. (You will not be able to draw any conclusions from moon-phase planting tests until you have repeated them several times, since the weather in the few weeks after you plant will exert a big influence on the crops, and this is not what you are testing. Only after you have tested the same crop repeatedly, probably over several years, will you be able to discern any pattern that occurs despite the weather.)

Throughout this book are ideas for simple experiments to help you gain new, reliable information specific to your garden. If you want further help in setting up an experiment, try contacting the Cooperative Extension office in your area or local community gardening organizations. *Improving Your Gardening With Backyard Research*, listed in Appendix VI, Sug-

Gardening diary entries

gested Reading, will also be helpful to you.

Gardening is a fairly recent phenomenon in our part of the world. So great was the area's natural bounty that the Native Americans who lived here didn't need to develop agriculture. Spanish friars were the first to till the ground. Then, as the population grew, small farmers began to supply the nearby towns with produce, making our area, including much of San Francisco proper, a major agricultural district. Most of these farmers are gone now, having sold their land for urban use often because they could not afford the higher property taxes that resulted from nearby development. Much of what they learned about growing food in this region went with them. Recently, new gardeners and organic truck farmers have begun reviving the idea that this is a good place to grow food, and what they learn will help us use our environment more successfully.

Many local gardeners who have experimented and kept records over the years contributed to the information in this book through interviews and questionnaires. Their records and those of other gardeners will continue to expand our knowledge. If you learn what you can grow in your particular microclimatic corner of the region, you can make valuable contributions to other gardeners who live nearby or in similar microclimates. New information on varieties that prosper here, ways to succeed with borderline crops, or unorthodox times to plant will make it easier for future gardeners to enjoy bountiful harvests. If you make discoveries, share what you learn with local gardening organizations, or write me a letter.

When Something Goes Wrong

Just as successes, even small ones, build confidence, failures rob us of that can-do, self-assured feeling. Beginners often jump to a too-hasty conclusion about what went wrong or keep themselves from analyzing the problem by denigrating themselves: "I just don't have a green thumb." Not only beginners but also experts have failures. One of the ways they became experts was to take failures as challenges. By setting out to find a solution, you will learn something about your current problem; at the same time, you are bound to discover techniques, skills, or other information to help you solve future problems.

First, carefully observe what went wrong and be prepared to describe the problem clearly. Reread anything you can find that might explain what happened, and if this doesn't set you on the right path, ask gardening friends or experts for advice.

Form a hypothesis: My cucumber plants are growing slowly and are pale green because the soil in which they are growing is short of nitrogen. I think this may be so because I know that cucumbers have a high need for nitrogen (see page 205) and that nitrogen deficiency is common in local soils (see page 73), and I suspect that I haven't adequately fertilized my soil. Also, I don't think the plants have an insect or other animal pest, because I used a magnifying glass to study the leaves and saw no pests on them. There is no clear sign of a disease, either. I wondered about a virus but doubt it is the problem, since the leaves are not mottled or oddly shaped in any way.

Then form a plan: I will make chicken manure tea (see page 80) and add it to the soil once a week when I water. If the leaves green up quickly, I will assume my hypothesis was correct. (To be absolutely sure that you are right, you will need a control. In this case, this means leaving a couple of plants unfertilized.)

Finally, apply your new knowledge the next time you grow the crop: Try the same cucumber variety the next year, this time adding more nitrogen fertilizer to the soil from the start. As a double-check, grow a couple of control plants in soil treated the same way but lacking nitrogen fertilizer.

THREE

WHAT CAN YOU GROW?

LTHOUGH SO MUCH IS possible in our mild-climate gardens, many gardeners use only a part of the year and try only a few of the potential crops. Even after limiting themselves, they still often have disappointing results. This happens because most gardening books and seed packets don't provide enough information to help gardeners deal with our climate. We can't figure out where our climate fits in those charts claiming to give planting dates for the whole nation. We wonder why so many crops don't do what the seed packet says they should do. Why does the patch of corn, planted at the time the packet suggested, take twice as long to bear ears as the packet promised or, in some cases, form no ears at all? Why do the tomatoes, which were supposed to taste as sweet as honey and grow as big across as a hamburger bun, taste bland and make slices no bigger across than a pickle?

Without proper information, beginning gardeners and gardeners new to the area may quickly get the idea that the local climate is hostile to vegetable crops in general. Actually, it is hostile only to a few inappropriate crops and to inappropriate planting times. True, it affects us right where it hurts, in the glamorous crops such as tomatoes, corn, and melons. However, we can grow many other desirable crops, some of which do not succeed in prime tomato and melon country. The moral is obvious: ignore our unique climate and you will encounter frustration; understand it and you will be on your way to year-round, bountiful harvests.

Microclimates

Did I say "climate"? I should have said "climates," because even within the limited geographical area covered by this book, there are a number of distinct microclimates. Newcomers commuting to a job as close as a mile away are often surprised to find that the climate there is very different from the one they left a few minutes earlier. San Francisco especially is famous for its several microclimates. The local joke is, "If you don't like the weather, just walk a few blocks." Unfortunately, the plants in our gardens are unable to take this advice. Crops that succeed in one garden may fail in a garden only a few blocks away.

The climate along the coast of our region is far more similar to the climates of other coastal locations, even those hundreds of miles away, than to places a few miles inland. The average maximum daily temperature for June, July, and August in Point Reyes, on the west coast of Marin County, tends to be within two or three degrees of that at Point Piedras Blancas, nearly two hundred miles south along the coast. During the same period the average maximum daily temperature in Point Reyes is an extraordinary twenty-three to twenty-seven degrees cooler than in Walnut Creek, which is less than thirty miles inland. As a general rule, the maximum daily temperature during these three months increases by four and a half degrees for every ten miles inland from the coast.

In general, the nearer you are to the coast, the foggier and colder the summer, the wetter the fall and spring, and the less likely that there will be

CROPS THAT WILL GROW IN COASTAL CALIFORNIA

All-region List: crops that are likely to flourish in all areas covered by this book.

Transition List: crops that need more heat & sunlight; will not thrive in the foggiest areas.

Sun Belt List: crops that will produce a satisfactory harvest only in the sunniest parts of the region. Even in the sunniest locations they will be slower and possibly smaller than if there were no ocean influence.

Borderline and Beyond List: crops for which a satisfactory harvest is unlikely anywhere in the region.

San Francisco Neighborhoods: local neighborhoods according to what climate is typical for that area.

All-Region List

Artichoke
Arugula
Asparagus
Bean, scarlet runner*
Bean, Fava
Beet
Bok choy
Broccoli
Cabbage
Carrot
Cauliflower
Celeriac
Celery
Chayote squash
Chervil
Cilantro
Florence fennel
Garlic
Greens (mustard, chard, collards, kale, etc.)
Herbs, perennial
Kohlrabi
Leek
Lettuce
Onion
Parsley
Parsnip
Pea (including snap and snow peas)
Potato
Pumpkin*
Radicchio
Radish
Salsify
Spinach
Spinach, New Zealand
Squash, summer*
Squash, winter*
Sunchoke*
Sunflower*
Turnip
Watercress

Transition List

Basil*
Bean, Snap (bush and pole)*
Corn (short-season varieties)*
Cucumber*
Tomato (cherry and very short-season varieties)*

Sun Belt List

Bitter Melon*
Corn (most varieties)*
Eggplant*
Tomato (midseason varieties)*
Pepper (especially cool-tolerant varieties)*
Winter melon*

Borderline and Beyond List

Bean, asparagus (yard-long bean)*
Cucumber (Asian varieties)*
Jicama*
Melon*
Spinach, Malabar*
Sweet potato*

*warm-season crop

San Francisco Neighborhoods

Fog Belt

Diamond Heights
Ingleside
Lake Merced
Richmond
Sunset/Parkside
West of Twin Peaks

Transition Zone

Eureka/Noe Valleys
Excelsior
Glen Park
Haight
Pacific Heights
Western Addition

Sun Belt

Bernal Heights
Hunters Point/Bayview
Mission
Russian/ Telegraph Hill
South of Market

SAN FRANCISCO MICROCLIMATES

Area 1   Cool temperatures, foggy to clear days, light winds, sandy and loamy soils

Area 2   Cool to moderate temperatures, foggy to clear days, light winds, sandy and loamy soils

Area 3   Cool temperatures, foggy, salt air, heavy winds, sandy soil

Area 4   Cool to moderate temperatures, foggy to clear days, light winds, sand, clay, loam, rock soil

Area 5   Cool to moderate temperatures, clear days with light fog, light winds, sand, clay, loam, rock soil

Area 6   Moderate to hot temperatures, clear days, light winds, sand, clay, loam, rock soil

Area 7   Moderate to hot temperatures, clear days, heavy wind, sand, clay, loam, rock soil

From the Division of Urban Forestry in the Department of Public Works

winter frost. However, the change of climate is not a steady and easily mapped one. It is modified by hills that block the wind from the ocean and by fog gaps, such as the Golden Gate, through which the cool, foggy ocean breeze can flow inland. The San Francisco Bay and other inland bodies of water also moderate the climate, making the areas around them cooler in summer and warmer in winter.

What Will Grow Here

The table entitled "Crops That Will Grow in Coastal California" (see page 12) lists most of the vegetables in Chapter 11 and some of the herbs in Chapter 12, according to how well they are able to grow in areas with cold, foggy summers. The All-Region List, fortunately lengthy, represents crops that are likely to flourish in all areas covered by this book. In fact, many of them grow *better* near the coast than they do in inland heat. Plants on the Transition List need more heat and sunlight, so they will not thrive in the foggiest areas. The Sun Belt List includes crops that produce a satisfactory harvest only in areas at least as warm and sunny as the warmest parts of San Francisco. Even in the sunniest locations, these crops will be slower and possibly smaller than they would be if there were no ocean influence. The Borderline and Beyond List contains crops for which a satisfactory harvest is unlikely anywhere in the region.

How do you adapt this information to your own garden? If you live very near the ocean, with no intervening hills, as in a neighborhood on the west side of San Francisco or in coastal Marin or San Mateo County, you should start with the All-Region List. If you live a few miles inland, but still to the west of coastal hills, or if your garden is unshaded and protected from the wind, add a couple of crops from the Transition List and see how they fare. In the path of a fog gap, the cool air and fog will extend farther inland. If you live several miles from the coast and out of the direct path of a fog gap, you can probably grow crops from the Sun Belt List.

The map on the facing page shows the area covered by this book, curving lines to indicate a climatic factor called the delay of the maximum. The numbers on the curving lines correspond to the number of days by which the warmest day of the year is usually separated from the longest day of the year, June 21. For example, in most of San Francisco the warmest day of the year is typically ninety days after the longest day—not until September 21!

I consider the area with a delay of maximum temperature of forty-five days or longer the area in which gardeners will find this book most useful. Appendix I provides further climatic data to help you predict your microclimate in locations from Mendocino to Monterey and as far inland as the fog and cool ocean breezes can reach.

The list of crops that will grow in our region was originally developed in the 1970s by the staff of San Francisco's then city-sponsored community gardening program. I have expanded and amended the list over the years, as I have learned more. The community gardening program divided San Francisco's neighborhoods into three growing zones to go with the lists. The roster of neighborhoods, including a couple that the program omitted, is included with the chart on page 12.

In recent years, a second attempt has been made to map San Francisco's microclimates, this one by the Division of Urban Forestry in the Department of Public Works. It divides San Francisco into seven microclimates (see preceding page) and lists relative amounts of fog, cool temperatures, wind, and salt air in each area.

I wish I could tell by your street address whether you can successfully grow cucumbers, but there is no magic line east of which they will bear a crop. Minor variations in the terrain make a great deal of difference. In any neighborhood there are pockets of wind and warmth that may create conditions typical of another zone. Also, the weather can vary enough from year to year to affect what you can grow. For example, gardeners in the foggiest areas may be able to grow corn successfully during a particularly sunny summer, but not every year.

The best you can do is to use the maps and lists to estimate your microclimate, notice how much fog and wind you actually get, and talk to other gardeners in your area. Then try to grow some crops and see how well they do. Take a few calculated risks and soon you will be the expert on what you can grow in your particular microclimate. You will learn a great deal by watching your plants. For example, if you can grow pole snap beans, you can probably also ripen short-season corn. Compare your successes and failures with those of friends gardening in nearby yards or other neighborhoods.

Because the microclimate boundaries are not sharp and because they vary from year to year, you will sometimes succeed against all odds. Although you should concentrate on crops that you know will do well where you live, you may sometimes want to

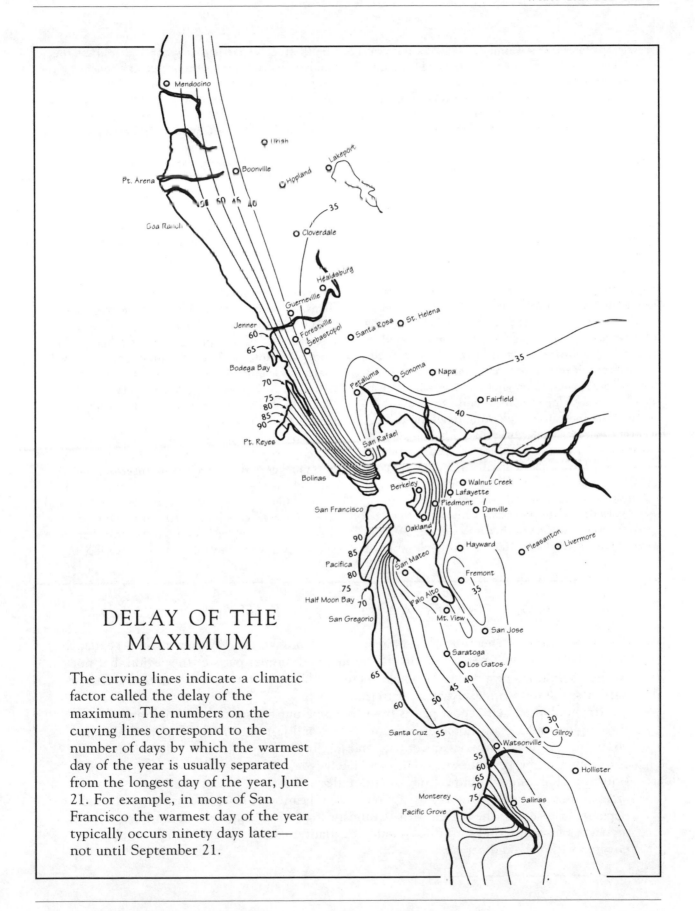

DELAY OF THE MAXIMUM

The curving lines indicate a climatic factor called the delay of the maximum. The numbers on the curving lines correspond to the number of days by which the warmest day of the year is usually separated from the longest day of the year, June 21. For example, in most of San Francisco the warmest day of the year typically occurs ninety days later—not until September 21.

15

grow crops listed for a warmer zone. If so, start with a very small planting. Consult Chapter 11, inquire at nurseries, and study seed catalogs to choose varieties most likely to succeed in cool, shady climates. Then give the plants the warmest, sunniest location you've got. If they don't even come close to succeeding, you will know that you were too ambitious. But if they almost succeed, try again next year with a different variety, a minigreenhouse (see page 59), or some other trick. You may find a way to succeed every year, or at least during especially warm years.

When to Grow It

To make full use of our mild climate, you must break out of the spring to fall gardening pattern and begin to see the year as continuous, overlapping seasons.

To use the full year, you need to know the range of times a crop can be planted, and the length of time a crop will need to grow before it is harvested.

I've provided two different planting charts (pages 18-21), one for foggier areas and another for sunnier parts of the region. In both, the heavily shaded bars indicate the planting times most likely to bring success. The lightly shaded bars signify that plantings at this time may succeed. Your particular garden may have a particularly warm or cool microclimate. Or one year may allow crops planted early or late to succeed while another may not. Also, some varieties of the crop may be adapted to certain planting times, while another may not be. Some crops have seasonal varieties—for example, you will

find lettuce varieties that withstand cold weather and others that are resistant to bitterness or flowering during warm summer weather. (For full details of possible vegetable planting times, see individual listings in Chapter 11. For information on when to plant herbs, refer to Chapter 12. For times to seed vegetables and herbs indoors, see Chapter 6. For edible and cut flower planting dates, consult Chapters 13 and 14.)

When it comes to planting times, there are advantages to gardening in both foggier and sunnier microclimates. For example, in gardens with cooler, foggier summers, carrots for a fall crop should be planted no later than July. More inland, they can be planted through August, since they will grow faster in the warmth of late summer. In foggier gardens, however, gardeners have the advantage of being able to plant such cool season crops as peas or broccoli late in the spring, when weather would turn too warm for them in sunnier areas. You will need to experiment a bit to learn how plants respond in your particular garden. Soon you will be learning about the microclimate of your garden by watching the plants.

To help you figure out how long a crop will occupy space in your garden, seed companies list the number of days required from seeding to the start of the harvest. These figures are frequently quite different for different varieties of a crop, and you will often choose a particular variety partly because of its number of days to harvest. For example, you will often select an early variety of a

FOG AND PLANT SIZE

You could map the effects of cool summer temperatures and fog by growing bell peppers or other plants that will bear a crop in the warmer and sunnier parts of the region, but not in the coolest, foggiest areas. Although there are differences in the responses of different varieties, the following is a typical pattern.

If you planted bell pepper plants from the same nursery six-pack on the same day in the foggiest areas, transitional areas, sunny areas, and just outside the fog-affected region, you would see clearly the effects of cold and fog. In the foggiest, coldest locations, the plant might grow 10 inches high but most likely would set no fruit. The plant in transitional areas might grow 1 or 2 inches taller and make few and small fruit. In sunny areas you might get a plant 15 to 18 inches high, bearing at least five or six good-sized peppers. Just outside the region with significant fog—for example, in Santa Rosa or even a pocket of warmth and sun in Oakland—the plant might reach 2 feet high and be covered with splendid peppers.

INTERPRETING SEED PACKETS

To guide a gardener to the right planting time, seed packets often bear the same standard recommendations. I have long thought of these common rhythmic phrases as little poems. One refrain advises planting "as soon as the ground can be worked in the spring." In an area with cold winters, this means planting the seeds when the soil has thawed and the mud from the melted snow has dried a bit. In our climate, the ground is never frozen under snow and, when the storms are not too close together, the soil is often dry enough to be worked in winter, although the soil temperature may be too low for even cool-season seeds to sprout. I usually interpret the seed packet instruction to mean that the crop can be seeded here in the open ground starting in February, when perhaps two-thirds of the winter rain has fallen and the days are significantly longer than they were in December and January. In fact, many such crops can be planted here much of the year.

Another standard phrase advises us to plant "as soon as the ground is thoroughly warm, and all danger of frost is past." This recommendation is more ambiguous in the context of our climate. Even though all danger of frost is past by the middle of February, the soil is usually not thoroughly warm until the beginning of May. Most crops labeled in this manner should not be planted outdoors until at least the middle of April, although earlier planting is sometimes possible. For example, summer squash may do just fine when planted as early as February—as long as the seeds managed to germinate. On the other hand, corn may be stunted if it sprouts in soil that is too cold for it, and the soil temperature may be too low for corn as late as April. Consult the charts on pages 18 to 21 and Chapter 11 for more information on vegetable planting times.

warm-season crop, since our summer cold and fog retard the growth of these crops. 'Early Sunglow' corn, listed in catalogs at fifty-five days, takes ninety days in a sunny San Francisco garden. A late corn, listed at ninety days, may not be able to ripen there at all. Cool-season crops, such as cabbage and broccoli, often take longer than the listed number of days when they are growing during the winter. This is less critical since they will eventually mature if they were planted early enough. Some of the best varieties take the longest to mature, but you will want to grow them anyway because they make up for their tardiness with taste.

The chart on page 22 shows some of the best times to grow selected vegetables and will give you a notion of how long crops need to stay in the ground and how long harvests last. (Note that these do not include all the vegetables you can grow or all the possible planting times.)

By referring to both the charts on Year-Round Production and on Microclimates, you can choose planting times that make certain sequences of crops possible. For example, peas planted in November will probably be harvested by the end of April. On May 1, you can plant 'Early Sunglow' corn in the same spot. The corn should be finished by July 30, in time to seed carrots for fall and winter harvests. If you had planted the peas in early March instead of November, they might not be finished until June. You could still plant the corn on June 15 and harvest it by September 15, but then it might be too late for carrots. Whatever sequence you choose, there is always *something* you can plant next. If your corn harvest runs into September, you can plant the space to garlic in the middle of October.

You make trade-offs when you choose planting times. For example, you may want to plant garlic, but a lack of space in your garden in October and November may prompt you to wait until December. You may even wait until February, when the days are a bit longer and warmer. The garlic might grow larger if planted in October, but the later planting may work out just as well. If it doesn't, that's a trade-off you won't make next year.

PLANTING TIMES FOR FOGGIER MICROCLIMATES

	January	February	March	April	May	June	July	August	September	October	November	December
Artichoke (rootstock)												
Beans, Fava												
Beans, Scarlet Runner												
Beans, Snap (bush)												
Beans, Snap (pole)												
Beet												
Broccoli (plants)												
Brussels Sprouts (plants)												
*Cabbage (plants)												
Carrot												
*Cauliflower (plants)										?		
Celery (plants)												
Chayote Squash												
*Chinese Cabbage							?		?			
Collards									?			
Corn (early)												
Cucumber												
Eggplant												
Garlic (sets)												
Kohlrabi									?			
*Leek												
Lettuce												
Melon												
Mustard				?						?		
*Onions (seeds)												
Onions (sets)												
Onions, top or bunching												

	January	February	March	April	May	June	July	August	September	October	November	December
Parsnip			■	■	■	■	■	■ ▒	?			
Pea	▒	■	■	■	■	■			▒	▒	■	
Pepper (plants)					■	■						
Potato tubers)			■	■	■	■	▒	▒	▒	▒	?	
Radish (small)	■	■	■	■	■	■	■	■	■	■	■	■
*Radish (winter)	■	■	▒	?			■	■	▒	?		
Rhubarb	■											■
Shallots (sets)	▒	?								■	■	▒
*Spinach		■	■	▒	?			■	■	▒	?	
Squash, Summer		?	▒	■	■	■	■					
Squash, Winter (and Pumpkin)					■	■						
Sunflower				■	■	■						
Sunchoke (Tubers)	▒	■	■	▒								
Swiss Chard	▒	■	■	▒	▒	▒	▒	▒	▒	▒	▒	▒
Tomato (plants)		?	▒	▒	■	■						
Turnip	■	■	■	■	▒	▒	■	■	▒	?		

KEY:

■   A heavily shaded area means it is okay to plant this crop at these times.

▒   A lightly shaded area means that these times will work for some varieties, in some locations and/or in some years.

?   A question mark (?) means that you may sometimes be able to extend planting times even beyond the end of the lightly shaded area, though not commonly.

*   An asterisk before the name of a crop (*) means that varieties of the crop have widely differing preferred planting times. For example, most winter radishes should be planted from mid-summer into fall, but some varieties can be planted in the spring.

PLANTING TIMES FOR SUNNIER MICROCLIMATES

	January	February	March	April	May	June	July	August	September	October	November	December
Artichoke (rootstock)	▨	■	■	▨	▨	▨	▨	▨	■	■	■	▨
Beans, Fava	▨	■	■						■	■	■	▨
Beans, Scarlet Runner				■	■							
Beans, Snap (bush)				■	■	■						
Beans, Snap (pole)				▨	■	■	■					
Beet		■	■	■	■	■	■	■	▨			
Broccoli (plants)		■	■	▨	■			■	▨			
Brussels Sprouts (plants)						■	■	■				
*Cabbage (plants)		■	■	▨	▨	▨	■	■	▨ ?			
Carrot		■	■	■	■	■	■	■	■	▨	?	
*Cauliflower (plants)		■	■	■	■		■	■	■			
Celery (plants)			▨	▨	■	■	■	■				
Chayote Squash	■	■	■									
*Chinese Cabbage	■	?		?				■	■			
Collards	■	■		?			■	■	▨	?		
Corn (early)				■	■	■						
Cucumber				▨	■	■	▨					
Eggplant					■							
Garlic (sets)	▨	▨								■	■	▨
Kohlrabi		■	■	▨	▨	▨	■	■	▨	?		
*Leek		■	■	▨	▨	▨	▨	▨	■			
Lettuce	■	■	■	■	■	■	■	■	▨	▨	▨	■
Melon					■	■						
Mustard	■	■	■				■	■	■	?		
*Onions (seeds)	■	■	▨						■	▨	▨	▨
Onions (sets)	■	■										■
Onions, top or bunching							■	■				

20

Crop	January	February	March	April	May	June	July	August	September	October	November	December
Parsnip			■	■	■	■	■	■	?			
Pea		■	■					■	■	■	■	?
Pepper (plants)				■	■	■	■					
Potato tubers)		■	■	■	■	■	■	▨				
Radish (small)	▨	▨	■	■	▨	▨	▨	■	■	▨	■	■
*Radish (winter)	▨	▨	■	■	?			■	▨	?		
Rhubarb		■	■									
Shallots (sets)	▨	?									■	■
*Spinach		■	■	?			■	■	?	■	■	■
Squash, Summer	?	▨	■	■	■	■	■	▨	?			
Squash, Winter (and Pumpkin)				■	■	■	■					
Sunflower				■	■	■						
Sunchoke (Tubers)	▨	■	■	▨								
Swiss Chard	▨	■	■	▨	▨	▨	▨	▨	▨	▨	▨	▨
Tomato (plants)		?	▨	▨	■	■						
Turnip	■	■	■	■	▨	■	■	■	▨	?		

KEY:

(■) A heavily shaded area means it is okay to plant this crop at these times.

(▨) A lightly shaded area means that these times will work for some varieties, in some locations and/or in some years.

? A question mark (?) means that you may sometimes be able to extend planting times even beyond the end of the lightly shaded area, though not commonly.

* An asterisk before the name of a crop (*) means that varieties of the crop have widely differing preferred planting times. For example, most winter radishes should be planted from mid-summer into fall, but some varieties can be planted in the spring.

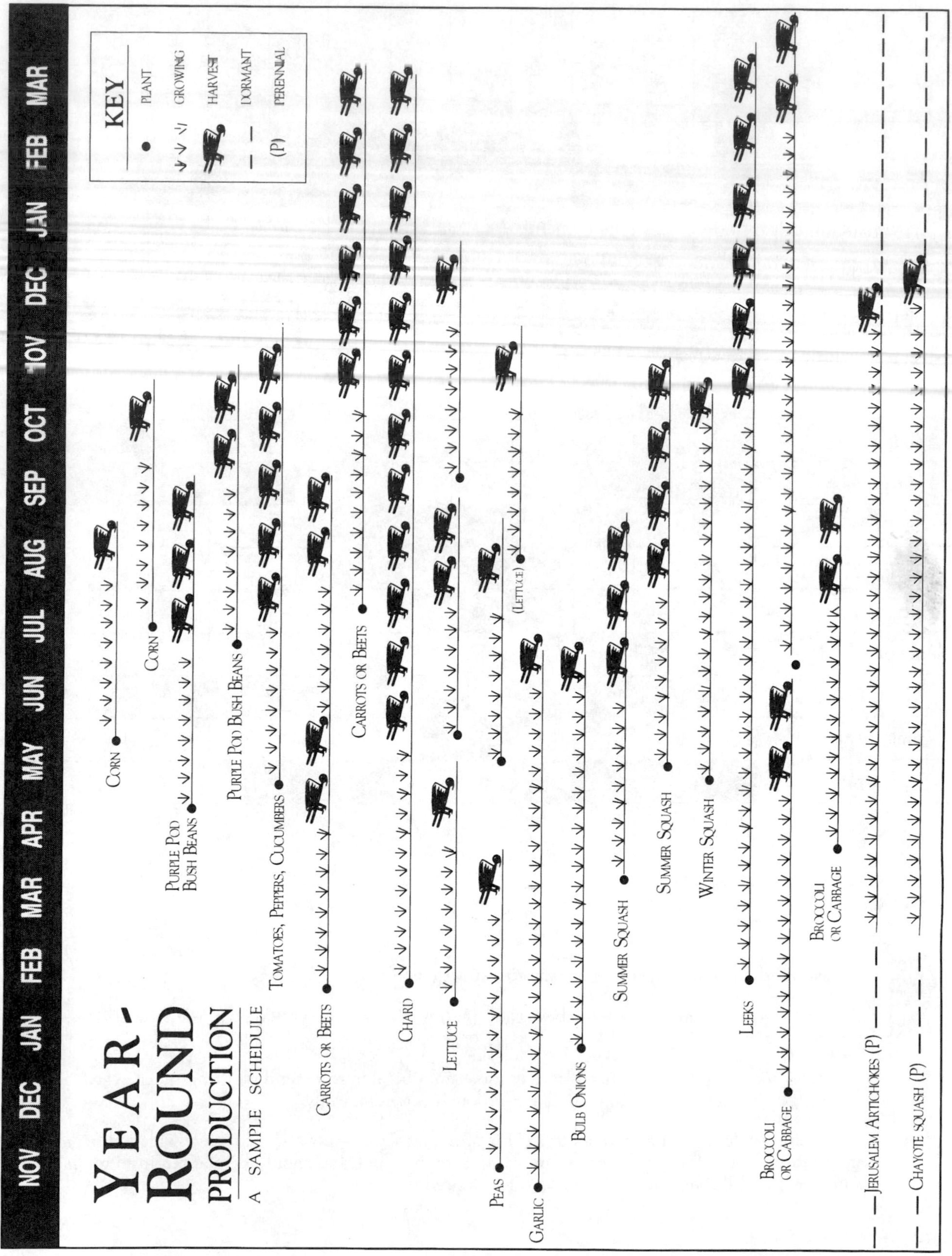

NOV DEC JAN FEB MAR APR MAY JUN JUL AUG SEP OCT NOV DEC JAN FEB MAR

YEAR-ROUND PRODUCTION

A SAMPLE SCHEDULE

KEY

- PLANT
- ∨ ∨ GROWING
- HARVEST
- – – DORMANT
- (P) PERENNIAL

Corn

Corn

Purple Pod Bush Beans

Purple Pod Bush Beans

Tomatoes, Peppers, Cucumbers

Carrots or Beets

Carrots or Beets

Chard

Lettuce

(Lettuce)

Peas

Garlic

Bulb Onions

Summer Squash

Summer Squash

Winter Squash

Leeks

Broccoli or Cabbage

Broccoli or Cabbage

Jerusalem Artichokes (P)

Chayote Squash (P)

You will not be able to try every crop or every possible planting time in a single year. Although the list of planting times suggests planting corn during four different months, that is something I rarely do. I may plant corn early one year, early and late the next, and in midseason the following year, and then I may skip a year altogether.

How Much to Plant

One of the skills that comes with gardening experience is the ability to grow just as much as you want of a crop, not too much or too little—at least most of the time. I've seen charts that purport to tell you how to do this, listing how much to grow to feed a family of four, assuming that everyone eats a standard (but unspecified) amount. Actually, no prepared list can reflect how much you and your family can or will eat of each crop.

Instead of relying on such charts, think about how well you like a crop, how much each plant will produce, and how long you will be able to harvest the crop. Then plant it, see how well you guessed, give away any extra, and estimate again next year. If you were planting a huge garden, you would probably want to be more accurate, but in a small space little is lost by a wrong guess.

Here is an example of how to estimate. Leeks produce one leek per plant. If you harvest only mature leeks, the leek season will last from September until about the end of February: six months. Decide how many leeks you will use in a month. Perhaps you will have potato and leek soup once a month, quiche once a month, and three quiches during the holidays. You may also want to use leeks occasionally in new ways, one of which may turn out to be a favorite. Assuming two leeks per soup or quiche, that is four leeks each for six months, plus six for the holiday quiches, or thirty leeks altogether. Add another half-dozen for good measure, for a total of thirty-six. This sort of estimate is rough, but it will save you from drastic underplanting or overplanting.

You are more likely to overplant if a crop has a short harvest season. Cauliflower and corn, for example, must be picked within a week or so of maturity. In these cases, you must be careful not to plant too much at one time. You should plant no more than you can eat in two or three weeks (which includes some refrigeration time). If you want to harvest the crop over a longer period, you must plant a successive crop every few weeks during the

FRUITING CROP PRODUCTION ESTIMATES

Bean, snap, bush: 1/4 pound per plant, over a few weeks.

Bean, snap, pole: a bit more than bush snap bean and for a little longer.

Bean, scarlet runner: even more productive than pole snap bean, and for 2 months or longer.

Corn: 1 or possibly 2 ears per plant, over a couple of weeks.

Cucumber: 10 to 12 per plant, over 2 to 3 months.

Pea, bush: 1/8 pound or less per plant, over several weeks.

Pea, pole: a bit more than bush pea and for longer.

Pepper, bell: 3 to 8 per plant, over 2 to 3 months; size varies on the same plant and by variety.

Pumpkin: 1 to 5 per plant, over 1 to 2 months; usually picked and stored for use in winter.

Squash, summer: 10 to 20 per plant, over 2 to 3 months.

Squash, winter: 2 to 5 per plant, over 1 to 2 months; usually picked and stored for use in winter.

Tomato, cherry: 30 to 100 or more per plant, over 2 to 3 months.

Tomato, paste: 50 to 100 or more per plant, over a month or so.

Tomato, standard size: 10 to 50 or more per plant, over 2 to 3 months.

crop's planting season. In the case of cauliflower, you may decide that your family can eat one head of cauliflower a week, or four a month, from April through July. Accordingly, you would start four plants from seed each month from January through April. You may want to start a few extra to allow for accidents, but this gives you the general idea.

As you read about the different vegetables in Chapter 11, you will learn more about how much each plant produces and how long it can be harvested. You will find it easy to grow enough of some crops and harder to grow enough of others, either because they occupy a lot of space or you eat so much of them.

The per-plant production of many crops is obvious, although size varies somewhat according to the variety and the health of the plant. Root crops such as carrots and beets produce one root per plant. Leafy crops make one plant, although many can be picked leaf by leaf while the plant continues to grow more leaves. In addition to root and leaf crops, there are fruiting crops such as tomatoes and beans. It is harder to guess how much fruit a fruiting crop will bear if you've never grown it before.

A Simplified Planting Schedule

The best way to get the most from our mild climate is to map out the planting year in advance. You will never be able to use all of your garden all year if you wait to see a bare spot in your garden before deciding what to plant next. If you are a beginner, a good way to learn to think in terms of year-round planting is to divide the year into four main planting seasons: April-May, July-August, October-November, and February-March. Even though some crops don't fit the format, and other planting times are possible for many of the crops, at least this method allows you to get a plan underway; refinements can follow later.

The simplified planting calendar, opposite page, lists appropriate crops to plant during these four seasons. Start by dividing your garden space into four equal parts. These could be only a few square feet each, and even if your garden space is large, limit the size of your first four beds to no larger than 100 square feet each. Decide which will be used for your first-year garden in which of the four seasons. A primary concern will be that the areas planted in October-November and in February-March will get some winter sun. Next, choose some crops that you would like to grow from each of the four lists. Don't try to grow too many crops, even if

you have lots of room and like to eat everything. Choose a season in which to plant the first bed, aiming for the earliest period in which you think you can have the soil in one bed amended and seeds or other starts ready to put in. Don't rush.

If it is November, for example, try for February-March. If the soil is still too wet in February, you can amend it in March.

Now move through your first year, planting another area in each of the four periods. By the time you plant your third bed, some of the crops from the first bed will be ready to harvest, so you will also have space there for crops from the third planting season list. Then, when you plant your fourth bed, you can also replant some or all of the second bed with crops from the list for the fourth season.

Beginning gardeners often do not get a fall garden in because in July and August, when they should be planting many fall crops, their whole garden areas is still tied up with the summer crops they planted, all at the same time, in April and May. Using the above plan, the area that was planted in February and March is vacant in time to put in late summer crops for fall. Then, February and March of the next year, these late summer crops will be finished, freeing area for another February and March planting. After a couple of years, you will probably no longer keep the four areas distinct, but hopefully you will still be planting all year.

As you carry out this plan, you will want to incorporate principles of crop rotation, as described on page 85, so that you won't exhaust your soil or spread diseases among your crops. To do this, just make sure that when you replant a bed, you choose a plant from the appropriate one of the four lists, that is from a different rotational group. For example, when replanting a bed that held October-November crops with April-May crops, you would want to follow peas with a crop that was not in the legume or the cabbage family, such as with carrot, to reduce the spread of pea powdery mildew.

Meeting the Challenge of a Winter Garden

Even with planting charts, many local gardeners find it a challenge to make full use of our winter gardening season. It is often hard to find time to go into the garden for very long during the short, cold, wet winter days. Night comes so early that we may

SIMPLIFIED PLANTING CALENDAR

FEBRUARY-MARCH

Asparagus (roots)
Bean, fava
Beet
Broccoli (plants)*
Carrot
Cauliflower (plants)*
Collards
Kale
Leek
Lettuce*
Mesclun (see page 221)
Mustard*
Onion (sets)
Parsnip
Pea
Potato (tubers)
Radish
Spinach*
Sunchoke (tubers)
Swiss chard
Turnip

APRIL-MAY

Basil
Bean, scarlet runner
Bean, snap, bush or pole
Carrot
Cauliflower (plants)*
Celery
Corn
Cucumber
Lettuce, leaf*
Pepper (plants)
Pumpkin
Squash, summer
Squash, winter
Sunflower
Swiss chard
Tomato (plants)

JULY-AUGUST

Bean, snap, bush (by mid-July)
Beet
Broccoli (plants)*
Brussels sprouts (plants)
Cabbage (plants)*
Carrot
Chicory
Chinese cabbage
Collards
Corn (by mid-July)*
Endive
Lettuce*
Potato (tubers)
Radish, winter
Rutabaga
Spinach*

OCTOBER-NOVEMBER

Artichoke (roots)
Bean, fava
Cabbage (plants)*
Garlic (sets)
Lettuce*
Onion (seeds)
Pea (during November)
Rhubarb (roots)
Shallot (during November)

* Check seed catalogs to learn about
which specific varieties are most
likely to do well if planted in this
season (see page 40).

still be in the middle of our commute when it falls. To enjoy stalking among the dripping leeks and Swiss chard takes a special hardiness, a tolerance of cold fingers and damp clothing, and perhaps a pair of waterproof boots.

To use winter well, you must sit down and make a plan for the entire year, so that you will remember to plant crops at the right time. This effort is well worthwhile and will allow you to eat a wide variety of garden-fresh produce all winter. In addition, some crops planted during the winter mature at other times, so you'll be limiting the number and variety of harvests during the rest of the year if you skip winter planting.

Overcome any reluctance to garden all winter by considering two important facts about winter gardening. First, fewer tasks need to be done at that time—for example, watering is rarely required in winter. Even in occasional dry spells, you won't need to water much since the soil will dry more slowly during the shorter, colder days. Also, crops need much less thinning, tying, staking, and other forms of attention, because they are growing at a slower rate. In addition, there are fewer pests. I seldom see any pests in winter except for some aphids on fava beans, garlic chives, and cabbage-family crops—and, of course, the ever-present snails and slugs.

The second fact to consider is that most of the work of preparing a winter garden is not done in

SOME VEGETABLES FOR A WINTER GARDEN

Artichoke, fava bean, garlic, and pea will grow vigorously through winter. Artichoke is best planted as the rains start; it will bear heaviest in February and April. Fava bean and pea seeds sown in November will germinate well despite the chill; both crops will bloom in February and produce pods in March or April. Garlic cloves planted in October will grow all winter to mature in June or July.

Cabbage and lettuce usually can't be seeded in the garden in midwinter. If planted out as seedlings, they will generally grow slowly to maturity through the coldest months. Some varieties handle cold better than others, and all will grow better during winters with several weeks of clear, mild days.

Broccoli and brussels sprouts will grow during the winter, but they will mature properly only if set out in middle to late summer so that they are half-grown before the coldest part of the year. Then they will continue to grow and produce good crops during the winter months (the timing of the harvest depends on the variety). However, if these crops are planted too late in fall, they will become stunted and produce short plants with miniature heads or sprouts.

Beet, carrot, kohlrabi, and parsnip won't grow much in the winter but will survive winter cold. To reach maturity by October or November, they must be planted in middle to late summer. No special protective mulch is required in our mild climate. 'Winter Keeper' beet and several carrot varieties are bred especially to hold flavor well into the winter months.

Leek and Swiss chard are best started the previous spring for harvest through the fall and winter. Both can be picked while young, leeks pulled as baby leeks and Swiss chard leaves harvested in summer. They reach maximum size by fall and may be harvested all winter.

Oregano, parsley, rosemary, sage, spearmint, thyme, winter savory, and winter tarragon are among the perennial herbs that grow slowly through the winter months, allowing light harvests. If you plan to harvest perennial herbs in winter, plant them in spring or early summer so that they will be large and well established by the fall.

winter. The key to a productive winter garden in our area is bit-by-bit preparation all year long. The broccoli, brussels sprouts, leeks, chayote, and carrots that you will be harvesting in winter were planted the previous spring or summer. As for crops that must be planted in winter, take advantage of the warmer days of early fall to dig and amend the soil. Wait for a couple of pleasant days in October and November to slip garlic cloves and artichoke roots into the ground.

Many gardeners only think about a winter garden in September, but by then their choices are limited. Some crops, such as beets and carrots, should already have been planted if you intend to harvest them during the winter. Planting times for winter harvests vary because some crops take longer to mature than others. Also, some crops can keep growing in cold weather, whereas others can't. In our mild-winter climate, more important than knowing frost hardiness is knowing how rainy, 40° F weather will affect a crop at different stages of its maturity.

Being Prepared for Frost

Although frost is rare here and many crops are hardier than you may suspect, it is a good idea to have a few antifrost tricks up the sleeve of your winter gardening jacket. Before the cold days arrive, use this technique to make your winter crops more resistant to cold: avoid adding nitrogen fertilizer during the last few weeks before the rains start. Nitrogen fertilizer will promote rapid, tender growth at the wrong time. Do any fertilizing of overwintering crops a bit earlier in the season. Also, plant the most frost-sensitive plants on the west side of an object that will shade them, as they will recover better from a frosty night if they can begin to thaw before the sun strikes them in the morning.

If you notice on a clear winter evening that the temperature is dropping toward freezing, beware. Frost is most likely when there is no night cloud cover to hold in the scant warmth of the winter sun. On such nights you can cover tender crops with a floating row cover (see page 50), straw, newspapers, plastic, or even old bed sheets to keep warmer air near the soil from radiating outward into space. Make sure the cover touches the ground all around the plants you wish to protect. If you use plastic, prop it up so that it doesn't rest on the plants.

When the frost is over, observe the plants for a while to assess the damage. In a few days you will be able to tell if annuals will recover. During the February 1989 frost, my celery plants were frozen for three nights in a row. When I harvested a few stalks, I heard the ice crunch as the knife cut through, so I thought the plants would surely die. But a couple of days later the plants were almost as good as new, the only damage consisting of dead tips on about one-tenth of the leaves. Perennials such as chayote and strawberries have the ability to die back and regrow, so even if they look dead don't give up on them until past the time they would normally grow back in spring.

Cold frames, cloches, and the like are small structures that stop the wind and hold in some heat. They let the sun shine through but keep heat from reradiating into the atmosphere. They can be used over single plants or an entire bed of seedlings. Although these structures can be pressed into action to avoid an occasional frost, they are best used to enable you to plant a bit later in fall, start cool-season crops a little earlier in spring, and seed winter lettuce and greens successfully in the garden. Coverings that are portable are most useful for protecting winter crops, since you may need them only sporadically. For more on cold frames, see page 58.

Dealing With Decay

Often a problem in a winter garden, decay first affects the last of the summer crops. At the beginning of the rainy season, tomatoes as well as winter and summer squash may rot on the bottom where the fruit touches the wet soil. Small boards or a drying mulch such as wood chips can save the last of the crop. In locations closest to the ocean, drying beans on the vine is chancy. If there are several cold, wet days together, the beans may decay before they dry. The best way to save them is to shell them and spread them out in a warm, dry place. (See page 170 for more on harvesting dry beans).

During very wet winters, decay of the leaves and stems of winter crops may be a problem. It is important to remove damaged and decaying leaves from plants before the decay spreads. When harvesting Swiss chard, tear the stalks from the base instead of leaving stumps that may rot. Even if a plant has some decay on it, the undecayed part is perfectly all right to eat. If the outer leaves of a cabbage head are decayed, just peel them off and eat the rest.

Roots may rot in winter if the soil is very clayey

and poorly drained. Any work you do throughout the year to improve clay soil pays dividends in your winter garden. A soil that drains well not only prevents decay but also is warmer.

Remembering to Harvest Biennials

After they overwinter, many vegetables go to seed, often surprising gardeners. Carrots, parsley, beets, Swiss chard, leeks, onions, cabbage, and collards are among the many spring seeders. Maybe you planted your winter carrots so late that they never grew very big but you thought they might grow more in spring. Perhaps you grew a few more leeks than you could eat before March. One day you notice that both are sending up tall stalks. In a few weeks the plants seem to have become nothing but stalk and flower—the carrots sporting little umbrellas and the leeks graceful minarets. Although these flowering plants are interesting to watch, they are not much use in the kitchen, since the carrot roots become pale and woody and the leeks wither around their tough seed stalks.

Carrots gone to seed

All of these spring-seeding crops are biennials, meaning they go to seed and die after being exposed to a certain amount of cold weather. If you grew them in a cold-winter area, you might never have discovered this, since the plants would have been harvested or killed by cold first. You will learn how to manage each crop later in this book but generally, come February, use up last season's biennial crop or lose it.

Year-Round Gardening Means...

- **You can eat fresh garden produce all year with little need for food preservation.**
  Although many local gardeners may preserve one or two favorites (I make green tomato chutney and freeze some basil in a pesto base), they don't spend much time preserving their produce. Instead, they eat whatever is fresh in the garden each month.

  Here are the reasons I don't preserve much

food. First, my garden space is limited. I would rather use valuable space in summer to start a bed of winter broccoli than plant twice as many tomatoes for canning. Second, there are winter substitutes for some summer crops. I prefer to grow winter-producing chayote rather than freeze zucchini. Third, the root cellar, the old standby of the cold-winter gardener, doesn't work well here because our climate is too mild. Carrots and beets store best in the ground and cabbage on the stalk.

- **Your gardening work will be spaced out over the year.**
  True, there is somewhat more work in spring, but even the spring planting season is spread out over several months. Harvesting takes place throughout the year rather than in one late summer blitz. Cleanup chores are staggered, because crops finish at different times. Since you usually have only small vacant areas at any given time, soil preparation is rarely done all at once.

- **Your soil will need more care because it is in continuous use.**
  When crops are growing all year, they remove nutrients the year around. Also, organic matter in the soil continues to break down throughout our mild winter months. It is probably best if you fertilize your soil and add organic matter not once, but twice a year.

- **You must attend to weeds all year.**
  There are summer weeds and winter weeds. The latter sprout in your garden when the rains start, just as the hills are greening up. It is tempting to ignore them, since they make the garden pretty, but some winter weeds, such as Cape oxalis, onion lily, and many perennial grasses are among the most invasive and must be controlled. Winter weeds go to seed in March and April, but the clever gardener never lets them get that far, having cut them or dug them in long ago. See page 98 for tips on winter weed control.

- **You have more leeway for mistakes.**
  Year-long gardening is more forgiving of failures than a single short growing season. When you see a crop has failed, you often have plenty of time to replant it. If it refuses to succeed, there are usually several other crops to try during the same or the next season.

FOUR

Planning Your Garden

EFORE YOU PLANT, PAUSE A while to study your yard with a gardener's eyes. Factors such as shade, wind, and slope will determine how much of the space is suitable for an edible or a cut flower garden, as well as which areas are best suited to particular crops. By arranging your garden well, you can make it more attractive and efficient to tend. And by fitting it into other uses of outdoor space, you can get more pleasure from your yard.

Finding Sunshine

The overriding problem of many local gardeners is shade. The inevitable fog and rain clouds, sometimes in combination with shadows cast by buildings and large trees, unfortunately make some yards impossible for vegetables. In our hilly terrain a yard may also sit on a steep and shady north-facing slope.

Leafy vegetables need four hours of full sun each day. Fruiting vegetables, such as beans and tomatoes, need at least six hours of sunlight daily. Since our summer days are so often foggy, it is best to have a site that is unshaded eight to ten hours a day during the summer. Generally, herbs require a fair amount of sunlight, although some, including watercress, chervil, and Japanese parsley, are suited to the shade. Most edible as well as cut flowers need as much sun as fruiting vegetables, but again there are exceptions. Flowers requiring part shade include forget-me-not, foxglove, and columbine. Most fruit-

ing trees and shrubs also need full sun, although deciduous trees can be in shade during the winter, when they are dormant.

What is the minimum sunny area for a vegetable garden? Although more space may be preferable, even 2 square feet receiving four hours of sun a day will grow a couple of dozen carrots or eight leaf lettuce plants. A 4- by 10-foot area is probably plenty to keep one or two people in salads. If you decide that too little of your yard gets enough sun for vegetables and there seems to be no way to let more sun in, first look up—to porches, roofs, and stairways—for sunny space. (See Rooftop Gardening on page 38.) If you can't find any, be content to plant shade-tolerant ornamentals in your garden and look for a sunny yard to borrow or a community garden to join. A community garden can be a satisfying choice, especially for a beginner, since you can watch other gardeners and learn by asking questions. Such gardens often have long waiting lists, but don't be discouraged; sign up right away and the wait will be shorter than if you put it off. (See Appendix V for community garden resources.)

If a tree in your yard is blocking sunlight from your garden, you can decide to remove it, or consult a licenced arborist about sound ways to prune it that let in more light. If you are planning a new landscape, plant only small trees, or keep them on the north side of your vegetable garden or in an area already shaded much of the time by a building. Some localities have laws that provide you a right to a view through neighbors' trees, and, by implication, sunlight; others do not. Search for such laws by calling city hall, the parks department, or the

---

USING SUNLIGHT
ABOVE GROUND LEVEL

Near the edge of areas too shady to plant are areas that are in shade at ground level longer than they are in shade at a level several feet above the ground. There are ways to use this upper-story sunlight. One is to plant vigorous, tall-growing plants such as sunchokes, sunflowers, and chayote. A second is to raise the soil level 1 to 3 feet; the increase in elevation may be just enough to make a difference for your plants.

---

public works department. In addition, housing associations sometimes have such rules, and your or your neighbor's property title may reveal an easement to allow a view. Research first, then talk to your neighbor; pursue mediation if necessary.

Summer shadows are shorter than those cast during the winter, because the sun is more directly overhead in the summer sky. The summer sun also reaches around to shine from slightly north of due east in the morning and north of due west in the afternoon, so the north side of a barrier, such as a hill, building, or fence, gets a bit of direct sun in summer.

Once you have determined which parts of your garden get enough sun to grow vegetables in summer, you must figure out where there will be enough sun for a winter vegetable garden. Because of the difference in the angle of the sun, areas of your yard will be unshaded for a part of the day in summer but will spend the winter in deep, cold shade. If you're lucky, there will be an area that is relatively unshaded all or most of the day during the winter.

December 21, the shortest day of the year, is the day of the longest shadows. Look at your garden at noon on or about this day; the area still in sun is the best place to plant winter crops, such as broccoli, peas, and garlic. If you find that your crops are struggling in too much shadow this winter, take note of the sunniest area and plant there next year. Another way to determine the amount of winter sunlight is to observe the shadows cast at midnight during a night of the full moon closest to June 21, the longest day of the year. The part of the garden that is bathed in moonlight will get the most winter sun. For information on finding and using tools that allow you to predict various seasonal shadows, consult *Designing and Maintaining Your Edible Landscape Naturally* by Robert Kourik (see Appendix VI, Suggested Reading).

Finding Shelter From the Wind

The region covered by this book is generally a very windy place. As a gardener, you must take wind into account because it makes a difference in what

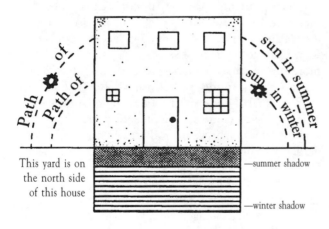

This yard is on the north side of this house — summer shadow — winter shadow

More of your yard will be in shadow in winter than in summer because the winter sun is lower in the sky. To determine the altitude of the sun at noon on the solstice, use the following formulas:

SUMMER SOLSTICE SUN ANGLE =
90° + 23.5° – your latitude in degrees.

WINTER SOLSTICE SUN ANGLE =
90° – 23.5° – your latitude in degrees

(For San Francisco, latitude = 37° 47′)

you can grow and when you can plant it. You will have a windier yard if you are in the path of one of the fog gaps between the mountains or hills. The narrower the gap, the stronger the wind. Although buildings may block the wind in an urban area, the wind is also intensified by being forced to flow around buildings. The arrangement of buildings nearby can make a yard or a group of yards protected and still, or it can make the air in it quite turbulent. For example, skyscrapers have created wind tunnels in many downtown streets of San Francisco. Gardens high on the north and west sides of the area's many hills will also be especially windy, since the winds come primarily from the northwest and increase at higher elevations. A report from a gardener high on the north side of one of San Francisco's central hills is that in the path of cold spring winds not even cabbage will grow before May.

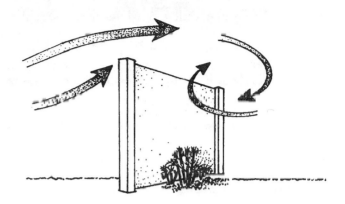

Wind effects with solid fence...

Many urban gardens are edged with a solid fence for privacy. Although a solid fence offers some protection from wind, the air just behind it will be turbulent. Shrubs or open fences that let a little air through do a better job of tempering the wind. Consider replacing a solid fence with either a partially open fence or an open, lightly vine-covered one. If you prefer the privacy of a solid fence, you may want to add a panel of semi-open, wind-baffling material to the top of the fence. Prefabricated redwood latticework or a plastic wind mesh designed for gardeners will slow the wind while still letting some light through. (The illustration shows how solid and semi-open fences affect wind flow, and Appendix V, Resources for Gardeners, lists sources of wind mesh.)

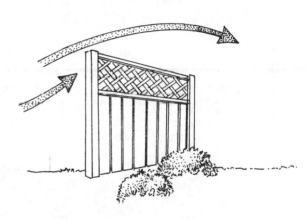

added panel...

Another approach is to use glass in your fencing. It doesn't prevent turbulence, but it does let light and heat through. One local garden has 1-1/2-foot-high glass panels atop the perimeter fence as well as several 4-foot-high glass walls within the garden area. These walls, placed parallel to each other and about 10 feet apart, create a near-greenhouse environment in the spaces between them. For such walls, use tempered glass fixed between 4 by 4 posts securely set in concrete.

Identifying Microclimates Within a Garden

Because of the desire to grow warm-season crops that may be borderline for our climate and to get

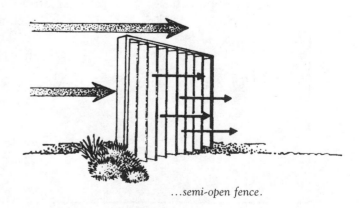

...semi-open fence.

the greatest variety in winter harvests, gardeners in our region tend to become fanatical about identifying different microclimates within a single yard. We want to find the warmest place in summer, the location least likely to get frost in winter, the spot with the least wind, and so on.

Although the center of your garden away from shadows cast by the house and any fences is probably the sunniest spot overall, the area south of a barrier on the north side of your yard may be warmer and sunnier in winter. A wall, fence, or

hedge on the north side of the garden doesn't shade the yard, because the sun shines mostly from the south. The area in front of a northern barrier gets more sun than areas in front of barriers on the other sides of the garden. It also gains some heat and possibly light because the barrier is there. Light-colored barriers reflect light back onto the planting area in front of them; dark barriers absorb and reradiate heat, as do dense materials such as stone, concrete, and bricks.

You can change the microclimate in front of a

SALT SPRAY

Within a few blocks of the ocean, the air contains a significant amount of salt spray. If you live very near the coast, you are probably well aware of the spray because it clouds your windows and makes your locks stick. Salt also settles on your plants and soil. There is less salt deposit and less corrosion on the sides of houses facing away from the ocean, so gardens are probably less affected when the ocean breeze is blocked by a house, fence, or trees.

Most of the salt will be leached by watering and rain, but some will remain. The effect is probably small, but it may be critical for sensitive plants. You can help salt-sensitive plants somewhat by occasionally spraying their leaves with fresh water, although you may have to weigh the benefit of spraying against the possibility of encouraging disease. The following is a list of the relative sensitivity of various crops to salt in the soil.

RELATIVE SALT TOLERANCE OF CROP PLANTS

VEGETABLE CROPS

High Salt Tolerance	Medium Salt Tolerance	Low Salt Tolerance
Beets	Tomato, Broccoli, Cabbage,	Radish
Kale	Bell Pepper, Cauliflower, Lettuce,	Celery
Asparagus	Sweet Corn, Potatoes (White Rose),	Green Beans
Spinach	Carrot, Onion, Peas,	
Swiss Chard	Squash, Cucumber, Cantaloupe	

FRUIT CROPS

High Salt Tolerance	Medium Salt Tolerance	Low Salt Tolerance
None	Fig	Pear, Apple, Orange,
	Olive	Plum, Almond,
	Grape	Apricot, Peach,
		Strawberry, Lemon,
		Avocado

fence or wall by changing its color. Either paint it directly, or attach a thin sheet of painted plywood. For a wooden fence, mount the plywood on a couple of vertical strips of 1x1s so that it won't trap water and cause the fence to decay. Sunlight reflected from a light-colored barrier stimulates fruit production. Here is the perfect place to put tomatoes or citrus trees. A barrier that is painted black or otherwise darkened will absorb heat during the day and radiate it back at night. Such a barrier will not stimulate fruit production, but it will help plants grow bigger and protect them somewhat from winter cold. The area in front of a dark-colored barrier is a good environment for winter greens.

A fence or wall on the east side of your yard creates the second warmest and brightest microclimate. Plants growing in front of it will receive morning shade and afternoon sun. Since afternoons are less likely to be foggy and are usually warmer than mornings, the area in front of an eastern barrier will get the best of the day's warmth and light, even if it does not get as much sun as the area in front of the northern barrier. Also, as mentioned in the section on frost protection (see page 59), plants growing in front of a barrier to the east have a better chance of surviving frosts, because the sunlight does not strike them in the morning when they are still frozen.

A barrier on the west side of a garden traps the cooler morning sun and provides protection from the prevailing west winds. Light and dark surfaces on structures located to the east and west will reflect and absorb light as on structures located to the north but the effect won't be as pronounced, since they will not receive as much total light or heat.

The worst place for a vegetable garden is on the north side of a barrier. For much of the year the barrier blocks the midday sun and makes the area just north of it shady, cold, and damp. The taller the barrier, the larger the affected area. The affected area will be even larger in the winter, when the sun is lower. The shadow from a tall house on the south side can cover the yard all day for several winter months.

A barrier with an overhang—such as a house with eaves—that faces south, west, or east will create a special environment. In summer, the area under the overhang will be shadier and cooler than the open garden, making it an ideal location for cool-season crops. In winter, it is a good site for tender crops.

The sun, lower in the sky during the winter months, will shine under the overhang. In addition, the overhang will block some of the rainfall and keep cold air from sinking onto plants below. Since drier soil tends to be warmer, the soil beneath the overhang will be warmer than soil in open areas of the garden. (Be sure to provide irrigation during winter dry spells.)

In a yard that is not level, consider the location of cold pockets—low areas where cold air collects as it pours downhill. Avoid putting frost-tender plants in these low spots, which can be several degrees colder than the surrounding terrain. Some gardening books suggest that you leave a gate open or build an open fence at the low end of a yard to let the cold air flow out; alas, research has shown that cold air moves more like porridge than water, and the opening would have to be much wider than most yards for appreciable amounts of cold air to depart!

Making Room for a Vegetable Garden

In our foggy region, unshaded garden space is at a premium. You may find that you have competing needs for the unshaded parts of your yard. Sun-loving ornamentals, picnic and social areas for adults, and play areas for children are likely to compete with vegetable gardening for unshaded space. After you evaluate your yard for sun and shade, consider all of your needs for sunny outdoor space. Think of ways in which special-purpose areas can overlap. Here are some ideas that may work for you.

- Intersperse vegetables among ornamental plantings, even in the front yard.

- Plant some ornamentals, especially edible flowers but also cutting flowers, in the vegetable beds.

- Design an attractive pattern of raised planting beds to contribute to the ornamental quality of your garden.

- Plant in hanging pots, containers placed on a stairway, and containers placed at the edge of a deck or play area.

- Place benches or a picnic table in the vegetable garden area. If you have a garden workbench or an outdoor sink in which to clean your harvest, let it double as an outdoor kitchen area during barbecues.

FOOD AMONG THE FLOWERS

Some vegetables and herbs are attractive enough to plant in ornamental areas of the garden. Such dual-purpose landscaping is especially useful in a small yard. When you use food crops ornamentally, treat annual vegetables as you would annual flowers, replacing them when they become unsightly. Some, such as lettuce, can be harvested and replaced with transplants several times a year. To avoid unsightly, yellowing foliage, you may want to pull others, such as beans, before the harvest is over. Plant annual flowers to screen perennial crops, such as artichoke and garlic, that go through a dormant or less attractive phase.

Vegetable crops grown ornamentally usually must be very healthy in order to be attractive. Well-grown lettuce is quite pretty, whereas lettuce left growing too long or with inadequate fertilizer or water can be downright homely. A level of pest damage that may be acceptable in a food garden may spoil the effect in a flower bed. You may want to practice growing edible crops in a less prominent setting before letting them star in an ambitious decorative scheme. Here are some ideas for growing vegetables decoratively.

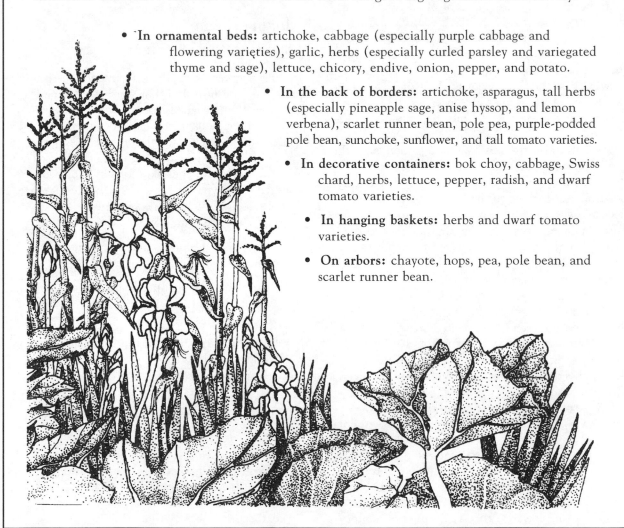

- **In ornamental beds:** artichoke, cabbage (especially purple cabbage and flowering varieties), garlic, herbs (especially curled parsley and variegated thyme and sage), lettuce, chicory, endive, onion, pepper, and potato.

- **In the back of borders:** artichoke, asparagus, tall herbs (especially pineapple sage, anise hyssop, and lemon verbena), scarlet runner bean, pole pea, purple-podded pole bean, sunchoke, sunflower, and tall tomato varieties.

- **In decorative containers:** bok choy, cabbage, Swiss chard, herbs, lettuce, pepper, radish, and dwarf tomato varieties.

- **In hanging baskets:** herbs and dwarf tomato varieties.

- **On arbors:** chayote, hops, pea, pole bean, and scarlet runner bean.

- Construct a bean trellis playhouse for children in their play area.

- Reserve a garden plot for children to use.

- Don't squander valuable sunny space for a compost pile; relegate it to a shady spot.

Gardening in Beds

Where I grew up, gardening was something you did in long rows with 2-foot-wide paths between. You stood or squatted between a row of carrots and one of beans, and you hoed or harvested. Now I plant in garden beds in which the plants grow very close together, and I tend the plants from paths between the beds. Generally, garden beds are 3 to 5 feet wide and 3 to 20 feet long, and the paths between them are 1-1/2 to 3 feet wide. The soil level in garden beds may or may not be raised above that of the paths, and the beds may be framed or unframed.

Bed gardening has become very popular because it makes efficient use of limited space and time. Production is often greater in beds than in the same area planted in rows. In part, this occurs because more plants will fit into the same space, since some of the path area between rows has been eliminated.

Another reason is that you can concentrate soil-building efforts on the soil in the beds, rather than in the whole area. This means you are more likely to go to the expense and take the time to build rich soil. You never have to walk on the soil in beds, so it stays light and fluffy, allowing plant roots to grow better. Another benefit is that gardens planted in beds conserve water, since only the beds and not the paths need to be watered.

You can discourage weeds on paths between beds with a sawdust or wood-chip mulch. When heavily mulched paths are packed down by walking, they are less likely to be muddy in winter and early spring. Paths can be made semipermanent and more handsome with crushed rock, unmortared bricks, or flagstones. Such materials will also collect and re-radiate warmth from the sun, possibly improving production in the beds.

Some garden beds are simply flat rectangular areas in which vegetables are grown. They may be raised slightly because a little soil from the path was tossed in or, in the case of double-dug beds (see page 83), because the loosened soil takes slightly more room. Other beds are framed, most often with boards. If you have a sandy or a well-amended and deep soil, a frame built of 2 by 4s is all that you

---

SLOPING YARDS

In a yard that slopes, even gently, planting rows should be arranged to follow the contour of the slope. If you build framed raised beds, make the downhill side higher and level the soil. A yard with a significant slope should be terraced, with wood, concrete, or stone retaining walls built to hold the soil.

Terracing can be done by the traditional method of cutting steps up the slope, putting in retaining walls, and using the soil removed to fill the area behind the next lower walls. However, modern urban terraced gardens are more often made by the less labor-intensive method of setting up retaining walls and depositing purchased soil behind them. Consult a book on garden construction to be sure you are providing the strength and drainage that retaining walls need. On terraces more than 2 feet high, the walls must be braced and anchored. A steep hillside should probably be left to a contractor, since a poorly constructed retaining wall could slide dangerously.

If you can do only part of the terracing at first, start at the bottom. Make the level areas wide enough so that you can work on them. If the slope is so steep that the terraces must be less than 4 feet wide, you could plan a vertical stairway path every 4 feet and plant in terraced strips between the paths.

As a bonus in a terraced yard, you get a little reflected light and radiant heat from the retaining walls, especially if the terrain slopes to the south.

SOME POSSIBLE FRAMED BED MATERIALS

MATERIAL	COST	DURABILITY	SAFE?	COMMENTS
Scrap lumber	Low	Low	Probably	Beware of lead paint (see page 75).
Pressure-treated Lumber	Medium	High	Controversial	Manufacturers claim it is safe; *Organic Gardening* magazine says no, definitive tests not done.
Wood treated with pentachlorophenol	——DON'T USE THIS MATERIAL——			Contains dioxin contaminants that poison humans.
Wood treated with cuprinol	Medium	Medium	Probably	You buy and paint on. Not well studied for safety.
Old railroad ties	Low	High	Probably	Creosote poisons plants, but much of it has leached out of old ties.
Redwood	High	High	OK	Heartwood is most durable. Stain or varnish it to make it last even longer.
Recycled Plastic "Wood"	Medium	High	OK	Weighs twice as much as wood, is more flexible.
Concrete blocks	High	High	OK	Hold heat—warm the soil.
Bricks	High	High	OK	Hold heat—warm the soil.

Pressure-treated wood contains arsenic compounds. Exact contents vary by brand. Some arsenic may leach into soil. Exactly how much, and how much is absorbed by plants, has not been delineated. If you do use it, wear rubber gloves and a dust mask while sawing it, sweep up and discard the sawdust. Don't save scraps for burning in the fireplace.

need. Its main function will be to delineate the edges of the beds.

Sometimes a taller frame is helpful. If you have a clayey soil, a frame 6 to 12 inches high will help the soil to warm faster. It will also provide lots of room to add organic amendments, which will increase the amount of air in the tightly packed clay and improve drainage. A high frame is useful if you must garden where there is no suitable soil—for example, where there is bedrock near the surface, in a place that was recently a salt marsh, or even where there is nothing but concrete. In such cases, you will need to bring in soil to fill the beds. (See page 77 for tips on when and how to buy topsoil.)

If you are building a framed bed on concrete or another surface that roots cannot penetrate, then the bed becomes a kind of container garden. Refer to the information on container planting (next page) to find out the soil depth required to grow various crops. Plants in a raised bed may succeed in slightly shallower soil than they would in individual pots, since the roots can spread laterally.

You may want to construct a tall bed if you have difficulty working at ground level. An 8- to 12-inch-high bed with a ledge to sit on allows you to work sitting down; a 2-foot-high bed can be used from a wheelchair. See books in Appendix VI, Suggested Reading, that contain many other ideas to make gardening easier for disabled persons.

Bed planting, and especially framed-bed planting, has additional bonuses for beginners. Beds help to define the garden space. They demarcate areas where the soil should be improved to support plant growth and areas that can be made into paths. If

HOW DEEP SHOULD IT BE?

In constructing container beds you'll want to consider the necessary root depth for your crops. The following is a list of depth requirements for many common vegetables, herbs and flowers.

6 10 INCHES DEEP: Basil, Beet, Carrot (short or round), Chervil, Chives, Cilantro, Lettuce (butterhead, looseleaf), Onion, green, Parsley, Peppermint, Radish, Spinach, Thyme, Tomato (dwarf cherry), Watercress
Larger herbs, such as oregano, sage, and marjoram, will be stunted, But they will still produce a small crop.
Flowers: small flowers such as alyssum, lobelia, pansy, dwarf marigold, or small types of dianthus.

10–15 INCHES DEEP: Carrot (longer), Celery, Chinese cabbage, Garlic, Leek, Lettuce (crisphead, romaine), Mustard, Oregano, Potato, Strawberry, Swiss chard, Tomato (dwarf or patio)
Flowers: taller flowers such as godetia, calendula, salpiglossis, cornflower or cosmos.

15–18 INCHES DEEP: Beans (all kinds), Collards, Cucumber, Kale, Pea, Pepper, Squash (summer and winter), Tomato (short vines)
Flowers: most annual and perennial flowers.

18–24 INCHES DEEP: Broccoli, Brussels sprouts, Cabbage, Cauliflower, Corn, Tomato (any kind)
Flowers: floribunda roses, small hybrid tea roses, sunflower.

Extra fertilizer and water will allow crops to grow in slightly smaller containers.

you start your garden with a framed bed, you will see one neatly planted bed, not a few lonely plants in a corner of your yard. My first garden as an adult was in a neighbor's otherwise untended backyard, and I remember thinking that it looked insignificant, almost accidental—a small island of crops floating in a sea of weeds. In a neatly framed bed, it would at least have looked intentional.

By drawing up a plan before you start to build, you can put the first bed in the right place to begin an attractive pattern of beds. This attention to design will help to inspire you to garden and will make your edible plantings more attractive so that even nongardeners will appreciate them.

Raised beds should be narrow enough so that the shortest person helping with planting and harvesting can reach the center. Length is not important, but don't make them so long that you get tired of walking all the way to the end when you want to get to the other side. Paths should be at least 1-1/2 feet wide; 2 feet is a little less crowded, and 3 feet is spacious. You will come to resent the wasted space if you make them too wide, but remember that from time to time you may need to maneuver a wheelbarrow to each bed. By making every other path wider, you can compromise between space and convenience.

Frames for beds can be built from various materials. The considerations are cost, beauty, durability, bulkiness, and safety for food crops. If your garden is small, you may regret very bulky materials, like concrete blocks. Wood is a popular choice, although eventually it will rot from being in contact with soil that is alternately wet and dry. Various wood treatments make it last longer, but may not be safe for food crops. Redwood, untreated, is among the most durable of woods. A new option, and one that re-uses waste materials, is "lumber" made of recycled plastics. The table on page 36 compares a few of the materials you may encounter.

Arranging Your Crops

Although what you will learn later about individual vegetables will help you decide the best way to arrange your crops, here are a few general tips. Plant tall crops, such as corn and pole peas, to the north so that they won't shade smaller plants. Plant perennials, such as herbs and artichoke, away from the areas that you will be turning each season to plant new crops. If you are planting in rows or beds that are longer than wide, orient the planting areas east to west for the greatest exposure to the sun. If your garden is on a slope, orient the rows or beds to follow the contour of the terrain.

Rooftop Gardening

To avoid shade and to maximize your garden space, you may decide to grow plants in contain-ers on a deck, porch, stairway, or roof. These areas can produce good crops, but there are special considerations. If you are plan-ning an extensive roof garden, you may want to consult a structural engineer to find out how much additional weight your roof can bear and whether or not the surface can withstand regular foot traffic without springing leaks.

Containers can consist of wooden planters, clay pots, plastic buckets, or even sturdy plastic bags filled with planting mix. Be sure they are large enough for the plants you want to grow (see the table on the previous page). The containers will need drainage holes. Don't risk rotting your wooden deck or stairs by placing planters directly on them. Use small wooden blocks under the containers or devise other methods to raise them so that the wood underneath stays relatively dry.

Soil for use in containers needs to be porous and moisture retentive. On a roof or stairway, it also needs to be as lightweight as possible. Ordinary garden soil is too heavy and it is also too difficult to keep evenly moist in containers. Use a potting mix or compost. The high content of organic matter in either substance will make it weigh less and hold moisture better. The moisture-holding capacity is important because water evaporates more quickly from small volumes of soil. In a mix that holds wa-ter well, the moisture level does not fluctuate as much between waterings.

Because container plants require more water, fertilizers must be applied more often. Even if you plant in pure compost, you will probably need to add liquid fertilizers, since the constant watering that containers require will leach nutrients out of the soil. (See Chapter 8 for more information on soils and fertilizers.)

As you plan your container garden, consider where the water to maintain it is to come from. Try to get a hose to the planting area, since your willingness to carry water in buckets may not last the season. For a back porch or stairway, a house-plant hose that attaches to a sink faucet may be the answer. Drip irrigation is also a great idea for a container garden; use one drip emitter for each container or one for each plant in larger containers.

As you garden higher up, you are likely to en-counter stronger winds. The cooler air and the dry-ing effect of wind will be more serious for container plants not only because soil in containers dries out faster, but also because it heats up and cools off faster and reaches more extreme temperatures than soil in the ground. The wind can also shred and break plants.

Some plants need protection from the wind only until they are past the seedling stage. One method of protection is to plant several inches be-low the top of the container, then stretch a piece of floating row cover (see page 50) over the rim. Or cover the seedbed with any of the protectors men-tioned in Chapter 6, anchoring them to keep them from blowing away. A floating row cover can also be used on plants that have grown taller than the edge of the container; be sure to place the cover over a frame so that the wind doesn't cause the plants to rub against the material. Once the plants are established, mulch the soil in the containers to reduce evaporation. You may find that you can't grow vegetables in some sites without installing a windbreak. Plastic wind netting, which is light-weight, lets light through, and takes up little space, is a good choice for a deck or roof garden.

FIVE

OBTAINING SEEDS & OTHER STARTS

NCE YOU HAVE DECIDED which crops to grow, boost your chances of success by getting the best seeds, transplants, or other starts that you can find. The plant material should be vigorous, well adapted to our climate, and free of diseases and other pests. Since some pests can spread swiftly through a planting or even the whole garden, take sensible precautions. Never plant potatoes, onions, or garlic from grocery stores, as grocery produce doesn't have to be free of plant diseases to be sold as food. Be cautious about accepting plants from someone else's garden. Don't save and grow seeds from a diseased plant, because the disease may be seed borne. Read the individual crop listings to find out about pests that can spread by seed, in the soil, or by other methods.

Buying Seeds

Local seed racks are a handy source of garden seeds, but the selection is limited. Some very desirable varieties are available only through mail-order seed catalogs. Appendix IV lists mail-order seed companies, that I have found useful. My favorite catalogs are those that provide the most information about the seeds they carry, include varieties especially suited to our climate, or offer the unusual. Many of the seed companies have a wide selection, but some are specialists. A few concentrate on only one or two crops, offering many varieties, including some that are well adapted to our climate. Others specialize in crops and varieties that grow in areas with climates similar to

ours—for example, the Pacific Northwest, areas of Great Britain, or the Mediterranean.

Study the seed catalog descriptions carefully and warily, since they tend to paint a rosy picture. Read between the lines to see what is not being said. For example, the description of one variety may focus on appearance, whereas another variety may be described as the best tasting one that the seed company carries. The pretty variety may not taste very good, but you won't be told that. If you compare the descriptions of different varieties of the same crop in the same catalog and then compare the same varieties in several different catalogs, you will get a clearer picture of the differences among them.

Beware of novelty items that have little accompanying information. Often the description focuses on one very desirable trait but ignores other important features. You may end up with a tomato variety that has an unusual color of fruit but produces little and late before succumbing to a disease to which it has no resistance. Or it may be a "wonder" variety that is quite productive, but when you taste it you decide the real wonder is that anyone would ever want to eat it. (I immediately become suspicious of any crop that I'm told to "cook like asparagus." Very few steamed vegetables taste anything like asparagus. To me, this is nothing more than name dropping.)

Novelty crops are not necessarily unsuitable, however. For example, the purple-podded bush bean is delicious and very useful in much of our region. Try to find out as much as you can about a novelty crop before ordering it, and consider your planting an experiment, backed up with other crops that have a good chance of success.

When selecting cool-season crops, such as lettuce and broccoli, look for varieties that are suited to planting in certain seasons—for example, a particularly heat-tolerant variety in late spring and an especially cold-tolerant one in late summer. When selecting warm-season crops, such as tomatoes and corn, look for varieties that mature early, tolerate cool weather, or have a proven track record in similar climates. Varieties developed for short, hot, northern summers may or may not thrive here; although longer, our summers are cooler, many of our days are foggy, and at this latitude our summer days are shorter. If a crop is susceptible to certain plant diseases that are prevalent here, check for resistance when you are evaluating varieties.

What About Treated Seeds?

Some seeds have been treated with a fungicide to help them survive in cold, soggy soils—a desirable ability in our region. The seeds most commonly treated are large ones, such as corn, beans, and peas. Though the amount of fungicide on a seed is minute when compared to the full-grown size of the plant, it is still toxic, and some choose to avoid it. If you choose not to use treated seed, you will find that most varieties are available untreated. Many of the mail-order seed companies listed in Appendix IV sell all or mostly untreated seed, or will send only untreated seed if you request.

One of the several fungicides commonly used to treat seeds is captan, a chemical which has been

---

STORING AND TESTING SEEDS

At the end of the year, you will probably have leftover seed packets as well as seeds saved from your plants. All of these can be stored for planting next year. Of the common vegetables, only corn and onion seeds lose significant viability after the first year. Most seeds last three to five years.

Make sure that packets and other seed storage containers are labeled with the crop, variety, and current year's date. Store them in a cool, dry place. Keeping seed packets in closed glass jars with a commercial desiccant provides extra protection. A little powdered milk wrapped in a paper towel will also work if you change the milk after opening the jar a few times. (Bean seeds keep best in a less tightly sealed container, such as a yogurt tub.)

A simple test will determine whether or not seeds are still viable. Fold a paper towel in thirds and place a row of 10 or 20 seeds of a single variety along one short side of the rectangle, stopping 1 inch from one end. Beginning at the seeded edge, roll the towel up and fasten the ends with wire twist ties. Set the rolled towel in a drinking glass, placing the end without seeds at the bottom. Keep a little water in the glass so that the towel stays moist. After the normal germination period has passed, check to see how many seeds sprouted. If 90 percent or more germinated, the seeds are healthy. If fewer than 50 percent sprouted, discard the seeds. If the percentage is in between, use the seeds but sow them thicker than usual.

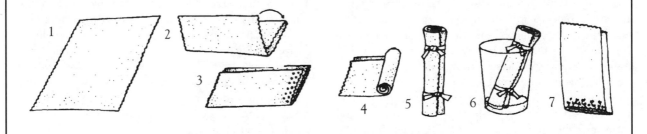

shown to cause cancer in rats and mice. In 1986, the Environmental Protection Agency (EPA) reported that this chemical is transported into plants and, in 1989, suspended its use on many food crops, but left seed treatment as a permitted use.

If you choose to use treated seed, be sure to wear gloves when you handle it. If you use untreated seeds, just plant them a bit more thickly in cold or clayey soil to make up for the losses to decay.

Saving Seeds

If you grow an open-pollinated variety (see page 44) that you particularly like and if the plants are free of seed-borne diseases, you may want to save seeds to grow next year. Our mild winter climate makes it easy to grow many crops for seed production, but other conditions complicate the process.

In a garden that is small or lies near other gardens, cross-pollination may cause undesired variability or even crosses between different related plants, such as beets and Swiss chard. You may plant what you thought were beet seeds and end up with something closer to Swiss chard! Also, damp weather may force you to harvest seeds as soon as they have matured and to dry them indoors before they decay. Here are some facts about saving seeds from vegetable crops. (For more information, see various books in Appendix VI, Suggested Reading about seed saving.)

- The best seeds for a beginner to save are bean, pea, lettuce and tomato, since these are mostly self-pollinating. The seeds of many other plants, such as squash and plants in the cabbage family, must either be pollinated by hand under a protective covering or isolated from other varietes in order to prevent unwanted crosses.

- To collect pea and bean seeds, you need only remove the mature seeds from the dry pods. Tomato seeds need a ferment to free them from the ripe fruit. Scoop seeds and pulp from ripe tomatoes, and mix them with a little water in a clear drinking glass or jar. Stir two or three times a day. When the seeds sink to the bottom after two to four days, add water and pour off the pulp several times until the seeds are clean, then spread them on a plate to dry. Lettuce seeds are among many seeds that must be separated from small lightweight dead flower

parts, known as chaff. Rub the seeds between your finger and thumb to separate them, then blow gently to make the lightweight chaff fly away. As an alternative, shake the seeds through a screen.

- Bean, pea, lettuce, and tomato plants ripen seeds in a few months, but certain other crops may take a year or more.

Buying Transplants

Growing from nursery starts is easy, fast, and rewarding if you buy plants in good condition. There are times when both beginners and busy experienced gardeners appreciate the shortcut of purchasing transplants. Beginners are especially delighted to be able to create an almost instant garden.

Transplants fulfill an important role by allowing you to plant when the weather is too cold for outdoor seeding. Gardeners in our region must usually wait until May for the soil to become warm enough for tomato seeds to germinate. But if tomatoes aren't seeded until May, very little of the fruit will have time to ripen. Another example is lettuce—gardeners in this area often use lettuce transplants in winter, when the soil is too cold for lettuce seeds to germinate well, but not too cold for the plants to grow.

Transplants are less vulnerable to pests than germinating seedlings are. Tiny basil seedlings can disappear in a blink, but 6-inch-high transplants aren't as much of a pushover. If something does start chewing on them, at least you have a chance to notice the damage and take action before the plants disappear. Snails love to eat squash seedlings until the plants grow three or four leaves—that's when the leaves and stems develop unappetizing prickles.

Transplants save garden space. When you use them, you can grow more plants and produce larger harvests, because you are not taking up space getting crops from seed to the transplant stage.

What to Look For

Buy seedlings that are in the best possible condition. If you don't have much experience shopping for seedlings, get them at a reputable nursery rather than a store that keeps a few seedlings as a sideline. Examine the plants carefully. Vegetables, in particular, grow so quickly that they can't be left in tiny seedling pots for very long. When the roots begin to grow in circles and through drainage holes, the plant is said to be pot bound or root bound. Another result of sitting too long on the nursery shelf is that the seedlings use up all the nutrients in the soil. The bottom leaves turn yellow and begin to drop, a sign of nitrogen defi-

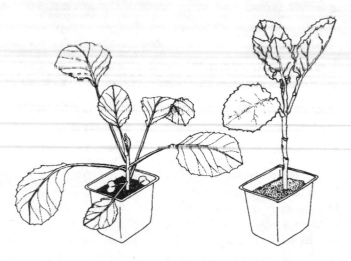

A good nursery plant.   A poor nursery plant.

ciency. The remaining leaves may take on a purplish or reddish tinge, a sign that phosphorus is lacking. New leaves don't develop fully but stay small. Plants in such poor condition may be permanently damaged.

Look for plants with a fresh green color (unless another color is normal) that do not have long roots growing out the bottom of the pot. Reject any seedlings with many leaf scars on the lower stem, indicating where leaves have fallen off. If you aren't sure, ask a nursery employee to show you seedlings that arrived within the past week and you will soon learn to recognize fresh stock.

Paradoxically, young plants in small containers are often the best buy when it comes to transplants. Young plants are better able to handle the shock of transplanting than older plants are. Plants that have not yet bloomed or formed flower buds have more energy to recover from transplanting, and they will grow larger and produce more generously. Although little marigold or zucchini plants in bloom may look cute, resist the temptation to buy them. Early flowering is often a sign that the plant is stressed for water or nutrients.

There are exceptions. Tomato is such a fast-growing, almost weedy crop that larger plants, even those with flowers, often produce earlier harvests. Try planting a smaller and a larger tomato plant of the same variety on the same day to see if you really are gaining an advantage. Much depends on whether the larger tomato plant was growing in a big enough pot with adequate water and fertilizer.

Beware of buying plants that will not do well in your microclimate. You can't always assume that a plant will succeed just because it is available locally. A nursery may carry melon seedlings, simply because their customers ask for them, even though the chance of a melon crop in nearby neighborhoods is slight. Likewise, the nursery may stock seedlings of certain crops much earlier than they can thrive without protection in your garden. If in doubt, refer to the growing instructions for each crop in this book, or discuss the crop and its timing with a nursery employee. (See the instructions for handling transplants, beginning on page 57.)

Right Name, Right Plant

The most common vegetables have become so familiar that you can be pretty sure of getting the right crop without knowing its scientific name. Almost everyone refers only to the common name of the crop and to the variety or cultivar name, such as 'Early Girl' tomato. Knowing the scientific name can be important when you are looking for an unusual crop or an herb, and it is often helpful even when the plant is well known. Scientific names show relationships among plants, and they can help you understand how to grow a plant when you see how similar it is to another, related plant. (For more on scientific names, see Appendix II.)

Common names seem easier, but they are often confusing because they are not subject to any rules. The same common name may be used for several different plants, or one plant may have several common names. For example, the names oregano and marigold are applied to more than one species of plant. You will often read that marigold is an herb used in medieval cooking, but the marigold used was *Calendula*, the pot marigold, not *Tagetes*, the Mexican marigold that brightens so many summer flower gardens. *Tagetes*, which tastes very different from the pot marigold, was unknown in the Old World during the Middle Ages. In the case of oregano, there is a labyrinth of common and scientific names between you and the plant that you want to use to season your pizza. When you know the scientific name of a plant, you know that it will be the plant described by that name in books and that all seed packets and nursery seedlings that are correctly labeled will produce the same kind of plant.

Beginning gardeners are often put off by scientific names, probably because they can't figure out how to pronounce them or remember how to spell them. Rest assured that it isn't important for you, as a gardener, to know how to do either. Just copy the name of the plant that you want and check it against the name on a nursery label or in a seed catalog.

When it comes to vegetables, fruits, and herbs, gardeners usually want to find not only a particular species, such as tomato, but a particular variety of the species tomato. In nature, varieties are commonly formed when a group of plants in a certain species gets isolated from the main species, as they would on an island or in a mountain valley. After a period of time, they become somewhat different from the rest of the species, though they could still interbreed with it if their isolation were to end.

Humans have created many plant varieties through selective seed-saving and plant breeding, and when a variety is manmade, it is called a cultivar (short for cultivated variety), though the terms variety and cultivar tend to be used interchangeably. Most of the varieties you find in seed catalogs are cultivars. For example the tomato variety 'Early Girl' is, properly speaking, the tomato cultivar *Lycopersicon lycopersicum* 'Early Girl'.

Open-Pollinated Cultivars

Most of our common food crops have evolved from less desirable wild plants because gardeners and farmers selected seed from the plants that they thought were the best. Over the years, and over the centuries, carrot roots and tomato fruits got bigger, and green beans more tender with less "string" to remove.

When gardeners are selecting for desirable traits, they often reach what they think is the best possible selection. That is, they decide that they like the plants they have been growing just as they are. Then, instead of trying to change the crop, they just save seeds from the plants most like the parent plants, so they maintain the cultivar in a more or less steady state. Cultivars that are produced this way—by selecting seed from the plants most like the desired ones—are called open-pollinated cultivars.

These days you often hear the terms "heir-loom seed" or "heirloom variety." An heirloom variety is an open-pollinated one that gardeners have liked and preserved by saving seed each year for a long time. They may have been commercially available for all of their history, or they may have been maintained only by gardeners, passed through the generations. Recently, many of these heirloom personal favorites have been rediscovered and made available for sale through seed businesses and seed-saving nonprofit groups. Now we can have treats such as 'Romanesco' broccoli or 'Green Zebra' tomato.

Hybrid Cultivars

Loosely speaking, a hybrid is a plant or an animal with unlike parents. We have all heard about the mule, which is a "hybrid" of a horse and a donkey—two different species of animals. And we know that a mule is sterile; it generally cannot produce offspring. While there *are* plant hybrids created by crossing different plant species, most hybrid vegetables are created by crossing two different varieties within the same species of vegetable.

When you see the word "hybrid" used to describe a plant cultivar, it almost always means that the cultivar is an F_1 hybrid. F_1 means first filial generation. To understand what that means, we have to back up just a bit.

To create an F_1 hybrid, plant breeders start with a number of open-pollinated plants. They select two plants that they think are potentially good parents for their hybrid and breed each of the parents in isolation, selecting for offspring that have only the desired traits. Then, when the genetic material of each of the parent lines is uniform, they cross the parents. The seed from this cross will be the F_1 hybrid seed that they will sell.

Plant breeders use the same parents each time they want to produce more of the same hybrid seed, producing the same combination of desirable traits each time. Because certain genetic traits are more dominant—or stronger—than others, they will be expressed each time the cross is made. For example, if large fruit, mild taste, and disease resistance are dominant traits, and one or the other parent has each of them, all of the F_1 hybrid plants from that cross will have those traits.

Breeders create F_1 hybrids because growers, especially farmers, have found them useful. Hybrid seeds have been custom bred for certain combinations of traits, and the seeds tend to be uniform, all having the same traits. Also, they offer an advantage known as hybrid vigor, a special vigor that often results when plants or animals with very different genetic material are crossed.

Which Is Best?

Some gardeners grow mainly open-pollinated or mainly hybrid seed. I grow some of each, choosing certain cultivars for specific reasons. Here are some of the advantages and disadvantages of the different types of seed:

On the plus side, a hybrid cultivar is uniform. An 'Early Girl F_1' tomato from one seed company should be genetically the same as from any other. It also means that the plants you plant should all behave in the same way. If the cultivar has disease resistance or an early ripening date, all plants should have these traits. You also benefit from the extensive testing breeders do for hybrids, such as for disease resistance. Finally, hybrid vigor may make it easier to produce a crop if the crop is borderline for our climate.

On the minus side, you can't save seed from a hybrid cultivar. That is, you can certainly collect the seed, and you can plant it, and, unlike the less viable mule, it will probably grow, but the offspring will show every possible recombination of the traits of the parents. Only about a fourth of the plants are likely to resemble the parents. That is, the F_1 hybrid is unstable. If you keep selecting the best plants from each generation and growing them out, year after year, you could eventually create your own open-pollinated cultivar based on the genetic material in the hybrid, but most of us don't have the space and time to do that. So, if we buy hybrid seed, we buy it again each year.

Another minus is that if everyone bought only hybrid seed, some very good open-pollinated seeds would be likely to be lost.

When you buy open-pollinated seed you contribute to maintaining genetic variability—keeping many old cultivars alive and well. And many of these varieties are very good. They introduce a wider variety of colors, forms, and flavors. They may even have disease resistances, though they have not been formally tested for them. They show more variation among plants grown from the same seed package. This can be good if it means that

they don't all ripen at the same time, since home gardeners often prefer, for example, a few weeks to eat up the cauliflower.

Open-pollinated seeds can be saved and replanted, so you don't have to rebuy seed every year. (Though if the crop you are growing can be cross-pollinated, you will have to make sure that no pollen from other cultivars has reached your crop's flowers; for example, you don't want pumpkin pollen to reach your zucchini flowers. For more information see page 41, page 249, and books on seedsaving in Appendix VI, Suggested Reading.)

On the minus side, you may not be able to find an open-pollinated cultivar with just the traits you want. Most of my favorite cucumber cultivars are F_1 hybrid crosses between regular slicers and Asian-type cucumbers. These cultivars have the mild flavor and tender skin of the Asian cukes, but are much better at coping with cool weather.

An interesting aside concerning open-pollinated cultivars is that, because they are not totally uniform genetically, strains may develop among plants of the same cultivar being maintained in different places. Thus the seeds of "Yellow Sweet Spanish" onions that you get from one seed source may be slightly genetically different from the ones you get from another source. This can work to your advantage if one strain is better adapted to your growing conditions. To find out if open-pollinated strains are different and how they differ, talk to an expert, such as a seed company professional or a plant breeder who has worked with them, or try the different strains yourself and compare them.

Compare Cultivars

Whether you grow hybrid or open pollinated cultivars or both, it is a good idea to keep trying and comparing new ones. This will help you find the very best ones for your growing conditions—and the ones you like best to eat.

To run a simple variety trial, grow a minimum of four plants each of at least two cultivars or two different strains of an open-pollinated cultivar. Plant all of the seeds on the same day and grow them under similar conditions. Compare the time to the first harvest, the size of the plants or the amount of harvestable fruit, the flavor, and other traits. When you find a favorite, grow it each year, but keep trying new alternatives.

SIX

GETTING PLANTS STARTED

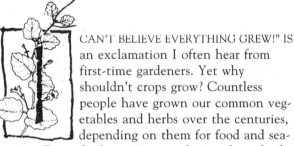

CAN'T BELIEVE EVERYTHING GREW!" IS an exclamation I often hear from first-time gardeners. Yet why shouldn't crops grow? Countless people have grown our common vegetables and herbs over the centuries, depending on them for food and seasoning. From the beginning, gardeners chose food plants partly for their easy natures. Through selection and breeding they created plants that were even more dependable. Although the history of domesticated flowers is shorter, we can still choose from a rainbow of easy-to-grow flowers.

From the time that growing fields were first cultivated, gardeners have figured out the most efficient ways to get plants started. Some plants grow better when they are direct-seeded—sown where you want them to grow in the garden. These plants include fast, vigorous growers, such as mustard greens, and crops that transplant badly, such as carrots. For crops that can be easily moved, such as cabbage, the use of transplants means earlier starts and better protection from pests. Plants whose growth from seed is impossible, unreliable, or very slow are usually grown in ways that bypass seeding—for example, onions grown from sets or herbs grown from cuttings.

Sowing Seeds Directly

Seeds are designed to spring into action as soon as conditions are right for growth. These conditions—warmth, moisture, oxygen, soft soil, and protection from pests—are more difficult to control when you direct-seed in the garden than when you sow indoors in seeding trays. If you follow these planting guidelines, however, you should have little trouble getting outdoor-sown seeds off to a good start.

Making Sure the Soil Is Warm Enough

The seeds of most warm-season plants require a minimum soil temperature of 60°F for germination. The seeds of most cool-season plants need at least 40°F, although a few crops can sprout at 35°F. These include lettuce, onions, spinach, and parsnips. All seeds germinate faster and better in soil that is warmer than the minimum: 80° to 90°F for warm-season crops and 70° to 80°F for cool-season crops.

If the temperature of the top 2 inches of soil, where seeds are planted, is going to rise above 70°F in our climate, it will generally do so by May. (You can be pretty sure that the soil is above 70°F when it feels warm to your hand.) The soil temperature begins to drop by October, falling into the forties or even the thirties by December, then rises slowly as the days lengthen.

Most gardeners don't know the temperature of their soil or the temperature that their seeds require. Instead, they make rough judgments about how warm the soil is and rely on trial and error when seeding. This imprecise approach is sufficient —I know that it worked for me. If you want to experiment with planting at a precise temperature, however, get a soil thermometer from a garden shop or nursery. To find out how warm the soil is where seeds will germinate, insert the thermometer 2 inches deep.

Preparing the Soil

Work the soil when it is moist, but not soggy. If the soil is too dry or too wet, you will damage its structure by digging—and the seeds may not come up anyhow. Soggy soil packs tightly, cutting off oxygen and suffocating the seeds. Dry soil is difficult to moisten thoroughly without washing away the seeds; also, seeds that are surrounded by dry pockets won't be able to germinate.

Allow soggy soil to dry a few days. If the soil is bone-dry, as it may be in midsummer, soak the planting area for two hours, then let it dry for a day or more before you plant. (To tell whether the soil is ready to dig, see page 82.) Never water the soil on the same day that you plant until after the seeds are in the ground.

Loosen the soil by turning the top 6 to 8 inches with a garden fork or shovel. Walk backward as you dig to avoid stepping on the freshly dug earth. Break up the biggest clods and remove any large rocks and perennial weed roots. If you are adding soil amendments or fertilizers that can be mixed into the soil on the day that you dig, spread them evenly on the surface before you turn the soil.

Use a rake, a hoe, or your hands to form a fine seedbed in the top 3 to 4 inches of soil. Crumble small clods and remove stones or chunks of organic matter. The seedbed needs to be finer for small seeds than for larger ones; a piece of undecayed bark that a bean seedling can easily push aside will stop a carrot seedling in its tracks. Smooth and level the soil, using your hand in a small area and a garden rake in a larger area. The bed should be level so that water doesn't collect on one side, although a very slight slope will help clay soil to drain.

How Deep? How Far Apart?

Use the information on the seed packet as a general guide to planting depth and spacing, but take into account that the directions may refer to row plantings. For a bed, use the spacing suggested for plants within a single row. For example, if the packet recommends planting 2 to 3 inches apart in rows 18 to 30 inches apart, then space all the seeds 2 to 3 inches apart in a bed. When you switch to seeds of another kind of plant, add together $\frac{1}{2}$ the proper distance for each, and leave that much space between the two plantings. When you plant in hills, or small groupings, don't put all the seeds in the same spot; leave the suggested space between them.

Even if you don't have garden beds, scatter-sowing in a wide band will give you some of the space-saving benefits of bed planting. Growing small leafy or root crops in bands a foot or more wide, instead of single file, uses space more efficiently and still lets you easily reach in to tend

---

ADDING AMENDMENTS AND FERTILIZERS

Rock fertilizers and well-decayed organic matter, such as compost, rotted manure, and peat moss, can be mixed into the soil on the day that you dig it. Soluble commercial chemical fertilizers and high-nitrogen organic fertilizers such as blood meal can also be applied the same day that you plant, but they should not be mixed evenly into the soil. To keep the concentrated chemicals from burning plant roots, apply these materials 2 to 3 inches to one side of the seeds. As an alternative, place them 2 to 3 inches below the seeds. The fertilizers will dissolve and move downward when you water, and the roots will grow into the fertilized area without being burned.

You must wait several weeks before planting an area where you have turned a cover crop or other undecayed organic matter, such as fresh manure, kitchen garbage, or weeds, into the soil. Fresh manure can harm plants by burning them. All fresh organic matter deprives plants of nutrients, because it is broken down by soil microorganisms that devour the nutrients to fuel their activity. (These microorganisms are different from the ones that release soil nutrients for plant use, which will be less active at this time.) In addition, some of the microorganisms and soil insects that feed on fresh organic matter may attack the roots of living plants.

PRE-SPROUTING CROP SEEDS

Sometimes you can improve your success rate by pre-sprouting the seeds—that is, getting them to germinate before you plant them. Carrot, celery, and parsley seeds are sometimes pre-sprouted to shorten their long germination periods. Corn is often pre-sprouted to be sure that the seeds have the warmth they need while germinating. Other seeds can be pre-sprouted, although it will not help beans and peas—in fact, experiments have shown that pre-sprouting lessens their vigor.

Arrange the seeds between two dampened paper towels placed on a plate or tray. Keep the towels moist until the seeds swell and the root tips just begin to push their way out. Large seeds can be uncovered and planted individually. If you were careful to space small seeds the right distance apart, you can plant them, towels and all, at the recommended seeding depth; the roots will grow through the towel, which will soon disintegrate in the seedbed.

and harvest the plants from paths between the bands.

Large seeds can be planted individually where you want them. It is possible to plant small seeds the same way, but scattering them is easier and just as effective. Decide how many square feet to devote to a crop and sow the seeds over that area. You may want to sow small seeds thicker than usual as insurance against seedling loss, but you don't want a solid mat of seedlings. To prevent this, mix small seeds with sand, sieved compost, or damp milled sphagnum moss before scattering them.

Gardeners with limited space often try to squeeze in as many plants as they can. Most plants should be spaced far enough apart so that at maturity their leaves just touch those of the next plant. There should be at least 1/2 to 1 inch between the mature roots of a root crop. Some crops, such as kohlrabi, are very sensitive to crowding and will not mature properly when spaced closer than the seed packet suggests. Other crops, such as bush beans, don't mind being a little jostled.

Closer spacing will give you more plants in the same area, but generally, each plant will be less productive. If the plants are only moderately crowded, the total harvest will be bigger than if you had used the recommended spacing. However, each crop has a point beyond which crowding will decrease total yield. You can jam in more plants when you are planning to harvest them young—for example, baby beets or mustard greens. Another special case is the seeding bed. Close spacing doesn't

matter, since you'll be transplanting the seedlings to another, permanent bed when they are still small.

For planting depth, follow the advice on the seed packet. The rule of thumb is to plant at a depth two to three times the diameter of the seed. In very sandy soil or during one of our uncommonly warm spells, plant a bit deeper to lessen the risk of the seeds drying out. In clay soil or during cold weather, plant a bit shallower. Seeds that must struggle to find the surface, especially in cold soil, may rot before they break through.

Putting the Seeds In

When planting individual seeds, use your finger or a small stick to make each planting hole the recommended depth. When planting seeds in a row, open a furrow with a trowel or other tool, then drop the seeds in and gently firm the soil back on top.

To scatter-sow, skim off a thin layer of soil and pile it on one side of the planting area. Working in 1- to 4-square-foot blocks marked off with stakes will help you keep track of your progress when you are sowing a large area. After scattering the seeds, sprinkle soil from the pile until the seeds are covered to the desired depth.

The soil used to cover seeds should be fine and well pulverized, with no rocks or large pieces of organic matter that may block the emerging seedlings. If your soil is clayey, you will get better results by covering the seeds with dampened sifted compost, potting mix, or milled sphagnum moss.

MAKING A SEED GLASS

If you are new at gardening or are growing an unfamiliar crop, you may have trouble recognizing the tiny seedlings when they emerge. The seed leaves of most plants look very different from the true leaves. To the inexperienced eye, weed seedlings may look like crop seedlings—or worse, the crop seedlings may resemble weed seedlings and get pulled! Here is a method that will help you identify the seedlings that you are growing.

You will need a paper towel and a straight-sided clear drinking glass or wide-mouthed jar, 1-1/2 to 2 1/2 inches in diameter. Fold the towel roughly in thirds, so that it is as wide as the glass is tall. Roll it into a tube that is about the same diameter as the glass. Insert the towel tube and push it against the inside of the glass so that it opens a bit and rests on the glass in several places. Pour an inch or so of water in the bottom of the glass. When the towel has absorbed water to the top, pull it back in several places and drop a seed in, until there are five to ten seeds resting partway down around the glass. Place the glass in a warm room and check it daily to be sure that there is water in the bottom.

You can start a seed glass anytime, but if you start it on the same day that you sow the seeds outdoors, you will get an idea of what is happening beneath the soil. The seeds in the glass will probably germinate ahead of the seeds sown outdoors if your house is warmer than the garden soil. Notice that the roots grow before you see shoots; this tells you that the garden-planted seeds are active before you see them break through the surface. When shoots begin to form on the seedlings in the glass, move the glass to a brighter place for a few days, so that the seedlings will develop normally enough to be identified. Seedlings germinated this way will not transplant well and should be discarded.

Fold a paper towel in thirds, then roll it into a tube with about the same diameter as the glass.

Moisten the towel and plant seeds between it and the glass—the seedlings will show you what to expect in your garden.

Use your hands to firm the soil over the seeds, but don't walk on the seedbed. (I remember Dad asking me as a small child to walk barefoot down the just-planted rows. It only took one try as an adult to realize why he had asked *me* to do it!) The soil should press against the seeds, but not so tightly that the seeds can't push out.

Use small sticks to mark off the area that you planted. If you are planting several crops at the same time, put in plant labels or draw a map so that you will remember what you planted and where you planted it. Water the seedbed thoroughly, using as fine a spray as possible so that you won't disturb the seeds. Keep the soil surface moist with frequent, light waterings for several weeks, until the seedlings are a couple of inches high.

Protecting Seedlings

Germinating seeds and small seedlings demand special attention during their first few weeks, when they are especially vulnerable to pests and to competition from weeds and from other crop seedlings growing too close to them.

Clear potential pests from the seeding area before you plant, and consider using barriers to protect your seedlings until they are growing well. If snails are your worst problem, you can reduce the hazard considerably by nailing copper strips around the frame of a planting bed. Sprinkling weed leaves on the seedbed may discourage cats. (For more information on protecting seedlings from pests, see the individual pest listings in Chapter 10.)

For severe pest problems, a floating row cover provides maximum protection. Place the cover over a large planting or cut it into pieces to protect individual plants or small groups of plants. Start with a piece larger than the area you wish to protect so that you can gather the material to form a loose center, giving the seedlings a little room to grow. Tuck the edges firmly into the soil all around. For convenience in tending the seedbed without having to remove the row cover and tuck it in each time, stretch the cover over a wooden frame. A rectangle built from 1x4s will protect seedlings. To protect taller plants, build an open-sided frame made of 1x1s. Let the row cover extend below the frame, then staple it to the

TROUBLESHOOTING

What if you wait twice the number of days suggested on the seed packet and still nothing comes up? What could have gone wrong? Consider these possibilities, keeping in mind that there may be more than one cause. Plant again, this time taking precautions and watching more closely.

- The seeds may have dried out in the middle of germination. Did the weather suddenly turn hot, or did you forget to water? Did you neglect to firm the soil in the seedbed?

- The seeds may have rotted. Did you plant much earlier than recommended? Did you plant too deep? Did you water clay soil too much, especially during cold weather?

- The seeds may have been too old to germinate. Did you keep the seeds too long before planting them? Corn and onion seeds last only a year or two; others last up to five years if they are kept cool and dry.

- The seedbed may have been damaged. Cats often ruin seedbeds because they love to dig in freshly turned soil. Sometimes people accidentally tread on unmarked seedbeds, crushing the seedlings before they come up.

- An insect or other animal pest may have eaten the seedlings before you even noticed that the plants were up. Snails, slugs, cutworms, earwigs, pillbugs, sowbugs, birds, and rabbits are among the local pests that eat seedlings. Sometimes they gobble young plants so quickly that you are positive that nothing came up. If you keep close watch, however, you will see the tiny seedling stems, shorn of their leaves, standing for a day or so before they wilt to nothing.

FLOATING ROW COVERS

These translucent lightweight materials, similar to nonwoven interfacing used in sewing, offer many benefits to gardeners. Pests can't get through them, but light and water can. The air under them is several degrees warmer than the surrounding air. They also reduce evaporation, keeping the soil beneath them more evenly moist.

Floating row covers have other advantages over clear plastic sheets. When you use a floating row cover in spring or fall, you should never have to rush out and lift it to keep the plants from scorching. In our cool, foggy summers, only rare heat waves will necessitate removal of the cover. A floating row cover can usually rest directly on the plants, without any stakes to hold it up—although in very windy sites it may require support to prevent injury to seedlings.

The drawbacks are minimal. The area under a floating row cover receives somewhat less light. The covers are available in different weights, and if pest protection is your main goal, use a lightweight material that blocks as little as 5 percent of the light. Floating row covers may make your garden look like a laundry after a windstorm has blown through, but the untidiness is a small price to pay for sneaking tender seedlings past hungry snails and other pests. (The Resources Appendix includes suppliers of floating row covers.)

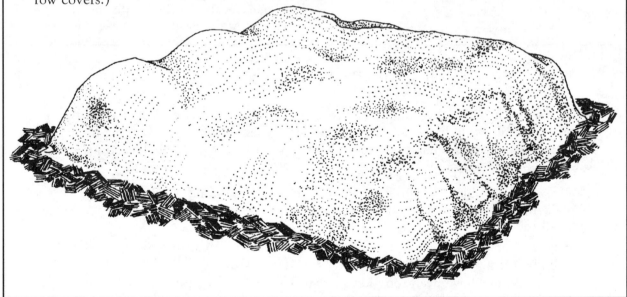

inside of the wood. To prevent entry by pests, press the frame partway into the ground.

Weeds compete with tiny crop seedlings for water, nutrients, and light. See Chapter 9 for information on weed control, including methods of presprouting weeds to clean up a seedbed before you plant.

As damaging as weed competition can be, competition from other seedlings is just as serious, because they are vying for the same nutrients in the same tier of soil. The result is smaller, weaker plants. Unless you are growing a crop for harvest when it is very young, thin the plants when they are still small, before they have begun to crowd each other. Use scissors to cut the unwanted seedlings at ground level so that you don't damage the roots of the remaining plants. Seed packets usually provide instructions for thinning. For example, a packet may recommend sowing seeds 2 to 3 inches apart and, when the plants are 2 to 3 inches high, thinning them to 4 to 6 inches apart. Also look for any special instructions for individual vegetables in Chapter 11.

Growing Your Own Transplants

Although raising transplants takes time and care, it is cheaper than buying nursery starts and it gives you many more options. Homegrown transplants, just like purchased ones, allow earlier planting, withstand pests better than direct-seeded plants, and save garden space. You can start transplants indoors anytime, or you can sow seeds in a special garden bed during warmer weather. In June you can use a square foot of space as a seeding bed for growing beet and broccoli transplants, which you can move to a permanent spot in your vegetable garden in July after you harvest garlic or a spring lettuce crop.

When you produce your own transplants, you have a wider choice of varieties. Nurseries can't possibly carry all the new varieties developed every year. The public expects to find the most common varieties at the nursery, which leaves little room for less familiar varieties that may be better suited to our area. Sometimes the best choices for your microclimate are available only as seeds. The broccoli transplants in nurseries are almost always short-season varieties, not the long-season, overwintering ones that do so well in our mild winters. Pepper seedlings are likely to be 'Yolo Wonder,' whereas several other varieties, such as 'Gypsy' and 'Early Cal Wonder,' bear more fruit in a borderline microclimate.

Another advantage of growing your own transplants is greater control over timing. I often find that the seedling I want is not available at the nursery when I want to plant it. I want broccoli transplants in July, but they usually don't arrive in nurseries until a month or so later. You don't have that problem when you grow your own.

Finally, it is fun to grow seedlings because there are almost always some to share. I start more than I need, because who knows how many will grow? Usually, most of them come up and reach transplanting age. After moving as many as I want into the garden, I wait a week for any disasters to happen. Once the cutworms or hailstorms have taken their toll, I fill in with some of the extra seedlings. Any that remain are for friends, to let them try new varieties and to celebrate nature's generosity.

You may choose to grow seedlings indoors because it's easier to keep an eye on them. I always start celery, parsley, leek, and onion seeds indoors, because they take so long to germinate and the plants are so slow in their initial growth that I am afraid I will overlook them in the garden.

It is important to know the best times to sow each kind of seed and how long it should grow before it is ready for transplanting. The seeding chart on the next page provides information on growing transplants for various vegetable crops.

Notice that there is often a range of times when seeds can be sown for transplants. When crops have a short planting season, as do cucumbers and brussels sprouts, it is a good idea to sow seeds at the beginning of the period suggested in the chart; if the sowing isn't successful, you can try again before it's too late. When the planting season is longer, as it is for beets or lettuce, you can start seeds every few weeks for a series of harvests.

Few crops benefit from being grown indoors longer than the time given in the seeding chart. Peppers and tomatoes may profit, but only if they are moved into large enough containers and given adequate light, water, and fertilizer. To grow them indoors for more than six to eight weeks, you would probably need a greenhouse, a large sunny window, or artificial lighting suitable for growing plants.

To start transplants indoors you will need a sterile potting mix, containers, drip trays, a warm place for germination, and a cooler, well-lighted place where the seedlings can grow.

Choosing a Seeding Mix

There are many recipes for seeding mixes, and no single right choice. The easiest course is to buy a seeding or potting mix. In addition to being sterilized, purchased mixes are formulated to hold air and moisture. Most mixes are adequate for seeding, but at the nursery you can request one with a finer texture. Or, if you already have a coarse mix, just sieve out the large particles before using it for small seeds. Although most commercial mixes work fine, occasionally you will run into a problem. I don't know why, but very few seeds came up in one mix that I tried some years ago. (Currently, potting mix manufacturers aren't required to reveal information such as nutrient analysis, pH, or salt content, but they may have to disclose it in the future.) Try planting a few seeds in a bit of the mix; if they

GROWING YOUR OWN TRANSPLANTS

When to seed:

These are the months during which it is most useful to start seeds to grow transplants. When there is more than one useful time to start seeds, I have listed it.

Reason:

I've given the most important reasons for growing your own transplants of each crop. There are often different reasons to grow transplants of a crop at different times of year. I've used the following codes to describe possible reasons:

EM=easier to monitor than in garden   PP=pest protection
ES=to get an early start   SS=to save garden space
NN=not in nursery at time needed   DV=to get different varieties

When more than one reason is given for planting at a particular time, they are listed in order of importance, with the most important reason first.

Time Required:

This is the number of weeks you should allow between seeding the crop and transplanting seedlings into the garden. It includes time for hardening off.

Pot Up?:

Here is an indication of whether or not the crop is easily, or usually, or even can be, moved to a larger pot before it is planted out in the garden. Yes means it can be and often is done. Possible means it is possible but not usually done. No means it's not done.

Starred (*) crops are the ones you may find most useful to grow as transplants. These are the crops that transplant best and give you the greatest benefits in terms of an early start and/or protection from pests.

Except for leeks and onions, seedlings that you are about to transplant to the garden should be roughly as wide as they are tall. Be especially careful not to let your bean, pea, squash, cucumber, pumpkin, or corn seedlings get overgrown before you transplant them. It is best in most cases to sow seeds of those crops directly in the garden, but if you do choose to grow seedlings for transplanting, plant them out when they have only 2 or 3 true leaves.

GROWING YOUR OWN TRANSPLANTS

CROP	WHEN TO SEED	REASON	TIME REQUIRED	POT UP?
Asparagus	Feb–April	EM, SS	8–12 weeks	yes
Basil*	March–May	PP, DV, ES	3–4 weeks	possible
Bean, Snap	Late March to Mid April	ES, PP	3–4 weeks	no
Beet*	Jan–Feb	ES	4 weeks	no
	April–July	SS	4 weeks	no
Broccoli*	Dec–Jan	ES, DV, NN	5–7 weeks	yes
	Feb–July 1	DV, NN, SS	5–7 weeks	yes
Brussels Sprouts*	May–June	DV, NN, SS	5–7 weeks	yes
Cabbage*	Dec–Jan	DV, ES, NN	5–7 weeks	yes
	April–July	DV, SS	5–7 weeks	yes
	Aug–Oct	DV, ES, SS	5–7 weeks	yes
Cauliflower*	June–Aug	DV, SS	5–7 weeks	yes
	Jan–April	DV, SS	5–7 weeks	yes
Celery*	Jan–Feb	EM, ES	8–12 weeks	possible
	July–Aug	EM, SS	8–12 weeks	possible
Chard	Dec–Jan	ES	4 weeks	yes
Chayote*	Nov–March	EM, ES, PP	4–12 weeks	yes
Chives*	Dec–Feb	EM, ES	4–6 weeks	possible
Collards*	Dec–Jan	ES	5–7 weeks	yes
Corn	Early April	ES	3–4 weeks	no
Cucumber	March–April	ES, PP	3–4 weeks	no
	April–May	PP	3–4 weeks	no
Kale	Dec–Jan	ES	4–6 weeks	yes
	Aug–Sept	SS	4–6 weeks	yes
Kohlrabi	June–July	SS	4–6 weeks	possible
Leek*	Dec–Jan	EM, ES	10–12 weeks	yes
Lettuce*	Feb–Sept	DV, EM, PP, SS	3–6 weeks or more	yes
	Oct–Jan	ES, EM, PP, DV	3–6 weeks or more	yes
New Zealand Spinach*	March	EM, ES	8–12 weeks	possible
Onion seed (for globe onions)	Sept–Dec	DV, EM, ES	6–8 weeks	yes
Onion seed (for green onions)	Any time	EM	6–8 weeks	no
Parsley	Dec–Feb	EM, ES	6–8 weeks	possible
	March–May	EM, SS	6–8 weeks	possible
Pea	Oct–Nov	PP, SS	3–4 weeks	no
	Jan–Feb	ES, PP	3–4 weeks	no
Pepper*	March–April	DV, ES	6–8 weeks or more	yes
Pumpkin	March–May	ES, PP	3–4 weeks	no
Spinach	Feb–Mar	ES, PP	4–6 weeks	no
Squash (winter)	March–May	ES, PP	3–4 weeks	no
Squash (summer)	Feb–May	ES, PP	3–4 weeks	no
Tomato*	Dec–April	DV, ES	6–10 weeks or more	yes

sprout, proceed with the planting.

Many gardeners like to make their own seeding mix. Some start their seeds in pure horticultural vermiculite (the mineral mica treated with heat). Others make mixes using various purchased materials. One common mix consists of equal parts horticultural vermiculite, perlite (a form of volcanic ash), and milled sphagnum moss. Another popular mix calls for equal parts loamy soil, milled sphagnum, and sharp builder's sand (not beach sand, which is too fine as well as too salty).

If you use garden soil in your mix, pasteurize it first. Otherwise, your seedlings will be exposed to diseases—particularly damping-off, probably the most common cause of death of seedlings grown indoors. (For information on damping-off, see Pests, Chapter 10.) Also pasteurize any seeding mix that you are reusing (see below).

Make sure that the medium is moist but not wet when you plant the seeds. Seeding mixes can be moistened right before you plant, since they contain much more organic matter than garden soil and are less likely to compact. If your mix is bone-dry, pour it into a large plastic container or bowl and add barely enough water to moisten it, then stir well with your hands.

A seeding mix needn't contain nutrients, since the newly emerged seedling draws on nutrients stored in the seed. Add fertilizer only after the seedling develops its second set of true leaves. Many commercial potting mixes contain fertilizer, but that may not be indicated on the bag and nursery workers don't always know. I usually watch the seedlings for good healthy color and fertilize if the color fades. A good fertilizer for seedlings is fish emulsion or a liquid houseplant fertilizer, applied at half the recommended strength once a week.

Choosing Seeding Containers

Almost any container 2 to 3 inches deep can be used for seeding. Deeper containers use more planting mix than necessary, since the seedlings will be transplanted before the roots are 3 inches long. Individual containers are the easiest to use, since you won't have to separate the roots at transplanting time. Six-celled nursery containers, paper cups, margarine and yogurt containers, and plastic or clay pots are all suitable for seeding transplants. If a container doesn't have drainage holes, puncture the bottom. Beware of large flats, such as those used in commercial greenhouses, because they produce more seedlings than most home gardeners can use.

Half-gallon milk cartons are useful for starting transplants. Cut them in half lengthwise and use the halves as flats in which to start small seedlings. Or cut them in half the other way and use the bottoms as 4-inch pots and the tops as square rings for starting fast-growing plants with delicate roots, such as squash and cucumbers.

To use the rings, set them in a drip tray, fill them with potting mix, and plant the seeds. At transplanting time you will be able to lift the cardboard rings over the seedlings without disturbing the roots. Position the whole plant, cardboard and all, over the planting hole and ease the soil ball through the ring into the hole. Level the soil and tamp it lightly over the rootball. Replace the ring, pushing it slightly into the soil to deter snails, slugs, and cutworms.

I rarely use purchased options such as peat pots or peat pellets, because they are expensive and I have observed that plant roots don't always grow through them as they are supposed to. I do use an Accelerated Propagation System (APS)

PASTEURIZING SOIL

Soil can be pasteurized in a regular oven, but it will reek unless you take precautions. Keep the odor to a minimum by using a large plastic broiling bag, sold in supermarkets for cooking meat. Place about a gallon of moistened soil in the bag, fasten the bag as directed on the label, and heat at 275°F for 30 to 40 minutes. You don't want the soil temperature to exceed 180°F, because higher temperatures will kill more of the helpful organisms in the soil and will also release dissolved salts, which are toxic to plant roots. To check the temperature, insert a meat thermometer through the bag. Do this toward the end of the heating time, so that the odor escapes only briefly.

ENOUGH LIGHT?

If the seedlings become tall and narrow, with small leaves, your growing location doesn't have enough light. This is most likely when you are trying to start transplants during the short, dim days of December and January.

If you aren't sure what a light-starved plant looks like, grow two small containers of seedlings indoors at the same time that you are starting the crop in your garden. Keep one container in the brightest spot indoors and the other in a dimly lighted room. After a while, compare the three plantings—the two indoors and the third planted in the garden. Lettuce is a good seedling to try, since you can start it outdoors during most of the year. (Beans or cabbage will also give you a clear idea of the problem.) If you have enough light indoors to grow reasonably sturdy lettuce seedlings, then you have enough light to grow most other seedlings for at least a few weeks.

If everything you grow indoors looks spindly, you may need a cold frame, a window greenhouse, or an artificial lighting setup. A perfectly good lighting setup can be made from an inexpensive fixture and two fluorescent bulbs. The bulbs can be cool white or one cool white and one warm white. To keep the tops of the seedlings 6 inches from the lights, either raise the fixture using hooks on chains, or lower the plants, using piled up bricks or newspapers that you reduce in height as the plants grow.

seed starter, the most foolproof seed-germinating system I've found. It consists of a tray of styrofoam cubicles (my favorite has twelve) that waters itself by means of an absorbent mat—soil in the open-bottomed cubicles stays wet because the mat wicks water up from a reservoir. With this gadget, you can sow seeds and then go out of town for a week without losing a single plant. If you use an APS system to grow more than one type of plant at a time, be sure that their germination times are similar, so that you can transplant them all at once. (The APS seed starter is sold by Gardener's Supply; see Resources, Appendix V.)

Used seeding containers can be a source of damping-off, although I have often simply washed them in plain water and had no problem. If you want to be sure, or if damping-off has been killing your seedlings, run dishwasher-safe containers through a cycle. Scrub other containers thoroughly, then soak them for ten minutes in 9 parts water and 1 part household bleach and rinse well.

Planting the Seeds

In each container, plant two or three seeds at the recommended depth. Pat the seeding mix gently but firmly, leaving the surface flat and level. Label the containers and note what you planted in a journal or calendar. You can buy plastic labels at a nursery, cut your own labels from cottage cheese or yogurt cartons, or use popsicle sticks. Write with a water-proof marking pen or a number two pencil. When you use an APS starter, you can draw a map of what you planted in it. (I've found it helpful to put an indelible ink mark on one corner of the tray, so that I can quickly see if it faces the same direction as the map that I have drawn.)

Water well with a gentle trickle or soft spray, or set the container in a pan of water and let the seeding mix absorb water, remembering to drain the pan as soon as the mix is thoroughly moist. Although a greenhouse is designed for dripping pots, the rooms in your home are not. Set your seeding containers in shallow baking pans, styrofoam trays from grocery purchases, or cafeteria trays from a restaurant supply store.

Keep the planting mix just moist, since excessive moisture encourages damping-off. Covering the containers with a plastic bag or a sheet of glass will help keep the moisture in, but don't make the cover airtight or let it touch the surface of the mix.

Until the seeds break through the surface, keep the containers in a warm location away from direct sunlight, such as the top of a refrigerator, water heater, radiator, or stove that has a pilot light. Different kinds of seeds have different optimum temperatures for germination, but most perform best when given more heat than the average room temperature (see page 45). They will still germinate if your house is cool, but it may take a few days longer. If your house is often chilly and you can't find a source of gentle heat, consider getting a set of heating cables for starting seeds.

Caring for the Seedlings

As soon as the first plants come up, take off any covering and move the containers to a cooler, brighter spot. A window or protected porch, where the temperature is 60° to 65°F during the daytime and cooler (but not below 50°F) at night is ideal. Check the soil daily, making sure that it doesn't get too dry or too soggy. The seedlings will bend a little to reach for the light, but they won't develop a permanent crook if you turn the containers daily. When you see the first true leaves forming above the seed leaves, thin to one plant per container or one plant every couple of inches in a flat. Choose the sturdiest seedlings and use scissors to clip the others at the soil surface, since pulling them out may damage the roots of the remaining plants.

Watch the seedlings closely to be sure that they are continuing to grow. Slowed growth indicates that the plants are becoming root bound—their roots have filled the pot and are beginning to circle it. Seedlings that become root bound may never grow to full size, so it is important to get your little plants into the garden or, if advisable for that crop, into larger pots.

Some plants can or should be potted up—moved to a larger pot to grow a little more before being planted outdoors. If you are going to pot up, you can go ahead as soon as the seedlings have developed their first true leaves. Be very careful when handling seedlings; they are fragile, and a light touch is essential. The usual advice to beginners is to handle seedlings only by the leaves, since the plant can grow new ones, but not to

touch the stem, since the seedling will die if the stem is broken. Use an old spoon or fork to lift plants from a flat, getting as much soil as possible with each plant. With six-packs, push the plants out from the bottom. Move each seedling to a container that is 2 to 4 inches in diameter, such as a small plastic pot or the lower half of a quart or half-gallon milk carton with drainage holes punched in the bottom. Put some fresh potting mix in the container and set the seedling at the same level at which it was growing. Fill potting mix in around the seedling, press down carefully but firmly, and water well. Keep newly potted seedlings out of strong light for a day or two.

If a seedling is potted up twice before it is moved to the garden, add a little sieved compost or composted manure to the potting mix for the final pot. You don't need to pasteurize it, since seedlings become less susceptible to damping-off as they grow older.

Hardening Off the Seedlings

Plants can't be moved directly from your living room or kitchen to the more demanding environment of the garden. While they are still in their containers, they need gradual exposure to outdoor temperatures and light intensities—a process called hardening off. Prepare them by withholding fertilizer and keeping the soil on the dry side for about a week. When you begin this process, block off any seedlings that are growing in flats. Run a knife through the soil between the seedlings, forming 2-inch blocks with one plant each. Blocking off keeps the roots of seedlings separate and lets the cut ends heal before you transplant.

Every day for a week or more, leave the plants outdoors for gradually longer periods, but bring them in at night. Put them in the shade at first, then in a partly sunny place, and finally in a location as sunny as your garden plot. Don't leave them where they will be whipped around in the wind, and be sure to bring them indoors if frost is expected. If you can't harden off the plants as gradually as you would like, just do the best you can. As an alternative, place them in a cold frame in a shady spot; you needn't bring them indoors at night unless the weather is expected to turn very cold. (See page 58 for more on cold frames.)

Transplants from a nursery have already been hardened off before you buy them. Buy nursery starts no more than a few days before you intend to plant them. Keep them outdoors, but not in the hot sun, because the small amount of soil in the container will dry out quickly. Water them lightly to keep the soil moist. Don't add any fertilizer before you plant the seedlings in the garden, since you don't want to encourage rapid growth until the plants have more space for roots.

Moving Transplants Into the Garden

The best time to move transplants—either purchased or homegrown—is the afternoon or evening of a foggy or overcast day. I've broken the rules and transplanted seedlings on very hot mornings when I was pressed for time, but that makes the process riskier. Seedlings transplanted in hot weather need extra protection and careful monitoring for the first few days. The garden soil should be moist but not soggy. During late winter and early spring it may be a bit wetter than is ideal for seeding. This is all right for transplanting, if you are careful not to pack it down too much.

The space between transplants, as between seeds, should equal the diameter of a mature plant. Closer spacing is possible but there is a limit to how much a crop can be crowded. A recent experiment showed that you can get more heads of broccoli per unit of garden space by placing two plants in the same hole, although there must be adequate space separating each pair of plants from adjoining pairs.

Dig a hole as wide and as deep as the soil mass of the root ball. Use a trowel to mix any compost or powdered rock fertilizer into the underlying few inches of soil. Dig the hole a bit deeper if you are planning to add a commercial chemical fertilizer or a high-nitrogen organic fertilizer, such as blood meal. Mix it in well and place an inch of plain soil above the mixture so that the roots won't come in contact with the fertilizer right away.

Turn the pot over, supporting the plant stem between your first and second fingers, and tap the bottom. If the container is made of flexible plastic, push it enough to bend it and force the soil out. (You may have to run a knife around the inside of the container to release the soil, but usually this is not necessary.) Pull off the pot and set it aside, then use the same hand to cradle the soil ball. If the plant is root bound, gently open circling roots at the bottom of the root ball before planting. Set the plant in the hole at the right depth and use the other hand to fill the soil back in around it.

Most seedlings should be planted at the same depth as they were growing, but there are exceptions. If a seedling falls over despite careful planting, it probably developed with too much of the upper root exposed. Reset the plant deeper so that it stays upright. Tomatoes and cole crops, such as broccoli, cabbage, and cauliflower, should always be set a little deeper than they were growing (see details in individual crop entries in Chapter 11). Firm the soil around each plant, but avoid touching the stem.

Generally, soil around transplants should be level. Don't plant on a mound, or push soil up around stems, or plant in depressions. (Planting on a wide mound is sometimes useful in clay soil, but not little individual mounds.) If you want to sculpt soil to make watering easier, you may make a raised lip around the seedling and a few inches from the stem on each side. The lip will wash away in a couple of weeks, but won't be needed by then.

Sometimes you will find seedlings bunched together in a container. To separate them, tease the roots apart gently, then gently tug the plants apart. The roots of some may be damaged so much that the plants should be discarded. Still, buying or growing seedlings this way can be economical, as you can usually separate the majority successfully if they aren't too entangled.

When you finish transplanting, water the plants thoroughly, wetting the leaves (even those of tomatoes) but taking care not to knock over the plants. If you are going to stake the plants, drive the stakes now, before the roots spread out or the plants sprawl. You can apply a mulch now or later, remembering to keep it a couple of inches away from the stems. (See page 77 for information on when and how to mulch.)

Caring for Transplanted Seedlings

Although both nursery and homegrown transplants are usually less delicate than germinating seeds, they are still very vulnerable in the first week or two after transplanting. They can succumb to transplant shock—a combination of root damage and sudden exposure to a harsher environment. Also the tender young plants are so appetizing that they can be an overnight sensation with certain kinds of pests.

Transplants will always undergo some transplant shock, but it can be minimized by the skill with which you plant them. Treat the roots gently, since damaged roots mean that the plant can't take

COLD FRAMES

Small covering structures that provide a protected environment in which to start seeds and grow seedlings are known as cold frames. You can build a permanent cold frame—a raised wooden frame partially filled with soil—in a sunny corner of the garden, or you can make portable cold frames to place over seedbeds or transplants wherever they are growing.

A cold frame for a small garden typically provides 4 to 6 square feet of growing space. The top covering, which must let in light and hold heat, is usually set at a slight angle, lower on the south side, so that the sun will shine on it more directly. (In a permanent cold frame, you can also slant the soil to catch more sun.) Glass and plastic film are the most commonly used coverings. Since even our winter days are rarely very cold, and occasionally may be quite warm, glass- or plastic-topped cold frames must be ventilated.

You can buy a thermostatically operated cold frame opener, but the open lid can serve as a snail portal, locking snails in as the cold frame automatically closes. As an alternative, build a cold frame covered completely with a porous material such as a floating row cover. A compromise is to make an open cold frame, consisting of just a top and two sides. Snails will get in, but in no greater numbers than in the garden at large, and they won't be trapped inside to devour everything in sight. Neither a porous nor an open-sided cold frame is quite as warm as a glass- or plastic- covered one, but either offers some protection from the cold without inviting snail damage.

Another way to deter pests is to put the cold frame on a sturdy garden worktable. Treating the table legs with a sticky substance such as Tanglefoot™, which is available at most nurseries, will discourage insects from climbing up, and wrapping copper strips around the legs will keep snails away.

up as much water and nutrients. The shock will be even more severe if the transplant wasn't properly hardened off or if the weather turns unexpectedly hot, cold, or windy. Experience will tell you when transplants need special help adjusting to their move. You will probably lose a few plants as you learn, but soon you will develop a sense of when

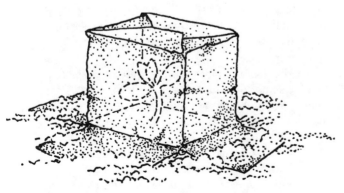

A paper bag will provide shade for new transplants.

and how to protect seedlings.

All transplants appreciate some shade during the first day or two to slow the loss of water from their leaves. A board or piece of cardboard stuck in the ground to the southwest of the seedlings and leaning over them may do the trick. A paper bag torn partway at the four corners, then inverted and anchored with soil on the flaps, is another option. Don't leave the bags on past the second day, or the plants won't be able to handle full sunlight and various pests may use the bags as feeding chambers. I often put weeds to work for my new transplants. I sprinkle a light covering of seedless and rootless weed clippings, such as dandelion or dock leaves, on the seedlings. The fresh weed clippings will shade the plants at first, letting more light in as they dry out. They will also humidify the air around the plants with the moisture they lose.

If the transplants were hardened off well enough and the root damage was not severe, the young plants won't need shade after the first couple

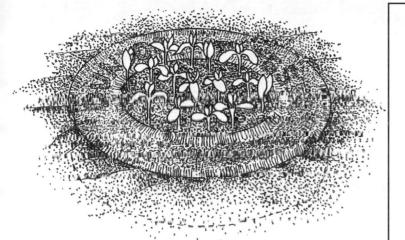

A tubeless tire will protect seedlings from the cold.

MINI-GREENHOUSES

A step beyond a cold frame, a mini-greenhouse is a structure for housing one or several plants through all or part of the growing season. It is most useful for protecting tomatoes, peppers, eggplants, and other crops that perform best in summers warmer than ours. Minigreenhouses must be tall enough to accommodate growing plants and either removable or easy to reach into to tend the plants.

One type of minigreenhouse consists of polyvinyl chloride (PVC) pipe arched over beds and covered with a floating row cover or clear plastic. Another type is an open-topped corral made by wrapping a piece of floating row cover or clear plastic over stakes placed around a plant. A third option is to construct a large framework of wood or PVC and cover its top and sides. One side covering can be attached at the top only and weighted at the bottom, so that you can lift it and place it on top of the frame when you tend the plants. The larger the frame, the harder it is to make it snailproof, so be prepared to hunt the pests.

Minigreenhouses are a good place to experiment. Start several plants of the same variety at the same time inside the mini-greenhouse and outside in the open garden; check their progress to see if the protected plants produce any faster than the unprotected ones.

of days. However, if plants weren't properly hardened off or if they were kept in a dimly lighted place too long after coming from the nursery, they may burn on very sunny days for the first week or two. Sunburned leaves either turn white or become brown and crisp. If you put the plants in partial shade when the damage is still minimal, you may save them. In the future, try to prepare transplants better for the outdoors.

Plants that are properly hardened off will have developed some resistance to cold and their growth probably won't be stopped by cold nights. Still, sometimes you may want to provide special cold protection—for example, when you plant warm-season crops extra early in spring. Any warmth that is gained from a protective device will help speed plant growth.

Portable cold frames, plastic jugs with the bottoms cut off, and purchased hot caps (little covers made of translucent paper) are among the common protectors.

Wall O' Water™ is a commercial product consisting of a ring of upright, water-filled plastic tubes that surrounds seedlings. Sometimes gardeners build low structures of stakes or arches with clear plastic over them. Floating row covers will also protect individual plants or entire rows and planting beds from the cold. Black plastic used as a mulch between plants will help warm the soil (see page 79). Old tubeless tires can also provide protection. Bury a tire on its side, leaving the upper side exposed to the sun, and fill the hollow with soil. The exposed black rubber will absorb some heat and radiate it back into the soil. Tomatoes, squash, peppers, and eggplants are good crops to plant in the soil-filled center.

The local pests most likely to attack new transplants are birds, cutworms, earwigs, the imported cabbageworm (on cabbage-family plants), slugs, and snails. Among the most vulnerable seedlings are basil, beans, cabbage-family plants, lettuce, and peas. For specific advice, read first about the crop that you are transplanting and then about the pests likely to attack it. However, only experience will teach you the problems of your particular garden. For example, the pea seedlings in some gardens may be eaten to the ground in fall and winter, whereas in other gardens they may grow unscathed. You neither want to spend hours building fortifications against pests that will not strike, nor do you want to forget about your seedlings for a week and return to find them gone. Experience gained in your particular garden—and only that—will show you the balance.

If you are just beginning to garden, you won't know which pests will attack. Plastic strawberry baskets placed over the transplants and weighted with a stone are a good light defense. This barrier will stop birds, rabbits, and large snails (after midsummer baby snails will crawl right through the mesh). An effective cutworm defense is a cardboard, plastic, or metal ring around the plant (see page 141).

Guard against pests when you use protective devices. For example, when planting in tires, set the tires deep enough and fill with soil to the top of the hollow to keep snails from crawling inside. Beware of devices that have openings only big enough to admit snails; once they get inside, they may be unable to find their way out and thus be forced to live on the only available vegetation—namely, your precious seedling.

Gardeners sometimes cut off the bottoms of plastic jugs or glass bottles so they can be set over seedlings. If you do this, exclude pests by covering the mouth of the container with a piece of cloth or floating row cover attached with a weatherproof plant tie. (You can't just screw the lid on a jar, because the lack of ventilation will cause the plants to fry in the sun.) If you use a floating row cover, be sure to tuck the edges firmly into the soil all around. Check your Wall O' Water™ every couple of days for snails, which can usually be found on the interior walls and in the water-filled tubes just above the water line.

As long as the transplants look fine, don't worry if they don't seem to grow much for a week or even several weeks. They are working hard to repair roots and toughen up. When you see new growth beginning, you will know that they, and you, have successfully weathered the delicate period.

Instead of Seeds: Other Ways to Start Plants

Some plants rarely or never produce seeds and must be reproduced by vegetative, or asexual, means—from underground structures, such as bulbs and tubers, or by division, cuttings, or layering. Even when plants can be seeded, they are sometimes reproduced more efficiently when you bypass the seeding process and use a vegetative method.

Although most vegetable crops are best grown from seed, a few are not. Potatoes rarely form seeds and are almost always grown from tubers, called seed potatoes, which are either planted whole or cut into pieces. Onions, garlic, and shallots can be grown from seed, but they mature much faster from small bulbs, known as sets. Artichoke and rhubarb also mature very slowly from seed and so are usually grown from divisions, made by cutting the thickened base of the plant into sections and allowing each to grow into a separate plant. Many common perennial herbs are rarely started from seed, because they grow *very* slowly as seedlings. Also, seedlings of the same type of herb often vary dramatically in scent and flavor; growing a new plant from a cutting, or piece of the parent plant, ensures that the new plant will have the same taste and smell. At least two perennial herbs, French tarragon and lemongrass, never flower and can be reproduced only by vegetative means.

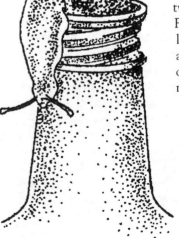

If you use a bottle to protect seedlings, cover it to exclude pests!

Many perennial flowers and fruit crops are also best propagated by vegetative means. Perennial flowers often grow into a clump that becomes so crowded that fewer blossoms are formed. When the clump is divided into several plants, each blooms more freely. Fruit trees are usually reproduced by cuttings or by grafting the stem of a plant that produces good fruit to the roots of a compatible plant that grows well in local soils. Most gardeners buy fruit trees already grafted, but you may want to try the technique. (For books about vegetative propagation and grafting, see Appendix VI, Suggested Reading.)

Division, stem cuttings, ground layering, and root cuttings are relatively simple techniques that allow us to make new plants from ones that are already growing. Novice gardeners are often reluctant to cut off part of a plant or plunge a spade into the roots of a plant to divide it. It may seem less natural than growing a plant from seed or too advanced for a beginner, but plants are more than willing to reproduce in these ways. Learning these techniques will reduce the need to purchase new plants when older ones need renewing.

Look up information about each type of plant that you want to propagate, either in this book or another reference, to see which methods are recommended, the best time of year to use them, and other important details. Hedge your bets: try several cuttings or layerings at a time but leave some of the plant, or several plants, intact in case something goes wrong.

Division

This involves cutting a large perennial plant clump into several sections, each with shoots and roots. You can divide clumps of small plants growing close together, such as clumps of chives, or multistemmed plants growing from underground runners, such as sweet woodruff or mint. If a plant grows from a thickened crown with a number of sites bearing smaller roots and shoots—for example, artichoke or rhubarb—you can cut the crown into chunks, each of which will grow into a new plant. Lemongrass is an example of another kind of clump that can be divided. It has many stalks, each of which has actively growing roots or the beginnings of roots.

Often you will want to divide the entire plant or clump of plants into smaller ones, but in some cases you may choose to remove one or more sections, leaving the parent plant to grow where it is. Just tuck the soil back around the base of the parent and keep it well watered for a few weeks while it heals and re-establishes roots.

Generally, divide a plant when it is dormant—when there is the least active growth occurring above the ground. In our mild climate, divisions are most often made in late autumn or late winter before new growth starts, typically in February. Plant the divisions right away in a well-prepared bed and keep them well watered, as you would transplants, for the first few weeks.

Stem Cuttings

This method of reproduction consists of cutting pieces of stem and inserting them in a potting mix, where they will grow roots and develop into new plants. Cuttings that are taken when the plant is actively growing, but not blooming, are known as softwood cuttings. Chrysanthemums, French tarragon, lemon-verbena, rosemary, sage, scented geraniums, and thyme are good subjects.

Snip off 3 to 5 inch stem tips and remove the leaves from the bottom half. Dipping the cuttings into a rooting hormone will increase your chances of success, but it's not always necessary. Bury the lower half (basal end) of the cuttings into a shallow container filled with ordinary potting mix or a purchased propagation mix. Typically, propagation mixes are very porous to reduce the possibility of decay, and to provide good aeration. They usually have no plant nutrients, or very low levels of nutrients, as these may inhibit initial root growth and encourage decay.

Place a clear plastic bag loosely over freshly planted cuttings, lifting it briefly every day or two to let in fresh air. Keep stem cuttings out of direct sunlight until roots have formed. Regularly check the cutting mix to be sure that it is moist, but don't keep it soggy. Once rooting begins, add half the recommended number of drops of liquid houseplant fertilizer to the water when you water the cutting mix. A cutting may succeed even if the leaves wilt or if some leaves drop, but you will know that the cutting was too immature to succeed if the stem wilts.

Expect to wait at least three to six weeks, and perhaps several months, for the cutting to develop into a rooted plant. You will know that it has rooted when you see new growth. Let the plant grow a bit longer to make sure that it is well established. Transfer each rooted plant to its own container and water it right away. Keep the plants out of direct sunlight for the first few days, then gradually expose them to conditions similar to those in the garden. When you see that they are growing well, plant them in the garden.

Ground Layering

The process of burying the stem of a growing plant so that roots form along it is known as ground layering. The rooted stem, which can be cut from the parent plant, will grow into a new plant. Layering works best in spring or summer, when the plant is actively growing. Any plant that can be grown from cuttings can also be reproduced by layering, which has the advantage of using the energy of the parent plant to nurse the new plant as it begins to grow.

Choose a low branch that can be bent to the ground and bury a section that is about 6 to 12 inches from the tip. You may improve your chances by preparing the stem: Remove any leaves on the part that will be buried. If the stem is thick enough to do so, notch the underside shallowly just below a leaf attachment point, then dip the notch into rooting hormone and insert a small twig or pebble to keep it open.

Dig a hole 3 to 4 inches deep and wide enough to bury the stem without breaking it. If the stem is too springy to stay buried well, weight the buried part with a rock or use a U-shaped metal irrigation bracket to hold it down.

Leave several inches of the branch tip above the soil. If it lies flat on the ground, tie it to a small stake to hold it more upright.

Keep the soil moist and watch for new growth, which signals that the propagation was successful. The process will take from several months to more than a year. Cut the old stem, then dig up the new plant and move it to a well-prepared garden site.

Root Cuttings

Some plants can be reproduced from root cuttings—pieces of root that sprout shoots and additional roots to become whole plants. Plants that will grow into new plants from root cuttings include comfrey, French tarragon, horseradish, and sea kale. Cut the roots into sections while the plant is dormant. You can either replant the cuttings directly in the ground or store them in containers in a dark place, replanting them during the season when active growth resumes. Either way, they should not be allowed to dry out.

Often the process is more successful if the roots are buried right side up, so conventions have developed for cutting the top and bottom ends of the roots differently. How you handle root cuttings depends on the kind of plant that you are growing; see the individual crop listings.

SEVEN

How to Water

INCE OUR WEATHER FROM April to October is essentially dry and our winter rains fickle, local gardeners must learn the best way to water a garden. Watering by the calendar—say, once or twice a week—doesn't work well, because the amount of water needed depends not only on rainfall but also on soil type, wind, sunshine, fog, temperature, day length, and the age of the plants. No one can give you a perfect watering schedule for your garden—but with a few guidelines and a season or two of practice, you can become so attuned to your garden's needs that you almost always water just right.

Here's the secret: for mature plants, water until the soil is holding all the moisture it can to a depth of a little more than 2 feet, then don't water again until the top 1 to 2 inches of soil have dried out.

Two inches of water applied to the surface (picture a 2 inch layer of water on the soil) will soak 2 feet deep in sandy soil; it takes 4 inches of water to penetrate to the same depth in clay loam soil. Water again when the top 1 inch of sandy soil and the top 2 inches of clay soil are dry. (The reason for the difference is that sandy soil is drier to a greater depth when its top layer has dried out.) When remoistening the top, you want to soak only 1 foot deep, so add only half as much water as you did to soak 2 feet deep.

This method may mean watering sandy soil as often as every two or three days during a hot spell and not watering clay soil for two weeks or more during foggy weather. It ensures that there is water deep in the soil where plant roots grow, and it allows air into the soil between waterings so that the roots can breathe.

Applying Water

You can water with a plain hose or one with a sprinkler or special nozzle attached, or you can use a soaker hose, drip irrigation, or various homemade soaking devices. A hose-end sprinkler is handy for watering seedbeds, but other methods are better as plants get bigger. Water on the leaves makes certain plants more susceptible to diseases and encourages snails and slugs. The weight of the water may pull some plants over. Also, sprinklers waste water, which evaporates from leaf surfaces and from droplets flying through the air.

A plain garden hose is perfectly adequate for watering a garden. Just leave it on the ground in one place while you work or relax, then move it to other areas of the garden. If the force of the water digs up the soil, tie a piece of burlap over the open end, or attach a soaker or fan-shaped nozzle.

A soaker hose, which consists of a long section of hose with tiny holes through which water seeps, will reduce the time spent moving a hose around. Screw the soaker hose into your regular hose when you are ready to use it. Plastic or rubber soaker hoses can be laid under mulch or buried as deep as 2 to 4 inches beneath the soil and left there all season. Or you may choose to leave the soaker hose on the surface, running it along a row or zigzagging it through a bed.

Today, the term "drip system" refers not just to

MAKING YOUR OWN CUSTOM WATERING DEVICES

Many gardeners use homemade devices to provide an even water supply to individual large plants, such as tomatoes and squash. One of the most common techniques is to sink a porous container—such as an unglazed clay pot or a plastic container with small holes punched in the bottom—into the soil next to a plant. Water poured into the container will seep slowly into the soil. These devices are particularly useful in sandy soil, since they get water deep into the soil, where it won't evaporate as quickly. Here are a few practical tips.

- When you use a clay pot, put a cork in the bottom hole and the entire pot will seep water.

- Use a hammer and a nail to punch holes in the bottom of a large empty can.

- If hammering a nail through a plastic container doesn't work, try heating the nail. Using a pair of pliers, hold the nail over a candle, then push the hot nail through the plastic.

- To avoid damaging roots, sink a watering device into the soil when the plant is still young. Locate it at least 3 inches from the plant.

- If you add a little manure or compost to the water, you can fertilize while you water. (See page 80 for directions for making manure or compost tea.)

polyethylene tubing with drip emitters attached, but to any low-pressure system that delivers water slowly. In addition to emitters that drip water, there are low-flow misters, minisprays, and minisprinklers. Drip is the most water-conserving method of irrigation and involves the least effort once it is set up. The slow delivery of water over an extended length of time keeps sandy soil from drying out and prevents irrigation runoff on clay soil. The disadvantages of drip are that it costs more than the other methods to install, and the tubing and emitters have to be worked around or removed when the soil is tilled. For larger plants, such as squash or artichoke, you can use a line with small side tubes to bring water to each plant. For small plants, such as radish or lettuce, you can use sets of parallel tubing with holes all along their length.

If you use a timer to automate drip or any other kind of irrigation system, don't just turn it on and forget it. Check occasionally to see that it is still working. With drip irrigation, you must also check for clogged emitters. An automated system must be adjusted to accommodate very hot spells or long foggy periods, and it should be turned off when there is a good rainfall. Don't let an automatic watering system get you into the habit of ignoring your garden. Your garden still needs other types of attention, such as weeding, staking, and harvesting.

How Much Is Enough?

You may wonder how you are supposed to divine what is going on under the ground. Is the soil wet only a few inches deep, or a couple of feet? Have you just added 2 inches of water, or 5 inches?

By late winter, the rains have usually saturated our soils to a depth of 6 feet or more. If you plant as soon as the soil near the surface is dry enough to work, you can assume that the deeper soil is still moist. At that time of year, you only have to worry about keeping the top layer watered. If you are starting a garden anytime from late spring to early fall in soil that has not been watered since the winter rains, you can assume that the soil has dried out and that you need to water thoroughly before planting. (Don't work the soil until it has dried a couple of days; to know when it is ready see page 82.)

Whether you are soaking dry soil or just moistening the surface, you will need to know how much water you are adding. The way to calculate this depends on your watering method. If you use a sprinkler, set out a coffee can or other flat-bottomed

---

CHECKING THE SOIL MOISTURE

You'll be more confident that you are watering correctly if you check the soil moisture before and after. Either dig a hole about 6 inches deep with a trowel or use a moisture meter. You can usually see a difference between dry and wet soil in the sides of the hole, or you can feel for moisture. When using a moisture meter, slowly push the probe into the soil to get readings at different levels.

Although you can get along fine without a moisture meter, you may want to buy an inexpensive one to use during your learning period. In fact, you may want to use both a trowel and a moisture meter the first couple of times, so you can *feel* what the meter readings mean. You will find yourself digging or probing a lot at first, but later you will need to do it only once in a while.

There are three times when a test with a trowel or moisture meter is especially useful: (1) to find out if the top 1-2 inches of soil are dry, (2) to make sure that you watered long enough so that you didn't leave a dry layer between wet layers (wait until the next morning to probe the soil), and (3) to find out if a light rain has wet the soil deeply enough so that you don't have to water.

---

container and measure the water accumulation after the sprinkler has run for an hour. From that, calculate how long it takes for an inch of water to collect in the container. When you run the sprinkler that long, you will be applying an inch of water. (By setting out several containers in different places and seeing if they fill at the same rate, you can tell if the spray pattern is well balanced. If the containers at the edges of the spray pattern didn't get as much water as the center, overlap the areas you water to give the edges extra moisture.)

If you water directly from a garden hose, either with or without a nozzle attachment, you can figure out how much water you are adding by measuring the time it takes to fill a gallon container. Put the hose into the container (attach any special nozzle that you plan to use), and turn on the water to a moderate flow. With a watch note how many seconds it takes to fill the container. To make the calculation easy, you can play with the flow until the container fills in thirty seconds. It takes 62 gallons to cover 100 square feet with a 1-inch layer of water. Of course, you will have to move the hose around to apply that inch evenly over the area. When your flow is adjusted to fill a gallon container in thirty seconds, it will take about thirty minutes to apply 1 inch of water to 100 square feet.

If it takes about thirty minutes to add 1 inch, it

will take 1-1/4 to 1-1/2 hours to add the 2-1/2 to 3 inches of water needed to soak clay soil 1 foot deep. By turning up the faucet, you can apply the water faster. If it takes fifteen seconds to fill the gallon container, you will be able to add 1 inch of water to 100 square feet in fifteen minutes, or 2 inches in thirty minutes. Don't apply water so fast that it runs off, as it almost certainly will in poorly amended clay.

Determining the flow from a soaker hose is much trickier, since a soaker hose may not emit water at the same rate as the garden hose alone, and it is difficult to measure the flow from all those holes. Your best bet is to run the soaker hose in the garden for a set period, such one or two hours, then check the soil moisture to see how deep the water has penetrated. From that, you can figure out how long to run the water in the future.

Drip and other low-flow emitters are made to emit a certain number of gallons per hour (gph). Drip emitters are usually available in flow rates of 1/2 to 4 gph. To figure out how long to run the system, either use the formula above (62 gallons = 1 inch over 100 square feet) or turn on the water for a certain amount of time and then check the soil moisture.

ANOTHER WATERING PHILOSOPHY

Despite what I've said about the benefits of deep, infrequent waterings, you will find that some gardeners believe in watering a vegetable bed a little every day or two so that the surface is constantly moist. This is a central tenet of French-intensive or biodynamic gardening. (See *How to Grow More Vegetables* by John Jeavons, listed in Appendix VI, Suggested Reading.)

Frequent, light irrigation may be fine if your soil is either sandy or very spongy with lots of organic matter, and it may be beneficial for fast-growing crops such as radishes and lettuce. However, it probably provides too much water for a garden planted in poorly amended clay soil. It is also inappropriate for slow-growing plants, including shrubs and trees, which grow better when given less frequent, deep waterings.

If you water frequently, you must not miss waterings since the plants will be more dependent on surface roots and thus more sensitive to a dry soil surface.

More Watering Wisdom

The rate of evaporation from the soil and from leaf surfaces is greater when the weather is dry, windy, warm, or sunny than when it is humid, still, cool, or cloudy. Large plants use and lose more water than small plants, and fast-growing, tender plants, including most vegetables, use more water than slow-growing, tough plants such as an established bougainvillea vine or a cactus. Plants are most harmed by a water shortage when they are growing rapidly—when seeds are germinating or when plants are forming large tender leaves, thickened roots, bulbs, tubers, flowers, or fruit.

Seedbeds are a special case. When the surface of a seedbed has been dry for half a day, water it briefly. Keep the surface moist until the seedlings have been up for a week or so, then gradually water less often as the roots grow deeper into the soil. Transplants also need plenty of water for the first week or two after they are in the ground.

Whenever you water keep the flow low enough so that the water soaks in as fast as it comes out of the hose. If water runs off the surface when you begin to water, turn the flow down. Runoff is often a problem in clay soil, since the tiny clay particles are so tightly packed that water enters slowly. The best remedy is to dig in plenty of organic matter before you plant. If water soaks in well at first but then begins to run off, you will know that you have watered long enough and no more water can enter until the water already in the soil penetrates deeper.

To help the soil absorb water some gardeners punctuate irrigation: they turn the water on and off in ten- or fifteen-minute cycles.

Since water runs off sloping surfaces, try to keep the beds and rows level or nearly so. If soil is slightly sloped, you can build raised lips around recent transplants to hold water until it can soak in (but don't plant in depressions). On a moderate slope, run planting rows along the contours rather than up and down. On a steep slope, make terraces (see page 35.)

Some gardeners sculpt the soil, even when there is no slope, to keep the water where they want it while it soaks in. They are following the lead of California agriculture, which often uses a system of raised rows with irrigation trenches between. Although I sculpt the soil for certain crops that require a lot of water, such as squash and cucumbers, my well-amended soil absorbs water so well that most crops don't need this special help.

Soaker hoses are an effective watering tool.

The Best Time to Water

You may read that the best time to water is the morning. It is true that early watering is appropriate if you are using a sprinkler, because it gives the plants plenty of time to dry before nightfall, when wet leaves are more susceptible to certain diseases. Also, there is less evaporation during the cooler, usually calmer early morning.

If you water at ground level and don't wet the leaves, you may do just as well to water a couple of hours before dark. Evaporation is low then because the sun is sinking and the sea breeze has usually died down.

Actually, the best time to water is when the plants need water and you have the time to provide it. Even midday watering (if that is your only available time and the plants are thirsty) is better than no watering. In some climates water might burn leaves in the midday sun, but this is not likely at the usual cool San Francisco temperatures.

Watering Through the Year

Your garden needs different amounts of water at different times of the year. With a little practice, you will learn to keep the soil moisture at the right level for your plants the year around.

Spring

You rarely need to water established plants before the end of February, but you may have to water to keep seedbeds moist. By April, most gardens begin to need regular watering. By May, don't count on nature to help water your garden: you're on your own until the fall storms begin.

Late spring rains can fool us. We may think that a light rain has watered our plants, when really it only moistened the surface. When you aren't sure, check the soil moisture with a trowel or moisture meter. Your neighbors may raise their eyebrows if they see you watering just after a rain, but you will know you are right to do so. I've even watered *during* a sprinkle! It was the only time I could get to my garden and I knew the sprinkle would let up before the soil was wet enough.

Hot spells, which often occur in April or May, can also surprise us. Our gardens may suddenly become very thirsty. When those glorious hot spring days come, remember to head to your spring seedbeds before you head to the beach or to the park.

SIGNS OF TROUBLE

Chronically underwatered plants are stunted. Their leaves lack a healthy luster and any fruit they make is undersized. Strawberries are small and rubbery. Carrots and other fleshy roots are smaller than normal and tough. Underwatered plants may show signs of nutrient deficiency, since roots take in nutrients from the soil via water. They are often more vulnerable to some pests, especially mites. Underwatered plants may wilt, and they will die if they've gone past the point where watering will revive them.

Overwatered plants suffer too. Their oxygen-starved roots often fall prey to fungus and other diseases. If rot sets in, the plants may turn yellow and they eventually wilt and die.

Wilting is a tricky symptom, because it may be due to dry soil, root rot caused by wet soil, or other damage to roots caused by pests and unrelated to soil moisture. Plants may wilt on an unusually hot day because the roots can't work fast enough to supply the plant with water. Squash plants often wilt on hot days but perk up in the cool of the night. If your plants are wilting from unaccustomed heat, help them out by sprinkling them lightly to cool the leaf surfaces.

Many vegetables respond badly to alternating periods of very dry and very wet soil. When moisture fluctuates too widely, carrots and cabbage heads split, and tomatoes develop blossom-end rot. Sometimes these problems develop when it rains heavily just before the crops are harvested. Adding plenty of organic matter to the soil and mulching will reduce the effects of fluctuating moisture.

Summer

The summer months are almost always rainless and the question is not whether to water, but how often. We typically have cycles of fog and sun, interrupted occasionally by a hot spell. It is often windy as well. Fog decreases the amount of water that your garden needs, and sun, heat, and wind increase it. Getting seeds and transplants started during the summer poses a problem, since the soil can dry out unexpectedly fast during hot, windy days. You can try planting at the beginning of a foggy period, but it is hard to predict how long these periods will last.

Heavy fog does occasionally turn to falling mist. While this doesn't moisten the soil much, it certainly reduces evaporation from soil and plants. Redwood forests in our region depend on fog drip as a major source of moisture. Fog condenses on tree leaves and then falls to the ground. However, if your garden is being dripped on by trees, it is probably in too much shade.

Summer is the vacation season. Before you leave on a trip, invite your garden sitter over to look at your plants. Point out where there are seedlings or recent transplants, or where maturing garlic should be left to dry. Draw a simple map of the garden identifying the plantings. If your sitter is not an experienced gardener, write out a regimen: "Water all areas except the garlic bed. Let the hose run with a low to medium flow, moving it often, for about one hour. Water on Tuesday and Sunday." Your schedule may not turn out to be perfect, but any schedule is safer than telling an inexperienced gardener to water when he or she thinks the garden looks dry.

As summer draws to a close, you may be tempted to ease off on watering, a typical gardening pattern in cold-winter regions. In those regions, many gardeners plant just once, in spring, and use up their harvest by the end of summer. They don't need to water as often because summer rainfall is common. If a dry spell comes late in the season, they may let it finish off the garden. They know that the first frost will do the same anyway. In our region, summer harvests often continue into November, sometimes even December, and crops for fall, winter, and spring harvests are actively growing in late summer, so we need to keep watering until the rains take over.

If you run out of energy to water your garden by the end of summer, stop to think why. Was it too hard to keep a poorly amended sandy soil watered?

If so, resolve to add more organic matter and to use a moisture-holding mulch. Did you grow vegetables that you didn't particularly like? Make note of the crops that weren't a chore to water and grow only those next year. Did you take on too much? Consider scaling down your vegetable, herb, and flower beds and planting some of the garden with low-maintenance, water-conserving landscape plants.

Fall and Winter

The early fall sprinkles may not be much help in watering your garden. Check the soil moisture, as you did in spring, with a trowel or moisture meter. Once the rains really get going, you may not have to water at all for several months, but then again maybe you will. If you are lulled into thinking that winter watering is unnecessary, one day you may find that your garden doesn't look as good or produce as well as it used to. (If you plan to be away during the winter, have a garden sitter ready to water, but only if little or no rain falls for more than two or three weeks.)

When you do need to water, you will find that there are fewer daylight hours in which to do it. Even during a dry winter, however, you will never have to water very often. The days are shorter and not as bright, since the sun's rays are dimmed by reaching the earth at a lower angle. The days and nights are cooler, evaporation decreases, and plants grow more slowly. Gardeners get to relax a bit.

Actually, in winter you must be careful not to overwater, especially if your soil has a high clay content. If there were fall rains, even if they were followed by a winter drought, the deep layers of your soil will probably still be quite moist. Water the surface layers, but don't overdo it: slowed evaporation in winter could leave your soil waterlogged for days.

Most vegetables that grow in winter, especially the cole crops, don't mind wet leaves. (Watch how rain rolls off cabbage or broccoli leaves.) The combination of cold and dampness can encourage rot, however, so try to keep moisture from collecting in plant crevices.

Trial and Error

You will soon get a feel for watering. You may be sitting in an office looking out a window and realize that it is the second warm day in a row, that you haven't watered for four days, and that your garden probably needs water. At first, you may guess wrong and find that your soil is drier or wetter than you expected. In time, you will become quite accurate.

Fine tuning your sense of how much to water various crops will take more than one season. For example, you may look back on your gardening year and realize that your strawberry plants were small and produced few berries. In reading again about strawberries and noting that ample moisture is needed, you resolve to provide more water next year. If you do and the result is a larger, more fruitful crop, then you will know that you have learned to water strawberries properly.

What If There Is a Drought?

Since central California is at the southern margin of a storm region centered in the Pacific Northwest, our rainfall is inconsistent. Some winters we find ourselves enjoying sunny days and listening to warnings that the snow pack in the Sierra may not be deep enough to fill our reservoirs for the summer. The luck of the draw means that this rarely continues for many years in a row, but it reminds us that it is risky building big cities and developing intensive agriculture in a semiarid region.

Drought or no drought, it is essential that we use water-conserving gardening methods every year: dig in plenty of organic matter, mulch, refrain from using sprinklers on windy days, and avoid runoff. When drought does come and water departments set quotas, it takes careful planning to have enough water for dishes, showers, flowers, and vegetables. Although vegetables and many flowers need quite a bit of water, you can still enjoy some fresh garden produce and bright blooms if you carefully plan your household water use and adopt water-wise gardening practices.

Conserve Household Water

Inspect your entire water system, indoors and outdoors, for leaks. Check your water meter for movement, over an hour or two, when no water is being used. (A water meter is usually located under a liftable cover in the sidewalk in front of the house.) Any movement at all indicates that water is leak-

ing. If food coloring dripped into the toilet tank colors the water in the bowl without the toilet having been flushed, you have found one leak to repair. Replace washers in any dripping faucets and hose connections, and install low-flow shower heads. Follow your water district's recommendations for reducing household water use.

Garden to Save Water

Decide on your gardening priorities to make the best use of your water allowance. Get rid of any thirsty ornamentals that you never liked much anyway. Don't grow more vegetables or flowers with high requirements for water than you can handle. If food crops went to waste last summer, plant a smaller area this year. Consider planting much of your nonedible landscape in drought-tolerant plants. Since all plants need extra water when they are first getting established, wait until fall so that the rains will help water the new plantings. (Several water districts in our area publish lists of drought-tolerant ornamentals.) Concentrate on gardening practices that make efficient use of water. Adding plenty of organic matter to your soil will mean less frequent watering, since well-amended soil is able to hold more water than soil that is poor in organic matter.

Broccoli leaves with water droplets

Compost, manure, and peat moss retain more moisture than barks or rice hulls.

Avoid deep turning of the soil; dig only when you are adding organic matter. Apply mulch around vegetables and ornamentals, and pull weeds before they can compete with desirable plants for moisture. You won't be able to stint on fertilizer for edible crops, but you can slow the growth and the water requirement of ornamentals and lawns by providing little or no fertilizer during the summer of a drought year.

Planting beds, raised or not, can save water, since the paths are left dry. When crops are planted close enough so that their leaves touch when the plants are mature, they form a living mulch that reduces evaporation from the soil. Form watering basins around plants or make channels between rows of plants to prevent runoff on slopes.

Take a good look at how you water. Water districts tell us that most gardeners overwater. Keep your garden moist enough to grow healthy plants, but make sure that you are waiting as long as possible between thorough waterings. Check the soil with a trowel or moisture meter (see page 65), and don't add water until the soil is dry 1 to 2 inches deep. Avoid overhead sprinkling, especially on hot, windy days. As a reminder to move your hose before you lose water to runoff or leaching, set an alarm clock or timer. You can buy a timer that attaches to the hose faucet and automatically turns off the water. Soaker hoses and drip irrigation, properly timed, can provide great water savings.

Use Gray Water

Used household water, sometimes called gray water, can help stretch your water supply but keep in mind possible hazards to human health and toxicity to plants. For health reasons, water containing bacteria and similar harmful organisms should be kept away from the edible parts of plants. These organisms generally don't live long in soil but there is no point in taking risks.

The cleanest used water is the water that runs out of the tap while you are waiting for it to get hot. Hold large plastic bottles under the tap or put a bucket or two in the shower. You can also save water used in washing, steaming, and boiling vegetables. Water from these sources is safe for all plants.

The next cleanest water is the water used for rinsing clothes. Some gardeners divert the final rinse water from their washing machines into the garden or a holding tank. Although this water will contain some soap and some bacteria associated with human beings, it is safe for ornamentals. Some gardeners use it for ground-level watering of plants like artichoke, corn, or fruit trees, which bear their edible parts well above the ground.

Wash water from the bathtub, shower, or washing machine will contain more soap and more bacteria associated with humans than water used only for rinsing. Direct this water only to ornamentals, freeing cleaner water for food crops. Don't reuse wash water at all if the wash contained diapers or if anyone in the household is ill with dysentery, infectious hepatitis, or typhus. It is probably best not to recycle dishwater.

Soap and detergent are relatively well tolerated by plants, but they are often formulated with other ingredients that may do harm. Avoid products that contain boron or borax. This ingredient may not be listed on the label, but often the name of the product will give it away. Don't water plants with gray water containing water softeners, fabric softeners, bleach, or any product that you aren't sure of. Phosphates are safe since phosphorus is a nutrient, but avoid them because they pollute waterways by encouraging rank growth of algae. (If your gray water contains toxic substances, you can still conserve by using it to flush the toilet. Pour it into the bowl, not the tank, until it has replaced the water that was in the bowl.)

Soapy water will lead to increased soil alkalinity and to a buildup of salts. Counter this by alternating soapy water and fresh water or by diluting soapy water with rinse water or clean water. Don't use soapy water on acid lovers such as citrus or on very salt-sensitive crops such as strawberries. (See page 32 for a list of crops that are sensitive to salt.) After a season of using gray water, check your soil pH (see page 72) and make any necessary adjustments.

Finally, be realistic about how much water you plan to carry around. A workable system is essential. For example, you can't leave wash water standing for more than a day or so, or it will start to smell. (For information on diverting and transporting gray water, see the publications listed under Ecology/Ecosystem Complexity in Appendix VI, Suggested Reading.) If you plan to invest in any water diversion equipment, check the local regulations to make sure that your plans are legal. At the end of the drought, store any reusable equipment for use during the inevitable next drought.

Down to Earth

OIL...EARTH...DIRT—WHATEVER we call it, we know what we want from it. We want it to be good and rich, so that the plants rising from it will be large and sturdy. Local soils rarely start out either good or rich, but we can usually make them so even when they don't seem to hold much promise for improvement. Only occasionally is a soil a complete bust, so yours is probably suitable for gardening but needs work. With enough effort, you can transform almost any patch of ground into a rich, crumbly garden soil in three to five years. In the first year alone, you can make a tremendous difference. To know how much work your soil needs you must look at it, feel it, dig into it, and possibly send it to a soil laboratory for analysis.

Evaluating Your Soil

First you must determine your soil type. When gardeners talk about this, they are referring to the soil *texture*—the ratio of sand, silt, and clay particles. In the area covered by this book, most soils either are very sandy or clayey, although there are stretches of loam.

Sandy soils, often called light soils, are made up primarily of large mineral particles with large spaces, or pores, between them. As a result, sandy soils are well aerated, but they drain so fast that it is hard to keep them moist in warm weather. Fertilizers wash out easily and must be replaced often. In their favor, sandy soils warm early in spring and are easy to dig.

Clay soils, also known as heavy soils, consist mostly of tiny mineral particles tightly packed together. The tiny pores hold water so well that little air can enter. Clay soils also hold nutrients better than sandy soils and any fertilizers you add will stay there longer. When overwatered, clay soils can easily become waterlogged, drowning plant roots. They warm slowly in spring and are extremely hard to dig. Silt particles are intermediate in size.

The ideal garden soil is loam, which consists of about 40 percent sand, 40 percent silt, and 20 percent clay. A soil that is close to the ideal loam proportions gets the benefits of both extremes. It has large pores, which drain quickly and fill up with air, and small pores, which hold onto water for a longer time. This means that plant roots have access to both water and air much of the time. Loam is a pleasure to dig.

To determine which type of soil you have, examine it when it is dry, then wet a handful and try to roll it into a snake. Dry sandy soil feels gritty and pours through your fingers. When wet, it still feels gritty and immediately crumbles when you try to roll it. Clay soil cracks when it dries and forms hard clods. Slippery and sticky when wet, clay holds together so well that it can be rolled into a snake several inches long. Loam doesn't crack and the clods are softer. When you roll loam, it crumbles before you can get it pencil-thin.

It's not easy to change your soil texture, since you would have to mix in large amounts of sand, silt, or clay to alter the ratio of particles. Sometimes gardeners try to change the texture of heavy clay by digging in sand, but not everyone agrees that this works. It is easier to change the *structure*, and thus

SOIL pH

The relative alkalinity or acidity of soil is measured on a scale from 0 (completely acid) to 14 (completely alkaline), with 7 the neutral point. Most soils in our region are near the middle of the scale, although there are extremes here and there. A plant will not be able to absorb nutrients from a soil that is too acidic or too alkaline for it. Most vegetables, herbs, and flowers listed in this book grow best when the soil is between pH 6.5 and 7, although they can tolerate a range from pH 6 to 7.5. Potatoes are unusual because they thrive in soil as acidic as pH 5.

All soils are more acidic at the end of the rainy season. Sandy soils tend to be more acidic than clay soils. Soils under trees that have acidic debris, such as oaks or redwoods, also tend to have a lower pH. Repeated use of ammonium or sulfur-based fertilizers will make any soil more acidic. If the site was used for acid-loving plants, such as fuchsias, camellias, or rhododendrons, it may have been acidified on purpose.

If your soil is too acidic, raise the pH by adding ground limestone or dolomitic lime. To raise the pH of 100 square feet of soil by 1 point (for example, from 5 to 6), add 5 pounds of lime to sandy soil, 7 pounds to loam, and 8 pounds to clay soil. (Avoid quicklime and slaked or hydrated lime, which can burn plants and injure soil life.)

If your soil is too alkaline, lower the pH by adding sulfur. To lower the pH of 100 square feet of soil by 1 point (for example, from 7.5 to 6.5), add 1 pound of sulfur to sandy soil, 1-1/2 pounds to loam, and 2 pounds to clay soil.

In general, the addition of organic matter, including compost, will bring any soil closer to the ideal of a slightly acidic 6.5, and keep it there through a buffering action. Peatmoss, cottonseed meal, pine needles, and oak leaves have a more acidic reaction, which is helpful if you are combatting alkaline soil or trying to acidify soil for plants that prefer a low pH. Animal manures often contain salts that raise pH, so it's best to alternate them with other amendments. Woodash raises pH, so it should be avoided in alkaline soils.

---

the characteristics, of either clay or sandy soil by adding organic matter (see page 74).

You can either test your soil for nutrients or assume that it is typical for the region—low in nitrogen, slightly low in phosphorus, and sufficient in potassium and trace minerals—and fertilize accordingly. For a rough analysis you can use a home test kit available from a nursery or garden center. For a more complete analysis and instructions for correcting an imbalance, have your soil tested professionally. California does not offer state-sponsored soil tests, so you must look for a commercial soil laboratory. (Try finding one through a local garden store or gardening organization.)

Your soil pH—the relative alkalinity or acidity of the soil—is probably all right but it could be too high or too low to grow certain crops, or even most crops, well. An inexpensive pH meter can quickly tell you your soil's pH. Laboratory soil tests also include pH, and the lab reports include suggestions for correcting pH. Once you have adjusted your soil pH, good gardening practices will usually keep it at the desired level.

Adding Organic Matter

Whatever soil you start with, you can improve it vastly by adding organic matter. If you are lucky enough to start with loam, you are ahead of the game, because organic matter makes loam even better. But if not—and most of us aren't that lucky—you will find that adding organic matter to

OUR LOCAL SOILS

The soils in our region vary dramatically. Some areas near the coast have very deep sandy soil. In some gardens, by the coast and elsewhere, sand may be laid over a heavier soil. Lowland areas around San Francisco Bay are often loamy, but with a high percentage of clay. Some of the deepest and richest loams are found near creeks or former creeks. Other areas are covered with very heavy clay called adobe. Although rich in minerals, adobe is hard to manage, turning rock-hard when it dries.

Because of our limited rain and mild winters, all our soils have a relatively thin topsoil. Rainier regions with cold winters, such as the Great Plains, the Midwest, and parts of the Northeast, favor the building of a thick, organic topsoil. The warm summer rains encourage lush growth, which is killed in winter and decays slowly. Here, lighter rainfall means sparser natural growth, which decays the year around due to our mild winters, and quickly dissipates.

Some soils, especially on eroded hillsides, are very shallow. Often they contain large chunks of shale, sandstone, serpentine, or granite. Although you can't garden in pure rocks, a few rocks aren't all bad. They absorb heat well and reradiate it to warm the surrounding soil. As they break down, they release nutrients, although this happens so slowly that it has no great effect on your garden. Avoid planting root crops, such as carrots or beets, in rocky soil as they will be stunted and deformed. If your soil is essentially gravel or if solid bedrock lies within a foot or so of the surface, you will probably have to import soil and fill a raised bed with it.

Garden plants languish in the excessively magnesium-rich soil that has developed over serpentine rock. Outcrops of this greenish rock occur here and there throughout the area. There are some in Sonoma County. In Marin County they reach to the top of Mount Tamalpais and to ground level on the Tiburon peninsula. In San Francisco outcrops occur in the Presidio, under and around the Mint, and elsewhere, and in San Mateo County they appear in the Crystal Springs hills. In areas of the Oakland-Berkeley hills, serpentine breaks the surface. Improve serpentine soil by adding 5 pounds gypsum (calcium sulfate) per 100 square feet. The calcium in gypsum will chemically displace the magnesium. In addition, fertilize well.

Some local soils may contain excess salts that will harm plants. Salty soils are more likely along the margins of the Bay, where land has been reclaimed from salt marshes. (Salt spray may get into soils very near the ocean, but this is not likely to be a large quantity.) There are different kinds of salt-laden soils and some are easier to fix than others. In some the salts are soluble and can be leached, but in others sodium is chemically bound to the soil and must be displaced (gypsum comes to the rescue again, providing calcium to supplant the sodium) before the soil is leached. If your plants are not growing well and you suspect that salts may be the problem, get a soil test and follow the recommendations. (See chart on salt tolerance, page 32.)

Many urban areas are no longer covered with the soil they had naturally. Some areas, especially at the edges of San Francisco Bay, are built on landfills. The Bay coast of San Francisco is built on fill that includes the hulks of sailing vessels abandoned during the Gold Rush! Soil in your neighborhood may have been hauled in from construction sites elsewhere. The contractors who built your home may have scraped off the original topsoil and poured a layer of presumably better soil over whatever was left in your yard. Transported soil differs from naturally occurring soil in that it has been piled topsy-turvy, usually burying the thin layer of topsoil. Your garden soil may bear little resemblance to your area's predominant soils, leaving you with unique difficulties to overcome.

Even if your yard has original soil, it may have been compacted to make the foundation firmer when your house was being built. If this is the case, you may need to rototill before you can install a garden—one of the few times that a rototiller is useful in a small garden (see page 83).

sandy or clayey soil creates the next best thing: a "made loam."

It is true that some plants, including many natives and most trees when they are establishing themselves, grow better in unamended soils. However, most of the plants discussed in this book need richer soil.

Unless you have inherited soil built up by a good gardener, you can assume that it is low in organic matter. (A notable exception is the organic soil of the Delta, where organic matter deposited over centuries by reeds and grasses decayed slowly because the soil was waterlogged. Drained, this soil is ideal for agriculture and is the source of local carrot, corn, and asparagus crops.)

If you add enough organic matter, you can physically change the structure of your soil. Organic matter breaks down into humus, a dark earthy substance that acts as a sort of glue holding sand, silt, and clay particles in little bunches, or aggregates. These aggregates give the soil a crumbly property, and enable it to hold both air and water well.

Pick up a handful of soil when it is moist and squeeze it. Then prod it gently with your finger. Without organic matter, sandy soil doesn't hold together at all and clay soil forms a solid lump. Soil that has a good crumb structure holds together lightly but will fall apart into fluffy loose aggregates. Because it holds moisture so well, it feels cool and damp whether it is wet or relatively dry. Don't expect to have a crumb structure unless your soil has been amended with organic matter for several seasons. If you need an example, find a longtime gardener in your neighborhood who will let you get the feel of well-amended soil. Holding it once is worth at least a thousand words.

Humus-rich soil is less likely to compact. That's why Dad was confident in asking me as a child to walk down his seed row. Even though I was small and light, I might still have compacted the soil had it not been so fluffy. Humus is colloidal, just like gelatin. If you smack a richly organic soil with your palm, you will see the surface quiver up to a couple of feet away.

When you add organic matter to sandy soil, you won't have to water or fertilize as often. A well-amended sandy soil can hold up to seven times more water than the same soil unamended. Humus also increases the ability of sandy soil to hold nutrients.

A few seasons of adding organic matter will make a clay soil easier to work and let water soak into it more readily. Plants will grow better because the soil contains more air. Seedlings will break through more easily, plant roots will grow deeper, and root crops will be well formed.

Although adding organic matter to a loam is not as crucial from the viewpoint of soil structure, it provides a nutrient reserve that cannot be matched by commercial fertilizers and it encourages healthy soil life. Organic matter offers these same benefits to sandy and clayey soils too.

Types of Organic Matter

A wide variety of organic materials can be used to amend soil. You can buy, scavenge, or produce your own organic amendment. Compost, homemade or purchased, is ideal but other substances will also serve.

You can purchase organic matter labeled *compost* or *soil conditioner*, or you can look for free sources. Some of the best organic materials are barnyard manure, green plants, and fallen leaves. Straw, sawdust, rice hulls, shredded bark, and peat moss can be used, but they are less desirable because they decay more slowly.

If the label on a purchased amendment says that the product was *composted*, that means it has sat around and decayed for a while, so that it is partway to becoming humus. Materials commonly composted are barnyard manure, sawdust, and fallen leaves (sold as leaf mold). A product sold as "compost" is usually a mixture of several different organic substances that have decayed together to a relatively stable state. When you dig in compost or any material that has been composted, you can plant right away.

After you dig in fresh material, such as kitchen scraps, fresh barnyard manure, or green manure (see page 76), you must let it decay for a few weeks before planting. Waiting may be worthwhile, since these materials are often free. Look around for organic matter that may be available for the asking, such as stable manure or pulp left over after making apple juice (pomace) or wine (grape pulp).

Kitchen scraps require planning because you usually obtain them in small quantities as you cook. Set aside a small area where you are not gardening right now and dig the garbage in, starting at one corner and methodically working across and then down the area. Chop large pieces before you dig them in. Leave the area unplanted for two months or longer after you finish. (One San Francisco gardener dug in all her kitchen scraps a couple of years before she planted. When she finally did plant, the crops practically leapt onto her table.)

Instead of tying up garden space while you wait for fresh material to decay, you can make your own compost in a small corner of the garden. (To learn how to make compost, see page 86.)

Straw and wood products such as sawdust, shredded newspaper, and ground bark, are low in nitrogen. Unless you add nitrogen, the soil microorganisms that break down fresh organic matter will devour the nitrogen in the soil to fuel their activity. If you buy any of these fresh products, check to see if they have been "nitrogen stabilized." This means

that a nitrogen source has been added. If not, you can add it yourself. Wood products that have been composted don't need to be nitrogen stabilized and neither does straw that was used as animal bedding, since the animal wastes contribute nitrogen. (The straw bedding is probably heat treated as fresh material and allowed to decay for a while before you plant. See page 77.)

Alternate amendments as much as possible to avoid adding too much of any type of material to the soil. Animal manure tends to have a high salt content. Some gardeners believe that redwood products inhibit plant growth, whereas others say it isn't so. To be safe, don't depend completely on any one

POLLUTED SOILS

The soils in urban areas usually contain remnants of the lives of people who lived there. I have found marbles, blue glass bottles, and bits of crockery. Once, in a new community garden in a vacant lot, we found enough bricks and concrete to make a small patio.

With the exception of broken glass, these findings pose no danger, but there could be a hazard from invisible pollutants. Virtually all homes built before World War II were coated with paint containing lead, which found its way into the soil nearest the house as the paint weathered or was scraped and sanded in preparation for repainting. The lead in the yard could be more widespread if a building burned down on the property. Paint made after 1978 is free of lead.

Lead has also entered the soil from the air, emitted by cars fueled by leaded gasoline. Because lead is heavy, it does not rise into the atmosphere but settles on surfaces near roads. Cadmium, a heavy metal in tires, may also pollute areas near roads. Soils in front and side yards next to busy streets and not screened by a fence or shrubbery are most likely to be polluted. The safest location for a food garden is 75 feet from busy streets, with a building, fence, or hedge to block the wind, but let a soil test be your guide.

Another possible source of lead is lead arsenate, once used as a pesticide in orchards but now banned. Consider this a possibility if your yard was once one of the area's many commercial orchards.

If you are new to the property and find that part of the yard is unusually bare, suspect that it may have been treated with a long-lasting herbicide. Test your theory by trying to germinate radish seeds. If several tries fail, have your soil tested professionally.

If there turn out to be low levels of pollutants in your soil, good gardening practices can reduce the hazard. The organic matter that you add to the soil will bind pollutants and keep them out of plant roots. If the pollutant levels are high, you will get instructions with your soil test, explaining what is safe to grow and eat. While it isn't probable, it could turn out that pollution levels are too high to garden safely. Then you might have to remove the soil and replace it, build raised beds and fill them with clean soil, garden in containers, or join a nearby community garden.

GREEN MANURE

One of the cheapest sources of organic matter is green manure, which consists of plants that you grow for the purpose of digging them under and allowing them to decay in the soil. Clover, grasses, buckwheat, and fava beans are commonly used this way. They decay quickly if you dig them in while they are still young and tender. You can also use weeds as green manure if you dig them in before they go to seed and if you avoid ones that will regrow from perennial roots. You must work a green manure crop into your planting plan, allowing at least four months for it to grow and then decay.

Some of the best choices for green manure in our area are fava beans planted in fall or winter, red clover planted in spring, and vetch planted in early to late fall. Since all these plants are legumes, they add nitrogen to the soil. Bacteria live in legume roots, usually fixing more nitrogen than they need to support themselves. When the legume dies, its roots release a large amount of nitrogen.

Some feel that you should purchase an innoculant from a seed company, to be sure of having the right bacteria, while others feel that the bacteria are probably already present, especially if there have been crops or weedy legumes in the soil recently. If you do innoculate your soil, the bacteria will probably remain active from season to season. (You can see if they are there by digging a legume plant and examining the roots for the nodules—small lumps on the roots.)

FIGURING OUT HOW MUCH TO ADD

Organic matter is commonly measured by the depth of a layer spread over the soil and then dug in. A minimum yearly layer is 1 inch but 2 to 3 inches are better and 6 inches better yet. If you garden the year around, add some in early spring and some in mid- to late summer or fall when you plant crops for fall and winter harvests.

You may not notice much difference over the years if you add only the minimum, but you will see a steady improvement if you are generous each time. Once your soil is in good shape, you can reduce the amendment to a maintenance level, maybe 1 or 2 inches a year. By that time you will know your soil well enough to be able to judge.

Organic materials are sold by the cubic foot in bags or by the cubic yard in bulk. To calculate how much material you need, figure out the area of the garden space you wish to cover, then multiply the area by the depth of the layer of amendment. Remember to express length, width, and depth in the same unit of measure.

For example, to cover a bed 10-1/2 feet long by 4 feet wide with a layer of material 3 inches deep:

10.5 feet x 4 feet = 42 square feet x .25 feet = 10.5 cubic feet

For four beds the same size you will need four times as much material: 42 cubic feet. Since there are 27 cubic feet in one cubic yard (3 by 3 by 3 feet), that comes to roughly 1-1/2 cubic yards.

material. One of the advantages of compost is that it consists of many materials.

Do You Need to Buy Topsoil?

Although it may be true that you lack topsoil—the richly organic top layer—and that you can buy substances called topsoil, what you will get is not likely to be the real thing since we just don't have much locally available rich topsoil. There is no legal definition of the term and what is marketed as topsoil is most likely subsoil, perhaps with some organic matter added. However if what you need is not just more soil, but better soil, put your money into organic matter instead.

On the other hand, if you do need to purchase soil—to fill raised beds, to substitute for salty or polluted soil, or for terracing—commercial "top soil" will do. In this case, look for soil that is loamy and well blended, or that, at the very least, contains roughly 60 percent sand and 40 percent clay. Make sure that it is weed-free. If organic matter was added, find out what it consists of and whether it would be cheaper to buy unamended soil and organic matter separately. This may be a good idea if you have a cheap or free source of organic matter. Be aware that a soil mix that is high in relatively undecayed organic matter will shrink considerably in size as the organic matter breaks down.

If you are adding purchased soil over existing soil, always dig a little of the purchased soil into the first few inches of the existing soil to reduce the abruptness of the interface, or change of soil texture. This is important since water may not be able to flow between two distinct layers.

Mulching

A mulch is a material that a gardener lays on the surface of the soil to conserve water, modify the soil temperature, prevent soil crusting, lessen erosion, keep weeds down, reduce diseases, and keep plant parts from touching the soil and decaying. A mulch can be organic, such as compost or cocoa bean hulls, or inorganic, such as black plastic or crushed stones. An organic mulch acts like leaf litter on the forest floor, decaying slowly into the soil to improve its structure and increase fertility. When you dig it in at the end of the growing season, you are adding organic matter to the soil.

The no-till method of gardening calls for cover-

USING WOOD PRODUCTS

Wood shavings, sawdust, bark, newspaper, and other wood products are so low in nitrogen that soil micro organisms will use up the nitrogen in your soil in the process of decaying them. Unless the wood products have been nitrogen stabilized, you will need to add 1/2 pound actual nitrogen per 15 pounds wood product. For example, that amounts to 10 pounds of a fertilizer that contains 5 percent nitrogen, such as 5-10-10, or 4 pounds of blood meal, which contains 13 percent nitrogen. (To interpret the numbers on a fertilizer label, see page 81.) A nursery worker should be able to help you calculate the proper amount of whatever nitrogen source you choose.

Both hardwood and softwood products are now thought to be safe, but avoid shavings or sawdust made from wood containing any toxic substance, such as a preservative (see page 36). Also avoid plywood sawdust, which contains toxic materials in the glue. Use caution when adding very fine sawdust from sanding, since pockets of it may compact, preventing water from passing through.

---

ing the garden permanently with an organic mulch, planting through it and never digging it in. This method, which controls weeds and produces a soft, fertile, water-retentive soil, was popularized by Ruth Stout, who gardened that way in Connecticut for some fifty years, many of them from a wheelchair. She planned her garden to save labor and her book *How to Have a Green Thumb Without an Aching Back*, (see Appendix VI, Suggested Reading), is well worth reading for her gardening wit and wisdom.

I have seen the no-till method work well enough in a sunny garden in the Mission district of San Francisco. The gardener grew many crops, including tomatoes, under a 6-inch layer of straw. However, warm-season crops will grow faster in our region if the soil is allowed to warm thoroughly before an organic mulch is applied. The foggier the site, the more critical this factor is. An organic mulch can cool the soil by as much as ten degrees—undesirable in a climate barely warm enough for some crops anyway.

Before laying a mulch, clear away weeds and water the soil well. Apply an organic mulch around seedlings only when the plants have several true leaves. Lay the mulch between young seedlings, leaving an open circle and drawing it up to the stems later, after they have toughened up. If you are using plastic, cut crisscross slits for the seedlings or lay strips between rows. Whenever you use plastic as mulch, tuck the edges into the soil or snails and slugs will cluster on the underside.

KEEPING YOUR SOIL ALIVE

Soil care is basically a kind of wildlife management. You want a large, active population of creatures, from beneficial bacteria to earthworms. Most of this soil life is invisible but it works wonders for the health of your plants. Various creatures in turn break down organic matter until the chemical nutrients are released into the soil for plant use.

Evidence is mounting that an active soil life plays a significant role in helping green plants fight diseases and other pests. Some microorganisms produce antibiotics that inhibit diseases, and others are actual predators of pests that damage plant roots. Some bacteria and fungi live in what appears to be a mutually beneficial association with the roots of green plants, using carbohydrates that the plants manufacture while releasing nitrogen in a form that the plants can use.

These helpful soil creatures need adequate moisture and air. They work best in warm soil, but some activity will continue as long as the soil is not frozen. Unlike green plants, which make their own food through photosynthesis, most soil creatures need to break down organic matter to obtain energy and carbon.

When the soil dries completely, the soil life dies, goes into a resting state, or moves to another garden. If you intend to plant but don't get to it in early spring, keep the area watered.

When the soil lacks air, many helpful soil creatures leave or cease activity. Creatures that are tolerant of low-oxygen conditions are likely to be the sort that attack plant roots. When soil gets waterlogged, as it often does in winter, disease organisms sometimes get the upper hand.

Digging and turning the soil lets in more air, enabling soil creatures to multiply more quickly. Turning clay soil, which is low in air content, is more useful than turning sandy soil, which already has plenty of air. If you dig sandy soil often, the soil microorganisms may digest organic matter faster than you can add it.

Organic matter must be replaced, since soil organisms will eventually digest even the humus. Dig more organic matter in at least once a year, and twice if you are gardening the year around. Dig it into the top 6 to 10 inches of soil, where there is enough air to support the helpful soil organisms. An organic mulch spread on the soil surface will serve as an additional food source for soil life.

Avoid chemicals that are toxic to soil life. Any fungicides or herbicides that work in the soil and even water-soluble fertilizers can kill helpful soil life. If you use pesticides that can harm these beneficial creatures, use them in ways that will cause the least damage (see page 135).

HELP FROM EARTHWORMS

If earthworms did nothing else, they would serve as an indicator of healthy soil. Their tunneling aerates the soil, improves drainage, and opens channels for plant roots. They eat organic matter and excrete it as castings, which soil bacteria and fungi can digest and break down into plant nutrients more easily than they can the original organic matter.

When you first start to garden, before you've improved the soil, you may not see many earthworms. After you add organic matter and begin to keep your soil moist, earthworms will migrate from neighboring yards and multiply in your soil. In addition to consuming organic matter in the soil, they will pull bits of organic matter from the soil surface down into their tunnels. When you thin vegetable seedlings or pull weeds, leave the pulled plants on the soil surface for the earthworms. (Make sure the weeds don't have seeds or roots that will regrow.)

Try not to injure earthworms when you are digging. A garden fork will cut fewer earthworms than a shovel or spade, and all hand tools are less damaging than a rotary tiller. (It is not true that an earthworm cut in half can regenerate to form two worms.) When you are digging, move to a safe location any earthworms you see wandering around in search of their lost tunnels. Loosen some moist soil in a shady spot and put them on it.

If you use water-soluble fertilizers in your soil, the earthworms will move deeper for a few days until the chemicals bind to the soil and become harmless. If you use these fertilizers often and over most of your garden, the earthworms will leave your yard.

Sevin™ bait, commonly used as an earwig control, is an example of a pesticide that will kill earthworms along with its intended victims, although a small amount used occasionally in a small area probably won't wipe out your entire earthworm population.

Most people just improve their soil and wait for earthworms to arrive on their own, but you can buy them. If your soil is inviting, a couple of dozen night crawlers should be able to colonize a hundred square feet or so in no time. (See also Earthworm Compost, page 90.)

If the mulch you plan to use is sold by the cubic foot or cubic yard, use the method described on page 76 (for organic matter) to determine how much you will need.

Local Mulching Plan

Between February and May you will be concentrating on gardening techniques that warm the soil. If you use an organic mulch, choose a dark material, such as compost, cocoa hulls, or rotted sawdust, and use only a thin layer to minimize the cooling effect.

Black or clear plastic will warm the soil. In fact, clear plastic may warm it too much in the sunnier parts of our region. Both types of plastic are best reserved for early plantings of warm-season crops. You may want to lay the plastic for a week or two

to warm the soil before you plant, then leave it on for a while to get the plants off to a good start.

By May or June you may choose to lay an organic mulch to reduce the need for water. If you do, don't lay it on top of plastic. The cooling effect of the mulch will be of less concern at this time of year, when the soil is as warm as it will get and the warm-season crops are well established. In fact, the cooling effect may actually work to your advantage if you are growing cool-season crops in summer.

Organic mulch will help keep the soil cool during hot spells. Experiment to see which crops will benefit from summertime mulching and which will be hindered where you live.

Avoid using gravel, pebbles, or large chunks of bark as mulch in a vegetable garden. They do not decay and add nutrients to the soil, and you would have to rake them out of the way every time you changed crops.

As you head into the rainy season, your mulching goals will change. The mulch will help cancel the damaging effects of heavy rain pelting bare soil. Mulch any areas that will be vacant for all or part of the winter, including areas between widely spaced plants such as broccoli. You can leave the area under vegetable leaf canopies bare, since the leaves will protect the soil and the bare places will catch and radiate more warmth. (See page 98 for tips on using weeds, either living or pulled, as a winter mulch.) If you have dormant perennial beds, mulch their soil lightly but don't pile up mulch over plants as you would in a cold-winter climate, since that will only encourage decay. At the end of winter dig the organic mulch into the soil.

Fertilizing

To grow a healthy garden, you don't have to be an expert in plant nutrition. Usually it's enough to know a few basic facts about the nutrient content of our soils. Of the major nutrients, nitrogen and phosphorus must be added routinely and potassium is rarely deficient in this region. If you don't know whether your soil contains adequate potassium, just add it as you do the other major nutrients. You can usually assume that organic matter is supplying all

---

MANURE OR COMPOST TEA

With very little effort you can turn manure or hot compost into a wonderful liquid fertilizer to add before or as you water plants. Put some manure or compost in a large container (a covered plastic bucket is ideal for concealing the odor) and fill it with water. Use about 2 cups solid material per gallon water. Let it sit in the garden for three days or more, stirring it a couple of times a day. Every two weeks or so apply the liquid around your plants. When the liquid is gone, pour the slurry in the garden in an area between plants and start over.

---

the trace minerals that your plants need. You're not likely to encounter obscure nutrient deficiencies but if you run into a problem, send a soil sample along with a description of the symptoms to a soil laboratory.

Surveys show that most gardeners don't fertilize their gardens at all the first year. This means that crops must mine the soil for nutrients left by decaying vegetation and dissolving minerals. Some crops may get by, but the soil will be depleted and will not support crops as well the second year. A regular fertilization program will return nutrients to your soil.

Nitrogen is the nutrient that must be added most often not only because plants use it in large quantities but also because it is easily lost from the soil. A lack of nitrogen causes slow growth and yellowed lower leaves. Adding too much nitrogen results in lots of lush growth at the expense of flowering and fruiting—this symptom is often seen on tomato plants that are fed too much nitrogen. Add nitrogen in a form that is released slowly or if it is quick-acting add it more than once during a growing season. You can supply nitrogen either with organic substances or synthetic fertilizers.

Phosphorus doesn't have to be replaced as often as nitrogen since it doesn't move in the soil. Essential for flowering and fruiting, phosphorus also contributes to disease resistance and a healthy root system. A deficiency causes stunting and poor fruit and seed development. The leaves turn dark green and there may be some reddening or purpling on the plant. Organic gardeners often add phosphorus in the form of bonemeal, rock phosphate, or soft or colloidal phosphate. Many synthetic fertilizers contain phosphorus as well.

Local soils are usually adequately supplied with secondary and minor nutrients, with the occasional exceptions of zinc and iron. A zinc deficiency, which may occur if you are gardening in subsoil, causes abnormally small leaves that are either mottled or pale between the veins. An iron deficiency often shows up in alkaline soils, since iron becomes tied up chemically in the soil as the pH rises. Although an iron deficiency is not usually a problem in growing vegetables, it can show up on citrus and other acid-loving plants. The main symptom is yellowing between the veins of the leaves. Both zinc and iron deficiencies can be corrected by using chelates—forms of minerals easily absorbed by plants. You can also correct an iron deficiency by acidifying the soil.

Types of Fertilizers

Fertilizers may be organic substances, natural inorganic materials, or synthetic formulas. They may be dry or liquid. Some contain a single nutrient and others contain many.

There are two types of inorganic fertilizers: rock fertilizers, which are mineral deposits ground to a powder, and synthetic fertilizers. Since rock fertilizers are not water soluble, they do not burn plants and are long lasting. Although these natural substances are inorganic, they are often used in an organic fertilizing program.

Synthetic fertilizers such as superphosphate or ammonium nitrate are manufactured materials. Many are water soluble, washing out of the soil easily. They can burn plant roots if they are used in concentrations that are too high or if the undiluted chemical touches plant roots. Some synthetic fertilizers are treated so that they release nutrients slowly; they are safer to use and last longer than the water-soluble types.

Organic fertilizers are natural organic materials. Sometimes, as with barnyard manure, the actual content of nutrients is low, but the fact that the material is applied in large quantities compensates. Some organic fertilizers, such as bonemeal, contain high concentrations of nutrients. Most organic fertilizers will not burn plants, although those with a high nitrogen content, such as blood meal or cottonseed meal, can do so if used in large amounts.

Well-made hot, or fast, compost (see page 87) is a superb organic fertilizer that supplies the major nutrients and plenty of trace minerals. Cold, or slow, compost, including most commercial, bagged composts, is variable in fertilizer value, depending on what was used to make it. A cold compost built with some attention to the ratio of carbon to nitrogen could be as rich in nitrogen as a hot pile. But many bagged commercial products are made with relatively low nitrogen materials and are best used as amendments, with some additional nitrogen fertilizer.

Organic gardeners argue that the heavy use of synthetic fertilizers kills soil life through chemical burning and harms the environment by seeping into the groundwater and contaminating wells. They also argue that the manufacture of these fertilizers consumes a high amount of energy, mainly from petroleum products, whereas organic fertilizers are renewable resources.

On the other hand, potassium is potassium whether it comes from kelp or potassium sulfate. Synthetic fertilizers are certainly better than no fertilizer and can help produce healthy plants in the short run, although I encourage you to rely

WHAT DO THE NUMBERS MEAN?

Whenever you buy a packaged product to use as a fertilizer, whether it is an organic product such as blood meal, a rock powder such as soft or colloidal phosphate, or a synthetic chemical fertilizer such as ammonium sulfate, you will find three numbers on the label. They stand for the percentages by weight of nitrogen (N), phosphorus (P), and potassium (K) listed in that order. For example, a fertilizer labeled 5-10-10 contains 5 percent nitrogen, 10 percent phosphoric acid (P_2O_5) and 10 percent potash (K_2O). The rest is filler material.

A fertilizer containing all three major nutrients is called a complete fertilizer, although of course it doesn't supply every nutrient that plants need to grow. If the fertilizer lacks a major nutrient, a 0 appears. For example, greensand (0-1-6) contains no nitrogen, 1 percent phosphorus, and 6 percent potassium.

You can use the numbers on the label as a guide to avoid using too much of a fertilizer. Nitrogen is probably the most harmful if overused. A general rule is not to apply more than 1/4 ounce actual nitrogen per square yard. If you know the percent by weight of nitrogen in the substance you are using, you can calculate how much is enough. For example if it is a 10-10-10 fertilizer, it is 10% nitrogen, or one ounce to 10 ounces of formulation. So you want to add no more than 2.5 ounces of 10-10-10 per square yard.

FERTILIZER FORMULAS

When you have your soil tested by a laboratory, you will get recommendations for fertilizing it along with your written report. This is the only way you can be sure of adding just the right amounts of fertilizer that contain just the amount of nutrients your soil lacks. (If you tell the lab you are planning to grow vegetables organically, you will also get recommendations for organic fertilizers.)

Without a soil test, gardeners often just choose sources of nitrogen, phosphorous, and potassium and add a moderate amount of each. This less exact approach works pretty well. Theoretically, you could add more than you need of one or more nutrients, because the soil might already contain them. However, nitrogen, the only one that could cause a serious problem (see page 81), is rarely abundant in unfertilized soil. The formulas below are just two out of many possibilities. Each includes both organic amendment and fertilizer.

Formula 1

Spread at least 2 inches of an organic soil amendment, such as cold compost, on the soil and lay 2 inches of well-rotted manure (nitrogen source) on top of the amendment. Over each 100 square feet sprinkle 5 pounds bonemeal (phosphorus source) and 1 pound kelp meal (potassium source).

Formula 2

Spread at least 2 inches of an organic soil amendment. Over each 100 square feet of bed sprinkle 5 pounds blood meal (nitrogen source), 10 pounds soft or colloidal phosphate (phosphorus source), and 10 pounds greensand (potassium source).

In both cases, dig the amendment and fertilizers into the top 6 to 8 inches of soil. Let the soil rest for a couple of days before you plant. All these nutrients, except for soft phosphate and greensand, should be replenished in six months to a year. The soft phosphate will last two or three years and the greensand as long as 10 years.

primarily on organic materials.

One time when synthetic fertilizers really can make plants grow better is during cold weather in early spring, when you are trying to get seedlings off to a rapid start. Organic fertilizers require the action of soil life to release nutrients, and the soil may still be too cold for that to happen.

Besides being dug into the soil, many fertilizers can be banded, or placed in the soil near where the roots of the young plants will grow. This is usually done on the day that you plant. A typical placement is 2 to 3 inches to the side or 2 to 3 inches below the seeds or seedlings.

If you want to give your plants an extra boost, you can use liquid fertilizers, poured into the soil or sprayed on the leaves. Fish emulsion and liquid kelp are organic liquid fertilizers commonly used this way, and so are chelated minerals. Use the kelp or fish emulsion about a month after planting and then monthly while the plant is growing. You can use manure or hot compost to make an excellent liquid fertilizer to water into the soil (see Manure or Compost Tea on page 80).

Digging

Before you dig, be sure that the soil is ready. It should be moist, but not soggy. Pick up some soil and squeeze it in your hand. If it is too dry, it won't form a clump. If it is too wet, it will remain in a

clump even when you prod it with your finger. At the right moisture for digging, the soil clump will fall apart easily.

Gardeners don't agree about how to dig. Some advocate digging the soil very thoroughly, whereas others think you should dig as little as possible. Most practice something in between these two theories. They dig to the depth of a shovel once or twice a year, mulch at least part of the year, and either dig the mulch in or add other organic matter when they dig. When digging in an amendment, they may turn it under completely or just turn it sideways so that whatever was layered on top is left in roughly vertical layers in the soil.

Among those who feel that you should dig very well are advocates of double digging, a central practice of French-intensive/ biodynamic gardening. Although there are many variations, double digging consists of three basic steps: (1) digging out soil to the depth of a shovel, (2) using a shovel or garden fork to loosen the soil at the bottom of the hole, and (3) replacing the top layer of soil. The digger works across the area double digging strips about a foot wide. You'll find complete instructions in *How to Grow More Vegetables* by John Jeavons, listed in Appendix VI, Suggested Reading, and in many other gardening books.

Double digging is most useful in heavy clay soil,

WHAT ABOUT ROTOTILLING?

Gardeners debate the wisdom of using a rotary tiller to turn the soil. In much of the country the gardening year begins with rototilling. This method is practical in large gardens that stand nearly empty in spring. However, hand digging uses less fossil fuel and is easier on soil structure and soil life. If the soil is sandy or loamy, you can probably hand-dig a small garden, less than 2,000 square feet easily. Expect to accomplish much less in clay soil. If you are gardening the year around, hand digging will be made easier by the fact that you are unlikely to be digging the whole garden at once.

You may choose to rent a rotary tiller to help you deal with compacted soil that you are trying to open up for gardening. Even sandy soil can become compacted and hard to work if it is bare and trampled often. Use the tiller with patience, going over the soil several times, digging a little deeper with each pass. You may only be able to dig an inch or so each time. Before starting be sure that the soil is the right moisture for digging. Also be careful not to spread perennial weeds by leaving their cut roots in the soil.

since it gets air into the soil and allows roots to grow deeper. If you have a sandy soil that is already loose and airy, double digging won't make much difference. But if you have a thin layer of sand over heavy clay, double digging will make the interface between the layers less abrupt and get air into the lower layer.

The no-till theory holds that soil rarely needs to be dug and that doing so disrupts natural cycles and damages the soil structure. Gardeners who subscribe to this theory may dig to the depth of a

SAMPLE ROTATIONS

Here are a couple of rotations for coastal central California gardens. They are not meant as recipes but as practice in thinking through a crop rotation.

PLAN A: In April or May work in compost and fertilizer, then plant tomatoes (heavy feeder). During the summer lay an organic mulch around the plants. By the middle of October, remove the tomato plants and dig in the mulch. Plant peas (soil builder) in November, adding a small booster of nitrogen when you plant. In May pull the spent peas and compost them, but don't add them to a cold pile unless they are free of powdery mildew. Dig in compost, then plant potatoes (light feeder). After harvesting the potatoes in August, add fertilizer and plant broccoli (heavy feeder, cole crop). As winter weeds come up, pull them and make a mulch of the ones that won't reseed or reroot. When you pull the broccoli the following February, dig in the weed mulch and plant carrots (light feeder). Harvest them by May or June, making way for beans (soil builder).

PLAN B: In February work in compost and fertilizer, then plant mixed lettuces (heavy feeder). In early May, when the lettuces have been harvested, plant scarlet runner beans (soil builder) with no additional soil preparation. In October add compost and plant garlic (light feeder). Early the following August add fertilizer and plant a fast-growing variety of cabbage (heavy feeder, cole crop). After harvesting the cabbage in November, plant fava beans (soil builder) and mulch them with pulled weeds in late winter. In April pull out the fava beans, move the stalks to a compost heap, and dig in the weed mulch. As an alternative, chop the stalks and add other organic matter to create a sheet compost (see page 88), then dig it in when it is ready. In May or June plant summer squash or cucumbers (heavy feeders) and side-dress the plants with fertilizer twice during the summer. After harvesting the plants in October, sow onion seeds (light feeder).

shovel and amend at the beginning, but from then on they rely on mulch to improve the soil from the surface down. They use a trowel to open up small planting holes or rows, then add fertilizer and plant. This was Ruth Stout's method (see page 77) and it seems particularly suited to sandy soil, which loses nutrients when you dig it, already contains plenty of air, and warms quickly even under mulch.

Rotating Your Crops

By not planting the same crop in the same place year after year you will use your soil more efficiently and prevent a buildup of soil diseases and other pests. Most rotation plans suggest that you follow a crop with another one from a different plant family. Members of the same plant family often draw on similar proportions of soil nutrients and share some

of the same soil-dwelling pests.

Gardeners often add fertilizer before planting a crop that is a heavy feeder, or they add organic matter before planting a crop that needs a loose, moisture-holding soil. They often follow a demanding crop with a less demanding one and plant it without adding anything to the soil.

The soil-building ability of legumes, such as peas and beans, is frequently put to work in a rotation. Used every third or fourth crop, legumes produce a plentiful supply of nitrogen. Many gardeners also plant green manure as part of their rotation, then dig it in to improve the soil during a break between food crops.

When the soil contains a serious disease organism or other pest, then pest control becomes an overriding issue in crop rotation. Since there is no chemical cure for many soilborne diseases, rotation plays an important role even in nonorganic agriculture. A rotation plan must leave enough years between plantings of affected crops for the pest to die out. In extreme cases, a garden or sections of a garden are left unplanted every couple of years to halt the buildup of soilborne diseases. Resistant plant varieties and good growing conditions are the best defenses against most diseases, but rotation helps too.

It isn't easy to carry out crop rotation rigorously in a very small garden, since there are so few locations to choose from. The distances between rotated crops may be too short to keep some pests from crawling over to find their favorite foods. Still, it is wise to rotate as much as you can.

A particularly serious problem in small urban gardens is the lack of sunlight. If you have only a certain area that is sunny enough to ripen tomatoes in summer, it is likely to be the same area that is sunny enough to grow cole crops in winter. Both crops are heavy feeders. If you have this problem, pay special attention to soil fertility. If you can afford the space, plant half of the area with a legume, perhaps beans in summer and peas in winter. If you are leaving part of the garden fallow over winter because it is too shady, be sure to cover it with an organic mulch or grow green manure so that you return some nutrients to the soil.

Crop rotation is a very old practice and you will come across many schemes, some of them developed to deal with local conditions, such as special soil problems or particular diseases. When you are reading about a rotation scheme, try to find out if the conditions for which it was designed are similar to yours.

How I Rotate My Crops

My first consideration is whether a crop is a heavy feeder, a light feeder, or a soil builder. I also classify mustard family crops, including radishes and turnips, as a fourth group and rotate them separately.

I draw a map of my garden twice or even three times a year as a reminder of what was growing where. I plant a heavy feeder, then follow it with either a light feeder and then a legume or a legume and then a light feeder. Next comes another heavy feeder. Occasionally, I plant two heavy feeders consecutively, but I choose them from different plant families and add enough fertilizer to support them. I am always sure to plant a light feeder or legume the next time around.

CATEGORIZING CROPS FOR ROTATION

When planning a rotation, refer to the following lists for guidance and also read individual crop listings in Chapters 11 and 12. This is only one way to categorize plants for rotation. Others are by plant family or by groups of crops that attract the same pests.

HEAVY FEEDERS

Crop	Family
Basil	Mint
Beet	Goosefoot
Celery	Carrot
Cole crops	Mustard
Corn	Grass
Cucumber	Gourd
Endive and chicory	Aster
Lettuce	Aster
Parsley	Carrot
Spinach	Goosefoot
Squash	Gourd
Tomato	Nightshade

LIGHT FEEDERS

Crop	Family
Carrot	Carrot
Leek	Amaryllis
Mustard	Mustard
Onion	Amaryllis
Parsnip	Carrot
Pepper	Nightshade
Potato	Nightshade
Shallot	Amaryllis
Swiss chard	Goosefoot
Turnip	Mustard

SOIL BUILDERS

Crop	Family
Bean, fava	Legume
Bean, lima	Legume
Bean, scarlet runner	Legume
Bean, snap (pole & bush)	Legume
Pea	Legume
Soybean	Legume

Traditional rotations, which were developed for cold-winter climates, may allow for up to two years before adding any organic matter or fertilizer. Since I am gardening the year around, I must add amendments twice a year to avoid exhausting my soil. I add extra fertilizer whenever I plant a heavy feeder, and sometimes I add even more while the crop is growing. I may not work in any fertilizer before growing a light feeder.

I rarely take the time or space to grow green manure, because I prefer to keep my garden in action. But I do use weeds as green manure, letting them grow briefly in unoccupied areas and then digging them in or composting them before they go to seed.

Winter legumes, such as peas and fava beans, are particularly useful in my year-round garden. Planting a soil builder in fall or winter leaves me free to plant heavy feeders, such as tomatoes and summer squash, in summer. Plan your rotation to allow fresh organic matter to decay in the soil for a few weeks before you plant. Don't plant carrots, parsnips, or salsify for six months after you dig in fresh animal manure, because it will cause them to develop badly.

In areas where the soil needs liming to make it less acidic, gardeners often add lime or wood ash just before they plant a cole crop (broccoli, brussels sprouts, cabbage, cauliflower, collards, kale, or kohlrabi). Cole crops don't mind slightly alkaline soil, and they can use the extra calcium in lime or the extra potassium in wood ash. My soil, like many local soils, doesn't need liming. Still, I sometimes have a little wood ash from the fireplace and I dig it in ahead of a cole crop.

To avoid soil diseases it is best not to plant tomatoes in the same place more than once every four years, but this is hard to do in a small garden. My mustard-family grouping is designed to reduce a buildup of the cabbage maggot and to avoid other mustard-family pests. If the onion root maggot has

been a problem, I try not to plant onions in the same spot more than once every two to three years.

Rotation may seem complicated if you try to figure it all out ahead of time. The traditional method called for dividing the garden into several sections and rotating crops through them in a preset order. Today most home gardeners who practice rotation do it in a more free-form manner. Rather than make a formal plan and try to stick to it, I just think through some possibilities for the crops I like to grow, sketch a simple map, and plan as I go.

Making Compost

I grew up in a composting household. Dad read *Organic Gardening* magazine in its earliest years and learned to compost. He made vast amounts in one end of our vegetable garden, and it seems to me that some of our best chats took place while he was back there adding garbage, turning the piles, and sifting the final product. While he worked he taught me to appreciate the beauty of compost. I love the feel, look, and smell of it. If you have never made compost, you probably think that organic gardeners are a little nutty over the stuff, but I encourage you to try making some and see the results for yourself.

Hot or Cold: What's the Difference?

Composting is done either by the hot, or fast, method or by the cold, or slow, method. Both methods produce an excellent organic soil amendment, but hot compost is more likely to contain enough nitrogen to satisfy plants. Although both methods recycle

Sifting finished compost

HOW TO MAKE HOT COMPOST

There are several methods for making hot compost, but they share some basic features.

1. Choose a good site.

Pick an out-of-the-way spot at least 3 by 3 feet, on bare ground, in either the sun or the shade. The pile should be a minimum of 3 feet high. Although a frame is not necessary, it makes the pile easier to shape and turn. Two frames side by side make it possible to turn the pile back and forth between them. Put a layer of coarse, dry organic matter, such as dry weeds, twigs, or straw, on the ground before you build the pile.

2. Provide the correct carbon-nitrogen ratio.

Build the pile all on the same day. It should contain roughly 30 parts carbon to 1 part nitrogen. You can come close simply by alternating 3- to 5-inch-thick layers of dry (low-nitrogen) and green or fresh (high-nitrogen) materials. You will know you added too much high-nitrogen material if the pile starts to smell of ammonia. Sawdust is a very low-nitrogen material—it contains 200 to 500 parts carbon to 1 part nitrogen. Other low-nitrogen materials include paper (170 to 1), straw (80 to 1), and corn stalks (60 to 1). High-nitrogen materials include fresh manure (20 to 1), grass clippings (19 to 1), and table scraps (15 to 1).

3. Don't include big chunks of material.

Since pieces thicker than 1/2 inch take too long to decay, either leave them out or chop them up. If larger chunks get in, screen the finished compost through 1/2-inch wire mesh and add the large pieces to the next pile.

4. Provide the correct moisture.

The microorganisms that make compost need moisture. Water the layers as you make them, then keep the pile about as moist as a wrung-out sponge. The pile is too wet if water runs out the bottom.

5. Provide air or, more accurately, oxygen.

If there is not enough oxygen in the pile, a different set of microorganisms will take over the pile, producing a compost that smells terrible and contains much less nitrogen than a well-aerated pile. Avoid too much fine sawdust since it can compact and exclude air. In rainy weather cover the pile with a waterproof tarp. If you use a bin, makes sure that air can enter through the sides (leave space between the wooden slats or use wire mesh for the sides).

6. Turn the pile frequently.

For the fastest compost turn the pile after three to four days, when the temperature should have reached 140°F to 160°F, then turn it every two to three days until turning doesn't stimulate more heat. Always turn from top to bottom and from sides to center. A pitchfork or garden fork works better than a shovel or spade. Turning allows the microorganisms to work on all parts of the pile and gives them oxygen.

7. Correct your pile.

There are two main signs of trouble in a hot compost pile: the interior of the pile doesn't heat up within two days and a strong smell of ammonia. Since every compost pile is different, it is impossible to be exact about how much corrective material to add, but you will soon be able to judge.

The interior of the pile doesn't heat up within two days.
- If the pile seems too wet, add thin layers of sawdust while turning.
- If the pile seems too dry, add water while turning.
- If the moisture seems right, assume that the pile lacks nitrogen. Sprinkle in a high-nitrogen material, such as blood meal or cottonseed meal, while turning the pile.

The pile begins to smell strongly of ammonia.
- The pile contains too much nitrogen. Add thin layers of sawdust while turning it.

garden and household waste, hot composting can handle more kinds of waste. The hot method takes as little as three to six weeks, whereas the cold method requires three months to a year.

Hot compost is a ferment, just as yogurt is, and requires close attention to the needs of the fungi and bacteria carrying out the process. You must mix everything together in the right proportions, then see that conditions remain favorable while the soil organisms partially digest your mixture. Unlike yogurt making, hot composting generates its own heat. The fungi and bacteria in compost raise the temperature in the center of the pile to 140°F - 160°F. This is hot enough to kill weed seeds, disease spores, and insect eggs. Also, unlike yogurt, hot compost must be stirred or turned while it is heating up. Turning moves the materials that were on the outside of the pile to the inside. When the organisms have done their work, the pile cools down, and the compost is ready to use.

If you don't have the time or energy to attend

to a hot compost pile, you can make cold compost. In fact, if you don't build the pile all on the same day, choose ingredients carefully, and turn it regularly, it will be a cold pile. Some or all of the pile will never heat up enough to kill seeds, spores, or eggs, so you should not add any materials that require sterilization. Helpful microorganisms are responsible for the slower cold process, but they are different from those operating at high temperatures.

Although you can't produce the highest quality compost without the careful layering and turning that makes a hot pile, you can improve a cold pile by chopping large materials so that they will decay faster, adding a nitrogen source along with dry material, and watering the pile occasionally. You can make a type of cold pile called a sheet compost (see this page), or you can use earthworms (see page 90) to speed a cold pile and improve the product. (To find out more about composting, see the publications listed under Soil and Soil Fertility in Appendix VI, Suggested Reading.)

SHEET COMPOST

Here is a style of cold composting you can use the first year that you garden or during a few months between crops on a small part of your garden. Layer different kinds of material up to a foot thick. Chop large pieces and avoid long, stringy material. As a nitrogen source include manure or freshly cut or pulled weeds without seeds or roots that may regrow. Keep the pile moist until it shrinks noticeably.

The composting process may take a month or several months, depending on the type and size of materials. A couple of weeks before you intend to plant, add manure, human urine, blood meal, or another nitrogen source. Dig the partially formed compost into the soil and water the area until it is just moist. If you are preparing the area for a seedbed, move any chunks of organic material that didn't decay to an area that you won't be digging soon.

Every Compost Pile Is Unique

Just remember that no single type of organic material has to be in compost. A gardener who lives near a cabinetmaker's shop may use lots of hardwood sawdust. Another gardener may collect trash barrels of spent hops from a nearby brewery, and yet another may gather used bedding from a local riding stable. All these materials will produce hot compost if the carbon-nitrogen ratio is correct.

Garden books written for other areas will stress locally available ingredients that may not be easily obtained here. They usually list fallen tree leaves and lawn clippings as main ingredients. Our lawns are not as extensive as those elsewhere in the country, and many of our trees are evergreen. Although evergreens shed some leaves throughout the year, the leaves are tougher and slower to decay than deciduous leaves. Some common evergreens, such as eucalyptus and juniper, contain resins that may poison microorganisms.

Keep your ears and eyes open for local treasures. Check with your local Recreation and Park Department to see if you can have some of their clippings. If there is a rice mill nearby, ask for hulls. If a nongardening friend has a rabbit, request the manure. I once accompanied a San Francisco community gardener on a compost hunt that took us to the waste bins of the wholesale produce terminal, a rice mill, a little-known horse manure dumping ground on the south side of San Francisco, and an industrial park where the gardeners had agreed to leave bags of pesticide-free grass clippings.

The Ins and Outs of Compost

When you are considering compost ingredients, you will want to know how quickly a material breaks down, and whether it contains toxic substances or attracts rodents or cats. Certain materials are fine for a hot pile but should be left out of a cold one. A truly hot pile will kill weed seeds, disease spores, and insect eggs, but a cold pile, or a sort of hot pile, will not.

You also need to consider local health regulations. For example, in San Francisco any compost set-up that includes kitchen scraps is required to be in a container with ventilation & drainage holes no larger then 1/4 inch. Gardeners in other areas should find out if similar restrictions exist in their locations.

Fine in All Piles

- Healthy vegetable or flower plants pulled from the garden.

- Weeds without ripe seeds or roots that will regrow. Freshly pulled green weeds are preferable, but add dried ones if you have them.

- Vegetable or fruit scraps, including citrus peels, from the kitchen.

- Crushed eggshells, nutshells, or shells of shellfish.

- Barnyard manure, hamster, rabbit, or gerbil manure, fresh or rotted, with or without bedding.

- Human urine from a healthy person. Dilute 5 to 1 with water.

- Fresh or partly rotted straw.

- Coarse sawdust.

- Grass or shrub clippings without pesticide residue.

- Fallen tree leaves, especially from deciduous trees.

- Rice hulls, coffee grounds, or tea leaves.

- Residue from making beer, wine, or apple cider.

- Seaweed, preferably rinsed to remove sea salt.

- Cottonseed meal, blood meal, or fish meal. Any of these purchased organic fertilizers can serve as a nitrogen source for a hot pile, but are not necessary if you have used enough high nitrogen materials, such as fresh grass clippings, weeds, manure, or garbage.

For Hot Piles Only

- Weeds with ripe seeds or roots that will regrow. (Avoid oxalis and wild onion bulbs, as they are too risky, though theoretically they would be killed.)

- Vegetable or flower plants that are diseased or contain insect eggs. Again, use caution.

- Bones, meat, or fish scraps. Add small amounts to the center of a pile if you are sure that you can get it to heat up. Otherwise, bury these scraps under at least 6 inches of soil in an unused part of the garden to avoid the odor and rodents.

- Feathers or hair. Although very slow to break down, they add considerable nitrogen.

Keep Out of All Compost Piles

- Blackberry brambles. Even if they don't reroot, they make prickly compost.

- Fats or cereal products, since they attract rodents.

- Sawdust from plywood, pressure-treated wood, or wood that may have been painted with lead-based paint or treated with poisonous materials (see page 36).

- Sewage sludge, since it may contain heavy metals.

- Manure from humans, dogs, or cats, as these can carry diseases.

- Glossy paper, bleached paper, or paper printed with colored ink.

- Branches or stems greater than 1/2 inch in diameter.

- Rocks, glass, plastic, or metal.

Controversial Items

- Old compost or soil. Some gardeners sprinkle a little of either in every other layer, but others think it is unnecessary.

- Pine needles or oak leaves. Use them in moderation since they will acidify the compost.

- Wood chips or leaves from acacia, California bay, eucalyptus, juniper, or pittosporum. They contain plant-inhibiting chemicals, which may or may not remain toxic to plants after composting.

- Purchased bacterial starters, herbal starters, or chemical fertilizers. They aren't necessary if you build your pile right.

- Lime. Definitely don't use slaked or hydrated lime,

EARTHWORM COMPOST

Earthworms from your garden soil, mainly the large "nightcrawler" types, will live around the edges of a hot compost pile, and can thrive throughout a cold one. Other types, called "redworms," can help you create a rich compost from kitchen wastes.

When I was a child in Indiana, we had earthworm compost in the basement all winter long. The compost didn't smell or attract vermin, and I rather liked knowing that the worms were down there working away on the compost that would enrich our spring garden, though I knew better than to talk about it in school!

In recent years, worm composting has become more widely known. And, while worms can work outdoors all year in coastal California, some gardeners prefer the convenience of a bin in the basement, under the sink in the kitchen, or doubling as a windowseat.

Use a plastic or plywood container with a lid (plywood is less likely to overheat). The container needs drainage holes (which must be under 1/4 inch in diameter to meet San Francisco health regulations for containers in which kitchen garbage will be composted). If the container is used indoors, it must have a drip tray.

Tear newspaper (without colored ink) into narrow strips and fill the bin almost to the top, sprinkle it with water, and toss it until it is as wet as a wrung out sponge. Add a handful of soil— to provide digestive grit—about 1,000 redworms (available at local nurseries), and a pound of kitchen waste, then stand back. After the first few weeks, a worm bin can handle a pound of garbage for each square foot of surface, each week.

In a worm compost bin, newspaper provides a carbon source, and garbage a nitrogen source. The worms digest both until nothing is left but a dark brown, pleasant-smelling compost that is higher in nitrogen than most hot compost. In fact, it is so rich that you should never dig in more than a one-inch layer of it at a time.

To renew a worm bin, trowel all of the worms and finished compost to one end and remake a newspaper bed in the rest of the bin. Add garbage, and, after a few days, when the worms have moved into the new bed, harvest the compost. You can go to the trouble of saving the worms that stay in the compost, or not, as you choose. To remove them, make small piles and brush off the surface. The worms will crawl away from light, so at the end you will have harvested compost and a ball of redworms to put back in the bin.

For much more on composting methods, including plans for making wooden worm bins, troubleshooting tips, and details of the worm life cycle, see the book *Worms Eat My Garbage* (listed in Appendix VI, Suggested Reading). Call local gardening stores or gardening organizations for information about local sources of wormboxes and redworms.

---

since it will kill the very organisms that you are trying to get to digest your composting materials. Dolomitic limestone can help if you are worried that the compost will make your soil too acidic, although this is unlikely.

• Newspaper with black ink. Gardeners have traditionally used shredded newspaper as a mulch and compost ingredient, but there are nagging doubts about the ingredients in the ink. Paper printed with colored ink should not be used at all.

Recently, there has been much publicity about dioxin in paper. It should be noted that dioxin is introduced by the bleaching process and most newspapers are not bleached. You can see this by leaving a newspaper in the sun for a few days and watching it turn yellow. There is very little dioxin in even bleached paper, and toxicologists doubt that plants take up much dioxin from the soil, so this is not a large worry for gardeners. However, the issue is not settled.

NINE

Growing Like Weeds

ARDENERS OFTEN ASK ABOUT an unknown green interloper, "Is that a plant or is it a weed?" Of course, we all know exactly what they mean; on the other hand, we also know that weeds are plants.

Before there were gardens, the Anglo-Saxons used the word *wèod* to refer to all small plants generally. As plants were invited into gardens they were withdrawn from the weed category, becoming instead such things as crops and flowers. Since then, the term *weed* has been reserved for any unmannerly wild plant that came into our gardens against our wishes.

Like gardeners of food crops and flowers everywhere, we must contend with many kinds of weeds: uninvited seedlings that blanket our seedbeds, wild vines that entangle our garden plants, and tough perennials that sprout each year from missed bits of root. We must control these weeds if we are to have productive and beautiful gardens. To save time and energy combating weeds, we need to understand the habits of these unwelcome plants.

Just What Is a Weed?

Some would have it that a weed is only a flower or vegetable growing in the wrong place, and this certainly can be the case. When you have carefully sown and tended nasturtiums, you call them flowers. With pleasure you watch them grow, enjoying their bright accents in your yard. You may even be charmed when nasturtiums reseed themselves, add-

ing their cheeriness to other parts of your garden. However, when these fast-growing seedlings crowd out your delicate baby carrots, you are right to consider them weeds. Other domesticated plants that can make pests of themselves locally include Algerian ivy, Cape oxalis, sweet alyssum, and our local wild onion. Our most common wild blackberry was once a domesticated plant, but it succeeded so well in this region that it is now one of our most familiar and hard-to-control weeds.

Another definition of weed is a plant that grows mainly in places markedly disturbed by humans. Nature rarely clears and churns up the soil as much as we do when we are about to plant a garden. Plants have to be tough to survive such conditions, which occur naturally only after floods, landslides, and other natural disturbances.

Many of these denizens of disturbed places, such as dandelions, lambsquarters, pigweed, and dock, have followed humans over most of the earth. Carried unintentionally in grain, manure, animal fur, implements, and vehicles, their seeds have proved adaptable to a wide range of climates. Although plants native to California turn up as weeds in our gardens, they are rarely among the most difficult to control, maybe because they have not had centuries to adapt to our gardening practices.

The imported, worldwide weeds have adjusted in many ways to human efforts to control them. Some have evolved seeds that closely resemble those of commercial crops—understandable, since those were the seeds most likely to survive. One Old World weed common in California, yellow starthistle, makes two kinds of seeds, one smaller

91

and darker than the other. The smaller seed is hard to separate from several kinds of commercial seeds, so the weed has been able to survive as a contaminant of crops. If you have ever tried to pull sowthistle, also called wild lettuce, from hard soil, you have encountered another adaptation. The stem will often break near the ground, then sprout again from buds near the soil surface.

The Pros and Cons of Weeds

There are many good reasons to control weeds. They can disrupt the design of ornamental plantings and make a vegetable garden look disorderly. They harbor pests, including diseases, that can spread to domesticated plants. Some weeds exude chemicals that slow the growth of plants around them, a process called allelopathy. They compete with intentionally planted vegetables and flowers for water, nutrients, and light—and if ignored for long, they will simply take over. Weeds can cover the ground in a solid mat that few vegetables or flowers can penetrate. Some weeds, such as fennel or blackberry, can eventually make your yard impossible to walk across, never mind using it for a garden.

On the other hand, there are reasons to tolerate weeds and even to encourage them. Some weeds are edible and make welcome additions to salads and omelets. As long as they haven't gone to seed, most weeds can be used to make compost, or they can be dug into the soil as green manure. Pulled before they go to seed, many weeds can be left on the soil surface to mulch it and to feed earthworms and other soil organisms. (Most weeds will not reroot if left on the soil surface in summer, but more care must be taken to avoid rerooting during the wetter winter months.) Certain weeds can even be tolerated for short periods as a living mulch. Many weeds also provide pollen for bees and serve as a refuge for certain helpful insects.

As Joseph Cocannouer explained in his classic *Weeds: Guardians of the Soil*, some deep-rooted weeds, which he referred to as deep divers, provide another crucial service—opening up the subsoil to water and to the roots of more delicate plants. Most of our garden crops have been bred for their tops and not their roots, and consequently they have relatively weak root systems that do not penetrate deep. Many weeds, because they have had to be tough to survive, have very strong, deep-reaching roots. These deep divers include lambsquarters, wild chicory, plantain, purslane, nightshade, sowthistle, and vetch.

You can use deep divers to improve your soil, growing them either before you plant your garden or while you are gardening. Of course, you mustn't let even these weeds take over. Lambsquarters and sowthistle are the easiest to control, because their flowers are mostly at the top and can easily be cut off as they form. Vetch is also a good choice, since it is rarely an aggressive spreader. Do not allow these weeds to grow close together, or their roots won't go as deep; one deep diver every few feet is plenty. When the weeds become large, cut them off at ground level, leaving their roots to decay in place. When added to the compost, the tops will enrich your garden with nutrients from deep in the subsoil.

Another reason to tolerate the occasional weed is that these intruders are interesting, adding a bit of serendipity to your garden. I had a friend who grew weeds in a window box in his San Francisco apartment, just watering and watching what came up. Learning to identify the plants that nature sends our way can be fun and educational, a little like bird watching. I let one plant of any unfamiliar weed grow in my garden until I am able to identify

---

THE USES OF WEEDS

FOR FOOD: chickweed, dandelion, dock, epazote, fennel, Himalaya berry, lambsquarters, miner's lettuce, mint, mustard, nasturtium, New Zealand spinach, onion lily, purslane, shepherds-purse, sorrel, and wild radish.

FOR ORNAMENT: calla lily, kennelworth ivy, nasturtium, and onion lily.

FOR DEEP DIVING: lambsquarters, sowthistle, and vetch.

FOR ATTRACTING BENEFICIAL INSECTS: fennel, mustard, wild radish, pigweed, and white sweet clover.

FOR LIVING MULCH: chickweed and other annual weeds before they flower.

FOR COMPOST: any weed that has not flowered and will not reroot.

it. Until you learn to recognize the most noxious weeds, however, it is better to err on the side of control.

Different Kinds of Weeds

Like your garden crops, weeds have varying life spans. Some are annuals, completing their life cycle in less than a year. Others are biennials, starting from seed one spring, overwintering, blooming the following spring, and dying the second year. (In mild-winter regions such as ours, biennials may act like winter annuals, growing during the fall and going to seed in spring.) Still other weeds are perennials, living for three or more years.

Annual weeds sprout only from seed, dying at the end of one season. Biennials also sprout from seed, and they may resprout from slightly thickened roots—although only once. Then they die, relying on seeds to carry on the generations. Perennial weeds sprout not only from seed, which most of them produce each year, but also from food storage structures—tubers, corms, bulbs, woody or starchy roots, or creeping stems—that stay alive in the soil from year to year. Because of these structures, perennials are much harder to eradicate than annuals or biennials.

In addition to the length of time that they live, weeds can be classified by the season of their most active growth. Some weeds grow the most in warm weather, sprouting as the soil warms and thriving on the water that you give your garden in summer. Common summer weeds include the annuals purslane, lambsquarters, mallow, and crabgrass and the perennial bindweed. Other weeds are most active in winter, encouraged by our mild, rainy climate. They sprout as the winter rains begin and go to seed in March and April. Winter weeds include many grasses, chickweed, Cape oxalis, and onion lily. Even if you don't plant a garden in winter, it is a good idea to keep winter weeds under control(see page 98).

How to Control Weeds

The following tactics are based on the premise that we are smarter than weeds, and if they have gotten away from us it is only because we have not been paying enough attention to them. Of course, being smart, none of us want to spend all our weekends weeding. Well, it isn't necessary. An hour spent reading about control strategies is likely to save many hours of actually pulling weeds.

Theoretically, if you killed every weed seedling that dared come up, soon you would have no weeds. However, weeds are not something you can ever completely eliminate. You will miss weeds here and there, and nature will bring new ones into your garden, so the struggle will always go on. Still, once you have eliminated the worst weeds, you will be able to stay in control with little day-to-day effort. (If you are facing a very neglected yard, see page 98.)

Eradication Versus Limited Tolerance

Gardeners differ about the degree to which weeds should be controlled. One style of gardening insists that all weeds be cleared away. In a clean-culture garden, only the plants that the gardener has actually planted are allowed to survive. An opposing style, what I call selective weeding, involves a certain amount of laissez-faire. Selective weeders may let some weeds live at some times while controlling others. They may even encourage certain weeds, but with a clear understanding of when control is essential.

The clean-culture method is a good idea for a beginner because it is simple to learn. Clear the ground completely before you plant, then remove anything else that comes up while your crops are growing. Period. Be thorough and stick with it. Selective weeding, on the other hand, requires knowing which weeds you have and how they are likely to interact with your crops. It also requires that you recognize flower and vegetable seedlings when they come up, whether you planted them or they seeded themselves. Perhaps the best approach is to practice clean culture when you are a beginner, then work toward a more selective approach as you learn more.

In my garden I tolerate some purslane, chickweed, and onion lilies as food plants, and I sometimes let chickweed grow for a while as a living mulch in winter. Also, I am very tolerant of volunteer flowers and vegetables that sometimes come up without being planted. Johnny-jump-ups, forget-me-nots, and nasturtiums are among my flower volunteers, and potatoes, arugula, collards, mustard, parsley, salsify, and garland chrysanthemum are among my vegetable volunteers. Depending on where they appear and if I have room for volunteers, I may pull them, thin them, or transplant them to other spots in the garden. My goal is to encourage volunteer vegetables and flowers and useful weeds while reducing undesirable weeds. In time, a good gardener can change the makeup of the wild flora of a garden, so that almost everything that comes up is useful in one way or another.

Timing Is Crucial

Crops are most damaged by competition with weeds in their first six weeks after seeding. It is not enough just to clear the bed of weeds before you plant. In the first month or so after planting, you must think as much about keeping the seedbed weed-free as you do about watering and thinning the crop seedlings. Even clean-culture gardeners often weed too late to protect their crops during this critical period. The little weed seedlings look so innocent that no internal alarms go off to warn you of the serious competition for food and water that faces your desirable seedlings.

As crop plants get older and larger, they are less affected by weeds. Crops that grow tall quickly, such as corn, and crops that spread out fast to form a solid leaf canopy, such as bush beans, can hold their own against weeds sooner than crops that are shorter or have a less solid leaf canopy, such as radishes and onions.

Some General Control Tactics

- **Mulching** Gardeners once hoed frequently between crops, not only to control weeds but also to maintain a dust mulch, which was believed to reduce surface evaporation. Hoeing was also supposed to open crusted soil so that water could penetrate more easily. However, it has been shown that dust is a poor mulch and doesn't prevent evaporation very well. Although hoeing will break up a crust, an organic mulch will accomplish the same purpose but with many additional benefits, including weed control, reduced evaporation, better water penetration, and improved soil structure and fertility. A thick organic mulch helps control weeds by reducing the germination of weed seeds beneath the mulch; also, any weeds rooted in the loose mulching material are easier to pull. However, mulching will not stop the sprouting of perennials weeds from their underground structures. Some perennials can even punch their way through a plastic sheet! (See page 77 for more about mulches.)

- **Shallow Hoeing** If you choose not to mulch, occasional shallow hoeing is a good way to control weed seedlings. To keep from damaging the roots of your crop plants, hoe no deeper than an inch. Choose a scuffle hoe, a hula hoe, or any other hoe with a blade that you hold parallel to the soil surface. This kind of hoe will cut weeds off just below the soil surface with minimal harm to the roots of crop plants.

- **Thick Planting** Another way to protect crop plants from weeds is to space them close enough together so that the leaves of adjoining plants touch at maturity. Fast-growing crops will shade out much weed growth.

- **Meeting Crop Needs** Growing your crops under the best possible conditions will give them an advantage when they compete with weeds. In general, provide loose and fertile soil, adequate water, and the proper amount of sunlight. Find out the special needs of each crop and try to meet them.

Controlling Annual (and Biennial) Weeds

Seeds are an annual weed's only means of continuity. Combating the weed by eliminating its means of reproducing itself seems simple enough until you learn how many seeds an annual weed can produce in a season. Consider purslane, which doesn't appear to be much of a threat, considering that it is squat, has small leaves, and is easy to uproot. But if you wait too long to pull it, purslane can drop fifty-two thousand seeds per plant! If you are wondering how so many seeds can germinate at once in a few square feet, they can't and they don't. What happens is worse.

The old adage "one year of seeds, seven years of weeds" is based on the fact that the seeds don't all germinate in the first year. The purslane that drops its thousands of little black seeds in your garden is ensuring that purslane seedlings will blanket your spring seedbeds for many years to come. Only 10 to 20 percent of the weed seeds will germinate each year. Assuming that 10 percent sprout yearly and that no new seeds are shed, 51 percent of the seeds will be left after seven years. At the rate of 20 percent each year, there will still be 21 percent left after seven years. In ten to twenty years, 1 percent of the original seeds will remain. So when you see your garden covered with annual weeds, understand that it is their seeding that you must prevent.

Many annual weeds bloom when they are quite young and some have flowers so insignificant that you hardly realize that they are blooming until you look closely. Still others continue to ripen seeds after they have been pulled. These traits have developed or persisted, because they allowed the weeds to survive eradication efforts. Here are some ways to control annual weeds before they take over your garden.

- **Hand Pulling** Start removing weed seedlings as soon as you can identify them. If the weeds are located right next to delicate crop seedlings, you can avoid harming the crop roots by cutting the weeds at soil level with scissors.

  Hand-pull larger weeds on days when the soil is moist and the weeds are easy to pull out. (Don't weed during soggy conditions, or you may damage your soil structure.) Reach down and grasp one or a few weeds near the base, gathering up all of its leaves. If you find that you are leaving the bottom of the plants in the ground, you are trying to pull too many at once or you are not reaching low enough. If a large weed is close to a crop plant, use one hand to hold the soil in place at the base of the weed as you pull, so that you won't pull up the crop plant too.

  As you gain experience gardening, you will learn the habits of various weeds and how to pull them, and you will be able to adjust your technique to different species. For example, you will need to hook a finger under crabgrass to pull out the base of the plant. Hand pulling will become easier as you continue to improve your soil. One day your soil will be so loose that you will pull out a really tough weed and realize that you did it with only a flick of your wrist!

- **Presprouting** Turning the soil even once before you plant will kill some weed seedlings. If your garden is heavily infested with weed seeds, however, a technique called presprouting will eliminate more weeds than just a single digging. This method works by tricking the weeds into using up their seeds faster. It takes some planning, but when you see the difference it can make for such hard-to-weed vegetables as carrots, you will agree that it is worthwhile.

  Begin by digging and amending your soil and raking it smooth. Water the soil and keep it moist, just as if you had sown crop seeds. In a week or two you will have a bed of little weed seedlings, mostly annuals. Kill the weeds by gently scraping the soil surface (it should be on the dry side) with a hoe or hand-weeding tool. Don't dig into the soil any more than necessary, because that will stimulate seeds that are deeper in the soil to sprout. If the plot is particularly weedy, water again, wait for more weeds to sprout, and destroy the seedlings before you plant. When you do plant, disturb the soil as little as possible to keep new weed seeds from sprouting.

  Weed presprouting must be done at a time of year when the weeds that you hope to control will germinate. Although some weeds will germinate almost anytime the soil is moist, others must wait for the soil to warm up in spring. I learned this the hard way presprouting weeds in an early carrot patch. The patch, which was perfectly clear in late March, was covered with tiny weed seedlings mixed with the young carrot plants by the middle of May. The late-starting weed seeds had escaped my hoe by remaining dormant. I presprouted in February and April the next time, and my June-planted carrot crop was practically weed-free. The earlier presprouting would have worked fine for a fast-growing crop, such as radishes, which would have been harvested before the weeds popped up in May.

  Even if presprouting doesn't work perfectly, it will reduce the number of weed seeds in your soil, hastening the day when a blanket of weed seedlings is a thing of the past. Presprouting also teaches you to recognize weed seedlings and helps you to distinguish them from crop seedlings. If you presprout weeds a couple of times a year, you will soon know most of the weeds that are likely to grow in your garden.

- **Postponing Delicate Crops** Even after presprouting, you may decide that an area is still too weedy for crops with delicate seedlings. If so, first plant a crop that quickly grows large, such as beans or potatoes. Keep the bed well weeded, and presprout again before you plant more delicate crops.

- **Planting in Rows** If there are still many weed seedlings coming up but you are impatient to start a delicate crop, plant the crop in rows. Rows are easier to weed than scatter-sown beds.

- **Avoiding New Infestations** Be aware of the

possible sources of new weed seeds that may enter your garden. Think twice when your neighbor offers a pile of weeds for your compost. Unless you make a hot compost, you may end up with your neighbor's weed species as well as the ones you already have. Notice whether the weeds in nearby vacant lots form wind-borne seeds; if so, cut them down before the seeds form and blow into your garden. Keep new weed seeds out of your garden while working to eliminate the weed seeds already there, and over time you will have to contend with fewer and fewer annual weeds.

Controlling Perennial Weeds

Although perennial weeds are sometimes big seed producers, they have an additional—and formidable—survival strategy of asexual reproduction from bulbs, corms, tubers, underground stems, or fibrous or thickened roots. When a perennial weed sprouts from one of these underground storage structures, it has more energy to draw on than if it were sprouting from a small seed. When you pull a dandelion and don't get the whole root, in a couple of weeks the part left in the ground can generate a

HERBICIDES—ONLY AS A LAST RESORT

Although nonchemical methods are safer, cheaper, and often easier for routine weed control, it can make sense to use one of the relatively safe herbicides to fight recurring infestations or very large areas of big, hard-to-stop perennial weeds, such as blackberry brambles.

Glyphosate (Roundup™ and Kleenup™ are two brand names) is a good choice for fighting perennial weeds. It is a general herbicide that kills most kinds of plants on contact. When sprayed on actively growing shoots, it is transported into the roots, killing the whole plant including any underground storage structures. When glyphosate comes into contact with the soil, it is deactivated. This means that the soil itself is not contaminated and that plants will grow in it as soon as a week after the dead plants have been removed. It also means that the chemical does not spread to the roots of nearby trees and shrubs. Although relatively low in toxicity to humans, glyphosate is still a poison, so read the label carefully and refer to the information on pesticide safety (see page 133) before using it. Check the label carefully to be sure that glyphosate (also called isopropylamine salt of glyphosate) is the only active ingredient in your product, since some formulas also contain other chemicals—often ones that are more damaging to the environment.

Apply glyphosate when the weeds are in a period of active growth, preferably when they are young or are about to flower. After the weeds have died, remove them from the garden. Some weeds may show resistance, and you may have to reapply the chemical, spot-treating the remaining growth. Bindweed, blackberry, horsetail, ivy, and mature mallow plants are among the perennial weeds that may not die after only one treatment. (See Appendix III for more information on glyphosate.)

Another product, a soap-based general herbicide called Sharpshooter™, is much less toxic than glyphosate to humans. Several applications of this product may be required to kill perennial weeds. It will work faster on all weeds in warm, dry weather.

Be aware that neither glyphosate nor the soap-based herbicide is registered for use in or around growing vegetables. If you intend to plant food crops in an area that you have treated with Sharpshooter™ soap spray, wait several days before doing so. After treating an area with glyphosate, wait at least seven days before planting asparagus, beans, beets, broccoli, cabbage, carrots, cauliflower, celery, chicory, corn, horseradish, kale, lettuce, Jerusalem artichoke, mustard greens, okra, onions, parsnips, peas, Irish and sweet potatoes, radishes, rutabagas, and spinach. Wait at least one year before planting any other vegetables.

plant that would have taken months to grow to that size from seed. Some perennial weeds almost never grow from seed, whereas others use both means of reproduction. If dock grows in your garden, you will soon learn to tell the difference between a robust sprout growing from a thickened root and the smaller, more delicate dock seedling.

The following techniques will help you prevent perennial weeds from gaining a roothold in your garden.

- **Digging Out** Although pulling and hoeing will remove perennial weed seedlings as easily as they do annual weed seedlings, these techniques are rarely sufficient to control more mature perennial weeds. You must also dig and remove the underground structure that allows the weed to spring back each season. Remember, most perennials will resprout from *every fragment* of runner or root that you leave behind. Yes, this digging can be hard work if the weeds have had several years to get a roothold. However, once you remove these structures, it is relatively easy to keep perennial weeds from ever becoming so well established again. After initial control efforts, keep pressure on perennial weeds by continuing to dig them whenever you see them and never letting them go to seed.

   Although you can dig out perennial weeds anytime in their life cycle, a particularly effective time is after they have just bloomed but before seed heads form. At that point, they are storing the least amount of energy underground. Another good time to dig them out is when they are just beginning to come up for the season, since you can use the technique of presprouting to find missed bits of root. Dig first, removing as many root pieces as you can, then water and wait for new sprouts to mark the location of the roots that you missed. Dig a second time to remove the sprouting fragments.

- **Cutting the Tops** When noxious perennial weeds are mixed with your crops, you won't be able to get into the soil to remove the roots, bulbs, or other underground structures. But at least you can keep the weeds from storing more food underground by cutting or pulling off their shoots. For instance, I try to pluck bindweed shoots before they are a couple of inches tall. You can do a more thorough job of removing the weeds during a break in crops.

- **Mulching to Smother** If your initial control efforts seem futile or if the area needing control is large, a smothering mulch may do the trick. To be effective against perennial weeds, a mulch must block light from reaching the soil and it must be difficult for weeds to penetrate. Ideally, the mulch will decay slowly into the soil to improve it. Finally, the mulch should be relatively attractive.

   Black plastic will block light and stop most weeds, but it doesn't let water penetrate, will not decay into the soil, and is unsightly. Both newspaper and corrugated cardboard from boxes meet the criterion of effectiveness against weeds and they will decay into the soil. (Although there may be some chance of contamination from newspaper ink, it is so slight that even *Organic Gardening* magazine approves the use of newspaper to smother perennial weeds. (For more information about newspaper as a gardening material, see page 90.) Commercially available weed mats can also be used, although they are more expensive and do not decay into the soil. On perennial weeds that are not very large, a layer of straw or wood chips at least 6 inches thick may be enough.

   Before spreading the mulch, clear an area as well as you can and water the soil thoroughly. If you are mulching with newspaper, use only paper with black ink, spreading it least six sheets thick. Double or triple the layer if you are dealing with very pushy weeds, such as fennel or blackberry. If you are using cardboard, spread a layer three sheets thick. Overlap the pieces of any smothering mulch material generously, so that weeds

Underground structures such as this runner, allow perennial weeds to resprout.

cannot grow between sections of the material. Weight black plastic, commercial weed mat, newspaper, or cardboard here and there with soil as you go. Cover any of these materials with 2 to 4 inches of an organic mulch, such as straw or wood chips, to improve its appearance.

Keep the mulched area moderately moist, unless you are using black plastic. You can dig in an organic mulch anytime from several months to a year after the normal sprouting time of the perennial weeds that you are fighting. (Remove any black plastic and any large pieces of newspaper or cardboard that have not decayed.) Straw, wood chips, newspaper, and cardboard are low in nitrogen, so if you dig these in you will have to add nitrogen before planting.

- **Avoiding New Infestations** Just like annual weeds, perennial weeds can come into your garden as hitchhikers. A plant from a friend's yard or a nursery can be a Trojan horse, bearing Cape oxalis corms or nutsedge tubers hidden in the soil. If you accept plants that you suspect are contaminated by perennial weeds, be on guard. Remove any visible weeds and weed storage structures from the soil around your new plants, then watch for new sprouts. As a precaution, you may want to keep the plants in containers for a few months until you are sure that the soil around the roots is free of perennial weeds.

How to Control (and Use) Winter Weeds

Our mild, rainy winters give local gardeners a special concern: winter weeds. As the hills turn green, so do our gardens. From our windows the green looks pretty, and the chilly, wet weather makes it easy to ignore the fact that those plants are weeds. Although the weeds offer the soil some protection against the pelting winter rains, they will lead to big trouble if they are ignored for too long.

As the days grow shorter and colder, winter weeds will outgrow most fall-planted garden crops. Soon they will be shading them and usurping scarce nutrients. By March or April, weed seeds will begin to ripen. If you wait for fine spring weather to begin weeding, you will be pulling large, tough weeds from drying soil. They will require more care and effort in composting because of the seeds and the woody stems. You will probably prefer to throw the weeds,

along with the nutrients they have removed from your soil, into the trash.

Winter weeding is the undoing of many clean-culture gardeners, who tend to keep summer gardens immaculate but fall down on the job in winter. It is important to continue weeding the year around. Even if you are a selective weeder, do not under any circumstances let winter weeds grow past January or February, when they begin to go to seed.

Although keeping winter weeds under control is crucial, there are also several ways to make use of the weeds. Sometimes I allow them to grow as a living mulch for a few weeks (I've let chickweed grow among cabbages, yanking it out in handfuls when it got too tall), but I do not tolerate aggressive perennials or let weeds overgrow my winter crops. Since garlic, onions, and winter legumes cannot endure competition from weeds, I always keep those beds weed-free. I often leave pulled chickweed and similar weeds on the soil surface as a mulch not only in summer but also in winter, even though the risk of rerooting is greater during the rainy season. Grasses are particularly likely to reroot and should be placed roots up after they are pulled.

Rerooting is less likely if you turn the weeds into the soil as a green manure. This should be done when they are still small enough to decompose easily and on a day when the soil is not too soggy from rain. If I have many weeds that may reroot or have grown a little too large for green manure, I use them to make a sheet compost (see page 88) to be dug under later in spring.

I find edible weeds more welcome in winter than summer, since summer weeds must compete for my attention with a greater variety of vegetables. For example, purslane comes up just as my cactus pads are ready and when there are large harvests of zucchini, cucumbers, and green beans. In winter I take great delight in tossing together salads of domesticated lettuce, endive, and sorrel along with bits of this and that weed, topped with a late nasturtium or two. Steamed dock leaves are a great treat when the last of the brussels sprouts are gone and the early spring greens are only just beginning to break through the earth.

How to Reclaim Neglected Land

After a garden is abandoned, the first weeds that appear are mostly annuals. In a few years the harder-to-control perennials take over. We have all seen abandoned lots in our neighborhoods. In win-

SOIL SOLARIZATION—
IF YOU HAVE ENOUGH SUNSHINE...

A relatively new technique to control most weeds and some soil pests, soil solarization involves covering the soil with clear plastic sheeting for six to eight weeks. If the days are warm enough, the soil near the surface will get hot enough to kill weed seeds, fungus spores, and other pests. Unfortunately, coastal gardens may never get warm spells that last long enough for this technique to be effective. Several consecutive warm spells may be enough to produce results in the sunnier parts of the region.

Soil solarization works work best in an area at least 6 by 9 feet. Clear the soil, then smooth it so that the plastic covering will be in contact with as much soil as possible. Water the soil thoroughly and cover it with one or two layers of sturdy clear plastic (recent studies showed that two layers are more effective than one). If you must piece together the plastic, use transparent tape, duct tape, or a heatproof and waterproof glue. Tuck the edges of the plastic into the soil—and hope for a lot of sunshine!

---

ter they are a riotous green, blanketed with grasses and small weeds. In summer only large, deep-rooted perennials, such as arching blackberries and towering fennel, remain green; the smaller plants turn brown, just as the small plants on the coastal hills do.

You can't expect to prepare an untamed, overgrown yard for planting in a day. You may not even be able to walk across it. Although I hope you won't have to face a badly neglected yard, especially if it is to be your first garden, the truth is that you may have to tackle one someday.

The following is a plan that, begun in fall or winter, will allow you to plant by early to midsummer. Begun in summer, it will allow you to plant by late winter or early spring. Be sure to put as much as you can into your initial attack. Enlist volunteer or paid help if there is too much work, since success or failure in the initial stages may mean the difference between an actual garden and a perpetual "someday" garden.

1 **Cut** Start by cutting and removing all the plants you don't want, including woody plants. Use hand pruners, loppers, or even a machete (if you are skillful with one) to cut the aboveground parts of blackberry brambles, fennel stalks, grasses, and other unwanted plants.

2 **Dig Out** Set about chopping and digging out what is left. Don't try to dig out weed roots when

the soil is dry. Water the soil thoroughly several days in advance, so that it will be moist but not soggy when you are ready to dig. A mattock or grub hoe is a good tool for cutting up and removing the base of tough weeds, such as fennel or wild pampas grass. (You can rent these heavy-duty tools inexpensively from a tool rental company.) A garden fork is a good tool for finding and removing trailing roots. If you have perennial weeds that spread by root fragments, don't be tempted to use a rotary tiller. Rototilling will make the situation worse by chopping the roots into fragments from which new plants can sprout.

3 **Discard** Although it is possible to compost some of the debris, it will contain many seeds and storage structures from which new weeds can grow. You would have to sort carefully and put any dubious material in a hot compost pile. Since you are probably impatient to finish clearing the yard, I suggest that you just put all the debris—the brambles, brush, grasses, rootstocks, runners, bulbs, corms, and tubers—into the trash and save composting for later.

4 **Presprout** Although the cleared area looks bare, there will be many seeds and roots lurking in the soil. Let them start to grow, keeping the soil moist during the dry season to encourage their growth. Turn the soil when the weeds are a few inches high but before they have a chance to go

to seed. Turn the seedlings under, and dig out any weeds that are sprouting from roots or other underground structures. Put these sprouting perennial weeds in the trash.

5 **Presprout Again** Wait for more weeds to grow, watering if necessary to encourage growth. When the weeds are a few inches high, kill the seedlings by lightly scraping the soil surface with a hoe. Keep presprouting, hoeing, and digging every few weeks for the next four to six months.

6 **Plant** Dig in organic amendments, add fertilizer, and plant. Having come this far, you may want to grow a cover crop, or a green manure (see page 76) or make a sheet compost (see page 88) before you plant.

7 **Keep Watch** Although this program will clear your garden well enough for you to start planting crops, you must be vigilant for the next couple of years. Watch especially for winter-sprouting perennials in fall and summer-sprouting perennials in late spring and early summer. A "rotation" of bindweed in summer and Cape oxalis in winter is a common one in neglected local gardens. Plan on continuing to dig out some underground structures for several years.

If you find yourself losing the battle against perennial weeds in your garden, either because the area is so large or you can't seem to dig out enough of the storage structures, consider using a smothering mulch (see page 97) or glyphosate (see page Appendix III). Use either only after the initial clearing steps have been completed. Put the smothering mulch on the cleared ground, or apply glyphosate when the weeds are actively resprouting. If your garden is in a sunny part of the region, you can try soil solarization (see page 99).

You are undoubtedly thinking, "Six months to a year is a long time to wait before I can garden. Can't I get something growing sooner?" For the understandably impatient would-be gardener, here are two good options. One is to garden temporarily in containers. A relatively inexpensive method is to plant in garbage bags filled with compost or a mixture of compost and a purchased soil mix. Unattractive at first, the bags will gain considerably in charm when they are bursting with healthy crops. When your garden is ready, just dig the planting medium into your soil.

Here is another good way to have your garden and prepare it too: Leave small openings, no more

than a foot in diameter, in the smothering mulch and set individual plants in them. In these openings amend the soil, making one more effort to remove perennial underground storage structures as you mix in the amendment. Plant and water thoroughly. When the seedlings are well established, lay on more mulch until it almost touches the stems. Large individual plants, such as tomatoes, cabbage, and broccoli, and hills of squash, corn, and pole beans are good choices for this treatment. You run a risk that perennial weeds will burst though the openings, but it's a controllable risk.

Weeds You're Likely to See

The chart on the next page lists the weeds that I have encountered frequently in my San Francisco garden or have heard are a problem in other gardens in our region. I have grouped annual and biennial weeds and listed perennial weeds separately. In addition to the chart are more detailed descriptions of weeds that are the most troublesome, the most useful, or just plain interesting. (Seed sources for some of the edible weeds are listed in code at the end of the descriptions. For an explanation of the codes, see Appendix IV.) The illustrations scattered throughout will help you to identify certain weeds, and the chart will allow you to make educated guesses about others.

If you need help identifying a weed, first show it to neighbors who garden, since they probably know the most common weeds in your neighborhood. If they can't help, refer to a good weed identification book (see Bibliography) or consult an expert. People who know local weeds include nursery employees, Cooperative Extension agents, instructors of horticulture classes, and staff members of various gardening organizations, such as San Francisco League of Urban Gardeners (SLUG) and the Ecology Center in Berkeley. If no one recognizes the weed, take it to an herbarium, where experts can identify it by comparing it with pressed specimens. (See Appendix V for a listing of herbaria.) You are much more likely to get a positive identification if your specimen has flowers on it; seedpods are helpful, but not crucial.

SOME WEEDS YOU MAY SEE

PERENNIAL WEEDS

COMMON NAME (LATIN NAME)	FAMILY	SOURCE	REPRO-DUCTION	COMMENTS	USE
*Bermuda Grass (*Cynodon dactylon*)	Graminae	Old World	Seed, rhizomes, stolons	Very invasive	Lawn grass
*Bindweed, Wild Morning Glory (*Convolvulus arvensis*)	Convolvulaceae	Europe	Taproot, rhizomes	Grows from root fragments	—
*Blackberry, Himalaya (*Rubus procerus*)	Rosaceae	Europe	Runners, seed	Very invasive	Edible berries
Calla Lily (*Zantedeschia aethiopica*)	Araceae	S. Africa	Rhizomes	Spreads slowly	Cut flower
Chicory (*Chicorium intybus*)	Compositae	Europe	Seed	—	Coffee substitute (roots)
Cineraria (*Senecio x hybridus*)	Compositae	Europe	Seed	Purple daisy	Ornamental
Coast Dandelion (*Hypochoeris radicata*)	Compositae	Old World	Seed, taproot	—	—
*Dandelion (*Taraxacum officinale*)	Compositae	Europe	Seed, taproot	Root breaks when pulled	Edible
*Dock (*Rumex crispus, R. obtusifolius*)	Polygonaceae	Europe, Asia	Rootstocks, seed	Grows from root fragments	Edible
*Fennel (*Foeniculum vulgare*)	Umbelliferae	Mediterranean	Seed	Large plants	Culinary herb
German Ivy (*Senecio mikanioides*)	Compositae	S. Africa	Seed, runners	Climber	Ornamental
*Grasses, Perennial (Various species)	Graminae	Various	Seed, rhizomes, stolons	—	—
Horsetail (*Equisetum hyemale, E. arvense*)	Equisetaceae	Native	Rhizomes	Probably poisonous	Ornamental
*Ivy, Algerian (*Hedera canariensis*)	Araliaceae	Canary Islands	Runners	Invasive	Ornamental
*Ivy, English (*Hedera helix*)	Araliaceae	Europe, E. Asia, N. Africa	Runners	Invasive	Ornamental
Judean Pellitory (*Parietaria judaica*)	Urticaceae	Europe	Seed	Leaves sticky	—
Jupiter's beard, Red Valerian (*Centranthus ruber*)	Valerianaceae	Europe, Mediterranean	Seed	—	Cut flower, ornamental
Kennelworth Ivy (*Cymbalaria muralis*)	Scrophulariaceae	Europe	Seed, runners	Small, nice in cracks	Ornamental
Mallow, Bristly (*Modiola caroliniana*)	Malvaceae	Southeast U.S.	Runners	Invasive	—
Mints (*Mentha* spp.)	Labiatae	Various	Runners	Invasive	Edible, tea
*Nut Sedge (*Cyperus esculentus*)	Cyperaceae	Old World	Tubers	Tough to pull	—
*Onion Lily, Wild Onion (*Allium triquetrum*)	Liliaceae	Mediterranean	Bulbs, seed	Invasive	Edible, cut flower

*means a particularly troublesome weed (common in gardens and hard to control)

SOME WEEDS YOU MAY SEE continued

COMMON NAME (LATIN NAME)	FAMILY	SOURCE	REPRO-DUCTION	COMMENTS	USE
* Oxalis, Cape, Bermuda Buttercup, (Oxalis pes-caprae)	Oxalidaceae	S. Africa	Bulbs	Invasive	Edible (small amounts)
* Oxalis, creeping (Oxalis corniculata)	Oxalidaceae	Europe	Runners, Seed	Invasive	Edible (small amounts
Pampas Grass (Cortaderia jubata, C. selloana)	Graminae	South America	Seed	C. Jubata is the worse spreader	Cut flower
Plantain, Narrowleaved (Plantago lanceolata)	Plantaginaceae	Europe	Seed	—	Edible
Plaintain, Broadleaved (Plantago major)	Plantaginaceae	Europe	Seed	—	Edible
* Quackgrass (Agropyron repens)	Graminae	Eurasia	Rootstocks, seed	—	—
Scotch Broom (Cytisus scoparius)	Leguminosae	Europe	Seed	Invasive	Cut flower
Sorrel, Sheep Sorrel (Rumex acetosella)	Polygonaceae	Europe, Asia	Rootstocks	Acid soil	Edible (small amounts)
Thymeleaf Speedwell (Veronica serpyllifolia)	Scrophulariaceae	Europe, Asia	Runners, seed	—	—

ANNUAL AND BIENNIAL WEEDS

Annual Bluegrass (Poa annua)	Graminae	Europe	Seed	Dormant in summer	Lawn filler
Bull Thistle (Cirsium vulgare)	Compositae	Europe, Asia	Seed	Sharp thorns Biennial	Ornamental seedheads
California Burclover (Medicago hispida)	Leguminosae	Europe	Seed	Clinging seeds	Soil improver
* Chickweed (Stellaria media)	Caryophyllaceae	Europe	Seed	Heavy seeder	Edible
* Quackgrass (Agropyron repens)	Graminae	Eurasia	Rootstocks, seed	—	—
* Cotula (Cotula australis)	Compositae	Australia	Seed	—	—
* Crabgrass, Hairy (Digitaria sanguinalis)	Graminae	Europe	Seed	Heavy seeder, summer weed	—
Cranesbill (Geranium spp., esp. G. Rotundifolium)	Geraniaceae	Europe	Seed	—	—
Cudweed, Pussy-toes (Gnaphalium luteo-album)	Compositae	Old World	Seed	—	Dry flower
Epazote (Chenopodium ambrosioides)	Chenopodiaceae	Tropical America	Seed	—	Culinary herb
* Groundsel, Common (Senecio Vulgaris)	Compositae	Europe	Seed	Heavy seeder	—
Hedge Mustard (Sisymbrium officinale)	Cruciferae	Europe	Seed	—	—
Horseweed (Conyza canadensis)	Compositae	U.S.	Seed	—	—
Ivyleaf Morning Glory (Ipomoea hederacea)	Convolvulaceae	Tropical America	Seed	Climber	Ornamental
* Pellitory (Parietaria hespera hespera)	Urticaceae	California	Seed	Leaves a little sticky	—
Lady's Thumb (Polygonum persicaria)	Polygonaceae	Europe	Seed	Matlike	—
Lambsquarters, White Goosefoot (Chenopodium album)	Chenopodiaceae	Europe	Seed	Leaf backs white–mealy	Edible, deep-rooted

* means a particularly troublesome weed (common in gardens and hard to control)

SOME WEEDS YOU MAY SEE continued

COMMON NAME (LATIN NAME)	FAMILY	SOURCE	REPRO-DUCTION	COMMENTS	USE
Lambsquarters, Nettleleaf Goosefoot (*Chenopodium murale*)	Chenopodiaceae	Europe	Seed	Leaf backs green=mealy	Edible, deep-rooted
* Mallow, Cheeseweed (*Malva* spp., esp. *M. parviflora* and *M. minicaensis*)	Malvaceae	Europe	Seed	Heavy seeder	Edible
Milk Thistle (*Silybum marianum*)	Compositae	Europe	Seed	Biennial	—
Miner's Lettuce (*Montia perfoliata*)	Portulacaceae	California	Seed	—	Edible
Mustard, Wild (*Brassica* spp., esp. *B. juncea, B. kaber, B. nigra, B. rapa*)	Cruciferae	Europe, Asia	Seed	—	Edible
Nasturtium (*Tropaeolum majus T. minus*	Tropaeolaceae	South America	Seed	Some climb	Edible–leaf and flower, cut flower
Nettle, Small (*Urtica urens*)	Urticaceae	Europe	Seed	Stinging hairs	Edible if cooked
New Zealand Spinach (*Tetragonia tetragonioides*)	Aizoaceae	New Zealand	Seed	Matlike	Edible
Nightshade, Black (*Solanum nodiflorum, S. furcatum*)	Solanaceae	Europe, S. America	Seed	Poisonous	—
* Petty Spurge (*Euphorbia peplus*)	Euphorbiaceae	Europe	Seed	—	—
Pineappleweed (*Matricaria matricarioides*)	Compositae	Probably California	Seed	—	—
Poison Hemlock (*Conium maculata*)	Umbelliferae	Europe	Seed	Poisonous Biennial	—
Prickly Oxtongue (*Picris echioides*)	Compositae	Europe	Seed	—	—
Prostrate Knotweed (*Polygonum aviculare*)	Polygonaceae	U.S., Europe, Asia	Seed	Matlike	—
* Prostrate Spotted Spurge (*Euphorbia maculata*)	Euphorbiaceae	Eastern U.S.	Seed	Matlike	—
* Purslane (*Portulaca oleracea*)	Portulacaceae	Europe	Seed	Heavy seeder	Edible
Rough Pigweed (*Amaranthus retroflexus*)	Amaranthaceae	Tropical America	Seed	—	Edible
Scarlet Pimpernel (*Anagallis arvensis*)	Primulaceae	Europe	Seed	Poisonous	—
Shepherds-Purse (*Capsella bursa-pastoris*)	Cruciferae	Europe	Seed	—	Edible
* Sow Thistle, Wild Lettuce (*Sonchus oleraceus*)	Compositae	Europe	Seed	—	Edible if young. Deep-rooted.
* Spiny Sow Thistle (*Sonchus asper*)	Compositae	Europe	Seed	—	Deep-rooted
Storksbill (*Erodium* spp., esp. *E. botrys, E. cicutarium, E. moschatum*)	Geraniaceae	Europe	Seed	—	—
* Swine Cress (*Coronopus didymus*)	Cruciferae	South America	Seed	Heavy seeder	—
Vetch, Common (*Vicia sativa*)	Leguminosae	Europe	Seed	—	Deep-rooted, improves soil
Wall Bedstraw (*Gallium parisiense* and probably *G. aparine*)	Rubiaceae	Europe	Seed	—	—
Wild Radish (*Raphanus sativus*)	Cruciferae	Europe	Seed	—	Young seed pods edible
Yellow Foxtail (*Setaria glauca*)	Graminae	Europe	Seed	—	—
Yellow Star Thistle (*Centaurea solstitalis*)	Compositae	Europe	Seed	Sharp spines under flowers	Poisonous to horses

* means a particularly troublesome weed (common in gardens and hard to control)

COMPENDIUM OF WEEDS

Annual Weeds

CALIFORNIA BURCLOVER

Medicago hispida
Legume Family ❖ *Leguminosae*

California burclover has clover leaves—little tre-foils—and small yellow pea-type flowers in groups of three to eight. As a legume, California burclover adds some nitrogen to the soil by forming root nod-ules with helpful bacteria. However, since it is a thin, rangy plant that becomes easily entangled with other plants, pull it out whenever you see it. Notice two of its interesting features. On older plants you may be able to see the little brown nitro-gen-fixing nodules on the roots. If the plant has gone to seed, examine the seedpods. They are min-iature bean pods, typical of a legume but rolled up in spirals with curved burrs along the outer edges for catching onto animal hair. (This method of hitchhiking ensures the distribution of seeds.)

CHICKWEED

Stellaria media
Carnation Family ❖ *Caryophyllaceae*

Sprouting mainly in the fall and greening up winter gardens, chickweed seems to grow every-where. It is a weak-stemmed, sprawling plant, with small bright green leaves and 1/4-inch white flowers (*stellaria* refers to the star shape of the blooms). Chickweed grows so fast that it often shades winter vegetable seedlings, but it is the most bothersome when it becomes entangled in perennial herbs and flowers. Growing through other small plants, it can be difficult to extricate and pull out. I have let chick weed grow as a living mulch under larger crops, such as broccoli, pulling handfuls

Chickweed

of it now and then and leaving them on the soil.

Chickweed is edible and, in fact, was sold in the markets of Old England as a potherb. It has a fresh, mild flavor. Try young plants in salads, either with lettuce or as the main green. Chickweed can also be steamed or cooked in just the water that clings to it when you wash it; season it with butter and a squeeze of lemon juice.

COTULA (OR AUSTRALIAN BRASSBUTTONS)

Cotula australis
Sunflower Family ❖ *Compositae*

Domesticated relatives of this aggressive little spreader are used as ground covers. Left alone, the weed will cover your garden with a low dense feath-ery mat. Before it blooms, cotula looks very much like swine cress (see page 113) and thus its seed-lings, like those of swine cress, are occasionally mistaken for carrot. However, you can distinguish cotula from swine cress by its flowers. Cotula has small flat greenish flower heads borne on wiry leaf-less stems, rather like those of English chamomile.

CRABGRASS (OR HAIRY CRABGRASS)

Digitaria sanguinalis
Grass Family ❖ *Graminae*

Hairy crabgrass germinates as the soil warms in spring. Its leaves are a light gray-green. On crabgrass seedlings, the leaves are almost as broad as long. Left to grow, crabgrass produces ro-settes of grassy leaves, then

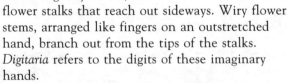

Crabgrass

flower stalks that reach out sideways. Wiry flower stems, arranged like fingers on an outstretched hand, branch out from the tips of the stalks. *Digitaria* refers to the digits of these imaginary hands.

If your soil is well amended, you can just scrape crabgrass seedlings off with a weeding tool. Once they have sent down their larger roots, they are hard to pull, even in loose soil. The trick is to hook a finger under each plant to make sure that you pull all of it.

GROUNDSEL, COMMON (OR SENECIO)

Senecio vulgaris
Sunflower Family ❖ *Compositae*

Many members of this genus—including florist's

cineraria (*S. x hybridus*), the pretty, spring-blooming purple daisy that grows wild in many local gardens—are cultivated as ornamentals. Common groundsel, however, has no redeeming value. It isn't pretty or edible. Also, it uses a great deal of nitrogen, competing strongly with crops. Seedling stands of common groundsel are often so thick that crop seedlings don't stand a chance. Furthermore, the weed blooms when it is quite young, and its flowers continue to ripen seeds even after the plant has been pulled.

Common groundsel is usually a small plant under a foot high, although it can reach 1-1/2 feet high. It is upright, with larger leaves at the base and gradually smaller leaves up the stem. Narrow with toothed edges, groundsel leaves resemble small, narrow chrysanthemum leaves. The flower heads, about 3/8 inch across, consist of many tiny yellow flowers. The seeds are carried on white fluff that floats over a wide area to assure a larger and thicker stand of seedlings next year.

Hoe or pull groundsel seedlings when they are still small. If a plant has flowers, remove it from the garden or put it in a hot compost pile right away.

JUDEAN PELLITORY

Parietaria judaica
Nettle Family ❖ *Urticaceae*

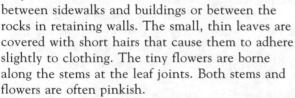

Judean Pellitory

This Old World weed and the similar native *P. hespera hespera* are widespread in our region. *P. judaica* and other native European pellitories are common in Mediterranean Europe, where they grow, as they do here, very successfully in the cracks between sidewalks and buildings or between the rocks in retaining walls. The small, thin leaves are covered with short hairs that cause them to adhere slightly to clothing. The tiny flowers are borne along the stems at the leaf joints. Both stems and flowers are often pinkish.

Pellitory isn't a major pest, but it can be hard to eliminate, especially when it grows wedged between bricks, concrete, wood, or other elements of garden construction. In such cases, it is difficult to pry out the whole plant.

LAMBSQUARTERS
(OR WHITE GOOSEFOOT OR FAT HEN)
Chenopodium album

LAMBSQUARTERS
(OR NETTLELEAF GOOSEFOOT)
C. murale
Goosefoot Family ❖ *Chenopodiaceae*

Several members of the genus *Chenopodium* are known as lambsquarters. They are upright plants with one main stem that can grow several feet high. Their leaves are roughly triangular with wavy or toothed edges, and their flowers are almost unnoticeable, resembling a cluster of tiny unopened buds.

Two species are particularly common in local gardens. *C. album* has a white mealy substance on the undersides of the leaves. The mealy coating is also on the upper surfaces of the leaves near the top of the plant, giving the growing tip a pleasant dusty white appearance. *C. murale* has a dull green mealy substance on the backs of the leaves, and a red tinge on the leaves, stems, and flower buds.

Both of our weedy species of chenopodium are ones that were widely eaten in Europe before the arrival of spinach from Persia in the 1500s. The edible seeds were also ground into flour. Similar species, such as *C. berlandieri*, are cultivated and eaten by native people of the American Southwest and Mexico.

If you want to try lambsquarters, try steaming the young shoots. You can buy seed of *C. murale* and *C. album*, and they are not so invasive that you will regret introducing them.

You will also find seed for *C. berlandieri*, *C. gigantium*, and *C. bonus-henricus*. The latter, known as Good King Henry, is a European species cultivated for its large, tasty leaves. *C. gigantium* has bright pink young leaves. And, if you like any of these greens, try also Orach (*Atriplex hortensis*), a related plant available with either green leaves, or with red-purple leaves that are dramatic in a tossed salad.

Lambsquarter is nutritious food for livestock. It can also be used as a deep-diving weed (see page 92), or dug in while young as green manure.

A drawback of harboring lambsquarters is that it is an alternate host for some pests—notably beet leafminer (see page 142).

Sources
C. *album* or *C. murale* seeds: ABL, DD, NSS, OBG, RH
C. *berlandieri* seeds: DD, NSS, RCS
C. *bonus-henricus* (good King Henry): DD, OBG, RH, SB
C. *gigantium* (magenta spreen): ABL, DD, SB
Orach seed: (green) ABL, DD, NGN, NSS, SB; (red) ABL, CG, DD, JG, JSS, NGN, SB, SOC

MALLOW
(OR CHEESEWEED)
Malva (various species)
Mallow Family ❖ *Malvaceae*

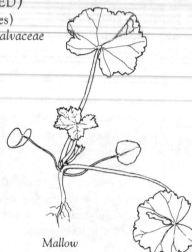

If your seedbed is covered with seedlings that have pairs of little heart-shaped leaves, don't ignore them—you have a mallow problem in the making. This is a plant to eliminate early on, because it can grow large and become extremely difficult to pull. At 3

Mallow

to 4 feet high, a well-rooted mallow can take the strength of two people to wrestle out. A specimen 6 to 8 feet high means hard work with a mattock—I know

Seed head

from experience. So, whenever I see the mallow seedlings with their pretty, dark green, elongated hearts, I become quite heartless and start cultivating.

The mature leaves of a mallow are more or less round and smooth with radiating veins and a toothed edge. They may have shallow lobes. The flowers, most often pinkish lavender, are borne where a leafstalk joins a main stem. The blooms are followed by intriguing seedpods that look like little cheese wheels, hence the name cheeseweed. The seeds are the wedge-shaped sections of the wheels.

The weedy mallows are edible plants (very high in vitamin A), although their flavor is not particularly interesting. The leaves can be used as a potherb and the immature seedpods are fun to nibble.

Closely related but less weedy mallows are among our favorite garden flowers: flowering mallows, lavateras, hibiscus, and hollyhock. (And for a closely related perennial weed, see bristly mallow on page 117.)

MILK THISTLE
Silybum marianum
Sunflower Family ❖ *Compositae*

Milk thistle is a common sight along our roadways, and you may very well see its rosettes of basal leaves getting a start in your garden. The weed is easy to identify, as the leaves have prickly edges and very noticeable white markings. A biennial weed, milk thistle usually does not bloom or mature its seeds until the second year, so you will probably have time to get it out. However, the bigger the plant gets, the pricklier it becomes, so you will be wise to dig it out when it is young. The dried flower heads, with their large recurved thorns, make spectacular additions to dried flower bouquets, but it is better to collect these from the roadside rather than let milk thistle invade your garden.

MINER'S LETTUCE
Montia perfoliata (Claytonia parviflora)
Purslane Family ❖ *Portulacaceae*

A California native, miner's lettuce is an attractive and unusual plant, clear green and up to a foot tall when it is growing in reasonably fertile soil with enough water. It is smaller and reddish when it is dry or in too much sun. The youngest leaves are straplike, the slightly older leaves are broadly triangular, and the mature leaves are nearly round with the flower stems growing unexpectedly right up through their centers. The small flowers are white or pinkish, and the tiny seeds shiny black.

Miner's Lettuce

Unless miner's lettuce is crowding your crop seedlings or mature plants, save some plants to harvest. One of the most succulent of greens, rather like a mild spinach, it is delicious in a green salad lightly dressed with a vinaigrette.

Miner's lettuce may properly be called a wilding instead of a weed. In fact, perhaps it ought not to be called a weed at all. Although it may come up wild in your garden, it can be rather difficult to get started there intentionally. You will see it in spring, growing wild on the north side of hills or among grasses in light shade.

Never overharvest greens or seeds from a wild stand. Just take a bit, being sure to leave plenty of seeds for next year. You can also purchase seeds (which you may find listed as claytonia) and sow them in fall or early- to mid-spring.

Sources

Miner's lettuce seeds: ABL, CG, DD, JSS, RCS

MUSTARD (OR WILD MUSTARD, FIELD MUSTARD, OR CALIFORNIA RAPE)

Brassica (various species)
Mustard Family ❖ *Crucifae*

Wild mustard is a general term for a number of similar plants in the genus *Brassica* that appear wild in gardens and fields. Many are escapees from gardens or wild relatives of the mustards that we grow on purpose. The flowers are like those of domesticated mustard: yellow, four petaled, and with four long and two short pollen-bearing stamens. The plants typically bear large leaves at the base and smaller ones higher on the flowering stems. Long narrow pods, each containing two rows of small round seeds, form along the stems behind the flowers. Mustards are most often winter annuals, blooming in early spring.

If you grow domesticated mustard, you will soon learn to recognize the reseeded or wild plants. I usually leave the wild seedlings alone, as long as they are not too close to my garden plants, and then pull them to eat when they are a few inches high. The leaves of most mustards are mild and tender when young, and tougher and more bitter when older.

Wild mustard may attract aphids, loopers, and other pests of domesticated members of the mustard family. However, their shallow-necked flowers may also attract predators of these and other pests. In general, tolerate wild mustards in small numbers, examining them to see if they are attracting many pests.

NETTLE (OR SMALL NETTLE)

Urtica urens
Nettle Family ❖ *Urticaceae*
Small nettle is a dark green, erect plant up to 2 feet high. The leaves, arranged alternately on the stems, are oblong, toothed, and pointed at the tips. Very small

Nettle (half-size)

green flowers form in little bunches where the leafstalks join the stems.

Small nettle makes a very good addition to a compost pile, and the young plant can also be cooked and eaten as a nutritious vegetable. However, from the time that small nettle is a couple of inches high, it is covered with hairs that are hollow and filled with an irritating chemical. If you brush against these stinging hairs, your skin will itch and burn for at least a few minutes.

Wear gloves when harvesting small nettle. You can usually avoid a sting if you reach in and grasp the plant at the very bottom, almost below the soil line. Cooking the stems and leaves destroys any trace of the irritant.

NIGHTSHADE

Solanum (various species)
Nightshade Family ❖ *Solanaceae*

Any rangy, upright weed with small round black berries is likely to be in the nightshade family, which also includes tomatoes, potatoes, peppers, and eggplants. The leaves of nightshade weeds generally are triangular with wavy edges, and they are sometimes lobed. The flowers, plain white or tinted with purple, look like tomato flowers but are usually smaller. The berries, quite soft when ripe, contain several seeds. The plants may reach 3 feet high and wide, or they may mature at a much smaller size if they are growing in the shade or in competition with other plants.

Several closely related solanums are considered part of the black nightshade group. These plants look so much alike that even botanists and farmers have trouble telling them apart. *S. nodiflorum*, known as American black nightshade or deadly nightshade, is common throughout California, especially along the coast. I have seen the similar *S. furcatum*, known as South American black nightshade, in San Francisco. There may be other species growing near you.

There is disagreement about which black nightshades are poisonous, how deadly they are, and which parts of the plants contain the poison. Black nightshades generally are known to contain nicotine and other poisonous alkaloids, traits they share with domesticated members of the nightshade family. Leaves of our local *S. nodiflorum*, have been suspected of poisoning livestock. However, poison is not necessarily spread evenly through plants. For example, potato tubers are a safe and healthful food, but all green parts of the plant and probably the fruit contain poisonous alkaloids. As far as wild nightshades are concerned, the research is not complete, but we should assume that all parts of the plants are poisonous until proved otherwise.

People do eat the berries and even the leaves of some wild black nightshades that grow in various areas of the United States and in other countries. If you have eaten nightshades elsewhere, you might assume that they are edible here, but they are probably different species. It is best not to experiment, not only because of the difficulty in identifying the plants, but also because the research into toxicity has not been completed and any harm suffered may not be immediately obvious. Suffice to say that I do not eat any local wild nightshades and do not recommend their use as food.

Despite this, seed of at least one kind of black nightshade is sold as an edible berry. You may see it sold under the scientific names *S. nigrum* or *S. melanocerasum* or under the common names wonderberry, sunberry, or garden huckleberry. Only fully ripe berries are edible, and I suspect that the other parts of the plant are poisonous. Although I have never grown it, I have read that some gardeners prize it as a pie fruit and others dismiss it as uninteresting.

Meanwhile, back in the garden, a good reason to get rid of wild nightshades is that they act as alternate hosts for spider mites and for many diseases that attack their domesticated relatives. It is advisable to rotate domesticated members of the family and to remove any doubtful or useless family members. For a discussion of the nightshade family and its edible members, see page 234.

Sources
Garden huckleberry seeds: DD, JG, SB

PIGWEED (OR ROUGH PIGWEED, GREEN AMARANTH, OR WILD BEET)

Amaranthus retroflexus
Pigweed Family ❖ *Amaranthaceae*

If you have ever seen domestic amaranth growing, you will recognize this common weed. Its leaves and bushy flower spikes look much the same. The leaves, arranged alternately along the stems, are oblong to roughly triangular and somewhat hairy. Although the flower spikes at the tops of the stems are clearly visible, the individual flowers are so insignificant that you have to look closely to see whether the plant is blooming or has already gone to seed. Domesticated amaranths often have red leaves or red flowers, or both. However, pigweed is completely green, its flower spikes a paler green than the leaves. The only touch of red appears at the top of the root, which characteristically is pink or reddish.

Pigweed is an upright plant that usually grows several feet high, with flower spikes up to 2 inches long. It has deep roots and can be used as a deep diver, loosening the soil for plants with shorter roots. Unless you are planning to use pigweed this way, it is best to pull it young because the deep roots will put up a fight later. When young, it is a good weed to dig under as green manure or add to your compost pile. Tender young plants may be eaten as a potherb. (In fact, you can buy pigweed in some produce stores and farmer's markets.)

You may come across other wild amaranths, either upright types or prostrate ones that trail along the ground. These can be used and controlled in much the same way as pigweed. (See page 163 for information about domesticated amaranth.)

POISON HEMLOCK

Conium maculatum
Carrot Family ❖ *Umbelliferae*

Although I had long known that *immaculate* means clean, I didn't realize that it literally means spotless—that is, lacking spots—and that the opposite, *maculate*, means spotted. That I discovered one day upon learning that poison hemlock's species name refers to the small purplish splotches on its stems. Semantics aside, this common weed of wild places and some local gardens is a very poisonous plant that is related to and resembles many of our domesticated vegetables and herbs.

A biennial weed, poison hemlock is in the carrot family, whose members have flat heads of flowers called umbels. Although poison hemlock has umbels similar to those of fennel, you won't mistake the two plants because fennel flowers are yellow and poison hemlock flowers are white. Hemlock flowers resemble those of carrot and parsley.

Although the leaves of poison hemlock could be mistaken for flat-leaf parsley or cutting celery, neither of these edible plants has spots on the stems. Also, poison hemlock has a pungent, unpleasant odor. (If you aren't sure whether a plant is edible, especially if you know it could be mistaken for a poisonous one, don't eat it unless someone can positively identify it for you.)

Incidentally, you may have thought that the hemlock with which Socrates ended his life was the tree, but it was this very weed. Its poison, an alkaloid called coniine, is contained in all parts of the plant. You needn't be afraid to pull or compost this plant—just don't eat it!

PURSLANE

Portulaca oleracea
Purslane Family ❖ *Portulacaceae*

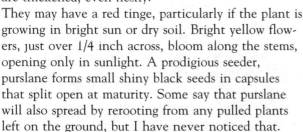
Purslane

Both the stems and the 3/4-inch, oval, dull dark green leaves of purslane are thickened, even fleshy. They may have a red tinge, particularly if the plant is growing in bright sun or dry soil. Bright yellow flowers, just over 1/4 inch across, bloom along the stems, opening only in sunlight. A prodigious seeder, purslane forms small shiny black seeds in capsules that split open at maturity. Some say that purslane will also spread by rerooting from any pulled plants left on the ground, but I have never noticed that.

Purslane seedlings usually begin to appear in May—a sure sign that the soil has warmed. They grow very fast in their first few weeks, so you must keep them from competing with your spring seedlings. Each plant forms a low mat a foot or more across. Only the central stems and not the side branches have roots. (If you have spent time in a climate with hotter summers, you may know *P. grandiflora*, a related ornamental flower known as portulaca or moss-rose. Forming a similar mat but with narrower leaves and large vivid red, orange, pink, or yellow flowers, it may succeed in sunnier parts of our region.)

Purslane is a weed that elicits varying reactions. Some gardeners would be happy if it disappeared from the face of the earth, and others enjoy it as a staple vegetable. At the San Francisco Farmer's Market you will find bunches of purslane sold as *verdolaga*, its name in Mexico. Purslane is eaten wild or cultivated in many countries of Europe and the Middle East as well as in India, Pakistan, China, and the Philippines. In Europe it is cultivated under various names including *portulaca* (Italy), *pourpier* (France), and *postelein* (Holland). In the United States, most gardeners don't even know that it is edible. In some areas it is called pusley—a name guaranteed to spoil anyone's appetite.

If managed properly, purslane can serve as a "free" summer green without intruding on your intentionally planted crops. Try adding the stems and leaves of some pulled seedlings to a green salad. Or let a few purslane plants that aren't too near your crops grow a bit longer, and harvest them when they are about 6 inches across but before they have bloomed. Eat the stems and leaves raw or cooked. Purslane is high in vitamin C and contains a moderate amount of oxalic acid, similar to that of domestic spinach. It has a pleasantly fresh, slightly tart taste.

Although you may be harvesting purslane to eat, you will still want to keep it from seeding itself widely in your garden. Even if it becomes a favorite green, pull it early or your garden will be blanketed with purslane next year.

Domesticated varieties of purslane are larger and more tender, but they probably spread just as freely as wild purslane. You may want to keep intentionally planted purslane in a separate planting box if you don't already have it as a weed in your garden. Purslane prefers sandy soil and needs only light fertilizing, although moist soil and partial shade will improve its size and tenderness. Grow successive plantings from May through August, harvesting young plants whole.

Sources
Purslane seeds: ABL, CG, DD, GG, JG, JSS, NGN, OBG, PTS, RS, SB, SC, SGS, TERR

RADISH (SEE WILD RADISH)

SCARLET PIMPERNEL (OR POORMAN'S WEATHERGLASS)

Anagallis arvensis
Primrose Family ❖ *Primulaceae*

Scarlet Pimpernel

This pretty little weed can be left alone if it is growing away from crop seedlings. A low plant spreading from a central stem, scarlet pimpernel has small leaves and tiny five-petaled flowers. The blooms are most commonly salmon, but they may be white or, in the case of one variety (A. *arvensis* var. *coerulea*), blue. A particularly common weed along the coast, where it blooms all year, scarlet pimpernel is poisonous.

Poorman's weatherglass refers to the weed's role as a weather indicator, since the flowers are reputed

BLACK BEAN TOSTADAS

This is one of the first recipes I learned to make after moving to California many years ago. To simplify last-minute preparation, you can cook the beans way ahead of time and reheat them before serving.

1 cup black beans
4 cups water
2 cups torn lettuce, spinach, and/
or edible weed greens
Edible flowers (optional)
2 tablespoons virgin olive oil
2 tablespoons red wine vinegar
1/4 pound jack or cheddar cheese

1 cup plain yogurt
1 4-ounce can chopped black olives
(optional)
1 medium to large avocado (optional)
Green taco sauce
Oil for frying tortillas
6 to 8 corn tortillas

Pick over and rinse the black beans. Soak them in water overnight, then put them in a saucepan with the four cups of water and bring to a boil over medium-high heat. Reduce heat and simmer for 2 hours, or until they are tender.

About 30 minutes before you plan to serve the tostadas, make a tossed green salad. Use lettuce, spinach and/or tender edible weeds, such as chickweed, young purslane, miner's lettuce, shepherds-purse or lambsquarters. Wash the greens, pat them dry, and tear them into pieces no bigger than 3 inches across. For color, you can add edible flowers, such as nasturtiums or pansies, if desired. Add the olive oil and toss to coat the salad. Sprinkle the salad with the vinegar and toss again. Refrigerate.

Grate the cheese coarsely and put it into a small bowl. Put the yogurt into a second bowl and stir it briskly with a spoon for about half a minute. Put the olives in another small bowl. Peel the avocado and slice it into strips. Put the avocado into a fourth bowl. Before you start frying the tortillas, put all four bowls of food on the table along with the salad, reheated beans, green taco sauce, and any utensils that might be needed. (Tortillas cool quickly and are best eaten immediately.)

Add 2 tablespoons of oil to a medium skillet and heat it until a sprinkle of water dropped into it jumps and sizzles. Add a tortilla and cook 1 or 2 minutes on each side. The tortilla should be crisp, but not brown. Remove it to a plate. As soon as the first tortilla is cooked, someone can begin to build a tostada on it. Here is a suggested order of ingredients, although some diners will have their own preferences, or even want to leave out some ingredients.

- 4 to 6 tablespoons of black beans
  (use a slotted spoon to remove beans from liquid)
- 2 tablespoons of yogurt
- 1/2 cup of salad
- 2 or 3 tablespoons of grated cheese
- 1 tablespoon of chopped black olives
- 2 or 3 strips of avocado

Serves three or four.

to close at the approach of bad weather. That's not much help in our region, since the plant doesn't distinguish between fog and storm clouds.

Yes, this is the plant for which the novel *The Scarlet Pimpernel* was named. In this turn-of-the-century fiction by a Hungarian countess, Scarlet Pimpernel was the code name for a Royalist hero who rescued nobles during the French Revolution.

SHEPHERDS-PURSE

Capsella bursa-pastoris
Mustard Family ❖ *Crucifae*

Shepherds-purse is a winter annual, sprouting mainly in the fall. The plant first forms a small rosette of coarsely toothed dark green leaves, which lies very flat to the ground. Then it forms a flowering stem, rarely over a foot high, with very small mustard-type white flowers. As new flowers open at the top of the stem, spent flowers form tiny heart-shaped pods below them. You will soon learn to recognize shepherds-purse by these distinctive heart-shaped "little purses."

A few plants are not much bother, although you wouldn't want to let them reseed until they formed a thick mat in your garden. If shepherds-purse appears, dig it in as green manure or eat the whole plant before it forms seeds. The plant has a mild, pleasant flavor and can be used in salads, omelets, curries, and casseroles. Late one November long ago it was among the wild plants that, together with leftover Thanksgiving turkey, saw me through a very lean week in fine style. I had only recently begun a garden and little was available to eat from it. However, I found shepherds-purse, chickweed, and onion lilies to combine with the few domesticated greens and herbs from my garden. Our meals included turkey and weed salad, turkey and weeds a la king, turkey and weed soup…

Apparently others agree that shepherds-purse tastes good, since several sources carry the seeds. I have never tried to grow it intentionally, but I think that you could do so without worrying that it would take over. Still, as a precaution, harvest the plants before they go to seed.

Sources
Shepherds-purse seeds: ABL, DD, RH

SOWTHISTLE, COMMON (OR WILD LETTUCE)

Sonchus oleraceus

SOWTHISTLE, PRICKLY

S. asper
Sunflower Family ❖ *Compositae*

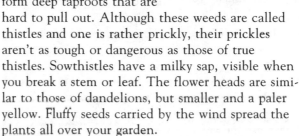

Prickly Sow Thistle with leaf miner damage

These are summer annuals that normally come up in late spring. Upright plants, they can grow 5 feet high, although mine rarely reach as much as 2 feet before I pull them. The leaves are several inches long, with toothed and lobed edges. The leaves of *S. asper* are dark green and quite prickly, whereas those of *S. oleraceus* are blue-green and much smoother. Both plants form deep taproots that are hard to pull out. Although these weeds are called thistles and one is rather prickly, their prickles aren't as tough or dangerous as those of true thistles. Sowthistles have a milky sap, visible when you break a stem or leaf. The flower heads are similar to those of dandelions, but smaller and a paler yellow. Fluffy seeds carried by the wind spread the plants all over your garden.

I have often been surprised by sowthistles growing up through my maturing crop plants. When I try to pull the plants, they frequently break off at the ground—a handy survival mechanism, since they can quickly regrow new side shoots to replace the missing central stem.

Hoe or pull sowthistle seedlings. Dig out larger plants if possible; if they are too mixed in with crops, just keep the top broken off so that the plants can't go to seed. Although their roots will provide the benefits of any deep-diving weed, sowthistles are large plants and should not be allowed to crowd your crop plants.

SWINE CRESS

Coronopus didymus
Mustard Family ❖ *Crucifae*

This low-growing, non-descript weed is common to both gardens and sidewalk cracks The flowers,which form at the tips of the stems, are tiny and without petals. The flat, rounded, light green seedpods are also tiny, and they spiral up the stem very much like those of sweet alyssum.

I once saw the vegetable bed of a beginning

gardener whose carrot seedlings had been completely shaded and crowded out by swine cress. She had assumed that the plants were carrots but began to wonder when they didn't act like carrots as they matured. It is certainly possible to confuse the two at first, as they have similar finely divided leaves. However, carrots soon grow upright, each tall stem holding aloft a feathery plume, whereas swine cress stems branch and remain close to the ground.

VETCH (OR COMMON VETCH)

Vicia sativa
Legume Family ❖ *Leguminosae*

Common vetch is a low, open, spreading plant with small bright magenta pea-type flowers. The leaves have a twining tendril at the end of the leaf stem and two rows of small leaflets arranged along the sides. The seeds are borne in small pods resembling those of peas.

I usually notice only a couple of these plants a year and leave them to mature out of respect for the nitrogen-fixing capacity of their roots. In fact, some farmers and gardeners sow common vetch as a cover crop. It makes an excellent addition to your compost pile, contributing nitrogen and other minerals. Don't assume vetch is edible, however, despite its resemblance to pea, it contains toxic substances.

If broad bean weevils have infested your fava or scarlet runner bean plants, eliminate weedy vetch, as it is an alternate host for this pest. You can see the little notches it eats in the edges of the vetch leaves (see page 172).

WILD RADISH

Raphanus sativus
Mustard Family ❖ *Crucifae*

I have never seen wild radish become a serious problem in areas that are actively gardened, but it does grow wild in abandoned lots and may sometimes appear in your garden. A winter annual, it sprouts during the rainy season and soon reaches 2 to 4 feet high. Blooming in spring and into summer, its typical mustard-family flowers, about 3/4 inch across, are white, pink, or lavender. The pointed green seedpods, which form along the sides of the flower stems, taste just like radishes. When they are still young and tender, pick them for a tasty nibble or add them to spring salads. No one grows wild radish as a crop, but podding radish, a domesticated relative, is raised for its large edible pods (see page 240).

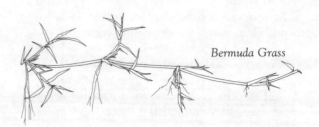

Bermuda Grass

Perennial Weeds

BERMUDA GRASS

Cynodon dactylon
Grass Family ❖ *Graminae*

When you realize how Bermuda grass reproduces, you will understand why it is so invasive. It spreads through the soil not only by underground stems, called rhizomes, but also by aboveground stems, called runners. Both types of stems may extend several feet from the parent plant, where the main roots are. Roots can form anywhere along these stems. And worse news—any broken pieces of stem can root to form new plants.

The stems are wiry, flat, and smooth. The leaves, 1 to 4 inches long, are rough on the upper surface and smooth underneath. There is a conspicuous ring of white hairs at the base of each leaf blade. Upright stems, 4 to 18 inches high, bear four to seven narrow flowering stems arranged like fingers. The flowering stems resemble those of crabgrass (see page 104) but are smaller.

This hard-to-control weed is a lawn grass that often escapes to overrun other garden areas. Except for tolerating drought and salinity, Bermuda grass is not well suited to our area. It does poorly in our cool weather and prefers sun to shade or fog. It also tends to turn brown in winter, unlike several other lawn grasses including bluegrass, ryegrass, and bent grass.

Mount an effort to eliminate Bermuda grass from your garden in fall or spring. Fork out all the stems, and take care to sift through carefully for any stem particles left in the soil. Water the soil and remove any new growth before you plant your crops. A smothering mulch is also an effective tool in destroying this weed.

BINDWEED
(OR WILD MORNING GLORY)

Convolvulus arvensis
Morning Glory Family ❖ *Convolvulaceae*

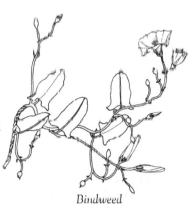
Bindweed

Bindweed can be recognized by its arrow-shaped leaves, 1/2 to 1-1/2 inches long, arranged alternately on stems that twine around any available support. All too often a new gardener is charmed by the pretty morning glory flowers, white on the inside and pink on the backs of the petals. Unfortunately, by the time you see bindweed blooming, it has already established a vigorous and persistent root system ready to send up shoots all over your garden. If you ignore it for even a month, you are likely to face a veritable sea of bindweed.

This is obviously a weed to which you should give no quarter. If it begins to invade your garden in the middle of a growing season, pull shoots whenever you see them. If you can get them before they are 2 inches high, the plant will be unable to enlarge its root system. When there is a break in crops, dig out as many bindweed roots as you can. Search for roots that look like dirty beige string. Some grow vertically, whereas others grow horizontally 6 inches or more beneath the soil surface. If you just pull up individual shoots with some vertical roots attached, the horizontal roots will soon send up new growth.

In a small area you can combat a heavy bindweed infestation with a thick newspaper mulch. Two years of summer fallow with once-weekly turning of the soil will also kill the weed.

If you enjoy bindweed's flower, you may like to know that bindweed is in the same genus as three very pretty, well-behaved domesticated plants. *C. cneorum*, bush morning glory, is a small perennial with silvery leaves and white or pink blooms. *C. mauritanicus*, ground morning glory, another small perennial, has soft blue flowers. *C. tricolor*, dwarf morning glory, is a 1-foot-high annual with striking flowers that have a yellow center and a white edge separated by a blue or magenta band. The first two

are widely available as nursery plants and the third as seeds.

The domesticated morning glory vines are members of the same family, but in the genus *Ipomoea*. *I. hederacea*, the blue-flowered ivyleaf morning glory, is included in the weed chart (see page 102), because it often escapes to spread weedily over large expanses of ground and fencing.

BLACKBERRY BRAMBLES

Rubus (various species)
Rose Family ❖ *Rosaceae*

The blackberry bramble in a neglected yard or vacant lot in our area is overwhelmingly likely to be *R. procerus*, Himalaya berry, a formerly domesticated plant of European origin that escaped from cultivation and is very common in the coastal areas of Northern California. Although you could encounter other kinds of escaped blackberries, few have taken to our local habitat with the vigor of *R. procerus*. *R. vitifolius*, the native California blackberry, is also found in the central coastal area. You are more apt to see it in less developed areas, such as native woods, coastal scrub, or open oak woodlands. *R. laciniatus*, the common blackberry sold in nurseries, may be a weed if it has been neglected and left to grow on its own.

Here's how to tell which blackberry is growing in your yard. If the flowers and fruit are borne sparsely in small clusters, usually along single stems, and the thorns are slender, the plant is California blackberry or another native blackberry species. If the flowers and fruit are borne in heavy bunches at the ends of the stems and the thorns are stout, the plant is an escaped domesticated type. In the case of *R. laciniatus*, the backs of the leaves are greenish. Also, the leaflets (five to fifteen to a leaf) are deeply cut, forming lobes. Himalaya berry leaves, which consist of three to five leaflets, have a whitish underside. A hand lens will reveal that this whiteness is due to a covering of short dense hairs.

Blackberries spread easily. They are carried to new sites by birds, which pass the seeds through their digestive tracts. Once a plant is established, it starts new plants quickly along underground rhizomes and from the tips of long (up to 20 feet) arching stems. Himalaya berry is particularly vigorous. Within a few years, its brambles can cover a neglected yard so thickly that the yard becomes impassable.

Himalaya berry will not politely share garden

TAMING HIMALAYA BERRY

Instead of removing all the wild Himalaya berry from your yard, you may have considered keeping some of it as a crop. The plant bears tasty fruit that ripens over a long season. Although it has been grown commercially to some extent, it is not very popular with growers, because it is a particularly thorny type. Also, aggressive pruning is required to keep the plants accessible for picking. You will probably be better off removing Himalaya berry and planting a domesticated variety, which will be much easier to control and may even offer the luxury of being thornless (see page 329). However, here are some tips for those brave souls who wish to tame the wild Himalaya berry.

At a minimum, you will need to make paths into the patch every few feet so that you can get to all the plants to pick fruit. Get rid of any that become rooted in the paths, and keep the others pruned so that they won't fill in the paths. Several times a year, cut aggressive root runners, prune back arching canes, and pull out seedlings.

Blackberries are a cane plant, meaning that they consist of many long stems that rise from the ground and arch up, then fall over. They branch very little. A blackberry patch is maintained by pruning out all the canes that fruited this year, since they won't fruit again, and preserving some of the new canes, which will fruit next year. Himalaya berry differs from the other domesticated blackberry plants in that some of the canes may become perennial, living more than two seasons, but it is still best to prune out any canes that have fruited and allow vigorous, new shoots to grow. In fact, Himalaya berry produces so many canes each year that it is more likely to form an impenetrable thicket than suffer for lack of its older canes.

Himalaya berry is considered a trailing blackberry. This type of blackberry is commonly trained by growing the fruiting canes along one or two wires stretched between posts 2-1/2 to 3 feet high. Because Himalaya berry is a heavy plant, it should be supported on 12-gauge wire, a heavier wire than is used ordinarily. Train the fruiting canes on the wire, but let the summer's new canes trail along the ground. When the new canes reach 8 to 10 feet long, cut off their ends. At the end of the season, cut all the fruiting canes to the ground. Save the four to seven strongest new canes and train them on the wire.

Himalaya berry begins to ripen in early July, and the best wild stands continue to ripen until the middle of August. In well-watered gardens, they will ripen a month or so longer and bear larger fruit. The berries are sour until they are quite ripe, when they suddenly become mellow and sweet. For pie, cobbler, jam, or any recipe to which you will be adding sugar, pick all the fruit that is black or almost completely black. For eating fresh, you want only the ripe fruit that is still shiny. Overripe fruit becomes dull.

space, so you must remove it completely from any area that you intend to cultivate. Pull seedlings when they are quite small, before they have a chance to develop a root system that can survive after the top is pulled. Cut back mature plants and grub out the roots. If your neighbors have blackberries that threaten to spread into your garden, several times every summer you will have to cut stems and dig out runners as they reach over, through, and under the fence and into your yard.

When cutting Himalaya berry, wear gloves to avoid the sharp, recurved thorns. Don't try to compost the plants. Even if they don't resprout, they will leave thorns in your compost. Remove all parts of the plant from your yard. I cut the canes into short pieces and stuff them into garbage bags. If you are trying to eliminate wild blackberry from a large area, glyphosate (see Appendix III) can be a big help in killing the rootstocks that resprout.

DANDELION

Taraxacum officinale
Sunflower Family ❖ *Compositae*

Although this widespread weed is more common in the eastern United States, where it spreads freely in lawns, it is also often seen here. The plant has a low rosette of smooth, irregularly toothed, bright green leaves. Each flower stem, which is hollow and produces a milky sap when cut, bears one bright yellow head. Winged seeds form a fluffy sphere atop the stem, before the wind disperses them.

Dandelion

If dandelions happen to be new to you, you may at first confuse them with some other local weeds. The biennial prickly oxtongue (*Picris echioides*) has similar flowers, although they are borne several to a stem, and its leaves are dark green, coarse, hairy, and dotted with raised glands. Another similar plant is the perennial coast dandelion (*Hypochoeris radicata*), which has hairy leaves and several flowers to a stalk.

Dandelions do not serve a vegetable garden well, and they are difficult to eradicate. They use much nitrogen and iron, robbing your crops of these nutrients. They also exude ethylene gas, which hampers the growth of nearby plants. Worse yet, they make many seeds and resprout from a broken taproot. When you try to pull a dandelion, its long thin taproot breaks partway down. Buds form on those broken roots, and soon the plant is growing merrily as if nothing had interrupted it. Control dandelions in your vegetable garden by digging them out, being careful to remove the entire taproot. Add the roots to your compost pile only if you are making a very hot compost. Otherwise, remove them from your garden.

Dandelions have a useful side. When I was a child, our midwestern lawn doubled as a dandelion farm. We ate dandelion buds and tender young greens every spring, and Dad made dandelion wine from the blossoms. At Thanksgiving and Christmas, he poured us all a sample of the wine—a sweet and often bubbly reminder of the sunnier times of year. In late winter or early spring, try young dandelion leaves steamed and flavored with butter or vinegar. Older leaves are likely to be too bitter, although you may enjoy the zest from just a few mature dandelion leaves in salads or mixed cooked greens.

To serve only the buds or make wine, you need more plants than most local yards contain. We plucked the flower buds from deep in the center of the plants or from stems that had grown no more than an inch or so, steamed them, and served them with butter. The milky sap stained our fingers in payment for this delicacy, but we always thought it a small price to pay. For wine, Dad had to pick at least a couple of quarts of blossoms.

Domesticated dandelion varieties are available for those who have developed a taste for the plant. These are bigger, somewhat milder versions of the wild kind. Domestic varieties may be forced, like escarole, for pale, milder leaves (see page 208). Domesticated dandelion is usually treated as an annual, and dug before it goes to seed.

Sources

Dandelion seeds: ABL, CG, DD, NGN, PTS, RH, SOC

DOCK (OR CURLY DOCK)

Rumex crispus

DOCK (OR BROAD-LEAVED DOCK)

R. obtusifolius
Knotweed Family ❖ *Polygonaceae*

Several species of *Rumex* are commonly called dock. The two listed here are common in our area. They resemble domesticated sorrel, although their upright leaves arising directly from the ground are darker green than those of sorrel. Dock leaves are also more leathery, and they are straplike rather than arrow shaped. Their tall spikes of tiny pinkish flowers are very similar to those of sorrel.

Dock grows through the winter months, blooming and setting seeds in summer. It spreads both by seed and root and is one of those persistent plants that regrows vigorously from even small bits of missed root. You will soon recognize the difference between a dock plant growing from seed and a root sprout. A seedling begins with small rounded seed leaves, flat to the ground, whereas a root sprout springs up with large, upright, elongated leaves. The first kind can be dealt with simply by pulling the plant and leaving it on the ground. To control root sprouts, you must dig out the whole root carefully and remove it from your garden.

Dock makes a good cooked green vegetable. When steamed, its leathery-looking leaves become surprisingly tender. Some people like to flavor the leaves with butter, others with vinegar. Eat them in moderation (once a week should not be a problem), because they contain oxalic acid. If you are going to leave a plant for greens, be sure to relegate it to an out-of-the-way area of your garden, and cut the flower stalks in summer to prevent seeding.

FENNEL (OR WILD ANISE)

Foeniculum vulgare
Carrot Family ❖ *Umbelliferae*

Although wild fennel may be an acceptable substitute for domesticated fennel and its flowers attract beneficial insects, it is too difficult to eradicate to be worth allowing in your garden. The huge clumps that develop over several years, such as those seen in untended lots throughout our region, require strenuous cutting and digging to remove. You are better off growing the less aggressive domesticated varieties or harvesting wild fennel from vacant lots. Pull any small fennel plants you find in your garden. For a description of the plant, and more information on using it as an herb, see page 285.

GRASSES, PERENNIAL

Grass Family ❖ *Graminae*

Besides Bermuda grass (see page 112) and quackgrass (see page 120), many other perennial grasses can become established in local gardens. Some spread by rhizomes or rootstocks, others have only a mass of fibrous roots, but they all reroot easily. If a grassy weed has only thin, fibrous roots, you can probably kill the roots by shaking off the soil, then putting the plant upside down for a while, or by putting them deep in a compost pile or under sheet compost (see page 88). However, if a grass has any kind of horizontal runner or rhizome, you should be very careful about composting it, putting it into only a very hot pile.

Be sure to pull grassy weeds before they can go to seed in the spring. If you look closely at newly formed flowering stems, you will be able to see the dangling stamens of the flowers, which lack petals. It is hard to tell when grass seeds are mature, but you know it will be at least a couple of weeks after the plants bloom.

HORSETAIL (OR SCOURING RUSH)

Equisetum hyemale and *E. arvense*
Horsetail Family ❖ *Equisetaceae*

These are ancient plant species that bear no flowers and reproduce by spores instead of seeds. They have hollow, jointed stems with slender vertical grooves. *E. hyemale* has many unbranched green stems, up to 4 feet high. The small black and tan fringed bands at each stem joint are primitive leaves. Spores are produced in the conelike structures, called strobili, at the tops of the stems.

E. arvense has two kinds of stems. Short, brown, unbranched fertile stems come up in early spring, make spores, and then die. Green branched stems follow and grow all summer. These are 1 to 3 feet high, with airy whorls of narrow, jointed side branches extending from each joint of the main stem.

In the wild, horsetail thrives along stream banks or wherever moisture is seeping. It prefers sandy soil. Although horsetail is very pretty as a wild plant and is sometimes used in ornamental gardens near pools, it is very invasive, spreading by perennial rootstalks. Be careful where you allow it to grow, because it is very hard to get rid of. Control horsetail by digging out all the roots and improving the drainage. Also, improve the fertility of your soil to help your crops compete successfully with horsetail.

Native Americans used horsetail to polish arrowheads, and the name scouring rush probably comes from the fact that these plants were used by early European settlers to scour cooking utensils. They are abrasive because of a high silicon content. *E. arvense*, and probably all horsetails, are poisonous to livestock and likely to people as well.

IVY, ALGERIAN

Hedera canriensis

IVY, ENGLISH

H. helix
Ginseng Family ❖ *Araliaceae*

Algerian ivy is the large-leaved, dark green ivy used frequently in public and home landscaping. English ivy has smaller leaves and is used in outdoor landscaping and as a houseplant. Both types of ivy spread by rooting along their creeping stems, and both can become pests, although Algerian ivy is probably the more common pest. If your garden is overrun with ivy, you will have to eradicate it before you can grow much else. If your neighbors grow ivy, you will have to fight it when it grows over, under, and through your fence. The stems will reach out over the soil and then root at every joint. The roots will anchor themselves to the fence, contributing to its decay if it is made of wood. If all that weren't enough, ivy patches are notorious as hiding places for snails.

To keep an intentional planting in bounds, you will have to prune the edges several times a year. To eradicate ivy, pull out all the aboveground stems and dig out all the roots. Remove all the plant parts from your garden, as they are likely to sprout and grow if left on the ground or composted. It is safer to use less invasive vines and ground covers in gardens; however, if you plant either kind of ivy, confine it to an area that it cannot easily escape or contain it in planters.

MALLOW, BRISTLY

Modiola caroliniana
Mallow Family ❖ *Malvaceae*

A creeping plant with rooting runners, bristly mallow has small salmon flowers and rounded leaves with shallow, toothed lobes. If you look closely you will see many similarities to the annual mallows (see page 106), which belong to a related genus. Notice the similarly shaped seedpods, which resemble cheese wheels. Bristly mallow is not usually hard to pull from soft soil, but it can be quite tenacious in firmer soil. It is all too easy to miss bits of stems bearing roots, and such fragments will easily replace the plant you tried to pull.

NUTSEDGE (OR YELLOW NUTGRASS OR CHUFA)

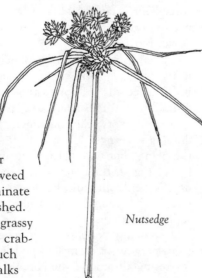

Cyperus esculentus
Sedge Family ❖
Cyperaceae

Nutsedge is another interesting, pretty weed that is hard to eliminate once it gets established. It has bright green grassy leaves—as broad as crabgrass leaves, but much stiffer. Its flower stalks

Nutsedge

Nutsedge seedling

remind me of papyrus: At the top of each stalk is an umbrella rib arrangement of small leaves and stems bearing brownish flowers. In fact, papyrus (*C. papyrus*), a member of the same genus, has escaped to the wild in some moist areas of our region from Marin County southward.

Although nutsedge doesn't spread as fast as some other weeds, it grows into a large plant that is hard to pull. I have never been able to hand-pull this weed once it matured. Instead, I have had to hack it out laboriously, even in fairly loose soil. Often my labor was for naught, because I missed some of the small tubers, which proceeded to grow into new plants. Your best bet is to learn to recognize this plant when it is small and pull it early.

Decaying nutsedge leaves have been shown to inhibit the production of corn and soybeans. Therefore, it would seem best not to use nutsedge as a green manure or mulch, although putting a little of it in a compost pile should be safe. However, even one tiny tuber will sprout a new plant, so discard all the roots.

Nutsedge isn't all bad: Its tubers are edible. The wild variety has tiny ones, but gardeners sometimes grow a variety bred for its large tubers. *C. e.* var. *sativus*, known as earth almond or chufa. It rarely flowers, and it produces many tubers, up to 3/4 inch in diameter, crowded on short underground stems. The tubers have a pleasant almond flavor and their texture is reminiscent of partially dried coconut. They can be eaten raw or roasted, or they can be ground into flour. I remember munching them in an aunt's Indiana garden.

You can order chufa seed (tubers) from Glendale Enterprises, Inc., 297 Railroad Ave., Rt. 3, DeFuniak Springs, FL, 32433, (850)859-2141. They sell them as food for wild turkeys, but also for human consumption. Although this crop could conceivably become a nuisance, the tubers are large enough that they could probably be removed easily. My one effort to grow it failed. That is, the plants grew, but I found no tubers, and the plant that I left to overwinter died out by spring. My guess is the chufa would do better in the warmer areas of our region than in a foggy San Francisco garden.

ONION LILY (OR WILD ONION)

Allium triquetrum
Lily Family ❖ *Liliaceae*

Onion lily sprouts in September from rounded bulbs less than an inch in diameter. The leaves are flat and reminiscent of leek leaves, although not as large and with a strong ridge, or keel, on their undersides. In late winter the flower stems appear, each bearing several nodding, bell-shaped white flowers. The flower stems, a foot or more tall, are triangular in cross section. When bruised, the entire plant smells strongly of onion. Each flower forms several black seeds in a roundish pod. The plant dies back in April or May, disappearing without an aboveground trace until next fall.

This wild onion of our urban backyards is not native to our part of the world but instead is a Mediterranean plant that has escaped to the wild in California. Although it is pretty enough to grace an ornamental flower bed and is edible, it bears controlling because it can seriously hinder a winter or spring garden.

To rid an area of onion lily you will need to dig up all plants and bulbs, as well as make sure that seeds don't fall. The best time to pull plants is in late fall or winter, when they are growing vigorously and the stems are sturdy. At this time you are likely to get the whole plant, and it may not have formed the dormant bulb offsets that will remain in the soil to reinfest the area next year.

All parts of onion lily are edible and once you get the plant under control, you may like to leave a patch behind for continuous harvesting. However, I advise preserving onion lily only in small numbers and in out-of-the-way corners, since left on its own it can blanket a garden. If you maintain a bed for eating, you will want to control seeding by

*Onion Lily
(Wild Onion)*

picking off the blooms as soon as they fade, before they fall over and shed their seeds.

Lately I have been experimenting with using my onion lilies. I harvested the leaves for salads and cooking throughout winter. The plants grow well even in deep winter shade, where scallions will not grow. In March, I pulled clumps of sprouting seedlings to use in salads. They made a wonderfully tasty and attractive addition, although I have decided not to let the plants seed anymore, since it is too easy to miss seedlings and end up with more plants than intended. In May, when the plants were just dying back, I harvested the bulbs, using some right away and saving the rest. They can be used in cooking much as you would use pearl onions. I served them in beef bourguignon, skinning them first by dropping them in boiling water for a few seconds and then popping their skins off. I also used onion lilies as houseplants. In the summer, I planted some of my saved bulbs in 6-inch-deep clay pots. They grew outdoors through the winter. In February, when they were about to bloom, I carried them indoors, where they made a graceful display, blooming prettily for several weeks.

OXALIS

Oxalis (various species)
Oxalis Family ❖ *Oxalidaceae*

O. *corniculata*, known as creeping oxalis, is a European native that has established itself throughout the United States. I called it sour clover when I was a child, and while at play I used to nibble its leaves. The leaves are rather like those of clover, with three heart-shaped leaflets, although the small, five-petaled yellow flowers could not be mistaken for clover blossoms.

Even though it appears delicate and not much in the way, creeping oxalis can make quite a pest of itself, especially if allowed to get a start among perennial herbs. This aggressive spreader can trail, rooting at every leaf attachment point, and climb, draping itself over low plants. It spoils the look of the plants, but more than that, it harms the plants by cutting off their sunlight. Removing the weed is unexpectedly difficult, because it is hard to trace the slender stems back to their origins through the supporting plant.

Creeping oxalis is a very successful seeder. Its seeds pop out of elongated pods when they are ripe, scattering all around the parent plant. I try to pull creeping oxalis while it is young, before it can show its skill at spreading and eluding the weeder's hand. I do not return pulled plants to the garden as mulch unless they are not yet blooming, and then only if the weather is dry enough so that the weeds will shrivel and die instead of rerooting.

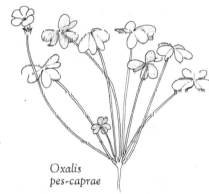

Oxalis pes-caprae

O. pes-caprae (*O. cernua*), known as Cape oxalis or Bermuda buttercup, is a larger plant than creeping oxalis. Introduced from South Africa as an ornamental, it escaped from gardens and spread so successfully that its showy yellow blooms are a common sight in late winter. It sprouts in September and dies back in May, although a few plants may hang on into summer in well-watered soil. An area infested with Cape oxalis can be used for a summer garden but is usable in winter and spring only if weeded frequently.

Cape oxalis leaves, which are larger versions of the cloverlike trefoil, grow from a common base at ground level, on stems 5 to 6 inches long. The leaflets often bear a few reddish dots. The roots are thickened and form scaly brown bulbs, shaped like teardrops, deep in the soil. The largest of these bulbs is almost an inch long, but many are quite tiny and easy to miss when you are digging. The best time to pull or dig plants is in late winter and early spring, since the bulbs are attached most firmly to the roots at this time. Still, some bulbs will always fall off and must be picked out by hand.

If you must pull instead of dig (because the weed is growing among desirable plants), be sure to grasp the plant below the point where the leaves are attached. If you just pull on the leaves, they will come off, leaving the plant base and the roots intact. The plant will grow new leaves from buds on the stem. But even careful pulling must be seen as a temporary control, until a break in crops lets you dig and remove the bulbs. Don't use the plants or bulbs in compost or mulch, as the chance of their resprouting is great. If you dig an area and sift through, removing bulbs, you will achieve reasonable control over this weed in a couple of seasons. If you don't have the pest yet, beware of accepting plants from gardeners who do, since tiny Cape oxa-

lis bulbs may well be hidden in the soil.

A less bothersome relative is redwood sorrel (*O. oregana*), a native of California and the Pacific Northwest. The leaves look like those of Cape oxalis, but the flowers are pink or white instead. It is less invasive, sometimes spreading in shade but generally stopping when it reaches a sunny area.

All these species can be nibbled in the garden or used as flavorings for salads and sauces. English cooks in the Middle Ages made a fish sauce from oxalis leaves. However, none should be eaten in large quantities, since the oxalic acid content is rather high. The acid interferes with the ability of our bodies to absorb essential minerals.

Many other, less invasive oxalis species are grown ornamentally, and some are treasured as miniature rock garden plants. Oca (*O. tuberosa*), a Peruvian species that forms an edible starchy tuber, is occasionally grown locally for food or as a curiosity. Check with your local chapter of the Rare Fruit Growers' (see Resources Appendix) for information on oca tubers.

PLANTAIN, NARROW-LEAVED (OR BUCKHORN PLANTAIN)
Plantago lanceolata

PLANTAIN, BROADLEAF (OR COMMON PLANTAIN)
P. major
Plantain Family ❖ *Plantaginaceae*

Both of these plants have rosettes of leaves with prominent parallel veins. As the common names indicate, one has broader leaves than the other. The leaves of broadleaf plantain lie flat on the ground, with a spread of 4 to 12 inches. Narrow-leaved plantain leaves are more upright, growing 3 to 12 inches high. Both plants have tiny flowers borne on the sides of leafless stalks. Narrow-leaved plantain flower heads, about an inch long, appear at the top of the stems, whereas those of broadleaf plantain cover several inches of stem.

Both plantains spread by seed and by new shoots growing from the roots. They don't spread as aggressively from their roots as many other perennial weeds, but their numerous tough fibrous roots can make them very hard to pull. Hook your fingers under the plants to make sure that you get the whole plant and not just the leaves. Otherwise, the base will be able to grow new leaves. Control light infestations by hand pulling. To fight heavy infestations, turn the soil and dig out each plant completely.

Tender young plantain leaves can be eaten raw in salads and slightly older ones are tasty when cooked. Don't bother harvesting the mature leaves, as they are bitter and tough.

QUACKGRASS (OR WITCHGRASS)
Agropyron repens
Grass Family ❖ *Graminae*

This perennial grass has some of the toughest roots I have ever seen. The plant itself is often small, short, seemingly insignificant, but growing underground are yards of horizontal, pale-yellowish, wirey rootstocks with sharply pointed tips. At each joint is a brown sheath, a ring of short roots, and the potential to grow a new above-ground plant. The rootstocks are so tough that they can grow right through a potato! And if you break up the rootstocks when you are digging, every fragment can grow.

Quackgrass thrives in cool, moist conditions, and is spreading in the coastal parts of California. Its seed can enter a garden as a contaminant in hay or straw.

Combat early infestations by removing as much as you can by hand, digging to get out all of the rootstocks. Their very toughness betrays them when you pry them up and tug on them, as they are more likely to come out whole than to break if your soil is reasonably loose. Smothering mulch made with cardboard doesn't stop quackgrass, but the rootstocks tend to grow near the surface in such a mulch, rendering it much easier to pull.

A quackgrass seedhead looks like a narrow head of wheat. Even seed that is immature can ripen and grow after it falls, so try to remove this weed even before it can form its flowering stems.

SORREL (OR SHEEP SORREL)
Rumex acetosella
Knotweed Family ❖ *Polygonaceae*

Sheep sorrel is a tiny wild relative of the domesticated French and garden sorrels (see page 244). Its leaves also resemble arrowheads, although it is a low-growing plant with a rosette of leaves only a few inches across. Sheep sorrel can be a serious invader, but in my garden it is only an occasional visitor in late winter and early spring.

If you see more than a few specimens of this plant in your garden, check your soil pH, since it is an indicator of acidity. To control sheep sorrel, dig it out and be sure to remove all the roots. Sheep sorrel has the same tart taste as its domesticated relatives, so I gladly add bits of it to my winter salads. Like any plant that contains a significant amount of the sour-tasting oxalic acid, sheep sorrel should only be eaten in small quantities, but a few of these small leaves in a salad now and then should not be a problem.

TEN

MANAGING BUGS AND BLIGHTS

THERE IS NO DENYING THAT pests can do horrible things to the plants we were hoping would produce food or flowers. Big holes in leaves or fruit, flowers eaten to shreds, ugly creeping gray mold all over the plants. Faced with these problems, most of us dislike the prospect of using pesticides. Why shouldn't we, since one of the joys of growing our own food is knowing that no dangerous chemicals have been used on or near it? I have decided that there is rarely a reason to use pesticides in a small home vegetable garden. I have found other ways to deal with the problems I encounter, and you can easily learn them. And, if you ever do use pesticides, this chapter will show you how to use them more effectively and safely.

Understanding Pest Outbreaks

Every garden has some pest problems. The first step in managing them is having an idea of which ones to expect and the factors that increase or reduce them. Why do some pests mentioned in gardening books never appear in your garden? Why are some crops relatively pest-free, while others are almost always attacked by one or more pests? Why are there worse outbreaks in some years than in others? While experience will teach you the answers, some general principles will help you begin:

- **Geography and Climate** If you read gardening books intended for the entire U.S., you will come across pests that never or rarely appear here. Some, such as the Colorado potato beetle, have not migrated this far west yet, and careful quarantine methods may prevent them from doing so. Others, such as the tomato hornworm or cucumber beetle, do appear occasionally, and although more common in nearby inland areas, seem to be deterred by cool, foggy summers.

- **Weather** Pests are more numerous when the weather of a particular year favors their growth, and less common when the weather is less favorable. Frequently, unusual weather brings unusual levels of pests. A very cold winter can result in fewer pests, if their overwintering stages were killed, or a very wet spring might support a larger population of pests that lived on spring grasses before they moved on to your garden's summer crops.

- **What you grow** Many pests only attack certain crops, leaving other crops entirely unaffected. The powdery mildew of squash and pumpkins will not infect peas, and powdery mildew of peas will not spread to squash, as these are different diseases (although each will attack certain other crops and some kinds of ornamentals). Onion root maggots, frustrating as they are, are limited to plants in the genus *Allium*. Sometimes particular crops of several unrelated crops are affected. In my garden the bean aphid, a charcoal gray to black insect, attacks only fava beans, artichokes, garlic chives, and nasturtiums.

  To have a crop wiped out by a pest is an

unnerving experience that calls for regrouping and new tactics. But you can at least keep from becoming discouraged by realizing that the problem is often self-limiting. While you plan a strategy to control the pest the next time you grow the susceptible crop, you can be enjoying harvests from the many other crops you planted that are immune to that pest.

- **How much food there is for pests to eat**
  If you clear an overgrown garden, but ignore the snails, and then put in tender vegetable seedlings, hungry snails will surely wipe you out. Conversely, when your cleared garden of early spring gives way to a lush summer garden, the same number of snails, earwigs, slugs and other chewing pests may eat the same amount, but less of each plant will be lost to them.

  Another aspect of this factor is how many nearby gardeners are growing a particular crop. Some pests, now rare in an area, could become more common if more gardeners begin to grow the crops they feed on. If new pests appear, gardeners can slow their spread considerably by acting to control them before they become endemic.

- **Health of the plants** Plants that are struggling against poor growing conditions are often more susceptible to pests. Poorly watered beans tend to get spider mites; tomatoes fed too much nitrogen are more likely to get aphids. Some crops are typically attacked by pests late in the season, when they are past their peak. Peas, for example, often fall victim to powdery mildew as they near the end of their bearing period, especially if the weather is also warm at that point. (However, while the health of your plants may make a difference in some cases, many pests are perfectly happy to attack healthy plants.)

- **Natural predators and parasites** Gardeners often notice only the insects that are eating a crop, but the garden is alive with insects, and a good many of them are busy eating the pesky ones. Not only insects, but also salamanders, snakes, spiders, and even birds, help control pests. In the soil, helpful micro-organisms destroy soil pests. If all of these creatures didn't help us with pest control, we would be in big trouble. You will have fewer pests if you garden in ways that encourage natural helpers. One of the best ways to do this is to reduce or eliminate use of pesticides, because pesticides are often more le-

thal to predators than to the pests.

- **Chance** Yes, of course, chance is part of the picture too. The soil around a plant given to you by a friend can carry pests to your garden, or pests and diseases may come to the garden on the wind. Insects can carry disease-producing organisms, the insects become infected while feeding on infected plants, then spread the disease throughout the neighborhood as they feed.

The Problems with Pesticides

Farmers had their first big successes using chemicals to control pests in the last century. Twentieth century chemists applied themselves to the development of pesticides and, beginning with DDT in 1939, introduced a host of new ones. In the past few decades, as modern chemical pesticides have become available, many gardeners, as well as farmers, have applied them on a regular, and even a preventive basis. In so doing they have run into some peculiar and unexpected difficulties. While pesticides seem to work fine in the short run, if they are overused they don't work as well in the long run. In fact, they sometimes seem to make pest problems worse.

- **Resistance** The first unwelcome surprise has been that hundreds of pests have developed resistance to chemicals that once were lethal to them. Gardeners, farmers, and professional pest eradicators have had to change chemicals, in some cases several times, to find ways to kill "super insects" or "super mites."

- **Resurgence** Another surprise has been that even when a pesticide treatment seems to have killed off a pest, it can soon reappear in much greater numbers. This effect, called resurgence, occurs because the pesticide has also killed the natural enemies of the pest. As soon as the pesticide wears off a bit, the few pests that either escaped or were resistant are able to multiply freely.

- **Secondary pest outbreaks** Sometimes after a resurgence is brought under control with a second spraying, another pest suddenly appears on the scene, one that was never a problem before. These secondary pest outbreaks occur because spraying has left the new pest free of competition and enemies.

ARE ANY VEGETABLE CROPS SAFE FROM PESTS?

Crops that are pest-free, or almost pest-free, in local gardens: Arugula, cilantro, endive, leeks, New Zealand spinach, parsnips, peppers, prickly pear cactus, salsify, sunchokes, Bolivian sunroot, and most perennial herbs.

Crops that rarely see damage other than by snails, slugs, earwigs, or cutworms: Beans, basil, cilantro, lettuce, spinach, and Swiss chard.

Crops susceptible to pests that sometimes—but not always—attack. (You may well be able avoid these pests by preventive measures and/or luck, but then again, maybe you won't): Artichokes, carrots, celery, corn, cucumber, garlic, onions, peas, potatoes, and tomatoes.

Crops almost always attacked by certain pests: Squash and pumpkin (they get powdery mildew almost without fail, though some squash varieties are more resistant than others) and cabbage family crops (rarely escape attack by cabbageworms—and probably by one or more other pests as well).

- **Residue** Yet another hazard of pesticide use, poisonous pesticide residues can injure your family, your pets, and non-pest wildlife living in or visiting your garden. Pesticide labels will tell you how long to wait after using the chemical before touching or eating the plant, but children, pets and birds can't read the label. And some kinds of pesticide stay toxic for a long time. If these get into groundwater or into streams and lakes, they can poison creatures in the world beyond the borders of your garden. Some types remain toxic long after they are ingested. These accumulate in the bodies of the animals at the top of their respective food chains, such as pelicans, eagles, and humans. A prime example is DDT, removed from the U.S. market due to this hazard.

A recent example of a large scale spray program illustrates some of the above principles. From 1980 to 1982 the insecticide malathion was sprayed over a large area in central California, to try to prevent the spread of the Mediterranean fruit fly, a pest of orchard fruits. Although it may have controlled the fly, the spray program had some impressive side effects. One of them was resurgence. There were dramatic outbreaks of whiteflies, aphids and mites in the treated area, because the spray had killed their predators. A secondary outbreak also occurred, in that the wild shrub, coyote brush, was seriously damaged by a gall midge, previously not a serious problem. And, either direct poisoning or residue killed so many honeybees that beekeepers were afraid their hives might not get through the winter.

Looking for Alternatives

Largely because of the above problems, pesticides have tended to become more expensive. Farmers may find they are using more, to fight resurgences and secondary outbreaks. Chemical companies find they need to develop new chemicals constantly to stay ahead of pest resistance and the discovery of unwanted side effects. When they have developed them, they find they must spend more and more to test and register the new chemicals.

A combination of cost, environmental awareness, and the willingness of the public to look at alternatives, has led to new interest in alternative pest management strategies. Some of these ideas are quite old, but have been neglected during the ascendancy of pesticides. For example, plant scientists have turned their attention to breeding more plant varieties that resist attacks by insects and diseases. And more beneficial creatures are being studied and bred in captivity, then sold to be released for control of pests.

Other pest control ideas are made possible by modern understanding of chemistry and biology. Summer oil is oil freed of a substance (sulfur) which was found to damage leaves. With this new product, we can apply oil to kill insect eggs in summer as well as on dormant trees in winter. "Pheromones" are insect sex hormones, which can be used to confuse insects so they won't breed.

Forming a Strategy

As the public has become more aware of the consequences of using pesticides, interest in alternative methods of pest control has increased. A new way of thinking and acting, Integrated Pest Management (IPM) has gained in popularity among farmers and other professionals who are combatting pests on a large scale. And you can adapt this successful method to protect your own garden from pest infestations.

What is IPM?

IPM *is a decision-making process that treats pest problems not as isolated attacks by the enemies of desirable plants, but rather as disruptions of a garden ecosystem.* Then, the solution is not just to kill the pest, but to modify the ecosystem in ways that reduce pest damage. And because you, your children, pets, the beneficial insects in your garden, the birds, the groundwater, the air, and the soil are also elements of the ecosystem, you will want to choose pest control methods that do not harm or pollute these elements.

The first decision that practitioners of IPM make is whether the pest damage is serious enough to bother with at all. They monitor the number of pests and the extent of damage carefully. Then, if the problem is deemed serious enough, either economically or aesthetically, they choose one or more management techniques, starting with the ones that least disrupt or damage the environment. IPM *does* include the option of using the more toxic pesticides, and pesticide marketers often imply that IPM is just a way to use pesticides wisely, but an IPM gardener can instead decide to use only other methods, avoiding polluting pesticides altogether.

Adapting IPM

The approach I use in my garden owes much to Integrated Pest Management, although I do not study each problem with the precision of the IPM farm advisor before I act. I don't need that much accuracy, as my livelihood is not at stake. So I make a decision based on my observations and experience, such as seeing white cabbage butterflies fluttering over my young broccoli plants in the spring, and knowing that if I ignore them, their caterpillars will destroy my crop. Or noticing that snails are particularly fond of basil seedlings, so unless I have controlled snails perfectly, I will need to protect basil while it is young. By using pest control methods based on the precepts of IPM, I am usually able to avoid or control a pest without using any chemicals. When I cannot, I usually either put up with some damage or do not grow that crop.

Examine Your Plants

Make a habit of examining your plants closely and often, beginning when they are quite small. You want to become aware of a pest when it first arrives, not after it has done serious damage. Look at different parts of the plants: the leaf tops and undersides, the older leaves, the young leaves and buds at the tops of the plants, the stems near the soil line, and the developing fruit.

If you see that your plants aren't thriving, your first question should be: Is a pest causing the problem, or is it just a symptom of poor growing conditions? If plants are smaller than they should be, are wilted, have yellow leaves, or are not setting fruit, but you can't find an insect or clear signs of a disease, carefully read over the entry for that crop in Chapter 11 to see if you planted it at the right time of year, whether it might have a nutrient deficiency, or might be receiving inadequate water. Some physiological problems resemble diseases. A common example is blossom end rot of tomato and summer squash.

Know Your Enemy

If you find signs that a pest is causing the damage, the next question you should ask is: Which pest is it? If you aren't sure which pest is the culprit, you can hardly take effective action to control it. Often you will see only the damage at first, and need to do some sleuthing to find out what caused it. You might see several insects or other creatures in the vicinity, and you don't want to incriminate the wrong one!

For instance, to find out what is chewing holes in leaves, look at both sides of the leaves. Look for feeding pests, and also for insect eggs. If you still don't see any pests, try examining the plants after dark, with a flashlight, as many chewing pests, such as slugs, snails and earwigs, are night feeders.

When leaves are puckery and distorted, or stippled with tiny light dots, the cause may be sucking pests, such as aphids, whiteflies, or mites. These pests often prefer to feed in the buds, flowers, the youngest leaves, and developing fruit. Examine distorted plant parts carefully, including leaf undersides. Use a hand lens, as some of these pests are quite small. If you still see nothing, suspect a viral disease, another cause of puckered leaves.

If a plant suddenly wilts, suspect damage to the roots. Pull away the soil at the base of the plant and check the upper part of the root for damage or pests. Cabbage family plants, carrots, and onions are often infested by root maggots.

Another symptom, spots on the leaves, can be caused by different types of diseases: bacterial, fungal or viral. For help identifying them, read descriptions of the most common diseases later in this chapter.

I have listed the pests I know often infest vegetable plants in this area, and this will be enough information to help you to identify most of the ones you will see. Look first at the ends of individual crop listings to see what pests commonly attack a crop, then see pest listings for more information on appearance, damage caused, and control. If you can't identify your problem from the information in this book, turn to other gardeners, other books (see Appendix VI, Suggested Reading), Cooperative Extension agents (see Appendix V, Resources), or gardening organizations to determine what is causing your problem.

Decide How to Control The Pest

Once you know which pest you've got, you can make effective decisions about controlling it. The first one you need to make is whether your problem is serious enough to require any method of control. In a farmer's field, this would be done with careful monitoring and recordkeeping, but in your small yard, you needn't be so formal. For example, I sometimes notice western spotted cucumber beetles in my garden—perhaps about six a summer. When I recognized the first one, I killed it immediately, and began to examine my cucumber and squash leaves for more beetles or for beetle damage every time I came to the garden. That first summer I was nervous, but now that I know there are never enough

beetles to do much harm, I ignore them. On the other hand, I have learned from experience that cabbage root maggots often infest spring-planted cabbage family crops, so I always take preventive measures against them. You will soon be learning from your own gardening experience when action is needed and when it is not.

When you decide that you do need to control a pest, you sometimes also have to select the right time to control it. To do this, read about the pest you have, or ask someone who knows about its habits. Often, as with imported cabbage moths, the answer is that you need to act as soon as you notice the problem. But your timing may also need to be related to the life cycle of the pest or of the plant it attacks. For example the right time to add mineral oil to corn ears (to repel corn earworms) is when the silks have wilted and just as their tips have turned brown.

When you read about an IPM program for management of a pest, you will often read a list of different ideas to try. You need to choose among them to create an effective strategy that isn't too expensive, doesn't take too much time, and that disrupts the environment as little as possible.

IPM theory divides these control suggestions into four categories: 1. cultural (what is grown, when it is planted, and how it is cared for), 2. mechanical (physical removal of the pest, or barriers to prevent it from having access to the plant), 3. biological (use of any living organism to prey on the pest) and 4. chemical (use of a chemical, usually one lethal to the pest).

For example, a list for controlling an imaginary pest called a tomato nastybug might read: plant a resistant tomato variety (cultural control), plant later than usual (cultural control), pick the nastybugs off the plants by hand (mechanical control), protect fruit with individual nylon net covers (mechanical control), buy and release nastybug-eating insects (biological control), spray your plants with commercial soap spray (chemical control), or, as a last resort, spray with a more toxic pesticide (chemical control).

In the pest entries later in this chapter, I divide tactics into the above categories, but you won't always find them in neat lists. Sometimes you will have to put together lists from several different sources, or add a newly discovered idea to a list you already have. Before you make decisions, you need to be able to recognize different categories of tactics. For example suppose that, halfway through the summer, you come across an entirely new idea for controlling tomato nastybugs: "Nastybugs have been shown to be susceptible to a spray containing the living bacterium *Nastybug getticus*." You would add this to your list as a biological tactic.

To help you place strategies in one of the four categories, here is a list of some common ones:

1. Cultural. This category includes a wide variety of basic preventive measures. They are particularly important to pursue if you hope to avoid chemical methods, or if there are no chemicals to kill the pest you hope to curb.

- Choosing varieties that have genetic resistance to the pest.
- Avoiding infected seed, sets, plants, soil, and containers, or treating them to kill any infections. Includes seeking certified disease-free starts.
- Choosing planting depth of seed or space between plants to discourage pests. Or, for indoor seeding, using sterile planting mix, appropriate temperatures and moisture levels.
- Taking better care of your plants by planting at a more favorable time of year, improving the soil, watering more effectively, fertilizing properly, or making sure the plants get enough sunshine.
- Growing plants that will repel the pest (companion planting, or intercropping).
- Eliminating pest breeding and hiding places, cleaning up plant debris.
- Rotating crops and seeding beds to avoid pest buildups.
- Not growing affected crops for a certain amount of time, or possibly permanently. This might become necessary if there are no adequate controls, or none you are willing to use, but you will rarely need to resort to this extreme.

2. Mechanical. Into this category fall many simple, common sense strategies that involve some degree of direct physical intervention. They may be free, requiring only some effort, or you may need to purchase materials to make barriers or traps.

- Handpicking the pest from the plants. This is the most direct method, and it works well for some pests as long as your garden is small enough to pick over relatively quickly.
- Washing pests from plants with a strong spray of water.
- Removing plants that have a disease or a pest

infestation from the garden.
- Creating barriers of various kinds, from paper wraps for seedling stems or copper strips to repel snails, to fences to keep out deer or rabbits.
- Using traps to catch pests or to lure them to places where you can gather them quickly. Sometimes traps are baited with food or beverage that appeal to the pest.
- Disturbing the soil to kill insect larvae.
- Handpulling weeds, presprouting them, or smothering them.

3. Biological. Helpful organisms can be as selective as careful handpicking, but they save you work by hunting the pests for you.

- Encouraging all kinds of natural predators in your garden by providing food, water, shelter, and by avoiding use of the pesticides that harm them.
- Buying beneficial creatures that eat pests outright, parasitize them, or kill them with a biological toxin. These may be insects, bacteria, helpful nematodes (microscopic worms), or even domestic birds. (Chickens and ducks can reduce insect and snail populations in a garden.)

4. Chemical. These range from the quite safe (soap sprays) to the most toxic of pesticides. They include repellents, baits, dusts and sprays. Pesticide is a general term that includes insecticides, miticides, fungicides, bactericides, and even herbicides (chemicals that kill weeds).

- Soap sprays. Various pesticidal soaps have been developed for use as insecticides, as fungicides, or as herbicides. All are relatively non-toxic to humans.
- Oil sprays (mineral oil or vegetable oil). These have most often been used when deciduous fruit trees are dormant, but new oils are available that are safe to apply to some vegetable crops.
- Chemical elements or simple inorganic compounds, such as those containing sulfur and copper. These are often used to treat plant diseases.
- Synthetic insect hormones used as lures for baits or to disrupt insect reproductive cycles. These are not yet used much in home gardens, but watch for developments.
- Pesticides derived from plant extracts. Examples are pyrethrum and rotenone. In general, plant-derived pesticides break down quickly, leaving no residue in the environment or on the crop, but they can be very poisonous when they are first

applied, so must be handled with caution.
- Synthetic pesticides, mainly manufactured organic compounds. These include Sevin™ (carbaryl), diazinon and malathion insecticides, metaldehyde snail bait, and glyphosate herbicide.

Very roughly speaking, cultural tactics are the least likely to harm you or the environment, and chemical tactics the most likely to do so, but there are some ambiguities. If the wrong beneficial creature is released in the wrong place, for example, it might eat something other than the pest, disrupting the environment in unexpected ways. And some chemical pesticides, such as soap sprays, although chemicals, are virtually nontoxic to humans.

Sometimes a list of possible tactics will contain only a few ideas, sometimes many. While the idea is to start with the least disruptive solution, in practice often several are relatively harmless to the environment, so you may choose to do more than one at once. If, however, the methods are costly and/or time consuming, you will probably want to try them one at a time, so you can see which works better for you.

Here's an example of an IPM decision-making process: "Well, I can't try a resistant tomato variety this year, because my plants are already half-grown, so I will table that idea till next year, and ditto for planting later in the season. Picking nastybugs by hand sounds quite unpleasant, but they are eating my tomatoes so fast that I think I will start picking them off right away. I know I have far too many plants to have time to tie netting on all of the fruits, so that's out. Since I would really rather not handpick these creatures, I will place an order for some of those nastybug-eating insects. If any nastybugs are still hanging around after I release those, I will spray my tomato plants with a soap spray. (I might change my plans if, for instance, I learn that the nastybug-eating insects are rather expensive, so decide to give the soap spray a try first.) I don't want to use anything more toxic, so if this plan of action doesn't do it, I will pull out this year's crop."

Assess the Results

While your program will probably work well, whatever the results of your efforts, you will enter the next season knowing more than you did earlier, having eliminated some possibilities, and you will no doubt have ideas to try next. Sometimes it takes more than one year to work out a really effective system, but when you have done it, you will feel *so* successful!

What are some reasons for failure of a pest management effort based on IPM principles? Assuming you identified the pest correctly, it could be that you had trouble carrying out a tactic effectively. Maybe there were really too many plants to handpick, and you fell down on the job. Maybe you didn't really spray with the soap twice a week as the label recommended.

Or, it is possible that you are trying a method that has not proven to be effective, but is often repeated in books and magazines. In their eagerness to avoid pesticides, gardeners try many tricks, and sometimes the trick appears to have worked, but didn't really. Then the gardener passes on the idea, by word of mouth or in print, although it has never been properly tested.

To continue the nastybug story, you may read that sprinkling paprika on tomato plants during the night of a full moon is guaranteed to drive the nastybugs away. But when you try it, your nastybugs just go right on feeding. If entomologists had been there to study the origin of this theory, they might have reported that the nastybugs disappeared when the gardener sprinkled paprika because they were all mature and entered cocoons for the winter.

Or you may read that a gardener in Florida repelled nastybugs by spreading coffee grounds around her plants, but when you try it, your California strain of nastybug is not repelled by, but is actually attracted to plants surrounded by coffee grounds. Or your uncle in Topeka may write to tell you of the perfect solution for tomato nastybugs, but when you ask him to describe his pest, you may realize that it is different from your bug despite the fact that it has the same common name.

Unfortunately, you can sometimes even buy products that do not work well, still on the market because folk wisdom says they work and because they are profitable to sell. Yes, watch for new ideas, but use some caution. Ask other gardeners and gardening experts to help you evaluate them. Also be sure to try unproven ideas one at a time and leave part of your crop untreated for comparison, so you can accurately assess the worth of the innovation.

Natural Reinforcements

When we think of biological pest management tactics, we often think mainly about the lady beetles and other helpers we can buy, but we get vastly more help against pests from creatures that occur naturally in our garden. As you spend time in your garden, you will become familiar with its helpful residents. If you encourage them, they will be delighted to help you reduce the numbers of pests. Generally, beneficial insects fall into two groups. The small, parasitic insects are more numerous in your garden, while you will find fewer of the larger predatory insects. The tiny wasps that parasitize aphids, you may never see, though if you see the mummified aphids they have killed, you will know they are there (see illustration on page 137). Others, such as the larger hunting wasps, are easy to identify as they cruise from plant to plant in search of prey. Besides insects, many other kinds of creatures help out.

As a beginning gardener, you may mistake some of your helpful creatures for pests. Many gardeners recoil from the large, black, soil-dwelling beetles that lift up their rears threateningly when you disturb them. But these are actually helpful rove beetles that devour pests in the soil. Another less familiar helper is a small, alligator-shaped, charcoal gray and orange insect. This is the larval (immature) form of the lady beetle, and it eats more aphids than the adult! You can see that it's a good idea to try to identify all of the creatures that live in your garden. Then you will not only recognize your pests, but will appreciate how much help you are getting from the other creatures that also call your garden their home.

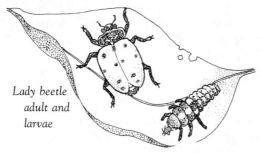

Lady beetle adult and larvae

Helpful Creatures You May See

Following are descriptions of beneficial creatures you are most likely to see in your garden.

LACEWINGS

You may see the 1/3 inch, buff-colored brown lacewing or the slightly larger common green lacewing. Lacewings eat aphids, thrips, caterpillar eggs, leafhopper nymphs, mealybugs, and mites. You are more likely to see the brown lacewing, as the green one (the one sold for pest control) requires warmer temperatures than our microclimates can usually provide.

LADY BEETLES

Lady beetles (or ladybugs), the best known of the helpful beetles, are represented by a number of local species. In general the larger reddish-orange ones eat aphids, while the smaller, blackish or gray ones eat such pests as whiteflies, scales, mealybugs, or spider mites. Many lady beetle species devour pests most actively in the spring, but some are more active in the fall. *Hippodamia convergens*, the convergent lady beetle, is the one collected in the Sierra mountains and sold to gardeners. It has red, or orange-red, wing covers, marked with black spots. The name "convergent" comes from the converging white bars, forming a V-shaped marking on the top of its thorax (the body part between the head and the wings). Convergent lady beetles are fairly common naturally, and do help out with pests, though most of the ones you buy and release will just fly away to feed in someone else's garden. Be careful to protect the gray and orange larvae of this and other lady beetles.

GROUND BEETLES

The small, shiny, black beetles that scurry about when you disturb debris at the soil surface are ground beetles. Some species eat small snails; others hunt and eat caterpillars. Some eat some plant material as well, and others live mainly on seeds. These beetles are unlikely to seriously damage your crops, and the seed eaters probably help by eating weed seeds.

ROVE BEETLES

These black beetles, with very short wings that leave their abdomens exposed, live at or near the soil's surface. They often raise their rears in the air as if to sting, though they cannot do so. One tiny local rove beetle eats mites. Other small ones destroy cabbage and onion maggots. You are most likely to notice the large rove beetle *Ocypus olens*, an insect inadvertently introduced to the Northwest in soil ballast brought in on foreign ships in 1931. While it is alarming in appearance, it relishes snails (even large ones) and slugs. It is black, lustrous (though not shiny), over an inch long, and is one

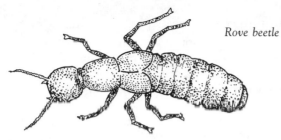

Rove beetle

of those that lift its rear in a threatening manner when it is disturbed. Protect immature ones as well. They are yellow-grayish and not yet lustrous.

SYRPHID FLIES

You will see these flies hovering like little helicopters over your flowers. They are often brightly marked in black and yellow, so that they look like bees at first glance. The larvae of most syrphid flies live on aphids, scales, leafhoppers and mealybugs. Adults require pollen from flowers before they can produce eggs. Syrphid flies tolerate cooler conditions than most predators, so they are likely to be a big help even in our cool summer climate.

TACHINID FLIES

This group of predatory flies looks so much like houseflies that you will probably not be able to identify them, but they are undoubtedly present in your garden. They are all parasites on various pests. Their larvae feed on other insect larvae, including those of many common caterpillar pests. One type attacks earwigs, beetles and the insect group known as "true bugs" (see below).

PARASITIC WASPS

Some thirty families of wasps are parasitic on other insects, or, more accurately, parasitoid, meaning they eventually kill the creature they parasitize. A number of these wasps are native to our area. Ichneumonid wasps, averaging one and a half inches long, parasitize caterpillars. The smaller brachonid wasps include *Diaeretiella rapae*, which is parasitic on the cabbage aphid and the asparagus aphid. This wasp is the one responsible

for creating aphid "mummies," and you are more likely to see this evidence of its presence than the wasp itself. Chalcid wasps are the tiniest wasps. Though you are not likely to see them, particular chalcid wasps control mealybugs, aphids, scale, and the larvae of beetles, moths and butterflies. Some are native, and several species are sold to control various insect larvae. Parasitic wasps do not sting humans.

HUNTING WASPS

Besides the parasitic wasps, other wasps are predatory, hunting and catching insects which they either eat themselves or feed to their young. Several of these wasps are common in local gardens. They are yellow and black, or a shiny blue-black. They may build papery nests to house their larvae, or they may dig small burrows in the soil. While you may want to remove wasp nests if they are on your house, do tolerate them in the less often visited parts of your property, as most are insect hunters. Yellow jackets are also hunting wasps. They may be a nuisance at a picnic, and their presence is not welcomed by those unfortunate people who are highly allergic to their sting, but I can testify that they catch insect pests, having once watched one fly away with a large cabbageworm.

BEES

Bees are important beneficial insects because they pollinate flowers, enabling fruit to form. In 1996-97, many wild honeybees were killed by two kinds of mites, so pollinating was largely taken over by bumblebees, leafcutter bees, and other pollinators.

ANTS

Ants have a mixed effect. They loosen and aerate soil by building nests in it. But ants can also disrupt the activities of various natural enemies of aphids, scales, and mealybugs, preventing them from eating the pests. See the listing for aphids for information on controlling ants.

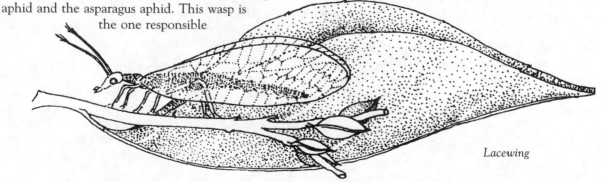

Lacewing

TRUE BUGS

The insect group known as "true bugs" includes squash bugs and other pests, none of which have caused me a serious problem. It also includes a small black and white insect, called *Orius*, that eats other insects. This is a fairly common predator, although so small and inconspicuous that few gardeners would notice it.

EARWIG

The common local earwig is a European species, *Forficula auricularia*. While it does often damage plants, it also eats some pest insects, notably some kinds of aphids. (More on earwigs as pests on page 141.)

PRAYING MANTIS

These strange-looking insects are well known as devourers of other insects. The species *Tenodeora aridifolia sinensis* was introduced to the U.S. from Asia to control garden pests, but it hasn't become established here, so you aren't likely to see it unless you or a neighbor released it. You can buy the egg cases, from which will hatch many small mantises. The praying mantis is no longer considered a very efficient means of pest control, as it is an unselective predator, eating anything in sight, including pollinators and other predators. Still, on the average it probably eats more pests than predators, because pests are usually more numerous.

SPIDERS AND MITES

These eight-legged creatures are closely related to insects. All spiders and some mites help control garden pests. Spiders eat all kinds of insects, including some beneficial ones, but on balance they eat more pests, including all kinds of flying insects and earwigs. Spiders make some gardeners nervous, but in my many years of gardening I have never been bitten by a garden spider. I enjoy watching the wide variety of spiders in my garden, from the tiniest lemon yellow ones to gawky daddy-long-legs, which look like spiders on stilts.

Some mites are also helpful, despite the fact that other species are serious pests. There are predator mites that devour pest mites, and others that eat insects called thrips. There are native predator mites, as well as ones you can purchase.

AMPHIBIANS

While they are not usually major contributors to pest control in a small garden, salamanders do help out. My garden has a number of California slender salamanders living under rocks and near the compost pile. They are brown, 2 to 5 inches long, with legs so small you don't notice them at first. They eat slugs, sowbugs, aphids, termites, beetles, and ants. If you uncover a salamander, gently cover it again.

You may see toads as well, particularly if you live near a creek or pond close to the edges of the San Francisco Bay—areas inhabited by the Western toad. This creature reaches 4 to 5 inches across, and is greenish-brown with a cream-colored stripe down its back. Like other toads, it is an unselective predator, eating just about anything that moves and is smaller than it is. It is best not to try to remove toads from their natural habitat, as they need water to reproduce. It is also illegal to collect them. However, if your garden is near a place where they live, you can encourage them to spend time in it by providing a moist, sheltered place made with coarse mulch materials, or maybe old boards.

REPTILES

Some gardeners will also see garter snakes and lizards, both harmless and at least some help in controlling garden pests.

BIRDS

Our region is home to many kinds of birds, most of which we welcome whether they help out with pests or not. At a minimum, they indicate that the environment is reasonably unpolluted. However some local birds, among them robins, mockingbirds and flickers, do help significantly against pests. Robins eat many kinds of insects, including wireworms, cutworms and caterpillars. Mockingbirds eat beetles, grasshoppers and other insects. Flickers eat ants, caterpillars, cockroaches, and ground beetles, and the presence of flickers may drive some of the pest birds from your garden. (For information on birds as pests, see page 150.)

MICRO-ORGANISMS

Pests, like all other creatures are attacked by agents of disease. Many kinds of naturally-occurring fungi, bacteria and viruses infect and kill pests. Helpful micro-organisms in the soil protect plant roots from soil pests.

Encouraging Your Natural Allies

The most important thing you can do to encourage beneficial creatures is to avoid using pesticides. This is because your natural allies are, unfortunately, often more susceptible to pesticides than your pests. First, there are fewer of them. Predaceous insects are the lions and tigers of the insect world, living on the great herds of plant eating pests. The deaths of relatively few predators allow bursts of increase in pest populations. Also, predators tend to be larger than pests, so they are more likely to be hit by spray. Then, of course, both predators and parasites must eat pests that have been sprayed, further poisoning themselves. Finally, pesticides also kill the many relatively harmless creatures that serve as the predators' alternative food, and that keep predators in the neighborhood at times when pests are inactive. An ideal garden, from a predatory creature's point of view, includes an ample supply of insect life. While you hardly want to be raising pests for your predators to eat, you don't want to kill every insect in sight either.

You can provide the predators with another source of nourishment besides pests. Many beneficial insects, especially adult wasps and flies, need pollen and nectar for quick energy during part of their life cycles. By providing these, you encourage such insects to spend their entire life cycle in your garden. And some predators, such as lady beetles, turn to pollen and nectar when the pests they eat are scarce.

Small, shallow-necked flowers attract predator insects best. Such flowers are common in many plant families—carrot, mint, mustard, onion, buckwheat, and daisy, to mention only a few. Encouraging insect predators is a good reason to let some crop plants bloom in your garden. I have, for example, seen many syrphid flies (whose larvae eat aphids and other pests) hovering around garland chrysanthemum blooms, and I notice hunting wasps feeding at my leek blossoms. Nearby weedy fennel, ornamental plants like candytuft, or natives such as coyote brush, can also serve this purpose. Attractant flowers are especially valuable in the late winter and early spring, when little is blooming. This is an area of active research, and no definitive plant list is available yet. But you can get a head start by planting, and letting bloom, plants of the above families.

You may notice advertisements for baits you can apply to attract beneficial insects. These can be useful as part of a program to encourage predators, but unless you know what you are doing, they may be no help. They are designed primarily for attracting the green lacewing and stimulating it to lay eggs, but chances are you won't have many green lacewings in your garden unless you've released them yourself. Lady beetles and the more common brown lacewings will eat this bait too, but will not come to the area because they are attracted to it. Late May or early June are the best times to spray such a bait, because there is usually a lull in aphid populations then. If you've released some green lacewings, spray in the evening to supplement their diet and encourage them to stay. Spray in the morning to feed native lady beetles.

To make your own bait, mix 1/4 pound of powdered food yeast (volume will vary by brand), and 1/4 pound (about 1/2 cup) of white sugar into one quart of water. Stir well. Paint it onto your plants with a brush, as it is likely to clog spray nozzles. You can store unused portions in the refrigerator for a few days.

Predators also need water in the form of droplets—called "free water"—from which they can sip. Fog drip and heavy dew can provide enough, but when the air is dry, insects appreciate water sprinkled on plants. Sprinkle only plants, such as the cole crops or parsley, that aren't made susceptible to diseases by having wet leaves. Or you can provide an "insect bath," using a medium-sized terra cotta saucer. Place rough rocks in the water, rising above the surface, to provide landing places and shallows where insects can sip.

A healthy soil will encourage helpful creatures that live in the soil or at the soil surface. Limit the use of soil pesticides and soluble synthetic fertilizers. And when you add plenty of well-rotted organic matter, you increase the likelihood that helpful soil creatures will outnumber harmful ones. However, if you are using undecayed organic substances such as green manure or fresh animal manure, as soil amendment, you should dig them in and then not plant for a couple of months, as some of the organisms that carry out the early stages of decay are also capable of attacking living plants.

Leave some dark, moist places on the surface of the soil to attract salamanders and predatory beetles. While you will be cleaning up your garden to avoid snails, slugs, and the like, it is wise to tolerate some easily checked flat rocks, pieces of wood, or mulched areas to offer predators safe harbor.

Hiring Helpers

The idea of bringing insects to the crops to provide biological control is not new. The first recorded success was in about A.D. 300. At that time, Chinese orchardists used predatory ants to control pests of citrus orchards. But until the past century, little organized research was done on biological controls. The first of the recent successes was the 1888 introduction of the vedalia beetle to control cottony cushion scale. Study and introduction of helpful creatures has continued since then, but recent years have seen a great increase of interest in this field so watch for new developments. For specific information on the purchased predators most likely to be helpful against your particular pests in your location, ask suppliers who sell them or consult your county Cooperative Extension.

The main problem with using purchased predatory creatures in a small garden, is that, if they are mobile, they tend to range further than the boundaries of the garden. In so doing, they help the neighborhood, but don't give the gardener who paid for their services his or her money's worth. (They are more efficient in a farmer's fields, where only the few that fly away from the fields' edge are lost, or in homes or greenhouses, where they are contained by the walls, with nothing to eat but the resident pests.) In view of this drawback, be cautious in spending money on highly mobile predatory insects. Concentrate first on keeping your garden attractive to native predators. This will provide a background level of help against pests and if you do try purchased ones, it will encourage them to stay in your garden. Also, look at the less mobile forms of biological control, such as predatory nematodes and other microscopic forms of life.

Long recommended, lady beetles and praying mantises are no longer considered ideal choices. It has recently been shown that, in the spring, at best only 10% of purchased convergent lady beetles stay where they are released—the rest will immediately fly away to feed elsewhere. When lady beetles are released in the summer, they are more likely to stay, but then they do not feed on pests—or on anything else. Also these lovely and beneficial insects are being decimated in their overwintering grounds by greedy commercial collectors who are able to quickly and profitably scoop up large masses of the hibernating bugs for sale in garden stores. Praying mantises are now known to eat predators and pollinators along with the pests, though they will probably eat more pests than predators, so you may want to purchase an egg case just to watch this odd-looking creature grow and feed.

Of the larger purchased beneficial insects, perhaps the most likely to succeed is the green lacewing (*Chrysoperla carnea*), a predator that will eat many pests, including aphids, thrips and mites. Although it prefers warmer nights than we get most of the year, it is potentially quite effective in our warmer areas or in the warmest times of year. Try releasing green lacewings (or lacewing larvae) in the warm spells of May or June, or during the month of September. Release them once a week, for three weeks, for best results. Another good bet is the spined soldier bug. This "true bug" will kill cabbage loopers and imported cabbageworms. It also eats Mexican bean beetles, but these are not a problem in California.

Microscopic organisms available for purchase can be very useful in small gardens. *Bacillus thuringiensis* (sold as Bt, Dipel™, or Thuricide™) is a bacterium that infects many kinds of caterpillars, including cutworms, imported cabbage worms and cabbage loopers. It doesn't affect their predators, nor does it cause systemic infections in humans. (It can, however, cause minor eye inflammations, so do treat Bt with caution and keep it out of your eyes.) Bt has to be sprayed while pests are actively feeding and usually works best when the feeding larvae are young. Wait for the first signs of damage, then spray both sides of affected leaves thoroughly and repeat as often as the label recommends.

Predatory nematodes are microscopic worms that live exclusively on insect larvae, never harming plants. Among the pests they kill are cabbage and onion maggots, wireworms, and carrot rust fly maggots. The nematodes are usually worked into the top few inches of the soil in the spring. To be sure of success, follow directions carefully, applying them when the soil is warm enough for them to survive, and at the time when the pest you hope to control is active. Apply them over only the area of soil suggested; if they are not numerous enough they won't eat all of the pests. And note that they must be reapplied each year, as they do not survive our winter temperatures. Predatory nematodes can also be used above ground, to kill insect larvae that live in plant crevices (for example, artichoke plume moth larvae; see page 138).

Wasp

Using Pesticides

If all of the nontoxic pest management alternatives have not succeeded in controlling a pest, you may choose not to grow that crop while you rethink your strategy. Or you may decide that it is worthwhile to try a pesticide. Personally, I find that using even moderately toxic substances interferes with my peace of mind. Since one of the main reasons I value working in my garden is for the peace of mind it can bring, I rarely use pesticides. Otherwise, there I am in my garden, poring over the fine print of a label, worrying whether the sprayer will leak, or how much of the stuff I will breathe. I soon realize I might just as well be driving in rush hour traffic as gardening!

Whether or not you decide to use pesticides, it could be important for you to understand the most effective and safest ways to use them. For example a tip to a neighbor could help him or her protect prize plants better, while reducing contamination to your garden. And if you ever do decide to try a pesticide in desperation, you don't want to spoil your usual environmental carefulness with a foolish blunder. For example, several pesticides will kill aphids, so you will want to choose the one that is least disruptive of the environment. You will want to know how to choose and use pesticides in ways that will minimize harm to beneficial insects and other nontargeted creatures—including yourself!

Reading Pesticide Labels

I know that pesticide labels are not inviting to read, starting with the fact that they use such small print. And it's true you may not find everything you want to know about a pesticide on its label. But everything that is written on the label is, nonetheless, very important. For one thing, the label is the law. The information on the label must appear there by law, and you are required by law to heed it. But beyond that, the label information will help you to apply the pesticide effectively, with the least hazard.

You should read the label carefully before you purchase a pesticide, and read it again every time you use, mix, store, or dispose of the chemical.

- **Toxicity to Humans:** First, look for one of the three signal codes—"Danger-Poison," "Warning," or "Caution"—which should appear prominently on the front and also under "Hazards to Humans and Domestic Animals" at the top of the fine print. These summarize the immediate, or acute, toxicity of the product, the amount that in short order killed half of the mammals (usually rats) used to test it. This is expressed as the LD_{50} (lethal dose for 50%) showing milligrams of poison per kilogram of body weight (mg/kg). If the label reads "Caution," the probable lethal dose for an adult human is over one fluid ounce. "Warning" means that the lethal dose is between a teaspoon and an ounce. Products bearing the signal word "Danger" can kill with less than a teaspoon, sometimes with as little as a few drops. Of course, smaller people, for instance, children, can be harmed by ingesting a relatively smaller amount of any pesticide.

While the signal codes on labels are good rough guides to toxicity, they do not include all kinds of toxicity. They reflect only the immediate danger of eating the chemical (oral toxicity), and sometimes include data on the immediate hazard of absorbing it through the skin (dermal toxicity). The dangers of breathing a pesticide (inhalation toxicity) is usually too poorly understood to be included, and the long-term toxicity, including ability to cause cancer (oncogenicity), mutation (mutagenicity) and birth defects (teratogenicity), is never considered at all in the rating. As a home gardener you should be using only products marked "Warning" or "Caution." More toxic substances, or more concentrated formulas, are not registered for use on food crops or are only available to professional pest eradicators licensed by the state. However, it is safest by far to treat all pesticides as though they were extremely toxic, since this is the surest way to avoid accidents, and since long term effects may result from repeated exposures to even relatively nontoxic chemicals.

Make note of any precautions for use and

advice to follow in the event of accidental poisoning. Have ready the number of a poison control center and your physician. Have someone else be aware of what chemical you are applying and where the container is located, as there is frequently a "Note to Physician" on the label.

- **Environmental Danger:** While potential environmental damage is not taken into account in the toxicity rating, you can learn something about this under the heading "Environmental Hazards." A common instruction is to keep the chemical out of waterways where it might harm fish. However there is no guarantee that the environmental information on the label is complete. For example, with the exception of honeybees, I've never seen mention of injury to beneficial insects. Pesticides that kill honeybees will also kill the beneficial wasps, which are close relatives of bees, and will probably also kill many other helpful insects. Also, it is possible that a chemical will harm the environment in ways not yet known. (When DDT was first released, no one anticipated its accumulation in mother's milk.)

- **Active Ingredients:** Next, look at the list of ingredients. Listed first will be the common names for one or more active ingredients—for example carbaryl or metaldehyde. (Notice that the pesticide usually has a different name at the top of the label. This name may be something such as "Lawn Weed Killer", or it may include a brand name for the active ingredient. For example, Sevin™ is one of the brand names used for the active ingredient carbaryl.) Knowing the name of the active ingredients of pesticides will help you find more information so you can decide whether or not to use a product. For example, it is by reading the active ingredients list that you will be able to learn if the pesticide contains pyrethrum or a longer-lasting synthetic pyrethroid. Or, when you are looking at herbicides, the active ingredient list will reveal which contain only glyphosate and which contain other, more toxic chemicals. (For more information and recommendations on a number of common active ingredients of pesticides, see Appendix III.)

  After the active ingredients, labels usually list the percent of "inert ingredients" in the formula. Inert ingredients include everything besides the active ingredients—the fillers, spreaders, solvents, etc. There has been no law requiring these to be identified, and most often they are not. Recently the Environmental Protection Agency has decided that, of the 1,200 possible inert ingredients, 56 are actually "toxicologically significant." Because of this research, inert ingredients are being tested and identified.

- **Effectiveness for Intended Purpose:** Of course a main consideration before you buy any pesticide is whether it is effective against the pest you want to eliminate. Check the label to learn for which pests the product is registered, and be sure that your particular pest is included.

  Next, find out whether the product can be used on the plant the pest is damaging. The label may list plants for which the product can be used, or simply state that it can be used on all plants in a certain group. It may also list plants for which it should not be used. Using a pesticide on non-recommended plants could cause them serious damage.

- **Use in Food Gardens:** In your food garden, be sure to use only pesticides registered for use on food plants. Other chemicals may also kill your pests, but they may leave residues on or inside the plant that would endanger you if you ate it. For example, some types of pesticides, called systemics, enter every cell of the plants on which they are sprayed. This means that they can't be washed off, and if they are still in the plant at harvest time, it will not be safe to eat. No systemic pesticides are registered for home use on food plants.

  If a product is registered for use on food plants, the label will tell you how many days you must wait between your application and harvest to be sure that the chemical is no longer present in a toxic form. Even when you wait this long, be sure to wash all food harvested from plants exposed to pesticide and also any food picked from nearby plants.

- **Directions for Use:** Pay close attention to the correct timing and placement of the chemical. It can make the difference between effective control and failure. For example wetting the soil before you apply snail bait makes it more likely that snails will crawl to the bait, but watering *after* applying the bait often renders it ineffective. As another example, soap spray kills only when it lands on the pest. It does no good to spray plants with soap when pests aren't present, or to spray the tops of the leaves when the insects are feeding on the undersides. And soap sprays must be repeated at several intervals, so that new pests hatching on or flying to the plants will also be killed.

Sparing Friendly Creatures

While pesticides often seem to work fine in the short run, they may not work as well in the long run. In fact they sometimes make pest problems worse. Leafminers, whiteflies, and spider mites are among the pests that are often more numerous when pesticides are used heavily. This is because these pests become resistant to the chemicals, and also because pesticides kill off natural predators. And some pesticides are so toxic to honeybees that pollination of fruiting crops decreases when these chemicals are used heavily in an area. Use the following checklist as a guide to minimize harm to beneficial insects and to the environment in general.

1. **Use toxic chemicals as infrequently as possible.** Use them after other less toxic methods have proven unsatisfactory. Use only when there are many pests present, never preventively, "just in case" pests might attack.

2. **Choose chemicals that are as specific as possible for the pests you wish to control,** not broad spectrum poisons that will kill everything in sight. When possible, choose formulations that affect pests more than predators. For example, snail bait containing metaldehyde and carbaryl will kill beneficial soil-dwelling insects, while bait containing only metaldehyde will kill only the snails and slugs.

3. **Choose formulations that are least harmful to beneficial insects.** For example, honeybees and wasps are least likely to be poisoned by granules. Sprays are more likely to harm them, and dusts even more so. The most harmful formulation for such insects is micro-encapsulation. Bees pick up poisons from these time-release capsules while pollinating. Then they eat the poison while cleaning their legs. No micro-encapsulated pesticides are currently registered for use on food plants, but their use on nearby ornamentals could harm the bees that pollinate your food crops.

4. **Choose chemicals that will not persist in the environment,** killing creatures you didn't intend to kill long after your particular problem is solved. If more than one chemical will kill the pest, choose the one with the shortest half-life. For example pyrethrum or pyrethrins break down more quickly than the synthetic pyrethroids. (See Appendix III.)

5. **Time pesticide applications to minimize harm to susceptible beneficial creatures.** For example, apply pyrethrum or pyrethrins in the evening, when honeybees are inactive.

6. **Use pesticides only in the area where the pests are found.** Never apply them to unaffected plants.

7. **Never use a higher concentration than the one recommended on the label for the pest and plant you are treating.** If you do, you won't kill more pests, but you will certainly harm more of the non-pest creatures in your garden.

Mixing, Using, Storing and Disposing With Care

Buy only the smallest amount of a pesticide that will do the job; don't buy the large economy size and save leftovers for later. If you buy more than you need, you will have more to store, and are more likely to end up taking leftovers to a toxic dump site later on. When you are treating only a small garden, you will most often be buying pre-mixed dilutions with built-in applicators. This gives you maximum protection from mixing accidents. If you ever do mix your own solutions, do it outdoors, away from areas where anyone might eat.

Wear rubber or neoprene gloves—unlined, since cloth linings can absorb pesticides and hold them against your skin. Make sure any measuring utensils are clearly marked "for pesticides only." Mix only as much solution as you need to protect your threatened plants: the extra will not keep. Also, make solutions only as concentrated as the label suggests. You will not kill more pests by making them stronger, but you will pollute more heavily and kill more neutral and beneficial life, and you are also more likely to damage the plants you are trying to protect.

If you mix herbicides, use separate utensils, clearly labelled "for herbicides only" and use different spraying equipment. This will protect your desirable plants from poisoning by traces of herbicide left in utensils or sprayers.

If a substance must be sprayed, protect yourself

while you do it. Spray only when it's cool and not windy—early mornings are most likely to provide such conditions here. Wear a long-sleeved shirt, long pants, socks, rubber boots or shoes, and a brimmed hat made of nonabsorbent material. Check whether a respirator is required when you are using either a spray or a dust. When you finish, wash your hands thoroughly before you eat or smoke. If there is any danger that any of the chemicals got on you or your clothes, shower immediately. Keep the clothes you wore when spraying separate from other dirty clothes and launder them separately. Line dry the clothes, to spare your dryer possible contamination. Run the washer on empty once before you launder uncontaminated clothing.

Store pesticides in their original containers with labels intact. Never put them in other containers, to avoid their being mistaken for something else. Store pesticides away from human and pet food, out of reach of children, in a cool place, and preferably in a locked cupboard.

Pesticide labels offer advice on how to dispose of the empty or partially filled container. You can dispose of empty containers in the garbage. However be aware that no matter what the label says, it is illegal in California to put unused pesticide in the garbage can. Partially filled containers should be taken to a toxic waste collection site, where they will be isolated from less toxic waste. Each county has its own arrangement for collecting such wastes, from toxic turn-in days to permanent toxic waste collection sites. For example San Francisco County now has a free toxic waste collection site for county residents. See Appendix V for information on how to find out what your county provides, as well as how to contact other resources offering advice on pesticide use and disposal.

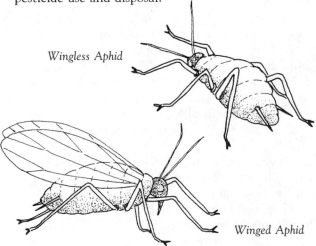

Wingless Aphid

Winged Aphid

COMPENDIUM OF PESTS

Pests and Strategies Against Them

I've compiled the following list of pests from my own gardening experience and that of local consultants. These are primarily pests of vegetables, and the list is as complete as I can make it for these plants. I have also mentioned some pests of fruits and flowers, but you should refer to other references for complete lists of the pests affecting those plants. I haven't much to say about herbs here, because herbs have very few pests.

If you need a checklist of pests that might affect a particular vegetable, you should turn to the listing for that vegetable. For cabbage family plants in general, see the "Mustard Family" page 181.

I have divided the pests into categories based on the type of creature that causes the damage, first insects, then other invertebrate animals (such as mites and snails), vertebrate animals (domestic and wild), and diseases (fungal, bacterial, and viral). Individual pest listings are organized in the following way: 1. What you will see, 2. What the pest is like, and 3. What you can do about it.

In general, management tactics are listed in the order I've suggested that you try them, earlier in this chapter: cultural, mechanical, biological, and then chemical. In practice, sometimes management tactics work better in a slightly different order, and so I will arrange them that way. I think the more toxic chemicals are rarely justified in a home food garden, but have included names of products registered for different pests, often suggesting the one least damaging to the environment or hazardous to your health.

Insect Pests

Insect pests primarily damage your garden in one of the following ways: They chew the stems, leaves, buds, or flowers of the plant, they suck sap from the plants, or they bore into the roots, fruits, or seeds.

Typical symptoms of chewing pests are holes in leaves and flowers or pockets in fruits. Leafminers chew out the insides of leaves, but the surface layers remain intact. Seedlings attacked by chewing insects may be eaten completely.

When sucking insects are involved, infested parts of the plant may become distorted, pale or stippled, due to a loss of chlorophyll. While sucking insects may be found anywhere on the plant, you should especially check rapidly growing places like stem tips and flower buds.

Root-chewing insects crawl through the soil to invade the roots. The symptoms are wilting (even when the plant is well watered), stunting, and yellowing leaves. Of course these symptoms could be caused by disease or other problems, but when you pull out an affected plant, you can generally see holes in the roots or the pests themselves. Plants may even be severed from their roots!

When you read about insects you will often encounter the names of different stages of their life cycles. Here is a brief review of how insects develop, and the terms used to describe the various stages. Some insects hatch from their eggs and just grow steadily, shedding skins, until they gradually mature into adults. The immature stages of these insects are called nymphs. Two of the many kinds of insects that develop this way are aphids and earwigs.

Other insect eggs hatch into larvae, which are wormlike creatures. An insect larva eats and grows, then rests, as a pupa. During its resting period (which may or may not be spent in a cocoon) the pupa metamorphoses into a very different looking adult. The larvae of particular kinds of insects are typically referred to by specific names, for example, caterpillars (butterflies and moths), grubs (beetles), and maggots (flies).

APHIDS

If your plants are infested with aphids, you may notice them on the plant. They are tiny teardrop-shaped, slow-moving creatures, usually feeding in clusters. Most will be wingless, though some will have two clear wings. They are most commonly gray, black, or light green. You may find them on the growing tips of the plants, on the flowers, or on leaves, especially on the undersides. When aphids are present, leaves may become twisted or rolled and may turn yellow. On woody plants, or on very badly infested herbaceous plants, a sooty black substance may cover leaves and stems. Ants may be crawling about on affected plants.

Aphids are sucking pests that insert a hollow beak and remove plant sap. After the aphid has digested the sap, it excretes a substance, known as honeydew, that still contains some plant sugars. This substance attracts ants, and also serves as food for the sooty mold fungus. Controlling aphids will control either of these attendant problems.

Our region is home to a number of aphid species, and they attack many kinds of vegetables, flowers, and woody plants. The cabbage aphid, a gray species, will be found on cabbage family plants, the light green pea aphid on peas, and so on. Despite the many different kinds of aphids, control methods are similar. For details about appearance and control of particular species, see information in the pest sections of various vegetable listings.

Aphid mummies

Just a few aphids will do little direct damage to your plants, but they do spread plant diseases, so you shouldn't tolerate many of them. And sometimes they multiply until the plant is severely stunted. Aphids reproduce very rapidly, making many generations in a season. Some winters are mild enough that they continue to feed and multiply, but, if not, they overwinter as eggs, glued to a plant.

Since there is some evidence that weakened plants are more likely to be attacked, attention to good growing conditions may pay off. Aphids may attack plants with roots badly damaged in transplanting, or those that have been given too much nitrogen fertilizer. Some crops, such as tomatoes, do not have a high need for nitrogen, so special care must be taken not to give too much.

A small percentage of aphids develop wings and fly to infest new plants. A mulch made of aluminum foil repels flying aphids, who become confused by the reflected sky. However, vigilance is called for, as this mulch also repels aphid predators, so any aphids that do land may multiply more rapidly. (The aluminum may also help plants grow larger, by reflecting more sunlight onto the them.)

Repelling flying aphids won't stop infestations that have already begun. If possible, crush aphids when you see them. If the aphids are lodged in places where it is difficult to crush them, or if you have many infested plants, wash them off with a strong spray from a garden hose. It won't do just to sprinkle the plants, you need to aim a fairly high pressure nozzle from many directions in order to knock aphids from their niches. Hold your hand behind the leaves and flowers as you spray, to avoid injuring them. The force of the water often fatally injures the pests that have their feeding parts attached to the plants, though those that are not feeding may survive to climb back on the plant. If a single leaf, or a whole plant, seems to be hopelessly coated with aphids, you may choose to remove it rather than fight a losing battle.

Aphids have many natural enemies, so efforts to foster these will pay off. Lady beetles, lacewings, syrphid flies, and others all eat aphids. You may see aphid "mummies" left by the braconid wasp *Diaeretiella rapae*. These are puffed up, pale brown, dead aphids, eventually with a single round hole where the hatching wasp emerged.

Ants protect aphids from their natural enemies. This is especially true of the Argentine ant, the small, dark reddish ant that comes into our houses so often. If you have large populations of the Argentine ant, consider using a boric acid bait to control them. One such bait, Drax™, is available through Harmony Farm Supply (see Appendix V, Resources).

When an aphid outbreak is heavy, you may choose to resort to chemical control. Many chemical pesticides, from soap spray to diazinon, will kill aphids, and you might as well use soap spray, as it is the least toxic. For best results spray as often as the label recommends. Other relatively safe chemicals that kill aphids, in order of safety, are neem, pyrethrum, and pyrethrins, sabadilla, and rotenone. If you have more than a few plants, it is best to use a pressurized sprayer, as you will tire of pumping a hand sprayer.

ARTICHOKE PLUME MOTHS

Often the first you will see of this pest is an unsightly, dark feeding trail in the scales or the heart of a harvested artichoke bud. If you are very observant, you might be warned earlier in the season, when irregular holes appear in the new leaves at the hearts of the plants. Sometimes you may see small light brown larvae in the damaged areas.

The moths responsible for this damage lay single eggs on the undersides of the lower leaves. The larvae feed first on the young shoots at the center of the plant and then move up to the flower buds. They pupate on the underside of the older, lower leaves and in the leaf litter. You may be able to grow artichokes without ever having this pest, but if it attacks, it can make your artichokes pretty unappetizing.

To prevent artichoke plume moths, begin by cleaning up dying leaves and leaf litter. Divide the plants often enough that they do not become huge thickets, difficult to search for signs of the pest. Cutting the plants back in the summer can help also, because this interrupts the pest's life cycle by removing its habitat for part of the year. Remove any nearby thistles, especially bull thistles, as they serve as alternate hosts for the pests.

Encourage native lacewings and parasitic wasps. These offer some help, although they alone can't control a serious plume moth outbreak. Purchased biological controls include Bacillus thuringiensis (Bt) and beneficial nematodes. Follow package instructions for using either. Both will be most effective if they are sprayed when the caterpillars are still small. To use the nematodes, spray when the caterpillars are 1/4 inch long. Use a total of three applications, one week apart. For more information on these products see page 132. For sources, see Appendix V.

CABBAGE ROOT MAGGOTS

When a cabbage or other cole crop plant wilts even though it is well-watered, suspect the cabbage root maggot. Eventually, infested plants may actually fall over, since the maggots have bored through the roots just under the soil. Radishes and turnips have thicker roots, so they may not be killed by the pest, but they are ruined by the many wormholes with small white maggots inside.

Cabbage root maggots are the larvae of a small fly which lays its eggs next to plant stems. When the maggots hatch, they enter the soil and begin to feed on roots near the surface. After feeding for several weeks, they pupate, emerge as adults, and breed to begin another cycle. The first larvae appear as early as late March, and there will be several life cycles during the warmer months. In the fall, the year's last pupae rest for the winter in the soil, emerging as adults the following spring.

Most references suggest protecting individual seedlings of the larger cole plants at planting time with tarpaper barriers. The paper is laid flat on the ground, with slits cut for the stems. However some gardeners have reported that the flies still get in. I've had the best results wrapping each stem with a small piece of grocery bag paper that extends a little over an inch above and below the soil. I remove the seed leaves, then tightly wrap the paper twice around the stem, holding it in place as I plant.

This method works fine as long as you are setting out transplants, but if you are sowing seed directly, as you always do radish or turnip, you can hardly wrap each stem. I'd read that wood ash in the soil would discourage root maggots, but when I mixed a large amount of wood ash into the first few inches of the soil where I planted turnips, root maggots still did a lot of damage. Instead, I've had good luck covering seedbeds with floating row covers, well tucked-in at the edges. Row covers or row covers on wooden frames can also be used to cover whole beds of the larger cole plants.

Another strategy is to grow susceptible crops when the pest is inactive. If you need to get a cabbage family crop started in mid- or late summer, use one of the above kinds of barriers until weather cools. Plant radishes unprotected in October through March. For "spring" cole crops, use short season cabbage or broccoli, set out as early as possible. Transplant cabbage seedlings into your garden as early as January and broccoli seedlings in February, wrapping the stems as you transplant them for extra insurance. Even without the wraps, early planting can help, as these older cole crop plants are less likely to be killed by the maggots than younger, later planted, ones. If you must plant in later spring, wait until late May or June, when there should be a letup of a few weeks duration while the first spring generation pupates.

Remove any infested plants from the garden, digging into the soil to try to get all of the pests that were in or near the root. Don't plant cabbage family crops in the same soil the next year.

Of the native predators, some small rove beetles eat cabbage root maggots, though they are not likely to provide control by themselves. You can help them out considerably by applying purchased predatory nematodes to your soil when you expect the first spring maggot generation. (See page 132 for a discussion of predatory nematodes and Appendix V for sources.)

The pesticide most often recommended to combat cabbage root maggots is diazinon. Applied at planting time, as soil granules or dust, it offers some relief, but usually doesn't provide complete control. As the predatory nematodes have a good chance at control without harming helpful soil life, I suggest using them instead.

CABBAGE LOOPERS AND IMPORTED CABBAGEWORMS

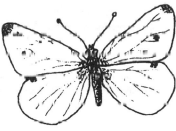

Cabbage butterfly

When there are irregular holes in the leaves of your cabbage family plants, look for either of these voracious pests. Both are smooth, green caterpillars, from very tiny to over an inch long, depending on their age.

Cabbage loopers, the larvae of a brown moth, move inchworm-fashion, a style of locomotion known as looping. They grow to 1 1/2 inches long, and have several fine, light lines down their sides and back. In addition to cabbage family plants, they may also eat beet, celery, lettuce, parsley, pea, potato, spinach, or tomato leaves.

Imported cabbageworms crawl without looping. They are the larvae of the white cabbage butterfly often seen fluttering about gardens in our warm months. Cabbageworms grow to about 1 1/4 inches, are a velvety, light jade-green, and may have faint orange or yellow stripes. They eat mainly members of the cabbage family, including ornamental and weed species.

Both pests are common in this region and one or both are almost certain to infest your cole crops. Both complete several generations in the spring and summer, overwintering in the soil as pupae, ready to strike again next year.

These caterpillars are most damaging when the plants are small, sometimes eating up whole seedlings. However, because the adult insects are inactive in cold weather, your earliest plantings of cabbage family plants may escape damage until they are quite mature, and the proportion of leaf damage is less significant. Then, midsummer and early fall plantings will need protection only until weather turns cool. It might be practical to use floating row cover on cole crop seedlings that are growing into the fall, removing it when the plants become larger and you no longer see cabbage butterflies in your garden.

In warmer weather, begin to inspect cole crop seedlings when they are quite small. Look for the pale yellow, dome-shaped eggs of the cabbage looper on the tops of leaves, and for the pale yellow to orange, rocket-shaped eggs of the imported cabbageworm on the undersides of the leaves. If you crush the tiny eggs about every 5 days, neither of these caterpillars will be able to hatch. Also check for the young caterpillars by inspecting both sides of the leaves and the heart of the plant. The imported cabbageworms are hard to see because they are almost the same color as the leaves, and can easily be mistaken for a leaf midrib. If you see deposits of greenish feces, you can surmise there is a caterpillar around somewhere. (While you are searching, you can also remove cutworms, slugs and snails and crush any incipient aphid colonies.)

Both cabbage worms have a number of natural enemies, including tachinid flies, spiders, wasps and yellow jackets, though these will not offer complete control. If you have a serious infestation and too many plants to handpick, you may want to use Bt berliner-kurstake (see page 132), sprayed every two to three days as long as the caterpillars are feeding. It will work better when the caterpillars are still small, and if you cover the leaves, including their undersides, completely with the spray. Both pests are also susceptible to neem, pyrethrum, sabadilla, rotenone, and other chemicals, although these shouldn't be necessary if you use Bt.

CORN EARWORMS

See information in corn listing on page 205.

CUCUMBER BEETLES

You may see either of two cucumber beetles in your garden. Both are shiny, black beetles, about 1/4 inch long, with markings on their wingcovers. The wingcovers of the western spotted cucumber beetle are yellow-green with twelve black spots, while those of the less common western striped cucumber beetle are yellowish with three black stripes. The adults do the most damage, chewing holes in leaves and flowers of many plants, but especially those of cucurbit crops, beans, and corn. They may also eat stone fruit, such as peaches or plums. The soil-dwelling cucumber beetle larvae eat roots. The larvae of the western spotted cucumber beetle feed on corn, sweet pea, and grasses. Those of the western striped cucumber beetle feed on cucurbit roots.

In the east, closely related cucumber beetles cause serious damage to cucurbit plants by spreading bacterial wilt disease. Neither western cucumber beetle species spreads wilt, but they can transmit cucumber mosaic virus. The adults can also cause serious damage to young cucurbit plants, though older plants are able to withstand some damage. The larvae of the western spotted cucumber beetle are less damaging to corn roots than are those of the spotted cucumber beetle common in the east. However, the larvae of the western striped cucumber beetle can seriously harm young cucurbit plants.

Both kinds of cucumber beetles overwinter as adults, most often in weeds outside your garden. In the spring they mate, and females lay eggs at the base of host plants. Larvae feed on the roots for a few weeks, then pupate and become adults. There are two or three generations a year.

If you see an occasional cucumber beetle, do handpick and destroy it. Also clean up plant litter and any fruit you don't intend to harvest, to reduce hiding places for the pest. If you only see one now and then, that is probably all you need to do.

Predatory nematodes applied at planting time will help somewhat in control of these pests, by reducing the number of larvae. Adults may be killed by neem, pyrethrum, or rotenone, but you will have to use either one repeatedly, since new adult beetles will continue to fly in from outside your garden. Probably the best protection is to cover young cucurbit plants with floating row cover until they are large enough to withstand some damage.

CUTWORMS

These pesky caterpillars kill seedlings by chewing through the stems of many kinds of vegetable and flower seedlings at the ground level. The seedlings fall over, and if they are very small, they may wilt so quickly that you think they simply vanished! You may find puffy, brownish caterpillars in the soil around your plants. They are usually rolled up in tight "C" shapes. You may also find cutworms climbing into older plants, or living in deep pockets they have eaten into young forming cabbage heads. Cutworms are the larvae of several species of drab-colored, night-flying moths. After passing through several generations in the warm part of a year, they overwinter in the soil as eggs, larvae, or pupae, depending on the species.

Cutworms have usually been a low-level pest in my garden, but they can be so numerous that they wipe out your plantings, so be vigilant. When you are digging your soil or transplanting, be on the lookout for cutworms or the golden-brown, torpedo-shaped pupae, and destroy them. If you know cutworms are present, protect transplants with brown paper collars (as above, for cabbageworms) or with half buried protective rings. Make the rings by removing the bottoms from containers such as yogurt cups, cottage cheese cups, or tin cans.

Bacillus thuringiensis will kill cutworms, but usually by the time they have eaten enough of the bacterium to harm them, they have already done a lot of damage. One way to overcome this problem is to make a bait of 1 or 2 parts by weight of Bt mixed into 6 pounds of apple pomace (apples with the cider pressed out). Bran can be substituted for the pomace, but it is worth looking for pomace, as it will work better. Perhaps a more convenient alternative is predatory nematodes applied at planting time.

EARWIGS

Earwigs eat leaves of seedlings and older plants. They may chew holes in the leaves, or may eat until nothing is left but the larger veins. They also often eat flower petals and even corn silks. If you suspect that you have damage caused by earwigs, look for shiny, dark brown insects, up to 5/8 inch long, hiding in the crevices of surface soil debris and of your plants. The insects have "pincers" on their rear ends and frequently hold these up in the air in a menacing gesture. To surprise them in the act of devouring your plants, try a night hunt with a flashlight.

Earwigs often live in gardens without becoming serious pests. Their preferred diet is decaying organic matter, plus some insects (including aphids, insect larvae, and snails). However, as I write this I can imagine the protests of gardeners who have had serious earwig damage in their gardens. The reason for the occasional serious problem is that when earwigs multiply very rapidly, sometimes there is not enough of their usual food sources. Then they turn to live plants.

You may have a sudden increase of earwig damage in the spring, when broods are hatching. They may also suddenly become pests after you clean up the decaying matter on which they have been feeding. If they do get out of hand, your goal should be to reduce the population until it can live on the amount of decaying matter available in your garden. Female earwigs tend broods of developing nymphs,

taking them on nightly feeding forays. If you use a trowel to investigate just under the soil surface from March to May, you may be able to find the developing earwigs in their daytime hiding places. Look especially near the boards of raised beds and in the drainage holes of pots. While earwigs look like they have hard shells, they are actually easily crushed. And, although I do work quickly just in case, none has ever used its pincers on me. If you are nervous about touching them, use a rock to crush them. Or if there are a number of them in one place, it can

Earwig

be efficient to quickly trowel them into a plastic bag for disposal.

You may find that certain objects stored in your garden area have become favorite earwig hiding places. For example they may hide in piles of clay pots or used plastic bags. Clean these up to reduce the infestation. You may also find them living in fruit or ornamental trees, vines, or weedy areas. Thinning too-thick growth in trees will reduce cover for the pests.

Traps of various sorts catch earwigs. Rolled damp newspaper traps, held with rubber bands, will catch earwigs seeking cover from morning's light. These traps must be removed daily and discarded in closed plastic bags. Earwigs will also drown in shallow containers of either beer or vegetable oil, and these traps have the advantage that they do not have to be emptied every day. Pour a half inch of beer or vegetable oil into shallow dishes, sunk so that the lip is even with the soil surface. Draw the earth right up to the edge so that it is easy for pests to walk to the edge without climbing. Empty traps when they fill up, and set them up again until the catch drops off. While the beer trap has been touted for snails and slugs, I find I rarely catch snails, and only a few slugs. But when my garden is infested with earwigs, I typically catch 50 of them in a beer trap in a single night. You may also decide to use floating row cover to protect small beds of seedlings.

Commercial insecticidal soap will kill earwigs too, but only if you can spray directly on them, so it isn't much help. Bait containing carbaryl is registered for use against earwigs, but it will also kill ground beetles, earthworms, and other harmless or helpful creatures. Therefore, since the above cleanup and trapping methods have a good potential for success, I recommend them instead.

FLEA BEETLES

If you have flea beetles, numerous tiny holes will appear in the leaves of affected plants. On examination, you will see small insects, reminiscent of fleas, leaping around the leaves. They may be black, dark green, or various other colors. They may be particularly serious on seedlings, or may attack older plants as well.

Of the several species of flea beetles, some are highly selective, while others attack a wide variety of plants. Taking all of the common species into account, many garden crops are susceptible, including all nightshade family crops, spinach, beets, sunflower, pumpkin, cabbage, and radish. Flea beetle larvae may feed on leaves, or may live in the soil, feeding on the roots of the preferred plants. The adults overwinter in the soil or in garden debris, then lay eggs. The pest may complete more than one generation each summer.

These pests do not appear in the whole region, and are probably limited to the warmer areas. I have only seen one kind in San Francisco, on arugula and radish. I know they appear in Berkeley and in the warmer inland areas of the peninsula and Sonoma County. If you do have flea beetle damage, cultivate the soil surface frequently, to disturb their eggs and larvae. Clean up garden debris, especially in the winter, so there are fewer hiding places for adults. Keep weeds under good control, particularly those in the same plant family as the affected crop plants. Use large, well hardened-off seedlings, and give plants very adequate supplies of fertilizer and water, for if they are healthy and fast-growing they can often survive the insect's attacks. Cover susceptible transplants or seedbeds with floating row cover until they are large enough to tolerate some damage.

If the flea beetle in your garden has soil-dwelling larvae, you may see some improvement if you apply beneficial nematodes to the soil. But you will need to learn when the larvae are in the soil, to be sure you are applying the control in time. For help identifying the species you have, and to learn more about its life cycle, try calling the Cooperative Extension service. Be sure you can report all of the affected crops, and try to study the pest long enough that you can describe it. If the infestation is very severe, you may want to try pyrethrum or pyrethrins, or rotenone.

LEAFMINERS

Gray, light green, or brown trails or blotches will appear on the leaves of vegetables or flowers when you have leafminers. You can often see the shadows of the small insects inside the leaves, feeding between the layers.

Leafminers are the larvae of various small flies. The serpentine leafminer eats winding tunnels in the leaves of many vegetables and flowers. Another, the beet leafminer, eats irregular blotches in leaves of beets, chard, spinach and the related weed, lambsquarters. The flies lay eggs on the surface of the leaves or under the leaves' epidermis. After the larvae eat and grow in the leaves, the pupae emerge through holes and fall to the ground to finish maturing. Their life span is highly variable, but may take as little as a month, which allows several generations to develop each season. Leafminers are usually only a minor problem, disfiguring a few leaves, rather than destroying plants. However when they attack plants, the leaves of which you hoped to eat, such as spinach, beet, or lettuce, they can be a serious nuisance.

As soon as you notice leafminer damage, either pinch the leaves to kill the visible larvae, or pick the affected leaves and remove them from the garden. Also remove dead leaves and debris under affected plants. If you are plagued by the beet leafminer, grow susceptible plants in the late summer so that they mature in the fall and winter when this pest is less active. A February planting might also escape damage long enough for a crop to be harvested young. Remove lambsquarters from gardens where beet leafminers are a problem and till the soil in the fall to kill overwintering pupae. Floating row cover is a good means of preventing leafminer infestations when you are growing crops while the flies are active.

STICKY TRAPS

These traps work on the principle that some insects are attracted to a certain shade of yellow. You can use them either to monitor certain pests in your garden in order to predict outbreaks, or to control the pests. For monitoring, use one trap per 1,000 square feet. Identify the pests with a hand lens, or find someone who can help you identify them. You can then count different pests, learn to correlate the counts with levels of damage, and see when the number of pests is rising or falling. Besides whiteflies, yellow sticky traps will catch winged aphids, leafminer adults, and possibly other small pest insects as well. Sticky traps painted white attract and trap flea beetles.

You can use purchased sticky traps, or make your own. To make yellow sticky traps, use either yellow paper plates, or 1/4 inch plywood painted with Rustoleum Yellow #659 paint. Then coat either of these traps with a sticky oil. You can buy materials to coat the traps, but if you do so, try to choose one that doesn't have a chloroflourocarbon propellent, to avoid further damage to the earth's ozone layer. Or, you can make your own from one part petroleum jelly to one part household detergent. In either case, use a thin coat, so the coating won't drip off. If your trap is made of plywood, you can wash the oil off periodically and renew it.

Hang sticky traps vertically on a stake at the level of the plants you're concerned about, facing the plant, and with the sticky surface out of direct sun. Avoid hanging them where wind will blow loose dust on them, as this quickly will render them useless.

Natural enemies, such as parasitic wasps, often are fairly effective in keeping leafminers from becoming serious pests. In fact, leafminer outbreaks often follow use of chemical pesticides that kill these wasps. Chemical control of leafminers themselves has been difficult in the past, because most of the insecticides registered for use on food crops will not kill leafminer eggs or the larvae hidden inside the leaves. However, the new botanical pesticide, neem, kills all stages of the pest. It also repels them for up to several weeks, though you will probably have to apply it more often if rains wash it off, or as new leaves form on fast-growing crops.

ONION ROOT MAGGOTS

When onions, shallots, or even leeks decline or die, pull one of the plants and check for root maggots. These 1/4 inch white maggots feed on the bulb and roots. They are the larvae of a small fly that lays eggs at the bases of the plants. Among onions, white bulbed varieties are the most susceptible. Yellow ones are less so, and red the most resistant, although they may still have damage. Shallots are more susceptible than onions, leeks quite resistant, although not totally immune. My plantings of walking onions and of garlic chives have never been infested by maggots.

One technique that may help combat this pest is to scatter your onion plants throughout the garden. To mature, these maggots need more than twenty onions, and if they can't find enough nearby, they will die. If you do find infested plants, be sure to remove them from your garden, removing all onion debris too, and check the soil around infested plants for maggots as well. Don't grow onions, shallots or leeks again for several years in the spot from which you pulled infested plants. One organic farmer reported that the onions he grew in his well-amended soil had far fewer onion maggots than those grown in his neighbors' non-amended soil—another incentive to add plenty of organic matter.

Native predators of the onion root maggot include predatory flies, wasps, beetles, and a parasitic fungus. Predatory nematodes will attack the maggots. Apply them in late spring when soil warms and the flies begin to hatch. If you are growing a crop through the summer, use the nematodes again in midsummer to combat later generations of the maggot. (See page 132 for more on predatory nematodes.)

TOMATO OR TOBACCO HORNWORMS

These large, green worms devour tomato and other nightshade family plants. They are easy to identify by the upright, curved "horns" on their rear ends and diagonal white markings on their sides. However they are not always easy to see on the also-green plants. Look for them hiding among the branches when you see serious leaf damage underway. They may also eat green or ripened fruit. Tomato hornworms may be distinguished from tobacco hornworms by the fact that the horn of the first is green with black sides, while that of the second is red. They are the larvae of two large species of sphinx moths.

In areas where they are common, hornworms often descend on tomato plants in large numbers and eat the leaves to their midribs. I have seen only about five of these caterpillars in all of the years I have gardened in San Francisco, and suspect they are limited by the cool weather of the region. However, as they are up to four inches long, even one on a plant in a season can do a certain amount of damage, and can certainly be an alarming discovery.

Handpicking should be quite sufficient here to control hornworms. When they are present in large numbers, they may be controlled by spraying the plants with the bacterium *Bacillus thuringiensis* (Bt), although this works best while the caterpillars are still small. A naturally-occurring braconid wasp parasitizes hornworms by laying eggs in them. The wasp larvae feed on the hornworm, then pupate in white cocoons, which protrude from the parasitized caterpillar. I have never seen such a parasitized hornworm here, but should you ever see one, do leave it alone so the hatching wasps can attack other hornworms too. Lady beetles, lacewings and trichogramma wasps will all help with control by eating hornworm eggs.

WHITEFLIES

You know you have whiteflies when you see tiny, snow-white, winged insects clustering on the backs of leaves and fluttering about when disturbed. The infested leaves may turn yellow, or seem dry and slightly curled. On careful inspection you may see small shiny spots on the undersides of the leaves. These are the larvae—flat, immobile discs fastened tightly to the plant. Whitefly adults and their larvae both suck plant juices. Beans, tomatoes, cucumbers, and squash are common host plants, especially when these plants have been given too much nitrogen fertilizer or are growing in otherwise poor conditions. Whiteflies are also serious pests of citrus, so check neglected citrus growing near your vegetable crops to see if they are serving as a source of this pest.

While just a few whiteflies do little harm, they reproduce quickly, and heavy infestations weaken or kill plants. On woody plants, or on severely infested herbaceous plants, whiteflies create the conditions that favor development of sooty mold, as do aphids (see aphid listing.)

Whiteflies lay eggs on the undersides of leaves. These hatch into "crawlers," which crawl around for up to two days, then settle down to become immobile larvae. (Larvae lack legs and antennae and are covered by a waxy shield, all traits they share with scale insects.) Whiteflies can complete a life cycle, from egg to adult, in 30 days, and will complete several overlapping cycles in a summer season. The plants are soon infested with a mixture of adults, larvae, crawlers and egg cases. Most control methods work on only some of these stages, making control difficult. If an annual vegetable plant has become heavily infested, it might be easier to pull it, clean up its debris, and discard all of it. But you can probably bring light or moderate infestation under control.

Check lower leaves for early signs of whiteflies, and remove the leaves if you see the pest. When infestations are very light, you can hold them down by treating both sides of the plants' leaves with a strong spray of water once a week. You can also use yellow sticky traps to monitor for the presence of this pest and to control light outbreaks, although be aware that this method only removes adults, leaving eggs, crawlers and larvae. To have any effect, you will need to use one trap for every two large plants.

Some gardeners use a small vacuum cleaner to remove adult whiteflies from plants. While this could be very satisfying, it, like sticky traps, removes adults only, so at best, it would have to be repeated every few days to have any hope of reducing the population. Still, if you have such a tool, you might want to use it in combination with other tactics.

A purchased predator, the wasp *Encarsia formosa*, is a parasite of the whitefly pupae. It is most likely to work in the early stages of an infestation, when there is a lower number of host insects.

It is relatively expensive, and must be released weekly over a period of four weeks.

Among chemical controls that kill whiteflies, soap spray and summer oils are the least disruptive to the environment. Apply either to the undersides of leaves every 4 to 6 days until control is achieved. Use caution in applying soap spray, as a high concentration is suggested for whitefly control and may damage some plants. Try a little at first, wait 48 hours, and if there is no damage, proceed. The botanical pesticide neem is effective against all life stages of whiteflies. It is best to avoid use of other chemical controls, as whiteflies tend to rapidly develop resistance to most pesticides.

WIREWORMS (CLICK BEETLES)

Wireworms are leathery, pale yellow larvae, 1/2 to 3/4 inches long, that turn up when you are digging the soil. They have a yellow-brown band at each end. They eat roots and tubers, killing young plants or stunting larger ones. They may attack root crops, potatoes, cabbage, corn, beans, lettuce, or onions. You might find one actually tunneling in a root crop or in potatoes, but it is more likely that you will just find them loose in the soil.

Wireworms are the larvae, or grubs, of the click beetle. You may also turn up pupae and adult click beetles. The pupae are pale yellow and you can see their developing beetle-like features—legs, wings, etc. The adults are narrow, brown beetles, up to about 3/4 inch long, that snap their bodies, making small clicking sounds when they are on their backs, trying to turn upright again.

If you just see a wireworm or click beetle now and then while you are digging, the damage is probably not severe, but destroy any you find. Also turn the soil anytime between midsummer and fall, whenever you are between crops, to destroy larvae and pupae that would otherwise overwinter. If you have a severe problem, dig the soil once a week for four to six weeks. Also amend your soil well, as the pest may be more severe in poorly drained soil.

Potatoes or carrots have been suggested as a trap for wireworms. I tried putting cut grocery store potatoes an inch or so under the surface, with a stick inserted in the potato to mark the spot. I waited the prescribed two days, and up to a week, however the wireworms in my garden were not attracted to this bait. Predatory nematodes should reduce the wireworm population (see page 132).

Other Invertebrate Pests:

MITES

There are many species of pest mites. They attack a variety of food-bearing plants from tomatoes to citrus. These spider relatives suck plant juices, eventually causing woody plants to drop their leaves, and often killing herbaceous plants. Typical symptoms are dull-colored leaves, stippled with pale dots. In some cases the leaf backs, or entire leaves, may be covered with a dirty-looking web. A magnifying lens will reveal tiny yellow, orange, green, black, or red creatures in the webbing. Or if you tap the leaves over a piece of white paper, the mites will fall onto it. You will see tiny specks that start to crawl about.

While mites are most common in hot, dry areas, you may see them in cooler coastal gardens, especially on plants that are underwatered. They are also common on plants grown indoors. In local gardens I have seen mites on tomatoes, beans, squash, eggplants, and strawberries.

Mite attacks often get out of hand before a gardener can identify the pest, because the creatures are so small. They first appear near the midribs on the undersides of leaves. And as they are not extremely common, you won't be checking the leaves of all of your plants for them. However it is worth checking the above listed crops and any kind of plant on which you have had mites before. Begin early in the season to check the undersides of the lower leaves of those plants.

At the first sign of the pest, spray the leaves, especially the undersides, strongly with water once every five to seven days. If mite numbers still increase, try an insecticidal soap registered for controlling mites, or sulfur used as a dust or a liquid spray. (For cucurbits, test your sulfur formulation on one leaf before you apply it to the whole plant, since it may damage them. It can also burn strawberry leaves, if applied too generously when it's hot out.) On woody plants, dormant or summer oil sprays can control mites. These work by smothering the pest.

Mites are preyed upon by native predatory mites, as well as a kind of ladybug, and some other kinds of beetles. And you can purchase green lacewing larvae as well as predatory mites to help control them. There are several species of predatory mites, so before a supplier sends a predatory mite, they will usually try to determine which pest mite you need to control. They may ask you what plant is affected and whether it is growing indoors or out.

Mites are one of the creatures whose infestations have definitely become worse since the advent of pesticides. Pest mites have become resistant to many pesticides and these chemicals, unfortunately kill mite predators as well. Carbaryl (Sevin™), in particular, kills mite predators while sparing the pest. This stimulates increased reproduction of the mites, so mite outbreaks often follow Sevin™ applications.

If mites have become a severe problem on annual vegetable crops, as they can in a neglected garden, I strongly suggest you pull all the unhealthy and infested plants, clean up the infected debris, and replant with a less susceptible crop.

I suspect that many local tomato plant deaths blamed on disease are really caused by a mite called the tomato russet mite. Infested plants have a yellowish or bronzed, greasy look. To identify these tiny mites, you need at least a 15x hand lens, and a 30x microscope would be even better. Tomato russet mites are shaped like longish cones, with legs at the wider (front) end. They are yellowish, tan or pink. If you are using a strong enough hand lens, you can often see larger, faster-moving, predator mites hurrying among the russet mites, devouring them. The predator mites have the more typical spiderlike shape, with four legs on each side.

It's best, in controlling tomato russet mites, to avoid killing the predator mites, since these can keep low populations of pest mites in check. An effective precaution, where russet mites have occurred before, is to apply sulfur dust (or spray) once, when plants are large, but have no symptoms yet, and once again in three to four weeks if symptoms appear. Also remove any tomato debris from your garden at the end of summer and don't let other nightshade family crops or weeds overwinter either. Purchased predatory mites *Phytoseiulus persimilis* will help control tomato russet mites, which are also susceptible to the botanical pesticide neem.

NEMATODES

Nematodes generally stunt plants, and may also cause knots on the roots, discolored or bumpy leaves, or various other malformations. Nematodes are tiny, primitive worms that either attach themselves to plants and suck sap, or live inside them. They are unrelated to earthworms. While most kinds of nematodes prefer warmer climates, some kinds may live in our area, and could attack your crops.

Root knot nematodes, which are fairly common in this region, attack many kinds of plants, including carrots, tomatoes and squash. They live on the roots, causing knobs to form on them and causing carrots to fork. The pest is more common in sandy soils than on other kinds.

Another common kind of nematode, the stem and bulb nematode, attacks all allium crops, miner's lettuce, parsley, celery, salsify and daffodils. You can identify an infestation by rubbing the leaves with your fingers to feel any rough spots. Affected onion plants will be stunted. If you cut the bulb in half crosswise, there will be dark rings in it. The basal portion of the bulb becomes swollen and spongy and may separate from the bulb.

A third kind, a cyst nematode, attacks cole crops, causing stunted plants. Also, they cause plants that would have ripened all at once to have a staggered harvest.

A number of kinds of nematodes damage roots, but do not leave readily identifiable symptoms. Even root knots, though identifiable as nematode damage, do not tell you which root-knot nematode you have. Stunting, the most common symptom of nematodes, could be caused by several other problems. Consider if your stunted plants might have lacked water, fertilizer, soil aeration, or sunlight. Try to improve any growing conditions that might not be optimum. If you still strongly suspect nematodes are causing your problems, ask a Cooperative Extension office for information about having your soil tested in a nematology lab. This will cost on the order of $5 to $25. Once you find out which kind, or kinds, of nematodes you have, you can ask about specific control techniques.

Nematodes often enter a garden in soil surrounding plants from other gardens. While nursery soil is probably pest-free, the soil in your friend's yard may not be, so accept gift plants with caution. When nematodes do enter a garden, they generally appear in one part of it first. Because they move only a few feet a year on their own, it is possible to keep them from spreading to your whole garden. Take care not to move plants or soil from infested to clean areas. On any particular day, work the infested area last. After working where nematodes are active, clean your tools with a forceful jet of water, then with 1 part household bleach in 9 parts water. Don't let the wash water run back into your garden.

If nematodes have become a problem in your garden, you will probably need to combine several methods to keep them at a level that allows you to grow crops. When you know which species of nematodes you have, you can often reduce their numbers by planning a rotation of non-susceptible crops and resistant crop varieties.

Do keep the level of soil organic matter high, adding 3 to 4 inches a year. This stimulates natural enemies of nematodes, including soil bacteria and fungi. Commercial products are becoming available that claim to be particularly effective at this. You may want to try them, but none has yet proven a miracle cure.

Plant as early as possible to give crops a chance to grow large before the pest becomes active. When you pull any plant, assume nematodes are feeding on its roots, and remove them as well. Remove infested crop plants from the garden.

If the infestation is severe, you might want to try leaving half of your garden fallow each year. This will reduce root knot nematode infestation in the fallow half by 80-90%. If you rotate garden halves each year, you should be able to have a garden that, though half the size, has only minimal damage.

During the fallow, don't let anything grow in the area unless you know it is immune to the nematodes you have. This generally means bare soil, with even weeds hoed out while tiny. You can grow an immune cover crop, but only if you keep weeds out of it.

If you are using a bare soil fallow, keeping it watered will increase its effectiveness, though this will encourage weeds, so increase the work of hoeing them out. Solarization during all or part of a fallow will also further reduce nematode populations, if you live in a microclimate warm enough for this technique to work (see page 99).

Marigolds can help reduce certain root-knot nematodes, but it will not help at all to just scatter them here and there among your crops. First, you must know which kind of nematode you have. (Marigolds are not effective against the northern root-knot nematode, for example.) If you have a susceptible nematode, plant the entire infested area solidly with French marigolds, *Tagetes patula*, for an entire season, being careful not to let anything else grow there.

Since home use of metam sodium (Vapam) has been cancelled, there are now no chemical nematicides available to home gardeners. (In any case, home gardeners did not find the highly toxic fumigant Vapam to be more reliable than non-chemical methods—probably because it was so difficult to apply correctly.)

Snails and Slugs

These pests should be strong suspects when your seedlings are partly or entirely eaten and your larger plants have holes in the leaves. However other pests such as earwigs or birds could be the culprits. To convict snails or slugs, look for shiny slime trails on the plants or on the soil. Then hunt for snails, which hide on smooth plant leaves or on other flat surfaces, or slugs, which hide in moist crevices in plants, as well as on and in the soil.

The snail that plagues our gardens is the brown garden snail, which was imported to Oakland from France in the 1850s as a food source. (They are indeed edible, being the smaller of the two French snail species used as *escargots*.) The much smaller California native snails are more common in wild areas than in gardens, and are not serious pests. The several species of slugs that eat garden plants are either natives or European species.

Snails and slugs easily rank as the number one enemies of local gardeners. They attack a wide variety of crops, rendering a garden difficult when they are not under control. (To learn if a crop is susceptible check under individual listings.) They are particularly devastating to seedlings, often sparing older, less tender plants. Sometimes the only preventive needed is to plant transplants, rather than sowing seeds in place. Squashes and cucumbers, for example, become much less appetizing to snails when they have grown two or three prickly true leaves.

The first step in controlling both pesky molluscs, and one that should be repeated at least once a year, is a general garden cleanup. Your goal should be to remove as many snails and slugs as you can find, and reduce the areas in which they can hide. These pests come out at night, and you will certainly find some if you pay your garden late night visits with a flashlight. You can even find quite a few still out and about on cool, wet mornings. But few of us relish gardening for very long in the dark, or even in the morning dew. You will find that a hunt for snails and slugs in their likely daytime hiding places can be much more thorough because the gardening conditions are more congenial.

Snails spend their days glued to smooth, dry surfaces in shady spots. They might choose a broadleaved plant, a fence, or a flowerpot. They are especially attracted to plants with strap-like leaves, such as lily-of-the-Nile, leeks, and irises. (Their only means of self protection is to draw into their shells and drop into the underbrush when they feel vibrations, so you will learn to reach for them quickly, before they feel the plants move.) They even climb trees in their nightly forays, then cling to the bark in the daytime.

You should be able to eliminate some snail hiding places, such as weedy undergrowth covering the edges of raised bed frames, but you can't expect to eliminate every hiding place. You won't want to pull your leek crop, for example, or take out the vine that makes your fence a shady refuge. But once you know which areas in your garden attract snails, you can hunt for them there. Continue to search snail hiding places, daily if possible, until your catch becomes noticeably smaller. Then continue hunts of their favorite hiding places once a week. Don't stop handpicking; keep it as a part of your ongoing control program even if you use other methods as well. It's your most effective weapon.

Slugs, which are much like snails, but without shells, have similar habits, except that they like moister hiding places. Clean them out as you clean out snails, just looking deeper for them into any moist crevices. While you will find many of your garden's slugs this way, they will be easier to miss than the snails. Some dig several inches into the soil, not even coming up every night to feed, so any hunting or trapping method you use for slugs must be repeated every few days for several weeks.

Beginning gardeners find it difficult to believe that they can control snails and slugs effectively simply by handpicking. One San Francisco gardener found this out by a roundabout route. One day a man I didn't know asked me what to do about his rampant and destructive snails. I suggested he search for and remove them, but he was reluctant and seemed discouraged. So I suggested he pay his small son to collect snails for him. Several years later, when he was hired to edit the SLUG newsletter, David Gilden reported the following story: He hadn't liked my second idea either, but, afraid that he would never have a successful garden, he negotiated to pay his son five cents per snail. His son was so zealous and his garden's snails so numerous that David soon realized the catches were proving too expensive. Driven by a need to economize, he be-

gan to hunt snails himself when his son wasn't home. Working together (sort of!), father and son soon brought the snail population down to quite manageable proportions—and his garden thrived.

As for the snails and slugs you collect, think of them as potential fertilizer. Crushed and buried, they add valuable nutrients to your soil. (Tossing them over the fence is not only rude, but doesn't work, since they are capable of crawling back the same night. And throwing them against the fence is likely to only injure them, so that later you will be collecting the same snails, but with healed over shell cracks.)

Slugs and snails feed all year and breed in the warm season. Snails are hermaphroditic, each individual animal capable of laying eggs. Slugs are either hermaphroditic or they change sex as they mature. You may find snail eggs, which look like white BBs, or the gelatinous slug eggs, near the soil's surface when you are digging or cultivating. If you do, destroy them by crushing them or by spreading them in the sun to dry.

A step beyond searching out sites where snails and slugs hide or lay eggs, is creating traps. Black plastic, wooden boards, and either clay or plastic flowerpots all work. Arrange them to provide shady hiding places for snails, or moister hiding places for slugs. Empty them daily if possible, but at least every couple of days.

Various barriers can stop snails or slugs. Gardeners often try spreading materials around plants in hopes that snails and slugs won't climb over them. Wood ash, diatomaceous earth, rice hulls, and cedar sawdust are examples. These may work for a while, but become less effective when you water the plants, wetting the barrier material. Also, even when fresh, they may not stop the pests if the seedling in the middle is a favorite, or if you have not reduced your population by handpicking first.

Overturned strawberry baskets, each weighted with a stone, can protect small seedlings from larger snails, before the year's tiny new snails have hatched. (Get your non-gardening friends to save their baskets for you.) If the snails are already breeding and hatching tiny snails, floating row covers, carefully tucked into the soil around plants, or covers made of window screen are more effective.

Snails and slugs do not like to crawl on copper, which does to them something akin to what a metal fork does to us when it touches a tooth filling. You can purchase copper strips to fasten around planter boxes, wooden frames of raised beds, or tree trunks.

To make the barrier most daunting, get the 4-inch-wide strip with flaps, attach it flaps up, and bend them outward. Be sure all of the pests are out of the enclosed area. Be aware that snails and slugs will take another route to get to your plants if they can find it. For example, they will climb a fence and then an overhanging tree branch, or will climb weeds that are growing over the copper strip. Copper snail strips do not work well as free-standing barriers, simply stuck into the ground around a plant or plants, because plants overgrow them too quickly.

Stale beer traps or yeast traps are often touted for snail and slug control. Though others report success, I have never caught a snail, and only an occasional slug in such a trap. (See directions for these traps in the listing for earwigs.)

Natural predators don't keep snails and slugs under good control, but the large black rove beetle, *Ocypus olens*, does eat them, and it is becoming more common in our area. The decollate snail, which eats brown garden snails, cannot legally be released outside of some southern California counties, so is not a method we can use here. It would not be of much use in a vegetable garden anyway, as it also eats tender leaves.

Domestic ducks are a possible biological control, as they are fond of snails and probably will eat slugs as well. But they need to be penned, because they are also fond of vegetables. (When ours nibbled our corn silks, that was the last straw!) And be sure the duck pen can be secured against raccoons and opossums at night, as these predators will kill ducks. You can pen ducks in temporary enclosures while they eat pests, or carry snails to them. Children often enjoy feeding snails to ducks, and in fact sometimes need to be given a daily limit to avoid overfeeding them. Chickens can be taught to eat snails too, but you will have to crush the shells of the larger ones for them.

Finally, I must mention human beings as potential snail predators. Should you be fond of escargots, or develop a taste for them, you can eat your garden's snails. If you plan to do so, do not use toxic baits. You will need to keep snails you plan to eat in a cage briefly while their digestive tracts clean out. (See references in Appendix VI, Suggested Reading, for complete details.)

Salting slugs and snails will kill them, however, it isn't a good strategy because salt is toxic to plants. If you sprinkle it on too many pest mollusks, you might add a lethal amount to your soil.

Avoid toxic chemical baits if at all possible. Bait alone will not bring total control, because young snails and slugs are not attracted to it. Also, pets and wildlife may be poisoned not only by the bait, but by the poisoned snails and slugs. If you do use bait, save it for stubborn problems such as inaccessible hiding places. Place bait at the edges of your garden, not in the center, where snails will be tempted to feast on your plants on the way to get it. Never put bait directly on food plants, to avoid contaminating them.

If the problem is just snails and slugs, a bait containing only metaldehyde will do the trick. Mollusk baits containing other chemicals are not registered for use around food crops. If you use pellet-type bait, put it in containers that snails must crawl into, both to keep the bait invisible to pets and small children, and also to keep it out of the soil. Small plastic containers with the lids on, and with snail-sized holes cut into the sides, serve this purpose well. These also keep the bait dry, which is important, since when bait becomes wet, fungi grow on it, rendering it unattractive to snails and slugs.

PILLBUGS OR SOWBUGS

These gray, many-legged and many-segmented creatures crawl about on the soil and on decaying debris. They look almost alike and both reach 1/2 inches in length. If they roll into a ball when disturbed they are pill bugs; if not, sowbugs. Neither are really "bugs" at all, but crustaceans, like shrimp. They usually prefer to eat decaying plant matter, but they may eat actively growing parts of plants if there isn't enough of their favorite food around. This is especially likely in two cases. One is in the late summer and fall, since their population has been increasing all summer. When summer's plants are starting to die, pill and sowbugs may climb up into them to eat decaying parts. They may also munch strawberries and young zucchini squash in the fall, when these fruits are maturing slowly. The second case in which pill and sowbugs are likely to eat living plants is in spring just after you have cleared the garden for planting. Because you have removed or dug most of their food into the soil, they are likely to munch hungrily on your tiny seedlings.

If you pay attention to actual damage, rather than just being alarmed by the sight of these pests, you will rarely feel a need to control them. I usually ignore them, as long as they are just going about their business of eating debris. But if I see a huge population in a sheltered place on the soil surface among my crops, and notice them on my living plants, I act to reduce their population. I read about and tried several kinds of traps, such as half citrus rinds cut side down set about the garden, but my pill and sowbugs ignored these. So I usually just crush some of them against the side of the garden bed frame or scoop them into a plastic bag, seal it, freeze it, and discard it. Often you can avoid the need to take action after you clear your spring garden if you just clear it a couple of weeks before you plant. This allows the hungry pill and sowbugs (and often some of the earwigs, snails, and slugs as well) to move to another location before your seedlings appear. Another way to discourage pill and sow bugs is by letting the surface of your garden's soil dry out between waterings.

Pill and sowbugs are among the creatures that break down organic materials in a cold compost pile, and live in the outskirts of a hot one. If you have an overpopulation of these creatures in your garden, you could reduce it by moving your compost pile further from your most susceptible crops or making sure it is a hot pile.

Vertebrate Pests

None of these animals are universal pests of gardens in our region, but each can make gardening very difficult when it is present. Methods of control center on exclusion or live-trapping, except in the case of gophers and moles, which are often killed. Call your local animal shelter for information on trap rental and live animal removal services.
If wild animals are involved, remember to keep your distance. A cornered raccoon can be a fierce fighter, and many of the animals described can carry disease. Don't handle any of these animals with bare hands, whether they are alive or dead.

BIRDS

You can suspect birds of doing the damage if seedlings are clipped, fruit is pecked, or sunflower seeds stolen before you can harvest them. Birds that are likely to be serious garden pests in this region are house finches, house sparrows, crowned sparrows and domestic pigeons. Blackbirds, starlings, jays, and crows also sometimes cause damage here to garden plants. Some of these birds do eat insects, but usually only in the spring, when they need extra protein for reproducing and raising their young.

In contrast, birds that eat large numbers of insects are welcome in gardens. Although there is no evidence that birds can successfully control any particular pest, robins, mockingbirds, and flickers are likely to make a significant contribution to pest control. (For information on what these helpful birds eat, see page 130.)

Of the common pest birds, house finches are gray birds slightly larger than sparrows. The males have rosy red crowns, breasts, and rumps; a variant form has yellowish markings. They eat mostly seeds, seedlings, fruit, flower buds, berries, and other soft fruits—although they do catch some insects to feed to their young. As with any seed-feeding bird, most of the seed they eat will be weed seed, simply because there is so much weed seed available.

An occasional house finch will likely do little damage, but if you live near a large house finch population, you can expect some trouble. House finches do not migrate, so they are here all year long. In the winter months, house finches feed in small flocks. In the spring they pair off and build nests in evergreens or on the ledges of buildings.

House (or English) sparrows are small birds with gray breasts and gray and brown markings on their heads, backs, wings and tails. Like house finches, they are nonmigratory birds that fly and roost in flocks of a dozen or so, when not paired for nesting. They live mainly on seeds, although in the summer they eat some insects as well. They may nest in trees, but instead often use the cavities and ledges of such urban structures as bridges, buildings, and billboards.

In contrast to house finches and house sparrows, crowned sparrows are migratory birds, usually here just in fall and winter. They move northward to breed in the spring and summer. Crowned sparrows have gray breasts and prominent black and white stripes on their heads. They may pull up and eat seedlings and may peck at mature plants. They will also eat some insects. They like to feed at the edge of deep brush or dense woods, so gardens in such locations are likely to suffer more.

The pigeon, or rock dove, is a common urban bird. This once-domestic species eats a wide variety of food. When people feed pigeons, the birds increase in numbers and in utilization of an area. They often congregate and nest on buildings, and if your garden is near one of these sites, they may feed on your garden seed and small plants.

You may have little or no bird damage in your garden, or tender lettuce plants may be reduced to ragged nubbins every time you set them out. It all depends on the nearby bird population. If birds are a problem, protect your plants with bird netting, a one-inch plastic mesh. You can just lay it loosely over the top of a bed of seedlings, only propping it up when the seedlings are too delicate for even such light material. The edges should touch the ground, but do not need to be tucked into it. Just weight the netting with a few stones. You can drape plastic netting over fruit trees too, or tie it over ripening sunflower heads. You can also build frameworks of plastic pipe, cover them with plastic bird netting, and place such structures as needed over beds of vegetables and flowers. These can be as low as one foot high for crops such as lettuce or strawberries, or they can be tall enough that you can enter and stand inside them.

Floating row cover will keep out birds, along with snails, slugs and other pests. And pigeons and other large species can also be discouraged by driving numerous small, brushy, leafless woody prunings into the ground around seedlings or even just laying them on the ground in seeded areas. Inflated plastic snakes may scare birds away, or fluttering shiny foil hung on strings along a row, but birds may return when they get used to these objects. Such scare tactics will be most effective if you put them up as soon as birds begin to eat in your garden, rather than after they have been around for a while.

It is against federal law to kill many kinds of birds, and others may be protected by local laws. Also, no pesticides are registered for use on birds by homeowners. Licensed pest eradicators will know the laws concerning bird control.

Cats

If you see your seed beds dug up, cats may have caused the damage. They leave earth piles with scratched-out soil depressions around them. Loose soil is, unfortunately, the original kitty litter. Cats dig up seeds and destroy seedlings with their digging and scratching. I've had only minor cat damage myself, despite gardening in neighborhoods with high cat populations. But a gardener will sometimes report that their particular garden plot seems to have become the favored W.C. of the neighborhood's entire cat population.

If the cat damage is light to moderate, try tactics that make your bare soil surface less obvious or inviting. I have repelled cats successfully by scattering my seedbeds with the green leaves of grass and weeds (avoiding seedheads), renewing these camouflages every few days until the plants are well up. Cayenne pepper, sprinkled on the soil, may also discourage some cats. Floating row cover or chicken wire laid over seedbeds will present a more formidable challenge to more determined cats. For bare areas among maturing plants, use a large-particled mulch such as straw.

If you have been bothered by many cats, or by cats of great determination, you may want to build a permanent structure of netting or wire to exclude them from your plantings. One gardener found that a fishing net of the type used to catch large bass (purchased from a fishing supply shop) was an effective barrier. He built a walk-in structure of this net against his garden fence.

Commercial cat repellents may work briefly, but can become quite expensive for extensive garden use.

Deer

When new growth or entire plants are eaten, and you live near wild land, deer are likely to be the culprits. As with all pests, the size of the population and the amount and preferences of available food play a role in what deer will eat in your garden. They will do more damage when their population climbs or when loss of their habitat or dry summer weather reduces what they have to eat. In some areas and in some years you may have only occasional damage, but deer can make gardening all but impossibe at other times and places.

A product called Deer-Away™, is reported to be a very effective commercial deer repellent, lasting about two months. It is sprayed directly on plants, though not on any plant, or plant part, you will later eat. It is a good way to keep deer away from your ornamentals and non-bearing fruit trees, and will offer some protection to herbs or vegetables if sprayed on an ornamental planting around the perimeter. Some gardeners have reported temporary success with small bags of human hair hung among their garden plants or sprinklings of blood meal, and these are certainly worth a try. All repellents need to be renewed regularly to keep their scent fresh, and also, deer may simply get used to one or another of them, so it is a good idea to rotate your repelling substances.

The only way to be sure that deer don't enter an area is to erect a deer-proof fence. This should be at least 7 or 8 feet high, and be made of woven wire mesh, with 4 inch square openings, supported by sturdy posts. The fence must be flush with the ground. Another option, if you have a lot of land, is to take advantage of the inability of a deer to jump both high and far at the same time: build two 5-foot fences, with a 5-foot space between them. (For an excellent article on the subject, and plans for deer fences, see *Horticulture* magazine, April 1987, pp. 66-73.) An ordinary fence may deter deer from entering, providing that you also keep an alert and noisy dog in your yard. To protect only small areas of favorite crops, you can build small cages of wire mesh over them or use floating row covers.

Though no plant can be considered deerproof, deer don't eat all plants with equal relish. *Sunset Western Garden Book* contains a list of plants deer rarely eat. Included are the annual flowers calendula, scabiosa and zinnia, and the perennial flowers foxglove, freesia, and tulips. The only edible crops *Sunset* mentions as being relatively safe from deer are artichokes, cactus, and chives. However I did once grow corn and squash successfully in an area inhabited by deer. (Alas, gophers ate many of these plants, but the deer left them alone.)

DOGS

Sometimes you need look no further than a dog when plants are knocked over and flattened, especially if there are also signs of digging and fresh animal feces present.

Gardens open to the street in densely populated areas require some fencing to avoid dog problems, something that all urban community gardeners learn quickly. Whether your home garden is safe from your own dog depends on how well trained he is and on whether his needs are adequately met. Remember that a dog needs adequate exercise and interesting activities. If you take your dog for walks and play with him, he is much less likely to wreak havoc in your garden.

Raised beds provide a pattern that many well-trained dogs can understand. Dogs can be taught to romp on the paths, not on the beds. Some dogs will not respond to such training, however, in which case your dog will need a separate fenced area. If you find that your dog lies down on your plants, he is probably looking for a cool place to sleep. You may be able to redirect him by planting something soft but resilient, such as mondo grass, in a shady corner in which he has slept before. Planted in the fall, it should be sturdy enough to take the abuse by the time days are warm enough for the dog to need it.

GOPHERS AND MOLES

Raised piles of earth are often the work of the underground-dwelling rodents, gophers and moles. Gophers leave crescent-shaped mounds when they surface, and moles pile up earth like small volcanoes. Moles sometimes also leave ridges of loose earth between their mounds as they channel about near the surface. Plants may wilt and die because their roots have been damaged or devoured, or may simply disappear, having been pulled underground to be eaten.

Gophers are small, thickset, brown rodents with small ears and big front teeth. They are almost entirely vegetarians, and will eat your garden plants with relish. A single gopher makes extensive underground tunnels. They will eat bulbs, roots, seeds, and whole plants. (Watching a corn stalk tremble, then slowly disappear down a gopher hole, was one of my most maddening gardening experiences!)

Moles are gray to nearly black furry creatures with hand-like forefeet, designed for efficient digging. They have pointy snouts, only sparsely covered with hair, and their eyes and ears are so small they are not easily seen. They are not rodents, but insectivores. They eat very little plant material, preferring earthworms, grubs, and other soil creatures. However they do disturb plant roots, by heaving the soil about, exposing the roots to the drying air.

Many strategies have been tried to repel gophers and moles. Gardeners sometimes still plant gopher spurge (*Euphorbia lathyrus*), with poor results. It's true that gophers don't eat it, but they will pass quite close to it on the way to other plants. You would need to plant a gopher spurge barrier several feet wide all around your garden to keep gophers out. Ultrasonic devices or small wind-turned noisemakers aren't likely to repel gophers and moles for long, as the animals soon become accustomed to the disturbance. And there isn't good evidence that any kind of sharp or smelly material placed in the tunnels will drive these pests away.

A recently arrived gopher, one whose burrow system is relatively incomplete, may be flushed out or drowned with water. However, where gophers have been present for some time, the use of water is ineffective.

You can keep gophers or moles out of your garden beds by installing gopher wire under the beds. While this strategy takes some time to carry out, gopher wire will last for years and is a certain deterrent while it lasts. Dig out your bed to a depth of a foot or more. Cover the bottom and sides of the hole with galvanized wire mesh. A mesh with 1/2 inch openings is best, but even galvanized chicken wire, which has about 1 inch openings, will be a big help. Overlap any pieces by a foot. If you have raised bed frames, cut the wire long enough so that it overlaps with the sides of the beds for a few inches. Some garden supply stores sell gopher wire by the yard, and also sell prefab gopher wire pockets, suitable for putting under individual perennial plants (See sources in Appendix V under Sources of Gardening Supplies and Books.)

Any efforts to decrease insect larvae in your garden's soil, such as treatment with beneficial nematodes, will discourage moles. If you have an earthworm compost pile, and moles in your garden, the earthworms may be attracting the moles. You can protect your earthworm composting set-up by installing wire mesh under it, as mentioned above for gophers. To be very sure moles can't get in, leave an aboveground extension 10 inches tall. (In some localities, including San Francisco, health rules require worm compost to be contained in a rodent-proof bin with air holes or gaps of no more than 1/4 inch, an arrangement that eliminates the chance of mole problems.)

Trapping is the most effective way to control moles. Be sure to use a trap that is designed for moles, as mole and gopher traps are distinctly different from one another.

Trapping is also an effective method of controlling gophers. Follow the instructions that come with the traps you buy. You need to be persistent, as gophers are likely to be wary.

There are also toxic baits effective against gophers. This is the method most used by licensed pest irradicators. Most of these baits contain strychnine, and can poison other animals, including cats, dogs and wild predators so if you do decide to use them, follow label directions carefully.

OPOSSUMS

These nocturnal animals are about 12 inches tall and 33 inches long, including a foot-long, naked tail. They have light gray fur and a pointed nose. Their diet is varied, including insects, reptiles, snails, small mammals, fruits, vegetables, and mushrooms. While they often change sites every two or three days, if they find safe harbor in a cranny of a building, they may stay longer.

As with raccoons, live trapping or killing opossums is no longer considered a wise or useful option. Discourage opossums from staying for long by preventing their access to hiding places in or under buildings, to garbage and pet food (see raccoons, below), and by picking up fallen fruit under trees.

RABBITS

If your garden is next to an open field, meadow, or brushy area, even in a city, rabbits (the larger jackrabbits or the smaller cottontails) may be a significant problem. You can exclude them with chicken wire fencing, three feet tall, which can be installed at the bottom of any existing fence. Fencing for rabbits should at least be tight to the ground. Ideally the wire mesh should extend 6 inches below the ground surface, and then be bent outward another 6 inches.

RACCOONS

Raccoons live even in the hearts of our big cities. I will never forget the night that one awakened me by walking on the roof of the porch outside my bedroom, then peered in at me, its masked eyes at human height! Like opossums, raccoons eat both animals and plants. They will attack domestic fowl, eat the fish in fish ponds, overturn garbage cans, and eat some garden crops. On the positive side, they do eat snails.

Your first defense is to remove temptations. Keep garbage cans tightly covered or put them in a tip-proof rack. Close off any openings that allow raccoons to take shelter in buildings and do not leave pet food outdoors. If raccoons dig in your lawn, treat it with beneficial nematodes to reduce the number of lawn insects they can find to eat.

Gardening books list many different tactics for repelling raccoons from vegetable gardens, but these smart animals often learn to ignore our efforts. Ideas include leaving flashlights or radios on all night, putting a couple shakes of ground red pepper on the silk of each ear of corn, and strategically placing dishpans containing ammonia-soaked rags. Persistent raccoons may need to be fenced out. A cage, such as suggested for deer, will protect a small area, but a low electric fence may be less expensive. Use two strands of galvanized wire, about four and twelve inches above the ground, connected to a commercial fence charger. (Don't let plants grow against the wires, or the fence won't work.)

Live trapping of raccoons is legal, with a permit, but is no longer considered a wise or effective means of control. There are so many raccoons in the state that there is no "area with fewer raccoons" in which to release trapped animals. And, while it *is* legal for a citizen to humanely kill a live-trapped raccoon, this is not recommended either. The concentration of raccoons in most areas is so large that the animal will quickly be replaced by others.

Plant Diseases

Most infectious plant diseases are caused by one of three kinds of organisms: fungi, bacteria, and viruses. Many of these organism will attack only certain species of plants or groups of related plants. For example zucchini yellow mosaic virus will attack squashes and cucumbers, but no other crops, and celery late blight attacks only celery, and, to a lesser extent, celeriac. Depending on the disease, it may be spread by one or more of the following agents: infected soil, seed, or plant debris, splashing water, the wind, or insects. If a disease is insect borne, it spreads by an insect feeding first on an infected plant, then on healthy plants. Some diseases are spread on contact, so gardeners spread them by touching diseased plants with their hands or tools, and then touching healthy plants.

Noninfectious diseases, or physiological problems, occur even though there is no pest organism present. They include, for example, conditions caused by not enough of particular nutrients or inadequate watering. They are treated by improving growing conditions. Sometimes certain varieties are better able to avoid particular noninfectious diseases than are other varieties. For example, some tomato varieties rarely develop catfacing, while others show this deformation often. See the tomato and summer squash entries in Chapter 11 for examples of noninfectious diseases. See also page 80, on nutrient deficiency symptoms.

Many infectious diseases either have no cure, or have no chemical treatment registered for home use, so prevention should be your main defense. First, try to get disease-free starts. If your garden is free of diseases spread by infected seeds, seedlings, bulbs, or tubers, seek out ones that are certified to be disease-free. Especially avoid growing potatoes, onions, garlic cloves, dry beans, or other starts that were sold in a grocery as food. Although they are wholesome to eat, these may spread diseases in your garden.

When you can find plant varieties that are genetically resistant to particular diseases common where you garden, it is always wise to choose them. Study descriptions on seed packets or in catalogs. Varieties described as *resistant* are usually able to avoid infection, although they may show symptoms if growing conditions are very poor. Varieties listed as disease *tolerant* are only somewhat resistant, often showing signs of an infection but not succumbing to it.

Any variety will be better able to resist disease if it has the best possible growing conditions. As with humans, a healthy plant can resist disease better than one suffering from deficiencies. For example, when the soil is too wet, so the plant roots lack air, plants are particularly susceptible to root disease. And plants grown too close together, so that the environment around them is humid with poor air circulation, may become susceptible to foliage diseases.

Sometimes you will want to avoid conditions that are usually not harmful, because you know they can spread specific diseases. For example, celery leaves are not harmed by being wet, but they should be kept as dry as possible to discourage late blight. Or, though a much shorter rotation cycle is usually fine, you might wait three to four years before replanting onions in a soil infested with spores of downy mildew. And finally, while you would ordinarily compost crop plants at the end of the season, remove any diseased plants from your garden.

I have listed the diseases most likely to cause serious problems here. If you see that a plant is seriously damaged by a disease, pull it out and discard it, even if you can't identify the disease. Clean up all diseased plant debris and remove it from your garden. If a problem spreads to a large part of a crop or appears repeatedly, and it is not described here, try to get it identified so you can learn the best ways to avoid it in the future.

Fungus Diseases

Fungi are typically made up of threads of tissue called mycelia that grow through the substance on which they are feeding. Then at some point they form fruiting bodies, relatively organized structures in which spores are formed. A familiar example is the mushroom, the fruiting body of a fungus that grows through soil or wood. While many fungi live on dead organic matter and are very helpful in our gardens and compost piles, some fungi attack living plants, the mycelia growing inside the plant cells and then producing spores on the plant surfaces. For example, powdery mildew spores cover plant leaves with white powdery growth. Some kinds of fungal spores live for many years in soil, awaiting a susceptible crop.

CELERY LATE BLIGHT

If, in the cooler months, older leaves and stems of your maturing celery or celeriac develop yellow spots that turn brown, your plants have late blight. Tiny black dots will appear in the brown spots. Infected leaves eventually wither and the plants may die. While celery will often escape this disease, it is common enough that you should take precautions against it.

Celery late blight is also sometimes called septoria blight, after the fungus that causes it, *Septoria apiicola*. It is spread by infected seeds and by water splashed from infected plants or plant debris from these plants. It can live for up to eighteen months in infected plant debris, and for two years in infected seed.

If your celery or celeriac plants show symptoms of this disease, remove them immediately, together with any plant debris they have left on the ground. Don't grow either crop in that location for at least two years.

Late blight probably came into my garden via some infected nursery plants. Now I prefer to grow my own celery seedlings from seed I've treated to make sure it's disease free. Here's how to treat seed: Soak it in water at 118°F for 30 minutes. First tie the seed into a small, thin piece of cloth. Use a

Celery late blight

meat thermometer to be sure the water temperature remains constant. Add more warm water if it starts to cool, but don't let it get over 120°F. Stir the water a little to keep the temperature even and to reach all the seeds. When 30 minutes is up, cool the seeds by dipping the cloth bag in cool water, then dry them.

Other means of prevention include using seed over two years old (sown more thickly, to compensate for the lower germination) and avoiding overhead watering. "Emerson Pascal" celery is tolerant to the blight, but that doesn't mean it won't get some of the disease if it is present, and I prefer to eliminate late blight altogether rather than tolerate it.

CLUBROOT

Clubroot fungus infects cabbage family plants, causing them to turn yellow and often to become stunted. Plants wilt on warm days. When you pull the plants, you find that the roots are enlarged into club-shaped knots, and may be split open and decayed. Club root fungus lives in the soil, and while I have never seen it in San Francisco, it is common in soils from Salinas to Half Moon Bay. It is encouraged by warm moist weather.

If your area doesn't have club root, avoid bringing plants, soil, or manure from affected areas into your garden. Obtain seedlings from a reputable dealer or grow your own. Amend clay soil well to improve drainage. You can also reduce the chance of an outbreak by raising your soil's pH to 7.2 (see page 72), using ground limestone as well as hydrated lime, as limestone alone is not enough to prevent the disease. Pull all mustard family weeds from your garden, as they may harbor the disease, and plan as long a rotation as possible between cabbage family crops.

Once plants are infected, there is no cure for this disease. If you find infected plants, dig them up and remove them, getting as much of the root as you can. As the club root fungus is long-lived, in order to clear a soil of it you must use a crop rotation in which no cabbage family crops are grown for seven years. No variety is resistant to all races of this fungus. Check with local garden stores and Cooperative Extension offices to see if there are varieties that will resist the types of clubroot prevalent in your area.

CORN SMUT

See description under corn in Chapter 11.

DAMPING-OFF DISEASE

This scourge of seedlings causes them to fall over and wilt. The first point of damage is just at soil level. Soon shriveling will be so complete that small, insubstantial seedlings such as lettuce and tomato can seem to simply disappear. Though it is a very serious problem, damping-off is generally preventable.

Damping-off is caused by various soil-inhabiting fungi. It is encouraged when seedlings are grown in too-moist soil, crowded too close together and grown at too high or too low a temperature. It also may be more likely to occur when the seeding mix contains ample fertilizer. As plants get larger, they become less susceptible, although mature plants can be damaged by damping-off also if growing conditions are extremely poor.

To avoid damping-off, start by using soil that is relatively free of infection. When starting seeds in containers, use a sterile seeding mix and sterile or well-cleaned containers (see instructions in Chapter 6). If you use a part of your garden as a seed bed, growing seedlings close together for later transplanting, rotate the area used for this purpose, to avoid a buildup of damping-off organisms.

A seeding mix for containers should be formulated so that it holds moisture without becoming soggy. In your garden, keep organic matter plentiful in seeding areas, especially if your soil has a high clay content. However avoid adding fresh, uncomposted material to your soil just before you plant seeds. Don't plant seeds too close together, and if you are growing them indoors, move them to a well-aerated spot as soon as the seedlings break the soil surface.

I once overheard a gardener at a nursery, lamenting that all his seedlings had wilted and died. The clerk nodded sympathetically and handed him a bottle of fungicide with which to treat his potting mix. I too have lost seedlings to damping-off from time to time, but I can assure you, if you follow the preventive measures outlined above, you will see this disease so rarely that you will feel no need to resort to fungicides. (See also Root Rots, below.)

DOWNY MILDEW OF ONIONS

All onion family crops, but especially onions and shallots, can get this fungal disease. The symptoms are sunken, water-soaked spots, either yellow or gray, on the leaves, followed by a coating of a dirty gray or violet-colored powder. This disease doesn't usually kill the plants, but leaf tips may die, and

bulbs of infected plants are small and soft. The disease is favored by cool, wet nights and warm, but overcast, days. While downy mildew is not very common, it is common enough and serious enough that you need to watch out for it.

Prevent downy mildew by reducing excess moisture: amend heavy soil to improve drainage, don't overwater, and plant widely enough to allow the air to circulate among your plants. Once the disease appears, it will stay in the soil and in overwintering plants, and will break out again whenever conditions are right. You may escape chronic infection, seeing the disease only for one season, or it may appear several years in a row. If your plants do become infected, remove them, along with any plant debris. Don't grow any plants in the genus *Allium* in the affected spot for 3 to 4 years.

FUNGAL LEAF SPOTS

Plants infected with fungal leaf spots have discolored, round spots on their leaves. This is not a single disease, but several, each affecting one plant or several closely related ones. Strawberries get one kind of fungal leaf spot in our region. The disease doesn't damage the fruit directly, but it reduces plant vigor, and if spots form on the green caps over the berries, they may not ripen properly. Beets, chard, and spinach are affected by another disease, beet cercospora leaf spot. This leaf spot disease doesn't damage the roots, but it can reduce the size of beet roots by stunting the plants. (Despite the fact that spinach is susceptible, I have never seen the symptoms on my spinach.)

Spores of the organisms causing fungal leaf spot diseases live on plants and on infected plant debris and garden tools, but not in the soil. Beet leaf spot spores are also carried on seed. Spots usually appear first on lower leaves. If you notice spots just beginning to form, pick off the affected leaves. If many spots have already formed, pick off the leaves with the most spots and any dead leaves, and clean up any dead plant material from the soil's surface. A mulch on the soil forms a barrier that will prevent spores from splashing onto plants when it rains or when you are watering. In severe cases, remove the affected plants from the garden altogether and rotate the problem crop to a new site next season, using the affected site for susceptible crops only once every two or three years. In the case of beets, chard or spinach, do not save seed from affected plants. Sulfur is registered for use against some leaf spot diseases. Check the label.

Strawberries often show fungal leaf spot symptoms early in the season, especially if they are growing very rapidly (perhaps following over-fertilization with nitrogen). They also often outgrow the infection. You can reduce the likelihood of strawberries contracting leaf spot by planting them in well-amended soil and in unshaded locations, and by keeping the beds well-weeded. Also, if your strawberries have become quite thickly massed, remove some plants until the remaining ones are no closer than 10 inches apart, or reset your plants, well-spaced, into a new bed altogether. When you are shopping for strawberry plants, ask about resistant varieties suitable for your location.

LATE BLIGHT OF POTATO AND TOMATO

This is the same blight that caused the Irish potato famine in the 1840s. Potato and tomato have different strains of the disease, but each can infect the other, and eggplant can also become infected. In all three, dark brown lesions appear on the stems, usually with green stem both above and below. Infected potato tubers have brown to purple surface patches with a dry, corky, reddish-brown rot underneath. Infected tomato fruit has greasy-looking brown areas on its shoulders, near the stem. On very damp days, white fuzzy fungal growth apears on brown areas on the stem, leaves, or fruit. Infected plants tend to rapidly turn completely brown and die.

This disease lives in infected living tissue only. It is spread by spores that blow great distances in the wind or are splashed by water, and is fostered by cool temperatures and high humidity. It survives in overwintering crops and weeds in the nightshade family, including husk cherry, tomatillo, and weedy solanums. It can be brought into a garden by infected potato tubers or by tomato or eggplant transplants.

To reduce the spread of this terrible disease, plant only certified disease-free potato starts. Grow your own tomato seedlings or get them from a reputable source. There are some resistant potato varieties now (see page 239) and resistant tomato varieties are being developed (watch for them).

Do not water potato, tomato, or eggplant from above. Remove all nightshade family crops or weeds from your garden from November to April. Remove all potatoes when you harvest. If the disease appears, do not replant homegrown potato tubers. If nearly mature potatoes have the disease, you may be able to save the tubers themselves from infection by keeping earth piled well over them and cutting the tops of the plants 1 inch below soil level 10 to 14 days before you harvest the tubers. If you plan to store the tubers, be sure they are dry first and keep them in a dry place.

The label on a fixed copper spray I purchased said to spray at the first sign of the disease and repeat every five days, but in my experience, this did not save infected tomatoes. Another source says that if the disease is expected, you can spray fixed copper from the time the plants are 6 inches tall, every 7 to 10 days. If you choose not to spray, or if plants continue to decline, remove them, including all fallen leaves and fruit, from the garden immediately.

ONION WHITE ROT

See page 228 under onion pests.

POWDERY MILDEW

You have powdery mildew when leaves of your crops become covered with a light gray or white powdery substance. Several different fungi cause this symptom, each affecting one crop, or several—often related—ones. Squash, pumpkins, and sometimes cucumber get one kind. Peas get another. Cole crops are susceptible to a third kind of powdery mildew fungus.

Powdery mildew diseases of fruit crops tend to infect growing tips of branches, destroying young leaves and damaging developing fruit. One disease infects apples and quince. Peach and plum can get either of two different powdery mildews, one of which also infects cherry. Strawberries and grapes each can become infected with still other powdery mildew fungi.

There is some cross-susceptibility with ornamentals. Pea powdery mildew *Erysiphe polygoni* infects sweet pea, lupine, and flowers ranging from California poppy to calendula. One of the two diseases of peach and plum is the same one that infects rose, and grape shares its powdery mildew with ivy. See references on pest control in Appendix VI, Suggested Reading, for more information on the hosts of different powdery mildew diseases.

One yellow squash variety, 'Park's Crookneck PMR Hybrid' is resistant to powdery mildew, and a couple of zucchini varieties showed moderate resistance in my small trial (see page 249). Winter squash of the species *Cucurbita moschata* are more resistant than other species of squash. You are likely to find resistant cucumbers, peas, and strawberries.

American grapes resist grape powdery mildew, while American/European crosses vary in resistance.

To prevent powdery mildews, plant where your crops will get enough sunlight, water them adequately, and don't overfertilize them. Plant peas in the cooler times of year, when the fungus is less active.

Unlike most fungus diseases of plant leaves, powdery mildew can be disrupted early in its development by washing the plants. Wash fronts and backs of susceptible leaves before the disease appears. This may not prevent it entirely, but will help reduce the infestation.

Cucurbit crop plants will survive and bear longer if you remove the lower leaves as soon as the disease appears on them. These older leaves don't photosynthesize as actively as the upper, younger ones, and do so even less when covered with a disease, so the plant won't be much worse off without them. Be sure to carry such leaves out of the garden to avoid spreading the spores. And don't overdo this strategy. Be sure that at least half of the leaves remain on the plant. (Don't wait until more than half have signs of powdery mildew before you act!) If plants are hopelessly infected, remove them from your garden to reduce the spread of the disease. Keep grapes and fruit trees pruned to an open habit to discourage powdery mildew. Prune out affected twigs and leaves.

One local predator, the lesser ashy gray lady beetle, eats spores of powdery mildew on cucurbits. This tiny insect is rounded in shape, with mottled wing covers in shades of light gray and brown. Its larvae resemble those of the larger lady beetles, but are ash gray. Although it is pleasant to watch these beetles grazing on the mildew spores, they don't seem to contribute significantly to control, as they only appear when the leaves are covered with spores, and the plants succumb despite their help.

Sulfur dust or sulfur spray can help if applied at the first sign of the disease. Check the label for the crop you intend to spray, then if it is listed, test a small area first, to be sure you will not burn the plants. If they do burn, try a more dilute solution. Spray when the temperature is below 80°F, as higher temperatures lead to burning of the plants.

ROOT ROTS

If plants are infected by a root rot, they wilt in the daytime, even though well watered, and are stunted. Leaves turn yellow and then die. The stem at the ground level and/or the root are dark brown and rotting. Root rots are caused by many different fungi, known collectively as water molds. Rhizoctonias are one common kind of root rot fungus. Many of these fungi are ones that also cause damping-off in seedlings.

Root rots can infect a wide variety of crops. The main way to avoid them is to make certain the soil isn't kept too wet. Be sure the soil drains well and be careful not to overwater. If plants begin to yellow, remember that root rot could be the cause, and don't automatically water before checking whether the soil is too wet already. Remove any infected plants from the garden when you pull them. Rather than try to cure these diseases with chemicals, better to prevent them next season with better growing conditions.

VASCULAR WILTS

Wilt diseases are infections of plants' water conducting cells. When these cells are plugged by a fungal infection the plant wilts and often dies. While a number of fungi cause wilt diseases of one crop or another, the ones you are most likely to see are verticillium and fusarium. Verticillium wilt is encouraged by our cool summer weather, and, once in the soil, it remains infectious for 20 years. There is no cure for this disease. The variety of fusarium that attacks tomatoes attacks only tomatoes. Another variety causes decline in asparagus. Tomato fusarium is less common along the coast because symptoms do not develop until temperatures are above 68°F and are worst at 80–90°F.

Verticillium infects not only tomato, but also apricot, avocado, blackberry, cabbage, eggplant, grapes, horseradish, New Zealand spinach, olives, persimmon, pepper, potato, radish, raspberry, spinach, peaches, plums, sunflower, and strawberry. It also affects a long list of ornamentals, including California poppy, chrysanthemum, dahlia, elm, foxglove, fuchsia, geranium, ice plant, lilac, marguerite, nandina, maple, privet, snapdragon, strawflower, and sweet pea. Even the common weeds dandelion and groundsel are susceptible.

Verticillium is a common reason for the decline of local tomato and strawberry plants. If a tomato is infected, the older leaves wilt, beginning at the edges. Leaves first develop a V-shaped yellow patch, which then turns brown. Often the leaves dry up completely. The plants remain stunted and do not grow even when well watered and fertilized. They may not bear fruit, or may bear small, malformed fruit with poor flavor. When you cut the main stem off near the ground, the water conducting tissue in the center of the stem appears brownish, instead of pale green like the rest of the stem section.

If strawberries are infected by verticillium wilt, the outer leaves turn brown along the margins and veins, then die completely. The plants lie flat to the ground, forming few new leaves. There may be brown streaks on leaf stems or runners. The plants may recover to bear good fruit the next year, or they may not.

Cultural controls can be of some help in fighting verticillium wilt. Don't slack off watering toward the end of the season, as this increases stress, making susceptible crops even more susceptible. Rotate nightshade family crops together, since they are all susceptible. Solarization, if you have enough sunny weather to carry it out, can destroy verticillium in the soil. Choose resistant tomato and strawberry varieties. (Look for a "V" after tomato variety names.) Among vegetables, some kinds are resistant to all kinds of verticillium. These include asparagus, beans, carrot, celery, corn, lettuce, onion, and peas. Of the flowers discussed in Chapters 13 and 14, the following are among those that are resistant: calendula, carnation, columbine, Johnnie-jump-up, pansy, ranunculus, sweet alyssum, sweet William, and zinnia. Alternate susceptible crops with resistant ones in your rotation, even if the disease has not appeared.

While tomato fusarium is less of a threat, a number of tomato varieties resist both diseases (VF), and you may as well use these. You can also reduce the likelihood of infection by not overfertilizing tomatoes with nitrogen.

Bacterial Diseases:

Bacteria are creatures that consist of single cells. They grow by dividing into more of the same kind of cells. As with fungi, many kinds of bacteria are helpful in soil and compost because they break down dead organic matter. In fact relatively few bacteria attack living plants, and you will see far fewer bacterial diseases than ones caused by fungi. Also, while many kinds of bacteria produce spores, the ones that infect plants do not, so they are not able to live outside of their host plants as long as fungal diseases. A practical result is that crop rotations to avoid bacterial diseases rarely require more than a year or two.

Bacteria cause some kinds of superficial rots, as when cut Swiss chard stems decay. When the rot is superficial, I remove the affected part and try to keep the plants less moist. As for more serious bacterial diseases, the best prevention is to reduce moisture. Look to the soil, being sure it has good drainage. Keep plant leaves dry when possible and plant susceptible crops where air circulation is good. Also, don't use too much fast-releasing nitrogen fertilizer, as this can foster bacterial disease.

If you identify a bacterial disease in a crop, rotate planting so that the susceptible crop isn't replanted in the same place for the next couple of seasons. Look for resistant varieties or certified disease-free seed.

One common bacterial disease, fireblight, attacks many fruit crops in the rose family, especially apples, pears, and quince, causing limbs to die suddenly, as if by scorching. The main means of treating fireblight is by cutting out affected limbs well below the area of visible infection. Prevent outbreaks by planting resistant varieties.

Bacterial Soft Rot

Like damping-off, this disease is caused by several different organisms, in this case by several bacteria. It consists of a watery, mushy decay of the fleshy parts of plants, usually accompanied by a foul odor. This may destroy tubers, bulbs or ripening fruit. Follow general instructions above for reducing moisture; keep your crops well-harvested; clean up plant debris and remove it from your garden to reduce the source of infection.

Virus Diseases:

When plants are infected with these diseases, their leaves often have discolored blotches. Leaves may also be puckered and misshapen, but no insect will be visible. Fruit may be blotchy or lumpy. Viruses are tiny living particles, not even complete cells. They can't usually live very long outside of a living creature, so they rarely survive in the soil. They are spread mainly by insects, by infected seed, and in some cases, by contact with plants, tools, or gardener's hands that have the virus particles on them.

Since there are no biological or chemical cures for these diseases, control must focus on cultural methods. Some of the possibilities are choosing resistant varieties, buying certified seeds, bulbs, or rootstocks, growing extra crop plants (in case you lose some to a virus), removing infected plants, and planting when the infecting insects are least active.

Of course it is also a good idea to control the specific insects that spread the viruses, but it is rarely possible to eliminate them completely. Aphids are the most common virus-spreading insects, and also one of the most common of insect pests. Other common *vectors* of viral diseases are leafhoppers, whiteflies, and mealybugs.

Many viruses cause symptoms known as mosaic. Mosaic is a streaking or mottling of leaves with shades of green and/or yellow. Other viruses cause mainly stunting, sometimes along with curled leaves. Symptoms of different viruses may overlap, and plants may also be infected by more than one kind of virus.

Your most likely encounter with virus disease will be to notice that one plant of a particular crop is seriously malformed, or that its leaves have very strange markings on them. And the most common control strategy you will use is to pull the infected plant. Often, that will be the end of that. However, several viruses are common enough to merit learning their specific symptoms and ways to prevent them from reducing your harvests.

When you bemoan the number of diseases your plants could get, take cheer in knowing that we escape at least one common virus of vegetable crops. The curly top virus, which commonly infects beets, beans, tomatoes, and other crops elsewhere in the West, is spread by the beet leafhopper, an insect that otherwise does little damage. Fortunately this insect is rarely seen in our foggy coastal areas, and so neither is the curly top virus.

CURLY DWARF VIRUS OF ARTICHOKE
(See description on page 166.)

TOBACCO MOSAIC VIRUS

Tomatoes get several mosaic viruses, the most common being the tobacco mosaic virus. Most gardeners have heard of this disease. And most know not to let smokers handle their tomato plants, as they are likely to spread the disease from infected tobacco in cigarettes. But many gardeners are not familiar with the symptoms of the disease. Tobacco mosaic does not, as one might expect, cause tobacco-colored spots on the leaves. (These are more likely to be a less serious leaf speck or spot caused by a bacterium or a fungus.)

The symptoms of tobacco mosaic are subtle and varied. On young plants, or in cool weather, the leaves are likely to be malformed. They will be long and narrow, commonly called "shoestring," or may be more pointed than usual. On older plants, look for mottling of leaves. It will most commonly be a subtle pale and dark green mottle (looking at the leaf with the light behind it will help you to see this), but some strains of the virus produce a bright yellow mottle. Plants may wilt severely on a very sunny day following a foggy period. They may be stunted, have dying leaves, or malformed and brown-spotted fruit.

Tobacco mosaic virus can infect soil briefly, but probably doesn't linger until the next season. In fact, waiting as few as 20 days to replace an infected plant will greatly reduce the chance of reinfection. However the disease is easily spread, not only by touching tomato plants after handling infected tobacco, but by touching infected and then uninfected plants. When you remove an infected plant, it is safest to also remove any tomato plants that were adjacent to and touching it. Then wash your hands and any tools that touched the infected plant with a 3% solution of TSP (trisodium phosphate). Use the solution to wipe off door knobs, hose valves, or other items you handled as well. Launder clothing that touched diseased plants.

Seek out resistant tomato varieties, identifiable by the initial "T" following their names. To be quite safe from reinfection by virus in the soil, wait a year before replanting a susceptible crop in the same location. Other tomato family crops can get tobacco mosaic virus as well, as can spinach, mustard, and tomato family weeds.

ZUCCHINI YELLOW MOSAIC VIRUS

This viral disease has become common only in the past few years, and is wreaking havoc in local gardens. Spread by aphids, it affects zucchini and other summer squash, cucumbers, and pumpkins. The leaves develop yellow blotches and become stiff and brittle. Plants remain stunted and the fruit becomes lumpy and misshapen.

It is best to halt the spread of this disease by removing infected plants from the garden. A good strategy is to plant a few extra seeds, to be sure you have enough plants left when the disease strikes. Also, if too much of your early planting is affected, remember you can replant cucumbers till late June and summer squash until mid-July. The aphids are less likely to spread the disease at these later planting times.

ELEVEN

Vegetables From A to Z

ROM THE TIME I BEGAN TO garden in San Francisco, I deliberately set about growing as many different vegetables as possible to see what would succeed here. I wanted to know how well a crop would thrive in summer fog, how much cold and wet it would tolerate in winter, the best times to plant it, and how to get a longer harvest. I've planted the common and the uncommon, from tomatoes to Bolivian sunroot, in search of crops that perform well and are worthwhile growing. I've tried many different varieties and growing techniques to coax more out of reluctant crops. I've talked with a diversity of gardeners—from those who hear the ocean's roar from their gardens to those who raise crops in some of the East Bay's sunnier pockets—and collected reports of successes and failures.

I discovered that we can grow a wide variety of vegetables and that warm pockets make it possible to grow even a wider assortment than I would have expected in some neighborhoods. I also found that certain crops are not likely to give satisfactory results in the foggier areas. I'm not saying that those crops are impossible to grow here, only that success may be the exception rather than the rule, a triumph to celebrate and not a harvest to depend upon.

For instance, a resident of the outer Richmond district of San Francisco, just a few blocks from the ocean, told me that her husband once harvested a watermelon from their garden. "Really?" I inquired. "How did it taste?" She replied, "I don't know. He

shellacked it and we had it around the house for years." My own melon triumph was the harvest of a single cantaloupe from my San Francisco Mission district garden. My noble melon attained a diameter of just over a couple of inches, but it was passably sweet.

The yard-long bean, also known as the asparagus bean, is a prime example of a crop that has trouble even getting to first base in our region. The plant grows to about a foot high, then declines and dies. From a plant that short, you can bet you won't get yard-long bean pods!

Even though we can't grow everything in our region, we can raise a great many crops. In fact, discovering what we can grow is half the fun of gardening in this climate. I encourage you to be adventurous!

The Vegetables

The listing for each crop includes the following information in the same order. If any element is missing, it is because there is nothing relevant to say—for example, when a crop has no significant pest problems or there is only one variety on the market.

- A brief introduction, including information on how the crop copes with the microclimates of our region.

- **Growing instructions** Here you will find details on how to start the crop, whether to plant directly in the garden or sow seeds indoors, when to plant, and so on. If the crop's watering need is not mentioned, assume that it is average for vegetables—about an inch a week in summer. If there is no mention of sunlight, assume that the crop needs a minimum of four hours if it is leafy and six to eight hours if it bears fruit. "Any good garden soil" or "average garden soil" means soil to which organic matter and fertilizer have been added.

- **The Harvest** This section includes tips on when and how to pick a crop, as well as how to cure, store, and prepare the harvested crop.

- **Varieties** Here are the varieties that I, or other local gardeners, have found to be especially well adapted to our climate, superior in production, particularly flavorful, or just plain interesting to grow. (In some cases, closely related species are cited as well.) Certain crops, such as lettuce and cabbage, are so well adapted to our climate that most types will succeed. For crops that require heat, such as tomatoes and corn, the variety listing consists of those that mature early and are tolerant of cool weather. A factor other than climate will sometimes limit your choice. Disease resistance may be the key consideration if a crop is susceptible to powdery mildew or verticillium wilt—two common diseases in our area. The number of vegetable varieties available to gardeners is too great to be described fully and is always changing, so many good choices are left for you to discover on your own.

- **Pests** The insects, diseases, and other pests that most commonly damage the crop are cited here. Many of these problems are described in greater length, and control measures given for them, in Chapter 10.

- **Sources** Many of the seed and plant sources that I have found useful over the years are listed in code at the end of each crop entry. For example, you will find that the purple tomatillo 'de Milpa' is available from RCS, the code for Redwood City Seed Company. For a list of mail-order seed companies and their codes, see Appendix IV. If a crop or variety is so common that you are likely to find it in nine out of ten seed racks, general seed catalogs, or nurseries, I simply say that it is widely available. (Although the listings were accurate when they were compiled, seed companies often change their offerings. Refer to the most current catalogs for up-to-date information.)

So Many Choices, So Little Time and Space

There are so many crops to grow, even in the foggiest areas, that a gardener must be selective. As you read this chapter or browse through a seed catalog, you may be tempted to try everything the first year. But think carefully before ordering. There is no sense in growing more plants than you have the time to tend or harvest. Also consider the amount of space you have. Plants are not polite to each other, and fast growers are not shy about shading out slow growers. I am still learning this lesson. Not too long ago I planted several kohlrabi seedlings between my summer squash hills and potato patch—a space that looked big enough but obviously wasn't. I was a little chagrined to see the squash and potatoes meet and intermingle over the tops of the kohlrabi.

Compendium of Vegetables

Amaranth
(or Tampala or Hinn Choy)
Amaranthus gangeticus
Pigweed Family ❖ *Amaranthaceae*

This domesticated relative of pigweed is valued as a leafy green vegetable in many parts of the world including China, where it is called hinn choy, and India, where it is called tampala. Farmer's markets in California often carry both this amaranth and closely related wild pigweeds. Although amaranth spinach doesn't seem quite as tasty to me as ordinary spinach, some people prefer its milder flavor. It is more nutritious, since it is high in iron and calcium and has only half the oxalic acid content of regular spinach. A warm-season crop, amaranth spinach grows well throughout the region, although it is taller in the sunnier parts. The plants, which reach 2 to 3 feet high if allowed to grow freely, may have green or red leaves.

Growing Instructions Sow your first planting of amaranth spinach at the beginning of May or even a few weeks earlier if the weather is warm. Plant the small seeds 1/4 inch deep. The crop doesn't demand an extremely rich soil, but it grows better when fertilizer and organic matter have been added. Provide plenty of water, as you would for any rapidly growing vegetable crop.

The Harvest Amaranth spinach produces upright leafy stems right away. You can harvest whole young plants and seed successive crops every couple of weeks. Or you can harvest from the same plants all summer—in fact, you must keep pinching off the stem tips if the plants are to produce leaves instead of flowers and seed heads. To get the most iron, don't begin to harvest until the plants are eight weeks old. Amaranth spinach declines in fall and must be resown the following spring.

Prepare amaranth spinach as you would ordinary spinach. Use it raw in salads, or cook the tender stems together with the leaves. Try cooking tougher stems as a separate vegetable, steaming them for eight to ten minutes. Information on grain amaranth is found on the next page.

Varieties and Related Species There don't seem to be any named varieties of A. *gangeticus*, although some seed companies offer red-leaved selections. In catalogs look for this crop under its various names or under headings such as *spinach* or *unusual vegetables.*

Several other species of amaranth are sometimes grown for greens. Some are also raised as ornamentals for their red or variegated leaves or their unusual flowers, and others are grown as grain crops. Although I suspect that all amaranths are edible, caution is in order. If you see an amaranth listed among vegetables in a catalog, you will know that it is edible. If it is among the flowers, inquire before you eat it. The following are some of the edible amaranths.

A. *caudatus* is used as a leafy vegetable, or the seeds are harvested as a grain. Commonly called love-lies-bleeding or tasselflower, it has long drooping ropes of red flowers. There are several common varieties. 'Green Thumb' has upright green flower spikes, 'Pygmy Torch' has deep maroon upright flower spikes, and 'Viridis' has graceful electric green tassels.

A. *cruentus* is another species used as both a leafy vegetable and a grain, particularly in tropical Africa. A red-leaved version is sold as blood amaranth.

A. *hybridis* also has edible leaves and seeds. There is a form with green leaves and upright spikes, and one with reddish leaves and red spikes.

A. *dubius* is a favorite leafy vegetable in much of the Caribbean. A good cultivar is 'Claroen.'

A. *lividus* leaves were eaten by ancient Greeks and Romans and by medieval Europeans. This low-growing species is called vleeta in modern Greece and norpa in India.

The red, yellow, and green streaked leaves of A. *tricolor (A. melancholicus)* brighten a salad. Common cultivars include 'Illumination,' 'Flaming Fountains,' 'Early Splendor,' and 'Joseph's Coat,' although you may find them under the common name tampala. These plants are sometimes sold as herbs.

Pests Slugs and snails may damage amaranth, but I haven't seen other pests harm it.

Sources
Amaranth seed:
Grain amaranth: ABL, DD, JSS, OBG, RCS, RH, SB, SOC
Leaf amaranth: ABL, DD, EV, JG, JSS, NGN, OBG, RCS, RH, SB, SOC, SGS, T&M
Tricolor amaranth: DD, SB, SOC

ARTICHOKE

Cynara scolymus
Sunflower
Family ❖ *Compositae*

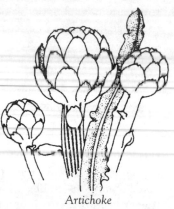

Artichoke

The Romans probably discovered artichokes growing wild in North Africa. These wild plants had small, tough thistles, but the Romans ate the leaf midribs, as they did those of cardoons. Introduced to rich soil and ample water, the plants responded with larger, more tender flower buds. By selecting the best plants, gardeners developed our modern vegetable.

Artichoke plants are very difficult to grow in areas with cold winters and hot summers, where they require the fuss and worry that we save for tomatoes. However, they are completely in their element throughout our region, the cool humid days fostering large, tender chokes. The suitability of this delicious crop for local gardens is attested to by the commercial artichoke fields lining the coast south of San Francisco into Monterey County.

Artichoke is a large perennial plant averaging 3 to 4 feet high but sometimes growing to 6 feet high. Young plants send up one flowering stalk each, whereas well-established plants can send up as many as twelve stalks. Each stalk bears at least three artichokes and sometimes as many as ten.

Growing Instructions The last living domesticated plant in an abandoned local vegetable garden is often an artichoke—a tribute to its arid ancestry. Such a survivor can be coaxed back with proper care, or it can be used as a rootstock to start new plants.

Artichoke plants are most commonly started from rootstocks purchased from nurseries. A rootstock is a division of the dormant base of a plant, including the stem base and the thick top of the root. Recently, artichoke seeds have also become available. If you want a lot of plants, starting them from seed is cheaper, although they will take from a few months to a year longer to bear.

Since an artichoke grows in the same place for several years, pay special attention to its site. Pick a spot away from annual vegetable and flowers, but make sure that it gets some winter sun. Control

GROWING GRAIN AMARANTH

Seeds harvested from grain amaranth species can be used as a cereal or ground into flour. Grain amaranth was a main crop of the Aztecs, but the Spanish conquerors forbade it because of its role in religious ceremonies. The ban slowed the spread of the grain, but recently it has regained popularity largely due to the efforts of Rodale Press, the company that publishes *Organic Gardening* magazine.

Gardeners rarely grow grains of any kind in small gardens, because the yield is usually too small for the trouble, but you may want to try grain amaranth as a novelty. The plants will produce a sizeable crop in the sunnier parts of our region. If you garden in a foggier area, start with a test planting. The maximum yield from plants that grow to 5 or 6 feet high is about a pound per square yard. When the seed stalks are mature and dry, cut them and remove the seeds. For small amounts loosen the hulls by rubbing the seed heads between your hands. For larger amounts rub the seed heads over a screen.

Although grain amaranth is interesting to grow, recipes for using it are not easy to find. For more on amaranth, see books in Appendix VI, Suggested Reading, under "Less Common Food Crops."

perennial weeds before you plant. Add plenty of organic matter and a slow-release fertilizer. A modern artichoke growing in poor soil with inadequate water will not revert to the original Mediterranean weed, but the plant will be stunted and it will produce only a few small chokes.

Although an October or November planting gives rootstocks the best start, nurseries may not receive rootstocks until December. Plant them whenever you can get them. Some nurseries pot up rootstocks in winter to sell as container plants throughout the year, and others obtain plants in containers for planting in late summer or fall. Plant these whenever you buy them. Whether you start with rootstocks or container plants, space them 3 to 4 feet apart.

If you decide to sow seeds, start them indoors in December or January or outdoors in a seedbed in February or March. Sow 1 inch deep and 4 inches apart, then transplant the best seedlings into a permanent site.

Container plants or plants grown from rootstocks may produce a small crop the first spring, but plants grown from seed probably won't produce until the following spring. In subsequent years, the plants usually bear from February through April, sometimes producing a second, smaller crop in fall. The plants may also surprise you with a stray stalk of off-season buds.

During periods of active growth, artichoke plants appreciate a monthly booster of high-nitrogen liquid fertilizer. Consistent watering is also important whenever the plants are actively growing. Be sure to water during dry spells in fall or spring. Although artichoke plants look sturdy, they collapse alarmingly when they wilt.

When the plant has finished bearing in spring, clean up the dead leaves and cut off the spent stalks at ground level with strong pruning loppers. (Don't twist or pull them out, because you may also pull out some of the developing shoots that will increase the size of your plant.) Allow any living leaves to grow until at least late spring. At that time local commercial growers often cut the entire plant down to or slightly below ground level and keep it on the dry side for several weeks. When the plant is watered again, it is more likely to rebound and make a fall crop.

As a plant gets older, it sends up many new whorls of leaves from the enlarging rootstock. It isn't necessary to divide a plant each year—do it when the clump becomes overgrown. Divide and replant rootstocks at the beginning of the rainy season, so that the plants can re-establish themselves during cool, humid days.

The Harvest   The buds are ready to harvest when they have stopped enlarging but before the scales begin to open. The best time to cut them is just as the tips of the lower scales begin to lift away from the bud. Each stalk will make one bud at the top. When that has been cut, the buds lower on the stem will enlarge, although they usually don't get as big as the top one.

When a bud opens, revealing its purple blossoms, it will inhibit the rest of the plant from making more buds. If you want to see the showy flowers, leave one plant unharvested or let some of the side buds bloom at the end of the season.

Varieties and Related Species   Most artichoke rootstocks available are 'Green Globe', and you can get seed of 'Green Globe' as well as improved strains of it that may bear more heavily than the original strain. 'Imperial Star' is a new variety that is said to consistently bear large buds the first year from seed, and 'Violetto' and 'Purple Sicilian' have purple bud scales that are green when cooked. See also Cardoon (page 190).

Pests   Two kinds of aphids, both of which attract ants, may sometimes attack artichoke buds. Bean aphids are dark green to black and oleaster-thistle aphids are pale yellow to green. A minor infestation does little damage, but a heavy outbreak may result in smaller, tougher buds. Aphids are difficult to wash out when they get under the bud scales. Another reason to control aphids is that they can spread diseases, such as curly dwarf virus (see below).

You may see the white foam that covers pale green spittlebug larvae on the leaves and under the bud scales. These sucking insects are rarely present in large enough numbers to cause much damage, but you may want to hose them off with a strong spray of water every few days.

The artichoke plume moth is a more serious problem, the larvae digging messy dark brown trails through the scales and right into the base of the chokes. Although I've had only occasional trouble, infestations are always possible. (See page 138.)

Slugs and snails occasionally do some damage, although they rarely make the buds inedible. Earwigs sometimes make a nuisance of themselves by living under the scales and emerging in the kitchen or, worse, getting cooked in the choke. If they invade your crop, shake the chokes firmly before you bring them into the house, then submerge them in water for a few minutes before you cook them.

Curly dwarf virus is a disease spread from infected plants to healthy ones by aphids and leafhoppers. When your plants are infected, you will gradually realize that they have become stunted and misshapen. Since there is no cure, prevent the virus by pulling any milk thistle (*Silybum marianum*) growing nearby (see page 106) by controlling aphids and leafhoppers. Pull any infected plants and start again with fresh roots from a source guaranteed to be free of the virus.

Sources
Artichoke seed:
Green Globe: ABL, BG, NGN, OBG, PTS, TERR, T&M
Imperial Star: GG, PS, SB, SGS
Violetto: PTS, TERR
Purple Sicilian: SB
Artichoke rootstocks: Available at local nurseries

ARUGULA
(OR ROCKET OR ROQUETTE)
Eruca vesicaria subsp. *sativa*
Mustard
Family ❖ *Brassicaceae*

Arugula is a quick, easy leafy crop with a sharp, or nutty flavor. It is a common ingredient in mesclun (see page 221) and is good both raw and cooked. Try a few leaves in a mixed salad or sauté it with onions and garlic, add a bit of goat cheese thinned with milk and serve it with pasta. The cream-and-violet flowers are also edible, and are pretty on salad.

Growing Instructions   Try planting this very hardy mustard-family green in early fall, again in February, and once more in spring. Scatter-sow the seeds, covering them 1/4 to 1/2 inch deep. Thin the plants until they stand 4 to 6 inches apart, and use the thinnings in salads.

The Harvest   You can harvest whole small plants or individual leaves. If seeds fall, arugula will regrow

the following season.

Varieties and Related Species   There are no named varieties of arugula, but a second species, *E. selvatica*, is now available. This "rustic arugula" has shorter, narrower leaves and a robust flavor. Keep the stems of edible yellow flowers picked to prolong the life of this tender perennial.

Pests   My arugula has had only one pest problem and that is flea beetle damage in warmer months. The damaged leaves are edible, though not so attractive. (See Flea Beetles on page 142.)

Sources
Arugula seed: Widely available
E. selvatica seed: CG, GG, JSS, NGN, SGS

ASPARAGUS
Asparagus officinalis
Lily Family ❖ *Liliaceae*

A native of marshy areas of Europe and Asia, asparagus thrives in cool, humid summers and so is well adapted here. Our winters are just cold enough to provide the necessary yearly dormant period.

Every spring asparagus sends up thick shoots from perennial roots. You can harvest these shoots for a certain number of weeks, depending on the age of the plant. Then you must stop cutting and let the last shoots grow into 3- to 5-foot-high feathery shrubs. The mature plants are attractive enough to grace the back of a flower border or to add to bouquets. After all, they are related to the lacy ornamental asparagus fern.

This is not a crop for the gardener in a hurry, because it requires careful soil preparation and takes several years to reach full harvest. In a few years, however, asparagus can be one of your most carefree and rewarding crops.

Growing Instructions   Because asparagus is a perennial that produces harvests for fifteen or more years in the same site, it needs a well-prepared permanent home away from areas that you dig up each season. The soil should be very rich and well amended. It is best not to plant an asparagus bed until you have gardened in a new site for at least a year. This gives you time to get persistent perennial weeds under control and to let organic matter mellow in the soil.

How many asparagus plants will you need? You can always grow a few plants for fun, but each plant

Asparagus unfolding

makes only a couple of stalks at a time, so it takes from five to twenty plants to supply one person with meal-sized portions all season long. Each plant requires a minimum area of 1-1/2 by 1-1/2 feet, so five plants need an area 7-1/2 by 1-1/2 feet, or 11-1/4 square feet. Twenty plants, an asparagus lover's dream, need an area 3 by 15 feet, or 45 square feet.

Asparagus is usually grown from crowns, or dormant rootstocks. One-year-old crowns are cheaper and transplant better than older crowns. Seeds are even cheaper, but they take more skill and effort. Research has shown that both seeds and crowns mature to allow a full harvest in the third spring after planting. And, though some newer varieties are advertised as being ready the second spring, caution is advised—previous research showed that harvesting plants before the third spring weakened the plants and could keep them from reaching full production.

In early spring presprout the seeds (see page 47), then sow them in a seedbed to which you added plenty of organic matter. Thin to 3 inches apart when the plants are still quite small. Tend the bed carefully to prevent weeds from taking over these slow-starting, wispy seedlings. You can start the seeds indoors, but you will need a setup that will accommodate the plants for two or three months. Transplant the seedlings to an interim bed in the garden until fall.

In fall, in an area that has already been amended and is free of perennial weeds, begin preparation for a permanent asparagus bed by digging in several more inches of organic matter. Transplant seedlings right away. Plant crowns anytime from January through March, being sure to put them in the ground the same day that you obtain them.

To plant either seedlings or crowns, prepare planting trenches as follows. On a day when the soil is dry enough to dig, make a trench 10 to 16 inches deep and 12 inches wide. Put 2 to 8 inches (2 inches if the trench is 10 inches deep and 8 inches if it is 16 inches deep) of compost or well-rotted manure in the bottom, mounding it slightly every 18 inches where the plants will be set. You may also want to work in another organic fertilizer, such as hoof and horn meal, or a slow-release synthetic fertilizer. Then place a 1 to 2 inch layer of soil in the trench. After you have done this, the trench should still be 6 inches deep at the top of the mounds. Set the seedlings or crowns in the trench, spreading the roots over the mounds. Fill in the trench so that the soil is level and the tops of the crowns are covered with 1 to 2 inches of soil. If you are using seedlings, pull 1 to 2 inches of soil around the base of each plant. The trench should still be about 4 inches deep. Fill it gradually as the plants grow taller, so that the soil is level by winter of the following year.

If your soil is heavy clay, you must modify this system to reduce the danger of decay. Dig the initial trench only 6 to 12 inches deep, then follow the other directions above. When you are finished, the asparagus plants will be planted in level soil rather than in a 4-inch trench. As the plants grow, mound soil around the stems, adding 2 inches by the next fall and 2 inches more by the next summer.

Keep the soil moist and free of weeds all year. When your plants are well up, you may want to apply a mulch. In early spring, before the plants begin to produce, apply a high-nitrogen fertilizer. If the plants appear healthy except that the ferns yellow or die back before fall, it is probably a sign that they need more fertilizer. When the plants die back for the winter, cut them at ground level and compost or discard them. It is always better to wait until the tops are dead before you cut them, but you can do it a bit earlier if they are an eyesore.

The Harvest Beginning the third spring after planting (whether you started from seed or crowns), you can harvest early spring shoots when they are 6 to 10 inches high. To avoid injuring the roots, just snap off the shoots right above the soil level. The first harvest should last no more than two or three weeks, since most of the plant's energy should go into forming fleshy storage roots. It is these roots that allow the plant to send up succulent shoots after each winter's dormancy.

You can harvest shoots for six to eight weeks in

the fourth year, and every spring thereafter you should get about two months of delicious asparagus spears. Never harvest after the largest spears become thinner than a pencil or you will harm next year's yield. If you pick any of the ferny stems for bouquets in summer, do it sparingly since they are supplying the roots with energy.

Varieties   The old varieties 'Mary Washington' and 'Martha Washington' are rust-resistant and widely adapted, with large spears. 'UC Davis 157' was developed especially for mild winter regions such as ours. It is tolerant to fusarium and plants are about 75% male, a good idea since female plants put energy into berries at the expense of more shoots. The 'Jersey' series is also mostly male, and various strains resist or tolerate fusarium and rust. Some European types are bred to be blanched (made white) by covering them with a thick mulch in spring, but they can be allowed to develop green as well. They should do all right near the coast. Purple-speared types might thrive, but would probably do better inland.

Pests   Given adequate care, your asparagus bed will probably reward you with years of pest-free harvests, but some pests are possible. To avoid rust, plant where air circulation is good and water plants at ground level.

The tiny light green asparagus aphid feeds on asparagus after it leafs out, giving the plant a blue-green cast and causing bushy "witches broom" growths. As a preventative, keep all shoots, even small ones, picked until the harvest is over. This may starve the aphids as they hatch.

Asparagus beetles, metallic blue-black ones with yellow to orange markings, may attack. The adult beetles live in weeds and plant debris in the winter, so clean up the garden to discourage them. Hand-pick the beetles. Rotenone, alone or with pyrethrum, will kill this pest.

Sources
Asparagus seed:
  UC 157: TERR
  Jersey series: PS
  Mary Washington: BG, PTS, SB, VBS
  "White" varieties: GG, JG, PTS, SB, TERR
Asparagus crowns:
  UC 157: BG, RSP, SGS, TERR
  Jersey series: BG, JSS, PS, PTS, RH, RSP, SGS, T&M

ASPARAGUS PEA
(OR WINGED PEA)
Lotus tetragonolobus
(Tetragonolobus purpureus)
Pea Family ❖ *Leguminosae*

Asparagus pea

Several legumes grown in different parts of the world produce pods with four high ridges known as wings. A great deal of research is being conducted on these plants, especially the goa or winged bean (*Psopho-carpus tetragonolobus*), an Asian legume that is being promoted as a good food source for tropical farmers. It makes huge pods up to 9 inches long, but it needs a tropical climate for proper development.

The asparagus pea bears much smaller pods, but it is more tolerant of cool weather than its larger cousin. A native of southern Europe, this low bushy annual does very well in our cool climate. In my garden in a sunny part of San Francisco, it began to bear pods in two months from an early June planting. I left it in the ground just to see what would happen. After three months of forming pods, it declined only to return and bear the following April and May.

Here is one more case in which the name asparagus has been called upon to imply that a crop is delicious. Even though I did not find the pods as tasty as promised, I still enjoyed growing this unusual crop with its attractive gray-green leaves and small scarlet blossoms.

Growing Instructions   Although I planted seeds in June, I think this plant would do better from an earlier planting, say in March. Direct-sow the seeds 1/2 inch deep and about 4 inches apart. This plant is very vigorous and will require little pampering, although it benefits from good garden soil and consistent watering.

The Harvest   Pick the pods when they are about an inch long, since they become stringy when they are larger. They will bear for up to 10 weeks in cool weather. Steam them or sauté them in butter or olive oil.

Pests   My plants declined in winter due to a powdery mildew attack, but they recovered in spring. I

LEGUME FAMILY

Beans and peas, which belong to the legume family, Leguminosae or Fabaceae, share many traits. They bear similar flowers, pods, and seeds, and they have similar habits of growth. Both crops have short bush varieties that grow only 1 or 2 feet high, and they also have pole varieties that reach 5 to 10 feet high and require a strong support. Both beans and peas add nitrogen to the soil by means of special nitrogen-fixing bacteria. It is possible to add a purchased inoculant to the soil to make sure that the right bacteria are present. (See Green Manure on page 76.)

Legumes need a good supply of phosphorus and potassium, but don't give them much nitrogen fertilizer, because it will inhibit the action of the nitrogen-fixing bacteria. I seldom fertilize beans or peas, instead planting them the season after a crop that was fertilized. If they are your first crop in a particular soil or if you are planting when the soil is colder than the seedlings like, fertilize lightly with nitrogen when you sow the seeds.

Legumes will grow in any soil, but they perform best in well-drained, organic soil with a pH of 6.5. Water adequately or the plants will become stunted and vulnerable to pest attack. Diseases can spread among wet plants, so avoid getting water on the leaves. If your plants were healthy, either compost them at the end of the season or cut the tops and leave the nitrogen-rich roots to decay in the soil.

Most gardeners harvest beans and peas before the seeds are mature. Snap beans are picked when the seeds are tiny and the pods succulent. Shell beans are harvested when the seeds are well formed but still tender and the pods leathery but not yet crisp. Most peas are picked at a stage similar to shell beans, although snow peas are harvested as very young, flat pods. When the pods are left unpicked until they are crisp, the hard, dry seeds are suitable for eating only after prolonged boiling.

Beans at the shell stage are a treat not often found in grocery stores. You can eat fava, lima, scarlet runner, and snap beans at this stage. Some types of snap beans, such as horticultural beans and French flageolet beans, are particularly good at the shell stage, but any snap bean will make a reasonably good shell bean. If you miss any bean pods that you intended to pick young, just shell the beans and cook them with the young pods.

To prolong the harvest of all but dry beans or dry peas, pick all the pods before they mature. If any pods form dry seeds, the plant will slow down or even stop production. Check the bottom of the plant, where the first pods form, to be sure that you didn't miss any. If you planted a bean variety that is used for both snap and dry beans, you'll get the biggest harvest if you pick all the young pods that form early in the season, then stop picking and let the rest mature as dry beans.

Beans and peas have fragile vines. Use both hands when harvesting, since it is easy to damage the stems and cut production short. Hold the vine with one hand and pick pods with the other hand. Of the two crops beans produce bigger harvests, although peas can be grown over a longer period. You can grow peas almost all year where summers are coolest. We usually think of beans as a crop to grow only in warm summers, but scarlet runner beans will produce well in foggy gardens and fava beans will make a crop in winter.

Once bean and pea seedlings survive snail attacks, they don't have many problems in our area. They may be bothered by aphids, mites, and whiteflies, but plants grown under good conditions can usually withstand the assault. A virus may infect an occasional bean or pea plant, but it doesn't usually wipe out a crop. Powdery mildew on pea is the only disease that may cause a serious loss of plants locally.

don't know if the disease would strike often, but apparently the plant can fight it off in the warmer months.

Sources
Asparagus pea seeds: T&M

BEAN, ASPARAGUS
(OR YARD-LONG BEAN)

Vigna unguiculata subsp. *sesquipedalis*
Pea Family ❖ *Leguminosae*

This is the yard-long bean used in Chinese cuisine. A close relative of the black-eyed pea grown in the South, it requires more heat than our area provides. I've never seen asparagus bean plants grow more than a foot high, even on the sunny side of San Francisco. They never get as far as a bloom, let alone a bean, so I doubt that this crop is possible anywhere in the region.

BEAN, DRY (INCLUDING KIDNEY, PINTO, AND BLACK BEANS)

Phaseolus vulgaris
Pea Family ❖ *Leguminosae*

Within the same bean species that is grown for snap beans (see page 176) are a number of types that are grown mainly to be ripened into dry or soup beans. In some of our microclimates where snap beans can be grown, it is less certain that dry beans will be able to ripen. Many of the most common kinds, such as pinto, black, and red beans, are iffy here. Cool weather slows their development, and damp fall days encourage decay. However, early ripening varieties are more likely to succeed. (See also Beans, Horticultural, page 172.)

Growing Instructions Choose a site that gets sun in early fall, and plant as early in the season as your site and the weather allow. In all other respects, grow dry beans as you would snap beans.

The Harvest Harvest the pods as soon as they are crisply dry—this will not be until at least six weeks after the pods begin to form. It is important not to leave drying pods on the vine so long that damp weather allows decay to set in. If your pods are brown but are taking a long time to become crisp, shell out some beans and see if they are hard. Even if they aren't quite mature, they will still be fine for eating after you dry them, although you probably won't want to save any to sow next year. If the pods are damp when you pick them, or if you aren't sure the beans are fully ripe, shell the beans right away. Throw away any flat, whithered beans or ones that have brown spots or other signs of decay. If you plan to store the beans before cooking them, spread then in a warm, dry place for a week or two to be sure they are well dried. Then store them in a cool, dry location.

You usually have to grow a lot of plants to collect a good supply of dried beans. Scarlet runner beans are the only type I've found to be remarkable for the amount of dry beans produced in a small space. However, you may have other reasons for growing dry beans. They are fun to grow. It always seems a miracle to put bean seeds in the ground at the beginning of the season and then discover more of the same handsome seeds inside the pods at the end of the season. Even shelling the beans is a satisfying activity. Perhaps you remember a certain kind of dry bean fondly from another time, place, or way of life. Even if our climate isn't favorable and the harvest is small, you may enjoy growing that type of bean just for the pleasure of holding a few of the newly harvested seeds in your hand again.

Varieties and Related Species An early variety is one rated at less than 85 days to harvest. Those listed as needing more days are borderline even in the warmer parts of our region, although I won't say it is impossible to grow them. Try small plantings of different types and see if they can ripen.

Territorial Seed Company has tested many varieties to see how they fare along the Oregon coast, an area with cool summers and a rainy season that typically begins a month earlier than ours. The few varieties that the company has chosen will also work in our area. In addition to early strains of kidney and black beans, it carries 'Soldier Bean,' which grows well through cool days even though it is not an especially early variety (Vermont Bean Seed rates it at 85 days).

Among other kinds of dry beans, mung beans (*Vigna radiata*), aduki beans (*Vigna angularis*), and black-eyed peas (*Vigna unguiculata*) mature in over 100 days and require a hot summer. Two dry bean types are worth trying here for harvest at the shell stage. Garbanzo beans (*Cicer arietinum*) are actually a cool-season crop, worth trying from a February or March sowing. In Mexican cuisine, they are used at the shell stage, added to soup. Experiment, starting with the 'Dolores de Hidalgo' garbanzos offered by Native Seeds Search. Soybeans (*Glycine max*), popular in Asian cuisines, will probably not succeed in the foggiest areas. In sunnier microclimates, try planting them a couple of weeks later than regular beans. They should bear a crop as days shorten in late summer. Test plant some of the varieties offered in seed catalogs.

Pests See snap beans.

Sources
Dry bean seed:
   Black Coco: ABL, SOC, TERR
   Soldier: ABL, RCS, SB, VBS
   Montcalm (Early Red Kidney): TERR
Vegetable soybean seed: ABL, DD, EV, KSC, PS, PTS, SOC, T&M
Garbanzo bean seed: ABL, DD, NSS, SOC, VBS

BEAN, FAVA (OR BROAD BEAN OR HORSE BEAN)

Vicia faba
Pea Family ❖ *Leguminosae*

The only bean known to early Europeans, the fava bean has been discovered among Iron Age relics in Britain and on the Continent. When you read that the Roman Army carried beans in its food supply, this is what the soldiers were eating.

Fava bean flowers, leaves, and pod

The fava bean is still widely grown in the milder regions of Europe and in the Middle East. It is seldom grown in most areas of the United States, because the summers are too hot and the winters are too cold for them. But they are perfect for our region, growing extremely well from fall to late spring and probably any other time of the year.

Favas are most often eaten as shell beans, either when the seeds are still small and tender or when they are larger but not yet dry. Favas can also be harvested after they are dry and boiled in soups or used salted and roasted. They are the large brown roasted beans in some kinds of Japanese party mixes.

Some people have a genetic metabolic disturbance that causes anemia when they eat fava beans or even inhale fava bean pollen. The problem, called "favism," is most common among those whose parents are from the Mediterranean area (particularly near Sardinia), Asia, or Taiwan. Symptoms are more common among men than women, and among adults than children. Some Americans of African descent also have the genetic defect, but they rarely show symptoms of the disorder.

The anemia results from destruction of older red blood cells, but not younger ones. Because younger blood cells are unaffected, it is usual for a person to recover fully once they stop being exposed to the beans.

Many people eat fava beans, including those in parts of the world where the problem is more common. There are seasonal outbreaks of favism in those places, and most victims recover. I have never heard of a case in the U.S., although they must occur. The prudent path is to ask questions of your family, then, if no evidence of a problem emerges, eat a small amount of the beans at first, followed by a few days break to be sure you feel O.K.

You are most likely to find seeds in a local nursery if there is an Italian-American population in the area, although the nursery will probably stock a single unnamed variety. For more choices, try seed catalogs.

Growing Instructions Plant the seeds 2 inches deep and 3 to 4 inches apart in blocks or in rows separated by 18 inches. Make sure that you will be able to reach the center of a block to pick the beans. The best planting times generally in the region are February and March for a late spring harvest and September through November for a winter harvest, although year-round planting is possible in the foggier areas. Like other legumes, favas add nitrogen to the soil. If you plan to use an inoculant (see Green Manure on page 76), purchase one specifically for fava beans.

The plants are handsome—the smooth leaves are gray-green and the flowers a dramatic black and white. They grow actively through the winter, reaching 2 to 4 feet high. They don't need much attention, but give them some support to keep them from blowing over in stormy weather. Form a grid by placing sturdy 4-foot-high stakes every 2 to 3 feet around and inside the planting, then connect the stakes at 1 and 3 feet above the ground with plastic garden tape or strips of rags.

The Harvest While the developing beans are small and tender, pick some to shell. Let some get a little bigger and see if you still like them. The bigger they get, the tougher and starchier they become. Some people cook the larger beans, then drop them in cold water for a few minutes and pop them out of their tough skins before serving them. You can also pick very young pods before the seeds form and eat them like snap beans. I thought that was a great idea, since the thick pods look very succulent, but I didn't find them very tasty. The foliage is a mild-flavored green that can be used in curries and other dishes in place of spinach. You can harvest leafy tops from young plants without harming later production. Older leaves are tougher.

Even if you don't find fava beans to your taste, there is still a good use for the plants. They make an excellent green manure. Sow the seeds in fall or late winter, then dig the plants under when they are 8 to 10 inches high, so that they will decay in time for your spring planting. As an alternative, compost the mature plants after you harvest the beans. Cut the plants to the ground, leaving the roots in the soil to rot, and chop the tops for your compost pile.

Varieties All varieties do well here. If the variety was developed to withstand warm days, plant it anytime from late winter to midsummer. There used to be only two types of favas—windsors, a short-podded bean with four or so large seeds, and longpods, which contain around eight smaller seeds. Now there are many hybrids, which fall into neither category. Although small-seeded varieties are said to be better tasting, I have not found any great difference among varieties—but I have never been a fan of fava beans.

Pests The only pest that I've seen on fava beans is the bean aphid, sometimes called the black fly, which attacks the tender growing tips of plants. Some gardeners wait until a good crop of pods has set and then remove the tops of infested plants, blooms and all, where the aphids congregate. This trick not only reduces the insect population and its favored habitat, but it also allows the plant to put its entire energy into ripening the beans that it has already set.

Sources
Fava bean seed (named varieties): ABL, DD, EV, JSS, KSC, NSS, OBG, PTS, SB, SOC, TERR, T&M

BEAN, FRENCH FLAGEOLET
Phaseolus vulgaris
Pea Family ❖ *Leguminosae*

French flageolet beans are a group of varieties that can be eaten at any stage from filet-sized (baby) pods to dry beans, but they are typically harvested as shell beans and dried—a stage called green dry. The shell beans can be dried indoors if the weather turns damp. The small pale green or white beans are similar to limas, but the plants are more tolerant of cool weather than limas. French flageolet varieties with pale green seeds are known as chevriers.

Growing Instructions See snap beans.

The Harvest For shell beans that you intend to eat fresh, harvest when the beans are fully formed and the pods are just beginning to become leathery. For green dry flageolets, pull up the plants when the beans are at the shell stage and hang them upside down in a dark, dry place. In France freshly picked shell beans or green dry beans are considered the perfect accompaniment to a leg of lamb.

Sources
Flageolet bean seed: CG, DD, GG, JG, JSS, NGN, SB, SGS, VBS

BEAN, HORTICULTURAL
Phaseolus vulgaris
Pea Family ❖ *Leguminosae*

This group of varieties consists of colorful, triple-use beans that are eaten primarily as shell beans but are equally good as snap beans or dry beans. They are particularly useful in our climate, since they are at least as tolerant of cool weather as the average snap bean and maybe a little more so. The pods start out light green, then become streaked with red as they mature. The beans are white or cream with red markings.

Growing Instructions See snap beans.

The Harvest Pick at any of three stages: when the seeds are beginning to form as you would snap beans, at the shell bean stage when the pods are leathery, or when the pods are crisply dry.

Varieties You'll find horticultural beans listed as such in seed catalogs, or look for them under colorful names like 'Wren's Egg,' 'Cranberry,' or 'Tongue of Fire' in other bean listings.

Sources
Horticultural bean seed:
Bush varieties:
   Borlotto: SGS
   Cranberry Bush: CG, PTS, RCS, SB, TERR
   Dragon Tongue (Dragon Langerie): OBG, PTS, SB, TERR, VBS
   Tongue of Fire: JSS, NGN, SB, VBS
   Dwarf Horticultural or Taylor's Dwarf Horticultural: ABL, BG, OBG, PTS, VBS, SB, TERR
Pole varieties:
   Cranberry Pole: ABL, VBS
   Gramma Walters: ABL
   King Mammoth: SB
   Wrens's Egg: SB, VBS

BEAN, LIMA
Phaseolus lunatus
Pea Family ❖ *Leguminosae*

Lima beans, the large flat beans in succotash, are very sensitive to cool weather. I had always been told that our climate wasn't warm enough for them, but I tried some in my garden in a sunny part of San Francisco anyway. I planted pole and bush lima seeds on the same day in late May that I sowed pole and bush romano beans.

Pods first appeared on the bush limas in early August, when the bush romanos were already halfway through production. The pole limas grew so intertwined with the pole romanos that I couldn't

BUILDING A BEAN TRELLIS OR TEPEE

If you have been growing bush beans because building supports for pole beans seems like too much trouble, consider this: Pole varieties bear more heavily and longer than bush varieties, and many supports last for several years.

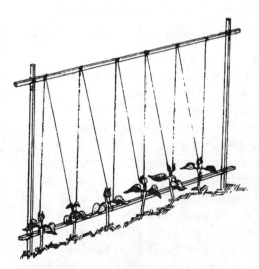

A sturdy wood fence will support simple growing strings or inexpensive nylon garden trellis netting. Drive galvanized roofing nails partway into the fence near the top, spacing them about 6 inches apart. Tie nylon or plastic string to them, or hook the nails through the openings of a purchased nylon trellis. If you use strings, tie the bottom ends of them to a long bamboo stake laid on the ground at the foot of the fence. If you use netting, anchor the bottom of it by tying it to short stakes driven into the ground a few inches from the base of the fence.

You can also hang strings or a nylon trellis from a homemade redwood frame attached to a raised bed.

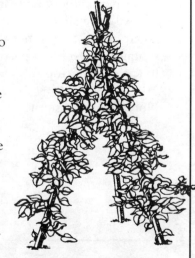

Nail 6- to 8-foot lengths of 1 by 2s to the bed, spacing the boards no more than 4 feet apart. Nail a 1 by 2 board across the top of the upright boards. Fasten the nylon strings or netting to the supports with a staple gun.

If you have enough space, you can make a bean tepee with three to eight bamboo or redwood poles. Lash 8- to 12-foot-long poles together near the top with nylon cord, then push them into the ground in a circle 1-1/2 to 3 feet in diameter. A larger tepee—one with a diameter of 4 feet or more—can also serve as a playhouse. Just leave an opening through which the children can crawl inside.

MINESTRONE

This is a wonderful, full-meal soup in the Italian tradition. Make a double batch and freeze half for later. Just be sure to remove the portion you intend to freeze before you add the pasta, as pasta doesn't freeze well.

Soup
3/4 cup dry garbanzo beans
1 medium carrot, thinly sliced
1 small onion, chopped
1 1/2 cups potato cut into large dice
1 cup green beans, cut in 1-inch pieces
2 1/2 cups tomato sauce, canned or
    homemade (see page 346 for recipe)
1 teaspoon chopped fresh thyme leaves
1 tablespoon chopped fresh basil
1 tablespoon chopped fresh parsley
2 small summer squash, chopped
1/4 cup small pasta (such as small shells,
    alphabet macaroni, or spaghetti broken
    into short pieces)
1 c. grated Parmesan cheese

Broth
1 1/2 pounds fresh (uncured)
    pork or beef hocks
1 1/2 pounds beef or pork
    soup bones
2 tablespoons vinegar
4 quarts water
1/2 cup coarsely chopped
    celery leaves
1 carrot, coarsely chopped
1 onion, quartered

The night before, put the meat, vinegar, water, celery leaves, chopped carrot, and quartered onion into a large pot and bring to a boil. Lower heat, cover, and let simmer for 2 to 3 hours, until the meat is very tender. Cool. Refrigerate overnight.

The next day, use a slotted spoon to skim off the hardened fat. Remove and discard the vegetables. Remove the meat and bones. Reserve all of the lean meat, discarding the bones, fat, and gristle. Cut or tear any large pieces of meat into bite-sized chunks and put them into a medium bowl. Pour the remaining broth through a sieve or colander into a large container. Scrub the pot well and put the strained broth and lean meat back in it.

Rinse and pick over the garbanzo beans and add them to the broth. Bring it to a boil, lower heat, cover, and simmer 1 hour, or till the beans are nearly tender.

Add the sliced carrots and chopped onion and simmer 5 minutes. Add the potatoes, green beans, and tomato sauce. Simmer 20 minutes more. Add the thyme, basil, parsley, summer squash, and pasta and cook 10 to 15 minutes longer. Serve with Parmesan cheese to sprinkle on top.

Note: You can substitute fresh beef hocks, but I like pork hocks better.

tell the plants apart at first. Finally, toward the end of August, when the pole romanos had been bearing for several weeks, I noticed the distinctive ridged edges of the first lima pods. By the middle of September, I began to see the shadows of small beans in the pods of both bush and pole limas. In the middle of October, I harvested the bush limas as shell beans. I got a grand total of 1/3 cup of shelled beans per plant. The pole limas reached the same stage by the last week of October and made about the same amount of beans per plant.

My conclusion is that, although the climate is not ideal, limas will ripen to the shell bean stage in the warmer parts of the region—good news for fans of this delicious bean. It would take several more weeks for the seeds to ripen to dry beans, and I'm not sure they would make it before the rainy season.

Growing Instructions In early May sow seeds in place 2 to 3 inches apart and 1 inch deep. Limas transplant so poorly that seedlings started indoors rarely catch up to plants sown in place. Otherwise, grow limas as you would snap beans.

Sources
Lima bean seeds: Widely available

BEAN, ROMANO

Phaseolus vulgaris
Pea Family ❖ *Leguminosae*

Romano beans, the broad-podded beans common in Italian cuisine, may be eaten as either snap beans or shell beans. They rarely appear in grocery stores, although they are quite delicious at either stage of maturity. I can vouch for the flavor and wonderful buttery texture of both 'Roma II' and 'Pole Romano'. 'Kwintus', a new European type, gets rave reviews for productivity, flavor, and tenderness even when pods get large. 'Sequoia' is a new purple-podded romano-type bean, which, like other purple beans, is green when cooked. 'Annelino' beans are a traditional Italian variety with short, crescent-shaped pods in yellow or green.

Sources
Romano bean seed:
Roma II (bush): BG, PS, SGS, VBS
Bush Romano: PTS
Pole Romano: BG, NGN, PTS, RCS, SB, SOC, TERR, T&M, VBS

Kwintus (pole): CG
Sequoia (purple, bush): BG, PS, PTS, SOC, VBS
Annelino Romano (pole): CG

BEAN, SCARLET RUNNER

Phaseolus coccineus (P. multiflorus)
Pea Family ❖ *Leguminosae*

This perennial plant owes its tolerance of cool summers to its origin in the highlands of Central America. It gives gardeners in foggy locations a good chance for success with a warm-season bean. And what a fine bean it is! The handsome seeds, usually mottled pink and black, grow into large vines that quickly blanket a fence or arbor. A profusion of flowers, red on most varieties, make the plants handsome enough to use as ornamentals. The flowers often attract hummingbirds, although the birds aren't required for pollination. The large pods are tender and tasty when they are picked young. When the pods are left on the vine, the seeds ripen into large, well-flavored shell or dry beans.

Scarlet runner bean

Growing Instructions Most runner beans are climbers that grow to 8 feet or more. Give them a 6- to 8-foot-high trellis or pole tepee. Since bean vines twine, vertical supports are more important than horizontal ones. Plant seeds 1 to 2 inches deep and 3 to 4 inches apart along a trellis and thin the plants to 6 inches apart. Or plant five or six seeds around each pole in the tepee and thin to the three strongest vines.

These beans can take slightly cooler soil than ordinary snap beans. Although they will succeed from a May planting, they can be sown in April or even earlier if the spring is unusually warm. The plants begin to bear in late June or early July and may continue to make new pods as late as the middle of October. Keep the plants well watered, since production drops if they get too dry.

You can often overwinter scarlet runner beans. Leave the plants intact in fall after you have harvested the beans. The tops may die back completely, or some vines may remain alive. When it is clear which parts are dead, remove them. Any vines that are still alive will leaf out in spring and begin to bear pods a few weeks before runner beans that are planted that same spring. I've had less success with overwintering vines during the third summer—typically vines on only about one-third of the plants make a comeback. But even if the vines themselves die or are cut back, the large tuberous roots will resprout. This will give you a crop after the first year, but without the advantage of earliness. (Some sources claim that the tuberous roots are edible, and others maintain that they are poisonous. The father of a friend sampled some from his garden and became very ill, so I suggest that you assume they are poisonous.)

The Harvest Pick runner bean pods to use as snap beans when they are 6 to 7 inches long, before the seeds have formed. Once the seeds begin to fill out, the pods become tough and unpalatable. If a pod escapes notice, you can harvest the seeds as shell beans. As an alternative, wait until the pods are crisply dry on the vine and save the seeds to cook as dry beans or to plant next year. The crop of both green pods and dry beans can be huge. From five plants I harvested enough pods for two people to eat and share with friends for almost three months, then picked enough dry beans to fill several quart jars.

PLANTING TIPS FOR BEANS

- Don't presprout bean seeds—it lessens the vigor of the seeds and may allow decay organisms to enter.

- For the best germination, plant bean seeds with the flatter narrow edge down.

- While all beans except limas may be started indoors, they should be planted out as soon as they have two or three true leaves or they may be stunted. Plant single seeds in each container and do not pot them up—plant from the original container.

Varieties Scarlet runner bean seeds sold as an ornamental may not be a variety bred for flavor or production. One year I grew some seeds from a mail-order vegetable seed catalog and some from the flower section of a local seed rack. The seeds sold as a vegetable produced pods a full month and a half longer than the ones sold as a flower. In seed catalogs look for a separate listing for runner beans in the vegetable section or check the broader category of pole beans.

In your search for varieties that offer good flavor and production you don't have to give up beauty. My productive vines had flowers just as colorful as those on the ornamental vines, and a lot more of them. Several varieties have white flowers (and white seeds). 'Painted Lady' has two-tone red and white flowers. If you can't give beans a place to climb tall, you might want to try a "half runner" or bush variety. Read catalog descriptions, as some of these need some support, while others are short enough to sprawl.

Pests Be on guard against earwigs, slugs, and snails when the plants are small, since these pests can do major damage. They are not likely to do as much harm to mature plants, although it is still a good idea to pick the plants over for snails as you harvest the pods. Whiteflies or spider mites may infest underwatered plants.

Sources
Scarlet runner bean seed:
Red-flowered varieties: Widely available
White-flowered varieties: NSS, OBG, SB, T&M
Red-and-white flowered varieties: OBG, TERR
Bush, or dwarf varieties: PTS, SOC, TERR

BEAN, SNAP (BUSH AND POLE)
Phaseolus vulgaris
Pea Family ❖ *Leguminosae*

Snap beans are the common green beans, such as 'Kentucky Wonder' and 'Blue Lake,' which are eaten when the pods are young and before the beans form. They used to be called string beans, because of the fibrous string that ran the length of each pod and had to be removed before the beans were cooked. Now that plant breeders have all but eliminated the string, the produce industry has popularized the name snap bean.

CHEESY ITALIAN SAUSAGE STEW

This dish is almost a full meal, needing only a green salad and maybe fruit for dessert to round it out.

6 Italian sausages, hot or mild (or turkey Italian sausages)
3 cups green beans, cut on the diagonal into 1 1/2-inch pieces
  (scarlet runner or Romano-type beans are especially good)
2 cups boiling potatoes, unpeeled, cut into 1-inch chunks
4 tablespoons butter or margarine
4 tablespoons unbleached flour
2 cups milk (lowfat or nonfat are fine)
1/4 cup grated Parmesan cheese
Salt and pepper, if desired

Put sausages in a saucepan of boiling water and simmer them for 10 minutes. Cut the cooked sausages into 1/4-inch slices and set aside. Steam the green beans and potatoes 10 to 15 minutes, until tender but firm, and set aside.

Melt the butter in a skillet over low heat, and stir in the flour. Turn the heat up slightly and cook the mixture for about 2 minutes, until it is bubbly. Turn off heat. Stir milk in very gradually, working rapidly with a fork to break up lumps and keep the flour dispersed. When all of the milk has been mixed in, bring the mixture to a simmer and cook till it thickens, stirring continuously and scraping the sides and bottom often to keep the sauce from burning.

Add the cheese to the thickened sauce and stir to mix it in well. Add salt and freshly ground black pepper to taste. Stir in the sausages and vegetables and serve hot. Serves three or four.

These beans appreciate our humid coastal climate, but they need warm days, so they may not thrive in the coolest, foggiest gardens.

Growing Instructions   Plant your first successive crop of bush snap beans after the soil has warmed, usually on May 1 but earlier during a particularly warm spring. Plant the seeds 1 to 2 inches deep and 2 inches apart in a small block or in rows spaced 12 to 18 inches apart. Thin the plants to 4 inches apart when they have two or three true leaves. Bush beans mature quickly, in just a couple of months, and produce for a few weeks. You can plant additional successive crops until the middle of July. 'Limelight', a super-fast variety, might mature from an August planting, but I found no current source for it.

Pole beans can be planted anytime from May 1 to early June. Sow the seeds 1 inch deep and 2 to 3 inches apart on one or both sides of a trellis, or plant five or six seeds around a pole. Thin the plants to 4 to 6 inches apart along a trellis, or keep the best three plants around a pole. Leave 1 foot or more between poles. Pole beans begin bearing a couple of weeks later than bush beans, but they produce longer.

The seeds may rot in the ground if they are planted too early, especially in clay soil. Their large seed leaves require a lot of energy to push through to the soil surface. Even if they manage to break the surface, the plants will not thrive if the soil is too cold. The leaves will turn yellow because they can't draw nutrients from the soil. The plants may succumb to pests that they might otherwise have outgrown. You may want to get a head start by sowing the seeds indoors three to four weeks before the garden soil is warm enough for planting.

The Harvest Pick snap beans while the pods are still flat and the beans not yet visible. When they are more mature, the pods are likely to be tough and stringy. How large they can get and still remain tender depends on the variety. Although pole beans are said to have a slightly better flavor than bush beans, they taste equally good to me.

Although you can pick any snap bean very young, you may get a more flavorful baby pod from French filet varieties, which were developed especially for picking at this stage. If you are growing these French delicacies, pick them when they are less than 1/4 inch (some say less than 1/8 inch) in diameter, steam them briefly, and serve them whole. They require daily harvesting to keep them from growing past their prime, and when they get past the baby bean stage, they may not be as tasty or tender as regular snap bean pods.

Varieties Bush and pole snap beans come in three colors of pods: green, yellow, and purple. Yellow-podded snap beans are also called wax beans. They have a firmer texture when cooked than other varieties. If you can grow any standard pole or bush bean, you can probably grow them all—although there is no point in trying to grow varieties bred to survive very hot weather when there are so many others to try. 'Blue Lake' and 'Kentucky Wonder' and their various strains are good bets here. And 'Kentucky Blue' is said to combine the best of both. Try others as well and compare your results.

The purple-podded varieties are tasty and are said to tolerate cooler weather and soil than most green or yellow beans. They can be planted a couple of weeks earlier or grown in a cooler microclimate. Their flowers are a lovely violet, and their deep purple pods turn an unexpected bright green when cooked. Common purple-podded bush varieties are 'Royalty' and 'Royal Burgundy,' and there are several pole varieties, including some that are called violet- or even blue-podded beans.

There are many French filet varieties, most of them introduced to American gardeners in the past few years. You may find them listed as baby beans or *haricot vert*, which is French for green bean.

If you find that all the varieties you try struggle in your microclimate, you may want to grow scarlet runner beans instead.

Pests Slugs and snails inflict great damage on snap bean seedlings, and earwigs do occasional damage. There are several strategies for protecting seedlings:

Plant twice as many seeds as you need and either thin the extras or transplant them to fill gaps when the pests strike; plant the seeds under a floating row cover; or start the seeds indoors and move them into the garden when they have several leaves and are better able to survive the pest damage. Late in the season the summer's baby snails may turn your bean leaves to lace, although they won't seriously reduce the nearly completed harvest. Still, crush as many small snails as you can to keep them from growing into the adult snails that will infest next spring's seedlings.

Other pests that I've seen on snap beans include aphids, spider mites, and whiteflies. All are more likely if the plants are grown under poor conditions, especially if they are underwatered. Beans also get aphid-transmitted virus diseases. Remove infected plants from your garden to keep such diseases from spreading.

In parts of the country that get summer rain, beans are susceptible to a number of bacterial and fungal diseases, so gardeners there are cautioned not to water with overhead sprinklers and not to work among wet plants. In dry-summer areas like ours, these diseases are rare, but it is still wise to water at ground level. It is also important to obtain disease-free seeds. Commercial bean seeds are the safest, and locally homegrown seeds are probably safe—but avoid using seeds saved from bean plants grown in wet-summer areas.

Sources
Snap bean seed:
Green-podded varieties:
　Blue Lake bush: BG, NGN, PTS, TERR, T&M, VBS
　Blue Lake pole: ABL, BG, NGN, OBG, SB, SOC, SGS, TERR, VBS
　Kentucky Wonder bush: PS, SB, T&M, VBS
　Kentucky Wonder pole: ABL, BG, NGN, PTS, SB, SOC, TERR, T&M, VBS
　Kentucky Blue pole: BG, OBG, PTS, TERR, T&M, VBS
Yellow-podded varieties:
　Bush varieties: ABL, BG, JSS, PTS, SOC, SGS, TERR, T&M, VBS
　Pole varieties: JSS, TERR, GOLDMARIE, VBS
Purple-podded varieties:
　Bush varieties: ABL, BG, JSS, NGN, PTS, SB, SOC, SGS, TERR, T&M, VBS
　Pole varieties: ABL, CG, JSS, OBG, PTS, SOC, TERR, VBS
　French filet beans: BG, CG, JG, JSS, PS, SB, SGS, TERR, T&M, VBS

BEET
Beta vulgaris
Crassa Group
Goosefoot Family ❖ *Chenopodiaceae*

At their best when daytime temperatures are 60° to

MARINATED BEETS

Make a couple of cups of these vermilion pickles and keep them at the ready in your refrigerator. They make a tangy, colorful addition to salads.

2 cups beets, cut into 1/8-inch strips, as described below
1/2 cup cider vinegar
1/2 cup water
2 tablespoons sugar (optional)

Scrub the beets. No need to peel them, but trim away any brown corky matter or hard-to-clean bunches of rootlets. Cut the beets into vertical slices 1/8-inch thick and then into strips 1/8-inch wide. Cut any extra long strips in half. Steam the beets until tender, 20 minutes or longer. Put them in a jar or plastic refrigerator container with a lid and set them aside.

In a saucepan, heat the vinegar and water (and optional sugar) to just below a simmer. Pour the hot mixture over the beets. If the beets are not covered, add a little more unheated vinegar and water till they are completely submerged. Chill overnight before using. They will keep at least a couple of weeks in the refrigerator.

65°F, beets thrive in all parts of our region. Like other root crops, beets make the best-shaped roots in either sandy soil or soil well amended with organic matter. They are almost always direct-seeded, but I have discovered that they can be transplanted successfully. Being able to transplant allows you to have beet seedlings growing while another crop is finishing production. You can start the seeds indoors, or outdoors in a corner of your garden.

Growing Instructions   Plant in rows or scatter-sow in small blocks. Plant seeds 1/2 inch deep and 1 or 2 inches apart. Since each beet seed really consists of several seeds, the seedlings must be thinned. If you sow the seeds in place, wait until the seedlings have two true leaves, then thin to 3 inches apart and to one plant per cluster. Use scissors to snip off the excess plants. If you grow seedlings to transplant, separate them carefully before planting and set them 3 inches apart. You must water regularly to produce sweet, tender beets with good color.

Begin sowing seeds outdoors as early as February, whenever the soil isn't too wet for planting. In areas closest to the coast, you can continue to plant until around the end of July. The July-planted beets will be able to mature in the warmth of late sum-mer, and they can be left in the ground to be dug up in fall and winter. In protected sites or farther from the coast, you may be able to plant a month or two later. If you plant too late, however, the beets won't have time to form big roots before they are stopped by cold weather. In spring you may be tempted to leave small beets in the ground hoping that they will get bigger, but they will go to seed instead and then die.

The Harvest   You can harvest beets for tender greens before the roots have even formed. The next harvest can be for baby beets, when the roots are only an inch or so in diameter. For regular use let them reach at least 2 inches in diameter, but check the seed packet to find out the optimum size for the variety you are growing. Some beet varieties remain tender when they get bigger, but most toughen up. Almost all beet varieties reach the size listed on the seed packet in about two months.

Varieties   When choosing a beet variety, don't limit yourself to early varieties, since beets aren't hampered by our cool summers. Standard round red beets, such as 'Early Wonder,' 'Detroit Dark Red,' and 'Ruby Queen,' do just fine here. 'Winterkeeper' (also called 'Lutz'), although not very shapely, is a good red variety for fall cropping, since it stays tender for a long time. 'Chioggia' is a novelty beet that shows alternating white and red rings when it is sliced. (This is normal for 'Chioggia,' but if other varieties show this trait, called zoning, it is because the days were too warm while the roots were maturing.) There are also yellow- and white-rooted beets. Both are reputed to germinate poorly, which I was quite relieved to hear after my first effort to grow 'Burpee's Golden' produced a very thin stand.

Pests   Spinach leafminers are my worst beet pests. The larvae tunnel inside the leaves, making unappetizing blotches. They don't harm the roots directly, but extensive leaf damage will stunt the roots. (For more on leafminers, see page 142.) Overwintering beets often get either cercospora leaf spot (see page 156) or beet rust. The same prevention methods help avoid both.

Sources
Beet seed:
Standard red varieties: Widely available
Chiogga: ABL, CG, DD, JSS, PTS, SOC, SGS, TERR, T&M, VBS
Winterkeeper (or Lutz): ABL, DD, NGN, PTS, SOC, TERR
Yellow varieties: ABL, BG, CG, GG, NGN, OBG, PS, PTS, SGS, TERR, T&M
White varieties: GG, TERR, T&M

BITTER MELON
(OR BALSAM PEAR OR FOO GWA)
Momordica charantia
Gourd Family ❖ *Cucurbitaceae*

A standard vegetable in Chinese cuisine, bitter melon is a vine that can be trained to climb a trellis in the same way that cucumbers are. The distinctive bitter flavor of this crop is due to quinine. Startling at first, the flavor appeals to many people once they get used to it. If bitter melon is new to you, buy it at a grocery store and make sure that you like the taste before you grow it.

Bitter melon is a borderline crop even in the warmer parts of our region. It may produce fruit in a sunny microclimate or a minigreenhouse (see page 59). Still, the plant is pretty, and even if fruit doesn't form you can use the young leaves and stem tips as a potherb.

Growing Instructions   Start seeds indoors in a bottomless milk carton, in the same way that you would start any other fast-growing plant with delicate roots (see page 54). Start the seeds during the

third week of March to plant out in early May. (The seeds will take two weeks to germinate, and the plants should grow indoors for three to four more weeks.) Fertilize your garden soil well and set plants 6 to 8 inches apart near a trellis. Keep the soil well watered and apply a booster of manure or compost tea (see page 80) or fish emulsion every two weeks.

The Harvest   Since bitter melon becomes too bitter to eat when it is ripe, it is only eaten green. Try the immature fruit while it is under 6 inches long. Sample larger fruit until it becomes too bitter for your taste. (The ripe fruit is interesting to look at, turning yellow and then orange and finally splitting open to show its red seeds.)

To prepare a bitter melon fruit, cut it in half lengthwise. Scoop out and discard the seeds, which are poisonous at any stage, and cut the melon into 1/4-inch slices. Drop the melon slices into boiling water and boil them for three minutes to reduce the bitterness. Bitter melon is often stir fried and served with fermented black bean sauce.

Sources
Bitter melon seed: EV, KSC, NGN, SB

BOK CHOY
(OR PAC CHOY)
Brassica rapa (*B. chinensis*)
Chinensis Group
Mustard
Family ❖ *Cruciferae*

Bok choy

This crop is the handsome white- or pale green-stemmed, nonheading Chinese green. It is a near relative of turnip, tendergreen mustard, and heading Chinese cabbage. Grown similarly to Chinese cabbage (see page 200), bok choy is somewhat easier. Since both crops attract slugs and snails in hordes, they should only be attempted if the pests are under control, or grown under a row cover frame (see pages 49 & 50).

Growing Instructions   Bok choy needs organic, fertile soil. Sow the seeds in place 1/4 to 1/2 inch deep. When the plants are about 4 inches high, thin them to 6 to 8 inches apart. Water bok choy regularly, so that it will grow fast and stay tender. It should be possible to grow bok choy from February through April and again from late summer into fall. You may be able to grow it all summer if your site is cool enough. Warm days will cause the crop to go to seed prematurely, or bolt, before it gets very big. It may also bolt during the longest days of the year, but it is less likely to do so than Chinese cabbage.

The Harvest Start by eating the small plants that you pull to thin the crop. Then harvest outer leaves of growing plants, or pull whole plants at any stage before the flower stalk has grown taller than the leaves. Eat leaves and stems in salads, in soups, or stir fried with sliced mushrooms in oyster sauce.

Varieties Tall, white-stemmed types used to be the main ones available, but now we can also grow the delicious short, or "baby", bok choys, including pale-green-stemmed types such as 'Mei Quing' or 'Ching-Chiang'. A similar Chinese green of the same species, 'Tah Tsai', has flat rosettes of shiny, dark green leaves with bok choy-like white stems. It is good in salads or stir-fried.

Pests Bok choy has the same pests, including clubroot, as other members of the mustard family (see page 183).

Sources
Bok choy seed:
Tall white-stemmed varieties: Widely available
Short green-stemmed varieties: CG, EV, JSS, KSC, NGN, PTS, SGS
Tah Tsai (or Tatsoi): ABL, CG, EV, JSS, KSC, NGN, OBG, PTS, SOC, TERR, VBS

BOLIVIAN SUNROOT
(OR LLACON OR STRAWBERRY JICAMA)
Polymnia edulis (Polymnia sonchifolia)
Sunflower Family ❖ *Compositae*

This is my latest discovery! It took me nearly three years to find a start of this plant, but the wait was worthwhile. Nearly pest-free, Bolivian sunroot produces a generous supply of large, sweet, juicy tuberous roots. A native of South America, it is grown for food in several Andean countries.

Bolivian sunroot leaps skyward to a bushy 8 feet or higher. Its huge triangular gray-green leaves are covered with soft hairs. Weighing up to a couple of pounds apiece, the edible roots are between jicama and watermelon in texture, and between jicama and sunchoke in flavor.

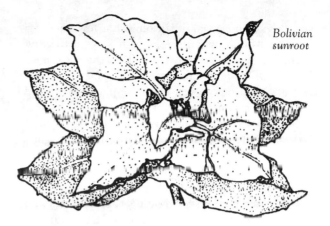

Bolivian sunroot

In fact, the plant is related to sunchoke (see page 251). You can see the family resemblance in the daisies, which on Bolivian sunroot are orange and a little over an inch across. Less impressive than those of sunchoke, the flowers are barely noticeable blooming atop the tall plants in fall.

Growing Instructions Bolivian sunroot is grown from rhizomes, which can be easily divided and transplanted during the winter when the plant is dormant. When you buy a crown, what you are getting is a rhizome division, usually one with several buds. Plant it in late winter, before the shoots start to grow, with the highest buds just at soil level. Leave 2 or 3 feet between crowns.

Bolivian sunroot needs good garden soil and deep watering while it is actively growing. Be especially careful not to let it dry out in late summer or early fall. (When the plant is thirsty, its leaves droop dramatically.)

The Harvest In mid- to late fall, the top of the plant dies back. Lop off the stems a foot or so above the ground, so that the stumps will clearly mark the site of your underground treasure. When the weather has cooled, dig around looking for the tuberous roots. The edible structure is not the rhizome that you see at the soil surface, but rather the large storage roots that have formed beneath them, each connected to the rhizome by a thin attachment root. You will find them by carefully digging in from one side of the plant. When you locate one, remove the soil around it until you can lift it out and detach it.

What you will have in your hands is a large, homely, brown object, either elongated and pointed at the ends or almost spherical. Wash it, cut off a portion, peel the thin brown skin, and enjoy.

You can harvest roots gradually or all at once. It is best to renew the plant each spring though, or

181

it will develop a mass of rhizomes but few new roots. By March, when the plantings begin to grow again, you should have harvested all the roots made that year. Divide the rhizome and replant a small start of them. Before you reset the plant, dig in some organic matter and fertilizer. You will have quite a few extra rhizomes, which you can use to grow more plants yourself, or share them with gardening friends.

So far I have only enjoyed Bolivian sunroot raw. The crisp roots enliven a bag lunch or make a good vegetable relish for dipping. The textures and flavors of Bolivian sunroot, romaine lettuce, and a jar of artichoke hearts with the marinade blend delectably in a salad. I suppose the next step is to look for recipes that include jicama and substitute Bolivian sunroot, but the truth is that I'm not looking very hard because I haven't tired of eating it sliced raw.

Varieties   Although there is probably more than one variety of this crop in its native South America, the local sources do not give any variety names.

Sources

Bolivian sunroot (Llacon) crowns: Floorcraft Garden Center, 550 Bayshore Boulevard, San Francisco, CA 94124, (415)824-1900.

BROCCOLI

Brassica oleracea
Italica Group
Mustard Family   ❖   *Cruciferae*

Our coastal climate is ideal for growing broccoli—and, in fact, Italian market gardeners who grew the crop in San Francisco and on the peninsula introduced it to the American market. If you time your plantings well, plant both short- and long-season varieties, and grow types that resprout when you cut them, you can harvest broccoli most of the year.

Growing Instructions   See Mustard Family (opposite page) for general growing requirements for cole crops. Unlike cabbage, young broccoli plants may stunt if the temperature approaches freezing, so I never set them out until the middle of February. There is also some risk of stunting when plants are set out after early September when fall is early and cold. July is the safest last planting time for fall broccoli, although you should experiment with your

microclimate. Nurseries sometimes don't stock fresh broccoli seedlings until September, so if you want them for a midsummer planting you will have to start them yourself. Start seeds indoors beginning in the middle of December and continue to grow more seedlings as you need them until the end of July. You can also start seeds outdoors in a seedbed between March and July. Transplant small varieties of broccoli to stand 8 to 12 inches apart and larger ones 18 to 24 inches apart.

Short-season varieties take 60 to 90 days from transplanting and long-season ones 90 to 120 days. When long-season broccoli is overwintering, it may take a month or two longer than listed. As with all cole crops, the long-season varieties are generally the old ones that have traditionally been cultivated in mild-winter areas of Europe. Short-season broccoli was developed in the United States for hot-summer areas. In much of the country they are planted in spring to mature before the summer heat strikes, or they are planted in late summer to mature in fall. I usually set out short-season plants in the middle of February or March for a late spring harvest. Then I usually seed both short- and long-season varieties indoors in early June and set them out in the middle of July. The short-season plants will mature in late summer or fall, and the long-season ones sometime between December and March. Either may mature earlier or later depending on the weather and the variety.

Broccoli plants that have stunted will bear small heads. The diameter of the main stem of a broccoli plant determines the size of the head it will be able to form. You can also judge if your plants have stunted by measuring their height when first heads form. Short-season varieties should be about 1 1/2 feet tall, and long season ones often exceed 3 feet, with a 4-foot spread.

The Harvest   Cut broccoli when the head stops enlarging and its flower buds are still tightly closed. If the variety is a sprouter (as most are), you can cut the stem several inches below the head and smaller heads will form from the base of the remaining leaves. You can keep cutting these heads, which become smaller and smaller, for months. I once cut a sprouter for a year and a half, just to see how long I could do it. Most of that time it yielded a large handful of very small sprouts twice a week, enough to add to a casserole or to stir-fry. It made more during cool spells and less when the weather turned warm. Remember not to let the flowers open on a plant kept for side

MUSTARD FAMILY

Many of our most common vegetables are members of the mustard family, *Brassicaceae*. (It is sometimes called the cabbage family.) Although the family members differ somewhat in leaf shape and general form, you can see that they are related if you study their flowers, which are cruciform or shaped like a cross.

The mustard family includes the cole crops—broccoli, brussels sprouts, cabbage, cauliflower, collards, kale, kohlrabi, and flowering kale—all of which belong to the same species. The family also includes arugula, cress, horseradish, mustard, radish, and turnip. All mustard-family plants thrive in cool weather. Although they tolerate slightly alkaline soil, they grow best when the soil pH is 6 to 6.8. They need ample water and plenty of nitrogen, calcium, and potassium.

Mustard-family crops are the ones most likely to be attacked by pests in local gardens, but there are effective controls for most of the pests and the harvest is well worth the effort. Common pests of mustard-family plants include aphids, cabbage loopers, cabbage maggots, cutworms, earwigs, imported cabbageworms, slugs, snails, and powdery mildew. In some areas clubroot, a fungus disease, poses a problem.

The big four cole crops—broccoli, brussels sprouts, cabbage, and cauliflower—grow well throughout our region and during most of the year. In fact, one or more of these crops can be harvested every month of the year. Their smooth, water-repellent leaves help them resist decay in our cool, damp weather. They are large plants, requiring 1 to 4 square feet per plant, depending on the variety.

Since cole crops often perform badly in hot weather, breeders have created small, early season varieties. In hot-summer areas they are often planted so that they will mature before the summer heat hits. We can also benefit from these quick varieties, planting them in spring, early fall, or—in microclimates with the greatest ocean influence—right through the summer. The larger, late-season varieties don't succeed in much of the United States, but they are ideal for our mild winters. They are the preferred varieties in England and other parts of Europe that have cool summers and mild winters similar to ours.

The big four cole crops are usually grown from transplants about six weeks old. When seed packets or catalogs give the "days to harvest" for these crops, note that the figures do not include the approximately six weeks to grow the transplants.

It is important to avoid stunting cole crops. A stunted plant produces an undersized crop—a wee head of broccoli or a few tiny brussels sprouts. Stunting follows a period of stopped growth due to cold, heat, lack of water, low soil fertility, or delayed transplanting. Cabbage is the least sensitive to these stresses and broccoli a little more so. Brussels sprouts and the prima donna cauliflower are probably best left until you have succeeded with one of the easier cole crops, although you can't rule out beginner's luck.

Crucifer flower

sprouts, since they will reduce sprout production. It's easy to overlook flower stems when you are harvesting side sprouts, so make a point of searching for them and snapping them off.

Some broccoli varieties do not make side sprouts. When you cut off the heading stalk, no more heads will form. You may be able to prolong the harvest of nonsprouting broccoli by cutting the outer spears first. Those nearer the center will continue to grow and you can pick several times before cutting the central stem. A catalog description usually tells you if a broccoli is a sprouter but rarely mentions if it's not. Some people would say that a nonsprouting broccoli is a green or purple cauliflower, but a nonsprouter like 'Romanesco' seems more like broccoli to me.

Varieties The most commonly sold broccoli varieties are short-season sprouting ones, such as 'Calabrise' or 'De Cicco', and they are fine choices. Also look for plants or seeds of new hybrids, such as 'Packman' or 'Premium Crop', that have been bred to increase the size of their heads. Look for long-season sprouters in seed catalogs. 'Shogun' and 'Umpqua Dark Green' grow into fall and make large central heads followed by smaller side shoots. 'Purple Sprouting' and 'White Sprouting' overwinter, making many small heads after a small central one. (The heads of 'White Sprouting' are light green.)

Romanesco is a long-season, nonsprouting type. In its nonhybrid form, it makes huge chartreuse heads of pointed spears that can be harvested from the outside, bit by bit. 'Minaret', a hybrid romanesco, has 5-inch heads. For my money, the non-hybrid is better, as each plant makes a larger crop. (Careful, Minaret isn't always identified, but the head size gives it away.)

Most broccoli varieties should thrive here, so try whatever sounds interesting. There is a continuum between broccoli and cauliflower, with some non-sprouting purple cauliflowers looking a lot like broccoli, and a broccoli-cauliflower hybrid looking like green cauliflower.

Pests Broccoli is subject to the usual mustard-family pests (see previous page). Aphids can be particularly troublesome if they get into the developing heads.

Sources
Broccoli seed:
    Short-season sprouting varieties: Widely available
    Long season sprouting varieties:
        Umpqua: ABL, TERR
        Shogun F_1: TERR
        Purple sprouting: ABL, CG, OBG, SOC, T&M
        White sprouting: OBG
    Long-season nonsprouting varieties:
        Romanesco: ABL, NGN, SB,
        Romanesco Minaret F_1: CG, JSS, OBG, TERR

COUNTING BACKWARDS FOR BRUSSELS SPROUTS

Plant brussels sprouts so that the crop begins to produce around the first expected frost. In San Francisco that's December 1. By then, the combination of cold weather and short days effectively slows growth, even if there is no frost. To calculate a transplanting date for a long-season variety that takes 150 days to mature, count back 150 days, or five months, from the first frost date. Five months before December 1 is July 1. Count back another six weeks—to May 15—for the last date to start seeds. Similar calculations for a short-season variety that takes 90 days to mature result in a last transplanting date of September 1 and a last seeding date of July 15.

Brussels sprouts

BRUSSELS SPROUTS

Brassica oleracea
Gemmifera Group
Mustard Family ❖ *Cruciferae*

These miniature cabbages grow up the stem of the plant, giving the impression of a plant creature from Mars. This crop thrives everywhere in our region. If you grew up eating (and hating) brussels sprouts that were picked too mature or boiled too long, give them another chance. Steam fresh sprouts until they are just fork-tender, then serve them with butter or a small dollop of a dipping sauce made from mayonnaise and soy sauce.

In addition to being a welcome winter crop, this big four cole crop is fun to harvest. The sprouts make a satisfying snap when you dislodge them from the sturdy stem with your thumb. It takes willpower not to harvest them all at once.

Growing Instructions See page 183 for general growing requirements for mustard-family crops. It is best to set out brussels sprouts transplants in late spring to midsummer so that, like late broccoli, they will mature into fall or winter. Unless your garden is very foggy, don't set out transplants any earlier, even if you see them in the nursery. Seedlings set out in March or April tend to produce small, strong-flavored sprouts.

Short-season varieties take 85 to 100 days from transplanting. They are sometimes called dwarf varieties, since they aren't as tall as long-season types, which take 100 to 150 days to produce. For a winter crop, seed long-season types in April or May and short-season types in June or July. Because the weather is warm when you sow this crop, you can start plants either in containers indoors or in a seeding bed in the garden.

Transplant short-season varieties to stand 12 to 15 inches apart and long-season ones 15 to 24 inches apart. If your location is windy or the plants begin to grow sideways, drive a 4-foot bamboo or redwood stake into the ground near each plant and tie the plant to it.

The Harvest Brussels sprouts can be harvested for two to four months, because they mature a few at a time from the bottom of the stem up. To get enough sprouts for a meal, pick a few from several plants. As each sprout matures, the leaf beneath it turns yel-low and eventually drops. When you pick the sprouts, pull off that leaf and any other yellowing leaves.

Sometimes it is hard to tell when sprouts are ready for picking. They should be like mature tiny cabbages—firm and even a bit shiny on top. The first ones to mature are usually smaller than the sprouts that will develop higher on the stem. A common error is to wait for the lowest sprouts to get bigger. You will know you waited too long if they begin to open. Discard any that open and pick the sprouts on the next three inches of stem. They will be ready to eat.

You may find that none of the sprouts get very big if the plant has stunted. Once you realize that this has happened, don't wait too long to harvest the small tasty sprouts. Keep checking their growth and pick any sprouts that haven't enlarged for a week or two. Try a different strategy when you grow brussels sprouts next year—perhaps choosing an-other variety, changing the planting date, adding more organic matter to the soil, or fertilizing or watering more often in late summer.

Varieties Most varieties should do well here. I have had good success with 'Early Dwarf Danish' and 'Valiant,' both of which produce plenty of fla-vorful sprouts. Try these and others until you find your own favorites. 'Rubine' has red sprouts that, like their larger cousin, red cabbage, hold their color when cooked. They are dramatic in the gar-den and on the table, though on my plants they were small and borne wide apart on the stems.

Pests A hazard of leaving sprouts on the stem too long is that aphids may get into them. The longer you allow the aphids to build up on the plant, the harder they are to eliminate. The best course of action is to spray them off with a strong jet of water and to harvest in a timely manner. The problem should lessen as cool fall days kill many of the aphids. The crop is also susceptible to all of the common mustard-family pests (see page 183).

Sources
Brussels sprouts seed:
Short-season variety:
    Prince Marvel F$_1$: CG, GG, TERR, PS, VBS
Mid-season variety:
    Valiant: SGS
Red variety:
    Rubine: GG, OBG, TERR, SB, VBS

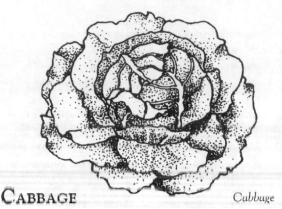

Cabbage

CABBAGE

Brassica oleracea
Capitata Group
Mustard Family ❖ *Cruciferae*

Cabbage heads are not much to look at in the produce market, but a maturing cabbage nested in a wide ring of unfurling leaves is one of the prettiest sights in a vegetable garden. If plain flat-leaved green cabbage is pretty, a plant with purple or savoyed (crinkled) leaves is spectacular. Sure you can buy cabbage cheap, but you don't have the pleasure of watching it grow! And freshly harvested cabbage is so sweet and crisp that I often cut a wedge and eat it right there in the garden. Fortunately, cabbage is in its element in our cool, foggy weather and can be grown nearly the year around in all parts of the region.

Growing Instructions Cabbage is the easiest of the big four cole crops. (See Mustard Family on page 183 for general growing requirements.) Still, although you can set out cabbage transplants during most months, doing so from November through January is risky. The plants won't be killed by frost, but they will grow very slowly during frigid weather and may become permanently stunted. They may also suffer snail and slug damage if they grow too slowly to replace damaged leaves.

Some cabbage varieties make a quick crop, whereas others mature more slowly. Short-season varieties are rated at 50 to 70 days from transplant size, midseason varieties at 70 to 90 days, and long-season varieties at 90 to 150 days. The long-season types are worthwhile planting out in June or July for harvests from December through March. Some of the seed catalogs have charts showing the best time to plant certain varieties in mild-winter areas.

I often start short-season or midseason cabbage seeds in the middle of November and set out a few of the plants in January. If the weather is mild and sunny, these plants will produce my first spring cabbage crop. I reserve some seedlings to plant in February or March, just in case the first ones don't make it. (I make sure the reserve seedlings are in 4-inch pots and that they get enough fertilizer and water so they won't stunt.) Although you can seed cabbage most of the year, you probably won't need enough to warrant starting plants every month. In addition to the November sowing, I often start cabbage in April or May for transplanting in June or July, and sometimes I start more in July for transplanting in August or September.

A cabbage plant produces a wide ring of open leaves before it forms a head. Thus each plant needs a space three to four times the diameter of the mature head. Plant small types 12 inches apart and larger ones 18 to 30 inches apart. You can allow the leaf tips of mature plants to touch, but if you crowd them much more your crop will suffer.

The head will split open if it grows too fast or the watering is uneven. Although splitting doesn't affect the flavor, it ruins the leaves for recipes like stuffed cabbage. As the spring days warm, keep the soil moist but don't overwater. If a head is mature and you aren't ready to harvest it, grasp the plant and give it a one-quarter turn. This will break some roots and slow the growth of the plant, making a split in the head less likely.

The Harvest When a cabbage head feels firm, it is ready to harvest, even if it hasn't reached full size. Once a head is ready, it can usually be left unharvested for up to several weeks depending on the variety. If the top of the head looks tight and shiny, however, don't wait much longer. Read the seed catalog descriptions to find out which varieties will stand longer in the garden before being harvested. To harvest the head, cut the stem with a sharp knife.

Varieties I've had good luck with all the varieties I've tried. 'Savonarch' is a new favorite that is reliable and tasty whether started in winter or summer. 'January King' is exceptionally beautiful in the garden. Its frilly, savoyed leaves have lavender highlights.

Read the seed catalog descriptions to learn the mature weight of a cabbage variety you are thinking of growing. Usually, but not always, the long-season ones make larger heads. If your household is small, you may not want to grow a large-headed type. I once grew a 15-pound head—and believe me, that's a lot of cabbage!

COLESLAW

I used to think this dish was called "cold slaw." Of course the word is really "cole," which derives from the Anglo Saxon word *cal* or *cawl*, meaning cabbage. Homemade coleslaw can be quite a different matter than the soupy, sweet stuff you get at a fast-food restaurant.

2 cups finely sliced cabbage
1/4 cup coarsely grated carrot
1/4 cup coarsely grated cucumber
1/4 cup coarsely grated or diced
   bell pepper
1/4 cup thinly sliced onion or leek
   (optional)
1 clove garlic, minced

Dressing
3 tablespoons brown sugar
3 tablespoons red wine vinegar
1 tablespoon cold water
2 tablespoons vegetable oil
1/2 teaspoon salt

Slice or grate the vegetables. I suppose a food processor would help, but you can make short enough work of it with a sharp knife and a coarse cheese grater. Peel the cucumber if it is a purchased one, since they usually are waxed. Mix the vegetable ingredients in a large bowl.

Combine the dressing ingredients and pour over the slaw. Toss to cover with dressing. Serve immediately or refrigerate several hours or even overnight before serving. Serves six.

Variation Instead of the vinaigrette dressing, use a dressing made of 1/2 teaspoon dried dill weed (or 2 teaspoons finely chopped fresh dill), 1 teaspoon cider vinegar, 1/3 cup prepared mayonnaise, and salt and freshly ground black pepper to taste.

Pests A cabbage plant should be examined regularly for insect pests. It is especially important to do this when the plant is young and also just as the head is beginning to form. The leaves and developing head may be attacked by aphids, cabbage loopers, cutworms, earwigs, imported cabbageworms, slugs, and snails. Generally, these pests do less damage as a cabbage head gets larger and firmer, although cutworms can burrow a short distance into a mature head. Damage by aphids, cabbage loopers, cutworms, and imported cabbageworms decreases in fall and may stop between October and March. Savoy and red cabbage varieties are more resistant to imported cabbageworms and cabbage loopers than are plain green cabbage varieties. Although you should keep leaf-chewing pests to a minimum, be aware that damage can look worse than it really is. A plant may look horribly chewed even though the head is still almost entirely intact. Cabbage is also susceptible to cabbage root maggots and to the fungus disease clubroot.

Sources
Cabbage seed:
Short-season varieties:
   Early Jersey Wakefield: ABL, CG, JG, JSS, NGN, T&M
   Copenhagen Market: SB
   Salarite F$_1$: NGN, PS
   Stonehead F$_1$: NGN, PTS
   Ruby Ball F$_1$: NGN, PTS, TERR, T&M
Midseason varieties:
   Savonarch F$_1$: TERR
   Savoy King F$_1$: NGN, T&M
Long-season variety:
   January King: ABL, DD, SB, TERR

STUFFED CABBAGE LEAVES

Variations of this dish are made throughout Eastern Europe.

1 head cabbage
1 pound ground beef or ground lamb
1 small onion, chopped
1 egg
1 cup cooked rice
1/2 teaspoon paprika
2 tablespoons chopped parsley
2 8-ounce cans tomato sauce (or 2 cups Quick Homemade Tomato
    Sauce, see page 346)
1/4 cup water
1 lemon, very thinly sliced (optional)

Carefully remove the leaves from the head of cabbage, trying to keep them intact. Start by cutting across the base of the outermost leaf, then gently pry it off, lifting the bottom first, then working the top loose. Repeat until you have 12 unbroken leaves. (Use the remaining cabbage and any badly torn leaves for another dish.) Cut a shallow V at the base of the good leaves, removing the thick stem end. Steam or parboil the leaves briefly, until flexible, but not fork tender.

In a medium bowl, thoroughly mix the ground beef, onion, egg, cooked rice, and paprika. Divide the meat mixture into 12 equal portions. To make the rolls, place a portion of the meat in the middle of a cabbage leaf. Fold the ends of the leaf over the stuffing, then fold in the sides, overlapping in the center. Fasten the roll with a wooden toothpick. Repeat to make 12 stuffed leaves.

Place the rolls in a casserole, forming a single layer, and pour tomato sauce and water over them. Arrange a lemon slice on each roll. Bake at 350°F for 40 minutes or until the cabbage is fork tender. Serves four.

CABBAGE, FLOWERING (SEE KALE)

CACTUS, PRICKLY PEAR (OR INDIAN FIG)

Opuntia ficus-indica or *Nopalea cochenillifera*
Cactus Family ❖ *Cactaceae*

Here is a crop that thrives in poor soil with little water. Great, you are probably thinking, but how can anybody eat it with all those prickles? I admit to an occasional ouch, but this low-maintenance crop is worth it. A common vegetable in Mexican cuisine, young prickly pear pads are cooked and used hot in egg, cheese, and vegetable dishes. The cooked pads are also served cold in salads. The canned nopalitos sold in the Mexican food section of the grocery store pale next to fresh ones picked from your own plant. In addition to the pads, prickly pear fruit (tunas) are eaten raw or cooked.

Although edible cactus is not a crop to interplant with standard vegetables, it may be just the thing for a corner of your garden. This large, striking perennial makes a lot of food for little work. It grows well throughout the region, isn't fussy about soil as long as the drainage is reasonably good, requires very little water, and is almost pest-free.

Growing Instructions Although prickly pear can be grown from seed, starting it from a pad is much faster. However, locating either seeds or pads may be difficult. Prickly cactus is rarely sold with other cacti, since it is not considered an ornamental. And it isn't grown often enough as a vegetable to be marketed by nurseries with the other vegetables. Still, persistence should pay off. If a local nursery doesn't stock rooted pads, ask if it can order them. If not, try to find a gardener who will give you pads, or ask a farmer who brings fresh nopalitos to a farmer's market. Friends in Southern California or the Central Valley may have or know of a plant from which you can get a start. The California Rare Fruit Growers (see Appendix V) may also have pads. If you get unrooted pads, start with two or three, since pads sometimes decay before they root.

Pads sold for eating are usually too young to plant and are apt to wilt and die instead of growing. You stand a good chance of success with mature pads, no matter when you get them. Pads cut in summer will probably root before winter, and pads cut in winter (a good time to prune and shape prickly pear cactus) should root in spring.

To root a pad some gardeners advocate burying two-thirds of the pad in soil, either in a temporary bed in the garden or in a pot. Others advise just laying the pad on the soil surface making sure the whole surface is in contact with soil. Both methods work. Even though well-amended soil isn't necessary later, adding organic matter to the temporary bed will help the developing roots grow better. Keep the soil moist, but don't overwater. Roots should form in a couple of months, but it won't hurt to allow extra time if the unrooted pad still looks healthy.

When a pad is well rooted, plant it in its permanent site. Since the cactus will eventually reach 6 to 8 feet high, choose the north side of an area suitable for growing sun-loving vegetables and flowers. Give it a minimum of 5 square feet—the smallest you will be able to keep the plant, even with careful pruning. Locate it where you will have maximum access for harvesting and pruning.

Once the plant is established, it will need very little moisture. I never water the soil under my prickly pear, since I am already watering nearby soil. In a very dry site, you can give it a couple of waterings in summer, but don't overdo it or the plant may rot.

Prickly pear plants enlarge slowly for the first few years. Every year one to several pads will grow from each of last year's pads until finally you have a sizeable plant. From then on, you must control the plant or it might develop into a huge, impenetrable thicket up to 18 feet high. Although that may be acceptable in a large garden, it isn't usually welcome in a small urban yard.

Control the growth of prickly pear by pruning. You can eat your prunings if you cut the pads when they are at the right stage. Be selective when you harvest: Remove wayward growth, crowded pads, or pads growing into the center of the plant. Eventually you may find that harvesting won't get rid of all the excess growth and that you will have to do additional pruning. When this happens, just lop off the unwanted pads at any time before they begin to bud again in spring.

Prickly pear with young pads and flower buds

The Harvest The year's first young pads may be ready to harvest as early as April, when they are at least 6 inches long. Some people won't eat them if they are more than 8 inches long, but I have found them tasty and tender as long as they are still a brighter green than the mature pads. The peak of the harvest is usually May and June, although a few new pads may develop later in summer. Use leather gloves or wrap a rag around the pad, then either snap the pad off at the base or cut it with a sharp knife.

You will notice that some buds stay small and cylindrical instead of flattening out. These flower buds open in summer, revealing cheery yellow flowers. The base enlarges and in late summer and fall forms fruit, which usually ripens to a bright red but may be paler. The interior is juicy and has many seeds. The surface is usually studded with tiny prickles, so beware when picking or eating.

I suspect that sweet fruit is a result of climate and genetics. I got my starter pads from an abandoned plant growing in San Francisco, and my plant has always made rather bland fruit. Try to get your

NOPALITOS IN TOMATO SAUCE

Nopalitos are strips of nopales, the prickly pear cactus pads. The fresh cactus has a slightly gelatinous quality. I don't mind it at all, but if you find this unpleasant, boil the cactus strips for 10 to 15 minutes, and rinse them several times in fresh water before adding them to the onion in the skillet. Serve this dish with Black Bean Tostadas (page 110).

1 or 2 pads young prickly pear cactus
2 tablespoons oil (olive oil is good)
1 small onion, chopped
1 8-ounce can tomato sauce (or 1 cup Quick Homemade Tomato
    Sauce, see page 346)
1/2 or more pickled or fresh jalapeño pepper, finely chopped

Cut the spines from the cactus pads, using a sharp knife, or, if you are good at such things, you can probably pinch out the spine-bearing bumps faster with your fingernails. Wash the pads. Cut them into 1/2 - by 2-inch strips. Parboil them if desired.

    Heat the oil in a skillet and sauté the onion until tender but not browned. Add the nopalitos and cook over medium heat, stirring occasionally, until they turn from bright to dull green. It will take about 5 minutes. Turn heat to low. Add the tomato sauce and jalapeño and cook a few more minutes, until the cactus is tender. Serves three or four as a vegetable.

---

starter pads from a plant that you know has sweet fruit, then cross your fingers and hope that the fruit will be equally sweet where you live. Wear leather gloves to pick ripe fruit. Roll it on firm, dry ground to remove the prickles. Wash it, cut it in half, and spoon out the pulp. In Mexico the fruit is eaten raw, cooked in desserts and preserves, and used to make a fermented drink.

Varieties and Related Species Edible plants of two different genera, *Nopalea* and *Opuntia*, are known as prickly pear. They aren't easy to tell apart, the main difference between them being that *Nopalea* has showier flowers. The most commonly grown species is *N. cochenillifera*, which in its native habitat attracts the cochineal insect. This is a kind of mealybug that produces a red dye used in cosmetics.

    The most commonly grown *Opuntia* is *O. ficus-indica*, which has sprawling as well as upright varieties. 'Burbank's Spineless Cactus,' a variety developed by Luther Burbank, offers obvious advantages but it may be hard to locate.

Pests I am not aware of any serious local pests of prickly pear cactus. The older pads, which lose most of their spines, provide a smooth, flat surface on which snails like to rest in the daytime. Although they may scrape at the pads, they don't do much damage. The main problem is that they attack nearby plants. To keep your cactus from becoming a snail haven, prune the center so that you can reach in to handpick snails.

Sources
Prickly pear cactus starts: See Growing Instructions above.

CARDOON (OR CARDONI)
Cynara cardunculus
Sunflower Family ❖ *Compositae*

Cardoon resembles its close relative artichoke. However, the part of cardoon that is eaten is the tender leaf midrib rather than the flower bud. Cardoon has been a favorite vegetable in the Mediterranean region at least as long as the artichoke and maybe longer. It is a favorite among Italians, who call it cardoni.

Growing Instructions Cardoon has requirements very similar to those of artichoke. Regular watering produces tender, mild flavored leafstalks. Cardoon does well in foggy weather, although it doesn't need cool days to produce a crop.

Although cardoon is a perennial, gardeners usually grow it as an annual to avoid having to provide space for the mature plant, which can reach 6 to 8 feet high and wide. Plants grown as perennials need the same careful site selection and preparation as artichoke, whereas those removed after one season can be mixed with other crops. As an annual, cardoon will grow in any organic, moderately fertile garden soil.

You can grow cardoon from a rootstock if you can find someone with a mature clump. The best time to divide the clump is early spring. Just dig it up and cut sections with roots and young shoots on them.

Cardoon can also be grown from seed. The plants should be up in February if you sow seeds in late fall. You can also sow seeds from the middle of February to April for a summer harvest, or in early July for a fall and winter harvest. Plant the seeds 1/2 to 1 inch deep and 2 inches apart in groups of five or six. Space the groups 2 to 3 feet apart if the plants are to be grown as annuals, or 5 to 6 feet apart if they are to be grown as perennials. When the seedlings are 2 to 3 inches high, thin to the best one in each group. Be wary of overplanting, since each plant will make a large harvest.

The Harvest A plant should bear in four months or sooner. You can begin to harvest the outer leaves when they are 1 to 2 feet long. For a larger proportion of tender stalks, blanch the plant when it reaches 3 feet high. To blanch cardoon, secure the leaves with string and fasten heavy brown paper or burlap around the plant. Pile soil around the base of the plant, then uncover it in about a month and cut the entire blanched plant at the base.

If you have space to allow the plant to mature, harvest only the young outer leaves and stop cutting when the plant gets over 3 feet high. You will get a tower of striking gray-green leaves, topped in fall by flowering stalks bearing small artichokelike flowers. Cardoon will die back in late fall, then sprout again in early spring. (Clean up the dead leaves and cut out dead stalks during the winter.)

Since the leaves are bitter, remove all traces of leaf from the stalks. Cardoon is always cooked. The stalks may take from twenty to fifty minutes to become tender, depending on their size and whether the plant was blanched. After the stalks have been steamed or boiled, cut sections can be served hot in a butter sauce, breaded and deep fried, or marinated in an Italian dressing and served cold in antipasto or salads. If you have never tasted cardoon, buy some from a produce store before you decide to grow it.

Varieties Although several cardoon varieties are available in Europe, the cardoon sold in seed catalogs in this country doesn't have a variety name.

Pests If you have trouble with the artichoke plume moth, that is a good reason not to let a cardoon plant mature near your artichoke planting. The plume moth caterpillar enjoys cardoon plants just as much as it does artichokes.

Earlier this century cardoon itself became a pest in an area at the edge of the region covered by this book. It had escaped to cover thousands of acres near Benicia on the Carquinez Strait. Although it has been controlled to some extent, there are still some infested areas. It looks so remarkably like artichoke that one local gardener collected the seeds, planted them, and grew the crop for a year before realizing his error.

Sources
Cardoon seed: CG, DD, GG, NGN, RCS, RH, SB, TERR

CARROT
Daucus carota
Carrot Family ❖ *Umbelliferae*

Carrots are a productive crop throughout the region. By sowing seeds from February through July (or even later in protected areas), you should be able to have carrots to pull almost every day of the year. Carrots grow best in sandy or fine loamy soil, often forming forked or otherwise misshapen roots in rocky or clay soil. If you don't have the best soil for carrots, here are a couple of strategies to try. Grow short carrot varieties, which need to push away only a little soil. Or improve your soil in just a small area and grow carrots there. Sieve out all rocks more than 1/4 inch in diameter to a depth of 6 inches. Then spread a 6-inch layer of compost or other organic amendment (but not fresh manure) and dig it in, mixing it with the sieved soil. You should be able to grow medium-sized carrots nicely in this bed.

Growing Instructions   Carrots have traditionally been grown from seeds sown in place. Although the plants may survive ordinary transplanting methods, the roots will not develop properly afterward. But now a special device called a Shadowbox, which was invented by a local gardener, allows you to transplant carrots successfully.

Sow carrot seeds from February though June for spring and summer harvests, and in July for fall and winter harvests. A crop sown later than July is a gamble. If the site is protected or fall is mild, the carrots may mature. Otherwise, they may never get very big and just go to seed in spring.

Carrot seeds can be sown in single-file rows, wide rows, or small blocks. The sowing depth—from 1/4 to 3/4 inch—depends on your soil type and the weather. For example, plant the seeds closer to the surface in clay soil during cold weather and deeper in sandy soil during warm weather. Carrots are usually sown thicker than needed and then thinned. Beginning gardeners are usually surprised to find out that carrots are tricky to get started. A tongue-in-cheek maxim is that if you sow carrots thickly they will all come up, but if you sow them thinly you'll be lucky to get any at all.

Carrot seeds take 10 to 17 days to germinate, which can seem like a very long time. You can hurry germination a bit by soaking the seeds in water several hours or overnight before you plant them.

Presprouting the seeds (see page 47) may improve your chances of success.

Another useful technique is to cover the carrot seedbed with some-

Carrot
seedling
(2x life size)

Swine cress
seedling
(2x life size)

thing that will hold moisture and prevent the soil from crusting. You may want to cover the seeds with sieved compost instead of soil, especially during warm weather. (Don't use bone-dry compost, which will be hard to moisten when you sprinkle the seedbed.) Another option is to lay a floating row cover or toilet paper on top of the soil or the sieved compost. You can water right through either material. Remove the covering once the seedlings are up.

It's easy to forget to keep the carrot bed watered after all your other plants have long since come up. To help you remember where your carrot bed is while you wait for something to appear, sow a few radish seeds mixed with the carrot seeds. The radishes will come up quickly, marking the place to water the carrots. The radish seedlings will also loosen the soil surface for the more delicate carrot plants. And, conveniently, when the fast-growing radishes are ready to harvest, the carrots will be ready for thinning.

The carrot seedlings are so tiny that they are easy to miss in the first few weeks, especially if they become covered by quick-growing weed seedlings. Try the weed presprouting technique described on page 95 to avoid this problem. A few weed seedlings, notably swine cress (see page 111) and cotula (see page 104), look very much like carrot seedlings. I once saw a garden in which a mat of swine cress completely covered what was to have been the carrot patch. But they are possible to tell apart: Carrot leaves always stand upright, whereas cotula and swine cress leaves lie flatter to the ground.

Once the carrot plants are about 2 inches high, they usually need to be thinned. You can wait until there are fingerlings and eat the largest ones as you thin, or you can ruthlessly pull the smallest plants so that the remaining ones stand 1-1/2 to 2 inches apart. With the first method you probably get more carrots to eat, but with the second you get bigger carrots faster.

All this worrying over getting carrots up and thinned will cease as soon as you have a little experience. Once you get the knack, carrot are an immensely satisfying crop, maturing quickly into plump, delicious roots that can be washed off and munched on the spot.

The Harvest   Carrots are mature two to three months after the seeds are sown. They can be eaten young as baby carrots, but they usually get sweeter as they get larger, attaining maximum sweetness when they are close to their full size. To check for maturity, brush aside the soil around the stem and see how wide the shoulders are. Pull up one of the larger roots and taste it. Seed catalogs and seed packets will show you the mature shape of the variety you are growing, but generally the bottom end of a mature carrot should be filled out rather than narrowly tapered.

Carrots that have overwintered should be pulled by February, because they will soon put all of their energy into producing tough seed stalks. On second thought, let one or two go to seed. The flowers attract helpful hover flies, and everyone seems to enjoy the rare sight of carrot flowers. They look very much like the flowers of wild carrot, or Queen-Anne's-lace, which are sometimes added to florist bouquets.

Varieties Most carrot varieties will do well here, but your soil may limit your choices. If your soil is rocky or a very heavy clay, start with an almost round variety, such as 'Kundulus' or 'Planet,' or any other very short type. If you have reasonably loose soil try 'Nantes' or 'Chantenay' (or related varieties), all of which make good medium-sized roots. Very long carrots, such as the commercial 'Imperator,' need deep, loose, well-amended soil and are not for a garden with poor soil or one in which you have just begun to improve the soil. 'Fly Away' is said to resist carrot rust fly, worth a try, but in my one trial, I didn't find it to have much less damage than other carrots.

Pests The parsleyworm, the larva of the black swallowtail butterfly, will occasionally munch on a carrot plant, but rarely in large enough numbers to cause significant damage. I see one or two of these smooth-skinned bright green, black, and yellow caterpillars a year. I either ignore them or move them over to a wild fennel plant, which they also enjoy.

The most serious local pest of carrots is the carrot rust fly. This spoiler lays eggs that hatch into maggots, which eat their way into the carrots. The only way to exclude the flies is to cover the plants with a floating row cover or a cage made of window screening. The flies are less active during cool weather. The only times my carrots fall victim to this pest is when they have been left in the ground too long in summer. If they get chewed, I just cut away the damaged parts and use the rest. Predatory nematodes, released after soil warms in spring,

will help control carrot rust fly.

Sources
Carrot seed:
Round and very short varieties:
Kundulus: T&M
Marche de Paris: GG
Parmex: CG
Thumbelina: BG, JSS, NGN, PS, PTS, TERR
Medium carrot varieties:
Chanteney (and related varieties): Widely available
Nantes (and related varieties): Widely available
Long carrot varieties:
Touchon: ABL, CG, JG, NGN
Imperator (and related varieties): JSS, SB, SGS, VBS
Fly Away carrot: TERR, T&M

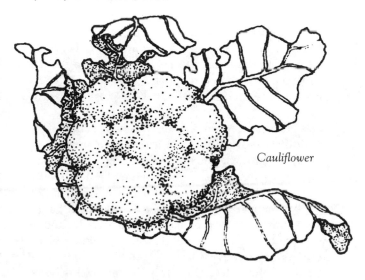

Cauliflower

CAULIFLOWER

Brassica oleracea
Botrytis Group
Mustard Family ❖ *Cruciferae*

When you first glimpse a pristine white head of cauliflower forming deep in the wide nest of leaves, you will know that this crop is worth the wait. Although cauliflower requires attention to timing and growing conditions, it is a reliable crop once you catch on to its needs.

Growing Instructions Like the other big four cole crops, cauliflower thrives in cool weather, but stunts and forms a small head if weather is too cold while it is growing. Cauliflower may also stunt if it is in a pot too long before it is transplanted, or is lacking in nutrients or water as it grows. In fact, cauliflower is so prone to stunting, that there is a special name for it—buttoning. (See Mustard family, on page 183 for general growing requirements for cole crops.)

The short-season types of cauliflower, which are rated at 45 to 70 days from transplanting, can be seeded between January and April for harvest between April and July. Try seeding the long-season types (70 to 200 days or more) anytime from June through August for harvest between fall and late winter. Allow 18 to 24 inches between plants.

Some cauliflower varieties need to be blanched or the sun will discolor the head, usually turning it pinkish. To blanch cauliflower, pull the leaves over the nearly formed head and tie them together. Break the leaves if necessary. Some types are self-blanching—that is, their leaves curl over naturally and shade the developing head. If you forget to blanch a variety that needs it, don't worry because a discolored head usually tastes just as good, although it may be received better at the table if it is blended in a cream soup or a soufflé.

The Harvest A long-season variety can take six months to form a head, and it may take another month or two when it is overwintering. That can seem like a long time. I once watched a neighboring gardener disgustedly pull her huge, seemingly unproductive summer-planted cauliflower plants in January. I interceded as diplomatically as I could, and we were both happy to see the one remaining plant form a fine large head in late March.

The other harvesting error I've noticed is leaving cauliflower heads on too long. As they do with brussels sprouts, gardeners hope that cauliflower heads will reach the size of the largest ones in the grocery stores. You may get heads that big, but smaller ones are more likely. Pick a head whenever it stops enlarging. Otherwise, it will begin to open up and the white florets will send up ungainly flower stalks. Although edible, the stalks are tougher and less flavorful than the head.

Varieties I haven't tried many cauliflower varieties but have had good success with the short-season 'Snow Crown' and the overwintering 'Armado Spring.' 'Snow Crown' matured a medium-sized head right on schedule about three months after seeding—in June from a March sowing and in July from an April sowing. It developed a pink tinge on the surface when the weather turned warm, just as the Territorial Seed Company catalog said it might, but it tasted fine.

Territorial offers several strains of the overwintering 'Armado.' It also offers 'Armado Spring Plus,' a mixture of seven varieties that mature at different times. Seeded in August, the plants are ready to harvest in January through March or even later. The staggered harvests are especially helpful if your family is small.

Try some other varieties, choosing heat-resistant ones for spring and summer harvests, and cold-resistant ones for fall and winter harvests. Purple cauliflower varieties are beautiful and somewhat easier to grow than white ones. Some purple cauliflower seems more broccoli-like to me. Breeders have recently made crosses between broccoli and cauliflower—which are really the same species—and have come up with chartreuse green cauliflower heads.

Pests Cauliflower has the same pests as other members of the mustard family (see page 183). Snails and slugs can make a cauliflower head less appetizing by munching away the surface.

Sources
Cauliflower seed:
Short-season variety:
    Snow Crown F$_1$: CG, JSS, NGN, PTS, TERR, VBS
Long-season variety:
    Armado Spring Plus: TERR
Short-season purple variety:
    Violet Queen: CG, JSS, T&M
Long-season purple variety:
    Purple Cape: DD, OBG, TERR
Short-season chartreuse green variety:
    Cauli-broc: PS
Mid-season chartreuse green variety:
    Alverda: JSS, TERR

CELERIAC (OR CELERY ROOT OR TURNIP-ROOTED CELERY)
Apium graveolens var. *rapaceum*
Carrot Family ❖ *Umbelliferae*

This variety of celery is grown for its globe-shaped taproot instead of its stalks. The root is sweet, has a mild celery flavor, and makes an intriguing salad. It is not grown much in the United States, although it is a popular vegetable in Eastern Europe. Well suited to our entire region, it has similar needs as celery but isn't as fussy.

Growing instructions Plant seeds from April through June to mature into fall. You can also try planting as early as February and as late as August, since celeriac is fairly adaptable. Seed in place or transplant with care to avoid damaging the root.

YEAR-ROUND VEGETABLE CURRY

Whatever the season, there are likely to be vegetables you can use to make this curry. Substitute whatever is available, making sure there are different colors among the ingredients. Rather than a prepared curry powder, this recipe contains a curry blend.

4 cups of vegetables, cut in 1/2-inch to 1-inch pieces (dice them if necessary)
2 teaspoons ground cumin seed
2 teaspoons black mustard seed
2 teaspoons turmeric
1 teaspoon ground coriander seed
1 teaspoon cayenne pepper
2 tablespoons butter or cooking oil
1 cup plain yogurt
1 tablespoon unbleached wheat flour or chick-pea flour

Steam the vegetables until they are just tender. If their cooking times are very different, you can steam the vegetables separately. Measure the spices into a small bowl. Heat the oil in a skillet, and add the spices all at once. Stir well for a minute or so, being careful not to burn them. Add the vegetables to the skillet and stir, heating them through. Add the yogurt and mix it in. Stir in the flour. Bring to a simmer and cook until the sauce has thickened. Serves four as a side dish.

Note: Just use what is available in your garden or try one of the following combinations:

- 1 cup each carrots, potatoes, broccoli, and peas (shelled, or cut-up snap pea pods)
- 1 cup potatoes, 1 cup carrots, and 2 cups green beans
- 1 cup carrots, 1 cup leeks, 1 cup Jerusalem artichokes, and 1 cup (or more, because they cook down) turnip greens
- 1 cup each broccoli, cabbage side shoots, green beans, and zucchini

CHAPATIS

Serve this simple fried Indian bread with the curry.

1/2 cup whole wheat flour
1/2 cup unbleached white flour
1 tablespoon butter, melted
About 3/8 cup warm water

Measure the flours into a medium bowl. Mix in the butter, using your fingers. When it is well blended, add water, a little at a time, mixing it in with your other hand. When you can form a ball of dough that cleans the bowl of flour, stop adding water. Knead the dough for a couple of minutes. If it is sticky, add a bit more flour.

Divide the dough into four balls. Put a bit of flour on a large cutting board and roll each ball of dough out into a thin even round, about 6 inches in diameter.

Heat just a little butter in a skillet. Fry the chapati about 30 seconds on each side, then repeat the procedure so you cook it twice on each side. If necessary, add a little more butter as you cook the chapati. The chapati may puff up as it cooks. If so, press it down with a spatula to flatten out the bulges and keep it in contact with the skillet.

POTATO LEEK SOUP

Have you ever pulled a leek while holding an umbrella? Hint: It is easier if someone else is holding the umbrella. Be sure to put some leeks in your garden so you can enjoy this simple, hearty soup on a cold, rainy, winter day. To make it, you will need one huge leek or two large ones.

2 1/2 cups diced unpeeled potato
2 cups water
2 cups leeks, cut in 1/4-inch slices (at least 2/3 should be the white part)
2 cups milk
Sprinkling of black pepper
1/2 teaspoon salt (optional)
1 tablespoon butter or margarine
1 tablespoon chopped fresh parsley
1/2 cup coarsely grated jack or cheddar cheese
1/4 cup chopped chives (or green onion tops or onion lily tops)

Boil the potatoes in the water until tender, about 15 minutes. Do not drain them. Mash them well in the cooking water, using a potato masher or the bottom of a clean glass. Add the leeks to the potato mixture. If there isn't enough water to cover the leeks, add a bit more, but the mixture should remain quite thick at this stage. Simmer, covered, until the leeks are tender—10 to 15 minutes.

Add the milk. Heat through, stirring occasionally, but don't boil. Stir in pepper, and salt, if desired. Melt the butter on the surface of the soup and sprinkle the parsley over all. Put the grated cheese and chives in separate bowls and pass them, so diners can sprinkle them on the soup as they desire. Serves two to three.

NASTURTIUMS WITH CURRIED CREAM CHEESE

Try this surprise at a picnic or a party. The flower is peppery and the cheese is spicy, but when you bite into the blossom's nectary, it releases a burst of sweetness. Thanks to Caroline Morrison for the recipe for these tasty tidbits.

20 nasturtium blossoms
1/2 cup cream cheese (or low fat cream cheese substitute)
1 teaspoon curry powder

Wash the blossoms and check them over for insects. Set them on paper towels to dry. In a small bowl, mix cream cheese and curry powder well.

Spoon a heaping teaspoon of cheese into each flower, and arrange the blossoms on a platter. If they can't be served immediately, cover them with a damp paper towel and refrigerate.

Plant the seeds 1/8 inch deep. Final spacing between the plants should be 8 to 12 inches. See below for other requirements. Although celeriac is less particular about soil fertility, than celery, it will probably grow larger roots in rich soil.

The Harvest   Encourage bigger roots by pulling soil from the tops of the roots several times as they are enlarging and removing yellowed lower leaves. You can begin to dig up roots when they are about 2 inches in diameter, but it is more common to harvest them when they are 4 or 5 inches across. Besides making a wonderful salad ingredient, celeriac roots can be added to soups, boiled and served hot with butter or a sauce, or mashed with potatoes. Celeriac leaves are strong flavored and the stems tend to be pithy, but they will flavor a soup stock nicely.

If the plants are left in the garden until spring, they will bloom. They become ungainly, growing 4 to 5 feet high, and their roots are too tough to eat though the flowers attract beneficial insects. If a plant forms seed, it will probably reseed itself, adding to the serendipity of next year's harvest.

Varieties   'Alabaster' and 'Prague' are two old, popular open-pollinated varieties, but there are many others including some new European hybrids.

Pests   I've found celeriac to be nearly pest-free. Although late blight doesn't affect celeriac as much as celery, it shouldn't be tolerated since it can live on celeriac waiting for the next celery crop to appear. Pull any plants showing evidence of a virus.

Sources
Celeriac seed: Widely available

CELERY

Apium graveolens var. *dulce*
Carrot Family ❖ *Umbelliferae*

I've had many successes with celery, but I've also had failures. During some winters homegrown celery stalks with peanut butter were a lunch staple. During other years I had to pull most of my crop in midsummer because it was going to seed prematurely or the stalks were bitter and tough. Although celery is a very demanding vegetable, it can produce a crop anywhere in the region.

Wild ancestors of celery were first cultivated in the Middle East, where they were found growing wild in the marshy lowlands. Modern celery is a much larger, milder, and more succulent version of those plants, but it has retained the need for constantly moist, very rich soil.

Celery likes cool, but not cold, weather. Our chilly night temperatures in spring and fall may cause young plants to go to seed before they make full-sized stalks. The safest period to plant out celery seedlings in areas nearest the coast is April through August, when normal night temperatures are at least 49°F. You may have to wait until May in inland locations, where the nights are slightly colder. Other planting times may work, but the crop will run a greater risk of going to seed early because of exposure to cold.

Growing Instructions   Celery can be seeded directly, but it is most often grown from transplanted seedlings. Start seeds indoors in January through March for transplanting into the garden in March through June. Sow the seeds 1/8 inch deep. Move the seedlings to larger containers when they are about four weeks old, then grow them for four to eight more weeks before setting them out. Be sure to give the seedlings ample water and fertilizer when you repot them. (See chart on page 53.)

As an alternative, you can sow seeds in a seedbed in the garden in spring, then transplant the seedlings to a permanent location when they are 2 to 3 inches high. Celery seeds will germinate in as little as a week at 60° to 70°F, but they can take up to three weeks in cooler weather. You may want to use the same techniques that were suggested for germinating carrot seeds (see page 192).

Set transplants 8 to 12 inches apart in organic, fertile soil (celery would like pure compost if it could get it). Celery may be the crop on which you use the most fertilizer. Fertilize at transplanting time, and give a booster of liquid fertilizer every two to three weeks during active growth. You will improve your chances for a large crop of crisp celery by keeping the soil constantly moist. Add a thick mulch to conserve moisture, especially if your soil is sandy. The stalks become pithy when the plants dry out.

The Harvest   You can begin to pick the outer stalks of a young plant when it is 6 to 8 inches high. Continue to harvest outer stalks until the plant begins to go to seed. Or you can harvest the whole plant at any time. Celery leaves contain more vitamins than the stalks. Use them, either fresh or as dried flakes, to flavor soups or to add in small amounts to salads.

Traditionally, celery was blanched to produce pale, tender stems, but this is rarely done today because modern cooks know that blanching drains vitamins. However, you may want to try blanching to rescue a crop that has become tough and strong flavored. To blanch celery, tie heavy brown paper around the plant, leaving a few inches of leaf at the top. Blanching takes about two weeks.

Varieties   The most commonly grown varieties today were developed to stay tender and mild without blanching. These include 'Golden Self-Blanching' as well as the 'Utah' types and their derivatives, such as the 'Crystal Jumbo' strains. (For celery varieties developed for seasoning, see Chinese Celery on page 280.)

Pests   Pick over celery for slugs and snails, which will eat holes in the stalks. Celery is susceptible to a number of other pests, including aphids, cabbage loopers, cutworms, leafhoppers, leafminers, parsleyworms, and spider mites. Luckily, I haven't had any serious problems with any of them.

Several diseases are also possible, although I have only seen one—late blight. A fungus disease occurring in fall and winter, it begins as spots on the leaves but can lead to the death of plants. Pink rot is another fungus disease affecting celery. It begins with a soft watery rot low on the outer stems, then moves up. A white to pinkish cottony mold with small black dots develops next, turning the affected parts of the plant a light pink. The disease is more common when the plants are overwatered, which can easily happen in poorly amended clay soil. Prevent pink rot by working in plenty of organic matter and watering carefully. Remove infected plants as soon as you see symptoms of pink rot.

Celery is also susceptible to several viruses spread by aphids. Since there is no cure, remove diseased plants and control aphids in the future.

Sources
Celery seed:
Golden Self-blanching: DD, NGN, OBG, PTS, RCS, SB, VBS
Utah types: ABL, BG, PTS, PS, SB, SOC

CELTUCE   (OR CHINESE LETTUCE)
Lactuca sativa var. *angustata*
Sunflower Family   ❖   *Compositae*

This variety of lettuce produces leaves for salads when it is young and a tender stem when it is mature. After the stem has been peeled to remove the bitter outer layer, it becomes a mild crisp vegetable that can be eaten raw or stir fried.

Growing Instructions   Celtuce is a very easy, fast-growing crop. Planted in February or March, it is ready to harvest before lettuce plants sown at the same time. Also try planting it in late summer to mature in fall or winter. Sow celtuce seeds as you would lettuce seeds (see page 218). If you are going to let the plants mature, thin to 8 inches apart.

The Harvest   Eat the leaves when the plant is young, since they toughen later. Plants grown for stems will be ready to harvest in about three months.

Pests   Celtuce seedlings may be nibbled by any of the pests that attack lettuce seedlings: birds, cutworms, earwigs, slugs, or snails. However, celtuce plants seem less susceptible to attack than lettuce.

Sources
Celtuce seed: EV, KSC, NGN, OBG, SB, T&M, VBS

CHAYOTE SQUASH (OR VEGETABLE PEAR)
Sechium edule
Gourd Family   ❖   *Cucurbitaceae*

Most types of squash are warm-season crops, producing fruit in summer, but there is one cool-season squash—chayote (pronounced shy-OH-tay), which bears fruit in November and December. It is firmer and sweeter than zucchini but may be used similarly. The young leaves and stems as well as the tuberous roots are also edible.

Chayote is a native of tropical America and its name derives from the Aztec word *chayotli*. The plant is now grown in most of the tropical and subtropical world, and it has picked up new names along the way. It is part of the cuisine of old New Orleans, where it is called mirliton. In Australia it is called choko, in Southeast Asia choco, and in India chow-chow. In the Philippines the name is pronounced sigh-OH-tay.

Once you learn to recognize chayote, you will notice it peeking over many backyard fences throughout the region, even in quite foggy microcli-

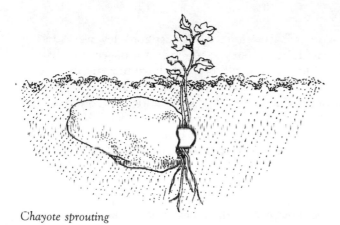

Chayote sprouting

mates. Since chayote is a plant of the tropical highlands, it can grow where the nights are cool—and, in fact, cool nights help production. Chayote is able to live from year to year wherever the soil remains unfrozen all winter.

Growing instructions This tropical plant grows from seeds that never become dormant, but just grow out of the mature fruit a few months after it falls to the ground. To start plants, get two or three chayote fruits from another gardener in December or January or buy some at a produce market. You are most likely to find them at a store that carries Central American or Filipino specialties. Choose fruit that is fairly large and free of blemishes. Keep the fruit in a warm room for a few weeks and watch for a seedling to emerge from the large end. The seedling sort of backs out of the squash, with the roots leading the way. The ends of the seed leaves remain inside, and the shoots grow sideways between the leaves and the fruit. As this occurs, the chayote shrivels up a bit. (If the seedling doesn't emerge by the end of March, the fruit is not viable.)

Sprouting chayotes can be planted in a pot or outdoors in the ground in March. I first learned to plant the fruit tipped, so that the emerging roots were beneath the soil surface and the shoot and most of the fruit were above the ground. However, Filipino gardeners bury the whole squash just below the soil surface. In a comparison planting, the Filipino way worked better. When you are growing seedlings in a pot indoors, don't let the plants become spindly. If a shoot grows more than a foot long before you can move the plant into your garden, cut it back to 6 inches or to three or four leaves.

Prepare your planting site well, adding plenty of organic matter and slow-release fertilizer, since

chayote is a perennial. Although there are male and female flowers on the same plant, production improves when there are two plants for cross-pollination. If no one near you is growing chayote, set out two plants. One San Franciscan of Central American origin refers to a neighbor's plant as his chayote's *novia*, or bride. Space your chayote plants at least 3 feet apart.

Water during the summer months and into fall. Typically, the plant grows rapidly, 10 to 15 feet the first season, but with few stems and quite possibly without any fruit. In subsequent years the plant grows larger, produces more stems, and bears increasingly larger crops that eventually total as many as 350 fruits per plant! Each winter the plant dies back. You will need to remove dead stems at least every couple of years to avoid a messy buildup. Robust growth begins again by about March.

Although the plant can become huge, it works in a small garden because it is attractive and a climber. Chayote can climb straight up a stairway, blanket a fence or garage roof, or cover a trellis to conceal a compost bin. It may be the only crop that succeeds in some shady pockets because it grows up to the light. The attractive leaves, similar to those of other types of squash, average 5 inches across. You can control the vines by cutting and eating young stems in spring and early summer. Later pruning will harm production, although you may choose to do it anyway to remove wayward stems and to curb runaway growth.

The Harvest In choosing a site, give some thought to how you will control the size of the plant. Given 30 feet to climb, the vine will make a run for it, so be sure you can reach the top. It will grow horizontally if there is no way to grow upward, so it can be trained on a fence or a wide trellis. But beware—chayote will hang over the other side of a fence, possibly bearing a good part of its crop there. Planted too near a tree, it will grow into the branches.

In Central America chayote is so plentiful that the spring harvest consists only of tendrils! Entire stem tips of about 1 foot, including tendrils and young leaves, are tender and tasty added to soups, sautéed lightly in butter and garlic, or stir fried. Stop harvesting tendrils, stems, and leaves by the end of May.

Small yellow-green flowers appear as early as July or as late as October. Look closely to see the male flowers, several to a stalk, and the female

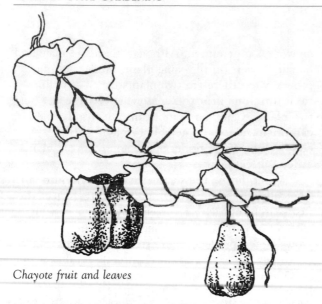

Chayote fruit and leaves

flowers borne singly where the leafstalk joins the stem. The first fruit may form as late as the middle of November. One of the pleasures of having your own chayote vine is being able to pick young fruit, which has a better texture and flavor than the more mature fruit usually sold in produce stores.

Another edible part of this versatile plant is the large tuberous root. Of course, you sacrifice the plant when you eat the root and I have not done so. After cooking one, my parents concluded that it was passable but not distinguished. "It was just another starchy vegetable," they reported.

Always eat the whole chayote, including the seed. The single large seed develops a nutty flavor as the squash matures. If the chayote is so mature that the skin has toughened, simply peel it. Young fruit may be eaten raw, sliced and served with a dip, or cut up in a salad. Mature fruit is best cooked.

In Mexico and Central America, the squash is served many ways. It is added to vegetable soups or cooked in a tomato sauce with onions and jalapeños. Cooked chayote is chilled and added to salads. In addition, the squash is sometimes treated as a fruit, as in Guatemalan chanclette—a sweet baked stuffed chayote (see next page). Other cultures that have adopted chayote treat it as they would similar vegetables in their cuisine. For example, cooks from New Orleans stuff it with sausage and shrimp, Australians braise it in a pot roast, and Filipinos stir-fry it with brine shrimp.

Chayote is comparable to scallop squash in nutritional content—not as vitamin-rich as many other vegetables but a solid source of minerals and fiber. The stems and leaves provide vitamins A and C.

Chayote squash will keep for a few weeks in the refrigerator, but a mature plant produces so much fruit that you will probably have to share the bounty just to get rid of it. Or follow the example of one gardener I know in San Francisco's Mission district and sell the fruit to a grocery. Chayote is one of the few vegetables still being raised in the city as a cash crop!

Varieties The fruit can be pale or dark green, round or pear shaped, thorny or spineless. The one sold most often in grocery stores is light green, pear shaped, and spineless. I have heard that the spiny ones taste better. If you see them in a market or are offered starts of them, compare them to the spineless ones first to see if you like them, since their spines will make them harder to prepare for dinner. (In one local community garden, spiny chayotes were a favorite not for their flavor, but because they were less likely than smooth ones to be used as baseballs by the local youths!)

Pests The plants I have grown had no pests except snails. Use a floating row cover to protect young plants. Snails don't significantly damage a mature chayote plant, but they can be a bother when they use the vine as a staging area for forays to other crops—a good reason to grow only as much chayote plant as you can reach. However, if you leave fruit on the vine too long or allow fallen fruit to lie on the ground, the seeds will begin to germinate. Snails will find them and eat the tender seed leaves, making the fruit useless for starting new plants.

Sources
Chayote starts: Local produce market or another gardener

CHICORY (SEE ENDIVE)

CHINESE CABBAGE (OR NAPA CABBAGE)
Brassica rapa
Pekinensis Group
Mustard Family ❖ *Cruciferae*

The upright heads of Chinese or Napa cabbage are mild, sweet, and never tough—they're delicious in salads, soups, and stir fry. This vegetable is a little harder to grow than its close relative bok choy, since it is more likely to go to seed prematurely, or

CHANCLETTE

This Guatemalan dessert is made with chayote squash. My good friend Maria-Marta Herrara taught me how to make it. She says it is not considered an elegant dish — that is, you wouldn't go buy chayote for it. You'd make it when your vine was so loaded that the chayotes were "falling on your head." The word *chanclette* translates to "old shoe."

    2 medium chayotes (best if they are not too mature)
    4 egg yolks
    2 tablespoons brown sugar
    1/2 teaspoon cinnamon
    2 to 4 tablespoons almonds, slivered or coarsely chopped in a blender
    About 20 raisins
    2 Mexican sugar cookies, crumbled (or 1/2 cup bread crumbs sprinkled
        with 1/2 teaspoon vanilla)

Cut the chayotes in half lengthwise, cutting in the direction of the crease in the large end. Steam them until they are barely tender. Remove from heat and cool a bit. Using a teaspoon, scoop out the centers, leaving a shell about 3/8 to 1/2 inch thick.

Place the removed pulp and seed in a medium bowl and mash them with a fork or cut into small bits with a knife. Beat the egg yolks and add them to the mashed chayote along with the brown sugar, cinnamon, almonds, and raisins. Stir to combine. Add the cookie crumbs and mix well. Spoon the filling into the squash shells, mounding it to get it all in. Bake at 350° F until set, about 30 minutes. Serves four.

bolt, during warm or long days. Like bok choy, it is very susceptible to attack by snails and slugs. And, because it stands a bit longer than bok choy and has more crevices in which pests can hide, there is more opportunity for damage. If you've never tried to grow Chinese cabbage, you may want to try bok choy first.

Growing Instructions Most Chinese cabbage varieties do best when they are planted after the longest day of the year, June 21, and allowed to mature as the days shorten. A long warm spell in late summer may cost you a crop, but planting too late may result in cold-stunted plants. July or August is usually a good time to plant, but experiment to find just the right planting time for late summer and early fall harvests. You can also try early spring plantings if you choose varieties selected for their ability to do well early in the season.

Chinese cabbage is usually seeded in place, since it transplants badly. Sow seeds 1/2 inch deep and 2 to 3 inches apart in very fertile, well-amended soil. Thin the smaller seedlings until you have a plant every foot or so. Water well to fuel rapid growth. Quick varieties mature in 45 days, late ones in as long as 90 days. Some late varieties may overwinter.

The Harvest It is best to wait and harvest whole plants after the head has filled out, though you can eat thinnings. The mature heads are solid, but not as firm as a European cabbage.

Varieties Most of the available varieties are hybrids, since hybrid vigor helps this crop grow quickly. Some varieties have been bred to withstand spring planting without bolting, and some of these can be planted in mid- to late- summer as well.

Pests   Snails and slugs love Chinese cabbage, so growing this vegetable will be difficult unless the pests are under control. The crop may fall prey to other mustard-family pests (see page 183), especially cabbage maggots, which cause the plant to collapse from the center and wilt.

Sources
Chinese cabbage seed:
Summer-to-fall sown varieties: Widely available
Spring-to-summer sown varieties:
   Nozaki Early: ABL
   Napa Spring Delight F_1: EV
   Summer Top F_1: JSS
   Taktis Spring F_1: NGN
Spring-or-fall sown varieties:
   Two Seasons Hybrid: BG
   Napa Super F_1: EV
   China Flash F_1: PS
Spring and Fall Harvester: KSC

COLLARDS
(OR COLLARD GREENS)

Brassica oleracea
Acephala Group
Mustard Family ❖ *Cruciferae*

Collards produce a lot of food for the space they occupy. The plants are easy to grow and produce nutritious greens most of the year, although I've found them to be

Collards

more tender and sweeter in winter and spring than summer and early fall. I have only recently come to relish the hearty flavor of this vegetable. Try it steamed until just tender.

Growing Instructions   Collards require the same growing conditions as other cole crops (see Mustard Family on page 183). The crop is usually seeded in place, although it can be transplanted if that's more convenient. You can seed collards in the garden from January until late summer. In summer sow by July if your microclimate is very near the coast; try as late as September in a more protected site. Plant seeds 1/2 inch deep. If the plants are to overwinter, space them 2 to 3 feet apart. For summer harvests space them a foot apart.

The Harvest   You can begin to pick outer leaves when the plants are about 15 inches high. At first, pick only one leaf per plant. In a few weeks the plants will be strong enough to withstand heavy picking, up

to one-half to two-thirds of the leaves at a time. Let them grow back for a week or so before you pick again. Leave one to three plants per person to overwinter. As a plant gets larger, begin to pick the medium-sized leaves near the center, leaving the outer leaves to feed the plant and the inner ones to grow a bit longer. You can pick until the plants go to seed, usually in February or March. Collards that are blooming and forming seeds develop tall stalks with small leaves. You can eat the tender stems and small leaves before the flowers open, but then pull the plants unless you are growing them for seeds. The seeds will take several months to mature after the plant blooms. They are easy to save, except that you may need to put a mesh bag over the stems to keep birds away.

Varieties   Almost any collard variety will do well here. My seeds, which were given to me by another gardener, surprise me with an occasional purple-tinged plant. Most varieties grow 2 to 3 feet high, with seed stalks reaching about 5 feet high. A tall perennial type, commonly called tree collards, may grow to 10 feet or more. Usually grown from cuttings, tree collards can be planted in February and picked whenever it isn't going to seed. Prune the stems in late summer.

Pests   Collards share all of the mustard-family pests (see page 183).

Sources
Collard seeds: Widely available
Tree collard plants: Ecology Action

CORN, SWEET

Zea mays
Grass Family ❖
Graminae

Corn is a warm-season crop that produces consistently in the sunnier parts of the region. It is border-line in the moderately foggy areas and is often a total bust in the foggiest gardens. If the summer is too cool and foggy, corn may respond by forming tassels and silks at different times. The tassels contain the male flowers and the silks are the female flowers. If they aren't ready at the same time, there is no fertilization and no corn. Once fertilization takes place, cool days don't seem to affect the sweetness of the kernels.

female flower

Growing Instructions Corn expects the red-carpet treatment—good rich soil and ample water. Dig in plenty of compost or well-rotted manure at planting time and some high-nitrogen fertilizer. Give corn a booster of nitrogen while it is growing, especially if there is any sign of yellowing in the lower leaves. If you let corn dry to a point where the leaves are dull and curled, it will be stunted.

Direct-seed corn anytime from April 15 to the middle of July. A foot between plants is the usual recommended distance. If corn varieties with standard-sized plants are spaced closer than 8 to 10 inches apart, they will bear fewer, and poorly filled out ears. Ample spacing is especially important when fog limits the amount of light. Plant the seeds 1-1/2 to 2 inches deep. I usually plant two kernels in each spot, spacing them 1 or 2 inches apart. When the plants are 3 or 4 inches high, I pull the extras or transplant them to fill gaps left by poor germination or pest damage.

Always plant corn in a block at least 4 by 4 feet. This is important because corn depends on wind for pollination. Grains of pollen from the stamens, which dangle from the tassels, must blow onto the ends of each individual silk. Every pollen cell then grows an extension that goes all the way through a silk until it reaches the ear, fertilizing one kernel. In a smaller or linear planting, much of the pollen is apt to blow uselessly over other crops.

A 4 by 4-foot block will produce twenty to forty ears of wonderfully sweet corn. Make the space even more productive by incorporating other crops. When the corn is at least 12 inches high, plant some beans to climb the stalks. As an alternative, plant a hill or two of cucumbers, pumpkins, or winter squash next to the corn planting and encourage the vines to grow under the cornstalks.

Corn seeds are most often sown in place. However, germination in cold soil (less than 60°F) may slow future growth. So if you intend to plant before the middle of May, when the soil is still cold, presprout the seeds (see page 47) or grow them in containers indoors for three to four weeks. You may also decide to start corn indoors to give it a jump on pests.

Gardeners used to remove the suckers, or the nonproductive little side shoots, in the belief that doing so increased yield. Recent studies have shown that these suckers either don't affect yield or may even increase it, so save yourself work by leaving them on the plants.

If you are trying to grow corn in the foggier

CORN THAT'S SWEETER THAN EVER

There has been much excitement over two new kinds of sweet corn that produce ears that are sweeter and stay sweeter longer on the plant and in the refrigerator. With this type of corn there is no need for the proverbial dash from the garden to the pot of boiling water. Much of the corn sold in markets is now one of these new hybrids.

I once harvested some ears of Kandy Korn, an Everlasting Heritage (EH) hybrid, stored them overnight in the refrigerator, traveled to San Diego with the ears in the bottom compartment of a Greyhound bus, refrigerated them overnight again, and served them to my parents for dinner the next day. The corn was still much sweeter than regular corn sold in grocery stores. These hybrids, which are also called Sugar Enhanced (SE), carry a gene that makes them sweeter, more tender, and able to hold their sweetness longer. They do not need to be isolated to prevent cross pollination.

The other new varieties, known as Super Sweets, or Xtra Sweets, carry the gene Shrunken 2, or sh_2 for short, which makes them even sweeter and able to hold their sweetness a week or more. Some gardeners even complain that they find these varieties too sweet! 'How Sweet It Is', a white-kerneled Super Sweet, did fine in my garden and wasn't too sweet for me. Super Sweet seeds are sensitive to decay in cold soil, so if your seed isn't fungicide-treated, delay planting till mid-May or start seed indoors. 'Northern Xtra Sweet' is said to have good germination in cold soil. Plant Super Sweets at least 25 feet from other varieties to avoid cross-pollination, as this will reduce the sweetness of your Super Sweet corn.

parts of the area, you can try to protect it in a minigreenhouse (see page 59). Using a short-stalked or dwarf variety, enclose a block of corn in a structure 5 or 6 feet high. When you see the pollen being released, shake the plants lightly to be absolutely sure that it falls on the silks. You can also try to time plantings so that the corn blooms during traditionally warm periods, either late May or the middle of September.

On more than one occasion I have found my corn in a horizontal position after a storm in late spring or early fall. You can usually save the plants by propping them upright, since most of the roots are still in the ground. However, it is much easier to put in supports before the damage happens. If your garden tends to be windy, build a corn corral. Drive in 5-foot stakes at the corners of the block and every 2 feet across the north and south ends, since the wind comes primarily from the west. Then tie rope or strips of cloth about 4 feet high around the perimeter and between the plants connecting each pair of north and south stakes.

The Harvest   Fertilized corn silks shrivel as the ear swells. When the visible part of the silks is dry and brown, the corn is ripe—or soon will be. To check for ripeness, make a small vertical slit in the husk near the top of an ear. Keep the slit small since it provides an entry for insect pests. See if the kernels have filled out. If they are still tiny, look a little lower down because kernels at the very top sometimes never fill out. Puncture a kernel with your thumbnail. If the liquid inside is watery, the corn isn't ready yet. If it is thoroughly opaque, you waited too long. Sweet corn is just right when the liquid is milky but still translucent. After a season or two you will be able to gauge ripeness by the appearance of the kernels without a thumbnail test. While you are harvesting try chewing on a fresh green cornstalk—it's as sweet as sugarcane.

Varieties   Seed companies rate corn varieties at 50 to 92 days, but don't be surprised if the crop takes half again as long to mature in our cool summers. Concentrate on the earlier, short-season varieties, especially if your microclimate is borderline.

The first corn I grew in San Francisco is still a good choice. 'Early Sunglow' is listed at 62 days but takes 90 days here and is said to be vigorous in cold weather. It makes two or more 7-inch-long ears on 4- to 4-1/2-foot-high plants. The leaves and husks bear attractive reddish markings. Don't be afraid to try other varieties, either hybrid or open-pollinated, including white and bicolored types. The varieties listed at 80 days or more are risky in all but the warmest areas, and even in sunny gardens they need to go in before the middle of June. Active breeding programs mean that new varieties appear every year. Look for ones that are early and tolerant to cool weather.

In addition to sweet corn, which is eaten immature, there are varieties that are harvested mature. Some of these are used for making cornmeal or cracked corn, others are used for popcorn, and still others are grown mainly to produce ornamental ears. These varieties take longer than sweet corn, since the seeds must be dry before the ears are picked. You run the risk of decay if the ears are still ripening on the stalks into the rainy season. If you live in a sunny area and want to try this type of corn, plant it in early May for the best chance of a successful harvest. Look for varieties that are said to mature early. For popcorn try 'Tom Thumb,' an early kind with 3-4 inch ears.

If you enjoy the miniature ears used in Chinese cooking, you may like to grow some. They are just tiny, unpollinated ears—corn flowers, if you will—picked when the silks first emerge. This crop has potential for moderately foggy areas, since no pollination is required. You can harvest any regular corn when it is tiny, before the kernels form, or you can buy a baby corn variety that produces several ears per stalk. I tried a baby corn variety thinking that it would take up garden space for a much shorter time than regular corn, but it took about as long. By the time the silks form, corn plants are pretty close to the end of their life cycle. After I stripped off the husks and silks and made my first little pile of tiny ears, I couldn't help thinking that it wasn't much food for all the time and effort, and it made me realize why baby corn is so expensive!

Pests   Various chewing pests eat corn seedlings: birds, cutworms, earwigs, slugs, and snails. Either plant the corn under a floating row cover, or sow the seeds indoors and move the seedlings to the garden when they are three to four weeks old and have a better chance of surviving pests. If birds are a problem, discourage them by propping a piece of bird netting over short sticks placed around the perimeter of the seedbed.

Maturing plants may become infested by aphids, which can get into the ears but usually get only as far as the tips by the time you harvest. They wash off easily.

Corn earworms may enter the ends of the ears and chew the kernels, although this has happened to me only twice in fifteen years of growing corn. If these small striped caterpillars catch you by surprise, just cut off the ends of the affected ears before you cook them. Next year start control efforts sooner.

Raccoons are notoriously fond of corn. There are plenty of raccoons in our area, even in the urban neighborhoods, but they aren't necessarily a problem. I know they live around my community garden, because they once killed our ducks, but they have never damaged a corn crop there.

Common corn smut is a fungus disease that produces galls on the ears, stalks, and leaves. Although it is more common in hotter regions, it sometimes appears in the warmer parts of our area.

Sources
Sweet corn seed:
Standard varieties
   Early Sunglow (yellow, early): BG, NGN, PS, SGS, VBS
   Platinum Lady (midseason, white): NGN, PTS, VBS
EH and Super Sweet varieties
   Kandy Korn (SE, midseason, yellow): BG, SGS, TERR, VBS
   Peaches and Cream (SE, early, bicolor): SGS, VBS
   Northern Xtra Sweet (sh$_2$, early, yellow): JSS, VBS
   How Sweet It Is (sh$_2$, midseason, white): NGN, PS, T&M, VBS
Early popcorn varieties
   Tom Thumb: JSS, OBG, SB, TERR
   Calico: PS, SGS, TERR
Baby Corn: EV, NGN, T&M

CORN SALAD
(OR LAMB'S LETTUCE OR MACHE)
Valerianella locusta
Valerian Family ❖ *Valerianaceae*

An annual valued in colder climates as a winter salad green, corn salad is a rather small plant with spoon-shaped leaves that have a buttery texture and subtle flavor. I have grown it but didn't think it was worth the trouble, since so many other domesticated and wild greens will grow in our winters. But if you want to give it a try, you may find that you enjoy this European favorite.

Growing Instructions Sow seeds in August for harvests throughout winter into spring, or sow in February for early spring salads. Plant the seeds in place, and thin the plants to stand 3 to 4 inches apart.

The Harvest Pick leaves individually from the low rosettes or pull whole plants. Plants will go to seed in a few months and may seed themselves in your garden.

Varieties Several European varieties are available and they should thrive here. Look for large-leaved varieties—a desirable feature in a plant so small.

Sources:
Corn salad seed: Widely available.

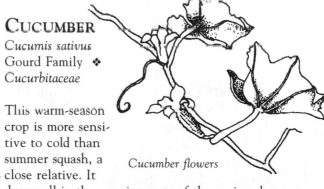
Cucumber flowers

CUCUMBER
Cucumis sativus
Gourd Family ❖
Cucurbitaceae

This warm-season crop is more sensitive to cold than summer squash, a close relative. It does well in the sunnier parts of the region, but not in the foggier locations.

Cucumbers need organic, nitrogen-rich, well-drained soil that is kept constantly moist but not soggy. Grown in excessively wet soil, cucumber plants may die from root diseases. They grow best when kept out of strong breezes, which are all too common in coastal gardens. In a very windy site, plant cucumbers where taller plants will protect them without shading them too much, or provide some other windbreak.

Growing Instructions Plant cucumber seeds outdoors from early May to the middle of June. A May-planted crop will start to bear in July and continue until the fall rains kill the vines. For a jump on the season you can use three- to four-week-old transplants started indoors as early as March (see chart on page 53). Indoor seeding may also allow you to avoid heavy snail damage.

I can't speak too strongly in favor of trellising cucumber plants. Trellised plants produce more and straighter cucumbers. The cucumbers are also more likely to escape snails and slugs, which can scar the surface of the fruit so badly that it is stunted. You can make a trellis from a length of 4- or 5-foot-high hog wire fencing or similar fencing with at least 2-inch openings. Mount the fencing on stakes that are either fastened to a raised bed or driven into the ground.

SOUTHEAST ASIAN CUCUMBER SALAD

A wonderful mix of flavors sets off the refreshing taste of cucumbers. I grind the peanuts in a mortar and pestle. Whatever you do, don't grind them to a powder. Just break them into several pieces each.

1 medium cucumber, peeled (if necessary*) and sliced thinly
2 tablespoons onion, cut into thin slivers
2 tablespoons rice vinegar
1 tablespoon water
1 teaspoon sugar
1/4 teaspoon salt
1/4 teaspoon crushed red chile pepper
1/4 cup coarsely chopped coriander leaves (or mint leaves)
1/4 cup unsalted dry roasted peanuts, crushed

Put the cucumber slices in a medium bowl. Sprinkle the slivers of onion and the red chile pepper over them. In a small bowl, mix the vinegar, water, sugar, and salt. Stir until the sugar and salt are dissolved. Pour the dressing over the cucumber and onions. Toss. Sprinkle with the coriander (or mint) leaves, and the peanuts. Serves two to four.

CUCUMBER RAITA

You can serve this Indian dish as a salad or as an accompaniment to curries.

2 cups grated cucumber (peeled, if necessary*)
1 1/2 cups plain yogurt
1 1/2 teaspoon cumin
1/2 teaspoon salt

Using a cheese grater, grate the cucumber into a medium bowl. Press the cucumber lightly and pour off the excess moisture, but don't try to squeeze all moisture out. Add the yogurt, cumin, and salt and mix well. Serve immediately or chill first. Serves six.

* *One of the joys of homegrown cucumbers is that they are not waxed and needn't be peeled as long as the skin is not tough or bitter.*

Plant a row of cucumber seeds 2 inches from each side of the trellis. Sow the seeds in pairs, leaving 4 inches between pairs, and thin to the stronger of each pair when the plants are 4 to 6 inches high. Although cucumber vines have tendrils, often they aren't very functional. Every few days as the vines grow I gently guide the growing tips through higher openings in the wire.

If you don't trellis, use a straw mulch under the vines to keep the fruit off the ground. When the cucumber vines are young, guide them in the direction you want them to grow.

The Harvest   It is important to keep cucumbers picked, since even a single overmature cucumber on a plant will slow down or stop production. That means harvesting as often as every two days at the height of the season. Overmature cucumbers turn yellow and become tough. Also watch out for partially fertilized fruit. You may see only the skinny, pale green undeveloped part near the stem and overlook the fat, yellow overmature tip.

Cucumbers are usually ready for harvest when they are between an inch and 1-1/2 inches in diameter. Cut open a seeded variety and taste it. The seeds should be visible in the cross section, and they should be just as tender as the rest of the cucumber. One of the joys of homegrown cucumbers is that they are not waxed and needn't be peeled as long as the skin is not tough.

Varieties   There are three kinds of elongated green cucumbers: slicers (the supermarket standards), picklers (harvested small for making into pickles), and long green ones, which include traditional Asian and Middle Eastern ones, greenhouse varieties, and hybrids that are called "burpless." The so-called "English" cucumbers in grocery stores are of this type, and probably greenhouse-grown.

In my search for delicious cucumbers, I tried the traditional 'Japanese Long' and Middle Eastern 'Amira', but they did not thrive. Then I discovered the hybrid "burpless" types, and have grown them exclusively ever since. They are long, mild-flavored, have thin skins that usually need no peeling, and are able to produce abundantly in warmer parts of San Francisco. Try 'OY200', 'Sweet Success', or 'Burpless Tasty Green'. (One year I planted a generic "burpless" variety from seed purchased in a local store, and the fruit quality did not approach that of the above, named, varieties.)

Bush cucumbers promise a crop in less space, but I have found that they are less productive per plant than vining types, and also less productive per garden area if the vining types are trellised.

Grow lemon cucumbers the same way you do other cucumbers. At first the small round fruit is pale yellow. Harvested at this stage, it is very mild and tender. When the fruit turns bright yellow it is tougher and has a stronger flavor. Some people prefer the cucumber mild and others like it more robust.

Pests   In addition to getting root rot when they are overwatered, cucumbers sometimes suffer from leaf diseases, such as powdery mildew. Although the crop thrives in our coastal high humidity, the damp air encourages many diseases. 'Burpless Tasty Green' and 'Sweet Success' are among the cucumber variet-

---

CUCUMBERS & THE BIRDS & THE BEES

Most cucumber varieties are dependent on bees for pollination. Some varieties have male and female flowers on the same plant, whereas others bear female and male flowers on separate plants. When you buy a variety that has separate male and female plants, the seed packet will usually contain mainly female plants with just enough male plants to provide pollen. Even without these pollinator plants, you would probably still get some fruit, since bees bring pollen from plants up to a mile away.

'Sweet Success' is a variety with only female flowers on all plants, and these flowers don't need to be fertilized to develop fruit. Thus the fruit is mostly seedless, although you may find an occasional seed due to chance pollination.

ies that resist powdery mildew.

Cucumbers are susceptible to several virus diseases, including beet curly top virus, cucumber mosaic virus, and zucchini yellow mosaic virus. There is no cure for these diseases, so look for resistant varieties and remove infected plants as soon as you notice them.

Sources
Cucumber seed:
Burpless varieties:
   GY200 F$_1$: KSC, TERR
   Burpless Tasty Green F$_1$: BG, KSC, NGN, PS, T&M, VBS
   Sweet Success: BG, NGN, PTS, VBS
Slicing varieties: Widely available
Pickling varieties: Widely available
Lemon cucumber: ABL, CG, GG, NGN, OBG, SB, SOC, SGS

EGGPLANT

Solanum melongena
Nightshade Family ❖ *Solanaceae*

A native of India and Africa, eggplant requires more warmth than either tomato or pepper, members of the same family. Cold nights will stunt eggplant, and temperatures under 60°F will keep fruit from setting when the plant finally blooms. The crop is borderline for our region—impossible in the foggiest areas and only a moderate producer in the warmest locations. In a sunny San Francisco garden, I once planted six eggplants and harvested a total of two small fruits. In a more favorable growing area, I could have picked as many as four dozen fruits from the same number of plants. In my garden, flowers dropped unfertilized all summer long and the plants didn't set any fruit until nearly the end of September.

Growing Instructions In the middle of May, set eggplant seedlings in a sunny, protected spot out of the path of strong winds. The crop grows best in organic, fertile soil. Lay a black plastic mulch and cut holes for the plants 18 inches apart. A floating row cover or minigreenhouse (see page 59) will help warm the air around the plants. Add a booster of compost or manure tea (see page 80) or liquid seaweed a month after transplanting.

The Harvest For the best flavor pick the fruit small, when it is one-third to two-thirds full size. No matter what size the fruit is, pick it if it stops enlarging. You will know you waited too long if the seeds are brown when you cut open the fruit. Don't pull up the plants until the weather turns chilly, since fruit may still ripen during a warm fall.

Varieties While choosing early, vigorous eggplant

varieties is of some help, no variety truly thrives when days and nights are cool. Some that have performed best in Pacific Northwest gardens are 'Dusky', 'Short Tom', 'Bride', and 'Bambino'.

Pests In the warmest parts of our region, flea beetles may chew tiny holes in the leaves. Spider mites may be a problem in any garden, especially if plants are underwatered. Eggplant occasionally develops verticillium wilt, and is also susceptible to tomato or potato late blight, so rotate eggplant along with other tomato family members to reduce the chance of spreading these diseases. Watch for the serious malformations caused by viruses, and remove infected plants from the garden if you see them.

Sources
Eggplant seed:
   Bambino F$_1$: NGN, PS, TERR, VBS
   Bride F$_1$: PTS, TERR
   Dusky F$_1$: NGN, PS, PTS, TERR
   Short Tom F$_1$: TERR
Eggplant plants: Available at local nurseries

ENDIVE (INCLUDES ESCAROLE, FRISÉ)

Chicorium endiva

CHICORY (INCLUDES RADICCHIO, WITLOOF CHICORY)

Chicorium intybus
Sunflower Family ❖ *Compositae*

Endive is a mildly bitter relative of lettuce. The broad-leaved varieties are known as escarole, while the narrow-leaved types are called frisé. You will find it in supermarket salad mixes, and frisé and lettuce alone dressed with olive oil, wine vinegar, salt, and pepper make a tasty salad.

Another mildly bitter lettuce relative is chicory. Some form heads, shaped like head lettuce or romaine. Two well-known heading types are the round-headed, red, radicchio and Witloof chicory (sometimes confusingly called Belgian endive), which, after forcing, has pale green, pointed heads. Another chicory variety is grown mainly for tender shoots, and others are grown for their roots, which are dried, ground, roasted, and used as a coffee substitute.

Endive and chicory grow well in cooler weather, and both are often blanched to reduce their bitter flavor. Some varieties are milder in flavor than others and some are self-blanching, meaning that the leaves form a tight head that is blanched inside.

Growing Instructions Both *Chicorium* species appreciate an organic, fertile soil. Sow seeds in place or start them indoors four to five weeks before transplanting. Space the seedlings 6 to 18 inches apart, depending on the variety. Keeping the soil constantly moist will produce plants with a mild flavor and also discourage the plants from going to seed prematurely, or bolting.

Endive and chicory are more tolerant of cold than lettuce, and it is satisfying to watch them grow heartily in our usual winter temperatures. Be wary of overplanting—a little endive or chicory in a salad goes a long way. Most varieties are planted in July or August to mature in the cool days of fall and winter. You can also try a quick crop from seeds started in January or February, but plants of most varieties will bolt if they are planted much later. Some newer varieties have been developed especially for planting in early spring, and some of these can also be planted into summer. As a component of mesclun (see page 221), chicory or endive may be planted most of the year and cut while it is still young and mild flavored.

The Harvest Although endive is a biennial and chicory a perennial, both are harvested for greens as annuals. Looseleaf endive as well as red- and green-leaved chicory varieties can be harvested unblanched by the leaf or by the plant. Self-blanching varieties form heads, which are harvested whole.

Looseleaf types of endive can be blanched to give them a milder flavor. If you are interested in blanching, here is a method that works well. On a dry day in fall or winter, tie the leaves of mature plants. Then cover the plants with overturned flowerpots and plug the bottom holes to exclude sunlight and rain. Check the plants occasionally: They should be blanched in two to three weeks. Whether blanched or not, endive heads placed in plastic bags will keep for months in the refrigerator if they are dry when you bag them. Storage reduces bitterness even more.

Forcing is a special kind of blanching in which the top of a chicory plant is cut off and the plant base is encouraged to resprout. This is most commonly done using special forcing varieties that are planted to mature in fall. In colder climates the mature plants are cut and the roots dug up in fall. The roots are then brought into the basement, where they are buried in moist sand. In our mild winters, however, a plant can be forced right where it is growing. In November or December cut mature chicory plants 2 inches above the ground and pile 6 to 8 inches of soil on them. Keep the soil just moist, but don't overwater. (If rains are heavy, cover the area with a tarp.) In late December dig cautiously and look for the pale shoots. Harvest them when they are 3 to 4 inches long. Cover the cut stumps with soil to let new shoots form. Use stakes to mark your place in the underground harvest as you move down a row or across a bed.

Varieties Choose an endive variety based on whether you prefer the broad-leaved escarole (also sometimes called Batavian endive) or the narrower, curled leaves of frisé.

There is more to think about in choosing a variety of chicory. If you are planning to force the plants, in order to form Witloof chicory, choose a variety intended for this purpose. Among non-forcing types, you will have a choice of green-leaved or red-leaved varieties. Be sure to check if you are buying seed meant to be fall-planted (which, in our area really means July or August), or one that can also be planted in early spring as well.

'Sugarlof', a green-leaved chicory planted in late summer, is said to be unusually sweet. It forms heads shaped like romaine lettuce. Harvest whole plants young and at more mature stages to see which stage you prefer. A good choice for spring planting is 'Crystal Hat'. It forms a romaine-shaped head that is said to be sweeter if it is rinsed in warm water before you eat it.

Radicchio, those pricy little heads of mildly bitter red leaves, are not the easiest of crops to grow, as even the best varieties tend to be a little erratic in behavior. A certain proportion of the plants tend to bloom before they form good heads. I have had the best luck with 'Guilio', a variety that can be planted February through July. My February-planted 'Guilio' even came back after I cut the tops to make a second, smaller, fall crop.

I haven't tried the Catalogna-type chicory grown for tender spring shoots—called asparagus chicory—and have my doubts about any vegetable claimed to rival asparagus, but you may want to try it. I did once try to prepare chicory root coffee and found it a lot of work for the amount of beverage, although the flavor was interesting. If you are curious, try some chicory coffee from an herb store to see if you like it before you grow your own.

Pests Endive and chicory are often described as pest-free and, in fact, I have had little trouble with pests. Snails and slugs may attack young plants but they pretty much ignore older plants, since they prefer so many other kinds of greens. Be prepared to control aphids if they appear.

Sources
Endive seed:
Broad-leaved varieties (escarole): ABL, GG, JSS, PTS, RH, SB, SGS, TERR, T&M, VBS
Narrow-leaved varieties (frisée): ABL, GG, JSS, PTS, SB, SGS, T&M, VBS
Chicory seed:
Varieties for forming Witloof chicory: CG, GG, JG, JSS, NGN, PTS, RCS, RH, SB
Green-leaved varieties:
Sugarloaf or Pan de Zucchero: OBG, SB
Crystal Hat: NGN
Red-leaved varieties (radicchio):
Giulio: CG, PS, SGS
Catalogna (asparagus) chicory: CG, NGN, SB
Chicory grown for roots: SB

FLOWERING KALE (SEE KALE)

GARDEN CRESS
(OR PEPPERGRASS OR UPLAND CRESS)
Lepidium sativum
Mustard Family ❖ *Cruciferae*

Garden cress is a mustard-family crop, similar in flavor and appearance to watercress. Since it doesn't require the moisture that watercress does, it can be grown in an ordinary garden bed. A fast-growing annual, garden cress makes a rosette of tasty leaves, then quickly goes to seed. It is best to make small plantings every few weeks.

Growing Instructions Garden cress is more likely to produce a good crop of leaves in cool weather. Scatter-sow the seeds in place in rich soil from February to April or from July to September. Provide part shade for the July to September crops, perhaps by planting the garden cress behind taller plants.

The Harvest Pick the outer leaves or pull entire plants.

Varieties and Related Species There are broad-leaved and curly-leaved varieties. Garden cress is sometimes called upland cress, which can lead to some confusion, since there is another plant, *Barbarea verna*, called upland or winter cress. It is a

biennial that overwinters, then goes to seed in spring. The two plants are grown the same way and their flavors are similar, so there isn't much practical difference.

Sources
Lepidium sativum seed: ABL, CG, DD, JSS, NGN, OBG, PTS, SB, SGS, TERR, T&M
Barbarea verna seed: ABL, BG, DD, JSS, NGN, SB, T&M

GARLAND CHRYSANTHEMUM
(OR SHUNGIKU OR SUKIYAKI GREENS)
Chrysanthemum coronarium
Sunflower Family ❖ *Compositae*

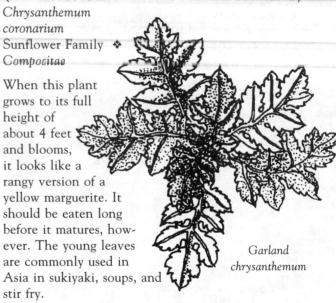

Garland chrysanthemum

When this plant grows to its full height of about 4 feet and blooms, it looks like a rangy version of a yellow marguerite. It should be eaten long before it matures, however. The young leaves are commonly used in Asia in sukiyaki, soups, and stir fry.

Growing Instructions Garland chrysanthemum prefers cool weather and can be grown most of the year throughout our region. It grows readily from seeds sown from February to September and is ready to harvest about a month and a half later.

The Harvest Begin to pull whole plants when they are about 5 inches high, or harvest by cutting the leaves. If you cut all the leaves an inch or so from the ground, the stubs will resprout for another harvest. The leaves have a distinctive, pungent flavor. Mild at first, the flavor becomes stronger as the plant matures, until it is too strong for many palates. Let some plants bloom. In addition to attracting syrphid flies and other beneficial insects, the flowers can be cut for bouquets. The petals can also be eaten in soups and other dishes. Garland chrysanthemum will seed itself, rewarding the gardener who spots it amid the weeds with early spring greens.

Varieties You can buy this chrysanthemum species as an ornamental, but any variety sold as a vegetable is probably more succulent. When you are looking in a seed catalog, try the Asian greens section.

Sources
Garland chrysanthemum seed: ABL, CG, DD, EV, JSS, KSC, NGN, RH, PTS, SB

GARLIC

Allium sativum
Amaryllis Family ❖ *Amaryllidaceae*

You can use a tiny corner of your garden in winter to produce an entire year's supply of garlic. One year I grew 6 pounds of this useful seasoning in a plot measuring only 3 by 3 feet.

Growing Instructions Start with purchased garlic bulbs, preferably from a nursery rather than a grocery store. Ask if they are certified disease-free; the nursery person should be able to find out. Plant the garlic in a bed that gets as much sun as possible in winter. Dig in a few inches of aged manure or compost and some fertilizer that provides more phosphorous and potassium than nitrogen. (For more on fertilizing, see page 80.)

To plant, gently separate the cloves and gather up all but the smallest center ones. Do not peel them. Set the larger cloves in moist soil, blunt (root) end down and pointy end up, with the top about 1 inch below the surface. Space the cloves about 4 inches apart. Don't water on the same day that you plant—in fact, wait until shoots emerge before watering for the first time.

You can plant anytime between October 15 and February 15, although fall-planted garlic will be the largest, since it has the most time to mature. The bulbs are ready to be harvested in late June or July.

When the plants begin to grow rapidly in late winter and early spring, add a fertilizer that provides more nitrogen than phosphorus or potassium. Watch out for dry spells, especially in spring, and water when necessary but don't keep the bed soggy. Between May and late June, the tips of garlic leaves will turn yellow even with adequate watering. This means that the bulbs are nearly mature and should be watered less frequently. In softneck varieties, the stem near the ground will begin to flatten and the mature plant will fall over. Hardneck types produce a flower stem, which is stiff, so it doesn't fall over.

When garlic is ready to dig, the leaves should be at least 60% brown. If you want to check maturity, dig a bulb. A mature bulb has well-developed cloves throughout and four to six dry leaves wrapped around the entire bulb.

Dig up mature plants carefully and brush off as much dirt as you can. Cure the whole plant in a warm, dry place out of direct sunlight for two to three weeks. Then clean the cured bulbs. Using the ball of your thumb, brush off dirt and the outer one or two layers of loose and broken skin. With scissors cut the roots to 1 inch. Braid the stems or cut them 2 inches from the bulb. Store garlic out of the sun in a cool, dry, airy place.

You can use fresh garlic leaves during the winter and spring. They are milder than the bulbs and higher in vitamins A and C. Eating leaves will limit the size of the bulbs, so this is a good use for the smallest cloves in the bulb. Plant them close together and use their leaves, saving the larger cloves for bulbs.

Varieties Softneck garlic is best adapted to our mild winters. It tends to have a spicier flavor than hardneck and stores for up to a year. The tops are good for braiding. Examples are: 'California Early', 'California Late', and 'Silverskin'. You may want to experiment with hardneck types such as 'Spanish Roja' and 'German Red', but they may perform badly or have less flavor and quality in our climate. Garlic sources don't always make clear the traits or names of the varieties of garlic they sell, so I have given a general category and listed varieties.

Pests The only insect pest that has attacked my garlic is a black aphid. Examine the plant bases and leaf undersides regularly for this pest. If you see it, begin twice weekly spraying with insecticidal soap (see page 126) until it is under control. Examine nearby bunching onions, garlic chives, nasturtium, and artichoke for black aphids and control them on these plants as well.

If your garlic rots before it matures, the cause could be overwatering. If there are white fungal mats on the bulbs, suspect onion white rot or lettuce drop. Dig out the affected bulbs and seek positive identification of the disease. White rot affects other onion family crops (see page 228) while lettuce drop affects lettuce and many other vegetables and flowers (see page 220).

Sources
Garlic bulbs: BG, JG, PS, RCS, PTS, SB, VBS
California Early: RSP, SOC
California Late: RSP, SOC, SGS
Silverskin: NGN, RSP, TERR
German Red: NGN, RSP, SOC, TERR
Spanish Rojo: NGN, RSP, SOC, SGS, TERR

GARLIC, ELEPHANT

Allium ampeloprasum
Ampeloprasum Group
Amaryllis Family ❖ *Amaryllidaceae*

This is the garlic that makes huge mild cloves. The whole bulb is about the same size as an ordinary garlic bulb, but it consists of only three to seven cloves.

Growing Instructions   Plant individual cloves in October or November and grow them in the same way that you would ordinary garlic. Although an elephant garlic plant looks like a robust version of an ordinary garlic plant, it has slightly different habits. In spring it is very likely to form a flower stalk, which should be cut before it blooms so that more energy is funneled into forming bulbs. Elephant garlic also forms small bulblets at the base of a bulb, and these will make mature bulbs in two or three years.

The Harvest   Collect the mature bulbs as you would ordinary garlic, but check for small bulblets. Separate them from the bulbs as you harvest. Refrigerate the bulblets for at least a month, then plant them in fall. They won't all come up (20 percent is considered good), but after one year those that do grow will make small bulbs resembling boiling onions. Leave them in the ground and during the third summer you will get the familiar bulbs with their several giant cloves.

Elephant garlic has a nice mild flavor that makes it very useful in cooking, but don't plant more than you can eat in a couple of months since it doesn't keep well.

Pests   Elephant garlic is subject to aphid attack, just as ordinary garlic is. It is also susceptible to white rot—a good reason to start with certified disease-free cloves.

Sources
Elephant garlic cloves: BG, JSS, NGN, PS, RSP, SB, TERR, T&M, VBS

GARLIC, TOP-SETTING
(OR ROCAMBOLE OR SERPENT GARLIC)

Allium sativum var. *ophioscorodon*
Amaryllis Family ❖ *Amaryllidaceae*

Here is a garlic that resembles top onions (see page 230), since it makes several bulblets on tall stems. The name serpent garlic comes from the way the stem tops curl picturesquely as the bulblets form. This plant also makes the usual bulb of cloves underground. You can eat both the top sets and the underground cloves, and you can replant either. The underground cloves make bulbs in a single year, whereas the top sets take one or two years. Grow top-setting garlic as you would ordinary garlic, being on the lookout for the same pests and the same diseases.

Sources
Top-setting garlic bulblets: NGN
Top-setting garlic bulbs: BG, JG

GOURD

Cucurbita species
Gourd Family ❖ *Cucurbitaceae*

Gourds, which are members of several cucurbit species, are used more for decoration than food. They require a long, warm summer to ripen fruit until it forms the rock-hard shell that is so attractive and useful. Don't let visions of large decoratively carved containers entice you beyond the very limited possibilities of this crop in our climate. The coastal central California region is not gourd country. However, you may want to try a packet of the smallest gourd varieties, which are strains of *C. pepo*. With a little luck, these may mature even in foggy areas.

Growing Instructions: Grow a gourd just as you would winter squash (see page 249). It forms a long vine that trails along the ground, but you can save space by trellising the plant. Check every few days and help weave the vines through the trellis if necessary.

Sources
Small mixed gourd seed: BG, CG, JSS, NGN, SGS, TERR, VBS

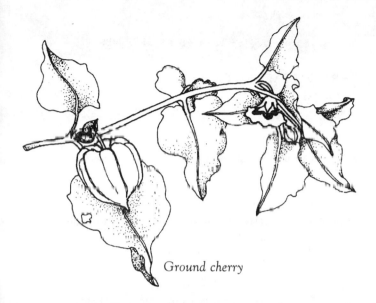

Ground cherry

GROUND-CHERRY (OR CAPE GOOSE-BERRY OR HUSK TOMATO)

Physalis peruviana (P. edulis) and *P. pruinosa*
Nightshade Family ❖ *Solanaceae*

When you pop a ground-cherry into your mouth for the first time, your eyes will probably open wide with surprise. This relative of the tomato can be used as a dessert fruit, although it may take a little getting used to. About the size of a cherry tomato, the yellow-orange fruit is very sweet but also tart and tangy. It is borne in little papery "lanterns" similar to those of the tomatillo (see page 255). The plants are rangy, with grayish green, softly fuzzy leaves and small pale yellow flowers. Ground-cherry is worth trying even very near the coast, since it will mature in a cooler climate than tomato will. It grows well in poor sandy soil.

Growing Instructions   Ground-cherry is easy to start from seed. It can be started indoors, but you may as well sow it directly in the garden. Thin or transplant the seedlings to stand 2 to 3 feet apart. Ground-cherry needs about three months to begin ripening fruit, then goes on producing for several months. Planted in spring, it bears into fall. My plants have seeded themselves to sprout in midsummer and bear fruit in spring, so midsummer sowing is a second option. An unusually cold winter may kill ground-cherry.

Some ground-cherry varieties sprawl on the ground and others grow up to 4 feet high. Taller ones should be staked or corraled. To corral a plant, surround it with several stakes, then tie strips of an old sheet or pantyhose around the stakes to keep the plant within bounds.

The Harvest   When ground-cherry ripens, its papery husk turns from green to brown, and the fruit inside takes on a rich golden color. Ripe fruit often falls to the ground. To harvest, start by picking up fallen fruit and peeking in the husks to be sure that it is still good, then pick over the plant, checking in the husks for full ripeness. I usually eat my ground-cherries right in the garden as a snack, but they can also be used in fruit salads, pies, and jams. If you are saving the fruit until you have enough for a recipe, you can store it in its husk for several weeks. Collect it when it is ripe, then spread it in a single layer in a cool, dry place. Once the husks are removed, the fruit will not keep unless it is frozen. Fruit that has been frozen and thawed tastes best cooked.

Varieties and Related Species   At least two separate species are called ground-cherry. You may also find either listed as husk tomato, yellow husk tomato, husk cherry, or even strawberry tomato.

P. peruviana, a perennial that grows 3 to 4 feet high, is sometimes sold as cape gooseberry or 'Golden Berry.' This plant is the source of poha jam, which tourists often buy in Hawaii. *P. pruinosa*, an annual that grows to about 1-1/2 feet high, is sometimes called dwarf cape gooseberry. Unfortunately, not all seed catalogs are clear about which species they are offering.

Pests   This crop seems to be completely pest-free, although it is a potential host for tomato russet mites and nightshade-family diseases. If your tomatoes have russet mites, don't let ground-cherries overwinter, since they will allow the pest to survive. Also rotate ground-cherry along with other members of the nightshade family to keep diseases from building up in the soil.

Sources
Ground cherry seed: DD, JG, JSS, NGN, SB, TERR, T&M

HORSERADISH

Armoracia rusticana
Mustard Family ❖ *Cruciferae*

If you enjoy the sharp taste of horseradish, you may like to grow it yourself and make fresh sauce. However, it is usually at its best only after several weeks of frosty weather—an unlikely occurrence in our region. Also the roots are thinner and not the best flavored here. Still, I know of several local gardeners who have grown horseradish and were satisfied with their harvests.

Growing Instructions   Horseradish will grow in
any well-amended, fertile soil. Add plenty of organic matter to sandy soil, since horseradish plants
need constant moisture for the best growth. Don't
use fresh manure because it will cause forked roots.
Also be sparing with nitrogen, since too much will
encourage leafy growth at the expense of roots.
Horseradish needs a large amount of potassium.
Although this nutrient is usually sufficient here, you
may want to add some kelp meal or greensand if
your soil is very sandy.

Horseradish plants are grown from root cuttings. The custom is to sell roots with the top cut
flat across and the bottom cut at a slant. In February plant the roots right side up and at a 45-degree
angle. The top of the roots should be 3 inches below
the soil surface. You may also find potted horseradish plants at a nursery. Plant them 12 inches apart.

The Harvest   Dig up the roots in November, after
cold weather has had a chance to add some bite. If
the flavor is still too mild, try again in a month or
so. Either dig up roots as you need them or refrigerate harvested but unprocessed roots in moist sand in
a plastic bag. Prepare the roots by cleaning them,
peeling them, and grating them finely. Mix any
unused grated root with vinegar and refrigerate it in
a closed jar. As an alternative, peel the roots and
run them through a blender with a little white
vinegar.

Horseradish is a sturdy perennial that will grow
from any root fragments left in the soil. If you harvest the whole crop and plan to grow something
else in that spot, try to get every root fragment. In
spring check again for missed pieces of root. You
can start a new planting with freshly dug roots or
roots that you stored in the refrigerator. (Be sure to
cut the ends of stored roots in the customary way so
that you won't accidentally plant them upside
down.) If you are leaving plants in the ground from
year to year, don't maintain any particular plant
more than two or three years, because the root will
become too tough to eat.

Pests   Horseradish may attract some mustard-family pests, such as cabbage loopers and imported cabbageworms. Although horseradish sometimes gets a
leaf spot disease, the roots are rarely affected.

Sources

Horseradish roots: BG, JSS, NGN, PS, PTS, RSP, VBS

JERUSALEM ARTICHOKE (SEE SUNCHOKE)

JICAMA
Pachyrhizus erosus
Pea Family   ❖   *Leguminosae*
These big crisp sweet roots (pronounced HEE-ka-
ma) require a warmer summer than we get in our
region. I once started some jicama seeds in my garden in the Mission district of San Francisco and in
my nearby apartment. The plants in the garden
grew less than a foot tall and died before the summer was over. The one that grew in a pot in my
living room made several twining stems, each bearing typical pea-family leaves with three leaflets
each. I put up string for the stems to twine on and
directed them around my living room window. They
framed it nicely, each stem growing about 10 feet
long. The plant was so dramatic that it got a lot of
comments, but when it died down in fall and I dug
up the root, I found that it was woody and only
about 2 inches across. I had to concede that we are
dependent on gardeners in warmer climates for this
delicious vegetable.

KALE (OR BORECOLE) AND FLOWER-ING KALE (OR FLOWERING CABBAGE)
Brassica oleracea
Acephala Group

SIBERIAN KALE (OR RUSSIAN KALE OR HUNGRY GAP)
B. napus
Pabularia Group
Mustard Family   ❖   *Cruciferae*

The plant most commonly called kale is *B. oleracea*,
the same species as collards. It even looks like
handsomely curled collard greens. *B. napus*, a related plant known as Siberian kale, is similar but
stays mild and tender enough to be eaten raw for a
longer period.

Several varieties of *B. oleracea* are grown mainly
as ornamentals. Called flowering kale or flowering
cabbage, they are grown for their decorative leaves.
The plants form a low cluster of leaves that look
like a big rose. The outer leaves remain green, but
the inner ones turn purple, white, or a combination
of purple, white, and green. Flowering kale adds

color to a winter garden, even in areas that get no winter sun. Use them for indoor decoration as well. Bring potted plants inside for a day, or cut the plants and stand their stems in water. Besides being beautiful, the leaves are also edible. Young leaves add a bright accent to winter salads, and older ones can be eaten cooked in hot slaws and other dishes.

Growing Instructions   Grow kale from transplants or seeds sown in place. Start seeds in midsummer for fall and winter harvests or as early as January for a spring crop. The final spacing depends on the cultivar and whether you want to harvest whole young plants or leaves from mature plants. Leave only a few inches for whole young plants, and 10 to 24 inches for mature plants. Grow Siberian kale the same way, but sow it in place since it doesn't transplant well. The final spacing for mature plants should be 18 inches. Like collards, kale plants become huge when they flower and go to seed, and they often seed themselves.

Start flowering kale seeds in mid- to late summer, sowing them in containers or a seeding bed for later transplanting. Young flowering kale plants are sometimes available in nurseries in late summer. For instant color, you can buy nearly full-grown plants.

The Harvest   Pull whole young plants, or pick leaves from plants as they grow. Try young kale leaves raw. Later, when the leaves have become sturdy and flavorful, cook them. In spring use the stalks of flower buds for stir fry.

Harvest flowering kale leaves during the winter when the color is fully developed. If you have room, you may prefer to harvest plants from a back bed while leaving untouched plants in a prominent spot to beautify your garden.

Varieties   All varieties of kale grow well here. As with collards, most of the available *B. oleracea* kale varieties are the shorter ones, which grow to 18 inches high at most. Tall varieties reach 3 or 4 feet. The name of the variety often suggests the height—such as 'Dwarf Scotch' or 'Tall Curled'. Look for 'Lacinato', an Italian variety that seems to be the same as the heirloom 'Braschetti' grown in San Francisco by Italian gardeners. It has dramatic, blue-green, straplike, crinkled leaves.

A very popular Siberian kale variety is called 'Red Russian' or 'Ragged Jack'. This type, originally introduced into Canada by Russian traders, has handsome red-tinged, lobed leaves and good flavor.

Flowering kale is usually listed under *kale* or *cabbage* in the ornamental section of seed catalogs. Some flowering kale plants have curlier leaves than others. You can also buy seed selections that produce only purple plants or only white ones.. Hybrid varieties may be more vigorous and develop earlier than the regular, open-pollinated strains.

Pests   All types of kale are subject to mustard-family pests (see page 183). Since you will probably be less tolerant of damage to flowering kale in an ornamental planting than in the vegetable garden, be ready to control imported cabbageworms and cabbage loopers until the colder fall days kill them. Handpick caterpillars or apply Bt (see page 132).

Sources
Kale seed: Widely available
Russian Red: ABL, JSS, ODG, PTS, SB, SOC, SGS, T&M, TERR
Lacinato: ABL, SGS
Ornamental kale seed: BG, JG, PS, SB, T&M

KOHLRABI

Brassica oleracea
Gongylodes Group
Mustard Family ❖
Cruciferae

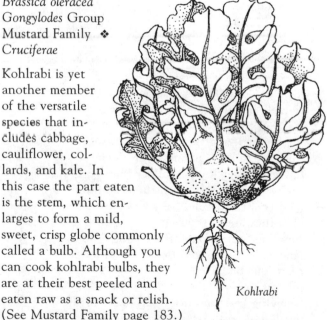

Kohlrabi is yet another member of the versatile species that includes cabbage, cauliflower, collards, and kale. In this case the part eaten is the stem, which enlarges to form a mild, sweet, crisp globe commonly called a bulb. Although you can cook kohlrabi bulbs, they are at their best peeled and eaten raw as a snack or relish. (See Mustard Family page 183.)

Kohlrabi

Growing Instructions   You can sow kohlrabi seeds in place or grow transplants. I have had the best results from a sowing in June or July, but plantings a month or so later or in early spring are also worth trying. (Bulbs that mature in very warm weather are likely to become tough and peppery.) The seedlings must be transplanted or thinned to stand 8 to 12 inches apart. Plants that are too close together simply refuse to make big round bulbs.

The Harvest Begin to harvest when the bulb is the size of a golf ball. This will take at least two months. You can let some bulbs get larger, up to about 4 inches across. Don't go for record-breaking bulbs, however, because they will be tough and tasteless. Peel bulbs before eating them.

Varieties Both green and purple varieties are available. Although the purple ones are pretty in the garden, all kohlrabi bulbs are white inside when peeled.

Pests Kohlrabi is subject to the usual mustard-family pests (see page 183).

Sources
Kohlrabi seed:
Green or white varieties: Widely available
Purple varieties: ABL, CG, JG, JSS, PS, PTS, SB, SGS, TERR

Leek

Allium ampeloprasum
Porrum Group
Amaryllis Family ❖
Amaryllidaceae

Leek flower buds emerging from bract

Leeks deserve wider planting in local gardens. They are easy to grow (largely because they are resistant to many of the pests and diseases affecting onions), and they produce a very welcome fall and winter crop. Their flavor is sweet—much milder than that of onions. Although they can be used young as tender baby leeks in summer, they are in their glory full grown and standing firm through the cold and rain, ready to be harvested for a soup or an elegant quiche.

Growing Instructions Give leeks organic, fertile soil and keep them well watered during the dry season. For the biggest leeks, plant seeds indoors from December through January or outdoors from January through March. Seeds planted later won't produce very large leeks before cold weather slows their growth. Although you can plant outdoors in fall, it is a gamble. The plants will probably go to seed in late winter or early spring of the next year, or if they are very small in winter they may con-

tinue growing into large leeks in spring and summer. Of course, if you plan to harvest them young, you can plant them almost anytime.

Sow the seeds 1/2 inch deep and 1/4 to 1/2 inch apart in a seedbed for later transplanting. Otherwise, direct-seed them slightly further apart and thin the seedlings to 3 to 6 inches apart. Another good option is to plant purchased seedlings. Nursery packs of leeks are usually a good buy, since they contain many seedlings for a low price.

I either sow seeds close together in a seedbed or start them indoors and transplant them to the seedbed when they have three or four leaves. They stay in the seedbed until they are approximately the diameter of a pencil. Whenever a large enough area of my spring or summer garden is bare, I transplant the leeks. Although some sources recommend clipping the leaf tops when you transplant, I never do. Since the leeks will be there all fall and often into winter, I don't interplant them with summer crops but instead give them their own out-of-the-way site.

The most tender part of the leek is the white portion of the shaft. Leeks are bred to make long shafts, which are tender and white only if they are blanched by being underground. Traditionally, gardeners achieved this by planting seedlings in a trench and gradually filling it in or by mounding soil around the growing plants. Since I don't have the extra soil to do either in my small raised-bed garden, I prefer a newer method of blanching that works just as well—burying the leek to the base of the first leaf joint when I transplant.

The Harvest Pull up baby leeks whenever you like. For mature leeks dig the plants when they are more than 1 inch in diameter, usually not until September. Harvest as needed during the winter, but finish picking before the middle of March or the plants will go to seed. Use some of the tougher but more nutritious green leaves in cooking, if only for flavoring broth. Don't add much, since you don't want to overwhelm the dish.

Varieties Some varieties are listed as winter leeks and others as summer leeks. Winter leeks are able to overwinter in climates that are colder than ours and would kill a summer leek. In my experience, all leeks overwinter very well in our mild climate. If you are growing the crop specifically for baby leeks, you may as well grow a summer leek, since this type is often more tender. For fall and winter harvests,

LEEK QUICHE

Quiches cost $12 and up at a delicatessen. They are really not hard to make and are great at a brunch or as a light supper dish, so why not make it yourself? Use the classic pie crust recipe below, or any unsweetened crust recipe that you prefer.

Filling
1 1/2 to 2 cups sliced leeks (at least 2/3 should be the white part)
3 tablespoons butter or margarine
3 eggs
1 1/2 cups milk (can be low or nonfat)
6 ounces Swiss cheese, grated (Gruyère is nice, or try Jarlsberg)

Pie Crust
1/2 cup butter or margarine (1 stick)
1 1/4 cups unbleached flour
1/2 teaspoon salt (optional)
2 to 3 tablespoons ice water

Preheat oven to 325° F and prepare the pie crust. Have ready a 9-inch pie pan, rolling pin and a clean rolling surface. (If your kitchen doesn't have a good rolling surface, use a sheet of brown paper cut from a large grocery bag.)

Put 1/2 cup butter in a medium bowl and cut it up with a knife until no piece is over 1/2-inch in diameter. Add flour and salt. Working quickly, rub the butter into the flour with your fingertips until the mixture looks like coarse meal. Try to keep the mixture loose; don't encourage the particles to stick to each other.

Put 3 tablespoons of water in a cup with an ice cube. Sprinkle half of the ice water over the flour mixture and begin immediately to try to form a ball of dough. Handle as little as possible. If some of the flour mixture is still not adhering to the ball, add just a bit more water until it does. (You may not need to add all of the water.) When the dough is ready, it should clean the bowl of the flour/butter mixture and it should not be sticky.

Sprinkle a little flour on your rolling surface. Place the dough in the center of it and flatten the top slightly with your hand. Sprinkle the dough with a little flour. Roll the dough out into a round slightly larger than the pie pan, adding just a bit more flour if needed to prevent sticking. Put the crust in the pie pan and use your fingers to make a thickened wavy edge. Cut any excess dough away with a knife. Set the pie crust aside.

Sauté the leeks in 3 tablespoons butter until tender but not browned. Spread them in the bottom of the raw crust. (For fewer calories, steam the leeks.)

In a medium bowl, gently beat together the eggs and milk, then stir in the grated cheese. Pour the cheese mixture over the leeks.

Bake at 325° F for 30 minutes, or until a knife inserted in the center comes out clean. Serves six to eight.

Variations:
• Blend 1 1/2 cups New Zealand or regular spinach with the milk and eggs in a blender. Stir in the cheese and pour the mixture over the leeks in the crust. Bake as directed.
• Spread 1/4 pound small cooked shrimp on the leeks before you add the milk, egg and cheese mixture.

choose a winter leek. I have no particular variety to recommend, since I have had great success with every variety I've tried.

Sources
Leek seeds: Widely available

LETTUCE
Lactuca sativa
Sunflower Family ❖ *Compositae*

Lettuce grows best and is most delectable when the days are cool. Our ocean-cooled climate allows us to grow lettuce virtually all year, although we may have to start it indoors during the coldest months and shade it during the warmest months. We can grow all the different kinds of lettuce: looseleaf, butterhead, romaine, and crisphead. Some varieties of each cope better with warmer days and some with cooler days.

Growing Instructions Lettuce needs soil that is fertile, loose, and well drained. It will grow very poorly in unamended clay soil. Give it plenty of water from the time it first sprouts until it is harvested. Chronically underwatered plants will be stunted, tough, and vulnerable to pests.

Direct-seed lettuce 1/4 inch deep from February to early July for crispheads such as 'Iceberg,' and from February to August for the others. Outdoor sowings from September to January are chancy—success depends on the variety, your microclimate, and the weather during that particular year. I sow lettuce indoors at this time, getting it off to a good start before putting it out to brave the elements. When you are sowing lettuce in containers, barely cover the seeds with fine potting soil. The ideal temperature for lettuce germination is 60°–75°F.

Although all lettuce varieties transplant easily, seedlings of looseleaf and some butterhead varieties are remarkably tolerant of being held in containers. They recover so well from being crowded and root bound that you can transplant seedlings as you need them and hold the rest in containers for several more weeks. Just add some weak fertilizer solution periodically and provide adequate light and water. Otherwise, the seedlings will become fragile and hard to transplant.

When you are direct-seeding lettuce, you can sow the seeds in single-file rows, wide rows, or small blocks. Try to sow thinly, or actually set each seed 1 to 2 inches from the next one. Cover the seeds

with 1/4 inch of soil. When the plants are 2 to 3 inches high, thin crisphead varieties to 12 inches apart and other types to 6 inches apart. If you like, remove the extra plants with a small trowel and plant them elsewhere. The transplanted seedlings will grow a bit slower, giving you a slightly staggered crop.

Our warmest and coldest days are difficult for lettuce. Look for varieties that cope best with the weather at the time of year you intend to plant. Even though our summers are relatively cool, even a brief hot spell may cause lettuce to become bitter, go to seed prematurely, or both. If you live in a sunny part of the region or are planting lettuce to mature in September or October, plant it where it will be shaded by another crop for part of the day. Don't expect it to remain at its prime for very long.

Local truck farmers grow baby lettuce the year around, starting it every two weeks in a greenhouse, planting it in raised beds kept free of snails and slugs, and harvesting it in four to five weeks. When I asked one farmer how his lettuce grows in winter, he replied dryly, "very slowly." During our dark, cool months, lettuce may grow so slowly that it can't keep ahead of pest damage. In warmer weather the stressed lettuce would just lose a leaf or two, but in winter it may actually diminish in size. If you can't eliminate snails and slugs, combat them by growing the lettuce under a floating row cover or in a pestproof cold frame (see page 50).

The Harvest You can begin to harvest lettuce by adding thinned seedlings to salads. When looseleaf, butterhead, or romaine have developed a number of leaves, you can take one or two outer leaves per plant. As these plants grow you can continue to pick them by the leaf, always leaving enough so that the plant can keep growing. You can also harvest by cutting or pulling the entire plant at any time. Harvesting by the leaf has the virtue of prolonging the harvest, but if you overplanted, you may prefer to take whole plants to reduce the total crop. Romaine lettuce is most often harvested either as whole baby lettuce or whole mature plants. Crisphead varieties are usually harvested at maturity, when the head is large and firm.

Cutting lettuces are varieties, usually looseleaf, that resprout vigorously from a cut stem. Just use a knife or scissors to cut the plant near the ground. These varieties are good additions to mesclun (see page 221) and, in my experience, are best cut and recut while they are fairly small.

Estimate how much lettuce you will use before you plant. Small successive plantings are usually better than a single large planting. When gardeners ask me what to do with lettuce besides making salads, I take it as a sure sign that they overplanted. Having said that, I offer two uncommon recipes from my father's childhood on a farm in Indiana. They won't take up much of your surplus (your nongardening friends are

looseleaf you can pick whole plants or leaves much earlier.

Romaine, or cos, lettuce is upright and columnar in habit, has a crisp texture, and is considered the slowest to bolt. Some references advise gardeners to plant it only in spring, but seed companies

Left to right:
Bibb, romaine, crisphead,
butterhead, looseleaf

probably your best bet for that), but they do offer variety. The first is Bibb or Buttercrunch lettuce with honey. This simple treat is nothing more than a bowl of very fresh young butterhead leaves drizzled with a little honey. The other is wilted lettuce (see page 220).

Varieties Looseleaf varieties are ones that form no heads. They include green-leaved 'Black Seeded Simpson', 'Salad Bowl', and 'Oakleaf', and red-leaved 'Red Sails' and 'Red Oakleaf'. Looseleaf varieties mature in only 45 to 60 days, though you will probably be picking outer leaves before then.

Butterhead varieties have a tender, buttery texture. They may not form much of a head, or may have a loose head and a blanched center. They include the old green variety 'Bibb', the newer 'Buttercrunch'—which is larger and more heat tolerant—and many other varieties. Red-tinged 'Continuity' and 'Four Seasons' (or Merveille des Quatre Saisons) are probably the same variety. Butterhead varieties mature in 60 to 75 days, but as with

offer winter varieties, and local market gardeners are able to grow some kinds through our winters. A good summer romaine is 'Little Gem,' a green-leaved type that grows only 6 inches high. For all seasons try 'Rouge d'Hiver,' a red-leaved type. Most romaine varieties take more than 75 days to mature, although dwarf ones may mature more quickly. 'Little Gem,' for instance, is listed at 65 days.

'Iceberg', commonly sold in supermarkets, is a kind of crisphead best suited to the Imperial Valley, where it is grown commercially. Try instead varieties bred for home gardeners. Two good new varieties are 'Diamond Head' and 'Summertime'. Batavian types, such as the red 'Sierra' have looser heads. Crispheads take about three months to mature.

There are a legion of lettuce varieties, and most will do well here, so try several a year. Try heirloom and new ones, redleaf and green. You will notice that the main types have strains with similar names or descriptions. For example, there is a 'Simpson Elite'—an improved 'Black Seeded Simpson'. And a number of varieties are really red oak leaf types, though they are called 'Purple Oak Leaf', 'Brunia', or 'Mascara'.

WILTED LETTUCE

Wilted lettuce reflects the German contribution to the Midwest melting pot and it's a dish I remember from my childhood there. The heated sweet and sour dressing wilts the lettuce, resulting in more of a vegetable dish than a salad. These days, I only make it when I've purchased some nitrite-free bacon at a natural foods store.

2 medium heads looseleaf or butterhead lettuce, torn into pieces (about 8 cups)
4 slices nitrite-free bacon
1/2 medium onion, cut into small pieces
3 tablespoons cider vinegar
2 tablespoons water
1 tablespoon white or brown sugar

Put the lettuce pieces in a large bowl, and set it aside. In a small bowl, combine the vinegar, water, and sugar, stirring until the sugar dissolves. Set this aside, too.

Fry the bacon in a skillet until it is crisp, then set it on a paper towel to drain and to cool. Crumble the bacon and set it aside. Measure out and reserve 1/4 cup of bacon drippings, and discard the rest.

Return the 1/4 cup of drippings to the skillet and fry the onion, over medium heat, till it is soft, but not browned. Stir in the vinegar mixture. Add the crumbled bacon. Heat this dressing to the boiling point, stirring all the while. Immediately pour the hot dressing over the lettuce, and toss it to mix. Serves four.

Variation: To make this even more of a vegetable dish, let the lettuce cook briefly in the dressing. Leftovers of either version are delicious.

Pests Lettuce seedlings are often the most tender morsels in a garden, so they understandably fall prey to birds, cutworms, earwigs, slugs, and snails. As lettuce plants mature they remain attractive to snails and slugs, and they may also attract aphids and spider mites. To the dismay of unsuspecting gardeners, slugs often live deep in the plants at the bases of leaves. Occasional night slug-picking forays, flashlight in hand, will reduce damage considerably. Earwigs often feed on lettuce, especially in the spring. Set out earwig traps among your lettuce plants and see what you catch (see page 141). If leaves are nibbled from the edges all around, suspect bird damage, and try covering the planting with bird netting. Cabbage loopers are potential pests, though they have not been so in my garden.

A fairly serious disease, lettuce drop, causes plants to collapse into a slimy mess. If this happens, check the base for white fungal mats and pea-sized, black resting bodies. Remove affected plants and as much of the debris as you can to halt spread of the disease. Soil solarization (see page 99) will control this disease. Corn is immune, but most other crops can get it.

Sources

Lettuce seed:
Looseleaf varieties:
    Black-seeded Simpson (green): Widely available
    Salad Bowl (green): Widely available
    Oakleaf (green): Widely available
    Red Oakleaf (red): ABL, BG, CG, DD, GG, JSS, NGN, SB, SGS, SOC, PS, TERR
    Red Sails (red): CG, JSS, NGN, OBG, PS, PTS, TERR, VBS
Butterhead varieties:
    Bibb (green): ABL, BG, CG, NGN
    Buttercrunch (green): ABL, BG, CG, JSS, NGN, OBG, PS, PTS, SB, SOC, TERR, T&M, VBS
    Continuity (Four Seasons) (red): ABL, GG, JG, NGN, OBG, PTS, RCS, SB, SGS, SOC, TERR

MESCLUN

In specialty produce departments you can now help yourself to pricey but delicious mixed young salad greens: green and red, frilly and plain, mild and piquant. They are chosen to delight the eye and the palate. This is really a very old idea—in Europe salad mixes were traditionally sown together and harvested young. The mixes may consist of several kinds of lettuce, or they may also include arugula, chervil, chicory, corn salad, cress, dandelion, endive, fennel, or any other fast-growing tender green.

Prepackaged mixes of cutting lettuce or more complex mescluns let you try the concept at minimal expense. Packaged mescluns are blended for matched growth rate and a pleasing mix of flavor and color, but you can also blend your own mix from seeds that you have.

Begin sowing seeds for mesclun in February, or even January if soil is dry enough to work. Be sure you have weeds reasonably under control, or can identify ones that might come up in the mesclun bed. (If not, better grow your mesclun in potting mix in a planter box.)

Broadcast the seeds in small blocks or sow them in rows 6 inches apart. Make successive plantings every week, sowing only as much as you think you will use in a week. Keep planting as long as the weather is cool enough to produce tender leafy growth. Take a break if the weather is too warm in late summer. Sow as late into fall as your microclimate permits, stopping if cold weather and dark days slow growth too much.

Harvest just a few weeks after you sow the seeds, when the plants are 4 to 6 inches high. The easiest method is to use scissors to cut a section of plants 1/2 inch above the ground. The cut bases resprout to give you additional crops.

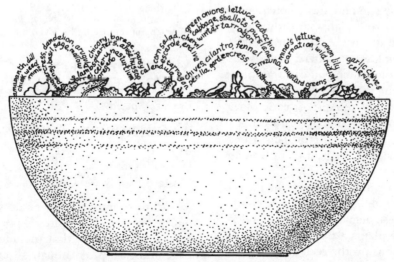

Even without sowing an actual mesclun, salads from your garden can have the same serendipitous look and mix of flavors. Throughout the year, but especially in winter and spring, you can use many domesticated and wild greens, herbs, and edible flowers to create a gourmet salad.

Sources
Cutting lettuce seed mixes: CG, NGN, PTS, SB
Mesclun seed: ABL, BG, CG, JSS, NGN, OBG, PS, PTS, TERR, VBS

Romaine varieties:
    Little Gem (green): ABL, CG, JSS, OBG, PS, SGS, SOC,
      TERR, T&M
    Rouge d'Hiver (red): ABL, CG, SB, SGS, SOC
Crisphead varieties:
    Diamond Head (green): TERR
    Summertime (green): BG, CG, PS, PTS, NGN, TERR
    Sierra (red): NGN, PTS, TERR
Lettuce seed mixes: BG, GG, NGN, PS, T&M, VBS

MELON (INCLUDES CANTALOUPE AND HONEYDEW)
Cucumis melo

WATERMELON
Citrullus lanatus
Gourd Family ❖ *Cucurbitaceae*

Every few years I come across a listing for a "very early" cantaloupe that is supposed to bear fruit even in cool weather. So far, my success has been limited to the 2-1/2-inch cantaloupe reported earlier in this chapter. And cantaloupe is probably the melon most likely to succeed here! Watermelon is even more heat-loving, although I have heard reports of small watermelons ripening in various San Francisco gardens. I expect I will be tempted again by another early melon variety.

Growing Instructions   If you garden in a protected, relatively sunny site and are tempted by melons, be sure to give your plants an early start indoors. In late March or early April, start melon seeds in 4-inch, bottomless containers, such as cut-off milk containers, from which you can transplant them without disturbing the roots (see page 54). Plant the seedlings out in late April or early May, when they have two or three true leaves. Do not be tempted to start much earlier and grow large transplants indoors, as these will not transplant well and are likely to be stunted.

Be sure the soil in which you plant the melons is well amended (to be able to grow in pure compost would delight these demanding plants) and well fertilized. Set the plants 3 to 5 feet apart (check recommendations on the seed packet). Water regularly but don't let the soil stay soggy or the flavor of the fruit may be ruined.

When Cooperative Extension researchers conducted melon variety trials in San Jose in 1987, they went to great lengths to provide good growing conditions. Several weeks before the planting date, they buried a drip irrigation line under the bed (you could use a soaker hose instead). Then they laid black plastic over the soil to warm it. They planted the seedlings in slits cut in the plastic, then placed a floating row cover over the whole bed to warm the air above the soil. (If you do this, remember to tuck the edges of the black plastic into the soil to keep snails from hiding under it, and then, when you add the row cover, tuck its edges into the soil outside the edges of black plastic.) They stopped irrigation as soon as they picked the first ripe fruit. Although these Herculean efforts don't guarantee a good crop in our cool region, they will improve your chances.

Varieties   In the absence of varieties that have succeeded in my garden, I will list top-rated melons in recent San Jose melon trials. These are early varieties, since San Jose is a bit cooler than melons like. ('Ogen' and 'Ha-Ogen', recommended in a previous edition of this book, have proven less reliable than the varieties listed below.)

Pests   Melons often fall prey to powdery mildew. Of the varieties listed below, 'Galica' and 'Gallicum' resist this disease. (See page 157 for information on combatting powdery mildew.)

Sources
Melon seed:
Galia (lime-green flesh): CG, SGS
Gallicum (lime-green flesh): NGN, PS
Snow Charm (orange flesh): CG

MUSTARD GREENS (OR SOUTHERN MUSTARD)
Brassica juncea

TENDERGREEN (OR MUSTARD SPINACH)
B. rapa
Perviridis Group
Mustard Family ❖ *Cruciferae*

All kinds of mustard greens do very well throughout our region. Some are *B. juncea* and others are *B. rapa*, the species that includes Chinese cabbage and turnip. Although all culinary mustards are probably Asian in origin, some have become staples in American cooking, especially in the South. Mustards vary considerably in flavor, tenderness, and susceptibility to snails and slugs, but most make quick, short-standing crops of greens. Experiment to see which ones you like and which do well for you.

Growing Instructions   Mustards often go to seed prematurely, or bolt, during long days and thus are best sown in late winter, early spring, or mid- to late summer. Since they vary in resistance to cold, some can be planted later than others in fall. Although they will succeed in any good garden soil, they grow faster in soils that warm quickly. (If your soil is clay, be sure to amend the area where you are growing spring mustards.)

All mustards are seeded in place, about 1/2 inch deep, and thinned as they mature. They are very quick crops listed at 20 to 45 days. If you plan to eat them young, sow a few more every couple of weeks. Most kinds go to seed soon after reaching maturity, so you must use them quickly. However, some will hold in the winter months from a fall planting, not bolting until spring. As with all quick-growing crops, be sure to keep mustards well watered.

The Harvest   Harvest whole plants or outer leaves at any stage, or cut young plants near the base and let them regrow. Use mild-flavored mustard in salads (young mustards are part of many mescluns) or stir-fries. Stronger-flavored leaves are generally cooked—boiled or used in stir-fries or soups. The key to preparing strong-flavored mustards is to use sturdy seasonings able to stand up to their strong flavor. In Southern cooking, the seasonings of choice are often onion, a little smoked bacon or ham, and a dash of bottled hot sauce. In a typical dish, the pork is sautéed with the onions, the mustard and some water added, the hot sauce tossed in at the end. Although this dish is usually cooked much longer, it is fully cooked and more nutritious boiled about 20 minutes. In Asian cooking, the seasoning for strong-flavored mustard is likely to be sesame oil and soy sauce. (See the recipe for Turnips, Noodle, and Tofu Sauté, page 262.)

Varieties and Related Species   The pungent mustard varieties are *B. juncea*. Their broad leaves, which are sometimes ruffled or lobed, may be green, red, or almost purple. The mild-flavored 'Mizuna' (also called kyona) so often found in mesclun, is probably also *B. juncea*. Its long, coarsely toothed leaves are nice in salad.

The most common *B. rapa* mustard is tendergreen, or mustard spinach. It is so mild that some find it bland. 'Tyfon Holland Greens' are a cross between genetic turnip and Chinese Cabbage.

Tsai tai, or taisai, is an Asian *B. rapa* grown for its young flower shoots. Those of hon tsai tai are purple. It is best sown June through early fall. Another *B. rapa* vegetable grown for its shoots of flower buds is broccoli raab, or rapini, a traditional Italian crop. Old strains of this had to be overwintered before they would bloom, but some new types will produce a fast crop from either early spring or late summer plantings. (Add chopped raab shoots to onion and garlic that have been sautéed in olive oil, add a few dry-toasted pine nuts, a sprinkle of lemon juice, and a dash of red pepper flakes.) To grow mustard seed as a seasoning, see page 293.

Pests   Mustard greens are susceptible to slug and snail damage, and can be infested by cabbage aphids. They often escape damage by cabbage maggots, though attacks are possible, especially in warmer weather.

Sources
Mustard greens seed:
B. juncea (green): ABL, CG, DD, EV, JG, JSS, OBG, PS, PTS, RCS, SB, SOC, VBS
B. juncea (red or purple): ABL, CG, DD, GG, EV, JSS, NGN, PS, PTS, RCS, SOC, SGS, TERR
Mizuna: ABL, CG, EV, JSS, KSC, NGN, PTS, SB, SOC, SGS, TERR, VBS
Tendergreen: ABL, NGN, PTS, SB, VBS
Tyfon Holland Greens: NGN, PTS, VBS
Hon tsai tai: EV, JSS, JG, NGN
Broccoli Raab: DD, PS, PTS, RH, SB, SGS, TERR

ONION, BULB
Allium cepa
Cepa Group
Amaryllis Family ❖ *Amaryllidaceae*
Bulb onions are a cool-season crop that can be grown successfully in all parts of our region. Yet gardeners often find that their plants go to seed before the bulbs form or that the bulbs never get very big. Onions are a bit ornery and some of your plants may misbehave no matter what you do. Still, you can increase your success rate dramatically if you learn what this crop needs: well-prepared soil, ample moisture, minimum weed competition, the right variety, and proper timing.

Growing Instructions   Amend your soil well for onions. This is especially important if the soil is very sandy or clayey. Without organic matter, you will find it too difficult to keep sandy soil moist enough, and in heavy clay soil onions often form small bulbs. Heavy clay also has a tendency to be come waterlogged—a condition that encourages soilborne onion disease. Be sure to fertilize when you plant.

Give onions plenty of water during their first few weeks of growth, since the surface roots that

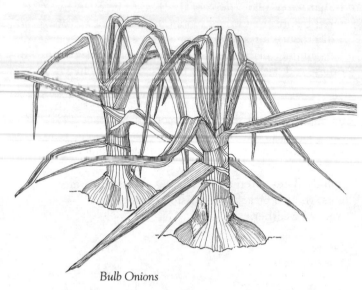

Bulb Onions

form during that time are essential to the future vigor of the plants. Keep weeds under control, because they will compete for water and shade out young onion plants.

Make sure that the variety you are growing will form bulbs in our region. Onions are sensitive to day length—that is, they begin to form bulbs when the days reach a certain length. If the variety you planted needs longer days than we get at our latitude, it will never form bulbs. (See opposite page for more information about day length.) Even when a variety is adapted to our day length, it still won't do well unless it is planted at the right time—either fall or late winter, depending on the variety. If it is planted too late, it will not be mature enough when the bulb begins to form and, as a result, will produce small bulbs. If it is planted too early, all or some of the plants will go to seed instead of making bulbs, since premature seeding is stimulated by low temperatures when the plant is half grown. (See page 227 for more details on why onions go to seed prematurely.) The most common way of starting bulb onions is from small purchased bulbs called sets. As an alternative, you can start your own seedlings, or you can buy seedlings or bare-root plants from a nursery. (Don't plant sprouted grocery store onions, because they will go to seed right away and never form good bulbs. Also, they may be diseased.)

Onions sets are a popular way to grow onions, since they are easier to handle than seeds or small plants. However, plants grown from sets are more likely to go to seed before they form a bulb than transplanted seedlings are. Another disadvantage is that the varieties available as sets aren't usually the ones best suited to our region.

If you are planting onion sets to produce bulb onions rather than green onions, choose sets that are less than 3/4 inch in diameter. Plant them, pointy end up, just below the soil surface, and leave 3 to 4 inches between sets. Plant onion sets in January or February to give them the entire spring to make big plants before the bulbs begin to form. March is risky, and sets planted in April or May definitely won't have enough time to make big bulbs. (Gardeners who plant late often leave the small bulbs in the ground hoping that they will mature into big bulbs next year, but that is unlikely to happen. The onions are more apt to bloom and go to seed the following spring.)

Starting onions from seed gives you the widest choice of varieties. If you are starting seeds before October 1 or after January 1, you can seed directly in the garden. From October through December start the seeds indoors, allowing ten weeks from the seeding date to the correct transplant time for the variety you are growing. If seedlings are getting their start outdoors in fall, allow an extra month or so, since they will grow more slowly as the days get shorter and colder.

Sow onion seeds 1/4 to 1/2 inch deep. You can plant them 2 inches apart and thin the seedlings to 3 to 4 inches apart. As an alternative, sow more thickly in a small area and transplant the seedlings to stand 3 to 4 inches apart when they have at least three leaves.

Some mail-order seed companies offer bare-root onion seedlings. Make sure that the variety is well suited to our latitude and that the company will ship it at the right time—January or February. Bare-root plants are usually sold in bunches of 150, so you will probably want to share your order with other gardeners. Container plants from local nurseries are also a good option, as long as you choose a suitable variety and plant at the proper time.

Keep the plants well watered through the spring, until the necks (the stems right above the bulbs) begin to be less firm. When this happens, stop watering. When the necks are quite flat, the bulbs are fully formed. At this point, most of the leaves are dead and the plants often fall over.

ONIONS AND DAY LENGTH

Most onions are sensitive to day length—meaning that their life cycle is geared to the amount of daylight they receive. Specifically, they begin to form bulbs when days reach a certain length. A short-day variety starts to form bulbs when days are 12-14 hours long. Intermediate-day onions begin to bulb up when days are about 14 hours long, and long-day types require between 14 and 16 hours of daylight.

Our goal as gardeners is two-fold. First, we want to choose an onion variety that can form bulbs at our latitude. If our longest day is too short for the variety we have planted, it will not form a bulb. Second, we want to have the onion plants growing in the garden as long as possible before the bulb-triggering daylength, because a larger plant can make a larger bulb. So this raises two questions: 1. What variety should we grow? 2. When should we plant it?

Before we can proceed, we need to know exactly how many hours of daylight we have on our longest day. This is determined by our distance from the equator. San Francisco is at latitude 37'5" north, where the longest day is 14 hours and 47 minutes. The longest days of Monterey and Mendocino, at opposite ends of coastal central California, are only a few minutes longer or shorter.

Therefore, we know that the longest-day onion types are not for us. A number of long-day onion varieties were bred for commercial onion growing areas such as Oregon, Washington, and New York, where daylight on June 21st is over 15 hours. However, some long-day onions will bulb at our 14 3/4 hour longest day, and if we can identify them, they are worth trying.

Short day onions will bulb up early, as early as March 21, when all of the earth's days are 12 hours long. This sounds OK, but raises problems of planting the onion early enough to be a large plant by that time—more on this in a minute, when we discuss timing. Our best bets are intermediate-day onions, ones that are best tailored to our day length.

Unfortunately, most seed catalogs don't mention the daylength needs of onions, let alone give the exact hours of daylight that trigger bulbing. If they do mention daylength, they may not separate out the intermediate daylength types. Furthermore, some varieties exhibit considerable variation, so seeds from one source may work better for you than seeds of a variety of the same name from another source.

Onion sets are even less predictable. Often, you won't know what variety they are. Try to find out, or at least try to learn where the sets were grown. Those grown in northern locations are least likely to do well here. Yellow and white sets are apt to be strains of 'Ebenezer', a long-day type.

Now, as for when to plant, the trick is to put the seed or set in early enough to get the biggest bulb, but not so early that cold weather will stimulate a flower stalk before the plant reaches its bulbing daylength (see Why Onions Bloom Instead of Bulbing, on page 227). To summarize planting times: plant seed for intermediate-day onions in mid to late fall, or in late winter (January or February), depending on the variety. Plant onion sets in January and February. Theoretically, if you wanted to try a short-day variety, such as 'Granex' or 'Bermuda', you would seed it in fall, but they are essentially a subtropical or tropical crop, so our winter cold could make them go to seed before they bulb. Much depends upon finding a hardier strain of short-day onion or having a particularly mild winter. It would probably be wiser to grow short-day onions indoors, or in a greenhouse, over the winter, setting them in the garden at the beginning of February. (Small pearl, or boiling onions, are short-day onions planted in spring and harvested young—see page 229.)

The Harvest You can eat onion bulbs fresh, digging them up when they are mature or nearly so. Or you can store them for up to several months—but if you plan to store them, don't dig them up too soon. Commercial onion growers keep the plants in the ground until they are completely dry, then leave them there for five to ten more days. Don't plan to put a summer crop, such as beans or tomatoes, in that spot next or you will be ⟍ tempted to dig the onions too soon. Instead, ⟍ plan to follow

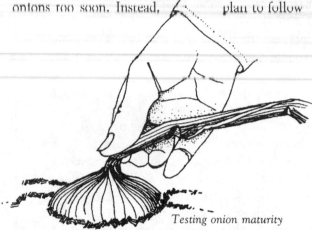

Testing onion maturity

onions with a late summer planting of a fall crop, such as carrots or a cole crop.

If you intend to braid the tops, do it immediately after digging up the bulbs. To cure onions, spread them in a single layer or hang them by their braids in a warm, dry place out of direct sunlight for a week or two. Check them every couple of days to be sure that they are drying well. When they are cured, gently brush off dirt and loose scales. If you didn't braid the stems, cut them 2 inches from the bulbs now.

Once onions have been cured, they keep best in a cool, dry place, ideally between 32° and 40°F. A refrigerator won't do, since the high humidity encourages sprouting and decay, and most local basements and garages are too warm. Hang the onions in the coolest, driest part of your home. If they are braided, hang the braids. If they are loose, hang them in mesh bags or in bags fashioned from panty hose. Store onions away from apples or bananas, since these fruits exude ethylene gas, which make onions sprout. Check stored onions often for sprouting, rooting, or decay—and eat undamaged parts of any affected onions immediately. Among onions of the same variety, use the biggest onions first. Also, use any onions that are more elongated than others of the same variety. Yellow onions are usually the best keepers, red intermediate, and white the worst. Other rules of thumb are that hotter varieties of onion keep better than milder ones, and long-day types keep better than short-day ones.

Varieties Read the catalog descriptions of onion varieties carefully. If an onion variety is described as *intermediate-day, midseason* or *grown in the north and south*, you will know that it is a good choice for our region. If it is listed as a *long-day type* or *grown in the north*, it may or may not grow well here. If a variety is listed as a *short-day type* or *grown in the south*, chances are that it will not do well here. But if you do want to try one of these short-day types, look for a variety that is said to resist cold.

The following are some of the varieties that we can grow. They are all intermediate or moderately long-day varieties, although I can't give you exact day lengths for them. I have not included short-day varieties, since I don't have any specific recommendations. It is, by no means, intended as a list of all varieties that may succeed. If you have questions

GROWING GREEN ONIONS

You can get green onions, or scallions, by planting bulb onion sets and pulling the plants when they are about six weeks old. For a continuous supply, plant sets every few weeks all year long, except possibly in December. For green onions plant the sets 3 inches below the soil surface, spacing them 1 to 2 inches apart. As an alternative, plant onion seeds close together and harvest when the stems are the diameter of green onions that you buy at the grocery store. (For other ways to grow green onions, see Bunching Onion on page 229 and Top Onion on page 230.)

WHY ONIONS BLOOM INSTEAD OF BULBING

All gardeners have had the problem of finding tall, inedible flower stems forming on onion plants that they had hoped would produce large, succulent bulbs. At the bottom of a blooming onion plant, there is a thinning, rubbery bulb, no longer good to eat, and by the time the seeds have formed, the bulb has disappeared altogether. A gardener needs to know why this happens, what can be done to make it less likely to happen, and whether the situation can be salvaged when it does happen.

Onion plants bloom, or bolt, when they are exposed to cold weather after they have reached a certain size. They are biennial plants, which, left to themselves, grow most of the year, rest as dormant bulbs, grow leaves again after winter, flower in their second spring, make seed, and then die.

Gardeners want the biggest bulbs possible, so they plant as early as they can, or even start with partly grown onion sets. But, if the seedlings, or the sets, have made plants with lower stems larger than a pencil in diameter when the grip of winter closes in December, the plants are likely to bloom before they can bulb up.

Some of your onion plants will probably always bloom. It is more likely to happen when we have a long, cool spring or one with alternating warm and cool spells. And onion varieties vary somewhat in how much cold they can endure before they are stimulated to flower. (You may find varieties that are said to be "bolt resistant.") But a general rule is that you can prevent most blooming by making sure that if onion plants are growing outdoors, their lower stems are less than 1/4 to 3/8 inch in diameter in December and January.

If you are planting seeds of intermediate-day onions outdoors in a site that is cool and foggy in late summer and fall, try sowing on September 1. If your site is warm and protected in fall, wait until October 1, as the onions will grow faster there and may be too big by December. If you are more inland, where winters get colder, start seed even later, maybe November 1, since the colder nights may make plants bolt while they are smaller than if they were in a more moderate microclimate. If your planting site is particularly cold, you might be better off starting seeds indoors in October and planting them out in January. Onions that need longer days, within the intermediate-day range, are best seeded outdoors in January or February and no later than March. If you want to give them an early start, sow them indoors from November through early January.

Wait until mid-January or February to plant onion sets. Fall planting is too risky, since plants growing from all but the smallest sets will by definition be larger than 1/4 inch in diameter when they encounter the colder temperatures of December and January. Sets larger than 1/2 to 3/4 inch are likely to bolt whenever they are planted, so look for packages with the smallest sets. When you get a number of larger sets mixed in, use these for growing green onions, or scallions (see page 226) and plant only the small sets for bulb onions.

Storage temperature also affects whether onion sets will bolt. Sets purchased in bona fide nurseries are more likely to have been stored correctly (either at 32° to 35° F or at above 65° F) than those purchased in mass-merchandise outlets or stores that sell plants as a sideline.

And what if your plants do form flower stems? One option is to dig up the plant as soon as you see the stem forming and eat the bulb before it shrivels. Another is to cut the flower stalk and hope that a usable bulb will still form. You will probably get a reasonably usable bulb if you do this. Or, you could let a few onions flower, as they are prime attractants for beneficial insects.

about any specific variety you find as seeds, sets, or bare-root seedlings, contact the seed company involved and ask for more information.

Mid-Keeper White and Yellow Types

- 'White Sweet Spanish' and 'Yellow Sweet Spanish' are long-day onions that are large, somewhat pungent, and store fairly well. There are numerous strains of these varieties, which vary in vigor, uniformity, yield, and storage life. If you find a good source, stick with it.

- 'Valencia' is a Utah strain of 'Yellow Sweet Spanish' that is a good keeper and has bulbs weighing up to one pound.

- 'Fiesta' is a hybrid of a sweet Spanish onion and 'Yellow Globe' that keeps pretty well and requires a slightly shorter day length than most sweet Spanish strains.

- 'Walla Walla Sweet' may be any of several varieties marketed under this name. Some will do well here, while others require longer days.

Short Keeper Reds

- 'Red Torpedo' is an intermediate-day type with an elongated light purplish-red bulb. It is sweet and mild. 'Italian Blood Red Bottle' is similar.

- 'Stockton Early Red' (also known as 'Fresno Red' or 'Early Red') is an intermediate-day onion that is bolt resistant, or less likely to go to seed before bulbing. It forms a large, mild globe.

- 'Early Red Burger' is intermediate-day, and similar to 'Stockton Early Red', but is a deeper red, slightly smaller, and a week or so earlier.

White and Yellow Storage Types

- 'Southport White Globe' is a long-day type that keeps very well. The medium-sized bulbs hold their shape and mildly pungent flavor well during cooking. One seed source has replaced it with 'Blanco Duro', which they say has better flavor, more uniform and heavier yields, and fewer thick necks, suggesting longer storage potential.

- 'Hi-Ball F_1' makes very solid ball-shaped bulbs weighing 10-12 ounces. The skin is yellow-brown, the flesh yellowish-white. These keep very well.

- For large keeper onions, try 'Giant Zittau' for its 4- to 5-inch bulbs that keep well.

Red Storage Types

- 'Mambo' is a large, round, red storage onion with good color on the interior rings. It is medium hot, and also sweet. It is a long-day type, but able to produce well at our latitude.

- 'Redman' is a week earlier, a round, deep burgundy onion that has redder interior rings after a few weeks of curing and keeps 4 to 5 months. It is moderately pungent.

- 'Southport Red Globe' is the red version of 'Southport White Globe', sharing its good keeping qualities and its suitability for cooking.

Pests If an onion plant dies suddenly, it very likely has succumbed to onion root maggots. Fortunately, snails and slugs show little interest in onions, but black aphids can be a problem. Downy mildew is a fungus disease favored by cool weather, especially when there is rain or heavy dew. The first symptom is yellow areas on the leaves. During very moist weather, the spores emerge and cover the leaves with a dirty gray or violet powder (see page 156).

Like garlic, onions are susceptible to white rot. The disease can be carried on sets or transplants, but not in seeds. Once white rot is in your soil, it stays a long time, so it is very important to use only certified disease-free sets and plants.

If you don't allow onion bulbs to dry thoroughly before you harvest them or if you don't cure them well, they can develop neck rot in storage. This decay works its way down from the still-moist stems. Poorly cured onions may also be damaged by black mold, which makes black spore masses between the layers of scales. Be sure the storage area is cool and dry, and check the bulbs often for signs of decay. Remove affected onions, which can still be eaten after you trim off damaged parts. Aphids may attack onions in storage. Keep aphids under control while you are growing onions, and check for the insects when you inspect stored bulbs.

Sources

Onion seed:
Spanish types:
    White Sweet Spanish or Yellow Sweet Spanish: BG, Lockhart, PTS, NGN
    Valencia: SOC
    Fiesta: Lockhart
    Walla Walla Sweet: GG, JSS, Lockhart, NGN, PTS, SB, SGS, TERR
Short keeper reds:
    Italian Red Burger: Lockhart
    Italian Blood Red Bottle: NGN
    Red Torpedo: CG, Lockhart, SOC

Stockton Early Red: Lockhart, SOC
White or Yellow storage types:
   Blanco Duro: Lockhart, PTS
   Hi-Ball F₁: TERR
   Southport White Globe: OBG
Red storage types:
   Mambo: JSS
   Southport Red Globe: ABL, Lockhart, OBG, PTS
   Redman: ABL, JSS
Bare-root onion plants:
   Walla Walla Sweet: CG, RSP, TERR, VBS
   White Sweet Spanish: RSP, TERR, VBS
   Yellow Sweet Spanish: BG, PS, VBS
   Stockton Red: RSP

A good source of onion seed for gardeners at our latitude is Lockhart Seeds, Inc. (Lockhart in the above listing), which sells many of these onion varieties and more. To request their vegetable seed catalog, write them at P.O. Box 1361, Stockton, CA 95205, or call them at (209)466-4401.

ONION, BUNCHING
(OR WELSH ONION)

Allium fistulosum
Amaryllis Family ❖ *Amaryllidaceae*

Each plant of a perennial bunching onion will form many green onions from a single base. The advantage of growing this type of onion is that you can harvest during most of the year. To get more green onions the next year, all you have to do is separate the remaining clump and replant the onions. Bunching onions are large sturdy plants that have been the main garden onion of China and Japan since ancient times. Although they are also known as Welsh onions, they have never been commonly grown in Wales. The plants look much like those of bulb onions, except that the leaves are round in cross section rather than indented on one side.

Growing Instructions Bunching onions are most often grown from seed. Plant them in midsummer to early fall for green onions in fall and spring. In winter the plant is so small and scraggly that you would only want to harvest it in a pinch. Mature clumps should stand 6 to 8 inches apart, but you can start seeds much closer together and either transplant seedlings or pull them to eat young. Remove flower stalks in summer before they have a chance to bloom. This will encourage the plants to put their energy into multiplying instead.

The Harvest Eat some plants when they are the size of small green onions and let others mature into clumps of larger onions. Pull individual green onions from the side of a clump. You may have to use a trowel to dig away a little soil next to a clump to remove plants without breaking them. You can maintain a planting for many years. Divide large clumps every two or three years in fall.

Varieties All varieties should do well here.

Pests Beware of the same pests and diseases to which bulb onion plants fall prey.

Sources
   Bunching onion seeds: Widely available

ONION, PEARL (OR BOILING, COCKTAIL, OR PICKLING ONION)

Allium cepa
Cepa Group
Amaryllis Family ❖ *Amaryllidaceae*

Seeds sold as pearl, boiling, cocktail, or pickling onions are short-day bulb onion varieties (see page 225) planted in spring so that they make very small bulbs in just a couple of months.

Growing Instructions Since these are simply varieties of bulb onions, they have the same growing requirements. Plant seeds in January through April and thin the seedlings to 1 to 1-1/2 inches apart, checking the seed packet instructions for the particular variety you are growing. Close planting keeps the bulbs smaller.

The Harvest You can begin to harvest pearl onions for fresh use as soon as they reach the desired size. Continue to harvest until they are ready for storage. Pearl onion tops are so small and weigh so little that they may not fall over as the leaves of larger onions do, so you will have to watch the plants more closely to determine when the bulbs are the maximum size. When the leaves die back, you can be sure that they are ready. Dig them up and store them as you would bulb onions.

To remove the skins of pearl onions, drop the onions in enough boiling water to cover them. Drain them immediately, dip them in cold water, and slip the skins off.

Varieties Most varieties should do well here. Round white varieties that I have seen listed include 'Barletta,' 'Crystal Wax,' 'Quicksilver,' and 'Wonder of Pompeii'. 'Purplette' is red, turning pink when cooked.

Pests Pearl onions are susceptible to the same pests as bulb onions.

Sources
Pearl onion seed:
Barletta White: JG
Crystal Wax: SB
Early Aviv: SGS
Snow Baby:
JSS
Purplette:
ABL, JSS, SB
Wonder of
Pompeii: NGN,
SB

ONION, TOP
(OR TREE, WALKING, OR EGYPTIAN ONION)
Allium cepa
Proliferum Group
Amaryllis Family ❖
Amaryllidaceae

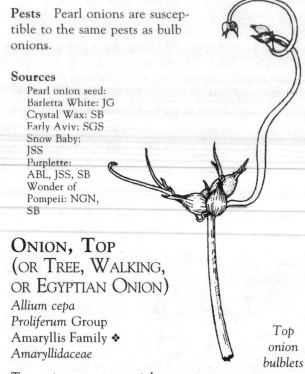

Top onion bulblets

Top onions are perennial green onions that multiply like bunching onions, forming new plants at the base. But they also make clusters of bulblets at the top of what would otherwise be flower stems. These bulblets, which are fully formed by about the middle of July, often begin to sprout into small plants while they are still attached to the stems. These little plants even make their own sets of tiny bulblets. The heads of sprouting bulblets are often quite picturesque with their tiers of bulblets and curving stems and leaves. The weight of the bulblets eventually pulls the stem over and the sprouting bulblets grow where they land—"walking" the onions to a new location. Like bunching onions, they offer the advantage of providing green onions for harvest much of the year with little effort.

Growing Instructions Either buy sets or plant harvested bulblets. Rather than letting the bulblets plant themselves, it is better to pick them as soon as they are fully formed, separate them, and plant them where you want them, either immediately or within a couple of weeks. Set them about 3 inches apart, or as close as 1 inch if you plan to harvest them as green onions. If you set bulblets at the bottom of a 4- to 8-inch trench and fill it in as they grow, you will have green onions with very long

white shafts for winter and spring harvests. The plants are undemanding, growing well in good garden soil with average water.

The Harvest Bulblets planted in July make tender green onions in fall. The same plants that you harvested in fall are tender and very mild when they start to grow again in late winter and early spring. Clumps of plants live for many years, eventually becoming crowded and unsightly. You need to find a balance among harvesting plants to eat, leaving some plants to produce summer bulblets for next season's green onions, and removing the oldest, least productive clumps.

Pests Top onions are susceptible to the same pests as bulb onions. Onion root maggots have never infested my top onions, but bean aphids have often attacked them in winter.

Sources
Top onion sets: JG, NGN, PTS, RSP, SB

OYSTER PLANT (SEE SALSIFY)

PARSLEY, ROOT (OR TURNIP-ROOTED PARSLEY OR HAMBURG PARSLEY)
Petroselinum crispum var. *tuberosum*
(*P. hortense* var. *radicosum*)
Carrot Family ❖ *Umbelliferae*

Root parsley has a parsnip-shaped root that tastes very much like celeriac, and the leaves are an acceptable substitute for parsley. Since the crop tolerates part shade and thrives in cool weather, it is a good choice for our region.

Growing Instructions Start root parsley from seed, either indoors in November or December or outdoors in February or March. Try a July sowing for harvests into fall and winter, especially in very cool areas nearest the coast. Plant the seeds 1/4 inch deep, and transplant or thin plants to stand 6 to 9 inches apart. Root parsley seeds takes several weeks to sprout. (You can use the same techniques recommended for starting carrot seeds; see page 192.) The crop grows best in loose, moisture-holding, fertile soil. Like other root crops, root parsley may make deformed roots in soil containing fresh manure or too much nitrogen fertilizer.

The Harvest   Harvest a leaf or two as the plant grows, leaving most of the foliage to help the plants form large roots. The roots take about three months to mature and are most tender when they are less than 7 inches long. They can be left in the ground to be dug up during the winter. Cold weather is said to improve the flavor of root parsley, but be sure to harvest before the plants go to seed in spring.

Scrub the root well before you cook it. You may want to peel it, although it will discolor if you peel it raw. Drop it into boiling water for about five minutes, then peel it. Use root parsley in soups, stews, and salads and as a boiled vegetable.

Pests   I don't know of any pests or diseases that attack root parsley in our region.

Sources
Root parsley seed: BG, JSS, NGN, PTS, SB, T&M

PARSNIP

Pastinaca sativa
Carrot Family ❖ *Umbelliferae*

Although these long white roots are not among the most commonly eaten vegetables, you may find that you're partial to them. They are tough when raw, but tender when baked or cooked in soups or stews. If you have never tried parsnip, prepare some store-bought ones first. Scrub the roots and halve them lengthwise. Add a little butter, some brown sugar, and a tablespoon of water, then cover and bake at 350°F for about 30 minutes.

Growing Instructions   A member of the carrot family, parsnip has many of the same needs as carrot (see page 191). Like carrot, it thrives in all parts of our region. I have planted parsnips in February, later in spring, and again as late as August, all with good results. The crop holds well in the ground in winter. In fact, parsnip is not only frost hardy but it actually gets sweeter after a frost.

Like carrot, parsnip needs a deep, fine-textured soil, and it makes inferior roots in rocky soil or poorly amended clay. Sow seeds thickly, 1/2 inch deep, and later thin the seedlings to 4 to 6 inches apart. Parsnip is even slower to germinate than carrot, taking 15 to 25 days. All the tricks that work to get carrot seedlings past their slow start will also help with parsnip (see page 192). Unlike carrot, however, parsnip will endure a careful transplanting while it is still very small.

The Harvest   Parsnip roots mature in three to four months, but a crop started in summer can be left to pull as needed through the winter. Pull the roots before spring growth begins, or they will become woody and the plants will go to seed.

Pests   Although parsnip plants are susceptible to bean aphids and to the carrot rust fly, mine have never been attacked by either. I have had some damage from a leafminer, presumably the parsnip leafminer, but since the damage is minor, and one doesn't eat parsnip leaves, picking damaged leaves should be a sufficient control.

Sources
Parsnip seeds: Widely available

PEA

Pisum sativum
Pea Family ❖
Leguminosae

Although a small garden can't produce a very large quantity of shelled peas, the pleasure of shelling the peas and eating them just picked is well worth the effort of growing this crop. Edible-podded peas, including snow peas and snap peas, produce a greater volume of food per plant. Snow peas are indispensable in stir fry dishes and salads. Snap peas have a thick, sweet, crunchy pod that makes them one of the garden's finest treats for eating fresh off the vine.

Peas

Like beans, peas need well-drained soil high in organic matter. Although they have the nitrogen-fixing root bacteria typical of legumes, peas will grow better if they get a little nitrogen fertilizer at planting time. (For more on the legume family, see page 169.) Also like beans, peas are available in bush and pole varieties.

Growing Instructions   Peas are a cool-season legume, typically planted in November and February in our region. Peas planted in November will bear their delicate blossoms after the worst winter storms have passed. A February-planted crop will bloom and fruit while spring is still cool. Peas planted from April through August may succeed in foggier micro-climates or during cool years, but they may stop production and die during a hot spell. Also, powdery mildew (see page 157) is more likely to strike in summer and early fall.

Peas are generally seeded in place, although they are occasionally sown indoors three to four weeks before being planted out. You may want to start them indoors to circumvent very wet weather or to escape the predation of snails. Plant all peas 1 to 2 inches deep. Sow bush peas in double rows 6 to 8 inches apart so that the plants can support each other, or sow them in a small block with 2 inches between plants. Pole peas can be planted 2 inches apart on either or both sides of a 6- to 8-foot-high sturdy frame.

Snow peas, garden peas, & snap peas.

When you are constructing a frame for peas, don't be tempted as I was one year to construct a flimsy one of wood scraps, or the spring winds will keep you laboring at repairs. Since peas use tendrils to climb, they need both vertical and horizontal supports. A well-supported wire or nylon mesh with 2- to 4-inch openings works well. Pea seedlings need some help finding the mesh at first. Gently guide them, perhaps tying wayward seedlings in place.

Bush peas grow only 2 to 4 feet high, but even they profit from some support. The British use pea sticks (brushy prunings from trees and hedges) inserted along the rows. If you don't have access to brushy twigs, make a mesh frame supported by stakes. Be sure that the frame or twigs are in place when you plant. Otherwise, the plants will twine on themselves, and you will damage them when you try to separate them and train them to climb something else.

The Harvest Peas will begin to bear in eight to ten weeks, or up to four months if they are growing during the winter. Their first pods will form at the bottom of the plant. Pick these as soon as they are ready, even if there are only a few. This will encourage the plant to grow and make more pods. Although bush peas are touted for small gardens, if you are looking for a good-sized crop, remember that pole pea plants will bear up to five times as much. If you are growing garden peas for shelling, you won't get much, even from a pole variety. In a small garden it is best to think of shelled peas as a salad garnish or an ingredient for a risotto or a soup, rather than providing large individual servings.

Young pea leaves and tendrils are edible, so be sure to try the seedlings you thin in a stir-fry. Evergreen Enterprises (EV) sells a variety that is popular in China where it is grown specifically to harvest the young shoot tips.

Varieties Home gardeners grow three main types of peas: old-fashioned garden peas, snow peas (sugar peas), and snap peas. Garden peas must be shelled, since the inner lining of the pods is too tough to eat. (Some people peel the lining before they munch the pods, but that's an arduous task.) Harvest garden peas when the peas are not quite fully developed. You will soon learn to recognize pods whose peas have become plump but not so mature that they are tough and starchy. Most varieties of garden peas should succeed here. 'Maestro' and 'Bounty' are resistant to powdery mildew. 'Novella' is one of the nearly leafless types that will twine firmly into each other, allowing you to grow a wide row of plants with no supports. Some of their tendrils can also be harvested along with the peas.

Snow, or sugar, peas are grown for their edible pods. They are traditionally harvested flat or with very small peas to use in salads and stir fry. 'Oregon Sugar Pod II' and 'Oregon Giant' promise powdery mildew resistance.

Snap peas revolutionized pea growing several years ago, when a breeder discovered in his trial planting a pea plant bearing thick, crisp, edible pods like those of a snap bean. The pods remained tender and sweet even as the peas filled out. The snap pea is delicious to eat out of hand and is a great addition to salads. The first variety on the market was the pole pea 'Sugar Snap,' which unfortunately lacks resistance to powdery mildew. However, many of the new varieties, including the pole 'Super Sugar Snap' and the bush varieties 'Sugar

Bon' and 'Sugar Mel' are resistant.

A footnote to the discovery and development of snap peas is that after the snap pea became popular, researchers discovered descriptions of just such peas in gardening books from a couple of centuries ago. Apparently, this is an example of an heirloom variety nearly lost but rediscovered by chance during a breeding program. Since then, an Amish heirloom pea has been discovered with the same traits.

Pests Slugs, snails, and other pests of seedlings love young pea plants. They are especially tempted by them in winter, when peas are among the most tender plants in the garden. Protect peas by starting them indoors, or grow them outdoors under a floating row cover until they are 6 or 8 inches high.

As weather turns warm, peas become susceptible to powdery mildew, which coats the leaves in a white dust. (Don't confuse it with the lacy, whitish, natural markings that appear on most pea leaves.) Fight the disease by planting resistant varieties or planting nonresistant ones only during the coldest time of year. If plants do get powdery mildew, let them bear until the disease becomes debilitating, then remove the plants from the garden. Sulfur can slow the disease, though it may not be worth the trouble for a few plants.

Control aphids that appear on pea plants; they sometimes spread viruses. Of the many possible pea viruses, one, pea enation, is common in the Northwest, and while I haven't seen it here, it is always wise to remove any plants that seem to be disfigured by a virus (more on viruses on page 159).

Sources
Pea seed:
Garden pea varieties
Bounty (bush): JSS
Knight (bush): JSS, PTS
Maestro (bush): ABL, JSS, PS, TERR
Novella (bush): CG, NGN, PTS
Snow or sugar pea varieties:
Oregon Giant (bush): NGN, SOC, SGS
Oregon Sugar Pod II (bush): ABL, BG, NGN, EV, VBS
Snap pea varieties:
Amish Heirloom (pole): OBG
Sugar Bon (bush): BG, PS
Sugar Mel (bush): PTS, SGS
Sugar Snap (pole): Widely available
Super Sugar Snap (pole): BG, NGN, OBG, SGS, VBS
Pea for leafy shoots: EV

PEPPER, SWEET AND HOT

Capsicum annuum var. *annuum*
Nightshade Family ❖ *Solanaceae*

These sweet or fiery delights are perennials in their native tropical America. Beyond the tropics they are grown as annuals, planted to mature in the warmest months. Occasionally, they survive a very mild winter to bear during a second summer. One plant I grew even came back a third year, but by then it had become woody and set only one or two small peppers.

In our cool summers, pepper plants rarely reach full size or maximum production. Pepper plants very near the coast are unlikely to set fruit at all, their blossoms falling unfertilized. In my foggy San Francisco yard, an unprotected 'Ace' pepper plant grew as large as the ones in my sunnier community garden but not a single blossom set fruit. Small harvests are possible in warmer microclimates. You can improve your chances by choosing varieties carefully and using aids to warm the soil and the plants.

Growing Instructions Because our climate is marginal for peppers, we need to pay special attention to the needs of this crop. They require a moderately fertile soil, so use a complete fertilizer at planting time. Compost made by the hot method (see page 87) will do nicely. Supplement with a high-nitrogen fertilizer when the blossoms open. Water pepper plants adequately, because water stress will cause blossoms and developing fruit to drop. Since pepper roots extend 4 feet or more into the soil, water deeply. Don't keep the soil soggy, however, or root rot may develop. Maintaining the right moisture level will be easier if the soil contains plenty of organic matter.

Since peppers are susceptible to cold, they are usually seeded indoors to give them an earlier start. Many local gardeners grow their own seedlings, since nurseries usually don't carry the varieties best suited to our climate. Plant seeds in March, but don't set seedlings out until May.

The ideal temperature range for pepper seed germination is 70° to 85°F. The plants grow best when daytime temperatures are in the low eighties and night temperatures are above 55°F. Try to give peppers the warmth they need while they are indoors, since they will have to contend with less favorable conditions soon enough. The minimum time required to grow pepper seedlings indoors is six to eight weeks. Some gardeners keep them indoors longer to get a bigger head start. You can start seeds as early as January, but you must be sure to give the plants enough light and fertilizer and move them to larger pots before their roots become crowded. If you can't meet these needs, you are better off with younger but

THE NIGHTSHADE FAMILY

The nightshade family, the Solanaceae, includes four well known crops—tomatoes, potatoes, peppers and eggplants—as well as a few lesser known ones, like tomatillo and ground tomato. All of the ones listed in this book are tropical perennials, native to tropical Central and South America. Species and varieties of species that are more cool-tolerant are probably related to ancestors that grew at higher altitudes, where the climate is cooler.

Potatoes are the most cool-tolerant of the group, growing best at 59 to 63°F. They can be planted from February through late summer in all of our region. Tomatoes, peppers and eggplants need progressively more heat. The most cool-tolerant varieties of tomatoes can succeed in much of the region, including protected areas nearest the coast. Even cool-tolerant varieties of pepper, however, need greater warmth than our region can generally offer for best production, and eggplants will be a disappointment in all but the warmest microclimates and the warmest summers.

If night temperatures are too cool, nightshade crops will drop blossoms unfertilized. This is not a problem with potatoes, since we are after the tubers instead of the fruit, but it does limit our ability to grow tomatoes, peppers and eggplants.

Tomatoes, peppers and eggplants are grown from transplants to give them an early start in a protected environment. As with cabbage family crops, the "days to maturity" rating on seed packets doesn't count the approximately six weeks to transplant size. Seedlings mustn't be set out too early either, since cool weather will stunt them. Still many gardeners do set tomatoes out early in hopes of getting early growth. If the spring is unusually warm, or if you use protective coverings to raise the temperature around the plants, you may get a jump on the season. But if it's too cool, your early plantings may end up no bigger, or even smaller, than later planted ones. Peppers are more likely to stunt in cool weather and eggplants even more so.

We may chuckle to remember that many people once believed that the tomato was poisonous, but do keep in mind that, except for the parts generally eaten, the rest of potato, tomato, eggplant and pepper plants, do contain toxins. Never eat any part of a plant from this family but the one you *know* is edible.

Solanaceous crops share the same pests, although the bugs that will eat these crops don't seem to be serious pests in at least some parts of the region. One disease, tobacco mosaic virus, can be spread by cigarette smokers if they do not wash their hands after smoking and before working in the garden.

healthier seedlings.

Wait until the weather is quite warm before you move transplants into the garden, since pepper plants may become stunted by cold. Temperatures hovering around 45°F, common on April nights in much of our region, can cause temporary shock. The nights are usually warmer by May. Still, the plants won't reach full size in most areas, since temperatures under 55°F (possible any night of the summer) will slow their growth.

Set the plants 12 to 15 inches apart. A protective covering will help peppers brave the hostile elements. In early spring try setting plants in a Wall O' Water™, or use a floating row cover to hold in heat and cut down on wind. Black plastic mulch will help warm the soil. If you combine black plastic with a floating row cover, be sure to extend the row cover beyond the edges of the plastic sheeting, so that both can be tucked into the soil to keep pests out. Later, try a clear plastic minigreenhouse (see page 59) to protect the maturing plants from wind and cold.

The Harvest The first peppers should be big enough to pick sometime in July or August. Plants may continue to bear through November if there are no heavy rains.

Pick sweet peppers as soon as they stop enlarging, which may happen before they reach the size promised in the seed catalog. You may have as few as three or four peppers per plant, although up to fifteen peppers are possible in favorable conditions. Cut the peppers with scissors or hand pruners to avoid damaging the plant.

All peppers start out green. Left alone, they mature into red or yellow peppers. (Some turn purple before they turn red.) Although red and yellow peppers are very pretty and have more vitamins than green peppers, the ripening process keeps the plant from setting new fruit—and peppers ripen very slowly in our cool climate. Since peppers are marginal to begin with, it is wiser to produce a good-sized crop of green peppers instead of trying to grow types that, given enough time, may ripen to exotic colors.

Hot peppers are picked green or red, depending on the variety. Green hot peppers are used fresh. Hot peppers picked red can be used fresh, or they can be dried and kept for later use.

Varieties The most common sweet pepper varieties available in local nurseries are 'California Wonder' and 'Yolo Wonder'. These are the big standard bells that thrive in the hot Central Valley. They may or may not succeed in your garden, depending on your location and the weather during a particular summer. Fortunately, pepper breeders have developed many varieties that produce earlier and are more tolerant of cool weather. Don't expect these varieties to make huge crops or to bear in the foggiest gardens, however. The large-fruited varieties 'Ace' and 'Early Cal Wonder' ripen to red, and 'Golden Bell F$_1$' turns yellow. Others trade fruit size for an ability to produce in cool weather. Among these are 'Cubanelle' and 'Gypsy F$_1$', which are yellow-green, and 'Jingle Bells,' which ripens to red.

Although theoretically it should not be so, I've often noticed hot pepper varieties bearing well in gardens where bell-types have fewer fruits. I've grown jalapeños and Thai peppers in my San Fran-cisco Mission District garden. Others that might do well are 'NuMex Big Jim' and 'Española Improved', both of which did well in trials in a cool-night part of New Mexico. 'Early Jalapeño' is very hot and able to set fruit under cooler conditions. But don't grow only very hot types, since a very small planting can produce enough fire to spike a year's cooking. Try a moderately hot variety such as 'Surefire F$_1$' (a Hungarian hot wax type) or 'Señorita Jalapeño' which is less than one tenth as hot as regular 'Jalapeño'.

Pests Peppers don't suffer much from diseases or other pests. About 70 percent of the varieties on the market are resistant to the most common diseases. If any of your plants seem discolored or misshapen from disease, remove them from the garden. Smokers should wash their hands well before handling pepper plants, since peppers can fall prey to tobacco mosaic virus.

Pepper plants are susceptible to attack by aphids and several caterpillars, including cabbage loopers and corn earworms. However, pepper is rarely the first crop these insects will attack.

Sources
Pepper seed:
Large-fruited early bells:
    Ace (New Ace): JSS, PTS, TT
    Early Cal Wonder: TERR
    Golden Bell F$_1$: TERR, T&M, TT
    Golden Summer Bell F$_1$: NGN, PS, TGS, TT
Smaller-fruited early bells:
    Cubanelle: ABL, PTS, RCS, SB, TT
    Gypsy F$_1$: BG, NGN, PTS, TERR, TGS, TT
    Jingle Bells: NGN, TERR, T&M, TGS, TT
Hot Peppers:
    NuMex Big Jim: SGS, TGS, TT
    Early Jalapeño: ABL, JSS, NGN, PTS, TT
    Española Improved: TGS
    Jalapeño: Widely available
    Señorita Jalapeno: NGN, PTS, TERR, TGS
    Surefire F$_1$: TERR
Thai pepper: BG, CG, EV, PS, PTS, SB, SGS, T&M, TGS, TT, VBS

POTATO
Solanum tuberosum
Nightshade Family ❖ *Solanaceae*

You may have read that potatoes aren't a good choice for a small garden because they take up a lot of space, and anyhow they don't cost much to buy. But I think they are a splendid choice: I enjoy growing unusual varieties, I like eating them fresh from the garden, and digging potatoes is one of the highlights of vegetable gardening. Moreover, fresh high-quality potatoes, especially unusual types, are no longer cheap items.

Native to the Andean highlands and to the cool Chilean coast, potatoes do well throughout our region. They thrive in our humid air and produce tubers best in cool weather—59° to 63°F is ideal. They prefer sandy soil, but they will grow in clay soil and actually help loosen it.

Growing Instructions   Potatoes are traditionally grown from pieces of tuber that have at least one bud, or eye. You can buy these pieces, known as sets, precut or you can purchase whole seed potatoes and prepare the sets yourself. Leave one to three eyes on each piece. Let the sets cure in a warm, humid place for a couple of days, so that their cut sides will harden a bit before you plant them.

You can also grow potatoes from small whole tubers, 2 to 3 inches in diameter. This is a common practice in England, and it often produces a greater yield than cut sets do. You can buy these small seed potatoes, or you can set them aside from your harvest. (But if you save your own, don't save the very smallest ones; egg-sized tubers will make a better crop.) Buy certified disease-free potatoes at local nurseries or through mail-order catalogs. If you plant potatoes from the grocery store, you take the risk that they may be diseased and that the disease might spread through your soil.

Some seed companies now offer gardeners a less

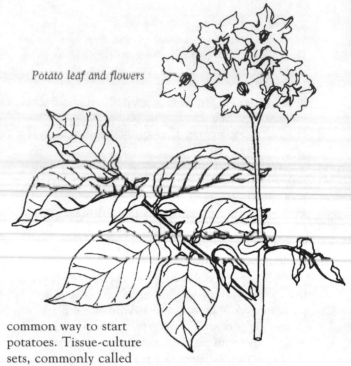

Potato leaf and flowers

common way to start potatoes. Tissue-culture sets, commonly called minitubers, look like very small potatoes. They are cloned from single potato cells in a laboratory so they are genetically uniform and disease-free.

Potatoes will grow the year around in our region, producing a crop in a little over three months, so several plantings are possible. Many gardeners plant spring potatoes on March 17, an easy date to remember given the historical link between the

POTATO TOWERS

You can grow more potatoes in a small space by planting them vertically in a tower of wire mesh. The potatoes will form in the tower, and you can harvest them simply by removing the tower.

To build a wire-mesh tower, construct a ring of fencing that is 3 to 4 feet high and 1½ to 2 feet in diameter. It should have openings at least 1 by 1 inch. Lay four or five potato sets on the soil surface 4 inches from the mesh frame. Add 10 to 12 inches of compost or compost-rich soil, then four to five more sets. Repeat until you get to the top of the mesh. The top layer of potatoes should be at least 4 inches below the top surface of the compost. The plants will grow out the sides of the mesh. This tower works best in late spring and early summer, when the sun is high in the sky and the north side of the tower gets some sun.

HIMALAYAN POTATO CURRY

This combination of flavors was unusual to my palate at first, but now I find it delicious.

4 medium potatoes (boiling varieties are best)
1/2 cup chopped tomatoes (or Quick Homemade Tomato Sauce, see page 346)
1 or 2 cloves garlic, minced
1 1/2-inch piece fresh ginger, quartered
1/4 teaspoon turmeric
Salt, to taste
1 medium shallot, chopped (or 2 tablespoons minced onion)
2 tablespoons olive or vegetable oil
1/2 teaspoon fenugreek seeds
1/2 cup thinly sliced bell pepper

Steam the potatoes for 15 minutes, then dice them into bite-sized pieces. Put the tomatoes, garlic, ginger, turmeric and shallot in a blender and purée to create a sauce. Heat the oil in a skillet and brown the fenugreek seeds, being careful not to burn them. Add the mixture from the blender, stir well, and cook over high heat for 1 minute. Pour the mixture over the potatoes and mix gently until well blended. Garnish with the slices of bell pepper. Serves four.

Irish and the potato, but the soil is often dry enough to plant a month earlier. If you plant in February, May, and August you will have three harvests a year. (Of course, plantings are also possible anytime between February and August.) Potatoes planted after September 1 will still be growing in December and January, when frost is possible. Ever since I lost a winter crop to a light December frost I have not made large plantings later than August, but it is fun to try to sneak a few potatoes past the winter. You can always cover them if frost threatens. (Seed potatoes aren't available for sale all year round, but you can save and plant your own.)

Gardeners often wonder about the wisdom of planting sprouting potatoes. If the sprouting potato is one you bought for food, the answer is not to plant it, because it is not certified disease-free for planting. However, some gardeners purposely let short sprouts form on their sets before planting them. This is OK, though mine always sprout fine without this extra help. If the sprouts get long and spindly, they will tend to break off during planting. Also, because the plant needs energy to make the maximum number of buds for new tubers in the first few weeks after sprouting, you really want it in the

ground, with access to water and nutrients during this period.

Potatoes will make the best growth in highly organic, moderately fertile soil. Dig in a few inches of aged manure or compost and some fertilizer that provides more phosphorous and potassium than nitrogen. (For more on fertilizing, see page 80.) Plant sets cut side down and 10 to 12 inches apart. You can bury sets or whole small tubers 4 inches under the level surface of the soil. However, there is much to be said for the practice of hilling potatoes—burying them deeper as they grow. Since tubers form only above the original set, hilling encourages more to form. A standard method is to dig a trench 8 inches deep and plant the potatoes at the bottom. Then fill in 4 inches of soil or compost. When the potato shoots have been up for a week or so, fill more soil or compost around them. It's all right to bury a few leaves, since the plants will just keep on growing. After about three weeks, pull soil up around the plants or add compost, burying part of the stem and making a mound. You can also cover the mounded surface with a thick layer of straw or other loose mulch.

However you grow potatoes, be sure to cover

any exposed tubers with soil or mulch. Otherwise, the exposed skin will turn green. The green parts of potato plants, including any green on the tubers, contain a moderately poisonous substance called solanine.

The Harvest Potatoes are ready to harvest beginning two weeks after the plant blooms. But often potato plants don't bloom. If you don't see the white or purple flowers or at least the small branched flower stalks at the tops of the plants, the next hint that harvest time is near is yellowing of the leaves despite regular watering. As soon as the plant blooms or begins to turn yellow, cut back on watering. You can dig potatoes from the time about 20 percent of the plant is yellow to the time it has completely died down. Don't leave plants unharvested long after that, since the tubers may decay.

Dig your potatoes on a day when the soil is relatively dry, so it won't stick to the potatoes. Use a digging fork if you have one. Insert your fork or shovel well back from the plant stem and dig straight down so that you won't cut across the tubers. You will find large and small tubers, which you can sort later to use for different purposes. If you plan to eat the tubers within a few days, just wash them well and store them in the produce section of your refrigerator. If you want to store them longer, leave the unwashed tubers outdoors for a while if it's warm. Otherwise, put them in a warm, dry room for a few hours. Then brush off most of the dirt and store the tubers in a dark, dry, cool (about 60°F) place for two weeks. After this curing period, move them to a dark, humid, cooler (40°F) spot with good air circulation. Most of us don't have an ideal potato storage location. Our basements are usually warmer, and refrigerators lack circulation. Still, potatoes will keep pretty well for at least a few weeks in either of these places.

Be very careful not to leave harvested potatoes in the light for more than a day, or the skins will begin to turn green. If this happens, peel away the green part. The rest of the potato is safe to eat.

If you plan to save your own seed potatoes for cutting into sets or planting whole, dig up the tubers when the plants are only partly yellowed or have just died down. Tubers left in the ground long after the plant has died won't be as vigorous. Choose tubers that weren't injured in digging—either large tubers for cutting into sets or 2- to 3-inch tubers for planting whole. Do not save any that show signs of disease or were harvested from plants that had a disease. Don't save the smallest tubers either. You may as well eat them, since they won't make a very big crop if you plant them.

Don't replant homegrown sets right away; they usually need a couple of months of rest before they will sprout. Store them in a plastic bag in the refrigerator. Insert a note to remind yourself when they were harvested and when to plant them.

Potato plants will also grow from tubers you missed while harvesting. These will sprout in spring and summer, having rested underground. When you see a potato seedling, you have the choice of discarding it, letting it grow, or moving it to a different location. If you move it, dig carefully with a trowel to get the tuber as well as the shoot and root. Although these volunteers often grow from very small tubers and may not produce prolifically, I have enjoyed many meals from such plants growing in out-of-the-way corners of my garden.

Varieties Potatoes are such fun to grow that I encourage you to try different varieties. The sets at your local nursery will probably be cheaper than those ordered by mail. Most nurseries carry old standard varieties, which may be sold by name or by color. 'Irish Cobbler,' or 'White Cobbler,' introduced to this country in the 1870s, is an early maturing, brown-skinned potato that is delicious baked or boiled. 'Kennebec' yields brown-skinned potatoes a little later, which are good for all uses. The oval, red skinned 'Red Pontiac' is easy, early, and very flavored. 'Bison' is a round, red treasure that is early and delicious.

Potato varieties with less familiar shapes and colors are becoming increasingly available. 'All Blue'—blue outside and inside—is great baked or boiled. 'Yukon Gold' and 'Yellow Finn' are yellow inside and out. 'Yukon Gold' is early, and great for french fries. 'Yellow Finn', which matures a bit later, makes wonderful mashed potatoes. Fingerling potatoes, such as 'Russian Banana', are long and skinny. You can steam them and serve them whole, or cut them into round chunks for potato salad or soup. There are many others for you to try. Some are more productive than others or better for certain uses than others. Read the descriptions and try out a few.

Pests Scab is a fungus disease that causes rough scabs on the surface of the tubers. Although unsightly, they are just surface blemishes that can be peeled off. Commercial growers keep the soil pH between 4.8 and 5.4 to prevent this disease, but lowering the pH for just one crop is awkward in a small garden. Besides, potatoes grow best in pH 6 to 6.5— so if you haven't encountered scab or have only an occasional spot of it, no heroic acidifying efforts is necessary. Reduce the chance of scab by starting with certified disease-free seed potatoes, planting in fertile soil, and watering well until the plants bloom.

Early and late blight are two fungus diseases that can cause plants to collapse before they mature and can make the tubers inedible. They are spread through diseased tubers, so the first defense is to buy certified disease-free tubers. Another precaution against both diseases is to avoid overhead watering. Late blight has been very prevalent in regional gardens in recent years. See page 157 for more on preventing it. Two varieties that have shown some resistance to late blight are 'Russian Banana' and 'Kennebec'.

We are fortunate to live in an area unaffected by the Colorado potato beetle, a common pest in most of the country. Slugs and snails—and sometimes earwigs—nibble on potato leaves, but they rarely decimate an entire planting. Wireworms may damage tubers.

Sources

Potato sets or small whole tubers:
  Irish Cobbler or White Cobbler (brown skin, white flesh): BG, RSP
  Kennebec (brown skin, white flesh): BG, JSS, PTS, VBS
  Red Pontiac (red skin, white flash): BG, VBS
  Bison (red skin, white flesh): RSP
  Yellow Finn (yellow skin and flesh): SB, SOC,
  Yukon Gold (yellow skin and flesh): CG, JSS, PTS, SB, SOC
  Russian Banana Fingerling (yellow skin, pale yellow flesh): CG, JSS, SB
  All Blue (blue skin and flesh): RSP, SB, SOC, VBS
Tissue-cultured potato sets:
  All Blue (blue skin and flesh): SGS, TERR
  Gold Rush Russet (brown skin, white flesh): SGS, TERR
  Kennebec: SGS
  Peanut Fingerling (brown skin, yellow flesh): SGS, TERR
  Redsen or Red Sun (red skin, white flesh): SGS, TERR
  Yellow Finn: SGS, TERR

PUMPKIN
(SEE SQUASH, WINTER AND PUMPKIN)

RADISH
Raphanus sativus
Mustard Family ❖ *Cruciferae*

Wild ancestors of the radish abounded from Europe through Asia, and domesticated versions were developed on both continents. Most American

gardeners grow the small-rooted types, but in Europe and Asia the large-rooted varieties are also popular. All offer a crisp, peppery treat, and as a gardener you can explore the many colors and shapes available.

Growing Instructions Radish seeds can be planted almost anytime, except during very wet periods or prolonged heat spells. Radishes appreciate organic soil, but they will make poor roots if the soil is too rich in nitrogen. They can take some shade in the sunniest sites. In foggier sites or during dimmer times of year, plant radishes in full sun.

Radishes are always direct-seeded in the garden. Sow the seeds thinly and 1/2 inch deep. To ensure room for the rapidly developing roots, thin the seedlings early to 1 inch apart for small radishes or to the diameter of a mature root for large-rooted varieties. (The thinnings are tasty in a salad or omelet.) Provide plenty of water for mild, juicy roots.

Small-rooted radishes are ready a month or less from the day of seeding. The larger radishes need 40 to 70 days to mature. Many of the larger types are best planted in mid- to late summer to mature into fall and winter—in fact, they are commonly called winter radishes. A few of the large-rooted varieties are also suited to spring planting.

Radishes become tough and woody if they are allowed to stand too long. For a steady supply of the quick-growing, small-rooted types, make successive plantings every two weeks. Larger radishes can be harvested for a longer time from a single sowing, since they keep better in the soil. Still, be careful not to overplant, since a single large-rooted radish can equal or exceed the size of three grocery-store bunches of the little ones.

Varieties Almost any radish variety will succeed in our climate, though some are more vigorous or more interesting to grow. Read the catalog descriptions if you are looking for one that is particularly mild or peppery. Besides the familiar small, round red types, you will find the French breakfast types, which are slightly elongated and two-tone—red at the top, white at the bottom. 'Flamboyant Sabina' is a particularly vigorous French breakfast strain. You will also find small white radishes, including round ones and the 5-inch-long "Icicle." For a novelty, you can grow 'Easter Egg', a mixture of small round roots in red, white, lavender, and purple.

Large-rooted types for summer planting vary

from 2-foot-long slender roots to short round ones up to 7 inches in diameter. For sheer mass try 'Sakurajima Mammoth,' reportedly mild and sweet and sometimes reaching 100 pounds—although I doubt if it is still mild and sweet at that size! In the grocery stores you may see the long white radishes that the Japanese call daikon. Shredded raw daikon is a traditional accompaniment to sashimi, and the root is pickled whole to make pungent yellow takuan, which is used as a condiment for rice. Although most varieties of daikon are for summer planting, a few can be planted in early spring as well. Most large radish varieties have white skin and white flesh, but consider some interesting alternatives: 'China Rose', which is rose skinned and white fleshed (5 inches long, slender); 'Misato Rose Flesh', which is red clear through (4 inches across, globe shaped); 'Green Meat', which is green clear through (5 inches long, oval); and the handsome 'Black Spanish Long', which is white inside with a matte black skin (7 to 10 inches long, slender). Nothing dresses up a salad more elegantly than thin slices of black radish.

Asian cuisine includes radish leaves, and you will find a variety especially for this purpose.

Podding radish (*R. sativum* 'Caudatus') doesn't produce thickened roots. Instead, it is grown for its young seed pods, which reach 9 inches long and can be eaten raw or used in stir fry. They taste much like a radish root, wonderfully sharp and crisp. All radishes produce edible pods, but no others approach the dimensions of the podding radish.

Pests Radishes often get cabbage maggots, which burrow into the roots, making them unappetizing. Radishes growing in fall and before the end of March are likely to escape damage, as the adult fly is inactive in this period. (For more on this pest, see page 138.) One note here: I tried a floating row cover frame over radishes, but in spring and summer, when the pest is active, it made the air too warm around the radishes, so they didn't form good roots.

Sources
> Radish seed:
> Small-rooted varieties:
>> Cherry types: Widely available
>> French Breakfast (red with white tip): Widely available
>> Flamboyant Sabina (French breakfast type): SGS, T&M
>> Icicle: BG, JSS, NGN, PTS, SB, SOC, TERR
>> Round white types: BG
>> Round, mixed colors: BG, CG, JSS, NGN, PTS, SGS,

TERR, VBS
> Large-rooted varieties:
> For spring planting:
>> April Cross Hybrid: NGN, PS, T&M, VBS
>> Mino Early: EV
>> Spring Leader: JSS
>> Spring Light: TERR
> For summer planting:
>> Black Spanish Long: JG, NGN, PS, PTS, SB
>> China Rose: KSC, OBG, PTS, SB
>> Green Meat: EV
>> Long white daikon types: Widely available
>> Misato Rose Flesh: NGN, PS
>> Sakurajima Mammoth: KSC, SB
> Podding Varieties:
>> Edible Longpod: DD
>> Rat's Tail:
> OBG, PTS
> Grow for
> Leaves:
> EV, KSC

Rhubarb

RHUBARB
Rheum rhabarbarum
Knotweed Family ❖
Polygonaceae

This perennial vegetable is a large plant with a small but enthusiastic following. Its long red stems are very tart, but they are used as a fruit, cooked with sugar, often in a pie. I don't grow it myself, because it bothers me to have to pour so much sugar into anything. If rhubarb pie is one of your favorites, however, you will be glad to know that we can grow rhubarb here.

A native of Siberia, rhubarb needs colder winters than ours to make the thickest stems. But narrow stems are still tasty, and it is such a big plant that even a few narrow stems constitute a sizeable harvest. You may also find that stems are paler here, since winter chill is needed for good red color.

Growing Instructions Rhubarb is grown from dormant roots or plant divisions, either of which are available in local nurseries in fall or spring. Pick a cold, unprotected planting site. (Rhubarb won't mind shade in winter or cool days in summer.) One plant is probably enough, and it will take up 3 or 4 square feet. As with other perennials, prepare the site well, mixing plenty of compost or aged manure deep into the soil. Plant so that the top of the dormant root lies 1 to 2 inches below the surface, or set a container plant at the same level it was growing in the container.

Each fall fertilize with manure. This will allow the plant to grow in the same spot without being divided for up to ten years. If it becomes too big to survive on the available nutrients in the site, rhubarb will produce big stalks of white flowers. Remove these as soon as they form and plan to fertilize well next fall. A plant may be ready to divide in as few as five years. You can dig the whole plant, separate it into two or more pieces, and replant the pieces—but you will have to wait two or three years for each to return to full production. To avoid the wait, use a shovel to detach and remove one or more rosettes of leaves with roots attached. This lets the parent plant continue producing while you wait for the new plants to get started.

The Harvest   Like asparagus, rhubarb is harvested only in spring, when it begins to grow again after winter dieback. (In our mild climate rhubarb plants don't die back completely, and the first flush of spring growth suitable for harvest is likely to occur in late winter.) Then it is allowed to replenish its energy during the rest of the year. Don't harvest at all the first year and only for two weeks the second year. After that you may take stems for two months every spring. Gently pull or twist the largest stems. Never yank so hard that you injure the crown, and never cut rhubarb because the stub may rot. Harvest when the stems are at their prime—just after the leaves open up and before they are completely flat. Remember that rhubarb leaves and roots contain poisonous amounts of oxalic acid. Eat only the leaf stems, making sure that no trace of green leaf blade remains.

Varieties   Local nurseries carry varieties suited to our region. 'Giant Cherry' has a low-chill requirement, important in our mild region. Or try 'Strawberry,' another variety that has done well here.

Sources
Rhubarb roots or plants: Local nurseries

RUTABAGA
Brassica napus
Napobrassica Group
Mustard Family ❖ *Cruciferae*

Rutabaga is a starchy root, a winter vegetable of the sort that you butter and mash. It is much like turnip in flavor and texture, but sweeter. The plants produce a lot of calories for the amount of garden space they use. Although rutabaga can be grown here, it is one of those crops that would be improved by a little colder weather in late fall.

Growing Instructions   Give rutabagas soil that is organic, holds moisture well, and is not too high in nitrogen. Sow the seeds 1/4 to 1/2 inch deep, and thin the seedlings to stand 6 to 8 inches apart. Sow in early spring, or wait until mid- to late summer so that the roots will mature in cool fall weather. If rutabaga is planted too late in summer, the roots won't attain full size before winter cold slows their growth.

The Harvest   Rutabagas are ready to dig about three months after you plant the seeds, when the roots are 3 to 5 inches in diameter. They hold in the soil over the winter, but they will go to seed in late winter or early spring.

Pests   Although rutabaga can succumb to the same pests as other mustard-family plants, it is not affected as often.

Sources
Rutabaga seeds: Widely available

SALSIFY, COMMON (OR OYSTER PLANT)
Tragopogon porrifolius

SALSIFY, BLACK
Scorzonera hispanica

SPANISH OYSTER PLANT
Scolymus hispanicus

Sunflower Family ❖ *Compositae*

Salsify

These three plant species, all of them known as salsify or oyster plant, belong to the sunflower family and are grown the same way. The name oyster plant derives from the flavor of the steamed or sautéed roots, which many people find reminiscent of oysters.

Growing Instructions
Since salsify does best when the temperature is between 55° and 75°F during most of its growing pe-

---

SAUTÉED GREEN BEANS

This is especially good when made with scarlet runner or Romano-type beans.

2 cups green beans, cut on the diagonal into 1 to 2-inch pieces
1 1/2 tablespoons butter or margarine
1 1/2 tablespoons virgin olive oil
1 or 2 cloves garlic, minced
2 to 3 tablespoons sliced shallots or white part of scallions (or fresh shallot
    tops, onion lily tops, garlic chives, or scallion tops, or any combination)
Black pepper

    Steam the green beans until they are about halfway to fork tender.
    In a medium skillet, heat the butter and olive oil. Keeping the temperature low, add the minced garlic and shallots or white part of scallions. Sauté gently for a few minutes, until they are tender but not browned. Add the green beans and stir to coat with butter and oil. Sauté over medium-low heat until the beans are tender. If you are using shallot greens, onion lily greens, garlic chives, or scallion tops, add them now and cook briefly, stirring, until they are limp. Serves four.

---

riod, it is a good crop for the entire region. Plant it with assurance from February through July. An August planting may also succeed.

    Although it differs botanically from carrot and parsnip, salsify is just as slow to get started and has similar cultural needs. It needs the same loose, rich soil and it abhors rocks and fresh manure. Sow the seeds 1 inch deep and 2 inches apart. Thin to 4 inches apart, or 3 inches if the soil is very loose and rich. Salsify seeds may germinate in as few as seven days, or they may take as long as twenty. The seedlings grow slowly at first and have linear leaves that can be mistaken for young grass. Like carrot, salsify makes poor roots if it is transplanted.

The Harvest   Salsify roots mature in four to five months. In cold-winter areas, they are harvested after a few light fall frosts. In our region, you can pull salsify whenever it is 1-1/2 inches in diameter at the shoulder. If your roots aren't that large in four or five months, you may have planted too late in the year, or perhaps you didn't supply enough nutrients or water.

    To preserve the flavor of all three species, peel the roots after, not before, cooking. Steam or boil them for forty-five minutes, then rub the skin off the cooked roots.

    Salsify blooms if the roots aren't dug up by March or April. I often leave one or two plants intact so I can enjoy the flowers and seed heads. The pretty lavender flowers of common salsify are the domesticated version of the wildflower goatsbeard. They are followed by large dandelionlike heads of pale brown winged seeds. You can collect the seeds to grow next year or let them fall to the ground. Some of the fallen seeds will germinate in spring, producing a free crop for gardeners who welcome such bits of serendipity.

Varieties and Related Species   Unlike the biennial common salsify, black salsify is a perennial. Larger than common salsify, it has yellow flowers and a black-skinned root. The root will continue to enlarge in the ground, obligingly remaining tender for over a full year. The biennial Spanish oyster plant has prickly leaves and a root that is longer, lighter colored, and milder flavored than that of common salsify. Unfortunately, I have not been able to find a source of seeds for Spanish oyster plant. But with so many imports appearing in seed catalogs, it may turn up one day soon.

Sources
Salsify seed: DD, JGG, NGN, PTS, SB, T&M, VBS
Black salsify seed: JG, JGG, NGN, RH, SB

SEA KALE
Crambe maritima
Mustard Family ❖ *Cruciferae*

A native of the sea cliffs and beaches on the English, Irish, and European coasts, sea kale is a large perennial plant with bluish green leaves and small white flowers. Before the plant was domesticated, people ate the wild spring shoots. In the eighteenth century they began to grow it in gardens, blanching the shoots to make them milder and more tender. Once a popular crop, it is now rarely grown.

Growing Instructions Sea kale is well suited to our climate, although it appreciates a sunny site. Sow seeds 1 inch deep in early spring in a temporary bed of good garden soil. When the seedlings are well up, thin them to 6 inches apart. The following spring move the plants to a permanent bed, spacing them 2 to 3 feet apart.

Sea kale can also be started from root cuttings taken in fall or spring. Cuttings are taken from the thongs, the long side roots growing from the main root. Roots used for cuttings should be 1/2 inch in diameter and 4 to 6 inches long. It is traditional, as with horseradish, to cut the end nearest the central root (the top end) level and the end away from the root (the bottom end) at a slant, so you will remember which end is up when you plant it. Since there are no commercial sources for root cuttings, you will have to get a cutting from someone who is growing the plant.

Try to plant the cuttings the same day that you get them, unless it happens to be very cold or wet. If the weather remains unfavorable, refrigerate the roots in a plastic bag. Cuttings obtained in winter should be planted during a dry period anytime from the middle of February to early March. Prepare the permanent bed with plenty of compost and well-rotted manure, and plant the roots or seedlings 2 to 3 feet apart.

The Harvest Begin to harvest sea kale the second spring if you planted roots, and the third spring if you planted seeds. When the shoots begin to poke through the soil, blanch them by placing large clay pots upside down over the plants. Plug the bottom holes. Pale shoots, with tiny leaf blades at the top, will continue to grow under the pots. Harvest outer shoots when they are 6 to 9 inches long. When leafier growth begins to appear, uncover the plants and stop harvesting.

Let the plants mature—the flowers are an airy addition to bouquets. However, you will probably want to cut the flower stalks back before seeds form, since you want the plant to direct its energy into forming storage roots for next year's crop. A plant should bear for up to ten years.

The flavor of sea kale is nutty and slightly bitter. Shoots can be eaten raw with cheese or in salads. They can also be steamed and served with butter. If you come across any recipes for cardoon, substitute sea kale for the cardoon.

Sources
Sea kale seeds: DD, OBG, T&M

SHALLOT
Allium cepa
Aggregatum Group
Amaryllis Family ❖ *Amaryllidaceae*

A shallot plant looks like a smaller version of bunching onions, except it makes small, usually elongated storage bulbs with a distinctive, mild flavor. The plants can be used fresh, leaves and all, like green onions, or you can dry the bulbs and store them for later use. Either way, shallots add a wonderfully delicate onion flavor to sauces and salad dressings. They are especially common in French and Southeast Asian cooking.

Growing Instructions According to a folk saying, you should plant shallot sets on the shortest day of the year, December 21st, and harvest them on the longest, June 21st. This is about right, but you should probably plant in November, before weather turns chilly. Plant shallot sets about 6 inches apart and no deeper than an inch.

The newly available shallot seeds should be sown outside in February, or inside 10 to 12 weeks earlier. Plant them 1/2 inch deep, and 1 to 2 inches apart for single bulbs, wider to get clusters. Shallots are sensitive to overwatering, so they are probably a poor choice for unamended clay soil. Keep shallots moist during dry spells, but leave them dryer in June, as the bulbs mature.

The Harvest You can cut shallot leaves to use like chives, dig up the entire plant to use like green onions, or wait until the tops fall over and the leaves begin to die back and harvest the bulbs for storage. Overusing the greens will reduce the size of the bulbs. Cure and store the shallot bulbs like onions (see page 223), being careful to check frequently for decay. Shallots do not keep as well as onions, so use them up by winter, or replant them to make next year's crop.

Varieties and Related Crops I've had the best crop so far with French shallots, but there are many kinds to try, both as sets and seeds.

Old-fashioned potato onions are the same species and variety as shallots, but they have a more oniony flavor. To grow them, plant a mixture of large (to 2 inch) and small sets; the small ones enlarge, while the larger ones multiply, so you have a harvest each year of green onion and bulb onions. Plant sets in fall or midwinter, and dig in early summer. The bulbs keep well.

Pests Shallots are susceptible to the usual pests affecting onion and its relatives. They are especially vulnerable to downy mildew and onion root maggots. Try to reduce the chance of disease by purchasing your shallot sets from a nursery rather than a grocery store.

Sources
Shallot sets: BG, CG, GG, JG, JSS, SB, SGS, T&M
Shallot seed: JSS, TERR
Potato onion sets: RSP, SB

SIBERIAN KALE (SEE KALE)

SORREL, GARDEN
Rumex acetosa
SORREL, FRENCH
R. scutatus

Knotweed Family ❖ *Polygonaceae*

Cool weather and fog are no hindrance to garden sorrel or French sorrel, perennial plants that bear tart, tender leaves the year around. As well as adding a kick to mixed green salads, sorrel is the key ingredient of some Old World soups and is an interesting addition to omelets and stuffing.

Growing Instructions Buy a small sorrel plant, which you will probably find among the herbs at your local nursery. Since you will probably only

need one plant, it is easier to buy it than to grow from seed. Prepare a planting site as you would for other perennials, controlling weeds and mixing in plenty of organic matter. Allow 1 to 1-1/2 feet between sorrel and neighboring plants. A fall or spring planting is best, but you can plant sorrel whenever you buy it. Keep the soil moist all year.

The Harvest Until the plant is over a foot high, harvest lightly. Once the plant is mature, it can handle frequent harvests throughout the year, although leaf production will slow in summer when the plant blooms. Cut back flower stalks to increase leaf production. The long stems of tiny pinkish flowers make an attractive if unconventional cut flower. Divide the sorrel clump in spring or fall if it gets too large.

Varieties and Related Species: French sorrel grows 1 to 2 feet high, whereas garden sorrel reaches 2 to 3 feet high and has larger leaves. You may or may not be able to tell which species you are getting. The situation is somewhat confused by the fact that garden sorrel is sometimes called French sorrel. However, the plants are so similar that the question is of minor practical importance.

Pests Although snails hide in my sorrel plant, they do only minor damage. I go to the trouble of removing them, because they use the sorrel as a home base from which to attack nearby plants.

Sources
Sorrel plants: BG, JG, NGN, RH, and local nurseries

SPINACH
Spinacia oleracea
Goosefoot Family ❖ *Chenopodiaceae*

Spinach is an annual plant, unlike its close relatives beet and Swiss chard, which are biennial. A fast-growing crop, spinach makes a low rosette of large, tender leaves in a little over a month. When the crop is grown in unsuitable conditions, it responds by making only a few small leaves and then rushing to form a tall seed stalk. Even spinach grown under good conditions is short-lived. Although it may keep producing leaves for several weeks in fall, it will often go to seed soon after reaching maturity.

Growing Instructions To grow spinach successfully, choose the best variety for the season in which you are growing it and apply ample organic amendment, fertilizer, and water. Spinach has very high nitrogen needs. One gardener even reported success from seeds spilled in fresh horse manure. If you are working manure or another fertilizer into your soil before planting spinach, add it to the top few inches only, since spinach has shallow roots. Spinach is usually seeded in place. Sow 1/2 inch deep and 2 inches apart in blocks or in wide rows separated by 8 to 12 inches. Thin the seedlings to stand 4 to 6 inches apart, and use the thinnings in salads.

Sow seeds from February onward, and experiment to see how long you can plant in your particular microclimate before spring warmth and lengthening days cause spinach to bolt to seed early. Start seeding again in mid-July and see how late into fall you can plant before cold weather slows growth too much. As fall progresses, it becomes too cold for spinach to grow large. It may overwinter and grow again in late winter, then flower when spring weather warms. A cold frame will allow you to extend fall planting.

Sow successive plantings of spinach every three weeks to a month for a more or less steady supply. Small plantings, just a dozen or two plants tucked in a corner, are best until you get a feel for the needs and rhythm of this crop.

The Harvest You can start picking the outer leaves of young spinach plants as soon as there are any reasonably large ones, or you can harvest whole plants when they are mature. While you are learning to grow spinach, the plants you harvest are likely to be much smaller than the ones in grocery stores. Just be sure to catch them before they form a seed stalk, and keep trying to improve conditions so the plants will grow larger next time.

Varieties Spinach has either flat or savoyed (crinkled) leaves. Flat leaves are a little easier to clean than the savoyed ones. As new spinach varieties appear often, I encourage you to experiment. My favorite spinach variety thus far is 'Wolter', which makes large, flat, mild-flavored leaves when planted spring or fall. The leaves of my August-planted crop remain sweet and tender enough for salads all winter, even when the plants begin to bloom. For spring-into-summer sowings try 'Nordic IV', 'Steadfast', or the semi-savoyed 'Tyee F$_1$'.

Pests Spinach shares leafminer problems with beets and chard (see page 142).

Sources
  Nordic IV: PS, SGS, TERR
  Steadfast: TERR
  Tyee F$_1$: JSS, PTS, TERR., VBS
  Wolter: SOS

SPINACH, MALABAR
Basella alba
Basella Family ❖ *Basellaceae*

Malabar spinach is a crop with thick, succulent, mild-flavored leaves that serve as a spinachlike crop in weather that is too warm for regular spinach. Alas, our climate is barely warm enough for it to survive, let alone thrive. In my sunny San Francisco garden it grew only 6 inches high, whereas in a warm Southern California garden it can sprawl or climb several feet. I kept one plant in my living room, where it grew over a foot long, but I fear the only way we will enjoy it in this region is by growing it in a greenhouse.

SPINACH, NEW ZEALAND
Tetragonia tetragonioides (Tetragonia expansa)
Carpetweed Family ❖ *Aizoaceae*

New Zealand spinach is not a true spinach, but a similar-tasting green that does well everywhere in the region right up to the beach. It can be found growing wild at the beach end of Golden Gate Park and even on the ocean side of the Great Highway in San Francisco. Although New Zealand spinach is one of the plants that saved Captain Cook and his crew from scurvy during their voyages of discovery from 1771 to 1775, no one seems to know whether the people native to New Zealand ever considered it edible.

New Zealand spinach is often advertised as a

hot-weather spinach. Although it grows well in hot temperatures, it also thrives in our foggy summers and often grows actively enough for harvests in winter. I have had tender young leaves from mid-winter plantings very near the coast. It also seems to be entirely pest-free.

Like regular spinach, it tastes a bit sharp and contains some oxalic acid. Rapidly growing young stem tips are the mildest. Enjoy New Zealand spinach in salads, as a steamed vegetable, or in a mixed dish such as quiche or spanakopita.

Growing Instructions Here is one crop that isn't choosy about soil, fertility, or watering regularity. Although it appreciates rich soil and grows faster when well watered, it matures in most soils and tolerates some drought.

In early spring plant the seeds after soaking them overnight for quicker germination. Use mail-order seeds, or collect seeds from wild plants or a friend's garden. Sow them 1/2 inch deep, either in flats or directly in the garden. Thin or transplant to 2 feet apart. Plants grow very slowly for the first couple of months, but once established they sprawl over several square feet. You may decide to keep just one or two plants, but it is a good idea to start extra plants to allow for accidents during the maturing process.

New Zealand spinach is a borderline perennial here. It will live through the winter in relatively frost-free areas, but it can be damaged by even a mild frost. If the seeds fall to the ground, some will probably come up next spring. Sometimes I just pull the old plant and let a couple of the seedlings have the spot. If volunteer seedlings pop up where I intended to grow something else, I dig them up and transplant them where I want them.

The Harvest Starting in early summer you can harvest small whole plants from spring-planted seeds. Or you can wait until the plants are larger and pick 3- to 4-inch stem tips, then pick some more when the plant has regrown. Once the plants have bloomed and the small knobby seedpods form, the stems are likely to be too tough and the leaves too strong for your taste. In late summer try cutting the plants back to 1 foot across to stimu-

late fresh growth.

Varieties Only one variety is available and it seems to be the same one that grows wild locally. You will often find it listed in seed catalogs under the heading *Spinach*.

Sources
New Zealand spinach seed: Widely available

SQUASH, SUMMER (INCLUDING ZUCCHINI, CROOKNECK, AND SCALLOP)
Cucurbita pepo
Gourd Family ❖ *Cucurbitaceae*

Like other members of the cucurbit family, summer squash is a warm-season crop that should be planted after the soil has heated up in spring. Both summer and winter squash are a good bet for the entire region, requiring less heat than other family members, which include cucumber, gourd, and melon. Summer squash requires a rich soil and ample water to produce good harvests. It makes large plants, each requiring 3 square feet or more. Although the plants will be smaller in cooler parts of the region, their fabled productivity makes them worthwhile even there. If you live in a foggy location or if you haven't improved your soil sufficiently, try zucchini first since it tends to be more vigorous than other types of summer squash.

Growing Instructions A summer squash planted in May will begin to bear fruit in July. It will continue to bear until it succumbs to the chill and damp in October or November—unless it falls victim to powdery mildew earlier. Planted as late as the middle of July, it will still be productive for a month or longer.

You can try starting summer squash outdoors as early as February. Many plants started before the soil and air are warm enough don't make it, but those that do survive produce early crops. To increase your chance of success with extra early plantings, try covering your seedlings with a floating row cover. Like the other cucurbits, summer squash can be

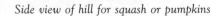
Side view of hill for squash or pumpkins

246

started indoors. Sow the seeds in a bottomless container so that you can transplant the seedlings without disturbing the roots (see page 54). Move the plants into the garden after about four weeks, when they have two true leaves.

Summer squash is usually planted in hills (a grouping of several seeds or plants), rather than rows. Although hills do not have to be actual mounds, they are commonly mounded for squash. Mounding creates a warm, well drained environment for the seeds. That allows the seeds to germinate faster and makes them less vulnerable to decay.

I plant summer squash seeds (as well as winter squash and pumpkin seeds) in a special mound I have designed to make the soil warmer, more aerated, and easier to water. Here's how to construct

Flowering summer squash

the mound. After preparing the seedbed, form a circular trench that is 3 to 4 inches deep and wide. Use the soil removed from the trench to make a 1-foot-diameter, flat-topped mound in the middle. Form a lip at the edge, press the lip to firm it, then plant five or six seeds in a ring around the level top of the mound. Water the top of the mound and the surrounding trench until the plants have a couple of true leaves. Thin all but the largest two plants, and from then on water only the trench. If you are using transplants, just make the circular trench and not the special mound. Plant two seedlings about 6 inches apart in the area circled by the trench.

At the same time you plant squash seeds consider planting a quick crop between the hills to mature before the squash grows over the area. Try radish seeds, lettuce seedlings, or onion sets for green onions.

Summer squash is a good candidate for the sunken-can technique of watering (see page 64). Periodically add a nutrient boost, such as manure or compost tea or fish emulsion, when you water.

The Harvest   One benefit of growing your own summer squash is that you can harvest the flowers, which are delicious in soups or fried. Squash plants have both male and female blossoms, which can be distinguished by the tiny squash fruit behind the female flower. A plant usually makes several male flowers first. You may as well eat them, since there is nothing for them to fertilize. Then it makes both male and female flowers at the same time. There are usually more male ones than necessary for pollination, so a judicious harvest won't slow production. Harvested female flowers have the added bonus of a baby squash. Of course, eating female flowers will limit overall production, but that may be just what you want to do.

We've all heard jokes about gardeners with too many zucchini and stories about fruit the size of baseball bats. It is best never to let the fruit get too big, not only because it is tough and bitter but also because production of tender new fruit slows and eventually stops.

The smaller the squash when you pick it, the better it will taste—and, almost as important, the smaller the total production of the plants. After years of dissatisfaction with too many big summer squash, for the past three years I have finally been able to pick all the fruit while it is small. I pick it as baby squash with blossoms, or I wait until it is 4 inches or slightly longer, but never more than 10 inches. This means picking it as often as every two or three days. If an occasional zucchini grows to 12 to 15 inches long, it can still be used for stuffed squash (see page 345). You may as well discard any zucchini fruit longer than that.

Varieties   I've had good luck with many summer squash varieties, including 'Black Beauty', 'Burpee Hybrid', various yellow crook and straight necks, 'Peter Pan' green scallop, 'Sunburst' yellow scallop, and the pale-green, Middle-East type 'Kuta'. Most of these do get powdery mildew, but with careful attention, yield a good crop before succumbing (see Pests, next page). 'Fiorentino' makes huge plants whose ridged fruits approach 8 inches long before they are even fertilized. Picked soon after, they are delicious sauteed or for stuffing. 'Zucchetta Rampicante' is a climber that makes long, curved, pale green squash with a firmer texture than zucchini, and a slightly different flavor. It thrives in my Mission District garden, but not in cooler parts of San Francisco.

PUMPKIN OR SQUASH SOUP

When you are cooking for Thanksgiving, freeze the cooked pumpkin that didn't fit in the pie. Make broth from the turkey neck, and freeze it with the neck meat. Then, when the fresh leftover turkey is gone, serve this soup as an echo of the feast.

3 cups cooked pumpkin (see directions below)
2 tablespoons butter or margarine
1 onion, chopped
4 cups turkey or chicken broth
Meat from turkey neck or chicken neck and back
1 cup or so of milk
2/3 pound grated jack cheese (2 1/2 cups, lightly packed)
1/4 teaspoon nutmeg
Freshly ground pepper, to taste
2 or 3 sprigs parsley, chopped

Cut the pumpkin into 2-inch chunks and peel them. Steam until tender, about 20 minutes. Measure out 3 cups, packing the cooked chunks into a measuring cup.

In a small skillet, sauté the onion in the butter until it is tender but not browned. Using a blender, blend the broth, turkey or chicken meat, pumpkin, cheese, and cooked onion, a little at a time. Pour the blended mixture into a large pot.

Add milk, stir, and heat through, but don't boil. Stir in nutmeg and pepper. Sprinkle with chopped parsley. Serves 3 or 4.

Variation: You can substitute butternut, hubbard, or other similar squash for the pumpkin.

Pests Some of the most common problems of squash are not actually caused by pests but by physiological factors—from inconsistent watering to lack of pollination. Gardeners sometimes have many squash blossoms but little fruit, or they have fruit that begins to form but never matures. If the female blossoms drop off without setting fruit or if the small fruit shrivels and turns yellow from the tip, your problem is probably lack of pollination. This can happen anytime, but it is more likely to occur very early or very late in the season, when bees are less active. For pollination insurance, you can hand-pollinate, using a cotton swab or even your finger to gather pollen from the center of male flowers and dab it on the yellow structures in the center of female flowers.

Squash may also remain unfertilized as a kind of natural birth control, setting fruit in several waves during the season with brief rests between. Also, if you've left large fruit on the plant too long, new fruit won't set. Sometimes, the stem end of the fruit is pollinated and swells, but the blossom end stays narrow. You must pick any half-formed fruit, because seeds can mature in the large end signaling the plant to stop making new fruit.

If the fruit begins to mature but the tip decays, you may have a condition similar to blossom-end rot in tomato. The cause is probably calcium deficiency caused by uneven watering. Root damage, heavy soil, or a nutrient imbalance could also be at fault. In our humid, foggy climate the problem may simply be a rot spread by blossoms that stay moist and stick to the fruit rather than drying up and falling off. Remove the blossoms as soon as the fruit begins to swell, carefully scraping away any decay on the end of the fruit. Do this soon enough and the fruit will dry, heal, and continue to develop normally.

Check summer squash blossoms and growing tips occasionally for aphids. Those found on squash are usually pale green. Zucchini yellow mosaic virus, a disease spread by aphids, is becoming more common in our area. See page 160 for more information on this disease.

Most summer squash varieties get powdery mildew, a fungus disease that covers the leaves with a white dust. Check the undersides of lower leaves for pale clusters of spores. (Don't confuse the normal white or silvery markings on the upper surface of the leaves of some zucchini varieties for powdery mildew. See page 157 for more on powdery mildew.)

In an attempt to find a zucchini with some resistance to powdery mildew, I located two that seem to resist zucchini yellow mosaic virus as well. I grew four plants each of four different varieties. Three of them—'Burpee Hybrid', 'Richgreen', and 'President'—had performed well in tests for powdery mildew resistance at the University of Florida. The fourth variety, which I planted as a control, was 'Zuchlong'. I lost all the 'Zuchlong' plants to the virus, and some of the 'Richgreen' plants were also infected. None of the 'Burpee Hybrid' or 'President' plants got the virus, and both thrived through light infections of powdery mildew.

A new yellow crookneck variety 'Park's Crookneck PMR Hybrid' offers resistance to powdery mildew. I have not yet tried it, but yellow crookneck is usually *more* susceptible than zucchini, so I'm hoping its resistance bears out.

Sources

Summer squash seed:
Zucchini varieties:
    Burpee Hybrid: BU
    Black Beauty: OBG, TERR
Yellow squash varieties:
    Park's Crookneck PMR Hybrid: PS
Scallop squash varieties:
    Peter Pan: BU, NGN, VBS
    Sunburst: CG, ISS, NGN, PS, PTS, SGS, TERR, VBS
Other summer squash varieties:
    Fiorentino (roman ridged): RCS, SGS
    Kuta: PS
    Zucchetta Rampicante seed: CG, PTS, SGS

SQUASH, WINTER AND PUMPKIN

Cucurbita species
Gourd Family ❖ *Cucurbitaceae*

Winter squash includes acorn, butternut, hubbard, and spaghetti squash. They are called winter squash because, although grown in the summer, they can be stored unrefrigerated to be eaten in winter. Pumpkin is grown in the same way as winter squash. Both have needs similar to those of summer squash. They differ mainly in usually taking up more space and in needing a longer period of growth before harvest. All prefer warm, sunny summers, but they are worth a try in foggier areas. Pumpkin generally

---

THE WINTER SQUASH FAMILY TREE

Both pumpkin and summer squash belong to the species *Cucurbita pepo*, and they can cross-pollinate. That explains why the seeds that you save from a pumpkin or zucchini or the seeds that sprout from a mature zucchini tossed into the compost pile may make plants with zucchini-shaped pumpkin fruit or pumpkin-shaped zucchini fruit. Acorn, delicata, and spaghetti squash are members of the same species.

Another species, *C. maxima*, includes many types of winter squash, such as banana, buttercup, hubbard, and turban. It also includes several varieties of squash that are more commonly called pumpkins, such as 'Atlantic Giant' and 'Big Max'.

C. mixta (*C. argyrosperma*) is represented mainly by cushaw, a type of squash native to the southern United States and Mexico. Cushaw is an elongated, curved-necked squash, often with a striped skin.

A fourth species is *C. moschata*, which includes butternut, golden cushaw winter squash, and winter crookneck. It differs from the other species in having softer fuzz on its leaves. Moschatas are the types I've found to be the most resistant to powdery mildew.

does well in the fog, and winter squash varieties vary in their ability to produce in foggy climates.

Growing instructions Plant winter squash and pumpkin anytime from the middle of April to the middle of June. Gardeners in the foggiest areas must get seeds in by May 15, so that the fruit has time to ripen on the vine before the weather turns cool.

Like summer squash, winter squash and pumpkin are usually planted in hills. The warm, well-drained environment of a raised hill (see page 246) is even more important to get these seeds off to a good start, since they need every available day in which to mature. You may want to sow them indoors to get the earliest start. Do it just as you would summer squash, planting them in bottomless containers to avoid disturbing the roots when you transplant. Move the seedlings into the garden in about a month. A few varieties form zucchini-like bushes, but most form long vines that can eat up a lot of garden space. Use the seed packet as a guide for the distance between hills. It will range from 3 feet apart for bush types to 10 feet for the largest vines.

You can guide winter squash and pumpkin vines as they grow to keep them from invading other plantings, or to direct them into a corn patch that has been given a head start. You can also train them up vertical frames. This may sound strange since the fruit is so big, but you can support it in cloth slings. Like cucumber, winter squash and pumpkin will need hand weaving every few days to help it climb. Make sure the frame is strong and has wide openings. If you're growing the vines on the ground, prop the developing fruit on a dry board or flat stone to keep the bottom from coming into contact with damp soil or decaying vegetation.

At Green Gulch Farm, which is quite near the west coast of Marin County, gardeners stop watering winter squash in the middle of August to hasten ripening and to keep the water content of the fruit down. Experiment with this, but be aware that the soil at Green Gulch is quite clayey. If your soil is sandy, you may find a total water cutoff too extreme.

The Harvest Only harvest male blossoms from winter squash or pumpkin plants when no female blossoms are present, as each plant makes only a few female blossoms, and if they don't get pollinated, you will have no fruit production.

Do not harvest pumpkins and winter squash until they have formed a hard shell. It's better to leave them too long than not long enough, since they will sweeten only on the vine. To be sure the fruit is ripe, leave it unpicked for a few weeks after it has reached maximum size and has stopped changing color. Also, wait for the stem to turn brown. Don't leave fruit on after the vines have died or into winter, since rain will foster decay.

When cutting a winter squash or pumpkin from the vine, leave a 2-inch stem and keep the fruit in a warm, dry place for a week or two. Then store the fruit, making sure that one doesn't touch another, in a dry, dark place as close to 50° to 60°F as you can find. If the shell is not damaged, pumpkin and winter squash will last at least two months and often much longer (although the sugar content will suffer by spring). If you are storing both pumpkins and winter squash, use the pumpkins first since they do not keep as well. Pumpkins and winter squash can be used interchangeably in many recipes.

Varieties If you plan to carve a big Jack-o'-lantern, choose varieties, such as 'Spirit Hybrid', or 'Jack-O'-Lantern' that are suitable for either cooking or carving. 'Small Sugar', weighing 5 to 6 pounds, is the traditional pie pumpkin, small and flavorful. 'Baby Bear' has a classic pumpkin shape, but weighs ony 1 1/2 to 2 pounds. It is good for pie, and has semi-hulless seeds for easy roasting. Even tinier, 'Jack-be-Little' is flattened and cute, useful for decorations or stuffing. 'Rouge Vif D'Etamps' makes big, decorative, "Cinderella-type" pumpkins, while 'Dill's Atlantic Giant' is among those grown for competition-size fruits. Both are really *Cucurbita maxima* and neither are best for eating, nor is their thick flesh ideal for carving.

Among winter squash varieties, choose ones with long vines and large fruit varieties for your main crop. That way, if cool weather limits the crop, you will at least have *something* to harvest. I have found production from bush-types, including acorn squash, to be disappointing.

Our best bets are butternuts and hubbards. Both types have thick orange flesh with excellent flavor and texture. Butternuts, which resist powdery mildew, have smooth, pale buff skin and are bottle-shaped or round. Among hubbards try the warty, blue-gray 'Blue Hubbard,' the similar Northwest favorite 'Sweet Meat', or the Japanese 'Blue Kuri'. Spaghetti squash, which has pasta-like threads inside, is not ideally suited for our climate, but often does bear a crop.

MARINATED SUNCHOKES

Serve these alone or toss a few in a mixed salad.

2 sprigs each rosemary, marjoram, and thyme
2 cups sliced sunchokes
1/2 cup red wine vinegar
1/2 cup water
2 to 3 tablespoons olive oil

Chop the herbs finely. Mix the vinegar, water, oil, and herbs in a jar or a plastic container with a lid. It's best to use a container that's just big enough to hold the sunchokes. Add the sunchokes and stir to distribute the herbs. Cover and refrigerate several hours or overnight.

Pests Powdery mildew seems to be the primary local pest of pumpkins and winter squash. Pumpkin vines may succumb before the fruit is even ripe—and once the vine is dead, the fruit stops maturing. For more on powdery mildew, see page 157. Another hazard is pillbugs and sowbugs, which will nibble fruit that has been in contact with soil and has begun to decay.

Sources
Pumpkin seed:
  Jack-O'-Lantern: ABL, VBS
  Spirit Hybrid: NGN, PTS, TERR
  Small Sugar: Widely available
  Baby Bear: CG, JSS, NGN, PTS,
  Jack-be-Little: Widely available
  Rouge Vif D'Etampes: Widely available
  Dill's Atlantic Giant: JSS, NGN, PTS, SB, VBS
Winter squash seed:
  Early Butternut: NGN, PS, PTS, SGS, VBS
  Ponca Butternut: DD, VBS
  Waltham Butternut: ABL, BG, GG, JSS, OBG, PTS, SB, SOC
  Blue Hubbard: JG, JSS, PS, PTS, SB, TERR, VBS
  Sweetmeat: NGN, TERR
  Blue Kuri: ABL, EV, KSC,
  Spaghetti Squash: Widely available

SUNCHOKE
(OR JERUSALEM ARTICHOKE)

Helianthus tuberosus
Sunflower Family ❖ *Compositae*

This native North American relative of the sunflower produces edible tubers. European settlers, who were introduced to the sunchoke by native Americans, carried some of the tubers back to Europe. They were grown there and renamed in several European languages. Eventually the tubers were reintroduced to the United States, where they became known as Jerusalem artichoke. Why Jerusalem? The most cogent theory I've heard is that it is a distortion of the Italian name for the plant, *girasole*, which means turning to the sun. Sunchoke is a newer name, meant to be more descriptive and less confusing.

The crisp, low-calorie tubers are very easy to grow in all parts of our region. They appreciate a sunny location, but because they grow 10 to 12 feet high, they will reach for the sun. If you plant them in a shady spot, such as next to a fence, their tops will soon be in sunlight, although they may lean out on the way up, reaching for just a bit more light. Sunchoke will produce a crop in relatively infertile soil. However, the crop is likely to be smaller and the tubers misshapen if they are grown in very heavy, poorly amended clay soil. The plants grow all summer, the tops dying back around October. The tubers can be dug from October to the following March.

Growing instructions You can plant a sunchoke you bought at the grocery store as long as the buds haven't been cut off. You can also buy tubers from mail-order seed companies.

The best time to plant sunchoke tubers is March or April. If you can't get them in the mail at the right time for our climate, just plant when you can. Planted in fall, the tubers should stay dormant until spring. Those planted in spring will get a late start this year but will sprout earlier next year. If the soil is too wet when your tubers arrive, refrigerate them in a plastic bag until the soil is the right moisture for planting.

Choose firm, unblemished tubers and plant them 2 inches deep and 1 foot apart. Sunchokes are very productive, so two or three tubers per person are plenty to plant, unless you know you will use them as staples. Put them where they won't shade shorter plants, then stand back and watch them shoot upward. Water well all summer.

The Harvest In late summer you may see groups of 2- or 3-inch sunny yellow daisies atop the plants. The flowers may not form if the summer is very foggy, but they are a bonus anyhow, since the plants don't need to bloom to be productive. When the leaves begin to turn brown in October, dig up the first crisp, mild tubers. What you don't need will keep best in the ground. You can break off the stalks, leaving just a little to mark the place, then harvest throughout the winter. If you need to store harvested tubers for a few days, put them in a plastic bag in the refrigerator. To prepare the tubers for eating, scrub them well. There is no need to peel them, even if they are green. (Green parts on a sunchoke tuber are harmless, unlike those on a potato.)

In March you will notice that the buds on your earth-stored tubers are beginning to swell. The tubers are still edible, but it is time to renew your sunchoke bed for the next year. Dig up the remaining tubers, add organic matter to the soil if you wish, then replant a few large tubers. When the new shoots appear, dig out any extra plants so that you have just the number you want to grow. A sunchoke bed tended this way once a year will not get overcrowded or spread out as the years go by.

Varieties Knobby branches on sunchoke tubers are a nuisance when you are cleaning them, and until recently all the available tubers were more or less knobby. Now, however, some new varieties with smooth skins have been developed from European stock. They include 'Fuseau,' which has tubers almost 4 inches long and 1 inch in diameter; 'Golden Nugget,' which has small, elongated tubers with a nutty flavor; and 'Smooth Garnet,' a red-skinned variety with an even richer flavor.

Another interesting sunchoke variety, 'Dwarf Sunray', grows only 5 to 7 feet tall. Sold as a dual-purpose plant, it blooms freely enough to find a place in your summer flower border. I don't know how well it will bloom in very foggy locations, but it is still worth growing if you want to fit this easy crop into a small garden.

Pests Sunchoke is practically pest-free. Although something chews a leaf of my plants now and then, it doesn't affect the productivity of the crop.

Sources
Sunchoke tubers:
Fuseau: SB
Golden Nugget: SB
Smooth Garnet: SB
Knobby types or shape unknown: JSS, NGN, VBS

SUNFLOWER
Helianthus annuus
Sunflower Family ❖ *Compositae*

Sunflower is a warm-season crop that tolerates some fog. Given organic, fertile soil and plenty of water, it will reward you with 6- to 10-foot-high plants that are topped with huge yellow flowers studded with deliciously munchable seeds.

Although sunflower isn't a very demanding crop, overconfidence can result in disappointment. If you are counting on the plant's tremendous vigor to help it survive wretched soil or severe underwatering, don't be surprised if you get pint-sized flowers on 3- to 4-foot-high stalks and only a few well-filled-out seeds. Sunflower may also respond to extremely foggy periods or to a too-late planting by producing hollow seeds.

Growing instructions Although unshelled raw sunflower seeds from the grocery store may grow, you will be more certain of good results if you buy seeds selected and packaged for gardeners. In early May sow the seeds directly in your garden in a place where the plants won't shade other sun-loving crops. Plant the seeds 1 inch deep, sowing groups of three seeds 1 foot apart. Thin to the best seedling in each group. Sunflower may succeed if it is planted as late as the beginning of July to mature in late summer.

A single sunflower is really many flowers. Each flat head is covered with hundreds of small fertile flowers, with a narrow fringe of infertile flowers forming the yellow "petals" around the edge. The seeds, which form under the fertile flowers, have creamy white hulls at first. Later, dark stripes become visible. When the flowers fall from the seeds at the brush of a hand, test a couple of seeds for ripeness. If the meat is well formed in them, cut the flower.

Keep cut seed heads in a warm, dry place for a few days, then brush the seeds out of the heads. The fleshy heads have a tendency to decay in our damp climate, so don't leave the seeds in them too long. You can crack the seeds and eat them immediately. As an alternative, spread them to dry for a couple of weeks, then store them in closed containers. Eat shelled seeds raw, or salt and roast them in the shell.

Pests Don't leave a mature flower uncut for too long, since birds may peck out the seeds and ants may crawl into the seed heads. Although ants don't do any damage, they make it unpleasant to dry a head indoors.

Sources
Sunflower seeds: Widely available

Sweet Potato
Ipomoea batatas
Morning Glory Family ❖ *Convolvulaceae*

Sweet potatoes are not related to Irish potatoes or yams. It has become customary to sell some sweet potatoes as yams, but the yam is a tropical root in the genus *Dioscorea* and is rarely seen in our grocery stores.

Also tropical in origin, sweet potatoes require a long, hot summer—a reason they are a popular crop in the South. I tried planting sweet potatoes one year to see how close I could come to success. Even on the sunny side of San Francisco, the plants produced about a pound of roots each—not much more than I had planted. Four pounds per plant is considered acceptable production for sweet potatoes. Still, it is a very pretty plant and the leaves are used in Filipino cuisine, so you may like to give it a try.

Growing instructions It is best to purchase certified disease-free starts. With care, you can also start your own slips from store-bought roots. Buy some medium-sized, unblemished roots in early November. Store them at room temperature in a light-filled room, but out of direct sunlight, until early February. Then in a container of sand or potting soil, bury most of the root at a 45-degree angle, leaving the sprouting end exposed. Each root will make up to a dozen sprouts, known as slips. Keep the sand or potting soil damp and the container in a warm place on a windowsill until the slips are 6

to 12 inches high.

Cutting the slips an inch from the root ensures that you won't transfer any diseases from the parent root to the soil, but it means the new slips will have no roots. Now you need to transplant them into clean soil and grow them indoors for six more weeks. Cover the slips with a plastic bag and keep them out of bright light for a few days after transplanting them.

In May plant rooted slips in rich, organic garden soil. Plant them 4 inches deep and 1 foot apart. For more warmth, try planting in raised beds or on mounds. Use black or clear plastic mulch to help heat up the soil.

The Harvest Dig sweet potato roots in late fall. You can eat them right away but they get sweeter after curing, because some of the starch turns to sugar. To store sweet potatoes, cure them in a warm, humid place (about 80°F) for two weeks. Then wrap each root in newspaper and store at 55° to 60°F. Take care not to injure the roots, since this will encourage decay.

Pests Sweet potatoes are quarantined, so you can't order sets from sources outside California. The cause of the quarantine is the sweet potato weevil, which has thus far been kept away from California sweet potato crops. Other pests of commercial sweet potatoes crops include two diseases—black rot and scurf. My plants didn't have any pests, although something might have found them had I grown them for several consecutive seasons.

Sources
Sweet potato plants: House of Alvarez, P.O. Box 474, Livingston, CA 95334 (209) 394-7065

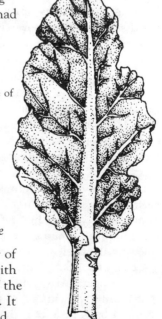

Swiss Chard
Beta vulgaris
Cicla Group
Goosefoot
Family ❖ *Chenopodiaceae*

Swiss chard, the ancestor of beets and a leafy green with no storage root, is one of the stalwarts of local gardens. It grows easily from seed and

BROILED TOMATOES
WITH HERBS AND CHEESE

This works well with tomatoes about 1 1/2 to 2 inches in diameter, such as are often produced by 'Early Girl,' 'Stupice,' or by the paste tomato varieties. Serve them as an appetizer or a side dish.

4 tablespoons grated Parmesan cheese
4 tablespoons chopped scallion, onion lily tops or garlic chives
2 tablespoons minced Italian parsley
4 tablespoons mayonnaise
6 small ripe tomatoes

In a small bowl, combine the cheese, scallion (or other onion-flavored vegetable), parsley, and mayonnaise. Cut the tomatoes in half. Cut a shallow depression in each half, removing some of the core. Cover each tomato half with a dollop of the topping, mounding it slightly and being sure it extends to the edges. Broil the tomatoes for 2 to 3 minutes, until the tops are golden brown. Serves three to four.

Variation: You can also use the topping on chunks of bell pepper or as a filling for mushroom caps. Broil them as you would the tomatoes.

provides ample greens for months. It is so at home here that it grows wild in some of the marshlands near San Francisco Bay.

Growing instructions   Swiss chard will grow all year. For the biggest plants sow seeds in spring, no later than April. Seeds sown in summer and fall will make shorter plants. Swiss chard is not fussy about soil, but it appreciates organic matter and fertilizer. Although Swiss chard can be transplanted, it is so easily started in place that direct seeding is more common. Sow the seeds 1/2 inch deep and 2 inches apart. Let the plants crowd each other a bit before thinning them to 10 to 12 inches apart. Eat the thinnings.

The Harvest   Cut whole young plants, or leave them to mature and harvest one or two outer leaves at a time. If you are harvesting by the leaf during rainy months, remove the whole leafstalk by pulling sideways. Don't leave a stub or it may rot and damage the rest of the plant.

Like beet, swiss chard is a biennial—meaning that it will overwinter and go to seed the following spring. I have been told that you can force the

plant to make more leaves by cutting back the flower stalk, but I have never found this to work well. Instead, I just pull out the blooming plants.

Varieties   Any variety of Swiss chard will thrive in our region. 'Lucullus' has light green stems and cream-colored stalks, while 'Fordhook Giant' has darker green leaves and broad white stalks. 'Rhubarb', 'Ruby', and 'Charlotte' with stunning red stalks and 'Golden' with deep yellow ones, are both pretty enough to feature in flower beds and bouquets. Or, for an interesting exploration, try 'San Francisco Wild', progeny of a variety brought here many years ago by Italian immigrants.

If you are not fond of the thick chard stem, grow spinach beet, a flat green-leaved variety with narrow stalks. It is sometimes called perpetual spinach because of its ability to produce for several months, a trait it shares with the other chard varieties.

Pests   Swiss chard is susceptible to the same leaf-blemishing pests (leafminers, cercospora leaf spot, and beet rust) as beet. (See pest chapter for more information on these pests.)

Sources
Swiss chard seed:
Fordhook Giant: ABL, BG, JG, JSS, PTS, SB, TERR, VBS
Lucullus: ABL, JG, OBG, RCS, SB, VBS
Rhubarb (or similar red-stemmed): Widely available
Golden: SB
Mixed colors: SB, SGS
Spinach beet: CG, OBG, PS, T&M
San Francisco wild: RCS

TOMATILLO

Physalis ixocarpa
Nightshade Family ❖ *Solanaceae*

Raw or cooked tomatillo is the main ingredient in Mexican green sauces. You'll find it in taco sauce, enchiladas, and many other dishes. Although a component of piquant dishes, tomatillo itself isn't fiery—in fact, it tastes very much like green tomatoes.

The tomatillo is a relative of the tomato and has similar needs. If tomatoes ripen very late in your microclimate, you may find tomatillos worth a try since they are harvested green. The 1- to 2-inch fruit forms in husks like that of another relative, the ground-cherry. The tomatillo plant is loose and sprawling like ground-cherry, but the leaves are smooth instead of furry. Also, tomatillo fruit bulges out of the husks instead of being neatly contained like ground-cherry fruit.

Growing instructions In May direct-seed tomatillo in a well-prepared garden bed. As an alternative, start the seeds indoors by the middle of March, then transplant the seedlings into the garden, spacing them 1-1/2 to 2 feet apart. Stake the plants if you want to economize on space. Keep the soil moist through the summer.

The Harvest When the husk has turned light brown and the green tomatillo begins to burst through, the fruit is ready to be picked. Tomatillos can be stored in their husks for at least a couple of weeks. Keep them in a cool, dry area spread out in a single layer.

To cook tomatillos, remove the husks and place the fruit in enough water to cover. Simmer for fifteen minutes or until the fruit is fork-tender. Pour off most of the water and whir the fruit in a blender for a few seconds. It is now ready to use in a sauce, or you can chill or freeze it for later use. Cooked tomatillos can be kept in the refrigerator for a few days or in the freezer for a few months.

Although tomatillos are most often picked and eaten green, they will ripen to yellow or purple, depending on the variety, if they are left on the plant and the weather is warm enough. Don't expect them to be as good as ripe ground-cherry fruit, but some varieties are fairly tasty. The ripe fruit will fall to the ground. If it is left there, it may reseed itself and sprout in spring.

Varieties As with many other uncommonly grown crops, there aren't as many tomatillo varieties available here as in the crop's place of origin. Most sold are simply "green tomatillos," but more types are beginning to appear. 'Toma Verde' has good husk coverage and is never pithy. Several small green strains are also available. 'Indian Strain' is early and more sweetly flavored than usual. 'Tepihuan' and 'Zuni' are two semiwild types grown by native peoples in Mexico and New Mexico, respectively. Finally, the also small-fruited purple tomatillos are said to have a sharper flavor than the green.

Sources
Tomatillo seed:
Green (variety unclear): ABL, BG, CG, JG, NGN, PTS, RCS, SB, SOC, T&M
Toma verde: CG, JSS, PS, SGS, TGS
Purple: ABL, NGN, SB
Indian Strain: TERR
Tepihuan: NSS
Zuni: NSS

TOMATO

Lycopersicon lycopersicum
Nightshade Family ❖ *Solanaceae*

Tomato is America's favorite home garden crop, so it's no surprise that it is the first crop that many beginning gardeners try to grow. It also comes as no wonder that local gardeners—novices and old hands—become frustrated by the typical performance of tomatoes in our region. At best, tomato plants bear later and produce lighter crops than they do in more favorable climates. At worst, they may produce no ripe fruit at all. The plants may not set fruit, set it too late to ripen, or succumb to disease before most of the green fruit can ripen. I used to think that you could predict success with tomatoes by your address, simply by knowing how far you live from the ocean.

Cherry tomatoes

But I've seen plants two blocks from the ocean outdo ones several miles inland. That tells me that a well-prepared, protected, unshaded spot with no tomato diseases in the soil can be more important than a neighborhood that gets very little fog.

A perennial tropical plant, tomato needs a very long, warm season to ripen fruit. The "days to harvest" ratings for tomatoes are from the time of transplanting six-week-old seedlings to the first ripe fruit. In my garden tomato seeds sometimes germinate from last year's fallen fruit, giving me a demonstration of what would happen if I were to seed them in place when the soil is warm enough. The seeds begin to grow in the middle of May, when I am often transplanting the last of the tomato plants from my windowsill. These volunteers never bear ripe fruit by the time the transplants do. Unless the fall rains are late, the fruit that does set on the volunteers may not ripen in time.

Cool days and nights will slow the growth of tomato plants, and fruit will not set if the nights are below 55°F. Tomato flowers are self-pollinating, with pollen falling from the male part (stamens) onto the female part (pistil) in the same flower. When the temperature is too low, the cells fail to unite and the unfertilized flower usually falls off. Unfortunately, our night temperatures can dip below 55° during any month of the year. If you observe closely, you may notice fruit set increasing and decreasing as cool and warm spells pass. Shaking the blossoms will get the pollen onto the pistil, but won't get the germ cells together. Fruit-setting hormones, such as 4-CPA, sometimes allow fruit to develop without fertilization, but are not always effective. Your two best strategies for aiding fruit set are doing what you can to increase night temperatures around your plants and choosing varieties that cope best with cool weather.

Growing instructions   Purchase tomato seedlings or grow them yourself. Among the easiest seeds to start indoors, they are ready to transplant into your garden in five to seven weeks. If you grow them indoors longer, be sure to move them into larger pots so that their roots aren't crowded. Put them in a very sunny window and provide adequate fertilizer and water.

It is warm enough to transplant tomatoes into the garden in early May. For the best results get them into the ground no later than the end of May. They can succeed when they are planted as early as February if the weather is particularly warm that year, the site is well protected, or you are using a special protective structure.

Choose the warmest, sunniest spot in your garden for your tomatoes—preferably one with a southern exposure. You may also want to try special techniques to generate more heat and light. Some of the best ideas include planting in front of a white wall, using mirrors or foil-covered boards to catch more light, mulching with black or clear plastic, planting in a tire, using a floating row cover or Wall O' Water™ to protect a young plant, or making a minigreen-house to hold the heat around a larger plant. If you are going to cage tomatoes for support (see opposite page), try wrapping black roofing paper around the bottom foot of the cage to absorb and reradiate heat back to the plants.

Before planting, work in plenty of organic matter. Dig planting holes 12 to 15 inches deep, and put a big shovelful of compost at the bottom of each hole. Tomatoes need soil that is fertile, but not too high in nitrogen, since too much will inhibit fruiting. If you are using a synthetic fertilizer, use one that has more phosphorus and potassium than nitrogen. Also avoid adding too much nitrogen-rich organic fertilizer, such as blood meal or cottonseed meal. Since tomato plants have an especially high need for phosphorus and calcium, you may want to add a handful of bonemeal if you haven't already used a fertilizer that provides these nutrients. Stir the bonemeal into the bottom of the planting holes, cover the amendments with an inch or more of soil, and set the plants into the ground.

Space tomato plants 1 to 4 feet apart, depending on the variety and whether they will be staked or caged. Unlike most transplants, tomatoes should be planted deeper than they were growing in the container. Pull off the bottom leaf, or several leaves if the plant is large, and bury about half the stem. This allows roots to form where the leaves were attached and makes for a stronger root system. If

STAKING, CAGING, AND PRUNING TOMATOES

When you are growing tall (indeterminate) tomato varieties, support them. Staked or caged plants take up less space and the fruit is more protected from pests and decay.

To stake your plants, at planting time drive one or two 6- to 8-foot-long redwood or bamboo stakes a foot into the ground about 4 inches from each plant. Use plastic plant tape or soft cloth strips to tie the plants to the stakes, making a figure eight with the plant in one loop and the stake in the other. Tie again when the plants are between 1 and 2 foot high, loosely encircling the whole plant and the stake. Continue to tie as the plants grow, keeping all the branches within the ties. Be sure to start tying the plants when they are young and do it regularly as they grow. If you try to tie plants after they have sprawled, you'll find it a difficult task and you'll probably break branches in the process.

Unless you prune staked tomato plants, they may become so heavy that even two sturdy stakes will not hold them up. Prune tomato plants by pinching off the suckers—the leafy shoots that grow where the leafstalks meet the stems. Let a sucker develop a couple of leaves, then pinch out the end of the shoot. If you do this from the time the plant is small, you can limit growth to one or a few main stems—three is typical. In order to keep a plant so drastically pruned, you must remove suckers every week or two.

Will this severe pruning decrease your yield? Yes and no. Each plant will bear fewer tomatoes, but the total production will probably be greater because you can grow more plants. Tomato plants staked and pruned to one stem can be planted as little as a foot apart. The tomatoes will be larger than those on unpruned plants, and they will ripen as much as a couple of weeks earlier. You may have more usable tomatoes, because fewer are lost to decay and other pest damage than if they were in contact with the soil.

Staking and pruning removes much of the foliage, exposing the soil surface and making it more difficult to keep the plants well watered. Inconsistent watering may lead to blossom-end rot. Lessen the problem by mulching under staked plants. Heavy pruning may also result in sunscald in the warmest microclimates. Prune less drastically, or erect a shade structure to protect the fruit.

Caging is less work than staking, and it causes less problems with water balance. It gets the fruit off the ground and allows tomatoes to be planted a little closer together than if they were sprawling. Although caging has the disadvantage of requiring a higher cash outlay, the cages will last several years. The best cages for tomatoes are made from 5- to 6-foot high galvanized fencing with openings large enough to reach through and pick fruit. To make a cage about 18 inches in diameter, you will need about 5 feet of fencing. For a cage about 24 inches in diameter, you will need about 6.5 feet of fencing. (Nurseries sell prefabricated wire tomato cages, but most of them are too small for indeterminate varieties.)

Tomatoes growing in cages need virtually no pruning, but you can pinch occasional suckers to let in light and air. Tuck the branches into the cage as the plant grows, lopping off the occasional wayward one. The wider plant base of a caged plant shades the soil, so a mulch is less important.

Gardeners often prune the tips of their staked or caged plants late in the season when no more fruit is likely to set. The theory is that the plant will then ripen the fruit that it has instead of continuing to grow taller. Try this in the middle of September and see how it works for you.

If you are growing short (determinate) tomato varieties, formal staking or caging is less important. If your site is windy, however, support may be necessary to keep the plants from blowing over or breaking. Some gardeners provide support in order to space plants closer together or to keep fruit off the ground. Here is a use for those 3- to 4-foot-high pre-fabricated wire cages sold at nurseries. As an alternative, insert two 4-foot-long bamboo stakes into the soil, and wrap the plants and stakes with soft ties at several levels as the plants grow.

A TOUR OF TOMATO TYPES

Cherry Tomatoes
Growing on rangy indeterminate plants, cherry tomato fruit is usually under 1 inch in diameter, although the largest may be nearly 2 inches. The fruit clusters may be quite large, often having twenty or more tomatoes per cluster. Although cherry tomatoes are not necessarily better than other types at setting fruit when the nights are cold, there is a better chance that some will set and ripen simply because the plant has so many more blooms. Cherry tomatoes tend to be very flavorful.

Standard-Sized Tomatoes
Although fruit size differs from variety to variety and even on the same plant, standard tomatoes are generally more than 2 inches in diameter. Some varieties react to our unfavorable conditions by making smaller fruit. In fact, none of the standard varieties in our San Francisco trials (see page 263) averaged more than 4 ounces, although catalog descriptions sometimes promised 8-ounce fruit. Our test plants typically made many cherry-sized tomatoes and a lesser number of bigger fruit, including a few that were quite large. Although they are usually round, standard tomatoes may be oblong or flattened and even irregularly lobed. They vary in flavor and texture. Among the best in the San Francisco trials were the ever-popular 'Early Girl' and a Czech-bred variety, 'Stupice'.

Beefsteak Tomatoes
These round, red varieties with very large meaty fruit are listed in the catalogs as reaching 1 or even 2 pounds each. Although most gardeners would love to grow them, beefsteaks aren't likely to perform well in our cool summer weather. The fruit is apt to be smaller and less flavorful than the beefsteak tomatoes you remember from some long-ago garden that was drenched in summer sun. Still, there are some early beefsteak varieties, which local gardeners report will bear fruit in reasonably warm locations. Try the determinate 'Bush Beefsteak,' which is rated at 62 days.

Container or Patio Tomatoes
Bred for growing in small containers, determinate patio types make early crops of smallish tomatoes that are sometimes as small as cherry tomatoes. Try them in a bright window indoors and in containers outdoors. A new class of container tomatoes, the Husky series, consists of indeterminate plants that are short and sturdy. They do need staking, but are well adapted to growing in containers in windy sites.

Paste Tomatoes
These tomatoes contain less juice than other types. Since you start out with a higher percentage of pulp, you get more tomato sauce from the same volume of fruit in less cooking time. Paste tomatoes are also becoming popular as salad tomatoes, because they make firm, tasty chunks. Most paste tomato varieties are determinate. Many bear oblong or pear-shaped fruit, typically 2 to 3 inches long. Others have round fruit that is 2 to 3 inches across. Early varieties of paste tomatoes will produce as well as early standard-sized varieties in our microclimates. The old standby is 'Roma,' but the newer hybrids 'Viva Italia' and 'Ropreco' performed better in our San Francisco trials.

Tomatoes of a Different Color
You may enjoy growing orange, yellow, or even pink tomatoes in addition to red ones. First check the earliness of a variety to see if it will ripen here. Some that are best suited are the light yellow, standard-sized 'Lemon Boy', the small, pear-shaped, 'Yellow Pear' and the delicious, golden, cherry-sized 'Sungold Hybrid'.

PHYSIOLOGICAL PROBLEMS OF TOMATOES

All crops have some problems that are not caused by insects, diseases, or other pests, but tomatoes seem to have more than their share. When a physiological problem is caused by something you can change, such as watering or soil fertility, you may be able to reduce or eliminate the problem. You can only do so much, however, when the cause of a problem is our unfavorable climatic conditions.

Sometimes the blossom end of the fruit (the end away from the stem) turns brown and begins to decay. This can happen even before the fruit is ripe. Blossom-end rot is caused by a shortage of calcium in the plant, seemingly hastened by uneven watering. To prevent the problem, work in plenty of organic matter and add bonemeal at planting time, don't let tomato plants dry out, and mulch plants that are staked and pruned. Some varieties are more susceptible than others, although you probably won't learn this from catalog descriptions. Just be aware that if the variety you grew this year was affected, a different variety next year may be fine.

Catfacing is another problem that appears most often on the blossom end of fruit. It shows up as rough, dry brown blotches or lines often accompanied by deformations, such as deep folds in the fruit surface. The brown lines often have little cross bars reminiscent of a zipper. Catfacing, which happens when the flower is first becoming a fruit, is believed to be caused by cool weather. There is little you can do to prevent catfacing. Many varieties will escape this blemish, although once again the problem is rarely mentioned in catalog descriptions.

Tomato fruit may crack, usually at the stem end. Cracking is most common when the plant has been very dry and is suddenly well watered. Cracked fruit does not keep well, since decay organisms can get in through the cracks. The best way to prevent cracked fruit is to water consistently.

You may notice that the leaves of your tomato plants have rolled up. If the leaves are not an unusual color, curling is not a serious problem. The disorder is more common on heavily pruned plants and some varieties are more likely to develop it than others, although it is so slight a problem that no one seems to pay much attention it.

Tomato fruit may also occasionally develop sunscald. Although it is not as likely to occur in foggier areas, it is possible, especially when plants are heavily pruned or losing leaves to russet mites or a disease. Sunscalded fruit develops a whitish patch on the side facing the brightest sun, usually the southwest. As the fruit ripens, the scalded spot often decays.

Although all these problems are a nuisance, affected fruit can still be eaten. Just cut away any unsightly parts and the rest of the fruit will be just as tasty and wholesome as an unblemished tomato.

you are going to stake your tomatoes, drive the stakes on the day you plant to avoid disturbing the growing roots. If you are going to cage them, it is best to set the cage the same day as well.

Tomato roots reach as deep as 4 to 5 feet into the soil, so they need deep watering. Diseases will get a foothold if you keep the soil soggy—but, on the other hand, don't let the soil dry out more than 3 inches deep. Underwatering is a cause of blossom drop, undersized fruit, and various fruit defects (see above).

Although tomato plants will produce a crop without extra fertilizer during the growing season, they are heavy feeders and will probably make more fruit if they get a couple of booster applications as they grow. Apply either an organic fertilizer or a synthetic one with a moderate amount of nitrogen (such as 5-10-10 or 5-10-4) when the first tomatoes have just formed and again about a month after that. If the stem 6 inches from the ends of major branches are thicker than your small finger, the plant probably has too much nitrogen; if the stems are smaller, the plant is lacking in nitrogen.

The Harvest Tomatoes ripen at least a month and a half after they set. A fast-growing tomato variety may produce its first ripe fruit in July, but don't be surprised if it takes until September in an unfavorable microclimate or during a particularly foggy summer. Some tomato varieties continue to grow taller and set more fruit until they are felled by winter rains and cold. They are called indeterminate varieties. Others, called determinate varieties, are short and bushy. They ripen fruit over a shorter period, then die.

Leave the fruit on the plant to ripen as long as you can, although you may have to pick some before it is totally ripe if you are having trouble with pests. Keep in mind that most tomatoes in the grocery stores are picked green and ripened with ethylene gas. The ones you pick red, although not absolutely ripe, should turn out better than any gas-ripened fruit.

When you pick tomatoes, try to break the stem at the natural separation point about 1/2 inch above the fruit, leaving the short stem and little green cap attached. This will keep you from tearing the fruit as you pick and allowing decay to enter. If you harvest more tomatoes than you can eat the same day, store them out of direct sunlight at room temperature. Refrigeration ruins their flavor.

Even the healthiest indeterminate tomato plant will usually die in October, or later if the fall has been dry. There will usually be quite a few green tomatoes left on the plant. They can be ripened indoors by a process called force ripening. One method is to pull the whole plant, hang it upside down in a cool place, and pick fruit as it ripens. Another method is to pick all the fruit that has reached full size, with stems attached, and wrap each separately in newspaper. Put the wrapped tomatoes in a dry place away from direct sunlight at a temperature of 60° to 70°F and check often for ripening. (Tomatoes gives off ethylene gas, which is needed for ripening, and the paper holds it near the fruit.) Don't give up on green tomatoes on a live plant—fruit has been known to ripen on plants in

the garden as late as February, especially when rain is scarce.

I often pick green tomatoes to eat fried during the summer and at the end of the season. When the plant is in decline in fall, I harvest all the green tomatoes that are too small to force-ripen and chop them up for chutney or relish.

Varieties If you are like most gardeners, by the end of summer you have forgotten which varieties of tomatoes you grew. By the time you are eating ripe tomatoes, the little tags that came with the tomato seedlings have long since disappeared. I encourage you to keep track of the tomatoes that you try, since the variety can make such a difference. Write their names in your calendar or datebook, with a little map of your tomato planting so you will remember even when the tag is gone, or use a hole punch on the tag and attach it to the plant or to the plant stake. Also notice what your neighbors are growing. (When you see one of their plants doing really well, you'll wish they had saved their tag.)

Here are some hints to guide you as you compare catalog descriptions of tomato varieties. If your garden is in a particularly foggy or windy location, choose only the earliest varieties. Early tomato varieties are those listed at less than 70 days from transplanting. Also watch for descriptions such as "bears well under adverse conditions" or "sets well in cool weather." Tomatoes said to be "good for short northern summers" may produce here, but they usually aren't the best choice for our shorter, cooler summer days. In warmer parts of the region, you can try midseason varieties, which are listed at 70 to 80 days from transplanting. Be wary of long-season varieties, which are listed at more than 80 days. They may make a crop, but it is likely to be small compared to earlier kinds.

Although you will want to know whether a tomato is a hybrid or not, this is not a deciding factor in whether it will produce well in our region. If you want to save seeds, get an open-pollinated variety. Otherwise, feel free to choose varieties based on other characteristics.

You may notice that some varieties are parthenocarpic. This means that the fruit is able to develop even though the nights are so cold that flowers cannot be fertilized. It does not affect the flavor or fruit size, but the fruit will have either no seeds or very few seeds. When you grow it from seed, you may find that you have to sow more

---

FRIED GREEN TOMATOES

1 to 2 medium-sized green tomatoes per person
About 1 1/2 tablespoons olive oil per tomato
A small bowl of water
About 1/2 cup whole wheat flour
Salt and freshly ground pepper to taste

Select firm, completely green tomatoes. Slice them 1/4-inch thick. Add enough olive oil to cover the bottom of a large skillet and heat the oil over medium heat. Dip each tomato slice in water and then in whole wheat flour. Fry, turning once, until the slices are browned and offer no resistance to a fork. Add more oil if necessary. Drain the tomatoes on paper towels, and serve immediately, with salt and pepper to taste.

---

thickly since some seeds will not be fertile.

Indeterminate varieties have the potential to make larger crops than determinate ones, because they grow taller and produce flowers over a longer period. They are more likely to have flowers ready for pollination during our sporadic warm spells in summer, and they are able to take advantage of warm weather in early fall to ripen the last fruit set. However, if a determinate variety is particularly good at setting fruit in cool weather, it is definitely worth a try. Look on plant labels and in seed catalogs for the designations *I* or *Ind* and *D* or *Det*. Occasionally a variety is called semideterminate, indicating that it falls between the two major types.

To compare varieties for resistance to diseases and other pests, look for the letters *V*, *F*, *N*, *T*, and *A*, which stand for resistance to verticillium wilt, fusarium wilt, nematodes, tobacco mosaic virus, and alternaria. For example, a tomato variety with the letters *VFF* after its name is resistant to verticillium wilt and two strains of fusarium wilt. It is a good policy to choose resistant varieties, especially if you are planting in soil where tomatoes have been growing for some time. Resistance to verticillium wilt is the most important type of resistance to look for in our region. However, infections are by no means universal so don't feel you must grow only resistant varieties. This is especially true if you are planting in soil that hasn't grown tomatoes recently, or if you have had no disease or nematode problems.

As for flavor, you probably can't learn much by reading the catalogs or seed packets. They will either tell you that the fruit is delicious, or they will decline to mention the matter. This points up an important truth: You can't really find out all you need to know by reading catalogs. That goes for productivity as well—rarely will the descriptions allow you to predict accurately how much fruit you will get in this region. Even earliness, although more reliably calibrated than flavor or productivity, is not entirely reliable, since different varieties may be affected to different degrees by our unfavorable conditions.

It was because of just such questions that I undertook—with the help of the San Francisco League of Urban Gardeners (SLUG) and many volunteers—tomato variety trials in San Francisco. On page 263 is a comparison of the varieties we tested. Although even three years of formal tests revealed only a limited amount of information, we did get some answers. The testing of standard-sized tomatoes bore out my prediction that indeterminate plants would be the biggest producers, even though not every indeterminate produced well. We were also able to see that some varieties produced a bit earlier, although none were remarkably early. Our trials also revealed that people differ widely in judging flavor. Some people liked every fruit they tasted, and other people panned them all. Some preferred sweet fruit, and others liked tart tomatoes. I am happy to report that we found some varieties that appealed to the majority.

I encourage you to try new tomato varieties often, since we only scratched the surface with the trials. There are hundreds of varieties and new varieties are constantly being developed, so maybe the next one you try will be the tomato of your dreams.

The chart on page 264 lists tomato varieties that I have grown or were recommended by other

TURNIPS, NOODLES, AND TOFU SAUTÉ

Here's a delicious dish that stars the small Asian-type turnips along with their greens. It can be made with mustard greens or other strongly flavored greens with equally good results. Chuka soba is a Japanese noodle made with wheat. Look for it in the Asian specialty food section of your grocery, or substitute ordinary ramen noodles. For a spicier dish, use sesame oil with chile oil.

4 cups water
6 ounces chuka soba (or 2 3-ounce packages ramen noodles, discarding the flavor packets)
3 to 4 cups small turnips and their greens (or use mustard, wild mustard, or young radish greens, or any combination of these greens)
3 to 6 tablespoons vegetable oil
1 pound firm tofu, cut into bite-sized pieces.
1 teaspoon toasted sesame oil (or sesame oil with chile oil)
Japanese soy sauce, to taste (use it freely)

Bring the water to boil in a saucepan. Add noodles and boil for 2 minutes. Drain them in a colander.

Slice the turnips and cut the greens coarsely. Heat 3 tablespoons of vegetable oil. Sauté the turnips a few minutes, until half-tender, not browned. Add the greens and sauté them until they are just limp.

Add the noodles to the skillet and fry them, turning them with a spatula as they cook. You want them slightly crispy and browned. Add more oil if the noodles stick. Add the tofu and heat through, turning frequently. Sprinkle the sesame oil over the top; stir it in gently. Serve with soy sauce. Serves two amply.

expert local gardeners as good choices for our region. The details in the chart are from seed catalogs or from other published descriptions. If a variety was among those included in one of my San Francisco tomato trials, I have marked it with an asterisk.

Pests Tomato plants often exhibit alarming symptoms: leaves that are spotted, curling, or dying, or fruit that is blotched or misshapen. Some symptoms are caused by poor growing conditions (see Physiological Problems of Tomatoes on page 259). Others are evidence of virus, bacterial, or fungus diseases, most of which are incurable. Tolerate minor spots and blemishes of unknown origin on tomato leaves while you learn what may be causing them. However, if it is clear that a plant is in very serious trouble and you can't find out why, it is best to remove it from your garden to avoid spreading the problem.

Verticillium wilt, one of the most common to-mato diseases locally, is spread by infected soil and encouraged by cool temperatures. The first symptom is the wilting of older leaves, followed by yellow, then brown V-shaped patterns on the edges of some leaves. The plants are small, despite ample water and fertilizer. If you cut a stem at soil level, you will see that the tissue inside is light tan instead of a healthy light green. (See vascular wilts, page 158.)

Late blight, another common tomato disease, causes dark brown stem areas, with green stem above and below, and brown, wilting leaves. Infected fruit has greasy, brown shoulders. Late blight is spread by spores that float in the air and splash in water. These spores don't remain alive in the soil or in seeds, but in living plants in the tomato family and in plant debris from those plants. (See late blight, page 157.)

Since tomatoes and potatoes are in the same family and share many of the same diseases, planting infected potatoes can spread diseases that will

SAN FRANCISCO
TOMATO VARIETY TRIAL RESULTS

When I started to write about tomatoes for this book, I realized that most San Francisco gardeners grow the same four or five varieties every year—even though there are many more varieties that will do well here. I found myself poring over seed catalogs picking out varieties that purportedly fruited early or shrugged off cool weather. With the help of volunteers, I set up variety trials. In 1987 we formally tested ten varieties and an additional four in 1988. In 1989 we put five paste tomatoes to the test.

STANDARD-SIZED VARIETIES

	Flavor[1]	Production[2]	Size[3]	Earliness[4]
Celebrity	Poor	Poor	Large	Poor
Early Girl	Very good	Good	Small	Good
Early Pick	Good	Fair	Large	Fair
Fantastic	Good	Poor	Small	Poor
Floramerica	Fair	Poor	Medium	Poor
Marmande	Fair	Fair	Large	Good
Nepal	Very good	Poor	Large	Fair
Oregon Spring	Good	Poor	Large	Very good
Quick Pick	Poor	Fair	Small	Fair
San Francisco Fog	Fair	Fair	Small	Fair
Santiam	Poor	Fair	Fair	Good
Siberia	Fair	Fair	Fair	Good
Stupice	Very good	Very good	Small	Very good
Visitacion Valley	Good	Very good	Medium	Very good

[1] Based on public and private tastings.
[2] Total production by weight ranged from about 3 pounds to 22 pounds per plant.
[3] The largest average size was just under 3 inches in diameter (fruit this size weighs about 4 ounces). All the plants were unpruned.
[4] Six-week-old plants were set out in early May. The first ripe fruit on the earliest varieties appeared by July 30. Most were bearing ripe fruit by the end of August, although some varieties in unfavorable sites took until the middle of October.

PASTE VARIETIES

	Fresh Flavor[1]	Paste Flavor[1]	Production[2]	Earliness[3]
La Roma	Good	Good	Fair	Fair
Nova	Fair	Fair	Fair	Good
Roma	Fair	Fair	Poor	Poor
Ropreco	Good	Good	Good	Good
Sprinter	Very good	Very good	Good	Good

[1] Based on a private tasting by food professionals.
[2] Total production by weight ranged from about 12 to 29 pounds per plant.
[3] Six-week-old plants were set out late, in the middle of June. (They were started in the middle of March, but they grew vbery slowly because of overcast, cool conditions.) Determinate varieties, they all produced at the same time—throughout October. The fact that the paste varieties are determinate and bear at the same time makes them ideal candidates for monthly successive plantings.

SOME TOMATO VARIETIES WORTH TRYING

Following are some tomato varieties recommended by local gardeners and gardening experts as good choices for our region. The information in this chart is from seed catalogs or from other published descriptions. If they were among those included in one of my San Francisco tomato trials, I have marked them with an asterisk (*). (See table of trial results, page 263.) Use these lists as a starting point, but don't be afraid to try other varieties, based on published descriptions or personal recommendations.

Variety[1]	Days to Harvest	Plant Size	Resistance[2]	Comments
Beefsteak Varieties				
Big Beef F_1	73-80	indeterminate	VFFNTA	10-12 oz. fruit, firm, juicy, old-fashioned flavor
*Nepal	78	indeterminate	——	From Nepal. Delicous, but probably needs East Bay warmth to set well.
Red Cherry Varieties				
Sweet Chelsea F_1	45-67	indeterminate	VFNT	1 to 1 1/2 inch fruits, tall vines, productive, tolerates 10 different diseases
Sweet Million F_1	65-75	indeterminate	FNT	As sweet and productive as 'Sweet 100', with added disease and crack resistance
Early Cherry	55	determinate	——	Especially good at bearing in adverse conditions, full tomato flavor
Red Currant	65	indeterminate	——	Tiny tomatoes with good, sweet tomato flavor; a different species—L. pimpinellifolium
Container or Patio Varieties				
Small Fry F_1	65	determinate	VFN	Huge crop of one-inch cherry-sized fruit on compact plants
Husky Red F_1	68	dwarf indeterminate	VF	Medium-sized fruit over a long period on 4 foot plants
Paste Varieties				
*La Roma F_1	62	determinate	VF	Said to yield 7 times standard Roma, but yielded only twice as much in my trials
*Sprinter	58	determinate	VF	Round fruit, very good flavor
*Ropreco	70-75	determinate	——	Angular, pear shape, productive
Viva Italia F_1	80-85	determinate	VFFNA	Not so early, but bears well and has good-flavored fruit

SOME TOMATO VARIETIES WORTH TRYING

Variety[1]	Days to Harvest	Plant Size	Resistance[2]	Comments
Standard-Sized Varieties				
Better Boy F$_1$	75	indeterminate	VFN	Large fruit, long bearing season, good, mild flavor
*Celebrity F$_1$	70	determinate	VFFNTA	Good-flavored 7 to 8 oz. fruit, multiple disease resistance
*Early Girl F$_1$	52-60	indeterminate	VFF	Great sweet-tart flavor, smallish fruit, very productive
*Early Pick F$_1$	62	indeterminate	VF	Developed by Burpee, good flavor
*Fantastic F$_1$	65-85	indeterminate	——	Flavor good, small fruit
*Floramerica F$_1$	70	determinate	VFFA	Tolerates or resists 15 diseases
*Marmande	67	semi-determinate	——	Old French variety, lobed fruit
*Oregon Spring	58	determinate	V	Nearly seedless, not large yields, may yield better with high soil fertility
*Quick Pick F$_1$	68	indeterminate	VFFNT	Smallish fruit
*San Francisco Fog	70	indeterminate	——	In S.F. trials, only fair in production and flavor
*Siberia	55	determinate	——	Supposed to set fruit at 38° F, but in S.F. trials, production was only fair
*Stupice	52	determinate	——	Developed in former Czechoslovakia, S.F. trial winner for production and flavor
*Visitacion Valley	early	indeterminate	——	Probably a local S.F. selection from 'Early Girl'; similar, but non-hybrid
Other Colors				
Lemon Boy F$_1$	72	indeterminate	VFN	Lemon yellow when ripe, has large, mild fruit, good production
Yellow Pear	78	indeterminate	——	Old variety with small pear-shaped yellow fruits
Sungold F$_1$	57	indeterminate	——	Orange cherry tomatoes with a remarkable tropical fruit flavor
Old German	75	indeterminate	——	Large, red-and-yellow-marbled fruit, 'Marvel Stripe' is similar
Black Krim	69-90	indeterminate	——	Moderate crop in S.F. of fragile fruit with wonderful texture and flavor, almost black shoulders
Green Zebra	75	indeterminate	——	Smallish fruit, green on green stripes when ripe, good flavor

[1] The symbol F$_1$ indicates a variety is a hybrid
[2] Code for disease resistance (see page 261 for discussion)

attack your tomato plants. That is why it is important to get certified disease-free potato starts. Once the diseases are introduced, they can be spread in soil or by wind and water. I first saw tomatoes with late blight in San Francisco in 1990, but now it is quite common (see page 157).

Tobacco mosaic virus can be spread by smokers, since it is usually present in cigarettes. The disease can also enter your garden on nursery transplants. Some diseases are spread by insects. Spotted wilt, a virus diseases spread by onion and flower thrips, turned up on a tomato plant in one of my experiments. The most obvious symptom is concentric rings of yellow, green, and red on the fruit. Several diseases are spread by splashing water, so avoid spraying the leaves of tomato plants when you water (see page 160).

Tomato diseases that live in the soil from year to year can end your efforts to grow tomatoes in your garden. If your plants succumb, try to identify the problem using books or enlisting the help of an expert. The next season plant tomatoes in a different location, try varieties with as broad resistance as you can find, add plenty of organic matter, and take care not to overwater. If the problem persists, you may want to try soil solarization (see page 99) if you are in a warm microclimate. Soil diseases eventually die out, but the wait can be long. For example, verticillium can live in the soil for twenty years or more, and it is carried by many other crops and ornamentals when tomatoes aren't being grown. When all else fails get some big containers, fill them with sterile potting mix, avoid contact between the potting mix and your infected soil and between the containers, and get on with your tomato growing.

Before you assume that your tomatoes have a disease, consider whether they may have tomato russet mites. I recently learned that these mites are probably a common cause of tomato plant death in our region. The mite infestations are often mistaken for a disease, however. The microscopic russet mites swarm over a plant sucking sap, soon turning the stems and leaves a greasy dirty yellow or bronze. The fruit is usually not attacked, but it may sunburn when the leaves die. If enough leaves die, that's the end of the plant—and the fruit (see page 146).

Damage to tomatoes from chewing pests is less common here than in many other parts of the country, although earwigs may do major damage to young tomato plants. You may find an occasional large green tomato or tobacco hornworm feeding on your plants, but they don't seem to be prevalent in cooler microclimates. Slugs may eat holes in your tomatoes, especially if the fruit is in contact with the ground.

Sources
Tomato seed:
Red beefsteak varieties:
Big Beef F_1: BG, NGN, PS, SGS, TERR, T&M, TT, VBS
Nepal: ABL, DD, TGS
Cherry varieties:
Sweet Chelsea F_1: PTS, TGS, TT, VBS
Sweet Million F_1: GG, NGN, PS, PTS, TERR, TGS, TT
Early Cherry: TERR
Red Currant: ABL, CG, DD, JSS, NGN, TGS, TT
Container or Patio Varieties:
Small Fry F_1: TGS, TT
Husky Red F_1: TGS
Paste varieties:
La Roma: TGS
Ropreco: ABL
Sprinter: TGS
Viva Italia: GG, NGN, TERR, TGS, TT, VBS
Standard-sized red varieties:
Better Boy F_1: PS, TT, VBS
Celebrity: JSS, NGN, PTS, TERR, TGS, TT, VBS
Early Girl: BG, NGN, PS, PTS, TERR, TGS, TT, VBS
Early Pick: BG, TGS, TT
Fantastic: TERR, TGS, TT
Floramerica: TGS
Marmande (or Super Marmande): ABL, GG, JG, OBG, SB, TGS, T&M (Super: ABL, OBG, T&M)
Oregon Spring: ABL, JSS, NGN, OBG, PTS, SB, SGS, TERR, TGS, TT
Quick Pick: PS
San Francisco Fog: DD, OBG, SB, TGS
Santiam: ABL, DD, TERR
Siberia: ABL, DD, TGS, TT, VBS
Stupice: ABL, TERR, TGS
Visitation Valley: ABL
Other Colors
Lemon Boy F_1: NGN, PS, TGS
Yellow Pear: ABL, CG, GG, JSS, PTS, RCS, SGS, TERR, TGS
Sungold F_1: CG, JSS, PTS, SGS, TERR, TGS, T&M, VBS
Old German: TT
Black Krim: OBG, SB, TGS, VBS
Green Zebra: ABL, CG, DD, SGS, TGS

TURNIP

Brassica rapa
Rapifera Group
Mustard Family ❖ *Cruciferae*

When someone mentions turnips, do you think of big starchy boiled roots and are you overcome by boredom? If so, I encourage you to try an Asian variety like 'Tokyo Cross Hybrid' or 'Tokyo Market,' or one of the other varieties meant to be eaten when the roots are small. They make small,

Turnip

crisp, mild-flavored white roots as quickly as radishes. They can be added to salads or used in stir fry (see page 262). If you have seeds for larger turnips, try harvesting the roots when they are only about 1 or 1-1/2 inches in diameter.

Growing Instructions The crispest and most tender turnips are produced in rich soil with plenty of water. Plant turnips every few weeks for successive crops from February to August. Direct-seed 1/2 inch deep and 1 to 2 inches apart. Don't let weeds compete with the rapidly growing seedlings. Thin the seedlings as soon as they begin to crowd each other, and eat the thinnings as greens.

Varieties 'Tokyo Cross F$_1$' can be harvested in 35 days, when it is about 2 inches across. It remains good at twice that size. Harvest crisp 'Yorii Spring' in 38 days at 1 1/2 inches across. 'Tokyo Market' and 'Hakurei F$_1$' make globe-radish-size white turnips in only 30 days. Shogoin is often grown for its large leaves, which are ready in 30 days. After 60 days, it has 4" roots.

Of the larger types, 'Gilfeather' is purported to be especially tasty and sweeter than most turnips. It is good for adding to casseroles, mashing with potatoes, or even eating raw with a dip.

Pests Turnips get cabbage maggots as often as radishes do, so they need protection when they are grown during the warmer months of the year. Try beneficial nematodes applied in mid- to late March, or plant under a row cover frame. Turnips also attract cabbage aphids.

Sources
Turnip seed:
Small varieties:
Yorii Spring: ABL
Tokyo Cross F$_1$: BG, EV, PTS, T&M, VBS
Tokyo Market: EV
Market Express: SGS
Standard varieties:
Shogoin: EV, NGN, TERR
Gilfeather: CG, PTS, SB, VBS

WATERCRESS
Nasturtium officinale
Mustard Family ❖ *Cruciferae*

Watercress grows wild in running streams, but you can grow it in your garden if you keep the soil very moist. It is a good choice for a site where water

seeps or near a hose attachment where you rinse vegetables. Since it does best in light shade, it is also a candidate for a shady corner. As a potted plant, it is suitable for growing in a bright north-facing window or an apartment light well. Watercress is happiest in the cool seasons and the coolest microclimates.

Growing Instructions Plant watercress in soil containing lots of organic matter. Sow the seeds directly, scattering them thinly and barely covering them with soil or sand. Thin the seedlings to 2 to 3 inches apart. When they are 6 inches tall, pinch the tips to encourage branching.

You can also start watercress from a purchased bunch. Cut off any injured or decayed stem bottoms. Cut the healthy stems in half and stand all the pieces in a small jar, with the bottom ends down. Add water to cover the stems halfway. Change the water daily until roots appear. The stem cuttings may also root well if you insert them in garden soil, burying them about halfway and keeping the soil very moist. Plant the cuttings, rooted or not, about 3 inches apart. Once the cuttings are well rooted and begin to grow, pinch the tips to encourage branching.

Watercress can also be grown in a pot of soil standing in a container of water. Be sure to put gravel in the bottom of the pot to keep the soil from leaking through, and change the water in the outer container daily to keep it fresh. Apply a liquid fertilizer once a week.

The Harvest When the plants have made substantial growth, harvest several inches of stem tips. Watercress seeds are rated at 50 days, but you will probably be picking before that. If you use cuttings, you may be harvesting in just two weeks. Pinch back any stems that are forming flower buds. Although the plant is a perennial and lives on after flowering, the flowering and seeding stems are too bitter to enjoy. Plants that form seeds may reseed themselves in moist soil. If the plants are becoming ungainly, just take fresh cuttings and reroot them to start again.

Pests Watercress sometimes gets aphids. Take them as a sign that something is wrong: overcrowding, inadequate fertility, not enough water, or too little light (possible in deep shade or indoors). If the infestation is severe, pull up the plants and try to improve conditions for the next planting.

Sources

Watercress seed: ABL, CG, DD, EV, GG, JG, JSS, NGN, RH, SB, SGS, T&M, VBS

WINTER MELON
(OR WAX GOURD OR DOAN GWA)

Benincasa hispida
Gourd Family ❖ *Cucurbitaceae*

An ingredient in Chinese cuisine, winter melon will mature in the sunnier gardens of our region. The plant is large and productive in warmer parts of San Francisco. It is a vine that can be trained on a fence or trellis, although you will need to support the fruit. Each pumpkin-shaped melon can weigh as much as 25 pounds.

Winter melon is not a sweet fruit; it is used as a vegetable in stir fry and soups. It is the basis for a classic Chinese dish in which the intricately carved melon shell serves as the soup tureen. In addition to using the mature fruit, you can also eat the immature fruit, young leaves, and flower buds.

Growing instructions   Give winter melon an early start, although it will not help to plant it out before the soil warms up, usually in early May. To gain four or five weeks, start the seeds indoors in a bottomless container to avoid disturbing the roots when you transplant (see page 54). Before you move the seedlings into the garden, add plenty of compost and fertilizer to your planting bed. Space the plants 8 to 10 inches apart and keep them well watered.

The Harvest   When winter melons are ripe, they are covered with a white waxy substance. Cut the fruit, leaving a couple of inches of the stems. Stored in a cool spot (but not under 50°F), the fruit will keep for six months to a year—hence the name winter melon.

Sources

Winter melon seed: EV, KSC, NGN, RH, SB

ZUCCHINI (SEE SQUASH, SUMMER)

TWELVE

HERBS FOR ALL SEASONS

OU CAN GROW MANY commonly used culinary herbs in our foggy coastal region and harvest most of them throughout the year. You will find herbs easy to grow, delightful to have in the kitchen, and thought-provoking as well—taking you through history, around the world, and into many of the world's cuisines.

Easy and Rewarding to Grow

Even if you have only a tiny plot to devote to food gardening, herbs are among the most satisfying plants you can grow. This is because many common herbs are among the easiest of crops. And also because an herb garden can be one you use every day. Think how many meals contain a bit of oregano, a little chopped parsley, a pinch of thyme. And it takes so little of an herb to transform a dish. One oregano plant is usually sufficient for a household. A few basil plants will keep you amply supplied with pesto sauce through the summer. And a half dozen potted herbs on a sunny porch can brighten your menu all year.

You'll be glad to know that some herbs will tolerate less than ideal garden conditions. Some don't mind deep shade, so can be grown in sites as shady as an apartment lightwell. Others will survive the extreme winds and sun of an exposed roof site. Most thrive in the foggiest areas and some tolerate fairly poor, dry soil. Herbs can even be grown indoors with some success, although they are not at

their best there.

You can easily integrate both annual and biennial herbs into your vegetable garden. A few parsley plants, some basil, a patch of cilantro make good neighbors to your other crops. (In a rotation, consider these fast-growing, succulent herbs to be heavy feeders.) Perennial herbs, on the other hand, are most commonly separated from the vegetables—at the corners of beds or grouped together in a separate area where they needn't be disturbed every time you replant annual crops. Many perennial herbs are light feeders, asking only reasonably fertile soil.

Annual or perennial herbs can also be used in ornamental plantings. Use annual herbs to fill in small spaces among more permanent plants in an ornamental border, replacing the herbs when they decline or when you have pulled them to eat. Perennial herbs, on the other hand, can provide the framework of an ornamental planting. They tend to stay green or gray-green all year. Many bloom for several weeks, and, though the flowers are usually small, they are an attractive background for your showier blossoms.

The most formal ornamental use of perennial herbs is to create intricate and carefully manicured patterns of low herbs called knot gardens. While these are lovely, they do take time to maintain. Also, you will often find the species used are herbs grown mainly for scent, rather than for cooking. This is probably because harvesting fresh leaves for cooking tends to disturb the uniformity of the pattern, whereas you can collect clippings for dried sachets whenever you need to prune for aesthetic reasons. And, consider that any ornamental pattern with many plants of the same culinary herb will probably produce far more of it than you can eat.

What's Included?

The chart on page 304 shows the herbs that are covered in this chapter. In deciding whether to include an herb, I considered first whether it would grow in all or at least most of the region. Many familiar herbs, such as sage, oregano, and rosemary, are right at home in our climate. Native to the European countries bordering the Mediterranean, they are accustomed to similar day lengths, winter temperatures, and patterns of rainfall. The main difference is that our summers are generally cooler. While it may be true that many of these herbs would be stronger-flavored if our summers provided more warmth, they still develop plenty of flavor in our part of the world. Other familiar herbs, like parsley, coriander, and garlic (see Chapter 11) originated in the Middle East. While that region has much hotter summers than ours, their winters are mild. This means that their winter herbs do well in our winters also, and they sometimes grow through our cool summer days as well.

Most of the herbs listed in this chapter will thrive in our entire region. (If I don't mention that an herb can grow only in one area, you can assume it will grow everywhere here.) But a few will have to struggle in foggier, colder gardens. Basil, in particular, may survive, but won't grow much, if summer temperatures are too low.

Among the many herbs that will grow here, I have included mainly the ones local gardeners grow most often and find most useful. But popularity wasn't my only criterion. Few have grown our native mint, yerba buena, a tasty and historically interesting plant. The hops vine is attractive and fun to grow, and could tempt you to try home brewing. Winter tarragon is a little-known but delicious herb, waiting to be more widely discovered. And, in at least one case, that of comfrey, I have explained why I do not eat or even grow a once popular herb any more.

Most of the herbs I've included are ones used in cooking, although I've described such uses as tea or sachets when they are common. And my cat insisted that I include catnip and similar feline favorites. I have not attempted to cover medicinal uses. I have also largely ignored the many claims that herbs can protect other crops from attacks by pests.

This is because other books have covered the subject thoroughly and because the verdict is currently out on so many of these claims (See Herbs and Pests on the next page.)

In cooking, herbs are generally the plants used as flavorings, while vegetables are the foods that might be flavored by them; but in truth there is no clear line separating herbs and vegetables. Onions and garlic, for example, are often used as seasonings, but can also be vegetables. Cutting celery, which belongs to the same species as regular celery, is used as an herb. One person may like strongly-flavored salads in which arugula or basil are a major green; another may see arugula or basil only as herbs to be chopped small and added sparingly. And sometimes what is an herb in one part of the world is a flower, or even a weed in another. For all of these reasons, any listing of herbs is bound to be a bit arbitrary. If you don't find a plant listed in this chapter, check the index—it might be among the vegetables, flowers or weeds.

Growing Herbs

Nursery herbs in their identical 2 inch pots tend to give the impression that all herbs should be treated in the same way. Sometimes herb garden plans or photographs also give that impression when they show herb plants all the same size, growing in tidy clumps. But to successfully grow herbs, you need to learn the differences blurred by those matching pots and neat arrangements. Some herbs never grow more than a few inches tall, others are trees. Some stay politely in one spot, while others spread rampantly by underground runners. Some are annuals, some biennials, some perennials. Some need sun, others suffer unless they are shaded. Some need rich, well-watered soil, and others actually taste better when grown in poor, sandy, dry soil.

Still, those nursery herbs in 2 inch pots are the best way to get many kinds of herbs started in your garden. They are almost as economical as starting plants from seed, since you usually want only one or a few plants of each herb. They are considerably more convenient, since many kinds of herbs grow very slowly from seed, while you can be harvesting from a nursery plant in only a few weeks. And, when you buy herb plants, you can decide if you like their scents before you buy them. This is important when you are buying an unfamiliar herb, and also because the scent is likely to vary among cultivars of the same herb or even among plants with the very same name. (Just gently rub a leaf and sample the aroma.)

Some herbs are so easy to grow from pieces of the mature plant that they are rarely grown from seed. For example, mint is usually started by planting a piece of stem, which then grows roots. And a few kinds of herbs cannot be grown from seed at all. You will never find French tarragon seed, because this tarragon cultivar never blooms. All French tarragon is started by cuttings from existing plants. (If you do buy tarragon seed, it will grow into the much less tasty Russian tarragon.)

At the other extreme, cilantro, chervil, summer savory and dill, are much more likely to succeed if they are started from seed, because they transplant badly. If you buy nursery seedlings of these herbs, not only will you be spending a lot for plants you could easily grow from seed, but you will also give them a poor start by subjecting them to transplanting.

In the listings, you will find advice on whether to grow an herb from seed or purchased plants, assuming that you are not planning to make a major project of herb propagation. The chart on page 304 lists whether an herb is best grown from seeds, plants, or if, given ample attention and time to grow, both are equally good. If you want to try more kinds of herbs from seed, either for the challenge or to have more plants, refer to the chart for general seeding requirements. For more information, see books in Appendix VI, Suggested Reading.

Keep perennial herbs tidy by pruning them back each year, as recommended under individual instructions. Many low growing perennial herbs thrive for several years, then decline. Some grow in clumps that can be dug up, then cut apart and divided, others need to be renewed by layering, or by root or stem cuttings, as described in Chapter 6. Replace any herbs that do not thrive or that have declined seriously.

Remember that each type of herb is a new plant to learn to grow and use. If you've never used fresh herbs in cooking at all, start with only a few that you already purchase and use as dried herbs. Introduce only one or two new herbs each season so you will learn to grow and cook with them, not forget them as you use instead, out of habit, the ones you already know. As you look through cookbooks for recipes using vegetables you grow, remember to look for uses for herbs as well (see page 352).

Some herbs you grow may never find a place in your kitchen. Many a gardener has brought home a wonderfully aromatic and mysterious treasure, only to find no way to use the mature plant that has now sprawled over a large part of the herb garden. Unless you are enjoying such plants as ornamentals, find the courage to toss them into the compost heap and give something else a try instead.

Herbs and Pests

Herbs grown out-of-doors tend to have few pest problems. Their aromatic oils often make them unattractive to insects. So unless an insect pest or a disease is mentioned for an herb, you can assume it is not likely to be affected by them here.

In fact, herbs are often mentioned as "companion plants." That is, it is said that they can save nearby plants from insects, disease, or general malaise. Scientific testing of these theories has shown mixed results. A few relationships seem to work, although most concern insects that are not common here. And when an herb does repel an insect, to do so it often must be growing so thickly that the protected crop is stunted by the competition. A more promising research direction has been using extracts of repellant herbs to spray on crops. (For more on companion planting research, see Appendix VI, Suggested Reading.)

A new and useful interpretation of companion planting is growing flowers to attract beneficial insects. Parsley family flowers provide nectar and pollen for beneficials; mint family flowers and borage attract pollinating bees (see also page 131).

Harvesting Herbs

We imagine that we will be able to pick the herbs we grow whenever we need them for a particular purpose. While this is true for many herbs, among them oregano, thyme, and chives, others are harvested according to other schedules. French tarragon can be harvested only in warmer months, as it is dormant in winter. Dill and basil are annuals that grow in the warm season. They die each winter and must be replanted every spring. Parsley is a biennial. It goes to seed in the spring (and sometimes at other times). While parsley can be harvested much of the year, you need staggered plantings to be sure of having it all year. A few herbs, like cilantro or chervil, must be replanted every few weeks to provide a steady supply of young plants.

Herbs that have groups of single leaves growing from a central point, like parsley, are harvested by cutting off entire individual leaves with their stems. Chives, which have grasslike leaves, can be harvested by clipping the tops of leaves, like mowing. Herbs with leaves borne on the sides of stems, such as basil or oregano, are harvested by pinching back the stem tips. (By pinching off ungainly shoots, you can also shape plants as you harvest.)

Because herbs are generally used in such small quantities, you are more likely to be underpicking than overpicking them, but there are limits to how much you may safely harvest. You can begin to pick when the plant is quite small, but even if you are picking only a little bit at a time, if the plant is getting smaller, you are picking too much. You may harvest larger plants quite heavily several times a season. A good rule of thumb is never to harvest more than 50% of the plant at one time, and if you do harvest that much, let it grow back before you harvest again. A few herbs, among them mint and chives, can withstand even heavier harvesting. Both will spring back even if they are levelled, as long as it is during a season when they are actively growing. However, you will probably not want to chop them quite so severely very often, as it will interrupt your harvest.

HERBS IN CONTAINERS

Herbs grow well in containers, so you can grow a few even if you have only a stair landing or porch. Choose tough, drought tolerant ones for windy spots, shade tolerant ones for shaded spots. Use a good potting mix, high in organic or other materials that hold moisture well, and plan to add some fertilizer regularly while the plants are actively growing. Choose 8 or 10 inch pots for most individual herbs, or larger boxes for several plants at once. Almost all herbs will be smaller when grown in pots, and perennials will be shorter-lived, but you will still be amply rewarded for your efforts.

Potting is one way to keep large herbs in bounds. Bay trees, for example, can be container-grown, keeping them well pruned so that they don't outgrow the pot too fast, and transplanting them to larger pots as they grow. Pots are also a good option for rampant spreaders, like mint, although you must remember that mint needs ample water. Use a very moisture-retentive soil mix, as large a container as you can arrange, water often, and don't try to grow potted mint on a windy roof.

If you want to try growing herbs inside, start by getting them out of their 2 inch nursery pots and into something more comfortable. Herbs do stay smaller when grown inside, but give them at least a 4 inch or 6 inch pot. Try them in your sunniest window— one that gets five or more hours of sunlight a day. If they still seem spindly, you may need to supplement with fluorescent lights. Just as for seedlings, the lights must be hung a few inches from the tops of the plants (see page 55). Also, wash your herbs in plain water once a week to avoid pests, which thrive indoors because there aren't enough natural predators there. Be sure to inspect and wash the backs of the leaves, too. If aphids, whiteflies, mealybugs, or mites do appear, use a soap spray to combat them. Check the source list in Appendix V also, for sources of the tiny predator insects or mites that are suitable for indoor release.

Gardeners who have any outdoor space at all can have the best of both worlds by alternating environments. Grow the herbs you use the most in two separate sets of pots. Bring one set inside for a few days of harvesting, then put it back outdoors and bring in the second set for harvests instead. (For more on growing plants in containers see page 38.)

Preserving Herbs

No matter how small your herb garden, you will occasionally grow more of something than you can use fresh. If you have time, dry some of your harvest, or freeze it. Most herbs dry very well at room temperature, in a few days to two weeks. Hang small bunches upside down in a well-ventilated room, or spread the herbs on a screen. Don't put them in direct sun or in a damp place. If you are drying seeds, like those of coriander or fennel, on their stalks, hang them with their tops in a paper bag. The bag will catch any seeds that fall from the stalks as they dry.

Oven drying is faster, from three to six hours. The oven temperature should be no higher than 150° F. Exceptions are basil and chervil, which should be dried at about 90°. Dry herbs until they are crisp. If they brown, you have used too high a temperature. Store dried herbs in a tightly closed container to keep their flavor in.

You can also freeze herbs. Either freeze whole herb leaves, in plastic bags from which you have forced most of the air, or put herbs in the blender with just a bit of water, and freeze the resulting paste in ice cube trays. When your herb ice has frozen, store the cubes in closed and labelled plastic bags until you are ready to use them in soups or sauces. You can blend and freeze a favorite combination of herbs together. And pesto base, frozen in the summer basil season, can extend that season to most of the year (see recipe, page 275).

We use herbs in such small quantities that you will often have a plant that is producing more than you can use. Extra home-grown herbs, fresh, dried, or frozen, make excellent gifts for nongardeners. Other ideas for easy herbal gifts include herbal vinegars, sauces, and mixes of dried herbs and flowers for use in fragrant potpourris or sachets.

Cooking With Fresh Herbs

Having a source of fresh herbs expands your options in the kitchen. For example, dried or fresh herbs can be used to season a salad dressing, but fresh herbs can also be chopped and added directly to the salad. Basil leaves in a tossed salad, cilantro in a salsa, mint in tabouli, or anise hyssop leaves and flowers in a fruit salad are delicious examples. Here is another advantage of growing herbs: their flowers are pretty, and scented as pleasantly as the leaves. See Chapter 13 for more on edible flowers.

When making a stock or broth for soup, use fresh herbs in a bouquet garni. This is a small bundle of herbs, tied together with a string. They are left in until the stock is cooked, or may be taken out earlier if they have imparted as much flavor as you desire. Dried herbs can also be used to make a bouquet garni, though they must be contained in a small cloth sack, since they are not in large, easily removed pieces. Basic herbs for this purpose are parsley, bay leaf and thyme, but you can vary the components as you desire. See the recipe for Homemade Chicken Stock on page 349.

In sautéed dishes, fresh herbs may be added to the oil, to flavor it, then removed. The fresh herb is better able to release its aroma for this style of cooking than are dried ones. Then, chopped fresh herbs can be added at the end of the cooking, especially ones that do not keep their flavor well when cooked, such as chervil or marjoram.

The possibilities go on: fresh herbs in scrambled eggs, omelets or fritattas, in sauces, casseroles, or breads. And, if you wish, try brewing tea with freshly picked herbs. Just put sprigs in a teapot or a cup, and pour boiling water over them. However you use the fresh herbs from your garden, you will enjoy the convenience and zest they bring to your kitchen.

COMPENDIUM OF HERBS

ANISE HYSSOP (OR LICORICE MINT)

Agastache foeniculum
(*A. anisata*)
Mint Family ❖
Labiatae

Grow this herb for the delicious, anisy-sweet tea that can be made from its fresh or dried leaves, and for its edible flowers. Although small, each blossom contains a burst of flavor. Use them in green or fruit salads or to ornament a dessert. Flowering stems are also handsome in bouquets. Anise hyssop is a native of the north central United States, where the Plains Indians discovered how good it tastes.

Anise hyssop plants are a bushy 2 to 3 feet tall. They resemble the related mints in having opposite pairs of leaves on square stems. However, they differ in their anisy or licorice flavor, and they clump rather than spreading aggressively by runners like mint. Purple flowers are most common, and a white-flowered variety is also available.

Growing Instructions   Start anise hyssop from a nursery plant, or, if that proves hard to find, you can also grow it easily from seed. Start seed inside in the spring. The plants will grow in any soil with good drainage, and will grow lushly in rich garden soil. Once you have anise hyssop growing, it may seed itself under the established plant, or you can get new plants by dividing established parent plants.

Sources
    Anise hyssop plants (purple-flowered): NGN, RH
    Anise hyssop seed (purple-flowered): ABL, BG, DD, GG,
        NGN, PTS, RH, SB, SGS, TERR
    Anise hyssop seed (white-flowered): RG, TERR

BASIL (OR SWEET BASIL)
Ocimum basilicum
HOLY BASIL (OR TULSI)
Ocimum sanctum
Mint Family ❖ *Labiatae*

I never saw much reason to grow basil until I tasted fresh garden pesto, a wonderful basil-based sauce for pasta. Then I became a basil evangelist. More basil, yes! Bigger basil leaves! Basil earlier and longer! And, while basil pesto is delicious, there is more; this is a wonderfully aromatic herb that can have many other uses in your cooking.

Basil does well in the sunnier parts of the region, but may not succeed in foggier gardens. If you are trying out basil in a very foggy area, include a dwarf variety like *O. basilicum* 'Minimum,' which may do better than the larger-leaved varieties. One fog zone gardener starts many large-leaved basil seedlings each spring, growing some in a small greenhouse and trying others in the garden. He reports that some years the plants outside fail, other years they thrive.

Growing Instructions   Basil is an annual plant that grows in the warm months. May is always warm enough to plant basil; earlier times may work out fine, but are speculative. Give the plants a protected spot that will be sunny on clear days.

To grow basil for occasional use as seasoning, start with just one or two plants. But to have enough for pesto, buy one or two six-packs of seedlings of a large-leaved variety. Basil is also relatively easy to start from seed. For an early start, seed your basil indoors. Sow March through May, maybe even as early as February if you have a good place to grow it till the weather warms, or if you are planting it out early into a very protected spot. The seedlings will be ready to transplant in three to four weeks, either into the garden or into a larger pot. I usually pot mine up and grow them to 5 or 6 inches tall before I set them out, to give them the best chance against slugs, snails, and earwigs.

Basil does best in well fertilized soil that has good drainage. Plant full-sized basil 8 inches apart, dwarf varieties 4 inches apart. When basil has three to four sets of true leaves, pinch out the tip of the plant. This will make side branches grow, creating a bushy plant. Keep basil evenly watered; it is not one of the herbs that thrives in dry soil.

The Harvest   To get the most production from

CALIFORNIA PESTO AND PASTA

I call my version of this classic sauce "California" Pesto because of the two changes I've made in the traditional recipe. First, I replace some of the olive oil with water. This reduces the fat content and lowers the calorie count, but still leaves plenty of flavor. Second, I substitute almonds for the traditional but more expensive pine nuts. (Sometimes I use pecans, which are also very good.) Try it and I'm sure you'll find that this pesto is as delicious as a traditional pesto. In this recipe, the pesto is served with spaghetti, but you can use it with any other pasta.

Spaghetti (a 3/4- to 1-inch diameter bunch per serving)
1/3 cup cold water
1/4 cup virgin olive oil
2 cups packed fresh basil leaves (no tough stems), coarsely chopped
3 cloves garlic
1/4 cup almonds (or pecans)
3/4 cup grated Parmesan cheese
1/4 cup or more spaghetti water, as needed

Let the spaghetti cook while you make the pesto. Bring a large pot of water to a boil and add the spaghetti. Bring the water back to a boil, turn to low, cover, and set the timer for 7 to 12 minutes, depending on the thickness of the spaghetti and how well cooked you like it.

To make the pesto sauce, pour the cold water and olive oil into a blender. Gradually add the basil and blend until smooth. Add the garlic and almonds and blend again. Pour the pesto into a medium bowl, and stir in the Parmesan cheese.

When the spaghetti is cooked, spoon boiling water from the pot into the pesto and mix. Add enough water to make a thick sauce. You don't want it either too solid or too runny. Drain the spaghetti and serve it with pesto to spoon on top, or toss with the spaghetti before serving. Serves two to four.

Variation: Pesto is most commonly used as a pasta sauce, but it has many other uses. For instance, you can stir it into soups, add a little to salad dressings, or use it as a pizza topping. You can even use it as a seasoning for baked fish: spread a 1/4-inch thick layer of undiluted pesto in the cavity of a trout, wrap the fish in aluminum foil, and bake at 350° F for about 20 minutes.

Note: Pesto sauce freezes well, but it will taste better if you do not add the cheese until after it is thawed. You can blend just the basil, cold water, olive oil, garlic, and almonds to freeze as a pesto base. When you need a pesto sauce, thaw the base, add the cheese, and spoon in enough boiling water to thin the sauce to the desired consistency.

your plants, don't harvest whole plants. Pick by pinching back the leafy stem tips, always being sure to leave at least half of the plant intact. Take 1 to 4 inches from each tip, pinching back to where there are small leaves sprouting at the base of a pair of large leaves. Keep harvesting tender tips all season.

Soon spikes of flower buds will begin to form at the stem tips. You can use these, or even opening flowers, just as you would leaves. However, if a plant blooms very much, and the flowers begin to form seeds, it will begin to lose its lower leaves and will not make many new leaves. Therefore try to keep flower buds picked before they open. After you have completed a day's harvest of leafy tips, check the plants over again for any opening flowers you have missed, and pick them off.

When weather turns wet and cold, basil leaves fall off and the plants eventually die. This commonly happens in October or November, but the exact time varies with the weather patterns of a given year. Watch your plants for a decline and try to pull them while the leaves are still usable. Strip the plants and either freeze or dry the leaves. Dry basil at no more than 90° F, just until crisp, or freeze fresh leaves in freezer bags, or in pesto base (see previous page).

Besides being used in pesto, basil is commonly used in dishes with raw or cooked tomatoes, in soups, in meat and fish dishes, and in salads and salad dressings. Try a few basil leaves in a green salad. Or make a salad of just tomatoes, avocado or cucumber, some chopped fresh basil and a sprinkling of pine nuts. Add basil to omelets or use it to season vegetables. A good combination is basil—either chopped fresh or crumbled dry—sprinkled on chunks of steamed winter squash.

Varieties and Related Species   Best for a traditional pesto are green-leaved sweet basil or its strains, such as 'Genovese'. For extra-large, green leaves to cut up in a salad or make "wrappers" for other foods, try 'Green Ruffles', 'Mammouth', or types sold as "lettuce-leaved" or "broadleaf." 'Purple Ruffles', 'Opal', and 'Red Rubine' have purple leaves. 'Minimum' and 'Piccolo' are rounded plants that are under a foot tall when full-grown, with small, tasty, green leaves.

You might like to try a scented variety, like lemon, cinnamon, or anise-scented basil. Lemon basil (*O.b. citriodorum*), has medium-sized green leaves with a lemony touch. Cinnamon and anise basil both have rosy pink flower stalks. An anise-scented basil known as Thai basil was introduced to the U.S. by Southeast Asian immigrants. Another favorite of that part of the world is the clove-scented perennial *O. sanctum*. Considered holy by Hindus in India, this plant is grown near temples and dwellings and is valued in Asian cuisine. *O. sanctum* may be sold as Holy basil or as Tulsi.

Pests   To protect basil seedlings from snails, slugs, and earwigs, grow them under row cover until they are 6-8 inches tall. A serious new threat is fusarium wilt. Fusarium-tested basil seed is just beginning to appear on the market. If your basil suddenly wilts and drops its leaves, remove it from the garden immediately.

Sources
Sweet basil seed (*O. basilicum*)
   Fusarium-tested basil seeds: RH
   Standard-sized, green-leaved varieties:
      Sweet basil (variety not specified): Widely available
      Genovese: ABL, CG, DD, JG, JSS, NGN, RH, SGS, VBS
   Extra-large, green-leaved varieties:
      Mammoth: CG, JG, TERR
      Green Ruffles: BG, CG
      Lettuce or Broadleaf: ABL, DD, GG, JG, NGN, PTS, SB, SOC, SGS, VBS
   Small, green-leaved varieties:
      Minimum: ABL, GG, JSS, PS, PTS, TERR, T&M, VBS
      Piccolo: ABL, CG, RCS
   Large, purple-leaved varieties:
      Purple Ruffles: BG, CG, GG, JSS, PTS, SB, TERR, T&M
      Red Rubin: NGN, SGS, TERR
      Opal: ABL, JG, JSS, PS, PTS, SB, T&M, VBS
   Scented varieties:
      Anise or Thai: ABL, BG, CG, DD, EV, JG, NGN, PS, RH, SOC, SGS, TERR, T&M, VBS
      Cinnamon: ABL, BG, CG, GG, JG, JSS, PTS, RH, SB, SOC, SGS, TERR, VBS
      Lemon: BG, CG, DD, GG, JG, NGN, NSS, PS, PTS, RH, SB, SOC, TERR, T&M, VBS
  O. sanctum (tulsi) seeds: ABL, NGN, PTS, RH, SOC, SGS, T&M, VBS
Basil plants: Many varieties are available in local nurseries.

BAY LAUREL
(OR SWEET BAY, OR TRUE LAUREL)
Laurus nobilis
CALIFORNIA BAY
(OR CALIFORNIA LAUREL)
Umbellularia californica
Laurel Family   ❖   *Lauraceae*

The bay laurel (*Laurus nobilis*) is the tree that bears the classic culinary bay leaf. It is also the tree from which laurel wreaths were made, in ancient Greece, to celebrate winners in the Pythian games, and in which Roman generals wrapped announcements of victories, before sending them to the Senate. And a striking tree it is, its branches covered thickly with lustrous, deep green leaves. Its small yellow flowers are sometimes followed by attractive (but inedible) berries. Although it naturally grows up to 40 feet tall, it can be kept much smaller by constant pruning and snipping. Gardeners without room for a large tree can keep a bay pruned as a shrub or grow it in a container. It can also be trimmed into fanciful shapes, a pruning style called topiary.

The California bay (*Umbellularia californica*) is a native plant from the same family. Its leaves are similar to those of the bay laurel, but a bit narrower. Californians often use them like bay laurel, although the flavor is decidedly harsher. In the wild, California bay can grow to 60 feet, often with several trunks. It thrives among the redwoods, its silhouette lovely in a soft fog. Under redwoods it grows long and narrow, reaching towards sunlight, often leaning so far that it falls over. In an open area it grows straighter and fuller.

There isn't the same tradition of growing California bay in containers for kitchen use, although it's probably possible, as it grows slowly, and is often used in ways requiring frequent pruning. For example, it may be trained as a street tree, or may be clipped to form a tall hedge.

Growing Instructions   Buy either kind of bay tree as a small potted plant. They are often sold in one gallon pots, and occasionally as even smaller plants. The California bay is the less commonly available of the two species. If you want to grow it, order it at your nursery, or contact a local chapter of the California Native Plant Society (see Resources Appendix).

Both of these trees will do well in partial shade. The California bay will even grow in deep shade. (Beware of planting either one where it can grow up and cast its shadow on your garden, as both create quite deep shade themselves.)

Soil for these trees needn't be rich, but both require good drainage. Mature bay laurels need little water. The California bay does well with moderate watering, though it will tolerate drought. However, if you grow either of the bays in containers, you will have to pay closer attention to watering it than you would if it were in the open ground, since neither should ever go bone dry. Use a good potting mix and mulch with well rotted manure. You may want to fertilize once in a while, but don't do so often or use too much fertilizer at a time, as you don't want to encourage rapid growth.

Either is guaranteed to outgrow its pot eventually, it roots reaching out the bottom. Before it gets potbound, repot it in a slightly larger container, adding fresh potting mix and trimming the roots back. (See page 325 for more on root pruning containerized trees.) You may be able to keep it in larger and larger containers for ten years or more, putting it in a half wine barrel when nothing smaller will hold it.

The Harvest   Prune either kind of bay frequently to keep it small. Harvest leaves when you are pruning, or break off a leaf or two as needed. Leaves can be used fresh or dried. Some cooks prefer to use the leaves dry, since the flavor is mellower, but dried bay leaves lose flavor if kept too long. Since the California bay is stronger flavored, use only one California bay leaf in place of two or three bay laurel leaves. In cooking, bay is used in soups, stews, tomato sauces, marinades, and as a pickling spice. Bay leaves are a standard ingredient in the French bouquet garni.

Varieties   If you prefer to grow the true bay laurel, there is one cultivar worth seeking out. *L. nobilis* 'Saratoga' was developed at the Saratoga Horticultural Foundation. It resists scale and another pest, the psyllid, and is a vigorous plant. It is worth a try as a container plant, although it has a slightly more open habit, so won't make quite the dense bush of leaves that the common bay laurel will.

Sources
Bay laurel plants: Widely available
Saratoga: Contact Saratoga Horticultural Foundation, (see Appendix V, Resources for Gardeners) or see if your local nursery can order it.
California bay plants: Often available in local nurseries or at plant sales or through the California Native Plant Society (see Appendix V, Resources for Gardeners).

BORAGE
Borago officinalis
Borage Family ❖ *Boraginaceae*

This is a big, exuberant plant with rough-hairy, grey-green leaves and striking blue flowers about 3/4 of an inch across. Borage grows wild in southern Europe and on the chalk downs of southern England. It also grows wild in my garden, reseeding itself in both the spring and the fall. I weed out, and sometimes eat excess seedlings, but let it mature here and there. I really don't use much of the mature plant, but I like the fact that it encourages bees to visit my garden.

Though it is not in the cucumber family, the whole borage plant has a definite, and very refreshing, cucumber flavor. You can use the seedlings in salads, the blossoms in salads or floating in iced tea or punches, and the mature leaves for tea. You may also want to try a stem or two of borage flowers in a bouquet.

Growing Instructions   Borage is an annual that grows 2 to 3 feet tall. It needs to be seeded in place, since it does not transplant well. It isn't fussy about soil, just growing a bit less tall if the soil is poorer. Sow in the late spring or summer, in full, or nearly full, sun. Thin so that mature plants stand a foot or two apart. Keep plants evenly moist.

Borage

The Harvest   The first time you see borage seedlings, you are likely to think they are squash seedlings, as they have similar big flat seed leaves. The true leaves of borage, however, are simple ovals, not lobed like a squash leaf. If you planted the seed thickly, do harvest the extra seedlings as you pull them. In subsequent years, the borage will self-sow, giving you plenty of extra seedlings to add that mysterious hint of cucumber to your salads. Use them when they have only seed leaves, or at most one or two small true leaves. After that, the true leaves become a bit too prickly for most people's taste.

You can eat borage flowers with or without their soft-furry sepals. (To remove the sepals, pull on the stamens.) For tea, harvest the blooming tops with their leaves. Use them when fresh or pick off the leaves and flowers to dry for later use.

Sources
Borage seed: Widely available

CAMOMILE, ENGLISH
(OR ROMAN CAMOMILE)
Chamaemelum nobile (Anthemis nobilis)
CAMOMILE, GERMAN (OR HUNGARIAN CAMOMILE, OR SWEET FALSE CAMOMILE)
Matricaria recutita (Matricaria chamomilla)
Sunflower Family ❖ *Compositae*

Two plants are championed as the true camomile. The English and the Germans have each historically preferred the flavor of one over the other, and you will still find opposing claims in modern books and seed catalogs! The flower heads of both are used to make a soothing tea with a strong apple-like scent.

English camomile is a creeping perennial groundcover, under one foot tall. It makes a thick, low mat of feathery leaves and, from the second year after seeding, small flower heads on wiry stems. These may have white-petalled flowers around the edge, like little daisies, or may be just yellow buttons. English camomile can be grown between stepping stones or even, with occasional mowing to remove its flowers, as a lawn.

German camomile, an annual, is a taller, much looser plant than English camomile. It makes no mat of leaves near the ground. In my garden it reaches only about 1-1/2 feet, but it is said to grow as high as 2-1/2 feet. Its flower heads are quite similar to the white-petalled form of English camomile.

Growing Instructions   Start English camomile from purchased plants, from either the herb or the groundcover section of your nursery. However, if English camomile plants are being sold as a groundcover, be sure the variety you buy is one that blooms, as it is the flowers that you will be harvesting. Grow German camomile from seed. It can be started indoors, and transplanted until it is 2 inches tall, but it is easier to sow it in place.

Both camomiles grow well in full sun. English camomile will tolerate some shade and prefers days that aren't too hot. Grow both in good garden soil, and keep them well watered.

The Harvest   Because the tea is made only from the flower heads, you will need to plant a number of plants. Plant a few square feet of either of the camomiles to get enough for a steady supply of tea. Harvest the flower heads when the yellow centers are taller than they are wide, but don't wait too long or they will be less flavorful. If you harvest more than you can use at one time, dry them at room temperature.

You can propagate English camomile by division, digging 1 to 2 inch diameter sections of the plant and transplanting them. Once you've let German camomile go to seed in your garden, it will probably continue to reseed itself. These volunteers can be a free source of tea, but they can get in the way of your other plants, so don't let very many plants drop their seed.

Varieties and Related Species If you are buying English camomile plants, beware of nonblooming cultivars. At least one, 'Treanague,' has been bred bloomless for use in lawns.

Two other locally common plants are also sometimes called camomile, but their flavor is clearly inferior to both English and German camomile. One is pineapple weed (*Matricaria matricarioides*), a low-growing plant with yellowish-green flower heads, often found growing wild in the cracks of the pavement. The second is Feverfew (*Chrysanthemum parthenium*) (see also page 316), a small-flowered perennial chrysanthemum that grows about 2 feet tall. It is used in landscaping, but often comes up wild in gardens. The flower heads of feverfew are white, usually double, with yellow centers. The leaves look like miniature chrysanthemum leaves. I tolerate wild plants of feverfew because they make nice cut flowers, but for tea, I choose one of the true camomiles.

Sources
English camomile plants: Local nurseries
German camomile seed: Widely available

Catnip
Nepeta cataria
Catmint
Nepeta mussinii
Cat Thyme
Teucrium marum
Mint Family ❖ *Labiatae*

These are herbs to grow primarily for your cat, although catnip also makes a passable, but not psychotropic, tea for people. Many cats enjoy these herbs, both fresh from the garden and dried. In fact, some cats enjoy these herbs so much that they will nibble them or roll in them until they kill the plants. (On the other hand, some cats are bored by all three herbs, and recent research has shown that

response or lack of it are genetic traits among cats!)

All three herbs are perennials. Catnip grows 2 or 3 feet tall, blooming in summer. Its small flowers are white with red or lavender dots. Catmint and cat thyme are prettier plants, worthy of a border or rock garden if neighborhood cat attention isn't too intense. Both are low growing, under one foot tall and sprawling. Catmint has blue flowers and cat thyme flowers are rosy pink to purple.

Growing Instructions Of the three plants, cat thyme is best grown from a transplant, while catnip and catmint can be grown from either transplant or seed, though for one plant, you would do best to use transplants. When you set transplants in the soil, you will bruise the leaves, releasing the odors. To keep cats from nibbling or crushing young plants to death, you may need to cover them with something firm, like a wire cage, while they establish themselves. In an extreme situation, you might need to resort to moving them to safety in a hanging pot. Sometimes plants grown from seed are more likely to escape cat notice, because if you don't touch the seedlings, and your cat doesn't walk through them, they won't give off much cat-attracting odor at first.

Plant any of these species in a sunny place. They all thrive in sandy soil, but will do well in any but heavy, unamended clay. Sun and good drainage will increase the strength of their scent.

The Harvest Cut leafy stems as desired. Cut the flowering stems before the seed sets to prevent plants from selfsowing and becoming a weed, or at least cut plants back once a year to improve their appearance.

You may decide to just let your cat enjoy these herbs fresh, or you can dry them. For drying, harvest the flowering stems. These dry easily if hung or spread in a dark, well-ventilated place. Give your cat a teaspoon or so of the dried herb or brush the dried leaves and flowers from the stems and sew or tie them into a piece of cloth, perhaps with a bell added for merriment.

Sources
Catnip seed: ABL, BG, DD, GG, JG, JSS, NGN, OBG, PS, PTS, RCS, RH, SOC, SGS, TERR, T&M, VBS
Catnip plants: JG, NGN,
Catmint seed: ABL, BG, NGN,
Catmint plants: Local nurseries
Cat thyme plants: RH

CHERVIL

Anthriscus cerefolium
Parsley Family ❖ *Umbelliferae*

Given a window box in Paris
big enough to grow only one
herb, many French people
would certainly choose
cerfeuil, or chervil. Chervil is
as common in French cooking
as it is rare in American. It
thrives in cool, shady places, so it
grows very well in our region.

Chervil is an annual plant that, like coriander,
makes a low leafy rosette, then a tall seed stalk.
Like coriander, the parts eaten are the young leaves.
Cool days, fog, and shade stimulate leafy growth,
while heat and sun stimulate seeding. I haven't
grown it long enough to be sure of all the planting
times that will succeed, but clearly it can be grown
more of the year in our foggier areas than elsewhere. I grew it in early spring in my foggy San
Francisco garden, and it reseeded itself in midsummer to make a plentiful harvest again in September.
Try plantings in late winter through midsummer,
and again in the early fall. Sow once a month for a
continuous supply of leaves.

Growing Instructions   Sow chervil seed in the
place where you want it to grow. Choose a location
that is partially shaded, especially in early summer.
Chervil will grow well in any good garden soil, but
if you have heavy clay, plant chervil only after you
have amended your soil for a couple of years. A
mulch can help keep the soil cool in warm periods.
Stimulate leaf production by cutting the plants back
to near the ground when they are 3 inches tall.

The Harvest   Thin small plants to 6 inches apart,
making use of your thinnings in cooking. Then, as
plants get larger, begin to harvest older leaves or
whole plants.

Chervil has a lovely taste, like a mild anise or
tarragon, with a hint of parsley. It is used particularly in omelets, but also with meat, fish, oysters, in
sauces, in sorrel or spinach soup, and in salads. Add
it at the end of cooking, or even after food leaves
the stove, to preserve its delicate flavor. It is almost
always used fresh since its flavor does not survive
drying well, but you can try drying it at 90° F.

Varieties   Two varieties of chervil, plain and
curled, are commonly available. If the variety is not
identified in a description, it is probably the plain-
leaved. Both are used as seasoning, with the curled
variety also favored for visual effect in a salad, or
for use as a garnish, instead of parsley.

Pests and Diseases   Chervil will be relished by the
various chewing pests, especially in the fall, when
small hungry snails and summer's larger sowbug
population are looking for something tender to eat.
See Chapter 10 for controls for these pests.

Sources

Plain chervil seed: Widely available
Curly chervil seed: BG, JG, RH, SB, VBS

CHINESE CELERY (OR KINTSAI, HEUNG KUN, SERI-NA CUTTING LEAF CELERY, OR CELERY DINANT)

Apium graveolens var. *dulse*
Carrot Family ❖ *Umbelliferae*

Ordinary celery is often used as a flavoring. Pieces
of stalk and leaves are boiled and then discarded in
the preparation of many soup stocks, and we also
value celery for the zest it can add to a variety of
salads. In China, and also in Europe, smaller and
particularly strong-flavored types of celery are used
exclusively as a flavoring ingredient, much as we
would use chopped parsley. These plants are left
standing in the garden, and their stalks, or sometimes only their leaves, are harvested as needed, to
use fresh.

Cutting celeries are strains of the same species
and variety as regular celery, and they are grown in
the same way. (See page 197.) While they are probably just as sensitive to cold as regular celery, and
need just as much water and fertilizer to thrive,
they don't have to be grown quite as perfectly, since
the leaves will be usable even if the stalks are not
very tender. Scan seed catalog herb listings under
its various names, or look for it under celery. While
cutting celery could be grown from purchased transplants, I have never seen them for sale.

Sources

Chinese celery seed: ABL, EV, KSC
European cutting celery seed: ABL, BG, CG, GG, JSS,
NGN, PS, PTS, SB, SGS

CHIVES

Allium schoenoprasum
Lily Family ❖ *Liliaceae*

Chives are smaller cousins of bunching onions. One of the most popular herbs, chives are easy for a beginner and quite useful in the kitchen. These perennial plants can be harvested with a pair of scissors, cutting back the tops and letting more leaves grow from the base.

Growing Instructions Chives can be grown fairly easily from seed, but are very slow to mature, usually growing to cutting size only in the second year. Because of this, gardeners usually save at least a few months by purchasing a clump or two of plants from a nursery. Chives will grow in most garden soils, doing best in a well-amended one that drains well and at the same time holds moisture well. Since they are perennial, you should choose a spot for them that is as free as possible from weeds. Grassy weeds are especially difficult to remove from an established chive clump. Chives also do very well in an 8 or 10 inch pot. They can live permanently in a pot near your back door, or they can be transplanted when you have prepared a garden spot for them.

Fertilize chives growing in the garden a couple of times a year to help them withstand heavy cutting. Fertilize potted chives every two weeks, while they are actively growing, with a liquid fertilizer at half the recommended strength. Divide your chive clumps every two to four years, replanting in groups of six to ten bulbs per clump, and leaving 8 inches between clumps. You can do this any time of year, but the spring or the fall is best. If you haven't developed a need for more chives by the time you thin your clumps, pot some up for budding gardener friends.

The Harvest Harvest chive plants by clipping their leaves with scissors. Cut leaves nearly to the ground, rather than just halfway down. This stimulates the plant to make more new growth, preventing flowering. If you would rather harvest smaller amounts more frequently, try cutting just a few plants in the clump each time, but cutting them low. Use your chives fresh, or freeze them, chopped small, to use in winter, when growth will slow.

Chive blooms are attractive lavender pompoms. They can be used in salad or to make an herbal vinegar (see French Tarragon Harvest, page 301), but unless you have a use for them, it is better to pick them off before the buds open. This lets the plants put more energy into growing leaves.

Chives are appealing snipped small into cottage cheese or sour cream, but try them also in omelets, scrambled eggs, creamed vegetable soups, and salads. Try sprinkling whole chives or at least half-length ones over a salad. While finely chopped chives will often migrate to the bottom of the bowl during tossing, these longer ones won't, and they add an intriguing visual touch to your salad.

Sources
Chive plants: Buy at a local nursery.
Chive seed: Widely available

CHIVES, GARLIC (SEE GARLIC CHIVES)

COMFREY (OR RUSSIAN COMFREY)

Symphytum x uplandicum (S. peregrinum)
Borage Family ❖ *Boraginaceae*

I have decided to stop growing comfrey, although it hasn't yet stopped growing in my garden. Once established, this perennial keeps coming back from missed bits of root. When I first planted it, I used the leaves or roots for tea, and found the very young leaves mildly pleasant to munch in early spring. Then recently, scientists discovered dangerous amounts of a cancer-causing poison, pyrrolizidine, in comfrey leaves so I stopped eating it. Comfrey is still a good ingredient for the compost, but I strongly recommend that you do not eat any part of it, make tea from it, or feed it to animals.

Comfrey has quite a reputation as a healing herb. It was used in the Middle Ages of Europe both as a tea and as a poultice for wounds. Comfrey has also been used as food for chickens and other livestock, and is considered an excellent addition to the compost pile. Modern study of the plant revealed a substance that does indeed aid healing. This has been named allantoin, and is now extracted from comfrey roots, as well as made artificially, for use in medicines.

Growing Instructions Should you wish to grow comfrey, it is best to start it from a 1 to 3 inch piece of root. Lay the root in the ground horizontally, 3 to 6 inches deep, 3 feet from any other plants. It will form a rosette of large, hairy leaves and, in the late spring and summer, tall stalks of small, bell-like flowers. The flowers are most likely to be purple, although white, rose or yellow flowers are also possible. Cut out the flowering stalks when they are spent. Plants will stop growing in the winter and may even die back if the weather is very cold. Tidy up by removing dead leaves each winter.

Varieties and Related Species   Russian comfrey is said to be up to 6 feet tall, common comfrey to 3 feet, a better size for a small garden. I have never seen a comfrey plant 6 feet tall, so I assume the comfrey I've seen growing here is common comfrey. Inquire about the mature height of the kind you are purchasing.

Sources
  Comfrey roots (variety not given): ABL
  Russian broadleaf comfrey roots: NGN, RCS
  Comfrey plants: NGN, RH, or buy at local nurseries

CORIANDER
(OR CILANTRO OR CHINESE PARSLEY)
Coriandrum sativum
Carrot Family ❖ *Umbelliferae*

Few people are neutral about the flavor of cilantro—the name by which most of us know the leaves of the coriander plant. Some find the flavor delectable, others, awful. I can testify that this can be an acquired taste. The flavor used to remind me of soap, but now I enjoy it and use cilantro in many delicious recipes. I also cook with coriander seeds, which have a different flavor from the leaves.

Gardeners' most common problem with coriander is that they expect it to stand all year like parsley, and they are surprised when it goes to seed after only a few weeks of harvest. Coriander is an annual plant, maturing seed in three to four months. For a continuous supply of young leaves, you must resow every few weeks. If you eat only a little of it, try sowing a dozen or two seeds at a time, as larger plantings may only go to seed before you can eat them.

Coriander

Growing Instructions   Coriander grows well in our cool temperatures, even in the winter months. Its maturation is slowed down when the weather is cool, or the garden site shady—which means a longer production of leafy greens before the inevitable bolt. In fact, plants that mature in a very warm period may send up seed stalks after producing only a few usable basal leaves.

Coriander will thrive in any moderately rich, well-draining garden soil. It needs even moisture to make lush growth. Since it is set back a bit by transplanting, it's best to sow your seeds in place. Plant them 1/4 to 1/2 inch deep, then thin plants to 4 to 8 inches apart. Each "seed" is really two seeds, so expect to thin out one each of a lot of plant pairs. You might want to use scissors to clip plants out, avoiding tearing the roots of the twins. Or, if you have good, loose soil, you might be able to separate and transplant pairs. To try this, work when the plants have only one or two true leaves.

The Harvest   Begin your harvest by using your thinnings. Continue to pick leaves, always letting some continue to grow. You can also pick and use the young flower stalks while they are in bud, and picking the stalk will delay flowering a bit.

Once the flowers open, the plants will offer little leaf for cooking. The lower leaves will soon turn yellow and die and the leaves on the mature flower stem will be very small and fine. Reseed as soon as you begin to harvest leaves from a young planting, so you will have plants to replace them before they decline.

Coriander flowers are pale lavender and are borne on 2 to 4 foot stalks, in the flat umbels typical of the carrot family. They make a pretty addition to a salad or to a delicate bouquet. I usually don't let the seeds form, because they are inexpensive to buy and I generally want the garden space for something else. However, seeds will ripen here easily. Harvest them when about two-thirds of them have turned from green to brownish. Cut the stalks and put their tops into a large paper bag. Tie it around them and hang them upside down to dry. If you harvest seeds on a damp day or in the early morning, the seeds will be less likely to fall before you can get the stalks into a bag. To harvest mature seeds for planting, let most of them reach the dry, brown stage before you cut the stalks, then cut carefully to avoid seed fall, and dry them as for culinary use. Or you can let a few plants drop seed in your garden, and let them seed themselves.

Both the leaves and seeds are used in cuisines

THAI FISH SOUP

I used to order a soup much like this at a Thai restaurant in the San Francisco Mission District. Sharply tart and wonderfully savory, it was just right on a cold winter evening before a bike ride home from work. I learned to make it by asking what was in it, and experimenting on my own. That restaurant is gone, but now I can make the soup myself. Fish sauce is a very common ingredient in Thai and Vietnamese cooking. It is made from an extract of salted fish. You can buy it at Asian grocery stores.

1 1/2 pounds red snapper or similar white fish
2 1/2 quarts water
3 or 4 fresh leaves lemongrass, cut in 1- to 2-inch lengths (or 1 bulbous leaf base, chopped)
1/3 cup lime juice
1/3 cup fish sauce
1/8 teaspoon crushed red chile pepper
1 14-ounce can coconut milk
1/3 cup fresh coriander leaves, chopped
1/4 cup green onion tops, onion lily leaves, or garlic chives, cut into 2-inch pieces

Cut the fish into 3/4- by 1 1/2-inch pieces, removing any bits of bone you find. Bring the water to a boil in a large pot. Add the lemongrass and simmer for 10 minutes. Stir in the lime juice, fish sauce, red pepper, and coconut milk and simmer the soup for a few more minutes. Add the fish, lower the heat, and simmer 5 to 10 more minutes. Just before serving, add the coriander leaves and onion greens. Taste and adjust seasonings, adding more lime juice, fish sauce, or crushed red pepper if needed. Serves four.

around the world. Alhough many Americans know coriander leaves only as the cilantro in Mexican salsa, they are also used in South America, the Middle East, through India, and into China, Southeast Asia and Japan. Middle Easterners use them in their vegetarian patties called falafel, and in the hot sauce traditionally served with it. In India, the leaves are an ingredient in many curries. In China, they are traditionally added to a stir fry near the end of cooking. Southeast Asians enjoy them in soups and salads.

Coriander seed, which is used in the U.S. mainly as a pickling spice, is used more widely in all cuisines of Arab and Arab-influenced countries in the Near and Middle East, North Africa, Spain and various New World cultures influenced by Spain. There, it is often used as a seasoning for fresh or cured meat. In India, coriander seed is a prime ingredient of curry.

Varieties   Until recently there was only one variety of coriander. Now there is a new one said to be slow to bolt. If you plan to grow coriander for its

leaves, look for this one. It doesn't seem to have an official name, but it is described in seed catalogs with terms like "slow-bolt" and "grow for leaves."

Sources
Coriander seed:
Regular types: Widely available
"Slo-Bolt" type: CG, JSS, NGN, PS, RCS, RH, PTS, SB, SOC, SGS, VBS

DILL

Anethum graveolens
Parsley Family ❖ *Umbelliferae*

Dill resembles its cousin fennel in appearance, but it is smaller. While fennel towers to a bushy six feet or more, dill is a thinner plant reaching only two to four feet. In fact, dill seems to be less than what most local gardeners expect. I think this is due to an incorrect assumption that it should grow as tall as the more robust wild fennel, in combination with the fact that dill may not reach its full size in our less than ideal conditions. Dill is a summer annual that requires full sun, warmth and some protection from strong winds. It will not grow well in a too foggy or too windy garden.

Growing Instructions   Soil for dill should be loose and moderately rich. Because dill transplants badly, sow your seeds in place, covering them only lightly. Sow the first planting in April, then, for a steady supply of dill leaves, sow more seed every few weeks through mid-July. Keep the soil evenly moist as the dill grows. Thin plants to stand 6 to 12 inches apart, depending on whether you plan to harvest plants small for leaves or let them grow to form seedstalks.

The Harvest   Dill leaves are best when harvested before the plant comes into bloom. The plants produce few new leaves once flowering begins. Sometimes cutting out the growing tip will delay flowering, but if the weather turns hot, flower stalks will form quickly anyway. To dry a leaf crop, cut plants when they are at least two months old, but before they bloom, and spread leaves to dry in a warm, shady place. The dried leaves are often called "dill weed."

Seeds ripen when the plant is four or more months old. To save dill seed for cooking, cut the heads before the last flower falls, and dry them well in a warm room, or in a paper bag, as for coriander (see page 282). Then knock the seeds from the stems. If you want to save seed for growing more dill, leave it on the plant longer, until it is brown. For pickling purposes, cut whole plants when the seeds are only half ripe, and bend these green plants to fit pickling jars. Plant dill for pickling in early May, for the best chance of making your dill harvest coincide with your cucumber harvest.

Dill is a popular flavoring in northern, central and eastern European cooking, as well as in Russia and Turkey. It grows wild in Southern Europe, but, except in Greece, it is not much eaten there. In the cuisines in which they are a popular ingredient, dill leaves are used to flavor many vegetables, especially potatoes and cabbage family vegetables. They are also added to meats, fish, eggs, salads, breads, and soups. Dill seed is used in cabbage and potato dishes, in fish dishes, and in breads.

Varieties   If you are growing dill for leaves, choose 'Dukat' or 'Fernleaf', varieties that are promised to be especially leafy. Fernleaf is a short plant, suitable for container growing.

Sources
Dill seed: Widely available.
Leafy variety seed:
Dukat: CG, GG, NGN, RH, PTS, SOC, SGS, TERR
Fernleaf: BG, GG, JG, JSS, NGN, PS, RH, PTS, TERR, VBS

EPAZOTE (OR JERUSALEM OAK PAZOTE, OR MEXICAN TEA)
Chenopodium ambrosioides
Goosefoot Family ❖ *Chenopodiaceae*

Epazote, an herb native to Mexico, is commonly used in Mexican cuisine as a seasoning for beans, hence it is known as the bean herb.

It's a perennial plant, closely related to the weed lambsquarters. The plant in my garden is quite vigorous, growing to 3 feet tall and almost as wide. The leaves are a rich green, to about 4 inches long. The green flowers that form late in the summer are so tiny that you won't notice them unless you look closely. The plant has a strongly pungent aroma.

My experience growing epazote began one day in early summer, when a Mexican-American family stopped during a stroll to ask me about my community garden. I invited them in and gave them some purslane and mint. When I told them I was trying to find some epazote, they offered to show me some that was growing in a nearby vacant lot. It was a small, struggling plant that I would have overlooked myself. I took several cuttings, and, though I'm not sure early summer is the best time to take cuttings, one of them did grow.

At the time, I didn't know where to buy epazote, but now you will find plants and seeds both locally and from mail-order sources.

Growing Instructions   One plant is enough for many a pot of beans, but if you want to grow more, it grows easily from seed. Grow from plants you purchase in spring or early summer, or sow seed in the spring. Epazote survives in the lean, summer-dry soil of local vacant lots, but it will grow much larger in more fertile and well-watered garden soil. I would expect it to suffer in poorly-drained, soggy soil. It grows well in full sun, but will also tolerate shade.

The Harvest   Cut leaves as needed and use them fresh or dried. The leaves dry well if spread in a dark, airy place. Look for epazote in Mexican recipes as an ingredient in dishes that contain tortillas and/or beans.

This herb can be so vigorous, and reseed itself so profusely, that you will want to spend some energy keeping it in bounds. It may grow so fast that you will want to prune it a couple of times during the summer to keep it from overgrowing other plants. My plant reseeded thickly, and it took considerable weeding to get rid of the extra plants. To prevent this, time one of your prunings to remove flowering stems before seeds can form. Cut the plant back one last time in the fall, to make way for fresh spring growth.

Sources
Epazote seed: ABL, DD, JG, JSS, NSS, OBG, RH, PTS, SB, SOC, SGS, TERR
Epazote plants: Purchase in local nurseries

FENNEL (OR SWEET FENNEL)
Foeniculum vulgare var. *dulce*
FENNEL, BRONZE (OR RED FENNEL)
Foeniculum vulgare var. *rubrum*
FENNEL, FLORENCE (OR FINOCCHIO)
Foeniculum vulgare var. *azoricum*
Parsley Family ❖ *Umbelliferae*

Wild sweet fennel is one of our most common and visible weeds. It grows in tall, dense thickets in many vacant lots or neglected backyards. The plants reach over 6 feet tall, with feathery leaves, and are topped in the summer with loose, flat heads of small, yellow flowers. You have probably heard it called "wild anise." Fennel does have a taste similar to that of anise, but the plant that produces commercial anise seed is another species.

Fennel originated in the Mediterranean region. Sweet fennel is a common weed there too, and is also widely cultivated as an herb. Some say that the flavor of wild sweet fennel is inferior to that of the domestic varieties, that it is bitter and hasn't much anise taste. Still, local cooks do use it, and the particular wild sweet fennel near my garden tastes strongly of anise to me. If you do like the flavor of wild fennel leaves or seeds, harvest them from vacant lots, but keep this plant out of your garden, as it is a nasty weed. (See page 116 for more on fennel as a weed.) If it is the sweet, white fennel bulb, that you want, you need to grow Florence fennel, a variety bred to produce it.

Growing Instructions   If you decide to grow sweet fennel, choose a domestic variety that meets your needs. Sow seed in place in February or March, or in midsummer. Sweet fennel will succeed in most soils, but will do best in one that is light and well drained, but kept moist. Fennel for bulbs will do best in a rich, moist, but well-drained soil.

Thin plants of varieties grown for leaves to 6-12 inches apart. Florence fennel must stand 10-12 inches apart, or bulbs will not form.

The Harvest   Collect sweet fennel leaves from the time of thinning on. Fennel leaves are famous as a seasoning for fish, and are also good with pork and veal, and in soups, salads, and salad dressings.

The plants are biennials or short-lived perennials that bloom in the second season or after exposure to cold weather. Seeds are used in sausages, breads, and cookies. In India, they are nibbled after a meal. If you want seed, cut off the seedheads when the seeds begin to turn brown and dry them in a paper bag as you would coriander seed.

Harvest Florence fennel bulbs when they are about 3 inches across by cutting the whole plant. You can use the leaves from these plants also; they may be milder in flavor than those of plants grown for leaves. If you want a more mildly flavored bulb, try piling earth up around it a week or two before you harvest it. The sweet, white bulb has a strong anise flavor when raw, and is used in salads. Cooked, it loses much of the anise flavor and becomes a sweet-flavored vegetable. It may be sautéed, roasted, or boiled.

Varieties   In addition to ordinary green sweet fennel, a variety with bronze or dark red leaves is pretty enough to use in an ornamental border. You may find Florence fennel listed in seed catalogs among herbs or among vegetables.

Pests and Diseases   Other than an occasional parsleyworm (see Parsley, page 295), which does little damage, fennel seems pest-free.

Fennel has a reputation for inhibiting the growth of other plants, however I have not tested this theory, and have seen no hard proof.

Sources
Sweet fennel seed: Widely available
Bronze fennel seed: ABL, DD, NGN, RCS, RH, PTS, SOC, SGS, TERR, T&M, VBS
Florence fennel seed: BG, CG, DD, GG, JSS, NGN, OBG, RCS, RH, PTS, SB, SOC, SGS, VBS

GARLIC

See the Compendium of Vegetables, Chapter 11.

GARLIC CHIVES
(OR CHINESE LEEKS, GOW CHOY OR NIRA)

Allium tuberosum
Lily Family ❖ *Liliaceae*

The first time I grew this herb, in a foggy garden on the coast side of the San Mateo County hills, was from a packet labelled "Chinese Leeks." I grew a whole row of them and let them stay for most of a year, hoping they would eventually get bigger. I thought they were awfully small leeks. Now I appreciate garlic chives for what they are, broad-leaved chives with a mild garlic flavor. The leaves of mature garlic chives are 12 to 15 inches tall and about 1/4 inch wide, with graceful curves at the tips. Attractive white flowers bloom in late summer, on stems as much as twice as tall as the leaves.

Growing Instructions   Nurseries sell small clumps of these perennial plants as potted herbs, and you can also easily grow them from seed. The best time to sow seed, either indoors or directly in the garden, is between January and April. The seedlings look like onion seedlings, little green threads, but they soon become sturdy and easy to transplant.

Garlic chives will grow in ordinary well-prepared garden soil. They are most productive if kept evenly moist. Grow a clump of them or plant them in a wide row.

The Harvest   You can harvest whole plants, then replant for the next year, or pick individual leaves as you need them, leaving the plants to grow. If you do let the plants grow year round, harvest fewer leaves in late summer, while the plants are blooming.

Divide perennial clumps every few years. Just dig the whole clump and cut it into two or more

parts with a shovel. Discard any plants badly damaged by the shovel, then replant the clumps at least 18 inches apart.

In China garlic chives are known as gow choy, and in Japan, nira. In both cuisines they are often used like scallions, the whole plant chopped in stir fries. They are also an ingredient in Southeast Asian cuisines. I use whole plants or just the cut leaves. I toss whole leaves, or pieces no shorter than 4 inches, in a salad, or add 2 inch lengths of leaf to soup just before serving, or chop the leaves finely in an omelet. I use the white flowers, too, in salad, to float in soup, or to add to a bouquet.

Pests and Diseases   Check low in the plants for incipient aphid infestations, especially in the winter. Cut or pull out any dead flower stalks that remain in the fall, to let the center of a clump get more light and air, and, incidentally to make it easier to see any aphids. (See page 137 for aphid control tips.)

Sources
Garlic chive seed: Widely available
Garlic chive plants: Available in local nurseries

GINGER

Zingiber officinale
Ginger Family ❖ *Zingiberaceae*

Ginger prefers warmer weather than our climate provides. Yet, while it is borderline if planted in the open ground, it grows well in a container. That way you can grow it in a bright room, or move it outside to a protected spot whenever days are warm. You can grow a significant amount of ginger in containers. In fact, ginger is so productive that if ignored for too long it will break the pot by simple root pressure!

Growing Instructions   In the spring or early summer, purchase ginger rhizomes from a grocery store. Look for plump, fresh-looking rhizomes, preferably with active buds. The buds begin as cream-colored bumps, then grow to minaret shaped protrusions. Either stage is fine for planting.

If you can't find rhizomes with active buds, buy the healthiest ones you can find and plant them anyway. Dig them up and check them in two weeks to see if buds are beginning to form. If not, just wash

SPICY SZECHUAN CHICKEN

It sounds complex, but the basic plan of this recipe is simple: Chop everything up, sauté the meat, sauté the vegetables, make the sauce, add the meat and vegetables, thicken the sauce. The cooking itself can be done in minutes. The secret is to prepare all the ingredients in advance and have them at hand before you begin. The hot bean sauce is sometimes called Szechuan chile sauce. It comes bottled or canned: store extra sauce in a closed jar in the refrigerator.

1 whole chicken breast
1 medium onion
1 large bell pepper
2 large cloves garlic, finely chopped
1 tablespoon grated or finely chopped ginger
2 tablespoons soy sauce
1 teaspoon sugar
1/4 cup chicken stock (or broth made with instant powdered mix)
3 tablespoons cooking oil
1 tablespoon hot bean sauce
1/2 teaspoon cider vinegar
1/2 teaspoon sesame oil
2 tablespoons cornstarch
2 to 3 green onions (or equivalent in garlic chives or onion lily leaves), cut into 2-inch pieces

Remove the skin from the chicken breast and lift the meat from the bones. Cut the meat into bite-sized pieces, removing any fat or tendons as you work. Put the meat into a bowl. Cut the onion and the bell pepper into pieces about 3/4 inch square and put them into a second bowl. Put the garlic and ginger into a third small bowl. Stir the soy sauce, sugar, and 3 tablespoons of soup stock together in a cup.

Heat 2 tablespoons of the oil in a wok, and when it is hot, add the chicken. Stir-fry at medium temperature for 2 minutes, turning until the surfaces are no longer pink. Remove the chicken from the wok and return it to its dish.

Add another tablespoon of oil to the wok. Heat the oil and then add the onion and bell pepper. Stir-fry at medium temperature for 3 minutes. They should be about half-cooked. Return them to their bowl.

Reduce the heat and add the garlic, ginger, and hot bean sauce. Sauté, while stirring, for 30 seconds, then stir in the soy sauce mixture. Return the meat and vegetables to the wok and cook over medium heat 3 to 5 minutes, stirring occasionally, until the liquid is simmering and the meat and vegetables are cooked. Sprinkle the vinegar and sesame oil over the food and stir again.

To thicken the sauce, mix the cornstarch with the remaining tablespoon of chicken stock, stirring until it is smooth. Pour this mixture over the meat and vegetables. Mix rapidly to avoid lumps, and simmer another minute or so until the sauce thickens. Sprinkle with the chopped green onions and serve immediately over rice. Serves two.

the rhizomes, dry them, and set them aside to eat—some ginger rhizomes just won't grow—and try rhizomes from another source.

If you find rhizomes with good buds, or if your buried rhizomes do begin to sprout, break off 3 to 4 inch pieces of rhizome with one or more good buds and plant them. A 10 inch terra cotta bulb pot should be big enough for three of these pieces. (Bulb pots are shallower than the standard kind.) Plant rhizomes horizontally, about 2 inches under the surface, in good potting mix, with some compost or well-rotted manure mixed in. Keep the container indoors in a warm place, as the rhizomes will rot if the soil isn't warm. However, keep the container out of direct sun, or where it will get only a little sun, until the shoots are well up. Even then, ginger prefers a warm, bright place to hot sun. It would actually not be bothered by our foggy days, if only they were warmer and less windy!

If the rhizomes sprout successfully, they will grow several stems up to 3 or 4 feet tall, each bearing two rows of fragrant narrow leaves. The plants may bloom on short stems near the ground, but this is not common. The closest mine has come so far was to form buds that then shriveled and fell off.

Keep the soil moist at all times, but not soggy, and never let the pot stand in water. Add liquid fertilizer, such as manure tea, fish emulsion, or 10-10-10, every couple of weeks. However if you plan to grow your ginger over the winter, cut back on fertilizer then to let it rest, fertilizing again when the plant begins more active growth.

The Harvest   You can dig ginger in four or five months and eat the young rhizomes, or let them grow eight or nine months to maturity. You can even wait a full year if you like. Whenever you harvest, be sure to save some of the rhizome to replant. If you are keeping a plant for a long time, harvest younger parts of the rhizomes to eat, as the older ones will become less flavorful.

Ginger rhizomes will keep for up to three weeks in the refrigerator. They can also be frozen, in which case the best way to use them is to grate what you need while they are still frozen, then return the rest to the freezer.

Varieties   Ginger has several varieties, but generally only one will appear in U.S. groceries. Ginger plants sold as ornamentals are not necessarily edible.

Sources
Ginger rhizomes: Buy in local grocery stores.

HOPS
Humulus lupulus
Hemp Family ❖ *Cannabaceae*

Hop vines can grow over 30 feet in a single summer if the summer is long and warm enough. Our cool summers may not allow for maximum growth, but the truth is that a full-sized plant would   be too big for many of our urban gardens anyway. Although references agree that hops need full sun, I know of two hops plants growing successfully in a shady backyard (in the northeastern corner of San Francisco). These plants grow over 10 feet each summer and produce plenty of hops, the fruits used in making beer.

Hop vines, with their attractive grape-like leaves, fit nicely into an ornamental garden. They are perennial plants, twining up their supports all summer, dormant in the winter, then sending up new shoots in February or March. If your garden gets enough sun to need summer shade, a hop vine will provide it very prettily. It will also create welcome privacy for summer entertaining.

Hops

Growing Instructions   Hops vines are often started by planting pieces of root, but the mailorder source I have located sells rooted plants, shipping them before they begin active growth in the spring. Plant roots or rooted plants 18 inches apart. Be sure the soil is rich and deeply dug. Keep moist and once growth becomes rapid, give ample water. Plants will need support a couple of months after first shoots appear, and will climb vertical supports more readily than horizontal ones. You will need a tall, sturdy fence, a tall trellis, or several tall poles. When plants die down in winter, you should remove dead vines. Omit the winter mulch suggested for cold-winter areas, as it will only encourage decay in our mild, wet winters. The clump of vines from a single hop root becomes more extensive each season. To keep a plant in bounds, dig straight down all around it in a circle one foot away from the stem. This cuts running roots. Dig out any roots outside of this circle.

Hops bear male and female flowers on separate plants. Only the female flowers produce the resins used in beer making. Because the flowers produce the resins whether or not they are pollinated, you don't need to grow any male plants. You can purchase female plants which have been started by rooted cuttings. Female blossoms are borne under green, papery bracts that make the flower bunches look like little cones.

The Harvest   Cones that are ready to harvest no longer feel damp to the touch, but instead feel papery and light. After touching them, your hand will pick up their odor and feel slightly sticky from the powdery, yellow resin called lupulin. (Wear long sleeves and gloves to handle the plant as you harvest; its hooked hairs may slightly irritate your skin.) Spread the cones of female flowers to dry in a sunny room or in an oven. If you use an oven, keep the temperature below 150° F and leave the door ajar. These dried fruits, called hops, are used to flavor beer. If you do make beer, be sure to return the spent hops to the compost pile.

In most places where hops are grown as a crop for beer production, people also eat the young shoots as a vegetable. They may not be vigorous enough the first year, but after that hop plants sprout so vigorously from the root in spring that you may have to thin out some of the later shoots to keep the plant under control. You can eat these extra shoots, or, if your plant is well established, you can blanch the first shoots to eat, let a few mature, and still eat some of the late ones. To blanch, pile earth over the roots in late winter and dig out the tender stems when the tips emerge through the mound. Sources say to eat these as an asparagus substitute, but a San Franciscan friend who tried them said they were OK, but not especially good.

Sources
   Hops plants: NGN

Lavender
English Lavender
Lavandula angustifolia (L. officinalis)
French Lavender
Lavandula dentata

Spanish Lavender
Lavandula stoechas
Mint Family   ❖   *Labiatae*

Lavenders are plants of the Mediterranean, native to the eastern Pyrenees, throughout Spain and into Portugal. Not much used as culinary herbs, they are grown in local gardens primarily as ornamentals, thriving in gardens that require little water. Lavender is a popular scent for soaps and a common ingredient in sachets and potpourris. The handsome plants have narrow, gray-green leaves and small lavender to purple flowers borne at the top of slender stalks. Lavenders prefer full sun, so should be grown in an unshaded spot; but they will grow and bloom in foggy areas too.

English lavender, the most widely planted species, is also the tallest–to 4 feet tall. Its leaves are up to 2 inches long, with smooth edges. It blooms in the summer, with flower heads an inch or two long. Several dwarfed cultivars are popular for small spaces and for edgings. 'Munstead' is only 18 inches tall with deep lavender flowers. 'Lady', a compact 8 to 10 inch tall plant, is the first type to bloom consistently from seed in the first year.

French lavender, as its scientific name, *L. dentata*, suggests, has toothed leaves. You can recognize it by the distinctively square-angled teeth on the edges of the 1-1/2 inch long leaves. Its flowerheads are topped by a prominent ring of bright purple, petal-like bracts. These plants reach 3 feet, and in areas with mild winters, they bloom almost all year.

Spanish lavender has tiny leaves, only 1/2 inch long, with smooth edges. It is 1-1/2 to 3 feet tall. Its flower heads are topped with a tuft of large purple, petal-like bracts. Flowers form only in the summer.

Growing Instructions   Lavender is best grown from purchased plants, since plants grown from seed will take a couple of years to reach full height. Herb nurseries sell several vaieties of lavender in small containers, and you will also often see larger, one-gallon cans of lavender in nurseries. Space the plants from 8 inches to 4 feet apart, depending on the mature size of the variety you are growing. Lavender will grow best in light soil, with good drainage, and does not require much fertilizer.

The Harvest   For dried lavender to use in sachets or potpourris, cut the stems just as color shows on the flowers, hang them in a dark, airy place, and then strip the dried flowers from the stems. You can also use fresh flowers in bouquets, eat them in salads, or use them to make lavender vinegar. (Chapter 13 for more on edible herb flowers, page 301 for herb vinegar recipe.)

Sources
English lavender plants: JG, NGN, RH, SGS
Munstead plants: JG, NGN, RH
'Lady' English lavender seed: JG, PS, VBS
French lavender plants: RH
Spanish lavender plants: NGN, RH, SGS

LEMON BALM
Melissa officinalis
Mint Family ❖ *Labiatae*

Lemon balm is a perennial with a fine lemon scent. It grows and is used similarly to mint. The leaves are oval, an inch or two long, with toothed edges. Its small white or pale blue flowers bloom in the summer. Lemon balm is well adapted to our climate, preferring cool days and not minding a bit of shade or some fog. One plant is usually enough for a garden, since the plants are up to 2 feet tall and rather bushy.

Growing Instructions   While lemon balm isn't hard to grow from seed, you will probably not want to bother for only one plant. Better to buy it already started. It's an easy herb to grow, although it requires a certain attention to grow it well. It needs a site with soil that is rich and kept moist. If it is grown too dry, its leaves will be pale and not as succulent.

The Harvest   Clip leafy stems as you need them, or shear the tops several times a summer, which will also prevent seed production. Lemon balm may seed itself and become a bit of a nuisance if the seeds fall. Harvest much less in fall and winter, since the plant will grow little then.

Lemon balm can be used as if it were just another kind of mint, good for a refreshing tea and in fruit salads, tabouli and mint sauce. It can be dried, but its lemon scent is much more potent when it's

fresh. You will probably like it, but if you plant too many herbs for tea, it may go to waste despite your best intentions.

Sources
Lemon balm plants: JG, NGN, RH
Or buy plants at local nurseries.

LEMON VERBENA
Aloysia triphylla (Lippia citriodora)
Verbena Family ❖ *Verbenaceae*

This is one of the best of the lemon scented herbs because it holds its scent when dried and also after cooking. Lemon verbena is a tropical shrub that can grow to 10 or more feet tall in its native Chile, Argentina or Peru, but is more likely to be about four feet tall in our cooler climate. Its 3 to 4 inch leaves grow from its stems in whorls of three or four, and it may bear small white to lavender flowers in mid to late summer.

Growing Instructions   Start your lemon verbena by purchasing a rooted plant, rather than starting from seed. Plant it in full sun, in soil that is well drained but fertile, and keep it moist. Avoid a windy site if you can, or stake the plant if wind makes it begin to lean. While our winter temperatures are not cold enough to kill this perennial, don't be surprised if it drops leaves or looks generally unkempt in winter: remember, it is tropical plant. It will look better come spring; or, to help improve its appearance, you can cut it back in late winter, thus encouraging fresh growth.

The Harvest   Tip pinch to use leaves as you need them during the summer growing season. The plant tends to be ungainly and you can improve its shape by your choice of places to pinch it when harvesting. For drying, harvest in August. In addition to using it for tea, try lemon verbena in poultry or fish dishes. It also makes an aromatic addition to potpourri.

Sources
Lemon verbena plants: NGN, RH, SHS
Or buy plants at local nurseries.

LEMONGRASS
Cymbopogon citratus
Grass Family ❖ *Graminae*

Lemongrass plays a central role in providing Southeast Asian dishes with their unique lemony taste. The grass is a native of Southern India and Ceylon and is frequently found growing in gardens throughout Southeast Asian countries. In the tropics this plant can grow to 6 feet tall, but in our area it grows to only a foot or two. Individual leaf blades are about 5/8 inch wide, and feel rough and dry. Groups of leaves grow from somewhat bulbous bases, each mature clump divided into many of these bases with their leaves. This plant will grow throughout the region, however it will grow faster and larger in warmer, sunnier microclimates.

Growing Instructions   Lemongrass rarely flowers, having been propagated by plant divisions for so many centuries. Get it started in your garden by buying a plant or two from the nursery. Or you might be able to root lemongrass stalks you buy at a grocery store. In the spring, look for stalks that are not too dried out, and that have some roots still attached. Put two or three of these in containers of seeding mix soil and keep them moist until they start to grow new leaves, then plant them in the garden.

Plant lemongrass in full sun. It is not fussy about soil, but since it is a perennial, it should be in a site that has been cleared of perennial weeds. Water evenly and moderately. Growth will slow in the winter and the plant may take on a reddish cast and look weatherbeaten. It will be damaged or killed by prolonged frosts. Trim out dead or unattractive leaves in the spring.

The Harvest   Usually the bulbous base of a section of leaves is cut up and added to a soup or other dish. Part of this is tender and can be eaten, and any part that is too tough is removed by diners as they eat. Use lemongrass to season soup, fish, or curries. (See Thai Fish Soup recipe on page 283).

To harvest the bulbous leaf bases, reach close to the ground and separate out a section of leaves joining one base. Use a knife to cut it near the ground. Cut off the leaf tops and peel outer, tough leaves.

Pests Lemongrass rust causes small linear lesions on the leaves. On leaf undersides, you may see the rust-colored spores bulging from the lesions. Remove any plants with rust from your garden and clean up all plant debris. Next season, plant lemongrass in another part of the garden.

Sources
Lemongrass plants: NGN, RH, SGS
Or buy plants at local nurseries.
Or try to root grocery store stems.

MARJORAM
(OR SWEET MARJORAM, KNOTTED MARJORAM, OR ANNUAL MARJORAM)
Origanum majorana (O. hortensis, Majorana hortensis)
Mint Family ❖ *Labiatae*

Marjoram is one of the easiest herbs to grow in our region. With very little care, it grows into a rangy, 2 foot tall, perennial plant. Its leaves are 1/4 to 1 inch long, oval, and gray-green. Its flowers are very small, usually white, although they may be pink. Marjoram is sometimes called knotted marjoram, because of the characteristic rounded "knots" formed by the green bracts of the flower heads.

Many gardeners grow marjoram but call it oregano, and this is not the only confusion surrounding this plant. First, you will sometimes find it sold under its obsolete names, *Origanum hortensis* or *Majorana hortensis*. Also, you may find it listed in gardening books as an annual, because winters only a little colder than ours will kill it. In fact, where winters are really cold, gardeners often substitute *Origanum onites*, a plant commonly, and confusingly, known as pot marjoram—and sometimes sold as oregano (see oregano listing, this chapter). In our region, however, marjoram lives through the winters very well.

Growing Instructions   To grow just a plant or two, purchased marjoram plants are certainly the easiest way to go, although marjoram is not hard to grow from seed. If you do use seed, sow it indoors in early spring. Plant seedlings or purchased plants in a sunny spot, in fertile garden soil and keep plants moderately moist. (This is not one of the herbs, like sage and oregano, that tastes better when it is grown hungry and dry.) Marjoram plants begin to look straggly after a few years and should be replaced or restarted by layering (see page 62).

The Harvest   For fresh use, harvest marjoram

leaves any time. Just cut some stems and strip the leaves from the somewhat woody stems. In our part of the world, marjoram grows most of the year and tends to outproduce our kitchen needs. To keep it from taking up too much space, and to reduce its woody growth, cut the plants to several inches above the ground when you first see forming flower buds. Then cut a second time when more flower heads are forming. Hang these bunches of stems to dry in a dark place with good ventilation.

The flavor of marjoram is strong and sweet and holds up well after drying. Cooking, however, may damage it, so it is often added near the end, or used in dishes that are not cooked long. Try in omelets or to season meats, or use it fresh in salads, salad dressings or herbal vinegar.

Sources
Sweet marjoram plants: RH
Or buy plants at local nurseries.

PEPPERMINT
Mentha × piperita (a cross between M. aquatica *&* M. spicata*)*
SPEARMINT (OR MINT)
Mentha spicata
APPLE MINT
Mentha suaveolens
PINEAPPLE MINT
Mentha suaveolens 'Variegata'
BERGAMOT MINT (OR ORANGE MINT)
Mentha × piperita var. *citrata*
CORSICAN MINT
Mentha requienii
Mint Family ❖ *Labiatae*

Yes, there really is a peppermint and a spearmint plant, though not a doublemint plant. The mints are easy to grow; in fact, some gardeners consider them too easy, since these perennials spread aggressively via horizontal underground stems. Though they can be a nuisance to keep in bounds, they offer plenty of interesting flavors for teas and for seasoning foods.

Oil of peppermint is used to flavor gum, candy and ice cream. While you probably won't go to the trouble of extracting oil from your plants, you can use fresh peppermint to flavor jellies or a sauce for meats, or make peppermint tea from fresh or dried leaves. Peppermint is the kind of mint tea that is most soothing to an upset stomach.

Spearmint can also be used for sauces and teas, and is the mint most commonly used fresh in the recipes of several cuisines. It is in the Middle Eastern tabouli, Indian chutneys, and in Southeast Asian cooking.

Besides these well known mints, there are a host of other mints with good, but less familiar flavors. Some of these are apple mint, pineapple mint, and bergamot mint. Gardeners often buy them, but sometimes can't think of ways to use them. Still, any of these might become personal favorites for any of the various mint uses. All mints make good tea, and a small amount of any mint is good in fruit or lettuce salads, especially if the salads have flowers in them or a dressing containing a bit of honey.

Corsican mint (*Mentha requienii*) differs from the others in that it is more often used as an ornamental groundcover than for culinary uses. It's under an inch tall, with tiny leaves—almost mosslike. It's especially nice between stepping stones, because if it is bruised by a passing foot it releases a very heady mint scent. It is probably not planted more widely because it is a delicate plant, hard to maintain at its peak all year. It may die back in the winter or during a warm spell. Corsican mint usually prefers 50% shade, but you can try it in full sun in foggy areas. Though its main culinary use has been to flavor liqueurs, it can be used as other mints. Try it as a tea, in combination with lemon balm.

Growing Instructions   Mints are best grown outside of your main garden area, since they will spread aggressively. At a minimum, keep mint out of the way of perennial crops like asparagus, and away from perennial herbs like oregano. You won't want to disturb the roots of these plants, but may have to do so in order to remove the competing mint plants.

You should be able to keep a mint under reasonable control by pulling out its runners as you work the nearby soil each season, but you will probably find mint coming up in unexpected places now and then. You might try sinking a section of terra cotta pipe, or a wood or metal barrier, at least 18 inches deep, around a mint bed to slow its spread, but even this may not totally contain it. The only sure way to confine a mint is to grow it in a container. If you do this, give your mint a pot 10 or more inches in diameter and be sure to keep the soil constantly moist.

Mint is most often started from a rooted stem

THE MINT FAMILY

Mint family plants (oregano, sage, savory, and catnip to name just a few) all share certain traits, and mint itself is a clear example. The stems are usually squarish in cross section, the leaves are arranged in opposite pairs, the flowers appear in whorls at the tops of stems. The flowers are small, and most often lavender, but sometimes white, pink or blue. They are two-lipped, the lower lip providing a convenient platform for pollinating insects. When you know these traits, you will discover many a wild or domestic mint relative on your own, although not all mint family plants have pleasant scents or can be used in cooking.

or runner. Plants started this way will grow to productive size much more quickly than plants started from seeds. Also, if you buy a plant grown from a cutting or runner, the scent you smell will be the one you get, while mint plants you start from seeds may be highly variable in scent. Buy your small mint plants in a nursery or get stems or runners with some roots on them from another gardener.

Soil for the mints should be rich and moisture-retaining, but with good drainage. Grown without enough water or in poor soil, the mints will be sorry-looking and slow-growing plants. Mints thrive in full sun in our foggy areas, as long as they get enough water. They prefer partial shade in sunnier areas. If they are not in containers, plant mints 2 feet from each other or from other plants.

The Harvest   Harvest mint stem tips or whole branches as needed. Mint grows more rapidly in the summer, allowing more frequent harvests. Cut off any flowers, to encourage leafy growth. Some mints, like spearmint, grow well enough in the winter to allow moderate harvests all year, while others, like peppermint, will decline drastically in winter and put out a flush of growth in the spring.

Pests and Diseases   Peppermint is subject to a rust, which does not change the flavor, and rarely kills the plant, but disfigures the leaves with rust-colored spots. Since mine got the rust, I just harvest leafy stem tips early in the season, before they are infected. Later, when rust spots appear on the upper leaves, I stop harvesting. Despite this, I am still able to fill my large tin with dried leaves each year from only one or two plants.

Sources
Peppermint plants: BH, JG, NGN, RH
Spearmint plants: BH, JG, NGN, PS, RH
Apple mint plants: BH, JG, NGN, RH
Pineapple mint plants: JG, NGN, RH
Bergamot mint plants: NGN, RH
Corsican mint plants: NGN, RH
Or buy mint plants at local nurseries.

MUSTARD SEED (BLACK MUSTARD)
Brassica nigra
FLORIDA BROADLEAF MUSTARD
Brassica juncea
Mustard Family   ❖ *Cruciferae*

Mustard seed is used as a seasoning in both Indian and European cuisines. Commercial mustard consists primarily of crushed mustard seed and vinegar. To produce mustard seed, just let either of the above mustards go to seed. Planted in the spring, they will mature seed over the summer. Grow them as you would mustards for greens, in rich, well-watered soil. Thin them to stand 8 to 12 inches apart. (See page 222 for more on growing mustards.)

Harvest the seed stalks when the pods are brown and some are just beginning to split open. You may have to cover the ripening seed stalks with mesh bags or other porous material to avoid sharing your crop with birds. After cutting the stalks, dry the seed pods for several days in a dark, warm place, then break them open and winnow out the seeds.

Use black mustard seed in curries and in Indian cooking in general, as well as in such European-style soups as split pea. In Indian cooking, it is usually used whole, just toasted slightly in oil before the other ingredients are added. In European cooking, mustard seed is usually crushed before it is used. Florida broadleaf mustard seed is sometimes mixed with black mustard seed to impart a slightly different flavor to mustard condiments.

Sources
Black mustard seed: GG, RH
Florida broadleaf mustard seed: JG, RCS, SB, SGS, VBS

OREGANO
OREGANO (GREEK OREGANO, SICILIAN OREGANO, WINTER SWEET MARJORAM)
Oregano heracleoticum (Origanum vulgare hirtum)
(OREGANO, SICILIAN OREGANO)
Origanum × majorana
ITALIAN OREGANO (OREGANO, WILD MARJORAM)
Origanum vulgare
POT MARJORAM
Origanum onites
Mint Family ❖ *Labiatae*

Plants of several separate species in the genus *Origanum* are called oregano. Complicating the picture, commercial oregano often contains several herbs, blended for flavor. It may contain more than one *Origanum* species, and may also contain leaves of sage and thyme, a Mexican herb called *Lippia graveolens*, or several other plants.

Greek Oregano

I can't tell exactly what is in your store-bought "oregano," but I can tell you that you will get good oregano flavor from plants of *Origanum heracleoticum*, sometimes called *O. vulgare hirtum*. As an alternative, try a new hybrid between oregano and sweet marjoram, which is in the same genus. It is sold as *Origanum × majorana*, or Sicilian oregano.

O. heracleoticum is a low plant, whose flower stems may grow to a foot or so. The leaves are oval to longish oval, less than an inch long, and a muted green. Flowers are small, in loose whorls at the ends of the stem, and are white. The leaves are somewhat hairy. *O. × majorana* also has white flowers and does not set seed.

Origanum vulgare is also commonly called oregano. It is often called Italian oregano, wild

marjoram, and sometimes even Greek oregano. It is very similar in appearance to *O. heracleoticum* when small, but grows to 2 1/2 feet tall. When it blooms, the flowers are born in heads that are loose and flat across the top. The bracts behind the flowers are most often purple, and the flowers lavender. The plant isn't much good as a cooking herb, though the flowers make a nice addition to a bouquet or, dried, to a wreath. The scent of this plant is much milder than Greek oregano, and many cooks think it is too weak to be of much use.

A third species, *O. onites*, is sometimes listed as oregano, sometimes as pot marjoram. It may be grown in cold winter areas as a substitute for sweet marjoram, or may be offered as oregano. In either case, its flavor will probably be less sweet than marjoram and less pungent than oregano.

You may see Dittany of Crete, *Origanum dictamus*, sold as oregano. It is grown mainly ornamentally for its pretty pink conelike blooms.

Growing Instructions All the oreganos can be grown fairly easily from seed sown indoors in the spring, but as the flavor of the seedlings tends to vary significantly, even within a species, this is not the recommended procedure. The most certain way to get the scent and therefore the flavor you want is to buy a plant you have been able to smell first. As you will not need more than one or two plants, this will not be expensive to do.

Plant your oregano in a sunny spot, in light, well-drained, not overly rich soil. Keep it moist at first, but don't overwater it as the season progresses. Too rich or too wet a soil will lesson the flavor of this native of the dry Mediterranean hillsides.

In fact, our cool, damp air probably reduces the flavor of oregano, but if you start with a good, strongly scented *O. heracleoticum*, you will still have an herb worthy of great pizza and lasagne.

The Harvest Harvest fresh leaves as needed and cut stems for drying as the plants come into bloom. Hang stems to dry in a dark, well-ventilated place. Besides in Italian dishes featuring tomatoes, use oregano in beef, lamb, fish, cheese or bean dishes, and in soups and salads.

Shape oregano plants as you harvest, by cutting back long, rangy stems. This will also encourage the plant to send up new shoots from the ground. Never cut off more than 50% of the leaves at one time, though, so it will have enough energy left to regrow quickly. Despite your pruning and shaping, oregano plants tend to become unattractive in a few years. If you layer a few stems, they will root and provide new plants to replace the aging one (see page 62).

Sources

O. *heracleoticum* plants: RH, SGS
O. × *majorana* plants: NGN
Or buy oregano plants at local nurseries

PARSLEY

Petroselinum crispum
var. *crispum* or *P.*
crispum var.
neapolitanum
Parsley Family ❖
Umbelliferae

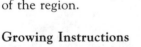

Even if you ignore the parsley sprig at the edge of the restaurant plate, there is still plenty of reason to grow parsley. Chopped fresh parsley is a great addition to many dishes, and is a major ingredient in the Middle Eastern cracked wheat salad, tabouli. You can grow enough parsley to replace dried parsley flakes with the fresh herb in your recipes throughout the year, in all parts of the region.

Parsley
flowering stem

Growing Instructions

Most nurseries carry small parsley plants, and these are the easiest way to get parsley started. Two to six plants are usually plenty. Parsley also grows easily from seed, but you must have patience during its long germination period. Folklore has it that parsley seed goes to the devil and back nine times before it sprouts. Actually, that seems an ambitious journey to complete in three to six weeks, but six weeks can seem like an eternity to water a flat in which no seedlings have appeared. It is probably safest to start parsley indoors, even when outside temperatures are warm, since it is easier to keep track of it in a container in the house than in a patch of the garden.

Sow parsley seed indoors in December through February for an early crop, as late as May if you forget to do it earlier. Seed you sow in late summer or early fall will grow fine too, but the life of the plants will be shorter, as they will probably go to seed in the spring, along with plants you started earlier in the year. You can get the seed to germinate a few days faster by soaking it overnight in warm water. After it has been soaked, pat the seed dry with paper towels, so it is easier to handle when you sow it.

Plant parsley in rich soil that you can easily keep moist. Choose a location either in full sun or in partial shade. Set your plants 6 to 12 inches apart. Keep them free from weeds.

The Harvest If your purchased or homegrown plants are ready to go in the ground in February, you can begin to harvest them beginning in March or April, as soon as they have ten or twelve leaves. Cut leaves at the soil level, even if you don't choose to use the stems. Biennials like parsley will usually produce leaves all year long, then bloom and go to seed the following spring. Though some references say that overwintered plants become tough and bitter, our cool, moist springs seem to bring out the best in even last year's parsley.

When a plant first begins to form flower stalks, they are still tender and you can cut them to eat. By cutting them, you stimulate the plant to make more leaves and flower stalks. Eventually the seeding process takes over. The stalks become too tough to eat, and the plant stops making new leaves. Even then, however, you can use parsley stalks to flavor soup stocks, discarding them before you use the broth (see recipe, page 349.) Occasionally, plants will go to seed in the first summer. When you see this beginning to happen, just purchase a few nursery plants to replace them.

If you let a parsley plant go to seed in your garden, it will often reseed itself, the new plants coming up the following winter or spring. You can move these volunteer plants to a different location, if you do so while they are very young. After the plants grow much over 4 inches tall, they will be set back seriously by a move. This is because parsley depends mainly on a tap root, one long, central root, like a carrot's but skinnier, which is easily damaged in a transplanting. (If you really want to move a larger parsley plant, do it like this: Holding a shovel at a slight angle, push it into the roots several times, cutting the tap root eight or nine inches below the surface. Water the plant, and leave it alone for 10 to 14 days, to let its side roots grow. At the end of this time, water it again. The next day, lift the plant and transplant it.)

Parsley may be added at the beginning of cooking, as when it is cooked to flavor broth. Or, it can also be chopped and sprinkled over food when it is fully cooked, just before it is served.

Varieties and Related Species The parsley most often used for a garnish is curled leaf parsley, *P. crispum* var. *crispum*. Several cultivars of curled leaf parsley are available, some more curled than others. While some people eat their parsley garnishes, and others ignore them, few realize that the traditional purpose of a parsley garnish was to sweeten one's breath after a meal. Certainly try eating it if you want to be rid of garlic or other strong odors. Curled leaf parsley is also decorative when cut coarsely and sprinkled over salads or cooked vegetables.

Flat leaf or Italian parsley (*P. crispum* var. *neapolitanum*) is more productive, and some cooks think it's better flavored. Its flat leaves are easier to chop than curled ones. Use it in salad dressings, sauces, soups, stuffings for poultry, and spaghetti sauce. Flat leaf parsley is also the better choice for drying, as it holds its flavor better when dry. To dry it, discard the thick stems and dry the leaves only. Dry them at 200° F to keep their green color. A third variety of parsley is grown mainly for its thickened root, although its leaves are also acceptable as a parsley substitute. This is *P. crispum* var. *tuberosum*, known as Hamburg or parsnip rooted parsley. For information on how to grow this vegetable, see Chapter 11.

Another plant very similar to parsley is Japanese Parsley (or Mitsuba). This Asian herb is really in another plant genus: *Cryptotaenia*. Directions for growing it are below.

Sources
> Curled and flat-leaved parsley plants and seed: Widely available
> Plants and seeds may also be purchased at local nurseries.

PARSLEY, JAPANESE (OR MITSUBA)
Cryptotaenia japonica
Carrot Family ❖ *Umbelliferae*

Japanese parsley looks like a cross between celery and parsley and tastes much like Italian parsley. This perennial plant grows to 3 feet tall. Here is a denizen of moist, shady places that actually suffers if it is exposed to too much sun. It should be grown in at least partial shade to prevent it from becoming pale and mottled, or in full shade if your garden gets a lot of sun.

Sow seed for Japanese parsley in rich soil in early spring, and keep the soil moist during the entire time it is growing. It is usually grown as an annual, sown as a succession crop, and harvested whole while young and tender. However you can harvest by the leaf from older plants. Leave a plant or two to produce seed for replanting. Chinese and Japanese cooks use the leaves and stems to add their distinctive flavor to stir fries. They can be used whenever you would use parsley or cutting celery. Try them with fish or shrimp, in an omelet, as a seasoning for vegetables, or in cucumber salad.

Sources
> Japanese parsley seed: ABL, EV, JG, KSC, NGN, RH

PERILLA, (BEEFSTEAK PLANT), SHISO (JAPANESE), JI SOO (CHINESE)
Perilla frutescens
Mint Family ❖ *Labiatae*

Here's an herb quite unfamiliar to Western palates, but common in Japanese and Chinese cooking. It tastes spicy, some cooks say like both ginger and cinnamon, but there is really nothing else like it. The plant is pretty, rather like a coleus with single-colored leaves, and can be nestled in among your flowers as well as your vegetables.

Growing Instructions Perilla is an annual grown from seed sown either indoors or in place. The seeds need light to germinate, so just press them into the surface of a well-prepared seedbed, then tamp the soil down around them. They germinate in a week to ten days, and are ready to plant out in 6 to 8 weeks. In the garden, plant perilla in any good, well draining garden soil. While it is tolerant of various types of soils, it may not do well in unamended clay. Plant it in the sun or in partial shade and keep it moist. Side-dress perilla lightly with manure tea or other fertilizer during the season, if you are harvesting heavily.

While perilla is generally considered a summer annual, it is tolerant of our colder temperatures and may actually do better in our colder months than in our summer, and in cooler locations rather than warmer areas. Try sowing a few seeds every couple of months from February on to see what works best in your location. Transplant or thin perilla to stand 6 inches apart.

MAIN DISH RISOTTO

Authentic Italian risotto is made with white rice and just a bit of Parmesan cheese, but this heartier version is a great vegetarian main dish and a showcase for the rich flavor of rosemary. True saffron is very expensive, so I use American saffron, which is quite reasonable. You can find American saffron in stores that sell herbs and spices in bulk.

2 tablespoons oil
1 medium onion, chopped finely
1 cup short grain brown rice
2 cups water or stock
1 teaspoon minced fresh rosemary or 1/2 teaspoon crushed dried leaves
3 tablespoons minced fresh parsley leaves
1/2 teaspoon dried American saffron (safflower)
1 1/2 cup grated jack cheese (or more)

Heat the oil and sauté the onion until soft but not brown. Add the brown rice and sauté, stirring constantly until the grains become translucent, only a couple of minutes. Stir in the rosemary, parsley, and American saffron. Add water (one of the world's noisiest cooking procedures), and stir once or twice. Turn the heat down and let the rice simmer, covered, until the water is absorbed and the rice tender. This should take about 30 minutes. Spread grated cheese over the top and put the lid back on for a couple of minutes to let it melt. Cut and serve. Serves four.

The Harvest   You can begin to harvest by using your thinnings, then pick leaves and stem tips from the time the plants are only a foot tall. They can reach 2 to 3 feet tall at maturity, but probably won't get that tall if you are harvesting from them. You should be able to pick leaves for at least a month, before the plants go to seed, at around 3-1/2 months.

A word of caution: perilla, like many herbs, is O.K. in small amounts, but should not be eaten in large quantities like a vegetable, as it contains potentially harmful chemicals called ketones. These substances are naturally produced in the body during the digestion of some foods, but they are harmful in large quantities, so are one of the byproducts the body eliminates. Too much perilla could introduce too much of them all at once.

Varieties   There are red-leaved and green-leaved perilla varieties. These are grown the same way, but used a little differently. The red ones are more pungent and contain more ketones. They are used medicinally, as a garnish, and also (sparingly) as a seasoning.

On the plant, the leaves are a very dark red-purple. When used as a pickling spice, they add a red color. In fact, they provide the red color of Umeboshi plums. Try a little red-leaved perilla chopped into black bean sauce, to season stir fried or steamed crab or shrimp. Red perilla is also pretty enough to appear in the ornamental border; it was a favorite of Victorian gardeners.

Green-leaved perilla can be eaten in larger amounts, has a milder flavor, and is more tender than red perilla, so it makes a nice addition to salads. When it is used as a seasoning, more is needed to make up for the mild flavor. Try two tablespoons of chopped green perilla in a pound of ground beef for meat loaf or patties. Another way to use it is to add the stem tips with flowers to a plate as an edible garnish.

Sources
Green perilla seed: ABL, EV, JG, JSS, KSC, NGN, RH, SB, SOC
Red perilla seed: ABL, DD, EV, GG, JG, JSS, KSC, NGN, OBG, PTS, RH, SB, SOC, SGS

ROSEMARY

Rosmarinus officinalis
Mint Family ❖ *Labiatae*

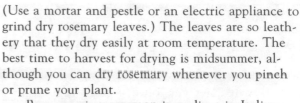

Rosemary is a woody shrub with deep green, leathery, needlelike leaves, 1/2 to 1-1/2 inches long. The small flowers are most commonly blue. The plant usually grows 2 to 4 feet tall, but may reach 6 feet. There are also prostrate types that creep along the ground or hang picturesquely over rocks and retaining walls. This is a good ornamental plant for all parts of the region, being tough and evergreen and requiring little water. While it thrives in full sun, it seems not to mind the fog. Once you learn to recognize it, you will notice it often in both private and public gardens.

Growing Instructions   One plant of rosemary is generally enough, or maybe more than enough, since it grows vigorously to a large size. It's best to buy a plant, because it grows so slowly from seed.

Rosemary is native to dry places along both the European and African shores of the Mediterranean. In your garden it will also grow best in light, sandy soil that is on the dry side. Though it appreciates occasional water in summer, overwatering may cause the roots to rot. If your soil tends to heavy clay, amend it well to assure good drainage before you plant this perennial herb.

The Harvest   Break off stem tips or branches when you need rosemary, as well as to shape the plant and control its size. An untended upright plant will send out ungainly branches and age to a large, oddly shaped shrub, fine on a windswept hill in Spain, or in a large garden, but maybe not what you had in mind for your small, tame herb garden. Prostrate types will be more attractive if you pinch them to keep the draping branches from completely covering the embankment. Thin them and stagger the ends, rather than cutting them all off in a straight line.

Whole fresh rosemary stem tips can be cooked in foods, to lend flavor before being plucked out and discarded. Fresh leaves, stripped from the stems, can be used chopped; dried ones need to be ground.

(Use a mortar and pestle or an electric appliance to grind dry rosemary leaves.) The leaves are so leathery that they dry easily at room temperature. The best time to harvest for drying is midsummer, although you can dry rosemary whenever you pinch or prune your plant.

Rosemary is a common ingredient in Italian cuisine. It is used more subtly in the cuisines of France, Greece and Spain. It's good with lamb, in fact with most meats, and with fish and shellfish. It is also used in soups, spaghetti sauce, in rice dishes, breads, and to season vegetables. One of my favorite uses is on the Italian flat bread known as focaccia. Just before baking, the dough is brushed with olive oil then sprinkled with rosemary. Don't add too much rosemary to any dish though, as the flavor, reminiscent of pine, can be overpowering. Some flavors that hold their own against it well are onion, garlic, parsley and wine.

Varieties   Check nurseries for different rosemary cultivars, all of which are fine for culinary purposes. Among full-sized ones, two attractive ones are majorca rosemary, with pink flowers, and 'Collingwood Ingram' with graceful branches and blue-violet flowers.

The creepers include 'Prostratus' and 'Lockwood de Forest.' The latter has deeper blue flowers and brighter green leaves than most rosemary varieties.

Sources
Rosemary plants: CG, JG, PS, SGS
Prostratus: NGN
Lockwood de Forest: RH
These and other rosemary cultivars are available in local nurseries.

SAGE
GARDEN SAGE
Salvia officinalis
VARIEGATED SAGE
(OR TRICOLOR SAGE)
Salvia tricolor
PINEAPPLE SAGE
Salvia elegans (S. rutilans)
CLARY SAGE
Salvia sclarea
Mint Family ❖ *Labiatae*

While there are hundreds of sages, only a few are used in

cooking. The sage commonly available in grocery stores is *Salvia officinalis*, garden sage. This is a perennial plant, a foot or two tall, which bears stems of bright violet, pink or white flowers in the late spring. The leaves are oblong, 1 to 2-1/2 inches, grayish-green, with a roughly textured surface. Garden sage is another of the Mediterranean herbs, a native of lands along the north and down the eastern side of the Mediterranean Sea, and therefore well suited to our similar climate. *Salvia tricolor* is a very similar species, with leaves mottled white, purple, and pink. It is so similar, in fact, that some sage sold as S. *tricolor* may actually be a similar-looking cultivar of S. *officinalis*.

Two other species of sage are used less commonly in cooking. The fruity flavor of *Salvia elegans* reminds some people of pineapple. This Mexican native is often grown for its vivid red blooms, which attract hummingbirds and bees. The perennial plant grows 3 or more feet tall and almost as wide.

Salvia sclarea, or clary sage, is the traditional flavoring, together with elder flowers, for muscatel wine. It's a biennial, but it is usually grown from seed in spring and kept only one year. 3 or more feet tall, it has strongly scented leaves and, in the second year, pale blue or white flowers.

Growing Instructions Although perennial sages are not difficult to start from seed, seedlings are so slow to mature that most gardeners buy plants in pots. Sages are adaptable to varied local conditions. They will grow in rock garden conditions of poor and dry soil. They will also grow in good vegetable garden soil as long as the drainage is adequate. They thrive in full sun, but will also do all right in foggy areas. In short, they are not very fussy.

The Harvest Gather sage leaves whenever you need them. They are best used fresh. If you do pick for drying, do it either just before the plant blooms or later in summer when the leaves are fully grown. Dry leaves quickly with ventilation, to prevent blackening.

Trim back your garden sage plant, or plants of S. *tricolor*, every spring, removing woody growth to stimulate more tender shoots. Replace these plants every three or four years when they get too woody. Buy new plants or try layering to propagate new plants from your old ones (see page 62). Also, look under the plants, as seedlings may sprout there from fallen seed.

Garden sage, like rosemary, is an herb of hearty flavor. Although it is said to taste even stronger in hot climates, locally grown sage is very flavorful. Sage is a traditional ingredient in poultry stuffing and in sausages. In fact, you can make a nice low-fat sausage for breakfast patties by working finely chopped sage, garlic powder, salt, and pepper into fresh, lean (uncured) ground pork. Sage is also used in various meat, fish and cheese dishes, as well as with peas and beans.

Harvest pineapple sage by pinching off leafy stem tips, shaping the plant as you harvest. Use the leaves to make tea or to flavor fruit dishes. The brilliant red flowers are striking in fruit salads or decorating a dessert. Clary sage leaves have a strong scent; they can be used to make tea.

Varieties and Related Species 'Holt's Mammoth' is a large-leaved cultivar of S. *officinalis*, great for big sage users. The variety *nanum* is a dwarf form for those who want just an occasional bit of sage. 'Icteria', has two-tone gold and green leaves; 'Purpurescens' has purple ones.

If you are shopping for clary sage, don't confuse it with Salvia horminium 'Claryssa', a pretty annual plant grown as an ornamental.

Sources
  Garden sage plants: JG, PS
  Holt's Mammoth: NGN, RH
  Icteria: NGN
  Purpurescens: NGN
  Nana: NGN
  Tricolor sage plants: GG, JG, NGN
  Pineapple sage plants: GG, JG, NGN, SGS
  Clary sage seed: ABL, RCS, SB, SOC, SGS, T&M, VBS
  Or buy plants at local nurseries

SUMMER SAVORY
Satureja hortensis
WINTER SAVORY
Satureja montana (S. illyrica, S. intricata)
Mint Family ❖ *Labiatae*

Summer and winter savory are herbs with small, bright green leaves and a peppery flavor. Summer savory, the annual, is milder in flavor than winter savory. Both are used in soups and stuffings as well as to season snap beans. Summer savory is mild enough to also be good as a seasoning for salads.

Growing Instructions Summer savory grows easily from seed. Plant it in the spring, 1/8 inch deep. Choose a sunny part of your garden with moderately rich, well-draining soil. Give the plants moderate water and thin them to stand 6 inches apart. They will grow rapidly to a maximum of 18 inches tall. Even though savory is so easy to grow from seed, gardeners sometimes buy plants, because one plant is often enough.

Winter savory is a perennial, somewhat woody, plant, 6 to 12 inches tall, spreading to 2 feet wide. It is most commonly started from small plants, though it can be started from seed in the same way you start summer savory. It doesn't need as rich a soil or as much water, and, in fact, will probably live longer in leaner, drier soil.

The Harvest   Begin to harvest summer savory by tip pinching when the plants are 6 inches tall. Continue to harvest stem tips all summer, thus preventing the plant from blooming as long as possible. When it finally is impossible to prevent blooming, wait for the lavender or white flowers to open, then pull the whole plant and hang it in a well-ventilated place to dry.

Our warm winters allow us to harvest fresh winter savory fresh all year, making lighter pickings in the winter months when growth is slower. Keep the plants well-shaped by trimming back any branches that become ungainly. Replace the plants every few years, or whenever they become unproductive. Use winter savory leaves fresh or dried. When dry, they are hard and except for use in a bouquet garni, must, like rosemary leaves, be crushed before they are used.

Varieties   Winter savory, with its preference for dryish soil, is nice spilling over the rocks of a rock garden. One cultivar, 'Procumbens,' only 6 inches tall, is particularly useful for this purpose.

Sources
> Summer savory seed: Widely available
> Winter savory plants: JG, NGN
> Procumbens: NGN
> Winter savory seed: ABL, BG, JG, NGN, OBG, PTS, RH, SB, VBS
> Or buy savory plants or seed at local nurseries

SWEET WOODRUFF (OR WOODRUFF)
Gallium odoratum (Asperula odorata)
Madder Family ❖ *Rubiaceae*

Although sweet woodruff doesn't have many uses, the fact that it is very pretty and has the ability to grow well in shady places, add considerably to its appeal. This perennial plant grows low to the ground, never over a foot tall, and usually quite a bit less. Whorls of six to eight leaves surround the stems at intervals, and small, four-petalled, white flowers bloom at the tops of the stems in late spring. The leaves have little scent when fresh; but surprisingly, when dry they release a subtle, sweet scent which has been described as a combination of sweet hay and vanilla.

Sweet Woodruff

Growing Instructions   Purchase woodruff plants, as seeding is not easy. (The seed may take 200 days to germinate.) Woodruff grows wild in European forests, particularly under beech trees. The soil there is moist, shady and rich with humus. You should imitate these conditions with well-amended garden soil, kept moist. Deep shade isn't necessary in our foggy area, but at least partial shade is a good idea in all but the foggiest microclimates. (And if you do have a shady problem spot in your garden, woodruff will grow there nicely.) Woodruff will spread, though the spreading plants are relatively easy to control by pulling them out where you don't want them. Still, do watch where woodruff is spreading, as it can be a bit of a problem if it gets mixed up with another perennial.

The Harvest   Pick small sprigs as needed, but make any major harvest just before the plants bloom. The leaves will dry quickly in warm shade. In Germany, a sprig of dried woodruff is traditionally added to sweet white wine to make May wine. You can make your own May wine by adding woodruff to a white wine, then restoppering and refrigerating it for a couple of days. The French add woodruff to champagne too, but I suspect this has to be done in the bottling process to avoid losing the bubbles. You can give apple juice a woodruff flavor by steeping the herb in it for a couple of days. Or, you might like woodruff tea. Finally, woodruff sachets will scent a linen closet pleasantly.

Sources
> Sweet woodruff plants: JG, NGN, PS, RH
> Or buy plants at local nurseries

TARRAGON, FRENCH

Artemesia dracunculus var. *sativa* (*Artemesia redowski*)
Sunflower Family ❖ *Compositae*

Many herbs have large variations in flavor within a single species. This is especially true of tarragon. One variety has an exquisite flavor; the others are quite unremarkable. I learned this difference the hard way. Someone planted tarragon seed in the herb bed of my community garden. After it grew into a typically ungainly Russian tarragon plant, I harvested some and tried to learn to love it. But try as I might, I couldn't develop any enthusiasm for its rather nondescript flavor.

If I had read up on tarragon first, though, I would have been suspicious as soon as I learned ours was grown from seed. True French tarragon, *A. dracunculus* var. *sativa*, rarely even blooms, let alone sets seed. It is propagated almost entirely by cuttings. So if you want to grow delicious tarragon, start with a French tarragon plant.

French tarragon has linear leaves, 1 to 3 inches long. The plant is quite variable in size. Most that I have seen locally are 6 to 8 inches tall, but plants 3 inches to 3 feet tall are possible. The stem bases lie on the ground, then turn upright. They also seem to vary considerably in vigor, some barely growing, others spreading rapidly. So if your plant seems very weak, you might try one from another source, or look for a friend with a vigorous one who will give you a start.

Growing Instructions   Transplant French tarragon into moderately rich soil, well amended so it can be kept moist without waterlogging. Plant in full sun or partial shade.

In its native range from Southern Europe to Asia, tarragon gets yearly periods of winter dormancy. Our mild winters may lead to a premature decline after a few years. Tarragon does get some rest in our winters though, in fact mine disappears completely for several months. If this happens to you, mark your plant's location with a stake and watch for it in the spring.

Plants may be reproduced by digging rooted stems, or with root cuttings. To take root cuttings, separate the roots with care, cut several 1 inch root tip sections and transplant them.

The Harvest   Pick tarragon stem tips and use fresh leaves as needed, being sure not to take more than half of the plant at once. Drying often damages tarragon's flavor, but it can be done if you do it carefully. Harvest leaves for drying in June, being careful not to bruise them, and dry them in a single layer in a warm room. Tarragon also makes a classic herb vinegar. Gather it in June and stuff fresh leafy stems into a bottle. Fill the bottle with white wine vinegar and cover it tightly. It will be ready to use after two months, when you can remove the herb if you wish. Try tarragon in salads and cream soups, and in dishes with chicken, fish, eggs or cheese.

Sources
French tarragon plants: CG, GG, JG, NGN, PS, RH, SGS
Or buy plants at local nurseries

TARRAGON, WINTER (OR MEXICAN TARRAGON OR SWEET MACE)

Tagetes lucida
Sunflower Family ❖
Compositae

Winter tarragon, a type of marigold, makes a credible substitute for true French tarragon. Its flavor is quite similar, although it lacks some of the subtle undertones of true tarragon. Use

Winter Tarragon

its fresh leaves in the winter when French tarragon is dormant. Winter tarragon is a half-hardy perennial, meaning that it should do well through all but our most severe winters.

Winter tarragon leaves are narrow, slightly toothed medium green, and up to 3 inches long. The plant grows a foot or two tall, bearing a few small, yellow, marigold-type flowers in the fall.

Plants are sometimes available in local nurseries. You may find seed, but starting with plants gives you the advantage of checking the scent before you buy. Seed or transplant it in the spring, in a sunny spot that has good garden soil with adequate drainage. Check the plant each spring for winter damage, and remove any dead leaves or branches. As with many other herbs, if the plant begins to look ungainly after a couple of seasons, replace it.

Harvest leaves as needed, especially in the fall and winter, but also in the rest of the year, to use any way you would use true tarragon (see above). They are especially nice in salads. This herb is far better used fresh, but does retain some scent if dried carefully and stored in a closed jar as soon as it is dry. Follow instructions for drying French tarragon.

Sources
Winter tarragon plants: NGN, or buy at local nurseries
Winter tarragon seed: DD, RCS, NGN, NSS, SB, SGS

THYME
COMMON THYME
(OR ENGLISH THYME)
Thymus vulgaris
LEMON THYME
Thymus x citrodorus
CARAWAY THYME
Thymus herba-barona
Mint Family ❖ *Labiatae*

Gardeners grow several species of thyme, some for culinary purposes, others as ornamental ground-covers. If it is a cooking herb you want, these three are your best bets. All are low-growing perennial plants that thrive in dry conditions–good candidates for a rock garden.

Common or English thyme, *T. vulgaris*, is the thyme you buy from a spice rack. It's a small plant, 6 to 15 inches high, with very small leaves. Whorls of tiny white or lavender flowers bloom along the upper stems in spring and summer. Lemon thyme, *T. x citrodorus*, is a cross between *T. vulgaris* and a thyme known as *T. pulegioides*. It has a lemony scent and can be used in the same ways as common thyme. Caraway thyme, *Thymus herba-barona*, grows only 2 to 5 inches high, forming a flat mat of leaves. It is valued for its caraway scent.

Growing Instructions   While thyme can be grown from seed, starting with plants is much easier and faster. Plant them in soil that is sandy, or well amended to make it very light. Keep established plants on the dry side.

The Harvest   Harvest thyme as needed, while allowing the plant to grow. You can shape the plant as you harvest, pinching off stem tips that are growing in ungainly directions. For drying, harvest most of the plant in the early summer, just before it blooms. Let the plant grow back, and don't harvest so heavily again until the same time the next year. The plants become woody with age and may die out in the center after three or four years. When this happens, replace them with a newly purchased plant or try dividing the plant.

The various culinary thymes are strongly flavored herbs and withstand cooking without losing their flavors. This trait made thyme one of the classic ingredients of a bouquet garni. Try thyme with any meat, fowl, fish, or with shrimp, and in soups or salads.

Varieties and Related Species   Common thyme has several varieties, with somewhat different scents, including one known as French thyme—the one most often used in French cooking. Other cultivars, with silver and golden leaves and two-tone green and gold, are not as predictably useful for cooking. Like common thyme, *T. x citrodorus* has golden and silver variegated cultivars, but these are good cooking herbs.

If a thyme is listed as "creeping thyme", it is not likely to be much of a cooking herb. There is some confusion in names here, but creeping thyme is likely to be *T. serphyllum* or one of several similar species sold under this name. They make nice groundcovers, but have little flavor.

Sources
Common thyme plants:
    English thyme: NGN, RH
    French thyme: JG, NGN, RH
Lemon thyme plants:
    Green-leaved: JG, NGN, SGS, RH
    Variegated leaves: GG, NGN, RH, SGS
Caraway thyme plants: JG, NGN, RH
Or buy thyme plants at local nurseries

YERBA BUENA
Satureja douglasii
Mint Family ❖ *Labiatae*

Yerba buena, which means "the good herb," is the Spanish name for a plant that was known and used by California Indians long before the Spanish came. Indians brewed it into a tea to calm the stomach. It was also one of the herbs that they rubbed on their bodies before a deer hunt, to disguise their human scent. Early European settlers used the plant for tea also, and Yerba Buena became

Yerba buena

the name of the Spanish colonial village located on the present site of San Francisco.

Yerba buena is a low, trailing plant. Its arching stems lace through other plants along the ground in coastal redwood country, especially in small meadowy clearings. Its leaves are arranged on the stems in opposite pairs, rounded in shape, 1/2 to 1 inch long, and wavy on the edges. Its flowers are typical two-lipped, mint family blossoms, white or lavender. The scent of the plant is minty, with a touch of lime.

In the wild, yerba buena thrives in moderately fertile, sandy soil. If it is not watered by seepage from a natural spring, it declines in the summer. It will look much fuller and prettier in a garden, where you can give it rich soil that's kept moist in the dry season. In sunnier parts of our region yerba buena can take some shade, but in foggier microclimates, plant it in full sun.

Harvest by clipping the stems partway back. Use leaves fresh or dried to make tea. As it is a New World herb, yerba buena isn't used in the Old World cuisines that are the basis of most of our cooking, but do try substituting it for other mints in your recipes.

Sources

Yerba Buena Plants: Best to look for plants in local nurseries, especially those specializing in native plants, or at plant sales of the California Native Plant Society. For help locating nurseries, see the book *Where on Earth*, listed in Appendix V, Suggested Reading. The California Native Plant Society is listed in Appendix VI, Resources for Gardeners.

HERB CHART

Herb	Type	Started by	Fertility	Water	Sun	Height	Veg Repro
Anise Hyssop	perennial	plant/seed	rich	moderate	sun	1–3'	division
Basil	annual	plant/seed	rich	moist	sun	8"–2'+	—
Bay Laurel	tree	plant	moderate	dry	s/ps	40'	cuttings
Bay, California	tree	plant	moderate	moderate	s/sh	60'	cuttings
Borage	annual	seed	most	moderate	sun/ps	3'	—
Catnip	perennial	plant/seed	rich	dry/mod	sun	2–3'	division
Camomile, English	perennial	plant	moderate	moderate	sun/ps	1'	division
Camomile, German	annual	seed	moderate	moderate	sun	1–2½'	—
Chervil	annual	seed	mod/rich	moist	ps/sh	2'	—
Chinese Celery	biennial	seed	rich	moist	ps/sh	2'	—
Chives	perennial	plant/seed	rich	moist	s/ps	1–1½'	division
Comfrey	perennial	root	moderate	moist/mod	s/ps	3'	root cuttings, division
Coriander	annual	seed	moderate	moist	sun	2–3'	—
Dill	annual	seed	moderate	moist	sun	3'	—
Epazote	perennial	plant/seed	moderate	moderate	sun	2–4'	stem cuttings
Fennel	biennial	seed	moderate	moist/mod	sun	5'+	—
Garlic Chives	perennial	plant/seed	rich	moist	s/ps	1–2½'	division
Ginger	perennial	root	rich	moist	ps	3–4'	root cuttings
Hops	perennial	root	rich	moist	sun	10–30'	division
Lavender	perennial	plant	low	moderate	sun	18"–4'	division, stem cuttings

Started by—Best way to get started. When either plant or seed can be used, they are both given in order of preference, i.e. plant/seed means best to start with a plant, although it isn't too hard from seed.

Fertility—(will thrive with poor fertility, moderate fertility is fine, rich fertility required, or most levels are fine)

Water—water requirements (dry, moderate, moist)

Sun—sun requirements (s-sun ps-part shade sh-shade)

Height—usual height (sometimes it varies by cultivar)

Veg Repro—means of vegetative reproduction, when applicable

HERB CHART

Herb	Type	Started by	Fertility	Water	Sun	Height	Veg Repro
Lemon Balm	perennial	plant/seed	rich	moist	s/ps	2–3'	divisions
Lemon Verbena	shrub	plant	rich	moist	sun	3–5'	stem cuttings
Lemongrass	perennial	plant	moderate	moderate	sun	1 2'	division
Marjoram	perennial	plant/seed	moderate	moderate	sun	1–1½'	cuttings
Mint	perennial	plant	rich	moist	sun/ps	1–1½'	rooted runners
Mustard	annual	seed	rich	moist	sun	2–3'	—
Oregano, Greek	perennial	plant	mod/low	rather dry	sun	1–1½'	cuttings, layering, division
Parsley	biennial	seed/plant	rich	moist	ps/s	6–12"	—
Parsley, Japanese	perennial	seed	rich	moist	sh/ps	1–3'	—
Perilla	annual	seed	moderate	moist	s/ps	1–1½'	—
Rosemary	perennial	plant	low/mod	rather dry	sun	6" to 4'	cuttings
Sage, Garden	perennial	plant/seed	moderate	dry/moist	sun	2'	cuttings, layering
Sage, Clary	biennial	seed	moderate	dry	sun	3'+	—
Sage, Pineapple	perennial	plant/seed	moderate	moderate	sun	3'+	—
Summer Savory	annual	seed	rich	moderate	sun	18"	—
Winter Savory	perennial	plant	low/mod	dry/mod	sun	18"	division, layering
Sw. Woodruff	perennial	plant	rich	moist	p. shade	6–10"	rooted pieces, root cuttings
Tarragon, French	perennial	plant	moderate	moderate	sun/ps	1–2'	division, root cuttings
Tarragon, Winter	perennial	plant/seed	moderate	moderate	sun	1'+	—
Thyme	perennial	plant/seed	moderate	dry/mod	sun	6–12"	cuttings, division., layering
Yerba Buena	perennial	plant	rich	moist	sun/ps	creeping	cuttings, layering

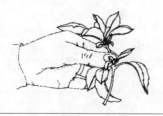

NASTURTIUM FLOWER SALAD DRESSING

Only the essence of the flowers will remain, but it flavors this salad dressing nicely. For this recipe, thanks to my friend Nick Latham.

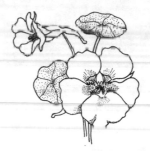

2 cups nasturtium blossoms
1/4 cup virgin olive oil
1/2 cup red wine vinegar
1/2 teaspoon salt
1/4 teaspoon pepper
1 tablespoon chopped onion
1 1/2-inch piece red chile pepper (optional)
1 whole clove garlic

Wash the blossoms and check them carefully for insects. Put the blossoms in a quart jar, add all the other ingredients, and shake well. Let stand two weeks at room temperature. Strain to remove the garlic, onions, flowers, and pepper. This dressing is good in simple tossed green salads. Leftover dressing can be stored in the refrigerator.

THIRTEEN

Eating the Flowers

LOWERS ARE NOT ONLY beautiful in your garden and on your dining table, they can also go right into your dinner. Edible flowers can lift your meals out of the ordinary, and the very best way to get them is to grow them yourself. The edible flowers in markets tend to be expensive and are not necessarily fresh. Also, they are sold in standard sized packages rather than in the variable quantities in which you are likely to need them. If you grow your own edible flowers, you can pick them as you need them, they cost very little to grow, and, as a bonus, they brighten your yard before they appear on your plate.

Using Edible Flowers

Sometimes edible flowers are used only for decoration. After all, form and color are their unique strengths. For example, flowers may be used on iced cakes, or as a garnish. While it is safest to use *edible* flowers for such purposes, they are often not actually eaten.

In other cases, flowers are an integral part of a dish. The range of edible flower flavor is from the delicious to the bland or even the bitter. You will need to experiment to see which flowers you like and how you like to prepare them. Herb flowers usually share the flavor of the leaves. Onion and chive flowers taste mildly of onion. Nasturtiums are pungent and peppery. Carnations are spicy, borage cucumbery, and bean flowers taste beany. Many

marigold blossoms have unpleasant flavors, but some, such as 'Lemon Gem,' are pleasant-tasting. Bland-flavored flowers, such as pansies, often make up for their lack of flavor with wonderful shapes and colors.

Often whole flowers are edible, for example herb flowers, nasturtiums, or squash blossoms. Sometimes only the petals are eaten, as is the case with marigolds, calendulas, or carnations. In at least one case, that of daylily, you must remove the stamens and pistils from the flowers before you eat them. Usually, when a part of a flower is not eaten, it is because it is bitter or otherwise unpalatable.

It is best to pick edible flowers just before you use them. Being able to have them in absolutely fresh, prime condition is one of the advantages of growing them yourself. Usually, to save a step in the kitchen, they are picked without stems. However, if you must pick them in advance of using them, you can leave the stems on and put the flowers in a vase. Or, if you have unused flowers that you picked stemless, put them in the refrigerator in a plastic bag. In either case, use within a day.

Always examine edible flowers carefully for insects, including looking down between the petals. Flowers are an unfamiliar food to many people and you especially don't want their first edible flower experience to be a crawly one! If you garden without chemicals, and your garden is away from the street and not dusty, you may choose not to wash your flowers. If you do wash them, do it quickly in cool water, shake them out, and dry them on paper towels.

SAFETY FOR FLOWER CONNOISSEURS

Never eat flowers bought from a florist, since they are likely to have been sprayed with chemicals unsafe for human consumption. Because they are not intended to be eaten, these flowers are often treated against pests with systemic poisons—poisons that are absorbed into the sap of the plants, and are impossible to wash off. If you buy a plant from a nursery, don't eat flowers from it for the first several months, to allow any pesticide to work its way out of the plant.

Beware too of flowers from parks or other people's yards, as these may have been sprayed. Roses and fuchsias are among the ornamentals that gardeners commonly put on a regular spray regimen.

Always be sure that the particular species of flower you are about to eat is an edible one. If you aren't absolutely sure of its identity, or have not seen it listed in a trustworthy list of edible flowers, don't eat it!

And, as with other new foods, consider the possibility of allergies to edible flowers. If a person has previously eaten other parts of the flowering plant, like beans, squash, or herb leaves, an allergy just to the flowers is highly unlikely. If however, the flower is the first part of the plant ever tasted, as is likely to be the case with pansies or day lilies, there is some question. While I have never heard of an allergy to an edible flower, they are possible. (One signal might be allergy to the flower's pollen.)

HERE ARE SOME COMMON **POISONOUS** FLOWERS. REMEMBER, **DON'T** EAT THESE FLOWERS!

Azalea, calla lily, crocus, daffodil, delphinium, foxglove, hyacinth, hydrangea, iris, lantana, larkspur, lobelia, lupine, oleander, poinsettia, ranunculus, rhododendron, sweet pea (*Lathyrus*), wisteria, tomato, potato, pepper, eggplant. This is not a complete list, only a list of some of the most common poisonous flowers. Contact your local poison control center for more information.

ADDITIONAL EDIBLE FLOWERS

Vegetable: arugula, mustard, beans, peas, squash, or pumpkin. (Baby corn are really corn flowers. Also, artichoke, broccoli and cauliflower are flower buds.)

Herbs: anise hyssop, borage, camomile, chives, coriander, dill, fennel, garlic chives, hops, lavender, mint, rosemary, sage, pineapple sage, clary sage, winter tarragon. Some herbs, such as thyme or savory, have flowers too small to use by themselves, though they often get eaten along with the leaves.

Weeds: wild radish, onion lily (*A. triquetrum*), dandelion (buds), oxalis, mallow.

FRIED SQUASH BLOSSOMS

There are many recipes for stuffed squash blossoms, and I'm sure they're very good, but I am always too impatient to get these tender morsels fried and onto the plate to take time to stuff them.

3 to 8 squash blossoms per serving (leave small squashes on any female blossoms)
Whole wheat flour
Oil for frying
Freshly ground pepper to taste
Salt or soy sauce

Check the blossoms over for insects. Sort out the male and female blossoms. If the young squash behind the female blossoms is over 1/2 inch in diameter, halve the squash and blossom lengthwise. Dip the blossoms in water, then in whole wheat flour. Fry in a thin layer of oil until they are light brown and a bit crispy. Pepper to taste. Add a light shake of salt or serve with soy sauce.

Growing Flowers for Eating

It doesn't take much space to grow enough flowers to bring forth many ooohs and aaahs at the table. With very little space and effort, you could go out on a whim and get, say, borage flowers and nasturtiums for the occasional salad, or to decorate an iced cake so dramatically that few would forget it. With only a little more space and time, you could have many different edible flowers awaiting your creative impulse.

And you should be able to grow a wide variety of attractive and tasty flowers no matter how foggy your garden. Many of the most choice edibles are flowers that bloom best in cool weather. Refer to the chart which begins on page 310 for more information on growing and using some of them. In this chart I have included the most popular edible flowers, with notes when a particular one is not among the best adapted to our region. Notice that many are also valuable as cut flowers. A second list, on page 308, includes plants with edible flowers that are discussed elsewhere in this book—as vegetables, herbs, or even weeds.

A number of mail order seed catalogs now indicate in flower listings whether a particular flower is edible. A few seed sources give you a little more help. Johnny's Selected Seeds uses a pictorial symbol to indicate which flowers you can eat. The Gourmet Gardener and Seeds Blüm group edible flowers together, and Seeds Blüm includes quite a bit of useful information about growing and using them. The Gourmet Gardener and Shepherd's Garden Seeds sell collections of edible flower seeds in separate mini-packets, and Thompson & Morgan sell a packet of mixed edible flower seeds.

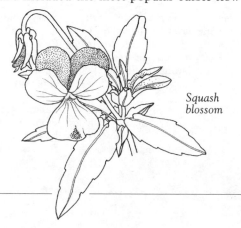

Squash blossom

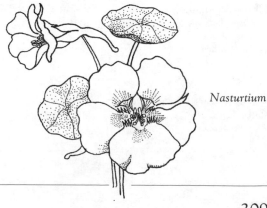

Nasturtium

EDIBLE FLOWERS

Annuals

Plant name	When to plant	When to harvest	How to propagate	Color(s)	How to use	Miscellaneous
Calendula (or Pot Marigold) *Calendula officinalis* (Compositae)	spring, summer, fall	summer, fall, spring, sometimes winter	seed	cream to orange	Use petals only, in salads, soups, rice dishes. Little flavor.	Very easy and dependable. Self sows readily.
Johnnie-jump-up *Viola tricolor* (Violaceae)	fall or spring	spring, summer	seed	yellow w/purple & white	Use whole flower to decorate salads or dessert. Slight wintergreen flavor.	Blooms profusely with little attention. Self sows.
Marigold, Signet *Tagetes tenuifolia* (Compositae)	spring, early summer	summer to fall	seed	yellow, orange, red, white	Use petals only, in salads. Many have unpleasant taste. "Lemon Gem" tastes lemony.	Other than Signet Marigolds, sample first. Also try "Tangerine Gem" & "Paprika."
Nasturtium *Tropaeolum majus Tropaeolum minor* (Tropaeolaceae)	early spring through fall	summer, fall, spring, sometimes winter	seed	yellow, red, orange, peach	Use whole flowers to decorate a salad, or stuff as appetizers. Chop flowers in omelets. Flavor is sweet and spicy.	Easy, dependable, one of the best flavored and most useful of edible flowers. Self sows.
Pansy *Viola wittrockiana* (Violaceae)	fall or spring	spring, summer, fall, sometimes winter	seed	many: both single color & bicolor	Use whole to decorate salads or desserts. Chop whole flowers in omelets. Little flavor.	Don't try to grow where snails, slugs and earwigs are not controlled.

Perennials

Plant name	When to plant	When to harvest	How to propagate	Color(s)	How to use	Miscellaneous
Carnation *Dianthus caryophyllus* (Caryophyllaceae)	spring	summer, spring	plant, seed,	red, orange, yellow, white, pink	Use petals only; trim away white bases. Try in salad, dessert sauces. Flavor is sweet.	Border types are easier to grow than florist types.
Chrysanthemum *Chrysanthemum morifolium* (Compositae)	early spring	summer, fall	plant, cutting, seed	yellow, rust, wine, white, etc.	Use petals only, trim away white bases. Use in soups, salads, cream cheese spreads. Subtle, aromatic flavor.	Pinch young plants to prolong bloom. Pick off smaller flower buds so the ones that open will make larger flowers.
Citrus flowers *Citrus* species (Rhamnaceae)	late winter	most of the year	plant	white	Use whole blossoms as a garnish or in fruit salad, citrus desserts and sauces. Flavor is tangy.	Lemon and lime bloom most freely, but you can eat flowers of any citrus.

EDIBLE FLOWERS (continued)

Perennials

Plant name	When to plant	When to harvest	How to propagate	Color(s)	How to use	Miscellaneous
Day lily *Hemerocallis* hybrids (*Liliaceae*)	early spring, late fall	spring, summer	division	yellow, red, orange, pink, etc.	Remove stamens and pistils. Use on the day they open. Use in soup, tempura, stir-fries, egg dishes, salads. Flavor nutty, a bit sweet.	Dried day lilies are the "golden needles" of Chinese cooking. They are soaked in water 90 minutes before they are used.
Fuchsia *Fuchsia* hybrids (*Onagraceae*)	any time	early summer to fall	plant	red, pink, white, purple	Use whole flowers as a garnish or in salads. Flavor is acidic.	Don't eat flowers of plants that have been sprayed for fuchsia mites. Grow mite-resistant varieties.
Geraniums, scented e.g. rose scented: *Pelargonium graveolens* peppermint scented: *Pelargonium tomentosum* (*Geraniaceae*)	fall or spring	spring to fall	plant or cutting	various	Line a cake pan with whole flowers to scent a cake, or use petals in fruit salads. Flavor is like the plant's scent.	Other pelargoniums are also edible, but their flavor is often not very good. Still, the brightly colored flowers are dramatic as garnishes.
Lilac *Syringa vulgaris* (*Oleaceae*)	spring	spring or fall	plant	lavender, pink, white	Use individual blossoms in fruit salads or desserts.	Some varieties do not bloom every year because they need colder winters. Other varieties are adapted to our climate.
Pineapple Guava *Feijoa sellowiana* (*Myrtaceae*)	spring or when available	May or June	plant	red and white	Use only the petals, in salads, on ice cream or as a garnish. The flavor is sweet.	If you remove the petals with care, the fruit will still ripen.
Rose *Rosa* species (*Rosaceae*)	all year	spring into winter	plant	red, pink white, yellow, etc.	Use petals in meat dishes, fruit salads, desserts. Flavor varies. Roses with the most scent have the most flavor.	In our climate, roses get rust, mildew—choose resistant cultivars; polyanthas are usually safe. Plant bareroot in winter, or from containers all year.
Tulip *Tulipa* hybrids (*Liliaceae*)	Nov-Dec.	March, April	bulb	red, yellow, pink, white, lavender, etc.	Remove pistils & stamens. Use as a container for dips or salads or chop petals into green salad. Vegetable flavor.	Tulips need colder weather to bloom well year after year. Here, gardeners usually plant new bulbs each year.

FOURTEEN

THE BACKYARD FLORIST

F YOU BUY CUT FLOWERS often, you may find you can save more money by growing bouquets than by growing vegetables. Besides, growing your own flowers allows you to create delightfully serendipitous bouquets. If you go to a florist's with a few dollars in hand, you are most likely to emerge with six or a dozen of the same kind of flower, or with a standard mixed bouquet. But you can easily grow enough flowers to make armsful of bouquets, featuring combinations for which you would have to pay dearly, assuming you could even find them to buy.

Imagine a vaseful of crimson red ranunculus and red sweet peas, combined with rose-red and pale yellow columbines, pale yellow nasturtiums, and white freesias—all set amidst airy, lacy columbine leaves. Pure fantasy! Every time I looked at my bouquet I thought of those French tapestries where unicorns pose in fields of flowers. Or imagine filling a vase with yellow marguerite daisies or garland chrysanthemums, together with blue cornflowers and wild grass seed stalks—you'd be creating a piece of summer meadow in a vase. Or try combining some of the small flowers of early spring—Johnnie-jump-ups, sweet alyssum, forget-me-nots, and grape hyacinths, for a small, tender nosegay. Or picture the dramatic accent in your fall kitchen of a single stem of the small, bright yellow "sunflowers" from a sunchoke plant.

The chart at the end of this chapter lists many annual and perennial flowers I've found to be both beautiful and reliable in our region. Most of these flowers prefer our cool days, and they do better here, blooming longer, than they would further inland. Of course the possibilities for cut flowers are endless, including the flowers of many shrubs, such as rhododendrons or flowering quince, not covered in this book. This list, however, will provide you with a more than ample start.

Besides the flowers you plant especially for cutting, many vegetables, herbs, and even weeds produce flowers, seed heads and foliage that you may find useful in bouquets. (See "Other Bouquet Possibilities," below.) But do be careful not to overcut foliage of crop plants, such as asparagus or artichoke, so as not to stunt their growth. And be sure not to let weeds take over your garden just because you are using them in bouquets. Nutsedge, for example, may be pretty, and you may as well use it if you have it, but it is too aggressive to tolerate in your garden.

Growing Flowers For Cutting

Many flowers grown for cutting thrive in the same full sunlight and rich garden soil, and with the same regular watering, that garden vegetables prefer. In fact, one way to grow them is simply scattered among the vegetables. There they can brighten your food garden as well as your home.

If your yard includes ornamental beds, you may choose to plant flowers for cutting there instead. If you do, you will need to consider their place in your decorative scheme, keeping in mind their height,

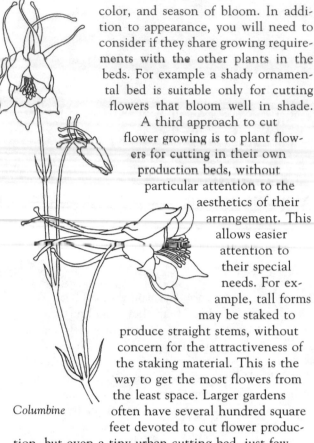

Columbine

color, and season of bloom. In addition to appearance, you will need to consider if they share growing requirements with the other plants in the beds. For example a shady ornamental bed is suitable only for cutting flowers that bloom well in shade. A third approach to cut flower growing is to plant flowers for cutting in their own production beds, without particular attention to the aesthetics of their arrangement. This allows easier attention to their special needs. For example, tall forms may be staked to produce straight stems, without concern for the attractiveness of the staking material. This is the way to get the most flowers from the least space. Larger gardens often have several hundred square feet devoted to cut flower production, but even a tiny urban cutting bed, just few square feet in area, can produce many bouquets.

As with vegetables and herbs, you will find it easier to keep annuals together, and to plant perennials where they won't be disturbed when you plant successive annual crops. Also, as with vegetables and herbs, you will find that some resow themselves. When the volunteers come up, you get to decide whether to weed them out, let them stay where they are, or transplant them to other sites.

Three techniques can improve the bloom of particular cutting flowers. The first is pinching, which means removing growing tips so that the plant will become more bushy. This is often done when a plant is young, so that it will make more flowering stems. Among the plants that will respond well to this treatment are stock, snapdragons, and painted-tongue.

A second technique is disbudding. If a plant makes several buds in one place, you can remove all but one of them. The fewer flowers left will be larger. Common flowers you might disbud are the dahlia and the chrysanthemum.

Third, many flowering plants will bloom longer if you remove the spent flowers every week or so.

Just picking the flowers for bouquets stimulates more flowers to form, but you should also prevent as many as possible of the remaining flowers from going to seed. Use this technique, sometimes called deadheading, to prolong bloom of marigolds, all kinds of daisies, pansies, sweet peas, and many other kinds of flowers.

Flowers grown from bulbs are some of the most dramatic of cutting flowers, from spring-blooming daffodils and tulips to summer's watsonias and lilies. Just remember to find out, before you grow a particular bulb, whether the bulb can remain in the ground from year to year, or whether it must be dug and stored—or even discarded—each year.

Many bulbs can stay in the ground from year to year, only needing to be divided when they get crowded. That is to say they will "naturalize." However others cannot survive if they spend the whole year in the ground. Gladiolus and ranunculus are usually watered less after they bloom. They are then dug and stored in a cool, dry place until winter or spring, although both may sometimes come back the next year even if they are not dug. Tulip and hyacinth need much more winter chill than our climate provides. If left in the ground, they will decline rapidly, blooming poorly or not at all after the first year. Local gardeners sometimes dig and store them, but the more common tactic is to discard them, buying new tulip and hyacinth bulbs each autumn.

Often the bulbs that will naturalize here are dormant for much of the summer. If a bulb has a dormancy period, and you want to it to bloom next year, heed this warning: Never cut back green leaves. Water the plants lightly until the leaves die back. Do not tie leaves in knots or knock them over. Just remove any that turn brown, and be patient.

Bulb plants in the process of going dormant can be a bit unsightly. Plan for this problem by planting summer-blooming flowers in front of them, to screen the foliage from view when the bloom is gone, or by blanketing the ground around the bulb plants with a small flowering plant like Johnnie-jump-ups or alyssum.

Love-in-a-mist

Creating A Simple Bouquet

If you are unfamiliar with flower arranging, a good beginning is a simple, but effective bouquet you build as you pick—the hand-held bouquet. Cut a few of a kind of flower you like and hold them as if your hand were the neck of a vase. Choose a stem length you can match with several kinds of flowers. Hold the first flowers you cut next to another kind of flower in your garden. If they look good together, cut a few stems of the second flower, too. Keep adding flowers until your arrangement pleases you and you have enough to fill a vase.

As you hold your expanding bouquet against each new flower, and before you cut it, move the bouquet up and down a bit. The stems don't have to be exactly the same length, and you will find that some flowers need to stand a bit above the others to look their best. Also, it often helps an informal bouquet to have several of one kind of flower, in the same color, in little groups throughout the arrangement, rather than having all of the kinds of flowers mixed evenly. And stems of foliage, such as fennel, columbine or spearmint, often look best around the outside, a bit lower than the flowers they are framing.

When making a hand-held bouquet, you don't need to cut all of each kind of flower at the same time. Take some time to wander about, comparing and visualizing, until a bouquet emerges in your mind's eye. Sometimes you will find that a certain color or shape is, after all, wrong for your bouquet. If that happens, don't be afraid to take it out. Chances are that flower will look fine in a small vase by itself.

Your color scheme choices will be limited to what is blooming, but, within that, here are some possibilities to consider. You may have all one kind of flower, but in several colors, or all one color, with several kinds of flowers. You might try analogous color schemes, like blue/purple/pink or yellow/orange/rust. A multicolor bouquet, with contrasting colors, can be either pastel (pink, pale blue, lavender) or bright (red, blue, gold, purple). A few stems of something white, or some greenery, will often show off your colors to better advantage.

This informal bouquet will be looser or tighter depending not only on the number of stems, but on the proportions of the vase you choose to hold it. A tall vase (or a small-mouthed one) will hold the stems closer together. A short vase (or a wide-mouthed one) will let them stand further apart. So as you are designing your bouquet, keep the proportions of your possible vases in mind too.

OTHER BOUQUET POSSIBILITIES

Flowers from Vegetables: artichoke, mustard, garland chrysanthemum, scarlet runner bean, sunchoke.

From Herbs: anise hyssop, borage, camomile (German), chives, comfrey, coriander, garlic chive, lavender, pineapple sage, garden sage, sorrel.

From Weeds: dock, fennel, onion lily.

Seed Stalks from Weeds: wild grasses, nutsedge, fennel.

Leaves from Vegetables: artichoke, asparagus, beet, carrot, celery or celeriac, ground cherry, Swiss chard (white, green, red, or yellow stemmed). **From Herbs:** lemon balm, mint, parsley, rosemary, garden sage, sweet woodruff. **From Weeds:** horsetail, wild fennel. **From Flowers:** columbine, nasturtium, feverfew, calla lily.

CUT FLOWERS

Perennials

Name	Bloom Size Plant Height*	Color	Fragrance	When to Plant
Calla Lily (*Araceae*) *Zantedeschia aethiopica*	4–6" 1¹/2–4'	White	Slight	Rhizomes: Fall Plants: As available
Chrysanthemum (*Compositae*) *Chrysanthemum × morifolium*	2–4" 1–3'	White, yellow, bronze, maroon, lavender, pink	None or pungent	Early spring
Columbine (*Ranunculaceae*) *Aquilegia* species & Hybrids	1¹/2–2¹/2" 1–3'	Blue, pink, yellow, lavender red, white (often bicolors)	None	Seed: Early spring Plants: Spring, summer
Coreopsis (*Compositae*) *Coreopsis lanceolata*	3" 2'	Yellow	Slight	Spring, summer
Crocosmia (*Iridaceae*) *Crocosmia × Crocosmiiflora* C. masoniorum	1–2" 2¹/2–4'	Yellow, orange, scarlet	None	Early spring
Daffodil (*Amarylidaceae*) *Narcissus* hybrids	1–3" 1–1¹/2'	Yellow, white orange, apricot (some are bicolors)	Sweet	Fall
Dahlia (*Compositae*) *Dahlia* hybrids	1–10" 1–6'	Many colors, but not blue. (some are bicolors)	None	Spring, early summer
Day Lily (*Liliaceae*) *Hemerocallis* hybrids	3–5" 1¹/2–4'	Yellow, orange, pink, cream, red, violet (many are bicolors)	Most have little	Early spring, late fall
Echinacea, Cone Flower (*Compositae*) *Echinacea purpurea*	3–4" 2–5'	Purple, pink, white	None	Spring, fall
Feverfew, Matricaria (*Compositae*) *Chrysanthemum parthenium*	³/4" 1¹/2–3'	White, yellow, white with yellow centers	Leaves are pungent	Fall, spring
Freesia (*Iridaceae*) *Freesia* species & hybrids	2" 1–1¹/2'	White, yellow, red, lavender, pink, purple (many are bicolors)	Some are very sweet	Fall
Gaillardia (*Compositae*) *Gaillardia × grandiflora*	3–4" 2–4'	Red, yellow, orange, bronze (many bicolored)	None	Spring
Gladiolus (*Iridaceae*) *Gladiolus hortulanus*	1¹/2–4" 1¹/2–4'	White, yellow, red, orange, pink, lavender, purple, green (many bicolors)	None	January to March
Iris (*Iridaceae*) *Iris* species & hybrids	2–4" 6"–4'	Blue, purple, yellow, white, wine, etc. (many are bicolors)	None	Midsummer, Fall, Spring
Lily (*Liliaceae*) *Lilium* species & hybrids	4–6" 2–5'	White, orange, yellow, red, pink, etc. (many are bicolors)	Some are sweet	Late fall, early spring

*See notes, page 320.

Perennials

When to Pick	Propagate by[*]	Growing & Cutting Tips	Miscellaneous
Spring, summer	Rhizomes	Sun or part shade. Most soils. Ample water.	Frequently grows wild. For less invasive callas, seek out species with colored flowers.
Late summer, fall	Cuttings, divisions	Sun. Soil with good drainage, well-amended and fertilized. Keep moist during growth and bloom.	Pinch plants often until midsummer to encourage branching. Stake plants. Fertilize 2–3 times in summer.
Spring, early summer	Seed	Sun, part shade. Soil with good drainage. Moderate water.	May self-sow. Sometimes attacked by leafminer, but this doesn't hinder bloom.
Summer, fall	Seed division	Sun. Soil with good drainage.	Pick flowers to prolong bloom. Divide plants when crowded.
Summer	Corm	Sun. Soil with good drainage, moderate fertility. Keep moist during growth and bloom.	Naturalize well. Some kinds are invasive.
Spring	Bulb	Sun, part shade. Well-amended soil. If rains fail, water while growing and blooming. Leave drier when leaves begin to die, in summer.	Bulbs are poisonous. Gophers don't eat them. Let leaves die back naturally; don't tie them in knots.
Summer into fall	Seed or tuberous root	Sun. Well-amended soil with good drainage. Moderate water.	Easy from seed. Tuberous roots can be dug and replanted in next spring. Snails and slugs eat the petals.
Spring, summer	Division	Sun or part shade. Well-amended soil. Water well while blooming. Cut while in bud.	Red ones need summer heat for best color.
Late summer into fall	Seeds, division	Sun, most soils if well-drained. Moderate water. Divide every 4 years or so.	One of two *Echinaceas* used medicinally; is also a good cut flower.
Spring, summer	Seed, division, cuttings	Sun or part shade. Most soils, good drainage, moderate water.	Cut back for rebloom. May reseed, be weedy. 'Golden Feather' has chartreuse leaves.
Spring	Corm	Sun. Soil with good drainage, moderate fertility. Let dry in summer months.	Freesias may naturalize.
Summer, fall	Seed, division	Sun. Soil with good drainage, poor or moderate fertility. Tolerates some drought.	Start from seed in May, or from nursery plants in summer. Divide in early spring each year to maintain its vigor.
March to May	Corm	Sun. Fertile, preferable sandy soil. Water while actively growing. Long-lasting cut flower.	Corms should be dug when leaves yellow and stored dry. Thrips may attack plants.
Spring, early summer	Bulb, rhizome	Sun. Some require rich soil, others are less particular. Moderate water while growing. Some should be drier after bloom.	Many kinds, some from bulbs, others from rhizomes.
Late spring, summer	Bulb	Sun, part shade. Fertile, well-amended soil. Keep moist during growth and bloom, drier when leaves yellow. Never let dry out completely.	Mulch soil to keep roots cool. Gophers eat the bulbs. There are many kinds. Most naturalize.

CUT FLOWERS (continued)

Name	Bloom Size Plant Height*	Color(s)*	Fragrance	When to Plant
Marguerite (*Compositae*) *Chrysanthemum frutescens*	1¹/₂–2¹/₂" 3–4'	White, yellow, pink (some with yellow centers)	Slight	Spring
Ranunculus (Persian) (*Ranunclaceae*) *Ranunculus asiaticus*	2–4" 1–2'	White, yellow, gold, orange, red, pink (many are bicolors)	None	September to November or Mid-February
Shasta Daisy (*Compositae*) *Chrysanthemum maximum*	2–6" 2–4'	White, pale yellow	None	Spring, fall
Tulips (*Liliaceae*) *Tulipa* species & hybrids	2–6" 6"–2¹/₂'	Red, yellow, white, lavender, near-black, etc. (many are bicolors)	Slight or none	Fall, early winter
Watsonia (*Iridaceae*) *Watsonia pyramidata*	2¹/₂" 4–6'	Species is pink to rose-red hybrids pink, white, lilac, red	None	Late summer, early fall

Annuals

Name	Bloom Size Plant Height*	Color(s)*	Fragrance	When to Plant
Calendula (or Pot Marigold) (*Compositae*) *Calendula officinalis*	2–4" 1–2'	Yellow, orange, cream, peach	Slightly pungent	Spring, summer, fall
Cornflower (or Bachelor's Button) (*Compositae*) *Centaurea cyanis*	1¹/₂" 1–2¹/₂'	Blue, pink, purple, white	None	Late summer, fall, or spring
Cosmos (*Compositae*) *Cosmos bipinnatus*	2–3" 3–6'	White to magenta, some bicolored	None	Spring to summer
Cosmos, Yellow (*Compositae*) *Cosmos sulphureus*	1¹/₂–2¹/₂" 1–6'	Yellow to orange-red	None	Spring to summer
Flowering Tobacco (*Solanaceae*) *Nicotiana alata*	1" 1–4'	White, greenish, red, mauve	Some are very sweet	Spring
Forget-me-not (*Boraginaceae*) *Myosotis sylvatica*	¹/₄" 6"–1'	Most are blue. Some are pink or white.	None	Late summer or fall, spring
Foxglove (*Scrophulariaceae*) *Digitalis purpurea*	2" 1–4'	Lavender, rose, yellow, white	None	Fall or early spring
Godetia (*Onagraceae*) *Clarkia amoena*	1–3" 10"–3'	Pink, red, lavender, peach (some are bicolors)	Slight, sweet	Fall or spring
Johnnie-jump up (*Violaceae*) *Viola tricolor*	¹/₂–³/₄" 6–8"	Purple/yellow/white (tricolor)	None	Early spring, early summer, or fall
Larkspur, Annual Delphinium (*Ranunculaceae*) *Consolida ambigua*	1¹/₂" 1–4'	Blue, pink, white, lilac, salmon	None	Fall or spring

*See notes, page 320.

When to Pick	Propagate by?*	Growing & Cutting Tips	Miscellaneous
Summer, fall, spring, sometimes winter	Plants	Sun. Well-amended or sandy soil. Moderate water. Replace overgrown plants every 2–3 years.	Succeeds very near the ocean. Dependable perennial daisies.
February to April	Tuber	Sun. Well-amended, preferably sandy soil. Regular water. After bloom, water less.	Tubers may overwinter successfully in the ground. For more certainty, dig and store till spring or buy fresh tubers each year.
Spring, summer, early fall	Seeds, division	Sun, part shade. Well-amended soil. Regular water.	Start seed late winter/early spring. Plant divisions fall or spring. Plant from containers any time.
Spring	Bulb	Sun. Fertile, well-amended soil. Regular water while growing and blooming.	Hybrid tulips do not naturalize here. Discard bulbs and buy new ones each year. Some species tulips do naturalize. Gophers eat the bulbs.
Spring	Corm	Sun. Well-amended soil. Keep moist while growing and blooming, drier after bloom.	These naturalize. Dig only to thin or replant crowded plantings. Do this in summer.

When to Pick	Propagate by?*	Growing & Cutting Tips	Miscellaneous
Summer, fall, spring & sometimes winter	Seed	Sun. Very easy to grow.	Self-sows freely. Gets powdery mildew, but generally blooms anyway.
Spring to late summer (sometimes fall/winter)	Seed	Sun. Fertile soil. Moderate water.	Tall varieties may require staking. Deadhead to keep looking tidy.
Summer to fall	Seed	Sun. Best in lean soil with little water. Easy to grow.	Self-sows. May break in strong winds.
Summer to fall	Seed	Full sun. Best in lean soil with little water. Easy to grow.	Self-sows. Look unkempt late in season.
Summer	Seed	Sun or part shade. Fertile, well-amended soil, kept moist. For reliable fragrance, try N. alata 'grandiflora.'	Some self-sow readily. Some open only at night or on cloudy days.
Late winter, spring, or summer	Seed	Part shade. Fertile soil; keep moist. Use in small bouquets.	Self-sows freely. Nice under spring bulbs. May get powdery mildew.
Spring, early summer	Seed	Light shade to full shade. Well-amended soil, keep moist.	May self-sow. Entire plant is poisonous.
Spring, summer	Seed	Sun. Grows well in poor, sandy soil.	May self-sow. Better for cutting than related clarkias, because flowers are at top of stem rather than on sides.
Spring, summer	Seed	Sun or shade. Fertile soil. Keep moist. Pick stems with leaves for small bouquets.	Self-sows freely. Sold as an edible flower more often than as an ornamental.
Spring, summer	Seed	Sun. Fertile soil. Moderate moisture.	Protect from strong winds.

CUT FLOWERS (continued)

Name	Bloom Size Plant Height*	Color(s)*	Fragrance	When to Plant
Love in a Mist (*Ranunculaceae*) *Nigella damascena*	1^1/$_2$" 1–2'	Blue, white, rose	None	Early spring
Marigold (*Compositae*) *Tagetes* (various species)	^{1}/$_2$–3" 6"–3'	Yellow, orange, white, rust, crimson (some bicolors)	None or pungent	Spring, early summer
Nasturtium (*Tropeolaceae*) *Tropaeolum majus* & *T. minus*	1^1/$_2$–2" 6"–6'	Orange, yellow, red, cream, pink (some bicolor)	Slight	Early spring through fall
Painted Tongue (*Solanaceae*) *Salpiglossis sinuata*	2–2^1/$_2$" 2–3'	Purple, crimson, lavender, yellow (contrasting veins)	None	Late winter, early spring
Pansy (*Violaceae*) *Viola* × *wittrockiana*	2–4" 6–8"	Purple, red, yellow, blue, white (some bicolor)	None	Fall or spring
Pincushion Flower (*Dipsacaceae*) *Scabiosa atropurpurea*	1^1/$_2$" 2^1/$_2$–3'	Lilac, pink, maroon, white	May have sweet scent	Spring
Shirley Poppy (*Papaveraceae*) *Papaver rhoeas*	2–8" 2–5"	Red, pink, white, salmon, yellow (some are bicolor)	None	Early to late spring
Sunflower (*Compositae*) *Helianthus annus*	4–15" 1–14'	Yellow, orange, red, burgundy (some are bicolors)	None	Mid-Spring
Statice (*Plumbaginaceae*) *Limonium sinuatum*	^{1}/$_4$" 1–2^1/$_2$'	Blue, lavender, rose, white, yellow	None	Early to late spring
Stock (*Cruciferae*) *Matthiola incana*	1" 1–2^1/$_2$"	Pink, lavender, purple, cream, white, red	Very sweet	Fall or spring
Strawflower (*Compositae*) *Helichrysum bracteatum*	2–2^1/$_2$" 2–4'	Yellow, orange, wine, rust, pink, white	None	Late spring
Sweet Alysum (*Cruciferae*) *Lobularia maritima*	<^{1}/$_4$" 4–8"	White, rose, lavender	Sweet	Late winter through fall
Sweet Pea (*Leguminosae*) *Lathyrus odoratus*	1–1^1/$_2$" 1–6'	Pink, lavender, purple, red, white, blue, salmon	Most are very sweet	Fall, winter, spring, summer
Sweet William (*Caryophyllaceae*) *Dianthus barbatus*	^{1}/$_2$" 6"–1^1/$_2$'	Red, pink, rose-violet, white (often bicolored)	Slight clove scent	Summer
Viola (*Violaceae*) *Viola cornuta*	1^1/$_2$" 6–8"	Blue, purple, yellow, white, apricot (some are bicolored)	None	Late summer or early spring
Zinnia (*Compositae*) *Zinnia* hybrids	1^1/$_4$–6" 3"–2^1/$_2$'	Red, pink, yellow, orange, white, greenish	None	Spring

*Notes to the Cut Flower Chart

Bloom Size/Plant Height: When there is a wide range of measurements, these refer to the range of cultivars of the flower. For example there are dwarf marigolds, to only 6 inches tall, with ^{1}/$_2$ inch flowers, as well as varieties that grow to 3 feet, with huge 3 inch pompoms. Consult references such as the Sunset Western Garden Book or seed catalogs to learn the names of different-sized verieties.

Color(s): Refer to catalogs or seed packets for colors of specific offerings. Some will contain flowers of all one color, others will be mixtures.

Propagate by?: Most kinds of flowers grown from seed are also available as nursery transplants or can be started indoors and transplanted. Check seed packets for information about indoor seeding.

When to Pick	Propagate by?*	Growing & Cutting Tips	Miscellaneous
Spring	Seed	Sun or part shade. Soil with very good drainage.	Dies in summer. May self-sow. Lacy seedpods also nice in arrangements.
Spring to fall	Seed	Sun. Most soils. Moderate water. Easy to grow.	Taller kinds may need staking. Deadhead to prolong bloom
Spring, summer, fall, sometimes winter	Seed	Sun. Sandy soil best. Moderate water. Rich soil inhibits bloom. Easy to grow.	Succeeds very near the ocean. Self sows freely. T. minus is compact; T. majus trails or climbs. 'Alaska' has variegated leaves.
Late spring to mid-summer	Seed	Sun. Fertile soil. Moderate water. Pinch when young to encourage branching.	Best to seed inside and transplant. If site is too damp and shady, blooms get gray mold.
Spring, summer, fall, sometimes winter	Seed	Sun. Fertile soil. Ample water. Pick stem with some leaves for bouquets.	Snails, slugs, earwigs eat blossoms. Deadhead to prolong bloom.
Summer, fall, sometimes winter	Seed	Sun. Fertile soil. Moderate water. Can grow in alkaline soil.	Taller varieties need staking. Deadheading prolongs bloom period.
Spring, summer	Seed	Sun. Well amended soil. Moderate water. Cut just as color shows on buds.	Red ones sold as Flanders poppies. Last longer in the vase if you dip end of stem first in boiling water, then ice water.
Summer, early fall	Seed	Average to rich soil, ample water. Cut flowers that have just opened; use a knife.	Protect seedlings from slugs, snails, and earwigs. Leave seedheads uncut—birds enjoy the seeds.
Spring & summer	Seed	Sun. Best in lean sandy soil. Moderate water. Use either fresh or dried.	Succeeds very near the ocean. All plants may not come into bloom together.
Late winter, spring, summer	Seed	Sun. Well-amended soil. Moderate water.	Scent is stronger on overcast days and in the evening.
Summer	Seed	Sun. Well-amended soil. Moderate water. Use fresh or dried.	Tall forms may need staking. To dry, cut before center opens, hang upside down.
Almost all year	Seed	Sun. Most soils. Moderate water. Good in small bouquets.	Self-sows. Cut back, to prolong bloom period.
Winter, spring, summer	Seed	Sun. Fertile, well-amended soil. Keep moist. Easy to grow.	Different varieties bloom in different day lengths. If a variety is fragrant, description will say so. Tall varieties need trellis.
Spring, summer	Seed	Sun. Fairly fertile soil. Moderate water. Long lasting cut flower.	Old varieties take nearly a year from seed. Some new ones bloom in as little as 10 weeks from spring sowing—check listings.
Winter, summer, spring, fall	Seed	Sun, part shade. Fertile soil. Ample water.	Like pansies, violas are really perennials, but treated as annuals.
Summer, fall	Seed	Sun. Fertile, well-amended soil. Ample water.	Zinnias prefer more heat. Look for varieties bred to withstand cool days. Avoid wetting leaves to prevent mildew.

Making Cut Flowers Last

The vase life of flowers is much improved by getting them into water as soon as possible. If your garden is far from home (as are many community gardeners), or if you are taking the bouquet to a friend, wrap the stems in a wet paper towel and put the stems or the whole bouquet in a plastic bag. Keep them out of the direct sun while in transport. When you are ready to put your flowers in a vase, always remove the lower leaves, so they won't decay in the water. If it has been more than a few minutes between cutting and putting your flowers in a vase, recut the stems, using clippers or a sharp knife to remove another 1/2 to 1 inch. For very delicate flowers, cut the stems while holding them under water in a bowl, then put the flowers immediately into a water-filled vase. If your cut flowers wilt despite these precautions, try this: As soon as you make an arrangement, put the vase in a cool room, away from direct sunlight. Keep a plastic bag over the flowers for a few hours or overnight, then remove the bag and move them to the place where you want them to be.

And don't forget your flowers after the first day. Changing the water every day or two and keeping your vases well filled with water will make your creations last longer.

FIFTEEN

FRUIT FROM THE FOG

 EMON TREES PRODUCE A steady supply of their tangy, bright yellow fruits in many a foggy local backyard and plum trees droop under their sweet burden every summer. These are among the most reliable fruit trees for our region. With attention paid to choice of variety and location, we can also grow many other kinds of fruit—from the deciduous fruit trees such as apples and pears, to subtropical evergreen trees such as avocado, figs, and tangerines, as well as bush and vine crops such as blackberry and kiwi.

The Limiting Factors

When a frost destroys all of a lime tree's half-ripe fruit, resulting in no crop at all that year, the tree has just encountered a *limiting factor*. Frost is one of several factors that can limit fruit production in local gardens. These factors affect some crops more than others. Some, such as certain plum varieties, can live pretty comfortably within all of our region's limits. Others, including oranges or peaches, tend to bump into one or more of these limiting factors fairly regularly, so they don't produce good crops every year or throughout the region.

Winters That Are Too Cold

While some parts of our region may stay entirely above 32°F during some winters, it is more likely that a garden will dip into the upper 20s at least once a winter. Tropical and subtropical plants are sensitive to frost, some being unable to survive temperatures below freezing even briefly. Among fruit crop plants, the entire plant may be damaged, or it may survive but bear no fruit. The mango is a tropical tree we can't grow because the slightest frost will kill it. Banana plants may survive light frosts, but they are not very likely to ripen fruit here. Avocado trees and some kinds of citrus will lose their fruit for the year if frost hits them at the wrong time. Deciduous fruit trees don't mind the cold at all, being natives of cold-winter areas.

When a plant is borderline in your location— hardy enough for all but the lowest likely temperatures—you may not want to waste space on it. But if you still want to try it, use the same principles you would for placing vegetables to avoid winter frost. Put the fruit plants where they will get the most winter sunlight and radiated heat, as well as the best protection from cold winds. When possible, plant them under an overhang, to provide a barrier to falling cold air.

Sometimes a deciduous fruit tree, like apple or plum, may be quite able to withstand frost while it is dormant, but not while it is blooming. It may be stimulated to bloom early by mild winter temperatures, only to lose its blossoms to a late frost. If you know a fruit variety may bloom very early, plant it where it will grow in a winter shadow, as this will cause it to bud out later, hopefully after the chance of frost is over. However, choose early ripening varieties for this, so the return of the shadow in late summer or fall won't cut short the ripening of the fruit.

Winters That Are Too Warm

A second limiting factor for fruit growing in our area is a lack of winter chill. Far from resenting an occasional frost, deciduous fruit trees such as apples, pears, peaches, nectarines, plums, and cherries require a minimum amount of winter cold to produce a good crop.

To calculate the amount of winter chill in an area, horticulturists add together all the hours in an entire winter during which the temperature is between 32 and 45° F. The total number of such hours is known as the *chill factor* for that year. Hours below 32° don't count, and hours over 60° get subtracted from the total chill hours. The chill factor in our central California coastal region ranges from fewer than 100 to 900 hours. Most coastal areas have up to 400 chilling hours. Areas more than a few miles from the ocean have 400 to 900 hours. If your location is blocked from the ocean influence by hills, or is shaded in winter, or is in a cold pocket, it will get more winter chill. Areas that get more winter "tule" fog may get additional chilling hours from the resulting cooler days, though not if warmer nights balance them out.

Some apple varieties need as many as 1,800 hours! Fortunately, researchers have found or developed varieties that can produce well with less chill. Thus, some apples succeed with a chill factor of 400 hours or even less. Of the above fruits, all but cherries have low-chill varieties. Figs, a deciduous tree from the Mediterranean, have a relatively low chill requirement—only 100 hours. Subtropical evergreen trees, such as avocado and citrus, have no chill requirement at all.

When a plant doesn't get enough winter chill, it does not end its dormant period in an orderly manner. It typically blooms late. Then the blossoms tend to open sporadically over a long period, rather than all at once. This reduces the chances of pollination because there are fewer blooms at a time. It also lessens the chance of cross-pollination, because the other trees that would have provided pollen may have already bloomed. In addition, the long bloom time weakens the tree, often leading to its early demise.

Although this is an important factor, it can be difficult to be exact in dealing with it. One uncertainty is that the chill factor rating for a fruit variety tends to be approximate—you will find published figures that vary by as much as 300 hours for the same variety. Also, you aren't likely to be able to find out the exact chilling hours for your garden's location. The experts who study this factor assure me that predicting winter chill with statistical methods is more difficult nearer the coast than it is inland.

And since there is little commercial fruit-growing in the region, there aren't likely to be efforts to record actual chilling hours here. Because of these uncertainties, local gardeners often do take risks, and sometimes these pay off in successful harvests. Despite the uncertainties, you should make an effort to guess your level of winter chill, and try to choose plants that require less, or only a little more, winter chill than the average you are likely to get.

Increase winter chill for borderline crops by planting them in spots where they will be in the shade much of the winter (on the north sides of structures or evergreen trees, or on north slopes of hills), or in low spots. Avoid planting them against heated buildings.

Summers That Are Not Warm Enough

Many kinds of fruits require summers warmer than ours to ripen fruit that is sweet. Fruit growers calculate summer warmth in terms of *degree days*. While the meaning of the term varies depending on the fruit you are growing, the principle is that degree days accumulate when the mean temperature for a day is above a certain minimum. For grapes, the minimum is 50° F. So, for example, if the mean temperature of a day is 70°, you would say it contributed 20 degree days toward the ripening of grapes.

As with the chilling hours, degree days are harder to predict for sites nearest the coast. But this factor is easier for us to guess at than the winter chill factor. When we feel chilly in the summer, chances are that heat-requiring fruit will not be getting enough heat. And we can pretty well assume that the degree day total is low in areas where the delay of the maximum temperature is great (see map on page 15). Our cool summers will limit our success with grapes, oranges, grapefruits, peaches, and pomegranates, among other fruits.

Sometimes we can find a variety of a particular fruit that can develop sweeter fruit than other varieties in a cool summer. But even then, it's a good idea to locate the plant in a favorable garden site to maximize warmth, using all the tricks you would use in locating a heat-requiring vegetable crop.

Too Much Humidity

Humid air fosters plant diseases such as fireblight, peach leaf curl, and brown rot of apricot. In foggier regions, peach leaf curl may be hard to control even with repeated treatments. To prevent these diseases, choose resistant varieties whenever possible and plant where the trees will get as much sun as possible. When you are pruning, thin the branches so that the trees don't have very dense foliage. Also avoid leaving a garden sprinkler set where it will spray water into tree branches.

Growing Fruit Trees in Small Spaces

Fruit trees used to require considerable garden space, as most grew to 25 to 40 feet tall, with similar spreads. Now we are fortunate in having smaller versions of these trees, so that we can have several kinds of fruit in even a small yard. And if we choose varieties that ripen at different times, we can avoid having the glut of fruit that a full-sized tree can produce. Sure you like apples, but just what would you do with 10 bushels of them, all ripe at the same time?

Growing Smaller Trees

Many dwarf and semidwarf trees have been created by grafting a full-sized variety onto a rootstock that stunts the tree. These can be highly satisfactory, bearing early and well. You can also often find dwarfs on rootstocks that offer resistance to local diseases and are particularly well-adapted to local soils. However the grafting process does tend to shorten the life of the tree, and you must take care to prune out any suckers that sprout near the ground from below the graft union, as these shoots will not bear good fruit.

More recently, a few natural, genetically dwarf trees have been discovered and developed. You may see them listed as either genetic dwarfs or miniature trees. These often bear even sooner than the dwarfs created by using dwarfing rootstock, and they seem to have considerably longer lives. Genetic dwarfs do not exist for all kinds of fruit trees and the quality of fruit they bear is not always as high as the best rootstock-formed dwarfs, but breeding continues, resulting in new and better varieties every year.

Aside from using dwarf trees, many kinds of full-sized trees can be pruned and otherwise treated in ways that control their size somewhat. When your deciduous tree, such as apple or plum, is approaching the size you want, you can slow its growth by shifting your major pruning from winter to summer. If it is a fig tree you wish to control, prune it while it is dormant. Evergreens, such as avocado and citrus can also be pruned to keep them in bounds, and this is best done when they are most dormant, neither sprouting new shoots nor flowering. Full grown avocado trees may sprout back and bear fruit even if they are chopped down to a three foot stump, something you might want to try if you have a too-large tree in your yard.

Dwarf trees of either kind can be grown in containers. Container-bound trees will inevitably produce less fruit than those in the open ground, but if you have only a roof or deck, you will welcome a chance to have even a modest crop. Half-barrels are a good choice of containers. These will last longer if they are spar varnished and have had their metal hoops bolted to the wood. Sometimes you can buy them already prepared in these ways. Drill 2 or 3 holes in the bottoms for drainage. Put each empty barrel on a small platform with wheels of the sort sold for house plants, so you will be able to move it about. Then plant the tree in a good potting mix. Water and fertilize your container trees often. Every couple of years, while they are dormant, remove them from their containers. Trim out circling roots and the fattest of the rest of the roots, leaving thinner, fibrous roots. Repot, using fresh potting mix.

Training Trees To Fit Small Spaces

A number of kinds of fruit trees can be trained and maintained in very small forms, such as espaliers, cordons, or Belgian fences. These are all two-dimen-sional trees, trained and pruned so that all of the limbs lie in one plane. They are generally grown against a fence or wall. These pruning techniques not only save space, but also provide a warm environment for the trees, because walls and fences radiate heat.

Espaliers may be pruned into very formal patterns, such as fans or candelabra forms, or they may be allowed to develop into a less formal, but still two-dimensional, pattern. A cordon is even more restrained than an espalier, being limited to a single stem, growing diagonally from the ground, with only very short side branches. Several cordons, grown in a row along a fence, allow the gardener to sample just a bit of several varieties or kinds of fruit while using minimum space. A Belgian fence is a row of

several fruit trees espaliered to single V shapes, with
their limbs overlapping, and maybe actually growing
together, to form a "living fence".

Fruits vary in their ability to adapt to formal
pruning and training such as the styles described
above. Apples, pears, figs, persimmons, and citrus
are among those that can be successfully treated
this way. And, among the varieties of a fruit, some
will adjust better than others. Some fruits, or varieties of a particular fruit, will take to an informal
espalier, but not a formal one, or to a fan, but not
to candelabra tiers. Ask an experienced grower
about the adaptability of a particular plant variety
before you purchase or create your own espaliered
tree.

All of these formally trained trees require careful pruning each year to create and maintain their
form. A cordon is probably the simplest to do, then
an informal espalier, with the more formal patterns
taking more attention and work. You can buy trees
already trained, several years old, ready to be set in
front of your fence, saving yourself much of the
trouble. Still, if you have never pruned fruit trees
before, and plan to do it yourself, get a guidebook
and study it well in advance of your first pruning
season.

Start with Plants, Not Seed

Notice that I have been talking about buying
plants, rather than starting your own fruit trees or
shrubs from seed. This is with good reason, as most
kinds of fruit do not come true from seed. That is, a
seed from a plant with good fruit often will produce
a plant with inferior fruit. It can be interesting to
start fruit from seed, and some seedlings may turn
out well, but after you wait several years for seedling
fruit trees to reach bearing age, you will not want to
find that a low proportion of your trees have high
quality fruit. For this reason, most fruits are grown
by grafting a twig of a known variety onto a carefully chosen rootstock, or by rooting cuttings.

Probably the most common homegrown fruit
seedling is the avocado, because it is such fun to
germinate the large seeds. All of the foregoing cau-
tions apply to avocados. While the chance of avocado seedlings maturing to trees with good fruit
could be as high as 50%, if you have room for only
one or two trees, those aren't very good odds. And
if they do not bear well, you will have on your
hands some large, heavily shading trees that are
expensive to remove. So enjoy the sprouting seeds

as house plants, but invest in a selected avocado
variety for your yard.

While buying already-grafted trees is clearly the
most practical route to good fruit trees, grafting
your own, or grafting other varieties onto the trees
you already have, is a pleasant exploration. Look for
workshops where you can learn the basics. If you
have a healthy seedling, you can use it as rootstock,
grafting onto it a twig (scion) of a variety that produces reliably good fruit. Some gardeners even graft
branches of several varieties, or even different fruits,
onto the same mature tree. This can work, though
it tends to exhaust a tree, especially when the different varieties develop fruit at different times. The
California Rare Fruit Growers Society (listed in
Appendix V), has scion exchanges that are open to
the public.

When you are ready to buy plants, try to purchase ones that have been grown as near as possible
to our region, as these are more likely to be on
rootstocks well suited to our climate and soils. You
can buy most kinds of fruits in containers, and if it
is a deciduous fruit tree you want, it is best to buy
these bareroot in the winter. Younger plants are
often a better buy than older ones, as they frequently become established faster, and so bear
sooner. Inquire carefully about the mature size of
the trees you are purchasing.

Choosing Fruit Trees and Shrubs
For Our Climate

Little or no fruit is grown commercially in the most
coastal parts of our area. And when commercial
interest is low, detailed information on how plants
perform is rarely compiled. What follows is based on
my experience, along with the recommendations of
the University of California Extension Service,
Sunset Books, several experienced fruit growers, and
fruit nurseries. Still, the whole picture will only be
clear when we have been able to make a formal
fruit tree census in our foggy area.

As nothing speaks stronger than proven success,
start by looking around to see what kind of fruit
your neighbors are growing. Talk to them about
their successes or failures. In many neighborhoods,
you can't see into backyards, but you may be able to
locate some of your neighborhood's hidden fruit
trees or shrubs by asking around, then trying to get
an introduction to neighborhood orchardists. Try to
get reports on the quality of fruits or fruit varieties

growing near you, or a chance to taste samples. Look for fruit tastings at farmers markets or produce stores. Contact the California Rare Fruit Growers and ask to talk to members who live near you. This organization often also has samples of different fruits and fruit varieties at their meetings. Send for the catalogs of mail-order fruit nurseries (some are listed in Appendix V), study them, and ask advice from these companies or from local nurseries that have been helpful answering your other gardening questions. Study listings in this chapter and in books listed in Appendix VI, Suggested Reading. Beware of the occasional local store that may stock standard apple varieties because the public requests them, even though they do not do well here.

COMPENDIUM OF FRUITS

The following entries will give you a general idea of how to grow each fruit—soil, watering, pruning, etc. When you have decided on the kind of fruit and the variety you want to grow, choose a book or two from Appendix VI, Suggested Reading and study in greater detail how to care for the plants you have chosen.

ALMOND

Prunus dulcis var. *dulcis*
Rose Family ❖ *Rosaceae*

Almonds are definitely not considered adapted to the most coastal parts of the region, as they need warmer summers for proper development of nuts. In fact, they are considered marginal at best in the entire region because of this problem. Still, there are bearing trees of the varieties 'Nonpareil' and 'All in One' growing in a very warm part of San Francisco, so I won't say never. Give almonds a deep soil with excellent drainage, and water deeply, but not often. They are susceptible to mites and to brown rot. Most need a pollinator.

APPLE

Malus species
Rose Family ❖ *Rosaceae*

Most apple varieties, including some of the most familiar, require 900 or more hours of winter chill. However, a substantial and increasing number of available varieties can produce well with only 300 to 400 chilling hours. A few even do well with as little as 100 hours. And many of these low-chill varieties bear fruit with excellent flavor and texture.

Apples require soil with reasonably good drainage, moderate fertilization and infrequent deep watering in summer. They also need some annual pruning and need thinning of young fruit to allow the remaining fruit to grow larger. Apples are available as full-sized trees, which grow 25 to 40 feet tall, as semidwarfs to 12 to 14 feet tall, or as dwarf trees only 4 to 8 feet tall. Apple trees are good subjects for espaliers, cordons, or Belgian fences. Most varieties of apples need cross pollination.

Apples may get fireblight, scab, mildew, aphids, codling moth worms, or various other insect pests, and may need treatments to combat these—most commonly with dormant oil or sulfur. While your apple trees may have any of these pest problems, they may also turn out to be relatively pest-free.

Fireblight is a bacterial disease of rose family plants that causes entire branches to die. In most cases, the leaves blacken, as though burned, but apple leaves turn dark brown. Fireblight is spread by splashing water, pollinating insects, and, some believe, infected pruning shears. High humidity encourages its spread. It can also be spread from ornamental rose family plants such as pyracantha. There are no cures, but some varieties are more resistant than others.

Fireblight will be less likely to occur if air can circulate amidst the foliage, reducing humidity. Consider this when you are pruning, and thin areas where branches are becoming crowded. A preventive measure for especially susceptible or valuable trees is to spray several times while the plant is in bloom with streptomycin or a copper fungicide registered for the purpose. Prune out any infected limbs out, cutting 18 inches below the dead area. It is recommended that you sterilize your shears between cuts by dipping them in 10% bleach solution to reduce the chance of infecting branches with contaminated shears. Some horticulturalists feel that this is an unnecessary or ineffective precaution. (If you do dip your shears, dry and oil them well after you are through pruning to prevent rust.)

There are too many suitable varieties of apple to list, but here are a few possibilities. The hours listed are the hours of winter chill required by each variety. The earliest apples ripen in early summer, the latest in October or even November.

Apple Varieties Anna: 200 hours. Very early. Yellow with red blush, sweet, crisp. Stores well. Needs pollinator.
Beverly Hills: 300 hours or less. Early. Pale yellow, red stripes, tender, somewhat tart. Self-fruitful.
Braeburn: 600 or less hours. Late. Medium to large, with a red blush over a yellow-green ground. Crisp and tart, good fresh or for pie. Good keeper. Self-fruitful.
Golden Delicious: 700 hours. Yellow, crisp, sweet, high quality. Self-fruitful. Resists fireblight. Stores well. Pollinator.
Gordon: 400 hours. Early to midseason. Red over green, sweet-tart. Self-fruitful.
Granny Smith: 600 hours. Very late. Green, crisp, tart. May ripen too late for cool coastal areas. Self-fruitful.
Gravenstein: 700 or less hours. Early. Red over deep yellow, crisp, juicy, aromatic. Poor keeper. Needs pollinator.
Hudson's Golden Gem: 600 or less hours. Late. Large, elongated fruit. Yellow with red-yellow, very sweet. Stores well. Needs pollinator.
McIntosh: 600 or less hours. Early. Deep red color, richly-flavored, aromatic. Keeps only fair when grown in mild climates. Self-pollinating but produces better with pollinator.
Mutsu (Crispin): 600 hours. Late. Pick green or yellow, very large, crisp, good flavor. Needs pollinator.
Pink Pearl: 600 or less hours. Early. Pink skin and pink flesh. Firm, rich-tasting apple that makes pink applesauce. Unusually dark pink blossoms. Stores well. Needs pollinator.
Red Astrachan: 600 or less hours. Very early. Medium to large fruit is yellow with red stripes. Crisp, juicy, tart flavor. Good raw, and very good for pies. Self pollinating, but produces better with pollinator.
Skinner's Seedling: 400 or less. Midseason. Greenish-yellow, sometimes blushed pink. Mild-flavored, good for both eating fresh and cooking. Reliable for coastal climates. Fair keeper. Needs a pollinator.
Winter Banana: 400 or less hours. Midseason. Large, pale yellow, blushed pink, tangy. Fair keeper. Needs pollinator.

White Winter Pearmain: 400 hours or less. Very late. Medium pale, green fruit, usually with one side blushed red. Mild and aromatic dessert apple. Excellent keeper. Needs pollination, and pollinates other varieties.
Yellow Newton Pippin: 700 hours. Late. Green to yellow, firm, crisp, slightly tart. Good for cooking. Stores very well. Self-fruitful.

APRICOTS
Prunus armeniaca
Rose Family ❖ *Rosaceae*

Apricots are considered unlikely to succeed in most of the region. Even when you choose low chill varieties, pollination may be inhibited by cold, rainy, or windy weather during their bloom time, and fruit will not ripen properly if a site is too cool in the summer. In addition our humid weather encourages fungus disease, brown rot, which spoils the fruit and weakens the tree. In some coastal sites fruit may develop purple blemishes known as "fog spots." Nevertheless, I have been told of three successfully bearing apricot trees in warmer parts of San Francisco, and these trees reportedly do not suffer from brown rot. I will list some low chill varieties for those with sunnier microclimates who wish to give them a try.

Soil, water and fertilizer needs are similar to apples. Apricots need annual pruning to stimulate new growth and they may be espaliered. Keep full-sized trees at 10 to 14 feet for ease of harvest. Some are self-fruitful; some need a pollinator. Unless you are extremely lucky, they will need dormant spraying with Bordeaux mixture to try to prevent brown rot.

Apricot Varieties Royal (Blenheim): 500 hours. Ripens June or Early July. Sweet, aromatic, flavorful. Self-fruitful.
Gold Kist: 300 hours. Ripens in May. Large, tart-sweet. Self-fruitful.
Flora Gold: 500 hours. Ripens June. Good quality. Self-fruitful.
Katy: 300 hours. Ripens May. Excellent flavor. Self-Fruitful.

AVOCADOS
Persea americana
Laurel Family ❖ *Lauraceae*

Some avocados are too frost sensitive for our region, others fare pretty well. In all cases, leafy growth is more frost-hardy than the flowers or fruit, so varieties that bloom and begin to ripen fruit in warmer months are more likely to bear full crops here. Varieties with Mexican avocado parentage are hardier than those from Guatemalan avocado stock.

Avocados are very sensitive to waterlogged soil. Plant where drainage is very good and don't overwater. Once established, irrigation every 4 weeks in the dry season is sufficient. Trees will grow best where soil has a pH of 5.5 to 6.5. They may require treatment with iron chelate to check iron-deficiency chlorosis. Full-sized trees reach 30 to 60 feet. Dwarf varieties reach 10 to 14 feet, but the currently available dwarfs, such as 'Wurtz', are Guatemalan in ancestry. Try 'Wurtz' in very protected sites or in containers on wheels so they can be wheeled inside in winter. Avocados don't require much pruning, but they can be pruned to keep them to a small-sized tree.

Most avocados are self-fruitful, however, if you plant an "A" type plant near a "B" type plant, both may produce better. I have identified these types when the information was available. Some varieties tend to produce larger crops in alternate years, but even the lighter crop is often sufficient for a home gardener.

Avocado Varieties   Bacon: Blooms in the spring and fruit matures in 18 months. It ripens around July, and then hangs on the tree for six months longer. Good quality fruit. Medium-large tree. Alternate year bearing.
Hass(A): Black-skinned, excellent flavor. Blooms in winter and ripens the next December-January. Hardy to 30°F.
Jim(B): Heavy producer of small to medium green fruit with very good flavor. Ripens September to January. Tree is medium-sized, upright. Hardy to 24°F.
Mexicola(A): Heavy producer of small, purple fruits with excellent flavor. Ripens August to October. Medium-sized, spreading tree. Hardy to 18°F.
Wurtz: Dwarf tree of Guatemalan ancestry. Bears medium-sized green fruit in the summer. Tree can reach 10-12 feet. Bears in alternate years.
Zutano(B): Heavy producer of medium-sized green fruits with good flavor. Ripens December to January. Medium-sized, upright tree. Hardy to 26°F.

BLACKBERRY
Rubus species, varieties, and hybrids
Rose Family ❖ *Rosaceae*

Trailing types of blackberries will succeed throughout the region, and should be planted in preference to the eastern upright varieties. Blackberries require a deep soil, moderate fertilization and plenty of water. Trailing blackberries must be trained on a trellis or on wires, and if they are not pruned and trained with care, will become a miserable tangle. See page 114 for a description of the pruning routine as modified for the very vigorous Himalayas, and Appendix VI, Suggested Reading for books with a more complete explanation of the process. Redberry mites sometimes attack, keeping fruit from ripening. Treatment is dormant spray with lime-sulfur. Some varieties get verticillium wilt.

Blackberry Varieties   Boysen and Thornless Boysen: Berries are large, soft, reddish and sweet-tart. High yield. Susceptible to verticillium wilt.
Himalaya: The common weedy blackberry. See page 113 for more on this plant. One virtue is its long season—mid-July to October with summer water.
Logan and Thornless Logan: Light reddish fruit, not as sweet as Boysen, wonderful in pies.
Olallie: Large, black, firm, sweet berries.

BLUEBERRY
Vaccinium corymbosum, V. angustifolium, V. ashei and *hybrids*
Heath Family ❖ *Ericaceae*

These wonderful berries are borne on long-lived and attractive shrubs. The plants bear small pink, bell-shaped flowers in the spring, berries in the summer, and often provide brilliant red or yellow fall color. Blueberries are marginal in the most coastal areas, but worth a try wherever you can give them full sun in a protected location. The varieties that succeed here are low-chill types, mainly highbush. (Rabbit-eye varieties, often advertized for southern locations, are low-chill, but not particularly well suited to cool summers.)

Blueberries require about the same soil as for rhododendrons—acidic, with good drainage. To create it, you must add acidic organic matter until the soil has a pH of 4 to 5.2, then continue to add acidic mulch, sulfur, and fertilizers over the years, to keep the soil from reverting to the pH of the surroundings.

Highbush plants typically reach 5 to 6 feet tall and need about as much space between plants. Blueberry plants are very bushy, not good subjects for espalier. Dwarf hybrids, which have recently become available, grow to only 1 1/2 to 3 feet. While I am not sure of their adaptability, I'm sure they are worth a try.

Don't prune blueberries at all for the first four years. Then they need only light pruning, which may include some tip-pruning to prevent the plants from setting more fruit then they will be able to ripen. You may need to put netting over the plants when fruit is ripening to foil birds. In most cases, if you grow more than one variety, you will get better pollination, but the new dwarf plants are self-fertile.

Blueberry Varieties Berkeley: Midseason. Large berries ripen in midseason on a tall, broad plant.
Bluecrop: 800 hours. Midseason. Superbly flavored berries on a tall, erect plant, with relatively low water needs.
Collins: Early to midseason. Large, very flavorful berries. Erect bush.
Earliblue: Early. Large, berries. Tall, upright plant.
Jersey: Berries only fair. Tall, upright plant.
Darrow: Late. The largest of blueberries: firm, tart, and flavorful. Upright bush.
Elliot: Late. Medium-sized, firm, and slightly tart berries. Upright bush.
Dwarf Blueberry Varieties:
Northblue: Midseason. Large, flavorful berries. Plant grows to 3 feet tall. Self-fertile.
Northsky: Midseason. Large, flavorful berries. Grows 18 inches tall and spreads 2 to 3 feet. Self-fertile.

CALAMONDIN

Citrus reticulata x *Fortunella mitis*
Citrus Family ❖ *Rutaceae*

This sour, orange fruit is popular in the Philippines, known in Tagalog as Kalamansi. It produces well, and, like the Rangpur lime, is very pretty on the tree. Full-sized trees are large, but dwarfs are a co-lumnar 8 to 10 feet. (See Citrus, page 333.)

CHERRY

Prunus species
Rose Family ❖ *Rosaceae*

No cherries are recommended for the coastal areas of the region, as they all require more winter chill. Nevertheless, I have seen one bearing sour cherry tree, of an unknown variety, in San Francisco's sunny Mission District in a location with winter shade. Cherries are more reliable producers further inland, east of the coastal hills.

FIG

Ficus carica
Mulberry Family ❖ *Moraceae*

Though figs are, in general, better adapted to areas with hot summers, some varieties will produce crops in cool coastal weather. Still, they may not succeed in the foggiest parts of the coast. Plant them where they will get a maximum of summer sun and warmth (but take care not to plant where the fall-ing fruits will stain pavement).

Figs are less particular about soil type than they are about good drainage. They need light to moder-ate amounts of fertilizer, and produce best with regular summer water. Full sized trees grow 15 to 30 feet tall, dwarfs to 10 feet. After initial shaping, prune mature fig trees, while they are dormant, to remove deadwood, to thin overgrown limbs, and to keep the tree in bounds. Figs are fairly amenable to severe size control. (In areas with moderately cold winters, they freeze to the ground and grow back each year as a shrub.) Full-sized trees can be held to 10 or even 6 feet tall, or can be trained into an espalier.

Figs typically make two crops a year, the *breba* crop, in late spring, and the larger, midsummer-to-fall main crop. Heavily pruned trees may not bear a *breba* crop, but you may consider this an acceptable price to pay for the pleasure of having a fig tree small enough for a very small yard or a large con-tainer. The commonly grown figs are self-fruitful.

Fig Varieties Black Mission (Mission): Purplish black skin, reddish flesh. Good fresh, dry or canned. Produces best if not heavily pruned. Fruit often not sweet enough near the coast.
Brown Turkey: Purplish brown skin, pinkish flesh. Best if eaten fresh. Grows in cooler areas than Black Mission. Bigger main crop if pruned heavily.
Osborne Prolific: Purplish brown skin, amber flesh. Very sweet flavor. Best eaten fresh. Very good for cool coastal regions.
White Adriatic: Green to yellow-green skin, flesh red, deeper red in cool areas. No breba crop. Good flavor and good for cool coastal regions.

GRAPE

Vitis species and hybrids
Grape Family ❖ *Vitaceae*

The limiting factor for grape growing in our coastal area is lack of summer heat. When summers are too cool, fruit ripens slowly and may not ripen properly at all. Most grapes require at least 1700 degree days, and the most coastal parts of the region do not provide this. However, the minimum is reached fairly quickly as you move inland, so if you live in a fairly warm microclimate, you may wish to try very early grape varieties. Note that no grape varieties are recommended for the most exposed locations near the coast.

Grapes do best in a soil rich in organic matter. They may need a little nitrogen fertilizer, added early in the season. They need excellent drainage, and require very little summer water. Most are self-fertile.

Training and careful annual pruning are necessary to keep grapes bearing well. And part of the purpose of pruning is to thin the crop, as a grape vine with too heavy a crop will not produce sweet fruit. Grapes are best grown on a trellis or fence.

A grape variety may be European in origin, American in origin, or a hybrid of the two. In general, American varieties have lower heat requirements. Also, European grapes are susceptible to mildew, while most American grapes are not. (I suspect that American/European hybrids vary in resistance.) If mildew strikes, it may be controlled by several dustings of sulfur. Without treatment, the mildew will often render a plant incapable of bearing fruit.

The grape leafhopper is a common pest in California grape growing areas, but I have not heard of this pest attacking San Francisco grapes. Whether we escape it because of the climate, or because there are too few grapes for the pests to locate, I don't know.

Table Grape Varieties Campbell Early: Early. A deep purple grape that resembles Concord, but is better for cool areas. American or hybrid.
Cardinal: Earliest red table grape. Large fruit, few seeds. Very vigorous and productive. Hybrid between two European varieties, Ribier and Tokay.
Concord: Midseason. Blue-black fruit with a distinctive, rich flavor. American.
Flame Seedless (Flame): Early. Light red, sweet and crisp. Dessert grape. European.
Moore: Early. Red grape. Vigorous, productive, disease resistant. American or hybrid.
Perlette: Early. Small, light green seedless grape. The earliest to ripen. Vigorous and productive. European.

GRAPEFRUIT
Citrus x paradisi
Citrus Family ❖ *Rutaceae*

Grapefruit is not likely to ripen well without considerably more summer heat than we get anywhere in the region. However, a cross between grapefruit and a similar fruit called a pummelo (C. *maxima*), has produced a variety known as 'Oroblanco', available as a dwarf, which may be able to produce acceptable fruit near the coast. (See Citrus, page 333.)

GUAVA (SEE PINEAPPLE GUAVA AND STRAWBERRY GUAVA)

HUCKLEBERRY, EVERGREEN
Vaccinium ovatum
Heath Family ❖ *Ericaceae*

If you've walked in the coastal redwoods in late summer, you may have tasted these small, almost black, berries that grow on decorative evergreen shrubs. (The plants are so attractive that the florist industry grows them for the shiny sprays of foliage.)

Huckleberries are adapted to the coastal climate, and need much the same soil as rhododendrons, camellias, and blueberries. They will do better with some shade in less foggy parts of the region, but may take full sun in the foggiest places.

Little attention has been paid to selecting and breeding these plants for fruit production. There are more and less productive strains, but finding a productive one still involves an element of chance. (Maybe you will discover a particularly fruitful strain and propagate it for others.) You will find plants at plant sales of the California Native Plant Society as well as in nursery catalogs (see Appendix V, Resources).

KIWI FRUIT
Actinidia deliciosa (*A. chinensis*)
Actinidia Family ❖ *Actinidiaceae*

It is possible to grow kiwi our region if you choose a low-chill variety and protect it from winds. Even so, where it is cool, fruit will ripen very slowly.

Kiwi fruit is borne on large, woody, twining vines, growing to 30 feet if allowed, and needing sturdy support on a trellis, fence or other structure. Plant kiwis in rich garden soil with good drainage, and don't let the soil completely dry out. You will probably have to water at least once a week. After the third year you can water them less frequently.

They must be pruned twice a year to keep them under control and encourage fruiting. In order to have fruit, you must plant at least two kiwi plants, one male and one female. These must have the same chilling requirements so they will bloom at the same time. The supplier selling you the female kiwi should be able to provide the correct male variety to pollinate it.

Kiwi Varieties (Female)   Hayward: 600 hours. One of the most common on the market.
Chico: Similar to, or possibly the same as, Hayward.
Vincent: 100 to 200 hours. Not common on the market, but worth seeking out if you live in a very low-chill microclimate.
Tewi: 100 to 200 hours. Another low-chill variety worth looking for.

KUMQUAT
Fortunella margarita and *F. crassifolia*
Citrus Family ❖ *Rutaceae*

Kumquats are the hardiest of common citrus fruits. They bear small, orange fruit, with a sweet, edible rind and more or less sour pulp. These can be eaten out of hand, or used candied or in marmalade. Non-dwarf plants vary in size from 4 to 25 feet tall. Dwarfs grow to 4 feet tall.

Kumquat Varieties   Meiwa (*F. crassifolia*): Neither the fruit nor the plant are found as commonly as Nagami kumquats. Fruit is larger, round, and a bit sweeter.
Nagami (*F. margarita*): Oval fruit, to one inch long. This is the standard, sour kumquat you will find in groceries, and the one more commonly sold in nurseries.

LEMON
Citrus limon
Citrus Family ❖ *Rutaceae*

All four common varieties of lemon will grow and produce well in our region: Eureka, Lisbon, Ponderosa, and Improved Meyer. While most citrus needs little or no pruning, lemon trees require occasional thinning of small branches and twigs to keep them from becoming too much of a tangle. They respond well to being cut back to keep the fruit within reach. Of the four varieties, I recommend any but Ponderosa, as the fruit of that variety, though quite large, is very thick-skinned, with little juice.

Lemon Varieties   Eureka: The common grocery store lemon. Bears throughout the year. Plant is somewhat thorny, sensitive to cold, and susceptible to insects, but should do well with reasonable care. It reaches 20 feet if full-sized, and is available as a dwarf. Easy to espalier.
Lisbon: Fruit similar to Eureka. Doesn't hold flavor well if left on the tree too long. More productive and frost hardy than Eureka, but thornier. Full-sized tree grows to 25 feet. Available as a dwarf.
Improved Meyer: Larger, rounder, and thinner skinned than Eureka or Lisbon, and still more frost-hardy than either of them. Has a unique, slightly sweet, taste that some think is superior to Eureka or Lisbon, while others perceive it as "wrong" for a lemon. Bears all year and from a very early age. If full-sized, it reaches 12-15 feet. Available as a dwarf.

LIME
Citrus aurantifolia
Citrus Family ❖ *Rutaceae*

It has been said that any dish you prepare with lemon will taste better with lime. And if you can grow a lemon in your microclimate, you can probably also grow a lime. The Mexican lime usually found in grocery stores is too tender to grow here, but Bearss lime is just as good. Or, for a slightly different flavor, try the Rangpur lime.

Lime Varieties   Bearss: Best true lime for the region, though it may not do well in locations that are both very foggy and windy. It has larger fruit than the Mexican lime, and is hardier. Most of its crop is ready in late winter and spring. Fruit is light yellow when ripe. Tree reaches 15 to 20 feet tall. Dwarfs are available.
Rangpur lime: Really a sour mandarin, the orange fruit of Rangpur lime hangs on the tree most of the year, giving it ornamental value. The flavor is interesting, different from both lemon and lime. Grows to a bushy 15 feet tall, dwarf to 8 feet.

LOQUAT
Eriobotrya japonica
Rose Family ❖ *Rosaceae*

Loquat is a subtropical, evergreen tree native to Southern China. Its large leaves have whitish,

CITRUS FRUIT TREES

Citrus trees are all subtropical evergreens. Their success is limited in our region by winter chill and lack of summer heat. The least hardy, such as Mexican lime and grapefruit, are least likely to succeed in our region because they will be damaged by an occasional drop to 28°F. The hardiest, such as Improved Meyer lemon and kumquat, will survive temperatures to 20°.

But even though most citrus will not be killed by our winters, many will not produce good fruit due to our cool summers. The sour-fruited crops, lemon and some kinds of lime, and the less familiar Rangpur lime, calamondin, and kumquat will ripen properly, but tangerines and oranges are borderline; grapefruits definitely need more heat. Tangerines, oranges, and grapefruits do not develop full sweetness unless the summers can provide consistent temperatures in the 70s and 80s.

While citrus types may differ in hardiness and need for summer heat, they otherwise have very similar needs. They will tolerate a pH of 5.5 to 8, but if soil is not acidic, all citrus is likely to develop iron or zinc deficiency. The surest cure is application of iron or zinc chelates (see page 80), but, for a longer term cure, you can use acidifying fertilizers and/or amendments to reduce the soil pH.

All citrus need a soil with good drainage, and enough irrigation to keep the soil moist down where the roots are. If not watered adequately, citrus will drop leaves—a problem especially common in container-grown trees. Even if leaf drop is severe, however, trees can usually be returned to health by beginning to water more frequently. All citrus trees respond to ample fertilization, divided into several applications a year.

As to pruning, most citrus do not require it to improve fruit bearing, though you may want to prune them for shape. They can be pruned to form trees, large informal shrubs, sheared hedges, or informal espaliers. They may also need pruning to remove dead twigs. Full-sized citrus trees range from 12 to 30 feet tall, while grafted dwarfs, at 4 to 10 feet, are available for most of the fruits. Most citrus is self-fertile.

If citrus is growing well, it may escape pests, but it can become infested with mites, scale, whiteflies or thrips. You can reduce the chance of infestation by occasionally washing the foliage with a vigorous spray of water. When you do this, spray both sides of the leaves, but do it briefly. Never leave a sprinkler on, drenching the tree for a long time, or you will encourage various diseases of the trunk or roots. Scale, aphids, and whiteflies all produce honeydew, which attracts ants and supports growth of the fungus Sooty Mold. Treatment for the insect pests will also control these secondary problems.

Another disease that is fostered by moisture is botrytis. If the plant is blooming during a rainy spell, blossoms may fall prey to this decaying fungus. Lemons and limes bloom several times a year, so a rain at the wrong time may cause only a short break in production. However oranges, which bloom in the spring, could lose a year's crop.

Snails sometimes climb into citrus trees where they rasp the leaves and fruit. You can stop snails by placing copper bands around the trunk if there are no low hanging branches that snails can use as bridges to bypass the trunk. Otherwise, pick them out of your trees periodically and control them in the garden at large.

woolly undersides. Its fruit is oval, an inch or two long, yellow to orange, and varies from bland to sweet. Loquats do well on the coast of southern California, where days are not too hot. But while they prefer cool days to hot, our central California coastal weather may be *too* cool for some varieties.

The trees are attractive and, as they can take the amount of water you give a lawn, they can be useful in landscaping. In fact they are often used ornamentally, for which purpose fruitless varieties have been bred. Be sure you are getting a fruit-bearing variety, and also, as the fruit is fairly low-key in flavor, you'll want to seek one that was selected for a good-flavored fruit. Look for grafted, named varieties. Loquats are hardy to 20°F, though flowers or fruit are damaged at 28°.

The plants are adaptable to various moisture conditions. They will grow through a drought if they are well established, though they will grow better if they get some water. They can take constantly moist soil, as long as the soil has good drainage, but too much water may make the fruit less flavorful. A moderate amount of fertilizer each year will encourage fruit production. For best flavor, let the fruits ripen completely on the tree. Loquats grow 15 to 30 feet tall. Prune them to shape the trees, and to let in more light, as they can make a rather thick canopy. They can be espaliered.

Loquats frequently get fireblight and are more likely to get it when there are late spring rains. Some experts would not plant them near apples and pears, for fear of spreading the disease. See apples for more information on fireblight.

Loquat Varieties Benlehr: White-fleshed, sweet fruit. Excellent flavor in southern California and recommended for central coastal regions.
Champagne: White-fleshed, sweet fruit. Probably needs more heat than foggier neighborhoods can provide.
Gold Nugget: Flesh is deep orange, sweet if fully ripe. Sweet fruit in May-June. Best for coast and commonly available.
Grant Road: An improved 'Gold Nugget' that may be hard to find.

MANDARIN ORANGE
(OR TANGERINE)
Citrus reticulata
Citrus Family ❖ *Rutaceae*

These fruits need a warm location if they are to make sweet fruit. Try them in sunny spots, protected from cold winds. Satsuma is the most cold-tolerant variety.

Mandarin Orange Varieties Satsuma: Has been reported to produce abundant and relatively sweet fruit even in somewhat foggy areas. Will become over-ripe if left too long on the tree, but stores well when picked. Full-sized trees 10 to 15 feet, dwarf to 6 feet tall.
Pixie: Matures later, but is relatively sweet near the coast.
Dancy: Can ripen acceptable fruit, but not as sweet as Satsuma and Pixie. Dwarf available.
Kara: Can ripen acceptable fruit, but not as sweet as Satsuma and Pixie. To 15 to 20 feet, half that as a dwarf.

NECTARINE
(SEE PEACH AND NECTARINE)

ORANGE
Citrus sinensis
Citrus Family ❖ *Rutaceae*

These are more sensitive to cold summer temperatures than mandarins. Try them only in protected sites in warmer parts of the region.
Trovita: Known to produce fruit with good flavor in this area. Relatively dependable in, for example, Oakland. Large tree when full-sized. Dwarf is available.
Washington Navel, Robertson Navel, and Valencia: Borderline, but worth a try in a favorable microclimate.

PASSION FRUIT
Passiflora spp.
Passion Flower Family ❖ *Passifloraceae*

Passion fruit is produced by large, vigorous evergreen or semi-evergreen vines. These are attractive plants with spectacular flowers. The most common edible passion fruit, *P. edulis*, has flowers that are white and purple, two inches in diameter. The fruit is purple with aromatic yellow pulp. Another, *P. mollissima*, has tubular red flowers and yellow fruit that makes a good juice. Both are among the passion fruit species that thrive in cool summers, but they do require a relatively sunny location.

Plant a passion fruit vine in soil that is rich in organic matter and has very good drainage. Keep the soil constantly moist, or fruit production will suffer. Fertilize regularly with a fertilizer that provides less nitrogen than phosphorus. Starting in the third year, prune plants annually just after the harvest, to keep them in bounds and to stimulate fruiting. You need to cut out dead inner branches and weak growth, then cut vigorous growth back by one third or more.

PEACH AND NECTARINE
Prunus persica (Nectarine is *P. persica nucipersica*)
Rose Family ❖ *Rosaceae*

Peaches and nectarines, which are the same species of plant, have very similar needs and problems. While low chill varieties of both are available, most require so much summer heat to ripen well that the fruit is likely to be a disappointment in all but the warmest, most protected sites in our region. Both kinds of fruit are highly susceptible to a fungal disease called peach leaf curl, and nectarines are highly likely to get brown rot as well (see Apricot listing for more on brown rot).

Peaches and nectarines require soil with good drainage, and will not grow well in heavy soil. Their water needs are not high, but they could need irrigation if a summer is especially warm. Fertilize them moderately. They are available as full-sized trees reaching 25 feet, as semidwarfs reaching 14 feet, as grafted dwarfs reaching 5 feet, and as genetic dwarfs reaching 6 feet. All peaches and nectarines, except the genetic dwarfs, require careful pruning each year. All need fruit thinning if the fruit set is heavy. They can be espaliered. Most are self-pollinating.

Peaches and nectarines will almost certainly get peach leaf curl. The treatment for this, and for brown rot, is dormant spraying with Bordeaux mixture, lime-sulfur or a micronized copper product. The common recommendation is to do this once, just before the buds swell, or twice—once in the late fall (when the temperature is above freezing) and again just before buds swell. However, in our climate, even repeated sprayings may not prevent the disease.

Perhaps our best bet, in the case of peaches and nectarines, is to grow genetic dwarf varieties in containers. After early attempts with mediocre flavor, newer varieties are reputed to taste better. Miniatures require only minimal pruning. If grown in containers on rollers, they can be moved to the most favorable protected spots as seasons change.

There is little data on which varieties of peach or nectarine do best in our cool summers. Check with local nurseries and with your neighbors. Here are a few possibilities for our warmer areas.

Peach Varieties Indian Free: 700 hours. Large freestone, red flesh. Must be fully ripe for good flavor. Late midseason. Needs another peach or nectarine for pollination.
Bonita: 100 or less hours. Midseason. Large yellow freestone, firm flesh, flavorful. Self-fruitful.
Honey Babe: 500 hours. Midseason. A genetic dwarf. Yellow freestone with sweet, rich flavor. Self-fruitful.

Nectarine Varieties Desert Dawn: 250 hrs. Very early. Semi-freestone, red skin, yellow flesh, rich flavor. Needs much pruning and fruit thinning. Self-fruitful.
Gold Mine: 400 hrs. Late Midseason. Tough skinned, juicy, sweet, white-fleshed freestone. Self-fruitful.
Nectar Babe: Midseason. A genetic dwarf. Freestone with red skin, yellow flesh, good taste. Needs any other dwarf peach or nectarine for pollination.

PEAR, EUROPEAN
Pyrus communis
Rose Family ❖ *Rosaceae*

Pears require, on the average, less winter chill than do apples, about 600 hours. Thus most should succeed in parts of our coastal region with the greatest winter chill. A few are rated at 500 hours, and one, 'Comice', requires only 200-300 hours. Several sources recommend against growing pears in foggier parts of San Francisco and San Mateo counties, and yet I know that there are productive Bartlett and Comice pear trees in the Richmond District of San Francisco, a couple of miles from the ocean. Even if they get enough chill, in areas with the coolest summers, nearest the coast in Sonoma or Mendocino counties, pears may need protected sites if they are to get enough warmth in summer to ripen well.

Pears are mainly available as full-sized trees, which can reach 30 feet tall, although there are a few semidwarf or dwarf varieties. One variety, 'Seckel,' is naturally somewhat smaller than most other pear varieties.

Pears can take wetter and heavier soil than most fruit trees, but do not need more than monthly deep watering in the dry season. Give them moderate amounts of fertilizer. After initial training, pears need only minimal annual pruning. They generally need cross pollination, and the pollen of some varieties is not compatible with that of others.

Some pears can be tree-ripened, but most need to be picked while still hard and ripened off the tree. Some even require cold storage, at lower than many refrigerator temperatures, to ripen properly, something to consider when choosing a variety.

Pears are quite susceptible to fireblight in our region, although some varieties are fairly resistant (see Apple, for more on fireblight).

Pear Varieties   Bartlett: 800 hours. Early midseason. Sweet and tender. Pick green and ripen off the tree. May require pollinator in cool coastal areas; any but Seckel will do.
Comice: 200-300 hours. Late. Excellent flavor and texture. (Ripens best after cold storage at 30-36°F for 2 to 3 months.) Self-fruitful, or plant with Bartlett to be safe.
Moonglow: 500-700 hours. Early midseason. Large fruit, good flavor, juicy, soft. The most fireblight resistant of the available pears. Needs a pollinator. Pollinates other pears. Not specifically recommended for this region, but widely adaptable.
Seckel: 500 hours. More fruit with 800 hours. Early midseason. Small but good dessert pear. Resists fireblight. Self-fruitful.
Winter Nelis: 700 hours. Late. Small, fine flavor. Requires pollinator.

PEAR, ASIAN

Pyrus pyrifolia

Rose Family ❖ *Rosaceae*

Asian pears are sometimes called apple-pears, as they are round and have a crisper flesh than many European or American pears. They are different from both pears and apples in texture and flavor. They also differ from pears in having a somewhat lower chill requirement, low enough for success just about anywhere in the region. Most require 450 hours of winter chill, though some need only 350 hours. However, like pears, they may not ripen well nearest the coast in the northern part of our region because of insufficient summer warmth.

Asian pears have the same soil, water, fertilizer and pruning requirements as European pears. Some are self-fruitful, while others are pollinated by other

Asian pear varieties or by European pears—check carefully for compatibility before you buy. Most reach 40 feet if unpruned, although you can prune them to control size. Asian pears have good resistance to fireblight.

Asian Pear Varieties   20th Century: 450 hours. Early August. Sweet, juicy, crisp. Self-fertile or pollinated by Shinseiki, Bartlett, others.
Shinseiki: 450 hours. Late July/Early August. Sweet, juicy, crisp. Self-fruitful.
Shinko: 500 hours. September. Very good flavor, crisp and juicy. Tree small and also available as grafted dwarf. Pollinized by Bartlett, Chojuro.
Tsu Li and Ya Li: 300 hours. September. Both are juicy, crisp; Ya Li is sweeter. They pollinate each other. Not specifically recommended for this region, but will probably do well here.
Chojuro and Shinseiki: now available as dwarfs.

PERSIMMON, ASIAN

Diospyros kaki
Ebony Family ❖ *Ebenaceae*

Asian persimmons can be grown in the warmer parts of the region, but are marginal nearest the coast because they need greater summer warmth to ripen properly. They do have some chill requirement, but cool summers are more likely to be the limiting factor. Of the two common varieties, Fuyu is slightly better able to ripen in cool summers than Hachiya.

I do have reports of two bearing Hachiya trees in San Francisco, one in a warm part of the city, one in a moderately warm spot. All I know about fruit quality is that the one in the warmer site had a successful first crop, but in the second year the fruit stayed unpleasantly astringent even when ripe.

For persimmons, a loamy soil is best, but good drainage is more important than soil type. When they are established, they need infrequent but regular deep irrigation. Fertilize them lightly. Trees reach 30 feet tall, though they can be controlled with pruning, or even espaliered. They do not need pruning to bear well and are relatively pest-free.

Persimmon Varieties   Chocolate: Very sweet fruits flecked with brown. Astringent (bitter) until ripe.
Fuyu: 200 hours. Flattened fruit is sweet even when firm. Takes less heat to ripen than Hachiya. Self-fruitful.
Hachiya: 200 hours. Dome-shaped fruit is usually picked while firm and ripened off the tree. Fruit

loses astringency as it ripens. Needs hot summer to ripen fruit, so may not succeed in foggy areas. Self-fruitful.

PINEAPPLE GUAVA
Feijoa sellowiana
Myrtle Family ❖ *Myrtaceae*

These attractive plants bear flowers with edible petals, then pineapple-flavored fruit. They will thrive in our area; in fact the cool weather seems to improve the flavor of the fruit. The evergreen foliage is handsome, the flowers a pretty red-and-white. The fruits, which drop to the ground when ripe, have a green, leathery skin, and pale yellow interior. They are typically cut in half, then eaten with a spoon, and their pectin content makes them a good fruit to use in jams and jellies.

Pineapple guavas are tolerant of various soils, but will produce the best harvests in a soil with good drainage and a pH of 5.5 to 7.0. While the plants are drought-tolerant once established, successful fruit production requires regular deep watering. They require little or no fertilizer.

Left to their own, pineapple guava plants grow slowly into multi-stemmed shrubs 18 to 25 feet tall. However they can take all sorts of pruning, including pruning to a low hedge or an espalier. The heaviest shearing and shaping will reduce fruiting, but shaping after the harvest will increase yields.

Pineapple Guava Varieties Nazemetz: Large fruit with a thin skin and sweet pulp. Self-pollinating, but produces better if another variety cross-pollinates it.
Trask: Medium-sized fruit of fairly good quality. Requires cross pollination.

PLUM (JAPANESE)
Prunus salicina
PLUM (EUROPEAN)
Prunus domestica
Rose Family ❖ *Rosaceae*

Plum trees are good choices for most of the region, with adapted varieties usually bearing large crops of good quality fruit. The ones that do best here are low-chill types, mostly Japanese plums. The chill requirement of Japanese plums generally ranges from 500-1600 hours, but that of our low-chill types is about 350 hours. Most European plums require 700-1800 hours, but still, some can get by with little

enough chill to produce well here.

Plums grow best in soil with ample organic matter and good drainage. They need moderate to high amounts of fertilizer and occasional deep watering in the dry season. Standard varieties grow to 20 feet, dwarf to 8 to 10 feet tall. After initial training, European plums need some annual pruning, while Japanese plums need, on the average, heavier pruning to keep vigorous shoots thinned out. Dwarf varieties can be espaliered. Some kinds of plums are self-fertile. Check compatibility carefully though, when a pollinator is needed—Japanese and European plums do not pollinate each other, although Japanese varieties can serve as pollinators for hybrids between American and Japanese plums. While plums can get various pests, they don't seem to be seriously plagued by any particular pest in our region. Many varieties will succeed here, so this is only a selection.

Japanese Plum Varieties Elephant Heart: 500 hours. Mid to late season. Large, dark red, freestone fruit with a rich flavor. Pollinate with Santa Rosa.
Howard's Miracle: 300 hours. Midseason. Yellow with red blush, flesh yellow with spicy flavor. Can be eaten while green, when it has an apple-like flavor. Pollinate with Santa Rosa.
Mariposa: 250 hours. Midseason. Nearly freestone, large, sweet, juicy. Pollinated by Santa Rosa, Nubiana.
Nubiana: 400-500 hours. Midseason. Dark purple skin, amber flesh, sweet, firm. Self-fertile.
Santa Rosa: 300 hours. Early. Red-purple skin, flesh yellow and red, juicy, with a pleasant tangy flavor. Self-fruitful. Pollinates Satsuma, Mariposa and many other plums.
Satsuma: 300 hours. Early midseason. Maroon skin, red flesh, mild, sweet flavor. Pollinate with Santa Rosa.
Weeping Santa Rosa: 400 hours. Early. Fruit similar to Santa Rosa. Weeping habit is useful in landscapes. Can be grown on trellis or espaliered. Height can be controlled at 8 feet. Self-fruitful.
European Plum Varieties Green Gage: 500 hours. Midseason. Green/yellow fruit with amber flesh. Rich flavor, juicy. Self-fruitful.

POMEGRANATE
Punica granatum
Pomegranate Family ❖ *Punicaceae*

Pomegranates are borne on a small deciduous tree,

hardy to 18 to 20°F. They will produce good fruit in the warmest parts of the region, but in areas closest to the coast they may set no fruit or only sparse fruit that doesn't ripen properly.

Soils too basic for most plants will support a pomegranate, but the plant will do better in neutral or slightly acidic loam. Good drainage with an occasional deep watering, light fertilization, and light pruning will keep the plant in good shape. It is relatively pest-free in our region.

'Wonderful' is the most common fruiting variety, but others are worth seeking out for their superior sweetness. Some of the names to watch for are 'Fleischman's,' 'Dewey,' 'Mae,' and 'Eve.' (Miniature pomegranate plants produce poor fruit.)

QUINCE
Cydonia oblonga
Rose Family ❖ *Rosaceae*

You probably know the ornamental "flowering quince," with its thorny branches and bright red, or pink, late winter flowers. Flowering quinces are plants of Asian origin, members of the genus *Chaenomeles*. Some of these plants do bear fruit, and can be eaten in preserves, but the quince more likely intended when cooks discuss the matter is a plant of the genus *Cydonia*. This is a shrub or small tree, to 25 feet tall, with thornless branches and white to pink flowers. (It can be pruned to keep it smaller.) Like *Chaenomeles*, it is handsome enough to be an ornamental, but the fruit is more useful. Though it is not good to eat raw, it adds a distinctive flavor to jams and jellies, as well as in cooking, either alone or with apples or other fruit. There are those who say that if a dish calls for cooked apples, it is usually better with quince.

Quince is recommended for even the foggy areas of the region. It is best grown in clayey soil with good drainage, but is relatively tolerant of wet soil. It needs only light fertilization. Pruning back about one-half of new growth of long, weeping branches will strengthen the tree, and you need to thin out bushy growth as well. Quince is self-fertile. It can get fireblight, especially if overfertilized.

Quince Varieties   Pineapple: 300 hrs. Rounded, yellow fruit, soft flesh, pineapple flavor, but not the best-tasting variety. Self-fertile.
Smyrna: Round to oblong, yellow, well-flavored fruit. Self-fertile.
Orange: Good-flavored variety. Self-fertile.

RASPBERRY
Rubus idaeus, R. strigosus, R. occidentalis and hybrids
Rose Family ❖ *Rosaceae*

The fruit of blackberries and black raspberries looks very much alike, however there are also red and yellow raspberries. An easy way to tell blackberries from black raspberries is that when you pick a raspberry, the core of the fruit remains on the stem, while if it is a blackberry, the core stays in the berry.

Raspberries are at their best in coastal Washington and the Willamette valley of Oregon, where winters are colder than our region, and spring is long and cool. However they can be grown in our area.

Grow raspberries in well-amended soil, with moderate fertilization and even moisture. They must be trained on wires or a fence and pruned carefully. Black raspberries and single-crop red raspberries are pruned differently from double-crop red raspberries. Consult your local nurseryperson for more information on locally adapted varieties, or find out what is growing successfully near you.

Raspberry Varieties   Canby: Large, red berries. Thornless plants.
Fairview: Early. Light red, good quality berries.
Heritage: Spring and Fall bearing. Flavorful, firm red fruit.
Sumner: Early. Firm, sweet, flavorful. Good in heavy soil.
Willamette: Midseason. Dark red berries are large and firm.

STRAWBERRY
Fragaria x ananassa
Rose Family ❖ *Rosaceae*

It turns out that most of what I once knew about growing strawberries is wrong for our subtropical area. I used to plant them in the middle of spring, mulch thickly with straw or pine needles, discard all fruit until the middle of summer during the first year, keep the plants for several years, and then get new plants by rooting runners. Wrong! This style of growing strawberries is more suited to colder climates.

I was right about some things. I chose a sunny spot, added plenty of organic matter, made sure that the bed was weed-free, and never let the soil get too dry. I added a nitrogen fertilizer in fall and pruned off dead leaves in spring. My bed of everbearing strawberries first ripened fruit in March and kept going into November. However, for the largest crop of luscious berries, we would do well to listen to the advice given by local Cooperative Extension agents.

The best time to plant strawberries here is November. (See below for the exact timing for each variety.) Cold improves the ability of strawberry plants to bear a heavy crop of fruit, and the plants sold in the nurseries during November were raised in areas with chilly early autumns. (Commercial growers in our area plant specially chilled strawberries in August, but these plants are generally only available in bulk to farmers and wholesalers.)

The best time to prepare soil for a strawberry bed is fall of the previous year. This gives you a year to get weeds under control. It also allows you to amend the soil early enough so that any harmful salts from animal manure, mushroom compost, or other materials can leach out before the salt-sensitive strawberry plants go in. If you are planting an ongoing garden, you can plan a rotation that puts strawberries in a bed one year after the last manuring.

Strawberries need good drainage. Sandy loam is best, but other soils are acceptable if they are well amended. If you have clay soil, add plenty of organic matter the year before and plant in a raised bed. Although the crop can grow in soil with a pH as low as 5, it will grow much better in pH 7 or even a bit higher. This probably comes as a surprise to most gardeners, who may have thought, as I did, that an acidifying mulch was just the ticket for this crop.

You may find strawberry plants sold in containers or bare-root. Container plants are easier to transplant, since you have only to set them at the same depth they were in the container. If you plant bare-root plants, be careful not to bury the base of the shoot, called the crown, or to expose the roots. Many nurseries supply a pamphlet showing the right way to plant. If there is no handout, ask the nurseryperson to show you how it is done. Spread the roots of bare-root plants in the planting hole so that they will grow out and down, rather than back toward the plants.

Whether you start with containers or bare roots, space the strawberry plants 10 inches apart. Don't set the plants in depressions or on individual mounds, but rather keep the soil level around them. If the plants are in depressions, soil often falls in and buries the crowns, encouraging decay. If the plants are on small mounds, they will dry out too easily. When you use a raised bed to improve drainage in heavy soil, make it wide enough so that the plants are at least 8 inches form the edges of an unframed bed, or 6 inches form the edges of a framed bed.

When you plant, apply a nitrogen fertilizer. Put some under each plant, making sure to keep it at least 1 inch from the roots. Either use a slow-release fertilizer that will last nine to twelve months, or side-dress four to five times a year with a faster-acting nitrogen source.

Commercial growers have found that using a clear plastic mulch greatly improves the yield and quality of strawberry crops. They apply it to the November planting right away, since it can stimulate runners instead of fruit if it is applied later. The plastic warms the soil, helping the plants to grow in cool weather and allowing the fruit to ripen better. It also protects the fruit from decay. Weeds must be under control if clear plastic is to do its job. Growers fumigate their soil, but I don't recommend that you do that. If your weeds are under relatively good control, lay the plastic and just lift it to remove weeds that begin to grow. Snails may congregate under the mulch, but not in the numbers that they do under black plastic, since clear plastic won't shade them. If you have a problem with pests living under the mulch, simply exclude them by tucking the edges into the soil. If you don't plan to use clear plastic, it is best not to use any mulch or to use a thin mulch of cocoa bean hulls.

Drip irrigation is ideal for strawberries, especially if it is used under a clear plastic mulch. It keeps moisture off the berries so they are less likely to decay, and it reduces weeds in areas that are not near an emitter. Water enough so that the plants don't dry out, but don't keep soil soggy. If you don't have a drip system, you can water carefully at soil level. If you are using a plastic mulch, water through holes in the plastic.

Most strawberries make at least a few runners—that is, arching stems that root to form new plants. You may have read about many styles of growing strawberries that include rooting these runners to make new plants. In our mild-winter area the hill system, in which all runners are removed, is your best bet. By removing the runners, you are encouraging the crown on the mother plant to develop, thereby increasing fruit production. Just go over the plants once a week and pick off any runners that form.

If you want to try growing new plants from rooted runners, chill them before you plant them. This procedure is a bit tricky. Start new plants in mid- to late summer, aiming for rooted plants in the middle of October. Don't let the parent plants make too many plantlets—cut off all but one or two. To root a plantlet, sink a small pot into the soil between strawberry plants and weight a runner so that a plantlet is resting on the soil in the pot. Sometimes a runner keeps growing to make another plantlet even further from the parent plant. If this happens, cut the extension off to keep energy directed toward rooting the first plantlet. When that plantlet has roots, sever the runner form the mother plant and lift the pot.

In the middle of October, remove the plants from the pots and gently shake off the soil. Store the bare-root plants in plastic bags at 34°F for two weeks. That sounds easy, but it isn't, since your refrigerator is probably between 38° and 42°F, and your freezer is well below freezing. Perhaps you can tolerate your refrigerator a bit colder for a couple of weeks, or you may have a second refrigerator at your disposal. Put a small thermometer in your refrigerator and experiment with the temperature dial until it registers 34°F. You don't ever want it to dip below 32°F, since neither the strawberry plants nor your other stored produce should freeze. Plant the strawberries in early November.

Don't prune November-planted strawberries at all the first year. If you keep them over for another winter, remove all the old or dead leaves in the middle of the second February. Commercial growers usually keep their plantings only one year, since production and fruit size tend to decline the second year. However, you can keep your plants for several years if you are satisfied with your production. If you have let runners root until the bed has become overgrown, thin the planting. Either pull our plants and discard them, leaving healthy plants no less than 10 inches apart, or dig up and move healthy plants to another bed.

Begin to harvest as soon as the first fruit ripens. Unless you are going to pop the berries into your mouth right away (not a bad idea), pick them so that the green caps and a little bit of stem stay attached. Then refrigerate them unwashed until you are ready to serve them. Only then should you remove the caps and wash the berries.

Varieties Get bare-root or container plants from a local nursery. Locally available varieties will be ones that will produce well here, whereas mail-order plants are likely to be more suitable for other regions. Many of the catalogs sell seeds for 'Sweetheart,' but resist the temptation to buy them, since the variety was developed for cold-winter areas.

Some strawberry varieties are sensitive to day length and thus bear during only part of the warm season. (See the discussion of day length sensitivity on page 225). Other varieties, which are called everbearers, are less sensitive to day length and produce from spring to fall. Some everbearers slack off during the long days in June, but others bear steadily all season.

Most of the strawberry varieties suited to coastal central California are introductions from the University of California. These are some of the best varieties currently recommended for local home gardens.

'Sequoia' is an early bearer with large, soft, very flavorful fruit. Although it has a long bearing season, it is not an everbearer. Plant it between November 1st and Thanksgiving. 'Chandler', which bears earlier, is a very good berry. Plant it between November 1st and 15th. 'Fern' is an everbearer that can be planted anytime from the middle of November to the middle of January, although it is best planted before December. The everbearer 'Seascape' is an improved variety of 'Fern' with larger fruit. Plant at the same

---

STRAWBERRY POTS

I have never seen a healthy, productive planting of strawberries in strawberry pots—those large pots with holes in the sides. I suspect that the plants need more root space (they need at least 4 inches in all direction) and that the plantings I have seen were not being given adequate water or fertilizer. If you decide to plant in one of these containers, get the largest you can afford, provide the best growing conditions, and don't try to keep them there for more than one season.

time as 'Fern.' A new variety 'Selva', the main commercial berry, is almost an everbearer, slowing just a bit with the longest days. Fruit is large and firm; pick it fully ripe. Plant 'Selva' in October. 'Hecker' is an everbearer that has small fruit, but resists verticillium wilt. Plant it anytime from the middle of December to the middle of January.

Pests   A number of pests enjoy strawberries as much as we do. Birds, earwigs, slugs, snails, and sowbugs may nibble ripe fruit. If birds are a problem, cover the planting with a net. Control the other pests as best you can and discourage them by lifting ripening fruit onto dry mulch or pieces of wood. (One gardener protected her small planting from slugs by using clean old socks to cover the nearly ripe berries.)

Strawberry plants are also susceptible to aphids and spider mites, especially when they are under stress, such as weed competition or inconsistent watering. Try to avoid aphids, which spread incurable and often fatal viruses to strawberry plants.

The crop is also susceptible to verticillium wilt, an incurable fungus disease. Infected plants wilt during warm weather, and their outer leaves turn brown starting at the tips and moving down between the veins. The plants may make a partial recovery during cool weather, but they seldom recover completely. If you have verticillium in your soil, grow the resistant variety 'Hecker.' Remove any plants that are infected by viruses or verticillium wilt.

Strawberry plants are vulnerable to powdery mildew. They may also get fungal leaf spots, which appear early in the season and can be recognized by spots with gray or white centers and purple edges. The fungus may also attack the fruit, causing one or two black spots on a berry.

Sources
    Strawberry plants: Local nurseries

STRAWBERRY, ALPINE
Fragaria vesca 'Alpine'
Rose Family ❖ *Rosaceae*

These wild European strawberries bear very flavorful fruit that is small and pointy. They tolerate more shade than ordinary garden strawberries and won't mind the fog as much. Give them partial shade in the sunnier parts of the region and full sun in the foggier areas. Otherwise, they have the same needs as other strawberries. They bear from spring to fall.

Growing Instructions   Alpine strawberries are most commonly grown from seeds, which take two to three weeks to germinate at 60° to 75°F. Sow the seeds indoors from February to April, and set the plants out whenever they are sturdy enough to transplant and the soil is sufficiently warm. Space them 8 to 12 inches apart. Alpines are less invasive than other strawberries, since they form few or no runners but they will self-sow. Try them as a border or at the edge of an ornamental planting.

The Harvest   You may be able to pick some fruit from alpines the first fall, and you will definitely get a full crop the following spring. They produce fruit for several years, as long as they don't succumb to virus diseases.

Varieties   There are a number of similar red-ripening varieties of alpines, some of which promise larger fruit. For an unusual treat, try an alpine variety that ripens to white—really pale yellow. The berries are very tasty, and their color may fool birds.

Pests   Watch your alpine planting for aphid infestations and for the virus infection that aphids can spread. Control aphids, and remove any stunted or malformed plants.

Sources
    Alpine strawberry seed:
    Red-ripening varieties: GG, JSS, NGN, PTS, RH, SB, T&M
    White-ripening varieties: SB
    Alpine strawberry plants (red-ripening): BG, RH
    Alpine strawberry plants (white-ripening): SGS

STRAWBERRY GUAVA (OR CATTLEY GUAVA)
Psidium catteleianum
Myrtle Family ❖ *Myrtaceae*

Strawberry guavas are one to two inch round, red fruits with a flavor reminiscent of strawberries. The plants are pretty in a landscape, growing slowly to 10 foot tall multi-stemmed shrubs. The evergreen leaves are glossy and the white flowers are fragrant. The fruit is very nice in jellies and jams, or blended with other fruits in juices. Given an unshaded location, this plant should be able to bear fruit throughout our area.

Plant in rich soil with good drainage and a pH of 5 to 7. It can withstand short periods of drought, but may drop fruit unless it gets regular deep watering. Fertilize moderately every month. The plants bear fruit on this year's growth, so pruning stimulates fruiting. They can be pruned to an informal hedge. There are no named varieties.

TANGERINE (SEE MANDARIN ORANGE)

WINTERGREEN (TEABERRY)

Gaultheria procumbens
Heath Family ❖ *Ericaceae*

If you like the flavor of wintergreen, you might like to try this pretty little plant. Both the leaves and the red berries of this Eastern U.S. native have the familiar wintergreen flavor. You can make tea from the leaves and eat the berries. This plant used to be the main source for oil of wintergreen, but now most of this flavoring is extracted from, of all things, a birch tree! (It's the cherry birch, *Betula lenta*, another Eastern U.S. native.)

Wintergreen is a creeping groundcover, to six inches tall. It will thrive in soil prepared for rhododendrons, with moderate summer water. Give it partial shade in sunnier microclimates.

I offer wintergreen in preference to the California native *Gaultheria shallon*, known as salal. Salal does have edible, black berries, but they haven't much flavor.

SIXTEEN

A Garden-Based Cuisine

HAT A TIME TO BE COOKING from your own garden! The past decade has seen a splendid celebration of garden-fresh produce. Many kinds of vegetables, herbs, and edible flowers that were formerly known primarily to gardeners have now become available in the average metropolitan supermarket. Maybe the trend started with the opening of "California cuisine" restaurants that served a lively garden-based cuisine, using food from their own gardens or from specialty truck farms. At the same time, increasing numbers of new immigrants came to our area from around the world, introducing their garden crops, condiments and recipes.

A new American cuisine is being expressed in many new cookbooks. It is playful and colorful, with recipes also selected for flavor, good nutrition and ease of preparation. It draws fresh inspiration from some of the world's best garden cuisines, including those from Central and South America, the Mediterranean, Asia, and Southeast Asia. It is not afraid of using less familiar produce, or combinations of produce. And it uses a wide range of the world's herbs, spices and condiments to create lively, complex, vivid or subtle flavors.

For the gardener, the results have been wonderful. You can find all manner of unusual crops in the produce markets, and try them to see if you want to grow them. Also, a wider variety of seed is available when you are ready to plant—including many heirloom and new varieties imported from other countries such as France, Holland, Italy, Japan, and

China. And, when you have your own harvests in hand, you can find a much wider variety of recipes using all of the crops you have grown.

Farm Cooking

Garden-fresh ingredients are currently in the limelight, the latest culinary fashion, but most of our ancestors, including many of our grandparents and some of our parents, raised plants and animals to feed themselves and their families. The cuisines they developed reflected the foods they could grow. They might be able to produce a very good diet. Especially before modern transportation, prosperous farmers often enjoyed a diet fresher and more varied than that of city dwellers. However, because a farm family depended on the land, there was always the lurking shadow of a failed crop, or a bad year. And on poorer farms no amount of planning and preserving would prevent a lean period every late winter and early spring.

Many of our agricultural ancestors were from other countries, as most living Americans are the descendants of peoples from other parts of the world. Some were farmers in this country. My father's parents, Frank Peirce and Pearl Fullhart Peirce, descended from families that had been farming in this country for roughly 225 years, so the family's cuisine, though basically European, had adapted itself to the crops of the New World, and had lost some of the crops, and especially the seasonings, of the Old.

My grandparents were farming at a time when new technology was beginning to improve the diets of many Americans. By the first years of the twentieth century, refrigerated railroad cars were carrying fresh meats and produce to many Americans. Commercial canning allowed many to buy ready-to-eat food and store it even without the aid of an ice box. By the 1920s, mechanical refrigerators were becoming common in middle class homes. These advances in transportation and preservation permitted a relatively varied and dependable year-round food supply.

But my grandparents were poor farmers, so their subsistence living in the first decades of this century had much in common with an earlier time in American history. For the most part the family ate only what they could grow. The stores they could reach in their horse and buggy had little or no meat or produce for sale, let alone ready-to-eat or commercially prepared food. And few in the area would have bought such foods in any case. As my father said "farmers had no money, only a living."

Still, they had a wholesome and varied diet including beef and pork in winter, and sausage or cured pork into the spring and summer; fresh produce, starting with the earliest wild spring greens, then summer's garden vegetables; wild walnuts and hickory nuts; fruit, including wild and domestic berries, apples, pears, peaches, plums, and grapes. There were enough potatoes to last almost all year, wheat to mill into flour, hard corn for cornmeal, popcorn, sorghum cane grown for a little molasses, and dried beans, harvested by the whole plant, to be shelled out of the pods on winter evenings.

The food eaten had to be balanced against some cash crops. For example, many of the eggs had to go to the grocery, "to be applied to the bill, past present or future." Butter, and later, cream, were sold to a creamery, and then, eventually, milk went to a cheese factory.

And the diet also had to be planned to cope with natural seasonal shortages. Meat was butchered when weather was cold enough to keep it. Then beef would be traded with neighbors, by the quarter, so that no one had more than they could deal with at once. Pork sausage was preserved under lard in stoneware crocks, and other pork sugar-cured. When the pork ran out, there would be little meat until the next fall butchering, except a few chickens (young roosters or old hens), young rabbits turned up during the haying, and a bit of other wild game, turtle, or fish caught nearby.

Fresh vegetables and fruits were mostly unavailable when not in season. A few could be stored or preserved. Potatoes, pumpkins, and root crops kept over winter in a root cellar, and sweet corn was scraped off the cob and dried. Apples could be stored for a while, or would keep longer if sliced and dried, and drying made prunes and raisins of some of the plums and grapes. Jellies and jams could be preserved under paraffin in stoneware crocks. Even with the best planning, however, winter could bring periods of mostly bread, gravy and potatoes.

Cooking was without the benefit of most herbal flavorings. Flavoring agents included home-produced salt pork, onion, molasses, and cider vinegar, as well as purchased sugar, salt, and pepper. Prepared dishes were mainly soups, stews, or fried foods. Bread was sourdough at first, as yeast was not readily available. There were rolls, biscuits, corn bread, fruit pies, and, occasionally, doughnuts.

By the time of World War I, the family had enough cash to buy canning jars. At first, they could can only tomatoes, fruits, and fruit juices, but later, as they learned cold pack and pressure cooker methods, they could can vegetables and have "delicious canned meat in any season."

Examples of recipes from the cuisine of Midwestern farmers such as my grandparents are Wilted Lettuce, on page 220, Fried Green Tomatoes, page 261, and Fried Squash Blossoms, page 309, although the tomatoes and squash blossoms would have been fried in lard rather than olive oil.

"Modern Convenience" Cooking

When I was a child, we had a large garden, typical of twentieth century gardens in that it was not expected to feed us entirely. We grew a profusion of fresh vegetables in season, as well as having apple trees, berries, and grape vines. I loved the fresh fruit and vegetables, but was less fond of the canned tomatoes, applesauce, and most particularly of the green beans that my mom and dad prepared each summer. My life experiences did not give me the same appreciation as my dad for the neat rows of glass jars on the basement shelves—lined up against hard times. I would eye the rows of preserved green beans with great dismay, knowing that one quarter of the total was destined for my plate.

When people enter mainstream twentieth century America from American farms or from other traditional cultures, they, or certainly their children, tend to seek out the mainstream diet. The old ways represent fearful memories of want, of periodic dietary boredom, and of the hard labor of growing,

STUFFED ZUCCHINI

One year a group of gardeners from my San Francisco community garden made a harvest feast. It featured big plates of sliced tomatoes vinaigrette, garlic bread, and stuffed zucchini. Delicious! (But don't ever let your zucchini get this big unless you are planning to stuff them.)

1 zucchini, 14 to 16 inches long
1 egg
1 cup lowfat or nonfat cottage cheese
1/2 cup diced mild cheese
1/2 teaspoon crushed dried rosemary (or 3/4 teaspoon chopped fresh rosemary leaves)
1 tablespoon chopped fresh parsley
1/2 cup chopped chard leaves (or other greens)
grated Parmesan cheese
3/4 cup cooked rice (brown or white)

Sauce
1 clove garlic, minced
1/2 cup finely diced onion
1 tablespoon olive oil or other oil
1 15 ounce can tomato sauce (or 2 cups Quick Homemade Tomato Sauce, see page 346)
1 teaspoon dried basil (or 2 tablespoons minced fresh basil)
1/8 teaspoon crushed red chili pepper

Halve the zucchini lengthwise, being sure any curve goes to the side, so the halves will lay flat. Scoop out the center rather deeply, leaving about a 5/8-inch to 1/2-inch shell. Steam or parboil the zucchini shells for 5 to 10 minutes. Do not overcook; they should be slightly cooked but *not* fork tender. (If you have no pot large enough, cut the halves into 4-inch pieces.)

Chop the removed zucchini centers into bite-sized bits. Mix these bits with the rest of the filling ingredients, adding the rice last. If it seems you will have too much filling, leave out some of the rice. (Put the extra rice in the sauce instead.) If you have added all of the rice and it looks like too little filling, add more cottage cheese.

Stuff the zucchini shells, mounding the filling high and smoothing and forming it with your hands or a spoon. Top with a sprinkling of Parmesan cheese. Bake in a 350°F oven until tender and the cheese is browned—about 30 minutes.

To prepare the sauce, sauté the onion and garlic in oil over medium-low heat until cooked but not browned. Stir in the tomato sauce and add the basil and red pepper. Simmer for 20 minutes.

To serve, cut the stuffed zucchini into 4-inch sections, put them on plates, and pour some sauce over each. Serves four.

QUICK HOMEMADE TOMATO SAUCE

There are fancier ways to make tomato sauce, but if you have an abundance of tomatoes and are in a hurry, this will do the trick. If you would rather not have seeds in your sauce, scoop them out before you put the fruit in the blender.

Wash ripe tomatoes and cut out the stem end and any blemished parts. Cut large tomatoes into several pieces, and halve the smaller ones. Purée the tomatoes in a blender, about 2 cups at a time. Pour the puréed tomatoes into a stainless steel or glass saucepan, bring to a boil, and simmer at least 15 minutes. Cool, then use in recipes or freeze in plastic freezer containers. The sauce will be rather thin for most uses, so if you have time, simmer it longer, until most of the water has evaporated, leaving a thick sauce. If you don't have time, freeze it as is and cook it down longer, if necessary, when you pull it from the freezer. Season as you desire.

---

preserving, and cooking the food. The new ways represent modernity: stores always stocked with food, escape from farm chores, and ease of preparation. Modern food technology offers wonders, from frozen foods to soup mixes, and it seems foolish not to partake. When I was a child, cake came out of one box, frosting out of another, and "whipped cream" out of a nozzle. Jello™ was the wonder ingredient that could make salad or dessert, and instant pudding and pie filling could be added to the cake from the box to improve its texture. It became difficult to talk about food without using brand names.

In the 1950s, in the Kroger supermarkets of the American Heartland, many ethnic ingredients, whether fresh or prepared, were unavailable and unimagined. In the 1970s, my dad's sister, Aunt Helen, wrote me a letter asking if I would like to submit a recipe for the volunteer fire department cookbook of Losantville, Indiana, the town near which my grandparents had farmed. I sent her a variation on a Mexican dish that contained eggs, a bit of oil, onion, Anaheim or bell peppers, and Jack cheese. Without consulting me, she decided that the ingredients were too weird (she had never heard of Jack cheese or Anaheim peppers), and entered instead, above my name, a recipe that I had never seen. It is "Casserole Bread," containing "1 pkg. hot roll mix, 1/2 cup warm water, 2 eggs, separated, 3/4 cups cream style cottage cheese, 1 envelope dry onion soup mix, and onion salt." Besides introducing a certain doubt in my mind about the authorship of the other recipes credited to my relatives

and their townswomen, this event illustrated to me their preference for recipes that contained prepared foods as well as their reluctance to investigate unknown ingredients.

Whole Foods Rediscovered

By the 1960s, there arose, out of this mainstream culture and cuisine, a widespread desire to return to whole foods. Many Americans who had been raised on processed foods now sought foods that had minimal processing, no food additives, and were preferably organically grown. Vegetarianism became popular as well, a trend that led to interest in a wider variety of vegetable foods.

In the search for whole foods recipes and vegetarian recipes, two major influences that emerged were peasant cooking and cuisines inspired by religious vegetarians. Many explored the simple, mostly bland, foods of zen macrobiotic diet, in which plain brown rice, perhaps sprinkled with a bit of ground-up sesame seed, is seen as the ideal food. They learned to make hearty whole grain breads and served stir-fried vegetables with brown rice. They tried using soy-based foods instead of meat in many otherwise familiar Western-style dishes. In some cases this exploration taught the pleasures of exploring fully the flavor of a food previously thought bland. It also resulted in the revival or creation of some very good recipes. Recipes reflecting this cuisine include Main Dish Risotto, page 297, and Stuffed Zucchini, page 345.

SOUTHWEST CHILE VEGETABLE SOUP

This soup is quick to make and very satisfying—great for lunch after a morning in the garden. You can vary the vegetables with the season, substituting other summer squash, chayote, leek, green beans, bok choy, sunchokes—whatever is available, but always include either leek or onion. Add the vegetables to the broth in order of the amount of cooking time they require. I like to make this with my own Homemade Chicken Stock (see page 349)

4 cups chicken stock (or broth made with instant powdered mix, or, if you don't have that either, just plain water will do)
1/4 medium head cabbage
1 large boiling potato
1 small onion
1 5- to 6-inch zucchini
1 8-ounce can tomato sauce (or 1 cup Quick Homemade Tomato Sauce)
2 tablespoons prepared chile powder

Bring the chicken stock or water to a boil. While you are waiting for it to boil, thinly slice the cabbage. Turn the heat down to maintain a simmer and add the cut-up cabbage. Leaving the peel on the potato, cut it into 3/4-inch dice and add it to the pot. Cut the onion into 1-inch chunks and add it to the soup. Cut the zucchini into 1/4-inch slices. When the other vegetables are almost tender, add the zucchini and cook 5 minutes longer. Add the tomato sauce and chile powder. Stir well and cook a couple more minutes to heat through. Serves two to three.

A New Cuisine

The garden-inspired whole foods cuisine that developed in the 1980s tends to be truer to the ethnic cuisines from which it draws inspiration than were the whole foods recipes of the previous two decades. For example, if an ethnic recipe uses white rice, white rice will be specified. And recipes often include ingredients, such as fish sauce, that are new items to most Americans. When spices are used, they are called for in amounts that are closer to those used in the original cuisine, rather than following the previous practice of catering to American tastes by drastically reducing the amounts of all but salt and sugar. Meat often appears, as it does in many of the world's cuisines, in small amounts, intended to be eaten with a larger amount of a starchy food such as pasta or rice. And foods have reappeared that are easiest to keep in supply when you have a garden, such as fresh herbs, wild greens, and edible flowers.

There is more emphasis on speed and ease of preparation, rather than an attempt to reproduce the home food processing of the subsistence farmer. And, finally, there is greater emphasis on presentation, on food for the eye. Foods are combined not only to taste good, but to look good together. They are chopped in ways that add to eye appeal, with special touches, such as sprinklings of fresh herbs, to increase visual impact.

A Local Garden Cuisine

When I read recipes from Mediterranean countries, especially country French and Italian recipes, I often think the cooks must have had a garden much like mine, though in a bit warmer climate. Because of my garden, a dish that would ordinarily require a lot of separate purchases of this and that, including expensive fresh herbs, becomes the natural dish to make when a particular crop and all of its supporting flavorings are available in the garden.

Our Mediterranean climate permits us to harvest many kinds of herbs year-round. Thus fresh herbs can become staples — always available for our kitchens. At any time we can have parsley, oregano, thyme, sage, marjoram, rosemary, tarragon (or winter tarragon in colder months), winter savory, spearmint, chives, and garlic chives.

And we can have at least some fresh vegetables all year as well. Our winter garden may offer more cole crops, and our summer more beans, squash and tomatoes, but there is generally *something* available to serve fresh. If we live in a foggier part of the area, our gardens will lack the eggplants, peppers and basil of those in southern France or Italy. And we will notice these and similar lacks also when we turn to other cuisines, such as Southeast Asian or Indian. But because we do not depend on our gardens for all of our food, we will be able to supplement our harvests with purchased food and go on to create great meals.

Since we do have so many foods available for purchase, and are not depending on our garden to be our only source of food, we can grow foods that emphasize quality and variety rather than quantity, delicacies rather than fillers. We do not have to worry what we will eat if the potato crop fails, and we don't have to can the green beans. We are free to maximize the feelings of accomplishment and joy that accompany sitting down to a meal containing

our own fresh, home-grown food.

When I grow my own food, following it from seed to table, I often feel a very close kinship with those who did so before me. I don't need the possibility of starvation to appreciate the concern that motivated the Navajo people to walk in their cornfields at specific times, from seeding to harvest, singing songs that coaxed the plants to produce a bountiful crop. Or to understand the feelings of frustration that led my grandfather to plant the watermelons in the middle of the corn patch, where they would be shielded from the eyes of would-be melon rustlers.

When I thaw a container of last summer's pesto on a stormy winter day, I can appreciate the pleasure my father must have had when he first tasted home canned green beans in a snowbound farmhouse. And when I pick a few wild and tame greens for a late winter salad, I can imagine the pleasure of doing that in late March after a winter of snow and ice — and after weeks of potatoes, biscuits, gravy. To intensify this understanding, I tried, for several years, to avoid buying anything that I could grow. I found I could eat fairly well, if a little oddly at times, from a few hundred square feet of garden. I did still buy a little produce, including apples and oranges, fresh mushrooms, and supplementary potatoes, carrots, and onions.

I enjoyed late winter's glut of artichokes—and I

GARDEN PLANNING TIPS

Learning to eat from a garden requires thought and practice. Here are some tips that will help you.

- At first, grow mostly crops that you would buy and eat even if you weren't gardening.
- Be aware of the yield and duration of harvest of the crops you want to grow.
- Be realistic: Don't plant more of a crop than you would normally eat.
- Look at your garden with recipes in mind. Are there recipes that use two or more crops you plan to grow? Maybe these crops can be planted so that they can be harvested together.
- Stay on the lookout for recipes that use your most successful crops.
- Check your garden, just as you check your refrigerator, before you go grocery shopping. Leave a note on the fridge, if others will be shopping, to let them know what **not** to buy.
- If you go on vacation, leave instructions not only for watering, but for harvesting. That way, you won't return to find that some crops, such as summer squash and beans, have matured fruit, and so stopped producing in your absence.

MAKING SOUP STOCK

Soup stocks, or broths, serve as the basis for many delicious homemade soups and sauces. They are made by boiling vegetables and, usually, bony meat or fish, for several hours. Then bones, fat, and vegetables are discarded, and only the liquid and any lean meat are kept. Gardeners often have just the sorts of odds and ends of vegetables needed to make interesting stocks. Most vegetables can be used, although a few, such as, New Zealand Spinach or mustard, will give the stock an unpleasantly strong flavor. The most common vegetable ingredients are onion family crops, such as onion or leeks, or carrot family ones such as carrot, celery, or parsley. Fresh or dried herbs are also often added.

Making soup stock may sound time consuming, but while the stock needs to cook a long time, it really takes very little of your time. You can simmer it while you eat dinner, and turn it off at bedtime, and let it cool overnight at room temperature or on a cool porch. In the morning, if you have time, strain out the solid ingredients, put any lean meat back into the liquid, and refrigerate it. That night, skim off and discard any fat that has hardened on the surface. Or, if you don't have time in the morning, pop the whole pot into the refrigerator before you leave the house, skim fat and strain the broth that night. Use the broth right away or freeze measured amounts for future use. You can freeze it with the meat in, or freeze some containers of meat just covered with broth, others that contain only broth.

A typical stock recipes follows. This Chicken Soup Stock can be used with the meat in it for Pumpkin or Winter Squash Soup, page 248, or with the meat strained out in Southwest Chili Vegetable Soup, page 347, or Spicy Szechuan Chicken, page 287. Once you begin to make stocks, you will find many uses for them.

HOMEMADE CHICKEN STOCK

I buy five chickens at a time when they are on sale, cut them up, freeze the best pieces in meal-sized portions, and make soup stock from the backs and necks.

> 3 pounds bony chicken parts (backs, necks, wings)
> 2 medium onions, chopped (or the equivalent in chopped green onions, onion lilies, or leek leaves)
> 2 medium carrots
> 2 stalks celery (or an equivalent amount of Chinese celery)
> 5 parsley stalks (or 5 root parsley leaves)
> 2 bay leaves
> 1/2 teaspoon whole black peppercorns
> 4 quarts water
> 1/2 teaspoon dried thyme (or several sprigs fresh thyme)
> 1/4 teaspoon marjoram or oregano (or 1 sprig fresh marjoram or oregano)

Combine chicken, onions, carrots, celery, parsley, bay leaves, peppercorns, and water in a large pot. Bring to a boil. Skim off the foam that forms on top. Add thyme and marjoram or oregano. Lower the heat, cover, and simmer for 2 to 3 hours. Cool the stock, then refrigerate it overnight. The next day, skim off the fat and discard it. Discard all of the vegetables. Strain the stock. If you don't plan to use it right away, freeze it in plastic freezer containers. (If you wish, save the lean meat, freezing it in a plastic container with enough stock to cover.)

BACKYARD OMELET

Here's an omelet made with the backyard gleanings of a chilly December morning. (If you feel nervous about making a proper omelet, you can scramble the eggs instead, and they will taste just as good.)

4 medium sage leaves
1 2-inch sprig rosemary (tender parts only)
6 nasturtium flowers
6 nasturtium leaves
6 garlic chive leaves (or onion lily or garlic leaves)
3/4 cup grated jack cheese (or other mild cheese)
4 eggs
2 tablespoons butter or margarine

Mince the sage and rosemary leaves finely. Chop the nasturtium flowers and leaves and the garlic chives into 1/2-inch pieces. Beat the eggs in a bowl and stir in the minced herbs, nasturtiums, and garlic chives.

   Melt the butter in a frying pan and pour in the eggs. Shake the pan back and forth to prevent sticking. As the eggs begin to cook, slip a spatula under the edges and tilt the pan so that the uncooked egg can run under the cooked part to the center of the skillet. When the omelet is almost set, place the cheese on half of it. Fold the omelet in half over the cheese and slide it out of the pan onto a plate. Serves two.

Note: For scrambled eggs, beat the eggs and stir in all the ingredients except the butter or margarine. Cook the eggs in the butter, mixing and turning until the eggs are set to your liking.

had enough of them that I also enjoyed the lull in production that followed. I loved the profusion of cucumbers, from midsummer to midfall. I liked the fresh cabbage, so sweet and crisp that I cut large wedges of it to eat raw. I also enjoyed my efforts to achieve year-round self-sufficiency in such crops as garlic and lettuce. Though of course I could never be self-sufficient overall, my limited successes gave me a feeling of satisfaction that was well worth the effort. They also gave me a stronger sense of connection with those who live from the land.

If you want to try self-sufficiency in some crops, or even a single crop, choose ones you can either produce year round or that you can store easily. Some good candidates are garlic, carrots, leeks, green onions, lettuce, or parsley. Don't worry too much about perfection. If you grow too little of a crop, buy some; if too much, give some away.

Whatever our food supply, we are always dealing with an abundance of some foods and a scarcity of others. In a market economy, abundance is reflected in a lower price, scarcity in a higher one. You can easily avoid having an oversupply of an abundant item on the market, simply by not buying too much no matter how cheap it is; and those with a larger budget can obtain more of a scarce food if they are willing to pay more.

The ruling factors in a supply of garden food are a bit different. Abundance and scarcity are affected by what a climate will let you grow, the size of your garden, your gardening skill, and a certain amount of chance. Sometimes you will find yourself harvesting an unexpected bounty. And you can't refuse garden bounty, because you already have it. If you stop picking a crop, it will just go on bearing. Letting it go to waste will probably leave you with an uneasiness that will reduce your pleasure in gardening—I know it does mine.

One solution is to pick crops as baby vegetables, a tactic that limits their total production.

Zucchinis picked with the flowers still attached, slender green bean pods, or young lettuce plants are all delicious. A warning though: getting yourself to pick young vegetables may take some determination. You may find yourself thinking, "Maybe it should get a bit larger," or "Seems a pity to pull that when I just put it in."

If a crop bears too much food for me to eat, I usually give it away. I may preserve some of it, though I make it a point not to preserve any food unless the result is truly delicious. If I can make dried tomatoes that are as good as the ones I can buy, then I will do that. If they turn out to be inferior, I will not try that again unless I learn a different technique. If I haven't picked a crop when it's small, can't give it away, and it doesn't preserve well, then I must look for more recipes for that crop and grow less next time.

Because of the fluctuations in the supply of garden crops, there are two kinds of recipes that gardeners love: 1. Ones that find yet another way to use up lots of whatever you have too much of, and 2. Ones that use a little of this and a little of that, whatever you have around. In the first category are recipes such as Zucchini Fritters, on page 353, Wilted Lettuce, page 220, or Southeast Asian Cucumber Salad, page 206. Look for salads or soups that are based on a single vegetable. Then look for unusual ways to prepare a crop, in dishes in which you wouldn't expect to find it, or with seasoning unlike that of dishes you already make — anything that will dispel the impression that you are eating the same thing every day.

If, instead of too much, you find yourself with only a little of this and that crop, you will find the second kind of recipe useful. Times you are likely to find yourself with these "wee bits" of any one item are when a crop hasn't done well, or at the beginning and end of a harvest. When you have only a little of several crops, make mixed soups or salads, omelets, casseroles, stir fries, or vegetable curries. One day in early summer you will go out and find that you have ready for harvest seven green bean pods, one baby zucchini, a few small side heads of broccoli, and a few leaves regrown from a cut cabbage head. These slim pickings can serve as the basis for a very nice Year-Round Vegetable Curry (see page 195). Other such recipes in this book are Backyard Omelet, on opposite page, Southwest Chili Vegetable Soup, page 347.

In many cases, you will have, for a given planting of a given crop, a cycle of scarcity as it begins to bear, then bounty, then scarcity again. This cycle will be most intense with crops such as corn, lettuce, or cilantro, that do not last long once they are ready, and do not keep very well in storage either. In such cases, you can reduce the production bulge by making a series of small plantings, rather than only one.

And sometimes you will find that you waited a bit too long, so a crop has become too mature, or has begun to go to seed. Soup stock is a handy use for any members of the carrot or onion family that are past their prime. Soup stock relies on vegetables for flavoring, then the vegetables themselves are discarded. For this purpose, it matters little if the vegetables are too tough to eat. (See Soup Stock, on page 349)

Notice that the availability of garden produce is not bound by the same principles that govern price at the grocery. Some crops that are often very inexpensive to buy never produce well in foggy gardens, so are always scarce in our gardens. And some that are generally high in price are easy to grow in great abundance. For example, fresh herbs are always pricey, but one of the easiest of crops. And edible flowers are extremely expensive, but most are not hard to grow. Baby vegetables cost more at the grocery than mature ones, but the only secret to growing them easily is knowing the time to pick. And there are still some crops, such as scarlet runner beans and Bolivian sunroot that you will see in a grocery only rarely at any price.

Trying Something New

You could just plan to grow foods you already like and know how to cook, but how do you know there aren't

ALLERGIC?

People sometimes discover they are allergic to new foods, and the effects of these allergies can be deadly, so if you know you are allergic to any food, test small amounts of new ones before you rush in headlong. It is probably also wise to let dinner guests know if unconventional foods are about to be served, in case they have allergies or a tendency to allergies.

MEXICAN VEGETABLES

In summer, substitute purslane for Swiss chard in this delicious Mexican dish.

1 tablespoon oil
1 small onion, chopped
1 clove garlic, minced
1 15-ounce can tomato purée (or 2 cups thick homemade tomato sauce, see page 346)
2 medium potatoes, diced
6 to 8 leaves Swiss chard, chopped, stems included (or 2 cups chopped young purslane)
1 cup cooked garbanzo beans
1/2 to 1 jalapeño pepper, pickled or fresh, finely chopped

Heat the oil in a medium skillet and sauté the onion and garlic until just tender, but not browned. Add the tomato purée or sauce, potatoes, and stems of the Swiss chard, chopped into 1/2-inch pieces. Simmer until tender, 10 to 15 minutes.

Add the chopped chard leaves (or all of the purslane if that's the green of choice), garbanzos, and jalapeño. Simmer another 5 minutes.

Serve as a main dish or a side dish.

---

wonderful surprises to discover? Especially if fog is limiting your choices of crops, you may as well find out if you like everything it is possible for you to grow.

Whenever possible, start by buying some of a new food at a good grocery, or get a friend to let you taste a crop they have grown. But if neither is possible, just put some in and see what you get. If a new crop requires preparation, start collecting recipes for it before you harvest it. Check for recipes in cookbooks; ask other gardeners; look in specialty seed catalogs, magazines and newspapers. Look for recipes with flavorings or secondary ingredients that you know you will like, to increase the chance you will enjoy them.

To sleuth out recipes for different kinds of produce in cookbooks, try very inclusive ones such as *Joy of Cooking*, books on cooking with vegetables, and books on regional or ethnic cuisines that might include the crop. For example, you might find recipes for chayote in cookbooks on New Orleans cuisine, or that of Mexico, the Philippine islands, Australia, or even Madagascar, as all of these make use of this versatile crop.

In each cookbook, try the index first. In recent cookbooks, with the new emphasis on authentic ingredients, you may not need to look further. But in older cookbooks, I have often had to also scan the recipes themselves for particular vegetables, because no one thought it important to index such things. While this is a frustrating process, it can turn up some gems. Try listings for soups, salads, main dishes, pickles, chutneys, and even desserts. To widen the possibilities for using new crops, think which familiar vegetable your unusual one resembles and try substituting it in recipes—as chayote squash for zucchini, garlic chives for ordinary chives, or Bolivian sunroot for jicama. The recipe for Mexican Vegetables (above) works just as well if purslane is substituted for the Swiss chard.

Staple Foods

When you try new foods, and new ways to prepare them, you will find the number of staples you keep in your kitchen will increase somewhat. A staple is any food that, when you notice you are out of it, you put on your shopping list. These are the foods you expect to find on your refrigerator or cabinet shelf when you are ready to make a favorite dish that contains them. For example, you probably keep some kind of fat or oil, a vinegar, salt, and pepper. In my grandmother's kitchen, the fats of choice were lard or butter, the vinegar homemade from apple cider, the salt, plain, refined salt, and the pepper was black. In my childhood, we used

ZUCCHINI FRITTERS

A delicious answer to the summer zucchini glut, these fritters are also good when they are made with any other type of summer squash, with chayote, sunchoke, or potato, or with combinations of any two of these vegetables. They can be served for breakfast, lunch, or dinner.

1 cup grated zucchini (or other summer squash, chayote, sunchoke or potato)
1 cup lowfat cottage cheese
2 eggs
1 cup whole wheat or unbleached flour
2 teaspoons oil plus extra for frying

Mix the zucchini, cottage cheese, eggs, flour, and 2 teaspoons oil in the order given. Heat oil in a skillet. When water drops sprinkled on the skillet jump, spoon in the fritter batter. Make fritters about 4 inches in diameter and 1/2 inch or so thick. When the first side is browned, turn and brown the second side. Serve plain or with butter and, if desired, plum jam, applesauce, or syrup. Serves two or three.

bacon fat or a solid white fat known as Crisco™, as well as butter, then gradually shifted to margarine and a refined, polyunsaturated, liquid oil such as safflower oil. We used purchased cider vinegar, or a white vinegar. Salt and pepper were the same white and black that my grandmother used.

In the 60s and 70s, the main changes in these staples were that wine vinegar appeared here and there, sea salt became popular, and the powdered red, cayenne pepper was sometimes substituted for black. Nowadays, I use less fat, but a wider variety of kinds. I fry less, but when I do, I often use a non-stick spray to replace all or most of the oil. When I use oil in cooking, it may be a polyunsaturated oil, or I may choose butter, olive oil, or sesame oil for the flavors they contribute. My cupboard contains not only cider vinegar, but rice vinegar, red wine vinegar, and often an herb-flavored wine vinegar as well. I may not salt food, having become more attuned to other flavors, but when I do, I use sea salt, or one of several condiments that are used primarily for their saltiness: soy sauce, Thai fish sauce, white miso (for Japanese miso soup), and yellow miso (for Indonesian cooking). For a fiery flavor in my cooking, I have black peppercorns in a pepper grinder,

cayenne pepper, dried red pepper flakes, dried red pepper pods, pickled jalapenos, sesame oil with chili oil, and Louisiana hot sauce.

Clearly I can't stock all of the world's condiments, but a more adventuresome cuisine requires a greater variety. It takes a bit of thought to manage the increased number of staples. A new staple often enters my kitchen as part of a new recipe (one I chose in order to have some way to prepare a new food, or to increase the ways that I can prepare a plentiful one). If I buy a new condiment and then do not like the first recipe I use it in, that one may not become a staple. But if I do like that first recipe, I will look for other recipes containing the same condiments. For example, if I like a cucumber salad with rice vinegar, I will look for other recipes containing rice vinegar. In my search, I use the same methods that I use to hunt recipes for a new crop, scanning the index in cookbooks, and the ingredient lists of specific recipes. The trick is to keep the number of containers on my shelf to manageable proportions, while developing an expanded set of staples that will let me explore the world's flavors.

AFTERWORD

ON WRITING ABOUT GARDENING

The way I garden is based on long experience, on familiarity with the fabric of soil and plant. To write about how to garden, I must begin by describing the threads and how they are woven. But describing the warp and weft is not the same as seeing the pattern whole.

I cannot teach the fabric of gardening through writing. Only gardening can do that. But I can add to my description of the threads a sketch of what the fabric looks like to me. I want those who read to know that there is a fabric to discover: a richness and a sense of wholeness and well-being beyond the textbook list of what to plant where.

Although I use the discoveries of science in the garden, I do not think in the rational and linear way of the scientist all the while I garden. There is a continuity between my garden and that of the earliest garden-ers. The Mexican *milpa* had no tidy rows. It was a tangle of vines climbing trees, of vegetables jumbled together.

And nobody wrote about how to garden at first. How did people learn to garden? From each other. From parents. People gardened in families, next to other families. Someone would try something new to see if it would make more of some food. If it worked they'd do it again and others would copy.

*   *   *

But after a few years we might slip and not do it just the same way. There would be no record. So we might make up songs to help ourselves remember and to teach the children. (It is the same thing.) Then we would go into the garden or the fields and sing together while we worked. Sometimes there would be a dif-ferent song for each stage of the growing. Besides teaching, it would make us feel happy and close to sing together as we watched our food plants grow.

At first everyone would sing together or, if the women were the gardeners, we the women would sing. But eventually the ways would become old and perfected and not so likely to be lost. Then song leaders might develop, who walked in the gardens and fields and did the singing. We would still love to listen to the old songs, which would remind us of the old magical feeling about how our ancestors discovered the way to grow plants to feed the people.

*   *   *

Now writing takes the place of the community, of sharing knowledge directly with the people whose lives I share. When I cannot sing with my people, I write.

Pam Peirce
San Francisco

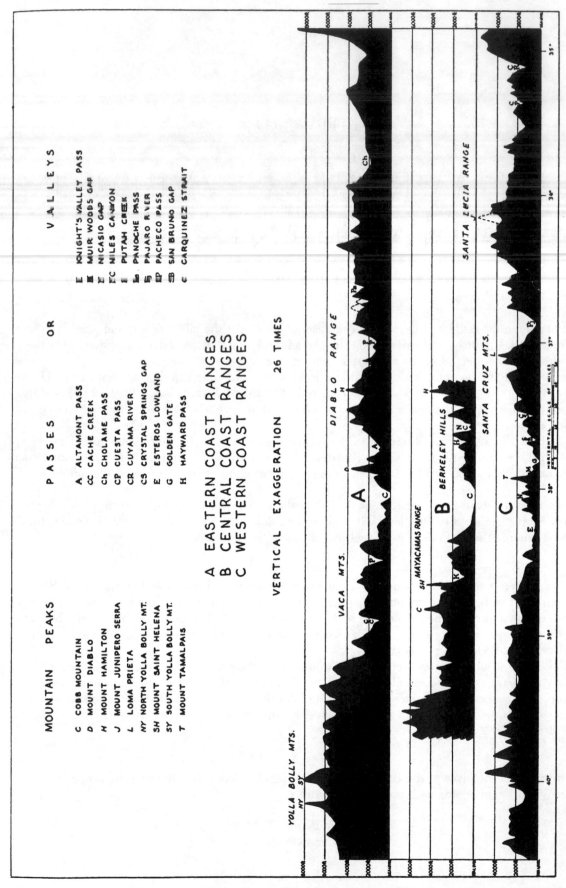

Crestline profiles of Coast Ranges in central California with names of passes and valleys. (Univ. of California Publications in Geography, vol. 7, 1951)

APPENDIX I

THE CLIMATE OF OUR REGION

■ Why do we get so much fog in the summer?

Summer fog is common because we are located between a very cold ocean and a very hot inland area. As the Central Valley warms, the heated air above it rises. Air from the west rushes in to fill the vacuum, creating an onshore wind.

Since the air carried by this wind has just passed over great expanses of cool ocean water, it is cool and humid. It is made even colder by the fact that there is a band of especially cold ocean water just off our coast. As the air passes over this cold water, it is cooled precipitously. The moisture it contains is condensed, becoming visible as fog. The pull of air from ocean to valley is often called the "fog pump."

■ Why is the ocean near our coast so cold?

The California Current flows parallel to the California coast, carrying cold water from the north and west. Then, deflected by the rotation of the earth, this water turns away from the California shore. It is replaced by an upwelling of deep ocean water that is 10 to 15°F colder than the already chilly surface water.

The band of cold coastal ocean reaches from Oregon to Point Conception (just below Lompoc, California), centering on the stretch between Cape Mendocino and Monterey Bay. It begins to appear in

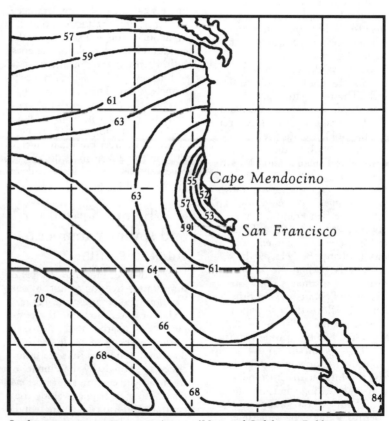

Surface water temperatures in August (Univ. of California Publications in Geography, vol. 3, 1931)

May, peaks in August, then tapers off. Ocean temperatures equalize by the following March.

■ Why does the summer fog build up for a few days and then go away for a few days?

After cold ocean air has been rushing into the Central Valley for a few days, the valley becomes cooler. When this happens, the fog pump stops, letting the onshore wind die down until the Valley warms up again. This process often takes a few days, but may take several weeks.

■ Is the summer so cold because of the fog?

No. The main reason for the cold is that the ocean breeze is cold. True, the fog blocks some sun, but on days when the breeze is not carrying fog, it is still a cold breeze.

■ Which areas get the most summer fog and why?

Areas nearest the ocean and those located along fog gaps get the most fog. Fog often covers a substantial swath of ocean off the coast and blankets the coast to the first hills. In the midsummer months, Point Reyes, on a long spit of land extending into the cold current, has the coldest summer temperatures in the continental U.S.

A fog gap is any place low enough for the fog to be able to flow through. The two main places through which fog can move inland are the San Francisco and Monterey Bays. The Golden Gate itself is narrow, but the whole distance between Mount Tamalpais and Mount Montara is lower than 500 feet. Marine air, often carrying fog, blows through this mega-gap, covering San Francisco, the San Francisco Bay, the southern tip of Marin and the central Bay coast of Alameda County (Albany, Berkeley, Alameda). On days when the fog is extensive, it continues to flow up the Carquinez Straits toward Stockton, and also flows through gaps in the East Bay hills.

Monterey Bay has a wide mouth, but has high mountains to the north and south. The fog moves inland against the hills, with Chittendon pass serving as a fog gap to let air into the Santa Clara Valley and the San Benito Valley. Fog sometimes spreads up the Salinas Valley, and Monterey Bay fog occasionally meets that from the San Francisco Bay at San Jose.

Outside of these two main entry points, there are also areas with narrower and/or higher gaps, and there are areas that are foggy at the coast with high hills blocking inland fog. (See map on page 360 for locations of main fog gaps and graph on page 356 for a view of the coastal mountains which block the flow of fog.) If a fog gap is parallel to the prevailing northwesterly summer wind, more fog will be able to enter it. Also, on the inland end of the gap, areas to the south and southeast will get more fog than ones to the north, since the wind will still be a more or less northwesterly one.

■ When it does get over a hill, why does the fog stop flowing and just hang there on the top of the hill?

The air does not stop flowing, but, as it passes the peak of the hill, it begins to fall. Falling air warms, a process called adiabatic warming. As the air warms, the fog evaporates. Sometimes, you will see fog on the coast, and at the peaks of the coastal hills, then more fog on the west side of hills on the east side of the San Francisco Bay. The ocean breeze carrying the fog has to rise to get over the East Bay hills, thereby cooling, so the fog condenses out again. This effect creates protected sites on the downwind sides of even relatively low coastal hills. Hills over 500 feet tall block much of the fog.

■ Why are our winter and summer temperatures so similar?

We owe our moderate temperatures, rarely freezing or hot, to our location next to an ocean. Large bodies of water moderate the temperature of nearby land, since water warms and cools more slowly than does land. Climates that are influenced so strongly by the climate over the nearby ocean are known as *maritime*. When, as happens along the central California coast, the wind most often blows from the ocean, the climate is very strongly maritime. The temperature of the San Francisco Bay/Delta Area is also moderated by the Bay and other inland waterways.

When the coast does get unusually hot or cold spells, you can be pretty sure that the source of the weather is not the ocean, but the land to the east. Only when the winds reverse for a few days do we get those warm summer nights in San Francisco, or coastal gardens blanketed in frost.

■ Why does it finally warm up in September and October?

Even though the most sun shines on the northern hemisphere on June 21 (the longest day of the year), there is a lag time before the warmest days occur, while the earth itself warms up. In the center of a continent, this takes about 30 days. But when winds blow from an ocean, especially cold, foggy winds like ours, the days of maximum temperature are delayed. The land can't warm up until the water temperature rises.

The longest delay of the maximum along the Central California Coast is 90 days—all the way to September 21! The warmest part of San Francisco has a delay of 75 days, which is the first week of September. The area in which this book will be most accurately useful to gardeners is that part of central California in which the maximum temperature is delayed 45 days or longer. That area is defined generally by the map on page 15.

You can judge the degree of marine influence in a particular location by seeing how long the maximum is delayed. San Francisco's warmest month is usually September, San Rafael's is August, and Walnut Creek shows a more continental July maximum. The warmest weather in more inland locations is also usually warmer than the warmest weather near the coast.

Incidentally, our warm days of late summer are not, strictly speaking, an "Indian Summer." This term is used in the central and eastern parts of the country to refer to a continuation of summer's warmth after continental cold fronts have brought fall's first chilly weather. Our climate has quite different sources, and our stormy fall weather usually hasn't yet begun when we finally get our warm days.

■ Why does it rain mainly in the winter?

We alternate between wet winters and dry summers because we are located between two large climate zones. One, centered off the coast of the Pacific Northwest, is stormy. The other, centered off the southern California coast, is calm. The stormy zone brings rain to Seattle most of the year, but it dips far enough south to soak us only in winter. The fair weather zone brings a semi-arid climate to San Diego, and gives us our dry summers.

A climate like ours, subtropical with summer drought and winter storms, is known as *Mediterranean*. It is named after the Mediterranean Sea, but climatologists now know that it is a climate typical of a zone 30 to 40° from the equator on the west coasts of continents. We share this climate not only with lands bordering *the* Mediterranean, but also with parts of the coast of Chile, of the southwestern tip of Africa and of western Australia.

■ Why does the amount of rain vary so much from year to year?

Our rainfall varies because we are on the southern edge of the rainy climate zone. Many storms hit in the center of the zone, in Washington and Oregon, but the storms at the edge are fewer and less regular. The normal annual rainfall in San Francisco is 19-21 inches, but there have been as many as 49.27 inches of rain and as few as 7.16 inches.

■ Why do different locations in our region get different amounts of rain?

Topography affects rainfall. Most of our storms originate over the ocean. The windward north or west sides of coastal hills get the most rain from these storms. Hills create rain shadows, with less rain falling south and east of them.

■ Why do we have fog in the winter?

Winter fog, called tule fog, after the tule reeds found in marshes, forms over damp land on clear, calm nights. It is the fog that makes Interstate 5 so difficult to drive in the winter. Tule fog forms in the Central Valley and slides down to the Delta on a weak wind that moves west from Carquinez. It forms up to 500 feet deep over the San Francisco Bay, and reaches onto the San Francisco peninsula and Marin. Winter days may see the reverse of summer—the coast clear, while inland areas are deep in tule fog.

Rarely, a marine fog forms in winter. It usually precedes a storm approaching the coast, unlike summer marine fogs that come with calm weather.

■ Why are some days so smoggy and others so clear?

The atmosphere further from the earth is ordinarily colder than that near the surface. A reversal of this normal condition is called a *temperature inversion*. When the cold ocean breeze blows onto the central California coast in summer, it passes under a layer of warm air, creating a temperature inversion. Inversions may also form in the winter, when the air is cooled by the cold land. These winter inversions usually last less than 24 hours, but summer inversions may last for days at a time. It is during summer inversions that we most often see smog increase for many days, filling the basin of air above the Bay and spilling into the valleys that open onto it.

When there is no inversion, pollution rises unhindered into the air, becoming more dilute as it spreads vertically into a larger volume of air. During an inversion, smog circulates within the cold air, but the cold air, being heavier than the warm air above it, does not rise. When the sun warms the land, the cold lower air is warmed, and only then can it break the inversion and rise, carrying away the smog.

■ Which are the smoggiest parts of the region?

The most urban areas, since the auto is the main polluter of the area's air. But urban areas closest to the ocean have fewer smoggy days than those inland, since the ocean breeze blows the pollution eastward.

■ What will air pollution do to a vegetable garden?

When you see a brown haze in the air, you are looking at nitrogen dioxide, which is mostly from auto exhausts. Some crops, including beans and tomatoes, are sensitive and will be weakened by exposure to this gas.

When smog builds for several days under an inversion and clear sky, the energy from sunlight causes chemical reactions in the smog, creating new chemicals that are often more damaging to both plants and humans. This is called "photochemical smog." It is particularly likely to harm lettuce.

Lead used to be a much worse air pollutant when all cars used leaded gas. Now all cars use lead-free gas, but soil near roads can still be contaminated. (For more on soil lead see page 75.)

While some of your crops may be somewhat harmed by air pollution, the current pollution level is not usually high enough for serious damage, and diagnosis is usually difficult.

Gardeners have a special interest in reducing particulate air pollution, since more of it could mean more, not less fog. Particulate pollution is any floating solid matter, like smoke, dust, lead, cadmium. While the heaviest of these don't float much, smoke and dust rise into the air. Such floating particles, as well as the salt that is in the ocean spray, serve as nuclei for the condensing water droplets that make up fog. While we can't prevent ocean spray, we can support efforts to stop any smoky polluters.

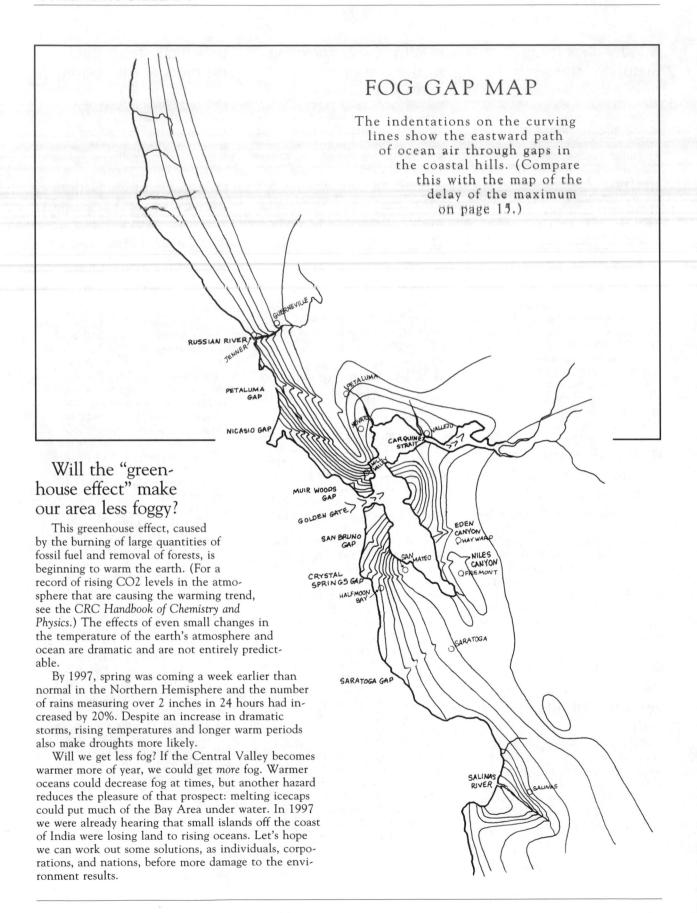

FOG GAP MAP

The indentations on the curving lines show the eastward path of ocean air through gaps in the coastal hills. (Compare this with the map of the delay of the maximum on page 15.)

GUERNEVILLE

RUSSIAN RIVER

JENNER

PETALUMA

PETALUMA GAP

NOVATO

VALLEJO

NICASIO GAP

CARQUINEZ STRAIT

MILL VALLEY

MUIR WOODS GAP

GOLDEN GATE

EDEN CANYON

HAYWARD

SAN BRUNO GAP

NILES CANYON

FREMONT

SAN MATEO

CRYSTAL SPRINGS GAP

HALFMOON BAY

SARATOGA

SARATOGA GAP

SALINAS RIVER

SALINAS

Will the "greenhouse effect" make our area less foggy?

This greenhouse effect, caused by the burning of large quantities of fossil fuel and removal of forests, is beginning to warm the earth. (For a record of rising CO_2 levels in the atmosphere that are causing the warming trend, see the CRC *Handbook of Chemistry and Physics*.) The effects of even small changes in the temperature of the earth's atmosphere and ocean are dramatic and are not entirely predictable.

By 1997, spring was coming a week earlier than normal in the Northern Hemisphere and the number of rains measuring over 2 inches in 24 hours had increased by 20%. Despite an increase in dramatic storms, rising temperatures and longer warm periods also make droughts more likely.

Will we get less fog? If the Central Valley becomes warmer more of year, we could get *more* fog. Warmer oceans could decrease fog at times, but another hazard reduces the pleasure of that prospect: melting icecaps could put much of the Bay Area under water. In 1997 we were already hearing that small islands off the coast of India were losing land to rising oceans. Let's hope we can work out some solutions, as individuals, corporations, and nations, before more damage to the environment results.

APPENDIX II

USING SCIENTIFIC PLANT NAMES

IN EACH HEADING FOR A PLANT discussed in this book you will find a scientific name. After the scientific name, you will find the common and Latin names of the plant family to which it belongs. For example, for potato (page 235), the scientific name *Solanum tuberosum* is given. On the following line, you see: Nightshade Family, Solanaceae.

The scientific name of a plant species contains two words. The first word is the name of the genus it belongs to; the second identifies the particular species within the genus. The two words of the scientific name are always written in italics. If the plant species has a naturally occuring variety or a subspecies, that name is also written in italics. (See, for example, celeriac, on page 194.) The genus name is capitalized, but the species and variety names are not.

If a species has a cultivar, or human-created variety, that name is also written after the species name. It is not in italics, but it is capitalized and in single quotes. For example, *Solanum tuberosum* 'Yellow Finn', commonly known as 'Yellow Finn' potato. (For more on cultivars, see pages 43 and 44.)

Sometimes a scientific name will be followed by another one, the second in parentheses. This means that the international body that decides plant names has changed the name. This can happen for several reasons, a very common one today being the use of genetic analysis

which shows plant relationships more clearly and reveals a plant to be misclassified. The name in parentheses is the former name.

When many cultivars have been developed from the same species, the cultivars are sometimes informally divided into groups of similar cultivars, such as "Sugar snap type peas" or "Beefsteak type tomatoes." Sometimes the cultivars are even divided into semiformal groups. For example, the onion species, *Allium cepa*, has been divided into the groups Cepa (common onion), Aggregatum (potato onion and shallot), Fistulosum

(bunching onions) and Proliferum (top onions). When this is the case, you will find these semiformal group names in the heading under the species name (see the various onion listings).

Knowing plant scientific names sometimes helps you to find the plant you want, as each plant has only one scientific name. It can also help you understand the relationships among plants. There are often similarities in the flavors of related edible plants, in how you grow them, and in the pests that plague them.

PLANT FAMILIES MENTIONED IN THIS BOOK THAT HAVE TWO CORRECT SCIENTIFIC NAMES

Common Names	Traditional Family Name	Modern Family Name
Carrot Family	Umbelliferae	Apiaceae
Grass Family	Graminae	Poaceae
Mint Family	Labiatae	Laminaceae
Mustard Family	Cruciferae	Brassicaceae
Pea Family	Leguminosae	Fabaceae
Sunflower Family	Compositae	Asteraceae

The names of some plant families have been changed recently. This was done because botanists wanted all plant family names to end in the letters "aceae" and this ending was not proper latin spelling for the old names. Though these names have been changed, the older names are still widely used and more familiar to many. I have used the older names most frequently, but here is a list of both the old and new.

APPENDIX III

PESTICIDE TOXICITY

A LIST OF COMMON ACTIVE INGREDIENTS

■ NOTES & EXPLANATIONS
ABOUT THESE LISTINGS
OF PESTICIDE ACTIVE
INGREDIENTS:

1. COMMON NAME. Name of active ingredient.

2. BRAND NAME(S). These are the common trademarks under which a chemical is sold. It may also be sold as part of products with names that are not trademarks, such as "Lawn Weed Killer."

3. CLASS OF CHEMICAL. Chemicals can be divided into groups, based on similarities of chemical structure. And sometimes generalizations can be made about a group of chemicals. For example we know that sugars are often sweet.

The simplest chemicals are the elements and simple compounds containing them. And they are perhaps the hardest to generalize about. Among those used as pesticides, some elements, like sulfur or copper, are actually plant nutrients when present in very small amounts. Others, like arsenic or mercury, are poisonous to life and accumulate in plant and animal material. They were used as pesticides until we understood that we were also poisoning ourselves.

Most pesticides are not simple inorganic compounds, but complex organic ones. (An organic compound can be one created by a living creature, or one created by humans based on patterns previously only present in living creatures.) Botanicals are organic compounds extracted from plants. Plants do contain anti-pest chemicals, and I think we have only begun to learn how to use them to our advantage. Examples of botanical pesticides are pyrethrum and rotenone. The main trait botanicals share is that they break down quickly, not remaining to pollute the environment. Contrary to common belief, they are *not* necessarily low in toxicity to non-targeted life forms, such as bees or people. Note that the botanical nicotine sulfate has one of the highest acute toxicities listed here. However one botanical is particularly selective for insects. Look for products containing neem, an extract of a tree native to India. This substance has a very low mammalian toxicity and, as it is used, does little harm to bees and other beneficial creatures. It kills 131 different insect pests, including some, such as leafminers and whiteflies, that are otherwise quite difficult to control.

The synthetic organic pesticides are chemicals created to kill. They enter a living creature masquerading as a normal chemical, but then make life systems go haywire. The earliest group of pesticides based on this kind of chemical were the organochlorines, of which DDT is an example. Speaking generally, these chemicals are relatively low in acute toxicity to mammals, but they bio-accumulate in fat tissue, moving up through the food chain to be particularly poisonous to humans, predatory birds, and other meat eaters. Because of this, some of the worst were withdrawn from the market, although some organochlorines, like methoxychlor and PCNB, are still available.

The next generation of synthetic organic pesticides were the organophosphates, which include diazinon and malathion. These do not bio-accumulate, but they are extremely toxic to humans and other nontargeted creatures. They are also toxic when they are absorbed through the skin, enter the body through a cut, or are breathed. They are nerve poisons, and a serious exposure can alter the brain waves for a year. Low doses may suppress the immune system. At least one organophosphate, parathion, is banned or restricted in many countries, though not in the U.S.

A third, more recently developed group is the carbamates. They do not bioaccumulate. They vary in acute toxicity to humans, but include a few that are more toxic than organophospates. They are quite toxic to honeybees, earthworms, and other beneficial creatures. Examples are carbaryl and the fungicide maneb.

There are other categories of synthetic organic pesticides, more than I can list here, but this list will give you an initial understanding of the possibilities.

4. CATEGORY OF PESTICIDE. Here I have listed the words used to describe what kind(s) of pest the pesticide will kill. Each term includes the type of pest followed by the Latin root [-cide] meaning to kill.

5. THE REGISTERED USES listed include only those pests most likely to be a problem in local food gardens. The chemical may be registered for other pests, and these will be listed on product labels.

6. ACUTE TOXICITY. LD_{50} is the scientific term for the amount of a chemical that proved to be a lethal dose for 50% of the test animals that were fed it or were otherwise exposed to it. The dermal LD_{50} refers to skin exposure, while the inhalation LD_{50} means the exposure came through breathing fumes in the air. Oral and dermal LD_{50}s are expressed in milligrams of active ingredient per kilogram of animal weight (mg/kg). Inhalation LD_{50} is often expressed in parts per million in the air inhaled. A lower LD_{50} means that a chemical is more poisonous—a smaller quantity will kill the exposed creature. (Also, because the oral and dermal LD_{50}s are expressed in mg/kg, a lesser quantity of any particular pesticide is lethal to a smaller person.)

The Roman numerals after the LD_{50}s refer to categories of toxicity, as expressed by signal words on the label. Category I chemicals would bear the signal word "Danger," Category II "Warning," and Categories III and IV "Caution." Notice that the rating for ingesting the chemical is often different from that for absorbing it through your skin.

This information refers to the acute, or immediate, toxicity of the *pure active ingredient*, not to that of any specific formulation containing the ingredient. The specific formulation will only have the same LD_{50} if it consists of 100% active ingredient. In most cases, the active ingredient will be diluted by "inert" ingredients. If, for example an active ingredient makes up 5% of the product formulation, the LD_{50} of that product (assuming the inerts don't increase toxicity) would be

$\frac{1}{20}$ of the LD_{50} given in the following list for the active ingredient. However, even if this calculation makes a chemical sound relatively harmless, long-term health or environmental hazards may increase its overall hazard and all pesticides should be handled with care. (See also "Reading Pesticide Labels" on page 133.)

7. LONG-TERM HEALTH HAZARDS AND ENVIRONMENTAL HAZARDS. Toxicity is a complex matter. The LD_{50}, or the combination of the several LD_{50}s, may sound like a relatively tidy summation, but they definitely are not! When you are thinking about how toxic a chemical is, do not think only about the acute toxicity ratings. Look further to see what other hazards the chemical may create. Just because you won't die if you drink a pint of a chemical, does not mean that it is harmless. For example you might, instead of becoming ill from acute exposure, develop a tumor years later. Or after long term, low level exposure, you might have a child with a birth defect. Pesticides can also poison other creatures in the environment. Because the toxicity to birds and fish is often quite different than that to mammals, pesticides are often tested on representative birds and fish. They may additionally be tested for their effect on aquatic invertebrates that serve as food to fish and water birds.

8. BREAKDOWN. The half-life of a chemical is the amount of time it takes for half of the chemical to break down into other substances. At the end of the half-life, half of the chemical is still intact; at twice the half-life one quarter of it is still intact. Therefore the chemical will continue to cause some environmental havoc until its half-life has passed several times. In some cases, the breakdown products of pesticides are also toxic.

9. RECOMMENDATION. Besides the suggestions in individual listings, I assume that if you do use a chemical pesticide, you will read the label to choose the correct one for a correctly identified pest, and will follow directions on the label when applying it.

CAPTAN

Brand Name(s): None.
Class of Chemical: Phthalate.
Category of Pesticide: Fungicide.
Registered Uses for Vegetables: Seed treatment (to prevent seed decay and damping-off of seedlings)
Acute Toxicity:
LD_{50} (oral): 9,000-15,000 mg/kg (IV)
LD_{50} (dermal): Unavailable.
Long-term Health Hazards: Despite the fact that it is relatively nontoxic in the short run, over time, captan has been shown to cause cancer in rats and mice, and is suspected of causing it in humans. For this reason the EPA has suspended the use of captan on many food crops and requested further proof from the industry that residues on treated seeds don't end up in the resulting crops.
Environmental Hazards: Highly toxic to fish, and moderately toxic to the invertebrate life on which fish feed.
Breakdown: Half-life in soil is about two weeks. Breakdown products are not known.
Recommendation: Captan is among the fungicides that may have been used to treat seeds that you buy. (The chemical that was used to treat seeds should be listed on their label.) Avoid treated seed as much as possible, though you may choose to use it when a choice variety of seed is not available untreated.

CARBARYL

Brand Name(s): Sevin®.
Class of Chemical: Carbamate
Category of Pesticide: Insecticide
Registered Uses for Vegetables: Flea beetle, imported cabbageworm, corn earworm, cutworm, earwig, tomato hornworm, pillbug, sowbug.
Acute Toxicity:
LD_{50} (oral): 500-800 mg/kg. (III)
LD_{50} (dermal): 4,000+ mg/kg. (IV)
Long-term Health Hazards: Suspected of causing cancer, mutations and birth defects. Proven long-term effects on the kidneys.
Environmental Hazards: Highly toxic to honeybees and other helpful insects that visit sprayed crops.

When applied to the soil, it kills earthworms, ground beetles and other helpful creatures. Mite outbreaks often follow applications of carbaryl, since predator mites are more sensitive to the spray than pest mites.

Breakdown: Half-life unavailable. Remains effective for one to three weeks.

Recommendation: Use in preference to diazinon but avoid use if possible.

CHLOROTHALONIL

Brand Name(s): Daconil®, Bravo, Termil.

Class of Chemical: Chlorinated isophthalic acid derivative.

Category of Pesticide: Fungicide.

Registered Uses for Vegetables: Celery late blight, squash and cucumber powdery mildew, onion downy mildew.

Acute Toxicity:
LD_{50} **(oral):** 10,000 mg/kg. (IV)
LD_{50} **(dermal):** >10,000 mg/kg. (IV)
While I can't provide an LD_{50} for inhalation, chlorothalinol is considered to be moderately toxic when inhaled. In addition, it damages eyes and skin. Some people have an allergic skin reaction to it. The eye and skin hazards are considered serious enough that some professional-use concentrations of this chemical are Category I.

Long-term Health Hazards: Suspected of causing kidney tumors, although the evidence is inconclusive and testing is continuing.

Environmental Hazards: In itself, it is not toxic to birds, but it is moderately toxic to fish. (See, however, breakdown information.)

Breakdown: Half-life is one to two months. One of its breakdown products is moderately toxic to birds and highly toxic to fish.

Recommendation: Concentrate on preventive strategies.

COPPER SULFATE
(TRIBASIC COPPER SULFATE)

Brand Name(s): One form of copper sulfate is sold as Microcrop.

Class of Chemical: Inorganic compound.

Category of Pesticide: Fungicide.

Registered Uses for Vegetables: Copper sulfate alone, or mixed with hydrated lime to make "Bordeaux mixture," is registered to control a wide variety of fungus diseases of vegetables. Check label for exact diseases and plants for which a formulation is registered. Copper sulfate is toxic to most plants, but Bordeaux mixture is less so. Bordeaux mixture was one of the first fungicides available to gardeners, and is still used today.

Acute Toxicity:
LD_{50} **(acute oral):** 15,000 mg/kg tribasic copper sulfate (IV).
I was unable to locate an LD_{50} for Bordeaux mix, and learned that it has proven difficult to establish, as ingestion of this chemical causes such nausea that animals can't eat much of it. However it is toxic, as shown by the reaction of rats to sublethal doses. When they ate 500 mg/kg rats showed weight loss, at 1000 mg/kg they showed damage to liver, kidneys and other organs.
Allergic?? Some people are particularly sensitive to copper-based materials, so be sure to wear a respirator mask and protective clothing when you are applying them.

Long Term Health Hazards: Symptoms of long term exposure include itching skin, weight loss, painful joints, and organ damage. It is suspected that this chemical is carcinogenic, mutagenic, and causes prenatal damage.

Environmental Hazards: Toxic to fish.

Breakdown: Some is bound to the soil, some leaches down through the soil, some reacts with oxygen to form other compounds.

Recommendation: Concentrate on preventive methods of controlling fungus disease. If you do decide to try a chemical fungicide, choose sulfur/copper sulfate or use Bordeaux mix, if sulfur is also registered for the particular disease, as sulfur is less toxic and less environmentally harmful.

DIAZINON

Brand Name(s): Spectracide.

Class of Chemical: Organophosphate.

Category of Pesticide: Insecticide.

Registered Uses for Vegetables: Aphid, imported cabbageworm, carrot rust fly maggot, cutworm, flea beetle, grasshopper, mite, whitefly, wireworm, pillbug, and sowbug.

Acute Toxicity:
LD_{50} **(oral):** 300-400 mg/kg. (II)
LD_{50} **(dermal):** 600-2,000+ mg/kg. (IV)

Long-term Health Hazards: Long-term exposure to diazinon can cause neurobehavioral effects.

Environmental Hazards: Highly toxic to birds—they fall dead when they walk on treated areas. Also highly toxic to fish and aquatic insects.

Breakdown: The half-life is under two days when it is exposed to sunlight; a week when not exposed to sunlight.

Recommendation: Avoid use of diazinon.

GLYPHOSATE

Brand Name(s): Roundup, Kleenup.

Registered Uses: All weeds.

Category of Pesticide: Herbicide.

Acute Toxicity:
LD_{50} **(oral):** 4,320 mg/kg. (III)
LD_{50} **(dermal):** 7,940 mg/kg. (III)

Long Term Health Hazards: A very weak carcinogen. Little or no tendency to accumulate in animals that consume it.

Environmental Hazards: Relatively nontoxic to birds and to most kinds of fish. Relatively nontoxic to marine invertebrates. Nontoxic to honeybees. Has only a low potential for contaminating groundwater, because it binds strongly to the soil.

Breakdown: Half-life of up to 19 weeks in sandy soil, or as little as 3 weeks in loam. Most of the breakdown is due to bacterial action. After the first one to two weeks, it no longer has herbicidal action in the soil. There are no known hazardous breakdown products.

Recommendation: Use nonchemical weed control methods as much as possible. Use glyphosate only in cases when nonchemical control of perennial weeds is not working. Do not spray it near food crops. Don't plant food crops in a treated area for at least six weeks after spraying.

LIME SULFUR
(CALCIUM POLYSULFIDE)

Brand Name(s): Orthorix, Security Lime Sulfur.

Class of Chemical: Inorganic compound.

Category of Pesticide: Fungicide, insecticide, miticide.

Registered Uses for Vegetables: Powdery mildew, overwintering insect eggs, mites.

Acute Toxicity:
LD_{50} (oral): 512-712 mg/kg (III)
LD_{50} (dermal): 2,000 mg/kg. (III)
Some people are particularly sensitive to sulfur-based materials, so be sure to wear a respirator mask and protective clothing when you are applying them. They can cause irritation of eyes, ears, nose, and skin. Direct contact with this chemical will cause skin irritation and eye damage.

Long Term Health Hazards: Only from exposure to near-lethal doses of the gas H_2S (see Breakdown, below).

Hazards to crops: Toxic to some plants including some members of the cucumber family, raspberries, apricots, and Delicious apples. May burn the foliage of other plants when the temperature is high.

Environmental Hazards: In mammals, causes eye damage and skin irritation.

Breakdown: Leaves a sulfur residue, which continues to have a pesticidal action.

If it comes into contact with acids, lime sulfur yields the gas hydrogen sulfide (H_2S), which is quite toxic. Low concentrations of this gas lead to eye irritation, sometimes to lung irritation as well, but recovery from this damage is almost always complete. Breathing air with high concentrations of H_2S can be almost instantly lethal, though such concentrations are not likely to develop during ordinary use of lime sulfur as a pesticide in well-ventilated areas.

Recommendation: Although it is a chemical, lime sulfur is considered a relatively less toxic alternative. Still, consider nonchemical strategies of preventing and controlling pests before you use chemical methods.

MALATHION

Brand Name(s): Cythion.
Class of Chemical: Organophosphate.
Category of Pesticide: Insecticide, miticide.

Registered Uses for Vegetables: Aphid, imported cabbageworm, cabbage looper, grasshopper, leafminer, red spider mite, onion maggot (fly), whitefly, pillbug and sowbug.

Acute Toxicity:
LD_{50} (oral): 1,000-1,375 mg/kg. (III)
LD_{50} (dermal): 4,444 mg/kg. (III)

Long-term Health Hazards: Reproductive toxicity. Repeated exposure may make a person more susceptible to the effects of this and related chemicals.

Environmental Hazards: Very toxic to the aquatic invertebrates that fish eat, to honeybees and to other beneficial insects. Often contains manufacturing contaminants which are more toxic than the malathion itself. With continued use, pests are highly likely to develop resistance to this chemical.

Breakdown: Half-life is one to four months.

Recommendation: Use in preference to diazinon, but avoid use if possible.

METALDEHYDE

Brand Name(s): Bug-Geta Deadline, Meta, Slug Death
Class of Chemical: This is the same material used as a fuel for camp stoves under the brand name Sterno.
Category of Pesticide: Molluscicide
Registered Uses: Slugs, snails.
Acute Toxicity:
LD_{50} (oral): 600-630 mg/kg (III)
Long-term Health Hazards: Possible spinal cord damage.
Environmental Hazards: Toxic to fish and wildlife. Birds feeding on treated areas may be killed. Can attract dogs, and it is poisonous to them. If you have a dog, put bait where the dog can't get it—maybe in a bait holder as described on page 149.
Breakdown: Half-life is unavailable. Said to remain effective in the environment for about two weeks, but it may be effective longer if it isn't washed away by irrigation or rain.
Recommendation: Base slug and snail control efforts on nonchemical methods. Only use bait where other methods fail, as where hiding places are inaccessible. See page 149 for some ideas that will increase safety when you use bait.

METHOXYCHLOR

Brand Name(s): DMTD, Marlate. Often sold in combination with other chemicals, such as captan, diazinon and rotenone.
Class of Chemical: Organochlorine.
Category of Pesticide: Insecticide.
Registered Uses for Vegetables: Effective against many pests, but not aphids.
Acute Toxicity:
LD_{50} (oral): 6,000 mg/kg. (IV)
LD_{50} (dermal): 6,000 mg/kg. (III)
Long Term Health Hazards: Liver and kidney damage, reproductive toxicity.
Environmental Hazards: None identified in available literature.
Breakdown: Half-life unavailable. Toxic gases and vapors may be released when it breaks down.
Recommendation: Avoid use of methoxychlor. Choose alternatives to other chemicals in the formulation that contain it.

NEEM OR AZADIRACHTIN

Brand Name(s): Bioneem, Neemazad
Class of Chemical: Botanical
Category of Pesticide: Insecticide, insect growth regulator, insect anti-feedant, miticide, fungicide.
Registered Uses: Aphid, corn earworm, cucumber beetle, cutworm, hornworm, imported cabbageworm, leafminer, looper, scale, thrips, weevil, and whitefly.
Acute Toxicity:
LD_{50} (oral) >5,000 [mg/kg] (IV)
LD_{50} (dermal) 2,000 [mg/kg] (III)
(Moderately irritating to eyes and skin. Gloves recommended during use.)
Long-term Health Hazards: None known.
Environmental Hazards: It is considered a water pollutant because it may harm aquatic invertebrates. It would harm bees and other beneficials if they acquired a large dose, but they usually don't because they don't eat the sprayed plants. Earthworms fed neem

leaves and ground neem seeds grew faster and survived better than ones fed a normal diet.

Breakdown: Breaks down in light or in water after 100 hours. Not likely to move very far in soil. In most soil or aquatic environments, microbes would readily digest neem.

Recommendation: Use neem in preference to all chemicals registered for the same purpose except soap sprays or summer oils. Still, try non-chemical strategies first.

NICOTINE SULFATE

Brand Name(s): Black Leaf 40.
Class of Chemical: Botanical.
Category of Pesticide: Insecticide.
Registered Uses for Vegetables: Aphid, imported cabbageworm, whitefly, earworm.
Acute Toxicity:
LD_{50} **(oral):** 83 mg/kg. (II)
LD_{50} **(dermal):** 285 mg/kg. (II)
Long Term Health Hazards: None mentioned in available literature.
Environmental Hazards: Very toxic to birds and other wildlife.
Breakdown: Breaks down relatively quickly once it has been sprayed, but is so toxic you must take special care not to harvest too soon after spraying. Read the label! Black Leaf 40 says to wait 7 days after spraying before harvest.
Recommendation: Avoid use of nicotine.

OIL, SUMMER
(SUPERIOR OIL, NARROW-SPECTRUM OIL)

Brand Name(s): Sunspray Ultrafine
Class of Chemical: Petroleum Product (unsulfonataed residue of paraffinic oil)
Category of Pesticide: Insecticide, miticide, fungicide
Acute Toxicity:
LD_{50} **(oral)** >15,000 mg/kg (IV)
LD_{50} **(dermal)** >5,000 mg/kg (IV)
Long-term Health Hazards: No information.
Environmental Hazards: Toxic to fish.
Breakdown: Time required to break down varies depending on the formulation.
Recommendation: Although it is a chemical product, summer oil is considered a least-toxic alternative. Consider nonchemical strat-

egies first, then use summer oils in preference to other chemicals. (Testing is underway on vegetable oils as pesticides, which, if they work, will provide even less toxic alternatives in the future.)

PCNB
(QUINTOZINE)

Brand Name(s): Terrachlor, Sanichlor.
Class of Chemical: Organochlorine.
Category of Pesticide: Fungicide.
Registered Uses for Vegetables: Club root of brassicas, damping off, rhizoctonia, onion white rot.
Acute Toxicity:
LD_{50} **(oral):** 1,750-12,000+ mg/kg. (III or IV)
LD_{50} **(dermal):** Unavailable.
Long Term Health Hazards: Liver damage. When ingested, PCNB is metabolized to other substances suspected of being responsible for prenatal damage and cancer.
Environmental Hazards: Toxic to fish and other aquatic organisms.
Breakdown: Half-life of four to ten months in the soil.
Recommendation: Concentrate on preventative measures to avoid soil diseases. Avoid using PCNB.

POTASSIUM SALTS OF FATTY ACIDS

Brand Name(s): Safer Insecticidal Soap, Sharpshooter.
Class of Chemical: Soap.
Category of Pesticide: Insecticide, miticide, herbicide. (The formulations for different purposes are different.)
Registered Uses for vegetables: Aphid, whitefly, spider mites, and earwig.
Other Registered Use: Nonselective weed killer, effective against annual weeds.
Acute Toxicity:
LD_{50} **(oral):** Virtually nontoxic to humans.
Long Term Health Hazards: None found.
Environmental Hazards: When high concentrations of soaps contaminate waterways, algae grow rapidly and are considered pollutants. However, as commonly used by home gardeners, soap-based insecticides and herbicides are much less likely to enter waterways than

are soaps used in cleaning.
Breakdown: Biodegradable.
Recommendation: Although they are chemical products, fatty acid formulations are considered a least toxic alternative. Still, consider nonchemical strategies before you decide to use them.

PYRETHRUM
(AND RELATED PRODUCTS)

Brand Name(s): See following note.
Class of Chemical: Botanical. (Or, synthetic pesticide based on a botanical one). Pyrethrum is an extract from a daisy (*Tanacetum cinerariifolium*) which kills or paralyzes insects quickly. It is often refined before being used as an ingredient in pesticides, and the refined extracts are known as pyrethrins. Also on the market are various synthetic compounds, called pyrethroids, that are structurally based on pyrethrum. Some of the many pyrethroids are: allethrins (brand name Pynamin), bioallethrin, cyfluthrin, flucythrinate, permethrin, phenothrin, resmethrin, tetramethrin, trihalothrin, and fenvalerate (Pydin, Belmark).
Category of Pesticide: Insecticide.
Registered Uses for Vegetables: Aphids, whiteflies, cabbageworms, cabbage loopers.
Acute Toxicity (for pyrethrum):
LD_{50} **(oral):** 263-1,500 mg/kg. (III)
LD_{50} **(dermal):** >1,800 mg/kg. (III) The above LD_{50}s are for pyrethrum. The LD_{50}s of synthetic pyrethroids vary widely. Both the natural and synthetic forms can cause allergic reactions, which may result in skin rashes or in more severe allergic symptoms. The acute toxicity effects of pyrethrins and of many of the pyrethroids have not been fully studied.
Long Term Health Hazards: Under "practical conditions," or as usually used, pyrethrum is considered one of the least toxic to mammals among pesticides. However, pyrethrum is often combined with piperonyl butoxide, to make it kill more effectively, and the long-term toxicity of piperonyl butoxide is unknown. Various pyre-

throids have been shown to cause enlarged liver, damage to the nervous system, and immune system suppression. Some pyrethroids have been shown to cause cancer. The long-term hazards of pyrethrins and several of the pyrethroids have not been fully studied.

Environmental Effects: Kills earthworms, toxic to fish, aquatic invertebrates and honeybees.

Breakdown: Pyrethrum breaks down quickly in the environment, especially in sunlight. The persistence of pyrethroids varies widely, as does their stability in sunlight. The behavior of the light stable pyrethroids has not been fully studied, but we do know that the half life of pyrethroids in soil ranges from 1 day to 16 weeks.

Recommendation: Avoid use of pyrethrin, synthetic pyrethroids and of pyrethrum formulations that contain piperonyl butoxide. Use pyrethrum in preference to malathion or carbaryl, but use nonchemical strategies first. If you do use pyrethrum, apply it in the evening, for maximum effectiveness and minimum exposure of beneficial insects.

ROTENONE

Brand Name(s): None found.
Class of Chemical: Botanical
Category of Pesticide: Insecticide.
Registered Uses for Vegetables: Aphid, imported cabbage worm, pillbug, sowbug, whitefly, earworm.
Acute Toxicity:
   LD_{50} (oral): 132 mg/kg. (II)
   LD_{50} (dermal): 1,000-3,000 mg/kg. (II or III)
Long Term Health Hazards: May cause liver and kidney damage as well as tumors.
Environmental Hazards: Toxic to fish.
Breakdown: Breaks down in one week or less in strong sunlight. Leaves no toxic breakdown products.
Recommendation: Use in preference to malathion or carbaryl, but avoid if possible.

SULFUR

Brand Name(s): None found.
Class of Chemical: Inorganic
Category of Pesticide: Fungicide, miticide.
Registered Uses for Vegetables: Powdery mildew, leaf spot, rust, most mites.
Acute Toxicity:
   LD_{50} (oral): Nontoxic to humans. Some people are sensitive to sulfur based materials, so be sure to wear a respirator mask and protective clothing when you are applying them. They can cause irritation of eyes, ears, nose, and skin.
Long Term Health Hazards: None found.
Hazards to Crops: Sulfur is toxic to some plants, including some cucumber family plants, raspberries, and apricots.
Environmental Hazards: Practically nontoxic to mammals. Not toxic to fish or honeybees. Kills beneficial as well as pest fungi.
Breakdown: Sulfur is an element, so does not break down. It enters biological compounds due to metabolic action of microbes. Some enters the air as sulfur dioxide.
Recommendation: Although it is a chemical, sulfur is considered a relatively less toxic alternative. Still, try nonchemical means of prevention first or along with its use.

APPENDIX IV

MAIL ORDER SEED COMPANIES

■ CATALOG CODES

The source codes given elsewhere in this book stand for various mail order seed and plant sources that I've found useful over the years, including some that are new, or that I've discovered since the first edition. Here is a list, for easy referral:

Abundant Life Seeds (ABL)
Burpee Gardens (BG)
The Cook's Garden (CG)
Deep Diversity (DD)
The Gourmet Gardener (GG)
Evergreen Enterprises (EV)
Le Jardin du Gourmet (JG)
Johnny's Selected Seeds (JSS)
Kitazawa Seed Co. (KSC)
Native Seeds/SEARCH (NSS)
Nichols Garden Nursery (NGN)
Organic Gardening with Bountiful Gardens (OBG)
Park Seed Co. (PS)
Pinetree Garden Seeds (PTS)
Redwood City Seed Company (RCS)
Richters Herb Catalog (RH)
Ronningers Seed Potatoes (RSP)
Seeds Blüm (SB)
Seeds of Change (SOC)
Shepherd's Garden Seeds (SGS)
Territorial Seed Company (TERR)
Thompson & Morgan (T&M)
Tomato Growers Supply Company (TOMG)

Totally Tomatoes (TT)
Vermont Bean Seed Company (VBS)

Treated seed: If the company says it offers some or all untreated seed (seed without fungicide coating), this will be noted in the description.

Phone Numbers: The phone numbers listed in the entries are for general information and ordering of catalogs. Some may also be customer order numbers, but, in general, you will get the order phone and FAX numbers out of the catalogs. Ordering is often possible through the internet on websites—see the websites themselves to learn more. (And remember, never give your credit card number on the internet unless you know that the system you are using will protect it from theft.)

SEED COMPANIES

Abundant Life Seeds (ABL)

P.O. Box 772
Port Townsend, WA 98368
(360)385-5660
http://csf.Colorado.edu/perma/abundant

This nonprofit foundation offers heirloom seeds, many grown by their seed growers network. Their offerings include unusual crops, small grains, herbs, flowers, and an interesting list of books. All vegetable seeds are untreated and open pollinated. ($1)

Burpee Gardens (BG)

W. Atlee Burpee Co.
300 Park Avenue
Warminster, PA 18991-0001
(800)487-5530
http://garden.burpee.com

One of the oldest seed companies, with a good selection of standard vegetable varieties, flowers, and common herbs. They use a bull's eye symbol to indicate crops suited for your local area, but the system is not infallible for our region. (Perhaps they have grouped us with an area that includes warmer inland locations.)

The Cook's Garden (CG)

Box 535
Londonderry, VT 05148
(802)824-3400
http://www.cooksgarden.com

Specializes in salad greens, lettuce varieties by season, and unusual salad crops, but they have expanded their list to include other vegetables, herbs, and flowers. They also carry some garden and kitchen supplies.

Deep Diversity Seed Catalog

P.O. Box 15700
Santa Fe, NM 87506-5700

A very special list of unusual and endangered varieties, including food crops, herbs, and dye plants. This catalog also presents a theoretical model for showing kinship among plant families and genera. $5.00.

Evergreen Y.H. Enterprises (EV)

Oriental Vegetable Seeds
P.O. Box 17538
Anaheim, CA 93817

A good selection of Asian vegetables and culinary herbs, with a few books on gardening and many cookbooks for various Asian cuisines.

The Gourmet Gardener (GG)

8650 College Blvd.
Overland Parks, KS 66210-1806
(913)345-0490
http://www.gourmetgardener.com

A small catalog specializing in French vegetable varieties and herbs. They also carry edible flower seeds and some herb plants.

Le Jardin du Gourmet (JG)

Box 75
St. Johnsbury Center, VT 05863-0075
http://www.kingcon.com/agljdg

Vegetable seeds, including French varieties, herb, and flower seeds, many available in special 25¢ minipackets. Also shallots, garlic, top onions, herb and ornamental plants, books, and various French gourmet foods. Send $1.00 for a catalog.

Johnny's Selected Seeds (JSS)

Foss Hill Road
Albion, ME 04910
http://www.johnnyseeds.com

Interesting selection of vegetable varieties including extra-early varieties, because Maine growers have to contend with a short growing season. Catalog contains good cultural information, also tools, ecologically safe pest con-

trols, and floating row covers. Most seed is untreated.

Kitazawa Seed Co. (KSC)

1111 Chapman Ave.
San Jose, CA 95126
(408)243-1330

Small flier offering ample packets of seed for crops used in Japanese cuisine. Includes a good selection of winter radishes, Chinese cabbage, and mustards.

Native Seeds/SEARCH

2509 N. Campbell Avenue # 325
Tucson, AZ 85719
(520)327-9123 (not for orders)
http://desert.net/seeds/home.htm

A nonprofit organization that seeks to conserve the traditional crops, seeds, and farming methods of the native peoples of the U.S. Southwest and northern Mexico. Their catalog offers seeds, books and native crafts. Inland gardeners will be able to grow most of these heirloom crops; coastal gardeners will find some treasures if they look carefully.

Nichols Garden Nursery (NGN)

1190 North Pacific Hwy
Albany, OR 97321-4580
(541) 928-9280
http://www.pacificharbor.com/nichols/

This was the first place I found some of the vegetable varieties that are still among my favorites. Many of their vegetable varieties are selected for adaptation to the Northwest climate. They also carry garlic and top onions, herb seeds and plants, small tools, ecologically safe pest control products, and books.

Organic Gardening with Bountiful Gardens (OBG)

Ecology Action
5798 Ridgewood Road
Willits, CA 95490

Vegetable seeds, as well as a good selection of herb and cover crop seed. (The catalog includes a two page chart on when and why to plant various cover crops.) This is John Jeavons' seed company,

and carries all of his own publications as well as many other good books. All seeds are untreated, open-pollinated.

George W. Park Seed Co. (PS)

1 Parkton Avenue
Greenwood, SC 29647-0001
(800)845-3369
http://www.parkseed.com

Like Burpee, one of the oldest seed companies, with a wide variety of fairly standard crops and cultivars, herbs, and flowers.

Pinetree Garden Seeds (PTS)

Box 300
New Gloucester, ME 04260
(207) 926-3400

A large, well-selected list of vegetable, herb, and flower seeds at low prices. They also carry bulbs, tools, and books. This catalog includes many choice varieties. They say that less than 2% of their seed varieties are treated, and if you get some that are, and don't want them, they won't charge you for them.

Redwood City Seed Company (RCS)

P.O. Box 361
Redwood City, CA 94064
http://www.batnet.com/rwc-seed

An unusual collection of food crops, herbs, and other economically important plants, including some wildlings and native plants. Most are untreated and open pollinated. ($1)

Richters Herb Catalogue (RH)

Goodwood, Ontario
Canada L0C 1AO
(905)640-6677
http://www.richters.com

A wide selection of herb seeds and plants, a short list of unusual vegetables, and a number of books on herb growing and herb use.

Ronningers Seed Potatoes (RSP)

P.O. Box 1838
Orting, WA 98360

A large selection of organically grown potato sets, standard and unusual varieties, including those with colored flesh and fingerling potatoes. They also now carry the complete line of garlic, shallots, and onions once sold by Kalmia Farm, as well as other perennial starts, cover crop seed, and books.

Seed Savers Exchange
3076 North Winn Road
Decorah, IA 52101

A membership organization dedicated to preserving heirloom varieties of vegetables and fruits. They publish a small catalog for nonmembers, listing a sampling of varieties, many of which are newly collected in the former Soviet Union and Eastern Europe. The catalog also includes information on membership.

Seeds Blüm (SB)
Heirloom Seeds and other Garden Gems
Idaho City Stage
Boise, ID 83706

Heirloom vegetable varieties and many of the less common vegetable crops. Also blue, yellow, and fingerling potatoes and several improved cultivars of Jerusalem artichokes. Vegetable listings give plant family and species names. Includes edible flowers and an extensive book list. ($2)

Seeds of Change (SOC)
P.O. Box 15700
Santa Fe, NM 87506-5700
(888)762-7333 (Toll Free)
http://www.seedsofchange.com

A relatively new seed company which sells only organically grown, open-pollinated, untreated seed. They also have a breeding program in which they develop new varieties for flavor and improved nutritional value. The catalog includes many useful vegetable varieties, herb and flower seeds, tools, books, and posters.

Shepherd's Garden Seeds (SGS)
30 Irene Street
Torrington, CT 06790
(860)482-3638
http://www.shepherdseeds.com

A selected list of vegetable varieties, many of which are imported from seedhouses in Europe or Asia. They also carry seeds of culinary herbs, edible flowers, cutting flowers, and flowers that attract butterflies.

Territorial Seed Company (TERR)
P.O. Box 157
80030 Territorial Road
Cottage Grove, OR 97424
(503) 942-9547
http://www.territorial-seed.com

"Seed that *grows* west of the Cascades" is their motto. They test vegetable varieties near the Oregon Coast. Though this region has colder winters and more rain than ours, it is similar enough that their varieties are often useful here. The catalog gives good growing advice for each vegetable crop, and also offers seeds for herbs, cover crops, and flowers, as well as pest control products, tools, and some books. They publish a second catalog for only the vegetables that succeed in a winter garden. About 2% of their seed is treated. If you don't want treated seed, notify them and they will substitute or refund your money.

Thompson & Morgan (T&M)
P.O. Box 1308
Jackson, NJ 08527-0308
(800) 274-7333

The American branch of a British company, T&M sells many vegetable crops and crop varieties useful in our region, like scarlet runner and fava beans, long season cole crops, and cool-tolerant peppers. They sell a spectacular list of flower seed too, but watch out for the ones that say things like "germination in 6 months to a year" until you master growing the easier ones.

Tomato Growers Supply Company (TOMG)
P.O. Box 2237
Fort Myers, FL 33902
(914) 768-1119

Tomatoes of all kinds, mainly, but they are now carrying tomatillos,

ground cherries, and many kinds of peppers as well. Some seed is treated. They will try to honor requests for untreated seed, but may not be able to do so for some varieties.

Totally Tomatoes (TT)
P.O. Box 1626
Augusta, GA 30903
(803)663-0016

A catalog that offers an extensive list of heirloom and hybrid tomato and pepper varieties. They say seeds are "with virtually no exceptions . . . all untreated."

Vermont Bean Seed Company (VBS)
Garden Lane
Fair Haven, VT 05743

A full range of vegetable seeds plus a very wide selection of beans and peas. Because they are located in Vermont, many of their cultivars are intended for short seasons. Almost all seed is untreated. If you don't want treated seed, let them know when you order.

APPENDIX V

RESOURCES FOR GARDENERS

USE THIS APPENDIX TO FIND:
- Sources of gardening supplies and books
- Sources of fruit trees, vines and shrubs
- Nonprofit education and advocacy groups
- Working and model farms with educational programs
- Gardening for schools
- Botanical gardens with edibles
- Herbariums
- Horticultural libraries
- Websites for gardeners
- Nearby colleges with departments of horticulture or agriculture
- Information on pesticides
- IPM information
- Community gardens
- Before you dig

SOURCES OF GARDENING SUPPLIES AND BOOKS

Acres USA
P.O. Box 8800
Metairie, LA 70011
(800)355-5313
http://www.acresusa.com
A mail order book catalog from the company that publishes the magazine *Acres USA*. While the magazine is about commercial scale organic farming, the books in the catalog include ones on both commercial agriculture and home gardening.

American Soil Products
2222 Third Street
Berkeley, CA 94710
(510)883-7200

565A Jacoby Street
San Rafael, CA 94901
(415)456-1381

200 Waterfront Road
Martinez, CA 94553
(510)228-8388

Carries a full line of blended soil mixes, organic amendments, and mulches. Wholesale and retail. Will make custom blends. Soil tests and personal consultation available.

Bell's Bookstore
536 Emerson Street
Palo Alto, CA 94301
(650)323-7822
A bookstore with a large and excellent selection of new and used books on horticulture and gardening.

Common Ground
Organic Supply Store
See Nonprofit Educational and Advocacy Groups, below.

Connecticut Street Plant Supplies
306 Connecticut Street
San Francisco, CA 94107
(415)821-4773
Organic garden supplies, including beneficial insects. Advice, especially on alternatives to pesticides.

Dirt Cheap Organics
3070 Kerner Blvd. Suite T
San Rafael, CA 94901
(415)454-8278
Organic fertilizers and soil amendments, composting earthworms, vegetable and cover crop seeds, biological pest controls and sprays, books, advice. Free catalog.

Gardener's Supply
128 Intervale Road
Burlington, VT 05401
(800)863-1700

http://www.gardeners.com
Mailorder gardening supply company that does a good job of selecting products for usefulness and quality. Among the products they carry are quality tools, child-sized tools, the Accelerated Propagation System (APS), floating row cover, wind netting, bird netting, a prefab wire compost bin, and a soaker hose irrigation system. *Best Solutions* catalog has core gardening products, and they put out several other catalogs as well.

General Feed and Seed

1900 B Commercial Way
Santa Cruz, CA 95065
(408)476-5344
Carries a wide selection of organic fertilizers, soil amendments, and organic pest control supplies. Also sells open-pollinated seed, including seed for green manure crops.

Harmony Farm Supply

Warehouse Store
3244 Gravenstein Highway North
Sebastopol, CA 95472
(707)823-9125
Mailing Address: P.O. Box 460
Graton, CA 95444
http://www.harmonyfarm.com
Sprinkler and drip irrigation systems, organic fertilizers, organic soil amendments, ecologically safe pest controls, gopher wire and root cages, beneficial insects, bareroot fruit trees, gardening books, vegetable and cover crop seeds. Soil tests, with recommendations for organic fertilization. Free educational workshops. Catalog costs $2.00, and is especially informative on the topics of drip irrigation and pest management.

The Natural Gardening Company

217 San Anselmo Avenue
San Anselmo, CA 94960
(415)456-5060
Organic amendments, fertilizers, pest controls, quality tools, seeds, seedlings, books, etc. Free classes and catalog.

One to Grow On, Inc.

P.O. Box 5372
Virginia Beach, VA 23471
(757)363-2240

A mail order source of ergonomic tools and tool adapters. These are ideal for those suffering problems of the hand, wrist, or arm, including repetitive motion injuries, carpel tunnel syndrome, tennis elbow, or arthritis. Ergonomic tools are also a very good idea to help you *prevent* injuries!

Peaceful Valley Farm Supply

110 Springhill Drive
Grass Valley, CA 95945
Mailing Address:
P.O. Box 2209
Grass Valley, CA 95945
(530)272-4769
http://www.groworganic.com
A mailorder source of organic fertilizers and soil amendments, ecologically safe pest controls, (including gopher-proof root cages), cover crop seeds, quality tools, floating row covers, watering equipment, and books. Free catalog.

Smith and Hawkin Stores

35 Corte Madera Avenue
Mill Valley, CA 94941
(415)381-1800

705 Stanford Center
Palo Alto, CA 94304
(650)321-0403

1330 10th Street
Berkeley, CA 94710
(510)527-1076

26 Santa Cruz Avenue
Los Gatos, CA 95030
(408)354-6500

2040 Fillmore Street
San Francisco, CA 94115
(415)776-3424

Smith and Hawkin carries quality gardening tools, books, seeds, less toxic pest control products, bulbs, ornamental plants, gardeners' clothing. Free catalog.

Strybing Arboretum Society Bookstore

Strybing Arboretum
Ninth Avenue and Lincoln Way
Golden Gate Park
San Francisco, CA 94122

(415)661-1316 Ext. 308
Located just inside the main gate of the Arboretum, this tiny bookstore is packed with books on plants and gardening. Although its collection on food gardening is relatively small, it is a wonderful overall resource for gardeners. Open 10-4 every day.

Urban Farmer Store

2833 Vicente Street
San Francisco, CA 94116
(415)661-2204

653 East Blithedale
Mill Valley, CA 94941
(415)380-3840

Urban Farmer Stores carry drip irrigation and sprinkler system supplies and installation, quality tools. Free catalog.

SOURCES OF FRUITBEARING TREES, VINES, AND SHRUBS

Four Winds

True Dwarf Citrus Growers
42186 Palm Avenue
Mission San Jose District
Fremont, CA 94539
(510)656-2591
http://www.mother.com/fourwinds
Look in local nurseries for citrus from Four Winds, or call them to find a local source of their trees. Free catalog for SASE.

Harmony Farm Supply

(See listing under Gardening Supply Stores.) Call or send for their winter catalog, showing their offerings of bareroot fruit trees and shrubs. While they will ship if absolutely necessary, they prefer that you pick plants up in person.

Raintree Nursery

Fruits, Nuts, Berries, and Bamboo for Northern California
391 Butts Road
Morton, WA 98356
(360)496-6400
This catalog carries many fruit varieties that should do well here

and includes much useful information on growing fruit, as well as a zonal map with recommendations for Northern California.

Sonoma Antique Apple Nursery

4395 Westside Road
Healdsburg, CA 95448
(707)433-6420
http://www.trine.com/gardennet/
Catalog Center
The catalog of this nursery offers apples, including many low chill varieties, as well as a number of other kinds of deciduous fruit trees. Free catalog.

Dave Wilson Nursery

19701 Lake Road
Hickman, CA 95323
http://www.sonnet.com/davewilson/
When this excellent nursery had a retail mailorder catalog, they published variety recommendations by climatic regions. Now they only sell wholesale, and no longer publish recommendations. However, it is still worthwhile to select their trees in local nurseries. You can contact them to see where they sell trees in your area. Ask at the retail source for useful, free pamphlets from Dave Wilson Nursery.

NONPROFIT EDUCATIONAL AND ADVOCACY GROUPS

Berkeley Ecology Center

2530 San Pablo Avenue
Berkeley, CA 94702
(510)548-2220
Promotes efforts toward a healthy environment. Garden-related information is available through their newsletter, library, bookstore, and classes. They sell organic fertilizers and compost and sponsor a seed exchange. The center serves as a clearinghouse for Bay Area gardening resources.

California Native Plant Society

1722 J Street Suite 17
Sacramento, CA 95814
(916)447-2677
http://www.calpoly.edu/

An organization whose principle aims are to preserve native flora and add to the knowledge of members and the public at large. Members receive the quarterly journal, *Fremontia* and a periodic *Bulletin*. They hold sales of native plants. Members join the state-wide organization and become affiliated with a local chapter.

California Rare Fruit Growers

The Fullerton Arboretum
P.O. Box 6850
Fullerton, CA 92834-6850
http://www.gardenweb.com/cyber-plt/society/crfg
This organization promotes growing of subtropical fruit, but also has information on unusual varieties of well-known fruits and vegetables. Members are often willing to give advice to non-members. You can join the state organization or a local chapter or both. The state organization publishes a yearbook, a quarterly journal called *The Fruit Grower*, and has a seed exchange. Local chapters may publish small newsletters, and they sponsor regular lectures and events, including scionwood exchanges and visits to nearby fruit plantings. Contact the state organization to learn the address of your local chapter.

Center for Urban Education about Sustainable Agriculture (CUESA)

1417 Josephine Street
Berkeley, CA 94703
(510)526-2788
This organization coordinates Open Garden Day, an annual spring self-guided tour of outstanding Bay Area community, school, and other and gardening projects, and publishes the *Bay Area Urban Gardening and Greening Resource Directory*. The Directory lists many resources of interest to gardeners, and to gardening, food, ecology and general science educators. Includes a list of farmers markets in the region. Directory is $3.00.

Committee for Sustainable Agriculture

406 Main Street Suite 313
Watsonville, CA 95076
(408)763-2111
http://www.csa-efc.org
This organization promotes ecological farming. The annual Hoes Down Harvest Fair held at Full Belly Farm in Yolo County provides family fun. You can also learn the latest information on sustainable agriculture techniques at the annual Ecological Farming Conference, held in January, and at regional workshops held throughout the year. Membership supports their activities and brings you information on upcoming events.

Common Ground Organic Supply Store

2225 El Camino
Palo Alto, CA 94306
(650)328-6752
This store and library is a project of Ecology Action of the Midpeninsula. This organization, directed by John Jeavons, promotes biointensive gardening. The store sells books, natural fertilizers, compost, bulk seeds, organically grown starts, tools, and ecologically safe pest control products, including gopher-proof root cages. It also offers gardening workshops.

Permaculture Institute of Northern California

P.O. Box 341
Point Reyes Station, CA 94956
(415)663-9090
http://pomo.nbn.com/people/pinc
Permaculture endeavors to provide as many needs as possible through design of environments, including food, shelter, energy, and recycling of wastes. This institute offers two week intensive courses, as well as shorter workshops. Call or write for a list of classes.

Saratoga Horticultural Research Foundation

15185 Murphy Avenue
San Martin, CA 95046
(408)779-3303
Since 1952 the SHRF has been

carrying out plant research for the California landscape. While most of their introductions have been ornamental, their 'Saratoga' bay tree is of interest to herb gardeners. Contact them for more information and their calendar of events.

San Francisco League of Urban Gardeners (SLUG)
2540 Newhall Street
San Francisco, CA 94124
(415)584-7584
http://www.slug-sf.org
An organization that supports and promotes community, home, and school gardening in San Francisco, and uses gardening and greening to employ and train at-risk youths and adults. Services for SLUG members include a quarterly newsletter the *SLUG Update*, discounts at garden suppliers, discounts on SLUG workshops, gardening information sheets, free seeds and supplies, and reasonably priced soil tests. A demonstration garden (The Garden for the Environment) at 7th Avenue and Lawton in San Francisco teaches environmentally sound gardening practices and is a site of free SLUG composting workshops. It is open every day during daylight hours. Call SLUG to find out about membership, workshops, and hours that the Garden for the Environment will be staffed.

Seed Savers Exchange
P.O. Box 70
Decorah, IA 52101
(319)382-5990
A grassroots preservation project of gardeners saving heirloom and endangered fruit and vegetable varieties from extinction. Nonmembers can order from a small catalog that contains many interesting vegetable and flower varieties as well as books. Members help maintain endangered varieties and have access to more of the varieties the organization preserves.

Strybing Arboretum Society
Ninth Avenue and Lincoln Way
Golden Gate Park
San Francisco, CA 94122
(415)661-1316 Ext. 301
This society is the private nonprofit organization created to support San Francisco's public botanical garden, the Strybing Arboretum. The society runs the Helen Crocker Russell Library (see Horticultural Libraries), a small bookstore (see Sources of Gardening Supplies and Books), classes, workshops, and tours for adults and youth, on gardening, including some on food gardening.

UNIVERSITY OF CALIFORNIA COOPERATIVE EXTENSION SERVICE

http://danrcs.ucdavis.edu
The University of California is a Federal Land Grant College. When the Federal Government gave land to the states for agricultural colleges, it stipulated that these colleges had to provide public education on agricultural matters. The agencies that provide this help are the county Cooperative Extension Offices.

The Coop Extension publishes many pamphlets and books, available at low cost by mailorder catalog. To get this free catalog, call any County Extension Office (except for the San Francisco and Contra Costa County offices, which do not sell publications).

In addition, the Coop Extension offices employ experts who do research, such as vegetable variety trials, and answer questions from the public. They are valuable sources of current and local information.

Some counties have a Master Gardening Program which offers training in gardening and then requires volunteer help from graduates. Another project, the 4-H program, offers classes for children on subjects ranging from raising livestock to plant propagation. Call to see if your local office offers a Master Gardening or 4-H program. (See also Elkus Youth Ranch, under Working and Model Farms.)

COOPERATIVE EXTENSION OFFICES

Alameda County
224 West Winton Avenue
Room 174
Hayward, CA 94544
(510)670-5200

Contra Costa County
75 Santa Barbara Road, 2nd Floor
Pleasant Hill, CA 94523
(510)646-6540

Marin County
1682 Novato Boulevard,
Suite 150-B
Novato, CA 94947
(415)899-8620

Mendocino County
579 Low Gap Road
Ukiah, CA
Mailing Address:
Agricultural Center
Courthouse
Ukiah, CA 95482
(707)463-4495

Monterey County
1432 Abbott Street
Salinas, CA 93901
(408)759-7350

San Francisco County
300 Piedmont Avenue,
Room 305A
San Bruno, CA 94066
(650)871-7559

San Mateo County
625 Miramontes Street, Suite 200
Half Moon Bay, CA 94019
(650)726-9059

Santa Clara County
1005 Timothy Drive
San Jose, CA 95133
(408)299-2635

Santa Cruz County
1432 Freedom Boulevard
Watsonville, CA 95076-2741
(408)763-8040

Sonoma County
2604 Ventura Ave. Room 100-P
Santa Rosa, CA 95403-2894
(707)527-2621

WORKING & MODEL FARMS OFFERING EDUCATIONAL PROGRAMS

Ardenwood Historic Farm
34600 Ardenwood Boulevard
Fremont, CA 94555
(510)796 0663
This demonstration Victorian farm is run jointly by the East Bay Regional Park District and the City of Fremont. It is open to the public and to school classes for day visits. Reduced public entrance fees on Tuesday and Wednesday, when the grounds only are open. Admission on Thursday through Sunday includes hayrides as well as demonstrations and workshops teaching old-fashioned farm skills.

Camp Joy
131 Camp Joy Road
Boulder Creek, CA 95006
(408)338-3651
Camp Joy is a small working French Intensive Biodynamic farm that offers tours and adult classes as well as an apprenticeship program.

Ecology Action
5798 Ridgewood Road
Willits, CA 95490
This is the research farm of Ecology Action, run by John Jeavons. They sponsor half-day tours and one day to three week workshops. Write for current dates and fees. See also Common Ground Store, in Nonprofit Groups and the Ecology Action seed catalog "Bountiful Gardens" in Appendix IV, Mail Order Seed Companies.

Elkus Youth Ranch
1500 Purisma Creek Road
Half Moon Bay, CA 94019
(650)712-3158
Mailing Address:
625 Miramontes Street Suite 200
Half Moon Bay, CA 94019
This working ranch can be visited by any of a wide variety of children's groups, from pre-schoolers up. Visits may range from a couple of hours to overnight stays.

The ranch is equipped for visits by persons with disabilities.

Center for Agroecology and Sustainable Food Systems (CASFS)
1156 High Street
Santa Cruz, CA 95064
There are three programs at this center: an apprenticeship program, public tours and workshops, and membership. Contact each through the above address and through the phone numbers and website listed below:

CASFS Apprenticeship Program
(408)459-2321
http://zzyx.csc.edu/casfs
This 6 month hands-on apprenticeship is offered through the University of California extension (not through U.C. Santa Cruz). Students gain experience on the 25 acre farm and 4 acre gardens. College credit is possible, but must be negotiated with the college you attend.

CASFS Workshops and Tours
(408)459-3248
CASFS offers workshops, events, and tours for the public. Call or write to obtain a current schedule. Ongoing events include tours for adults on Thursdays at noon and Sunday at 2 PM and tours for school children by arrangement. They also hold annual spring and fall plant sales and a fall Harvest Festival which includes activities for children.

CASFS Membership
(408)459-3376
Membership in CASFS helps to support its programs, and members receive a quarterly newsletter, *The Cultivar* that lists workshops, events, and resources, and includes articles useful to gardeners.

Green Gulch Farm Zen Center
1601 Shoreline Highway
Sausalito, CA 94965
(415)383-3134
This working farm associated with the Zen Center supplies restaurants and whole food stores. It

also serves as a Zen Buddhist retreat. Green Gulch Farm offers gardening workshops and apprenticeships, as well as workshops on topics relating to Zen.

Hidden Villa Summer Camp
26870 Moody Road
Los Altos Hills, CA 94022
(650)949-8650
Hidden Villa offers summer camp programs for children and teenagers, including both day camps and resident camps, that include involvement in a large garden and in the care of farm animals along with traditional camping activities. During the school year, they offer environmental education field experiences to school classes.

Prusch Park
San Jose Recreation and Parks
647 South King Road
San Jose, CA 95116
(408)926-5555
Prusch Park, run by the city of San Jose, is a demonstration farm including farm animals and an orchard of rare fruit trees. It is available for school tours and hosts gardening workshops. The site also includes some of the city-run community gardens.

Slide Ranch
2025 Shoreline Highway
Muir Beach, CA 94965
(415)381-6155
http://www.igc.org/slideranch
Children and teenagers can participate in programs at this working farm, exploring both the farm and the surrounding wild area. For children, there are one, two, or three day programs; for teens, "farmhand weekends" and summer camp. There are also spring, summer, and fall "family days." The garden, chicken coop, and farm animals are all wheelchair accessible.

GARDENING FOR SCHOOLS

Grow Lab

National Gardening Association
180 Flynn Avenue
Burlington, VT 05401
(800)538-7476
Grow Lab sponsors three major programs, which are described in their free catalog. First, they sell indoor light gardens with built in fluorescent lights, a timer, and a climate control tent, which can be used to teach about plants even when a school has no place for a garden. Second, they publish materials to help teach school gardening, including a teacher's guide to using an indoor garden, a separate curriculum guide for grades K through 8 with activities that can be used in any garden and a thrice-yearly teachers' newsletter called *Growing Ideas*. Third, their Youth Garden Grants program awards annual grants of gardening equipment and supplies. (See also, *National Gardening Magazine* in Suggested Reading, Appendix VI)

Let's Get Growing

1900 Commercial Way
Santa Cruz, CA 95065
(800)408-1868
http://www.letsgetgrowing.com
A mail order catalog of environmental science supplies, gardening materials, and related books for young people. They carry the books and curricula of both Life Lab and Grow Lab, indoor garden light systems, child-sized tools, root-viewing chambers, and small hand lenses for $.50 (or less in bulk).

Life Lab Science Program

1156 High Street
Santa Cruz, CA 95064
(408)459-2001
http://lifelab.ucsc.edu
This organization publishes curriculum guides for grades K through 6 that teach science and nutrition through gardening. Adaptable to a single planter or to an acre of flowers and vegetables. Life Lab will work directly in some schools. They also publish a more comprehensive book of curricula: The Growing Classroom (see Suggested Reading, Appendix VI).

San Francisco League of Urban Gardeners (see also the listing under Nonprofit Education and Advocacy Groups, above)

SLUG offers the Green Gardening Educator Training Program (GETTUP) which teaches participants non-toxic gardening methods, and the Community Compost Training program. Graduates of both work in the community, including with schools, to develop green gardening and composting projects. SLUG also provides technical support, in-class presentations, field trips, donated materials, and construction services to schools in San Francisco.

DEMONSTRATION GARDENS AND BOTANICAL GARDENS WITH EDIBLE PLANTINGS

Gamble Garden Center

1431 Waverly Street
Palo Alto, CA 94301
(415)329-1356
An historic home with gardens that include ornamental plantings, fruit trees (good examples of espaliers), vegetables, and herbs. The center also offers gardening workshops. The garden is open during daylight hours. The office and library are open 9 AM to noon on weekday mornings.

Garden for the Environment

7th Avenue and Lawton
San Francisco
This garden is a project of the San Francisco League of Urban Gardens (SLUG). It includes a drought-tolerant ornamental garden, a compost demonstration area, and demonstration edible plantings. See SLUG under Nonprofit Education and Advocacy Groups for more information.

Lakeside Park Demonstration Garden

Lakeside Park Garden Center
666 Bellevue Avenue
Oakland, CA 94610
This garden, located in a city park, shows East Bay gardeners the many possibilities for growing vegetable and fruit crops. It is gardened by a variety of local youth groups, and is open to the public daily from 10 to 3.

Mendocino Coast Botanical Gardens

18220 North Highway One
Fort Bragg, CA 95437
(707)964-4352
This coastal garden and nursery includes an herb garden, organic vegetable garden and an old orchard, as well as fine ornamental plantings.

U.C. Botanical Garden

200 Centennial Drive
Berkeley, CA 94720-5045
(510)642-3343 or (510)643-2755
http://www.mip.berkeley.edu/garden/
In addition to extensive and excellent ornamental planings, the garden includes a section called "Plants for Mankind," a collection of economically important species from around the world. There are samples of various fruit trees, vegetables, and herbs. Of course this part of the garden is most interesting in spring and summer, when trees bloom and annual vegetables grow.

HERBARIUMS

An herbarium is a library of pressed plant specimens. If you are trying to identify a plant, and having no luck elsewhere, the botanists who work at an herbarium should be ale to tell you what it is. Always call first.

Herbarium

Department of Botany
California Academy of Sciences
Golden Gate Park
San Francisco, CA 94118
(415)750-7187

Jepson Herbarium
University of California
1001 Valley Life Science Building
Berkeley, CA 94720-2465
(510)643-7008
Specializes in California native plants.

U.C. Santa Cruz Herbarium
Department of Biology
Sinsheimer Labs
University of California
Santa Cruz, CA 95064
(408)459-3674

North Coast Herbarium of California
Department of Biology
Sonoma State University
Rohnert Park, CA 94928
(707)664-2303

Davis Herbarium
Department of Plant Biology
University of California
Davis, CA 95616
(916)752-1091
One of their specialties is agricultural weeds.

Mendocino Coast Herbarium of College of the Redwoods
Teresa Sholars
Science Division
College of the Redwoods
1211 Del Mar Drive
Fort Bragg, CA 95437
(707)961-1011 Ext. 32

The Humboldt State University Vascular Plant Herbarium
Humboldt State University
Arcata, CA 95521
(707)826-4801
Regional herbarium, centering on plant communities of Northwest California and Southern Oregon.

HORTICULTURE LIBRARIES

Helen Crocker Russell Library
Strybing Arboretum Society
Ninth Avenue and Lincoln Way
Golden Gate Park
San Francisco, CA 94122
(415)661-1316 Ext. 303
A small, but wonderful horticulture library with helpful librarians

that is located within the Arboretum. In addition to a large collection of books and magazines on gardening and botany, it includes videotapes (viewable in the library), seed and nursery catalogs, and children's picture books. Open 10 to 4 every day except major holidays.

Bioscience and Natural Resources Library
Valley Life Sciences Building
Room 2101
University of California
Berkeley, CA 94720
(510)642-2531
This is a branch of the campus library. The public can use the books in the library, but can only check them out after paying an annual fee. This library has all of the research journals on horticulture and agriculture, in case you want to look up an article reviewed in, for example, the magazine *HortIdeas*.

GARDENING WEBSITES

See also websites listed under specific organizations, businesses, or magazines elsewhere in this appendix, and in Appendix IV, Mail Order Seed Companies, and Appendix VI, Suggested Reading.

The Bay Area Gardener
http://gardens.com
An online gardening magazine for Bay Area gardeners. It includes articles, columns, and a calendar of local gardening classes and events that is updated weekly. You will also find connections other websites of interest to local gardeners.

Garden Escape
http://garden.com
A national online gardening magazine with articles, gardening advice, an interactive chat line, and access to plants, supplies, and gardening accessories for purchase.

The Virtual Garden
http://www.pathfinder.com/vg
A Time-Warner website. Includes gardening articles, regional tips, a searchable copy of Barbara Barton's *Gardening by Mail*, and a plant selection guide that lets you choose plants by various attributes, then see a list with photos. A searchable database of gardening websites helps you locate them faster than through a general search engine.

NEARBY JUNIOR COLLEGES WITH DEPARTMENTS OF HORTICULTURE OR AGRICULTURE

In most cases, classes at these colleges are open to the public without prior enrollment in a degree program. Fees are low, and classes are often offered in the evening or on weekends.

Cabrillo College
6500 Soquel Drive
Aptos, CA 95003
(408)479-6241

City College of San Francisco
50 Phelan Avenue
San Francisco, CA 94112
(415)239-3236

College of Marin
835 College Avenue
Kentfield, CA 94904-2590
(415)485-9397

College of San Mateo
1700 West Hillside Boulevard
San Mateo, CA 94402
(650)574-6217

Foothill College
12345 El Monte Road
Los Altos Hills, CA 94022
(650)949-7427

Mendocino College
P.O. Box 3000
Ukiah, CA 95482
(707)468-3182

Merritt College
12500 Campus Drive
Oakland, CA 94619
(510)436-2418

Santa Rosa Junior College
1501 Mendocino Avenue
Santa Rosa, CA 95401
(707)527-4408

Solano Community College
4000 Suisun Valley Road
Suisun City, CA 94585-3197
(707)864-7155

FOUR YEAR COLLEGES AND UNIVERSITIES WITH PROGRAMS IN HORTICULTURE OR AGRICULTURE

California Polytechnic State University
San Luis Obispo, CA 93407
(805)756-1111
Offers undergraduate degrees in Environmental Horticulture, Crop Science, Plant Protection Science, Fruit Science, and Landscape Architecture.

Department of Environmental Studies
University of Santa Cruz
Santa Cruz, CA 95064
(408)459-3718
This department offers BA and PhD degrees in environmental studies, with an emphasis on agroecology and sustainable agriculture. (See also the Center for Agroecology and Sustainable Food Systems, listed under Working & Model Farms Offering Educational Programs.)

University of California at Davis
Davis, CA 95616
(916)752-1011 (main number)
(916)752-7645 (Student Experimental Farm)
Offers undergraduate degrees in Environmental Horticulture as well as many areas of Agriculture, including Agricultural Systems and Environment (sustainable

agriculture). Also offers graduate degrees in horticulture and agriculture. There is a summer course, "Introduction to Sustainable Agricultural Systems" (6 units), offered at the Student Experimental Farm.

PESTICIDE INFORMATION RESOURCES

California Poison Control System
(800)876-4766
Call for help in case of a pesticide poisoning.

National Pesticide Telecommunications Network Pesticide Hotline
(800)858-7378
Call for help reading a label, for information about particular pesticides, or for emergency information in case of poisoning or spills.

HOUSEHOLD HAZARDOUS WASTE COLLECTION FACILITIES

IN SAN FRANCISCO:

Hazardous Waste Hotline of the Household Hazardous Waste Collection Facility
(415)554-4333
This free service is for San Francisco County residents only. The hazardous waste facility is open Thursday through Saturday, and accepts most kinds of toxic household waste, including leftover pesticides.

IN OTHER COUNTIES:

There is a statewide mandate to develop hazardous waste facilities. To see what exists in your county, call your county Health Department.

*Pesticide Action Network of North America (PANNA)
116 New Montgomery #810
San Francisco, CA 94105
(415)541-9140
http://www.panna.org/panna/
PANNA is part of a worldwide network of organizations working to stop misuse of pesticides and to support reliance on safe, ecologically sound, alternatives. They publish a monthly newsletter *The Global Pesticide Campaigner*, which keeps you up to date on global pesticide issues and campaigns. Call for more information. You can also subscribe to a weekly Internet update called PANUPS. For more information on this, see their web page.

INTEGRATED PEST MANAGEMENT INFORMATION

Bio-Integral Resource Center (BIRC)
Box 7414
Berkeley, CA 94707
(510)524-2567
http://www.igc.apc.org/birc/
A membership organization promoting Integrated Pest Management and offering services to members.
The journals they publish are the *Commonsense Pest Control Quarterly*, a journal offering how-to approaches for solving pest problems in the garden and home, and the *IPM Practitioner*, aimed at professional pest control operators. Members receive the following:
1. Subscriptions to one or both of their journals (you pay extra to get both.)
2. Help locating or developing safe pest control products or services in their communities.
3. Practical advice on least-toxic methods for solving pest problems.
A free catalog of materials published by BIRC, including reprints of articles from the newsletters, is available. (See also Suggested Reading, Appendix VI, for their book *Gardener's Guide to Common-Sense Pest Control*.)

COMMUNITY GARDENING INFORMATION

San Francisco League of Urban Gardeners

(see listing under Nonprofit Educational and Advocacy Groups)

East Bay Urban Gardeners

1801 Adeline Street Suite 208
Oakland, CA 94607
(510)834-5342
http://www.geocities.com/RainForest/7586
A resource for community gardeners in the East Bay, primarily Oakland and Berkeley, EBUG offers technical assistance, classes, and workshops. Members receive their newsletter, the *EBUG Buzz*, discounts on workshops and at local nurseries, and discounted soil tests.

The Praxis Group

c/o Mark Westwind
2131 Tacoma Avenue
Martinez, CA 94553
(510)372-8486
http://www.ccnet.com/~westwind
This organization can put you in touch with a community garden organization in any area of California and can provide practical information about starting a community garden.

American Community Gardening Association

325 Walnut Street
Philadelphia, PA 19106
(215)922-2104
This is a national organization of professional community garden organizers, neighborhood leaders, and others who share an interest in community gardening. They publish a journal, *Review*, sponsor an annual conference, and offer a Community Garden Slide Show that would be useful in organizing a community. They can also help you locate nearby programs or give you advice on starting a garden.

BEFORE YOU DIG

USA (Underground Service Alert)

(800)227-2600
Our basic services are often supplied by underground pipes or cables, and it is entirely possible to damage these when you are digging a garden. Be prudent, and avoid this hazard, by calling the USA number two working days before you plan to dig in any unfamiliar area. Ask for the free "mark and locate service" for underground pipelines and cables.

APPENDIX VI
SUGGESTED READING

■ These are some books you may enjoy. Remember that gardening books not written for our particular region will not contain perfect descriptions of how to garden here. For example, the times for doing various tasks may be wrong for our region, or the pests described may not be the selection of pests you see in your garden. Use *Golden Gate Gardening* to anchor gardening instructions to our local growing conditions.

♠ indicates a book that is out of print, but still worth looking for in libraries and used book stores.

FOOD GARDENING IN GENERAL

Cabbage or Cauliflower? ♠
J. Eldridge
Godine Publishing Co., Inc.
Boston, MA, 1984
Clear drawings showing how to distinguish among the many small seedlings that appear in our gardens.

Gardening by Mail (5th Edition)
Barbara J. Barton
Houghton Mifflin
New York, NY, 1997
A fabulous reference book telling where to find everything for the garden and gardener—plants, equipment, plant societies, garden tours, etc.

Gardening: The Complete Guide to Growing America's Favorite Fruits and Vegetables
National Gardening Association Staff
Addison-Wesley Longman Inc.
Reading, MA, 1986
A good introductory book that includes instructions for growing fruits.

Growing Fruits and Vegetables Organically: The Backyard Gardener Guide to Growing a Great-Tasting, Problem-Free Harvest
Edited by Jean M. Nick and Fern Marshall Bradley
Rodale Press, Inc.
Emmaus, PA, 1994
Much useful information on growing vegetables and fruits. (I wrote the first chapter.)

Growing Vegetables the Big Yield/Small Space Way ♠
Duane Newcomb
J. P. Tarcher Inc.
Los Angeles, CA, 1981
An expansion of the *Postage Stamp Gardening Book* to include more tips for fitting lots of plants into small gardens.

How to Grow More Vegetables Than You Ever Thought Possible..., 5th Edition
John Jeavons
Ten Speed Press
Berkeley, CA, 1995
An explanation of the methods of bio-dynamic French intensive gardening.

How to Have a Green Thumb Without an Aching Back ♠
Ruth Stout
Simon and Schuster
New York, NY, 1955
Gardening under a permanent mulch allowed Ruth Stout to keep her garden after disabilities of age confined her to a wheelchair. Her book is wise, witty, and informative.

The Postage Stamp Garden Book ♠
Duane Newcomb
J. P. Tarcher Inc.
Los Angeles, CA, 1975
A good introductory small space vegetable gardening book.

The Salad Garden
Joy Larkcom
Penguin USA
New York, NY, 1996
How to grow salad ingredients, including herbs, flowers and wild plants. Includes inspiring photographs of each crop and recipes.

REGIONAL GARDENING BOOKS

Backyard Farmer ♠
Lee Foster
Chronicle Publishing Co.
Chronicle Books
San Francisco, CA, 1982
A small, personal book about using a city lot in Oakland to grow food crops.

The City People's Book of Raising Food ♠
Helga and William Olkowski
Rodale Press, Book Division
Emmaus, PA, 1975
Not ostensibly a local book, but this thoughtful introductory gardening book was written from East Bay experience.

Grow Your Own ♠
Jeanie Darlington
The Bookworks
Berkeley, CA, 1970
A small, charming, personal book on vegetable gardening in Albany, California, just north of Berkeley. An historical treasure.

Growing Organic Vegetables West of the Cascades
Steve Soloman
Sasquatch Books
Seattle, WA, 1989
The coastal region of Oregon has colder winters than we do, and seems to be about a month behind us in the spring, and the pests are somewhat different, but conditions are similar enough that this book makes very interesting reading.

Northern California Gardening: A Month-by-Month Guide
Katherine Grace Endicott
Chronicle Books
San Francisco, CA 1996
Key garden tasks, month by month, with separate listings for coastal gardeners. Helps you to integrate your edible and ornamental gardening calendars.

Strawberries in November: A Guide to Year-Round Gardening in the East Bay ♠
Judy Goldsmith
Heyday Books
Berkeley, CA, 1987
An East Bay gardening calendar, telling what to plant, fertilize, prune, and harvest, as well as what will be blooming, in each month.

Sunset Western Garden Book
Sunset Publishing Co.
Menlo Park, CA, 1995
An important reference for all gardeners West of the Rocky Mountains. Lists hundreds of kinds of ornamental and food-bearing plants and describes their growing requirements. Sunset divides the West into 24 climatic regions, and rates each plant for these regions.

Where On Earth: A Guide to Specialty Nurseries and other Resources for California Gardeners, 3rd Edition
Barbara Stevens and Nancy Conner
Heyday Books
Berkeley, CA 1997
Most of the nurseries listed sell mainly ornamentals, but some sell fruit trees, herbs and other edible plants. A wonderful resource.

Winter Gardening in the Maritime Northwest, 3rd Edition
Binda Colebrook
Sasquatch Books
Seattle, WA, 1989
The winter weather of Seattle is enough wetter and colder than ours, that some of the advice in this book will not apply here. Still the book is very inspiring for those who want to garden through the colder months, and shows that many of our winter crops can take considerably more severe conditions than those of our area.

LESS COMMON FOOD CROPS

Amaranth—Modern Prospects for an Ancient Crop ♠
Rodale Research Institute
Emmaus, PA, 1987
The history of amaranth, methods of cultivation, and over 80 recipes.

Cornucopia: A Source Book of Edible Plants
Steven Facciola
Kampong Books
Vista, CA 1990
A unique reference containing descriptions and sources for hundreds of edible flowering plants, fungi, algae, and bacteria.

Lost Crops of the Incas: Little-Known Plants of the Andes with Promise for Worldwide Cultivation
National Research Council
National Academy Press
Washington, D.C., 1989
Includes the history, methods of cultivation, nutritional value, and potential for wider use of many crops, including yacon (Bolivian Sunroot), oca, quinoa, amaranth, goldenberry, and different types of potato and pepper.

Oriental Vegetables: The Complete Guide for Garden and Kitchen
Joy Larkcom
Kodansha International
New York, NY, 1991
Explicit cultivation instructions based on the author's experience and observations in Asia. Traditional recipes and ideas for using these crops in Western-style cooking. Includes Chinese and Japanese characters for each plant, as well as English alphabet transliterations of the names in Mandarin, Cantonese, and Japanese.

The Random House Book of Vegetables
Roger Phillips and Martyn Rix
Random House
New York, NY 1993

Over 650 vegetable varieties and species, common and uncommon, described and discussed. Wonderful photos from around the world, histories of crops, cultivation information.

Taylor's Guide to Heirloom Vegetables
Benjamin Watson
Houghton Mifflin Co.
New York, NY 1996
A guide to historic vegetable varieties available to modern gardeners, with a large section of color photos.

Unusual Vegetables, Something New for This Year's Garden ♠
Anne Moyer Halpin and the Editors of Organic Gardening and Farming
Rodale Press, Inc.
Emmaus, PA, 1978
A really useful compendium of cultural and culinary information for some of the less familiar crops.

HERBS

Growing Herbs for the Maritime Northwest Gardener
Mary Preus
Sasquatch Books
Seattle, WA 1994
Focuses on the special growing conditions west of the Cascade Range, from British Columbia to northern California

Herbal Renaissance: Growing, Using, and Understanding Herbs in the Modern World
Stephen Foster
Gibbs Smith Pub.
Layton, UT, 1993
Full information on how to grow and use herbs.

The Honest Herbal: A Sensible Guide to the Use of Herbs and Related Remedies
Varro E. Tyler, Ph.D.
Hawarth Press
Philadelphia, PA, 1982
A modern, myth-free look at herbal remedies. Explains how

active ingredients work and what they can and cannot be expected to do.

Rodale's Illustrated Encyclopedia of Herbs
Edited by Claire Kowalchik and William H. Hylton
Rodale Press
Emmaus, PA, 1987.
Encyclopedic coverage of growing and using herbs.

FLOWERS

Complete Garden Guide to Native California Perennials
Glenn Keator
Chronicle Books
San Francisco, CA 1990
Information to help you grow over 500 species of native perennial flowers. Includes advice for using them in your garden plan.

Cutting Gardens
Anne Halpin and Betty Mackey
Simon and Schuster
New York, NY 1993
Good information on how to lay out a cutting garden, choose plants to grow, plant, maintain the garden, and tips for creating arrangements.

The Flower Arranger's Garden
Rosemary Verey
Little, Brown and Co.
New York, NY 1989
Guidance in designing a garden that produces cutting flowers. Includes many inspiring photos of flower arrangements.

Growing California Native Plants
Marjorie Schmidt
University of California Press
Berkeley, CA 1981
Detailed techniques of propagation and culture for more than 350 annuals, perennials, bulbs, shrubs, and trees.

Landscaping With Perennials
Emily Brown
Timber Press
Portland, OR, 1986

A wealth of detail about growing perennial flowers in our region from a gardener who gardened for many years at Filoli, the great public garden on the Peninsula.

When Does It Bloom? A Guide to Planning Seasonal Garden Color
Matthew J. Leddy
275 D Street
Redwood City, CA, 1996
This book give sequence of bloom in Sunset Zone 15. While it refers precisely to the area from Redwood City to Mountain View, bloom sequence will be very similar to that of other nearby areas. Lists flowers by plant type, color, height, and whether they need sun or shade.

EDIBLE LANDSCAPING

The Complete Book of Edible Landscaping
Rosalind Creasy
Random House
New York, NY, 1982
This book will help you design a beautiful garden containing a high proportion of edible plants. Includes an encyclopedia of food-bearing plants with growing and harvesting information as it relates to their use in the landscape.

Designing and Maintaining Your Edible Landscape Naturally
Robert Kourick
Metamorphic Press
Santa Rosa, CA, 1986
A book packed with information on the nitty-gritty of planning and constructing an edible landscape. Includes extensive information on choosing and growing fruit trees and a chart of flowers to attract beneficial insects.

FRUIT GROWING
(SEE ALSO FOOD GARDENING IN GENERAL, REGIONAL GARDENING BOOKS, LESS COMMON FOOD CROPS, EDIBLE LANDSCAPING, AND PRUNING)

All About Citrus and Subtropical Fruits
Maggie Klein, Paul Moore, and Claude Sweet
Ortho Books
San Ramon, CA, 1985
Information on growing and using all kinds of citrus and other subtropical and tropical fruits.

Backyard Berry Book: A Hands-on Guide to Growing Berries, Brambles, and Vine Fruit in the Home Garden
Stella Otto
OttoGraphics
Maple City, MI 1995

The Backyard Orchardist, 2nd Edition
Stella Otto
Ottographics
Maple City, MI 1995
A primer on growing deciduous fruit trees. It includes selecting, pruning, ongoing care, problemsolving, and pest control.

SEEDS
(SEE ALSO ECOLOGY/ECOSYSTEM COMPLEXITY)

Garden Seed Inventory
Kent Whealy
Seed Saver Exchange
Decorah, IA 1995
An inventory of seed catalogs listing all nonhybrid vegetable seeds offered in the U.S. and Canada. New editions are issued every couple of years. See also Seed Savers Exchange in Appendix IV.

The New Seed Starters Handbook
Nancy Bubel
Rodale Press, Inc.
Emmaus, PA, 1989
Detailed instructions for starting crops from seed.

Saving Seeds: The Gardener's Guide to Growing and Storing Vegetable and Flower Seeds
Marc Rogers
Garden Way
Pownal, VT, 1991

Crop-by-crop descriptions of how to avoid cross-pollination, collect the seed of vegetables and ornamentals and clean it for storage.

Seed to Seed: Seed Saving Techniques for the Vegetable Gardener
Suzanne Ashworth
Seed Saver Publications
Decorah, IA 1993
From personal experience, the tried and true details for successful small scale seed production of 160 vegetable crops.

Vegetable Seed Production in the San Francisco Bay Area of California and other Warm Winter Areas of the United States
Craig Dremann
Redwood City Seed Company
P.O. Box 361
Redwood City, CA 94064
A small, inexpensive monograph that presents the basic information you need to save seed.

SOIL AND SOIL FERTILITY

The Gardener's Guide to Better Soil ♠
Gene Logsdon
Rodale Press, Inc.
Emmaus, PA, 1975
Soils and garden fertility from an organic gardener's point of view.

Gypsum and Other Chemical Amendments for Soil Improvement
University of California
Division of Agriculture and Natural Resources Publication 2149
Revised Edition, 1980
Some clay soils benefit from the addition of gypsum. Don't buy gypsum before you use the test in this pamphlet to find out if your soil will benefit from it.

Hunger Signs in Crops: A Symposium ♠
H. B. Sprague
Longmans Publishing Group
New York, NY, 1964

Recognizing nutrient deficiencies is not always easy, since symptoms overlap with each other and with disease symptoms. That's why soil tests are so helpful. However, books such as this are good guides if you have a problem and want to try to identify the cause.

Let It Rot! The Home Gardener's Guide to Composting, 3rd Edition.
Stu Campbell
Story Communications
Pownal, VT, 1975
Humorous but effective introduction to composting.

Start With the Soil: The Organic Gardener's Guide to Improving Soil for Higher Yields, More Beautiful Flowers, and a Healthy, Easy-Care Garden
Grace Gershuny
Rodale Press
Emmaus, PA 1993
Thorough guide to soil improvement for many different kinds of plants, those growing in containers.

Worms Eat My Garbage
Mary Appelhof
Flowerfield Press
Kalamazoo, MI 1997
How to set up and maintain a worm composting system.

PRUNING

American Horticultural Society: Pruning and Training
Christopher Brickell (ed.), David Joyce
Dorling-Kindersley
New York, NY 1996
Great before and after photos and illustrations will aid you in learning how to prune over 800 kinds of ornamental and fruiting plants.

Espalier Fruit Trees: Their History and Culture ♠
Alan Edmunds
Pomona Books
Rockton, Ontario, Canada 1986
Espalier, from basic to fanciful. History, how-to, and many amazing drawings and photos.

383

How to Prune Fruit Trees, 18th Ed.

R. Sanford Martin
Martin Bio-Products
147 North Ontario Street
Burbank, CA 91505, 1997
A small book that contains brief but clear directions for pruning deciduous and subtropical fruit trees, berries, and grapes. Includes useful drawings.

The Pruning Book

Lee Reich
Taunton Press
Newtown, CT 1997
Good advice, well-illustrated, on pruning many kinds of plants, including fruit trees, shrubs and vines.

VEGETATIVE PROPAGATION AND GRAFTING

Growing Herbs from Seed, Cutting and Root: An Adventure in Small Miracles

Thomas DeBaggio
Interweave Press
Loveland, CO 1994
A small but thorough guide to propagating common culinary herbs, with color photo how-to sequences.

Plant Propagation, Principles and Practices, 6th Edition

Hudson Hartman, Dale Kester, Fred Davies, Jr., and Robert Geneve
Simon and Schuster
Upper Saddle River, NY, 1997
The standard textbook on plant propagation. It describes the techniques and explains why and how they work.

Secrets of Plant Propagation: Starting Your Own Flowers, Vegetables, Fruits, Berries, Shrubs, Trees, and Houseplants

Lewis Hill
Storey Communications
Pownal, VT 1985
Overview of propagation including seeds, cuttings, and grafting.

Specific methods for many kinds of plants, including fruits and nuts.

WEED APPRECIATION

The Flavor of Home: A Guide to Wild Edible Plants of the San Francisco Bay Area

Margit Roos-Collins
Heyday Books
Berkeley, CA 1990
Help locating, identifying, and using weeds, escaped domestic plants, and native plants that grow in the Bay Area.

My Weeds: A Gardener's Botany

Sarah B. Stein
Houghton Mifflin Co.
New York, NY 1994
Reading this book will give you an understanding of weeds, and a painless introduction to many aspects of botany—from plant anatomy to evolution.

Plants, Man and Life

Edgar Anderson
Missouri Botanical Garden
Saint Louis, MO 1997
A delightful exploration of the relationship humans have maintained with weeds and crop plants, newly back in print!

Weeds, Guardians of the Soil

Joseph A. Cocannouer
Greenwich, Devin-Adair Publishers, Inc.
New York, NY, 1980
The other side of the weed story, the value of weeds to the soil and as food and animal fodder.

WEED IDENTIFICATION

Growers Weed Identification Handbook

University of California
Division of Agricultural and Natural Resources Publications
No. 4030
Berkeley, CA 1992
Too expensive for the average

gardener to own, this set of sheets has color photos of each weed with a description on the back. Find it in a library.

Weeds of California ♠

W.W. Robbins, Margaret K. Bellue and Walter S. Ball
California Department of Agriculture, Printing Division, 1940.
Clear illustrations and vivid descriptions help to identify weeds. Entries include origins of the plants and their distribution in California at the time the book was published.

Weeds of the West

Tom Whitson
Western Society of Weed Science
University of Wyoming
Laramie, WY 1991
Full-color photos (3 for each weed) and descriptive text will help you identify over 350 weeds. Also available as UC Publication 3350 (See University of California Cooperative Extension Service in Appendix V, Resources for Gardeners.

Also, refer to local libraries for regional "floras", or lists of plants found in your particular region, to help you identify uncommon weeds.

PESTS AND BENEFICIAL CREATURES

California Insects

Jerry A. Powell, Charles L. Hogue
University of California Press
Berkeley, CA 1989
Pictures and descriptions of most of the insects you are likely to encounter—including color photos of 128 of them. Includes good introductory material about insects.

Cucurbit Diseases

Bernhardt, Dodson, & Waterson
Petoseed Company
Saticoy, CA 1988
A practical guide, with plenty of color photographs.

The Gardener's Guide to Common-Sense Pest Control

William Olkowski, Shiela Daar, Helga Olkowski
Taunton Press
Newtown, CT 1996
A selection from the larger Common-Sense Pest Control of information of particular interest to gardeners. Thorough and precise integrated pest management techniques from some of the pioneers in the field.

Insects, A Golden Guide

Herbert S. Zim, Ph.d. and Clarence Cottam, Ph.d.
Western Publishing Co., NY 1987
A guide to common North American Insects, with illustrations. Introduction is helpful for those beginning to study insects.

The Ortho Problem Solver, Fourth Edition

Edited by Michael D. Smith
Ortho Information Services
San Ramon, CA, 1994
Over 1000 pages of pest control information. Each entry includes a photo of the symptom you are most likely to see, a description of the problem, an analysis, and some solutions. The book lists mainly chemical controls, so you will usually need another reference to plan a control strategy. Look for reference copies in libraries and nurseries.

Pests of the Garden and Small Farm: A Grower's Guide to Using Less Pesticide

Mary Louise Flint
University of California
Division of Agriculture and Natural Resources Publication 3332
Berkeley, CA 1990
Here are excellent descriptions of problems and plans for integrated pest management of the pests of California vegetable and fruit crops. Includes great color photos and a troubleshooting table for each crop.

Pests of the West: Prevention and Control for Today's Garden and Small Farm

Whitney Cranshaw
Fulcrum Publishing
Golden, CO 1992
Clear, thorough, easy to find information on insects, diseases, weeds, and pesticides. Appendix on attracting insectivorous birds to your garden.

Rodale's Pest and Disease Problem Solver: A Chemical-Free Guide to Keeping Your Garden Healthy

Linda Gilkeson, Pam Peirce, Miranda Smith
Rodale Press, Emmaus, PA, 1988.
Includes entries for common plants and for common animal pests and diseases, listing organic methods of pest control. A section on "the healthy garden" describes garden methods that prevent problems.

Snails: From Garden to Table

Frances Herb
Illuminations Press
St. Helena, CA 1990
The only cookbook devoted to the savory snail, this covers the basics of catching, cleaning, and preparing *Helix aspersa*, the common snail that plagues us so.

Tomato Diseases

Jon Waterson
Seminis Seed Company
Saticoy, CA 1985
Like *Cucurbit Diseases*, a guide with many color photos.

COMPANION PLANTING

Companion Planting: Rodale's Successful Organic Gardening

Susan McClure, Sally Roth
Rodale Press
Emmaus, PA 1994
Mentions traditional lore, adds comments on scientific proof when available, and includes new information on growing companion plants that attract beneficial insects.

Companion Plants: Carrots *Really Detest* Tomatoes

Craig Dremann
Redwood City Seed Co., 1992
P.O. Box 361
Redwood City, CA 94064
A pamphlet reporting the author's experiments with traditional and other plant companion combinations. In most cases, the traditional combinations did not prove beneficial. He did find some one-sided companion pairs—that is only one of the pair benefited.

Good Neighbors: Companion Planting for Gardeners

Anna Carr
Rodale Press, Inc.
Emmaus, PA, 1985
Reviews traditional companion pairs in the light of current research.

PESTICIDES

The New Pesticide User's Guide

Bert L. Bohmont
Reston Publishing Co. Inc., A Prentice-Hall Co.
Reston, VA, 1983
A textbook on pesticide use. Includes discussion of laws pertaining to their use, environmental hazards, and methods of safe use, storage and disposal.

The Safe and Effective Use of Pesticides

Patrick J. Marer
University of Califorina
Division of Agriculture and Natural Resources Publication 3324
Berkeley, CA 1988
The best practical reference, covering every phase of pesticide use, emphasizing safety at every step.

GARDEN RESEARCH/ GARDEN SCIENCE

Botany for All Ages: Discovering Nature Through Activities for Children and Adults
> Jorie Hunken
> Globe Pequot Press
> Old Saybrook, CT 1994
> Fascinating introduction to botany for both children and adults.

Breed Your Own Vegetable Varieties: Popbeans, Purple Peas, And Other Innovations from the Backyard Garden ♠
> Carol Deppe
> Little Brown & Co.
> Boston, MA 1993
> Amateurs, who are often working with relatively unimproved crops, may have relatively rapid success creating new, more desirable varieties. Here is all you need to know to start, including specific genetic information for 801 edible plant species.

The Garden Explained: Discovering the Unexpected Science of Plants, Soil, Sun and Seasons
> Mia Amato and the Exploratorium
> Henry Holt and Co.
> New York, NY 1997
> Covers many aspects of garden science briefly and suggests experiments and observations you can use to "see for yourself."

Improve Your Gardening with Backyard Research ♠
> Lois Levitan
> Rodale Press
> Emmaus, PA, 1980
> You can find out what really works in your garden and what does not if you use logical methods to test your theories. This book will help you set up sound experiments.

Living With Plants: A Guide to Practical Botany, 2nd Edition
> Donna N. Schumann
> Mad River Press
> Eureka, CA 1992
> Presents botany—including plant structure and function, soils, propagation, and climatic adaptation—as needed to understand horticulture. Includes chapters on indoor plants, pruning, and garden design.

GARDENING WITH CHILDREN

A Garden for Children ♠
> Felicity Bryan
> Michael Joseph Ltd
> London, England, 1986
> How to create an attractive garden that children will also enjoy. Lots of great ideas for sharing a garden with children, including safety tips. The water color illustrations are an inspiration in themselves.

The Growing Classroom: Garden-Based Science
> Roberta Jaffe, Gary Appel
> Addison-Wesley Publishing Co.
> New York, NY 1990
> A source book of year-round garden-based science activities for grades 2–6. Meant to be used by teachers who have some training from Life Lab (see Appendix V, Resources), but useful for any teacher.

Grow Lab: Activities for Growing Minds
> Eve Pranis, Joy Cohen
> National Gardening Association
> Burlington, VT 1990
> Contains 45 lesson plans for hands-on indoor plant-based K–8 science lessons. Also includes activities for using indoor gardens to teach math, language arts and environmental topics.

Grow Lab: A Complete Guide to Gardening in the Classroom
> Eve Pranis, Jack Hale
> National Gardening Association

Burlington, VT 1988
A teacher's guide for using indoor gardening set ups. Complete plans for a grow lab garden, planning and planting, pest control, and special garden projects.

Let's Grow: 72 Gardening Adventures with Children
> Linda Tilgner
> Storey Communications, Inc.
> Pownal, VT, 1988
> Activities that will introduce children to the principles and joys of gardening.

National Gardening Association Guide to Kid's Gardening
> Lynn Ocone with Eve Pranis
> National Gardening Association
> Burlington, VT 1990
> More than 70 fun activities for young people ages 6–16. Also useful planning and gardening tips for school or community-based projects.

Worms Eat Our Garbage: Classroom Activities for a Better Environment
> Mary Appelhoff, Mary Frances Fenton, Barbara Loss Harris
> Flowerfield Press
> Kalamazoo, MI 1993

GARDENING FOR PEOPLE WITH SPECIAL NEEDS

The Able Gardener: Overcoming Barriers of Age and Physical Limitations
> Kathleen Yeomans, R.N.
> Storey Communications, Inc.
> Pownal, VT 1992
> Garden design, tools, and many special tips for making gardening easier. Includes a considerable amount of general gardening information, ideas for theme gardens, and a resource list.

Accessible Gardening for People with Physical Disabilities: A Guide to Methods, Tools, and Plants

Janeen R. Adil
Woodbine House
Bethesda, MD 1994
How to adapt an existing garden for use by persons with physical disabilities, set up container gardens, choose tools and plants. Resource list.

The Enabling Garden: Creating Barrier-Free Gardens

Gene Rothert, HTR
Taylor Publishing Co.
Dallas, TX 1994
Designing and constructing a garden for persons with special physical needs, choosing and adapting tools, tips for choosing and maintaining plants. Helpful illustrations, plans, and resource list.

RECIPE BOOKS

Chez Panisse Vegetables

Alice Waters
Harper Collins
New York, NY 1996
From a cook with a passionate desire to share her appreciation of fresh vegetables. The recipes for each vegetable are arranged from the simplest to the more complicated. Look for the unexpected combinations, such as butternut squash pizza or asparagus with blood orange. Includes information on the basics of handling each crop in the kitchen.

Classic Indian Vegetarian and Grain Cookery

Julie Sahni
Wm. Morrow & Co.
New York, NY 1985
Relatively easy recipes for everything from curry to dahl, with explanations of less familiar ingredients and spices. Vegans can substitute soy products for the dairy in this cuisine.

The Complete Book of Mexican Cooking

Elizabeth Lambert Ortiz
Bantam Books
New York, NY, 1985.
Includes great recipes for using tomatillos, cactus pads, coriander, epazote, chayote and other garden produce.

The Complete Vegetarian Kitchen: Where Good Flavor and Good Health Meet

Lorna Sass
Hearst Marine Books
New York, NY 1995
One of the best vegan recipe writers around. Her dishes are creative and taste good.

Cooking From the Garden ♠

Rosalind Creasy
Sierra Club Books
San Francisco, CA, 1988
Essays on planning, planting, and cooking from various theme gardens, such as heirloom, or Asian vegetables. The recipes are varied and delicious, and the photos of both gardens and recipes are beautiful.

Edible Flowers from Garden to Palate

Cathy Wilkinson Barash
Fulcrum Publishing
Golden, CO 1993
Recipes that use flowers. Includes color photos of the food and of the flowers in the garden as well as tips for growing each kind of flower.

Flowers in the Kitchen

Susan Belsinger
Interweave Press
Loveland, CO 1993
Recipes, large, inspiring photos of finished dishes, an edible flower garden plan and a chart listing 50 kinds of edible flowers.

From the Earth

Eileen Yin-Fei Lo
MacMillan General Reference
New York, NY 1995
Chinese vegetarian cooking. The author includes traditional recipes learned in her grandmother's kitchen in China as well as fresh personal creations. Included are a glossary of ingredients and explanations of basic techniques and tools.

Keep it Simple: 30-Minute Meals from Scratch ♠

Marian Burros
Pocket Books
New York, NY, 1981
Easy, tasty meals, each guaranteed to take no more than a half hour to prepare. This book includes many dishes using produce you can grow.

The Kitchen Garden Cookbook

Sylvia Thompson
Bantom Books
New York, NY 1995
This is very much a gardener's cookbook, with discussions of harvesting, using different parts of the plant than one usually buys, using up overproductive or slightly over-the-hill crops. Simple and interesting recipes for all kinds of vegetables and herbs.

Potager: Fresh Garden Cooking in the French Style

Georgeanne Brennen
Chronicle Books
San Francisco, CA 1992
Recipes for fresh garden vegetables and photos of gardens in the French potager style.

Recipes from a Kitchen Garden and More Recipes from a Kitchen Garden

Renee Shepherd
Ten Speed Press
Berkeley, CA 1991
(or from Shepherd's Garden Publishing, 7389 West Zayante Road, Felton, CA 95018)
Two collections of garden-based recipes that were developed to appear in a seed catalog. The second book has more recipes using herbs and chilies.

The Victory Garden Cookbook
Marian Morash
Alfred A. Knopf
New York, NY 1982
Lots of recipes for all kinds of garden produce. Includes information on translating pounds into cup measurements, ways to store and preserve, and many simple ideas for using up crops that you have grown.

The Yogi Cookbook ♠
Yogi Vithaldas and Susan Roberts
Pyramid Communications, Inc.
New York, NY, 1968
A small, charming introduction to Indian vegetarian cooking including curries, rice pilao, Indian breads, raitas, and chutneys.

ECOLOGY/ ECOSYSTEM COMPLEXITY

Forgotten Pollinators
Stephen L. Buchman, Gary Paul Nabham, Edward O. Wilson
Island Press
Washington, D.C. 1996
Essays on the plight of pollinators in the modern world. Teaches us to appreciate the importance and the diversity of pollinating insects and other creatures.

Gray Water Use in the Landscape: How to Use Gray Water to Save Your Landscape During Droughts
Robert Kourick
Metamorphic Press
Santa Rosa, CA, 1988
(Or order from Edible Productions, P.O. Box 1841, Santa Rosa, CA 95402.)
How to plumb for the diversion of gray water, and a list of cleaning products that are least toxic to plants.

Integral Urban House
Helga Olkowski, Bill Olkowski, Tom Javits, and the Farallones Institute Staff
Sierra Club Books
San Francisco, CA, 1979

The Integral Urban House was a demonstration project in Berkeley that showed how to maximize food production and energy conservation in an urban residence. This book explains how to do it—from vegetable and small livestock production, to solar heating and composting toilets.

Noah's Garden
Sarah Stein
Houghton Mifflin Co.
New York, NY 1993
As delightful as her first book, *My Weeds*, this one describes her efforts to recreate her ornamental garden into one which the native wildlife could inhabit. It's an Eastern garden, but they are lessons we can apply to California gardens.

Shattering: Food, Politics, and the Loss of Genetic Diversity
Cary Fowler, Pat Mooney
University of Arizona Press
Tucson, AZ 1990
Reviews the development of genetically diverse food crop plants over 10,000 years and exposes the loss of diversity in the past 100 years. Lays out what will be needed to stop the losses, including worldwide individual seed saving.

Weather of the San Francisco Bay Region
Harold Gilliam
University of California Press
Berkeley, CA 1962
A unique illustrated handbook about our weather patterns.

GARDENING MAGAZINES

HortIdeas
750 Black Lick Road
Gravel Switch, KY, 40328
http://www.pagestore.com/ideas/ hi-index.htm
Monthly summaries of horticultural research and news. Reports new ideas, new products, new plants, and includes book reviews. Sample articles appear on their web site.

Kitchen Garden
The Taunton Press
63 South Main Street, Box 5506
Newtown, CT 06470
http://www.taunton.com
A relatively new gardening magazine that covers growing, preserving and preparing food from the garden. Six issues a year. Their website includes articles, recipes, and many links to other websites of interest to gardeners.

National Gardening
180 Flynn Ave.
Burlington, VT 05401.
http://www.garden.org
Includes membership in the National Gardening Association (which used to be called Gardens For All) (See also the listing in Resources). Six issues a year. Their website includes articles, and information on other National Gardening Association programs.

Organic Gardening Magazine
P.O. Box 7304
Red Oak, IA 51591-2304
http://www.rodalepress.com
The oldest of the magazines for food gardeners, and still a good one. High quality articles, news, recipes, and garden tips. Eight issues a year.

Sunset: The Magazine of Western Living
Subscriptions:
PO Box 56653
Boulder, Colorado 80323-6653
http://pathfinder.com/vg/Magazine-Rack/sunset/
Though the total pages devoted to gardening are few, the information is local (there are regional editions) and is very good. Monthly. Look also for their *Garden Annual*, which includes the year's garden articles from the magazine, and for the twice-yearly *Garden Guide*.

INDEX

Page numbers in **bold (156)** refer to Compendium listings.

Page numbers in *italic (342)* refer to Sidebars.

A

Accelerated Propagation System™ (APS) seed starter   54
Actinidia
  chinensis. See Kiwi Fruit
  deliciosa. See Kiwi Fruit
Agastache
  anisata. See Anise Hyssop
  foeniculum. See Anise Hyssop
Agropogon repens. See Quackgrass
Air pollution damage to crops   359–360
Algerian Ivy. *See* Ivy, Algerian
Allantoin, in comfrey   281
Allelopathy, from weeds   92
Allergies   *351*
Allethrin   367
Allium
  ampeloprasum. See Leek
  cepa. See Onion, Bulb; Onion, Pearl; Onion, Top; Shallot
  fistulosum. See Onion, Bunching
  sativum. See Garlic; Garlic, Top-Setting
  Schoenoprasum. See Chives
  triquetrum. See Onion Lily
  tuberosum. See Garlic chives
Almond (*Prunus dulcis* var. *dulcis*)   **327**
Aloysia triphylla. See Lemon Verbena

Amaracus dictamnus. See Dittany of Crete
Amaranth (*Amaranthus gangeticus*)   **163**
  as a garden grain   *164*
Amaranthus retroflexus. See Pigweed
Amendments and fertilizers   46
Amphibian (beneficial)   130
Anagallis arvensis. See Scarlet Pimpernel
Anethum graveolens. See Dill
Anise hyssop (*Agastache foeniculum*)   273, **274**
Annual Marjoram. *See* Marjoram (*Origanum majorana*)
Ant (beneficial aspect)   129
  control of   138
Anthemis nobilis. See Camomile, English
Anthriscus cerefolium. See Chervil
Aphid   26, 125, 132, **137**, 160
Apium
  graveolens. See Celery
  graveolens var. *dulce. See* Celeriac;
  graveolens var. *rapaceum. See* Celery, Chinese
Apple (*Malus* spp.)   159, 325, 326, **327**, *344*
  need for winter cold   *324*
Apple Mint. *See* Mint
Apricot (*Prunus armiaca*)   158, **328**
  brown rot   325
Armoracia rusticana. See Horseradish
Arranging crops   38

Artemisia
  dracunculus var. *sativa. See* Tarragon, French
  redowski. See Tarragon, French
Artichoke (*Cynara scolymus*)   4, 5, 26, 60, 121, 123, 152, **164**, *348*
Artichoke, Jerusalem. *See* Sunchoke
Artichoke Plume Moth   **138**
Arugula (*Eruca vesicaria* subsp. *sativa*)   123, **166**, 221, 270
  as volunteer   *93*
  rustic (*Euruca selvatica*)   166
Asparagus (*Asparagus officinalis*)   **166**
Asparagus bean. *See* Bean, Asparagus
Asparagus Pea (*Lotus tetrago-nolobus*)   **168**
Asperula odorata. See Sweet Woodruff
Atriplex hortensis. See Orach
Australian Brassbuttons. *See* Cotula
Avocado (*Persea americana*)   158, 324, 326, **328**
  pruning   325

B

Bacillus thuringiensis   132
Backyard Omelet (recipe)   *350*
Bacterial disease   159
Bacterial soft rot   **159**
Balsam Pear. *See* Bitter Melon
Basella alba. See Spinach, Malabar
Basil (*Ocimum basilicum*)   3, 123, 269, 271, 273, **274**, *348*
Basil, Holy (*Ocimum sanctum*)   **274**

Bay, California (*Umbellularia californica*) **276**
Bay Laurel (*Lauris nobilis*) **276**
  culinary bay leaf 273
  topiary 277
Bean 24, 41, 123, 157, 160, 348
  planting tips *176*
  trellis or teepee *173*
Bean aphid 121
Bean, Asparagus (*Vigna unguiculata* subsp. *sesquipe* **170**
Bean, Dry (*Phaseolus vulgaris*) **170**
Bean, Fava (*Vicia faba*) 4, 26, 121, **171**
  crop rotation 84
  green manure 76
Bean, French Flageolet (*Phaseolus vulgaris*) **172**
Bean, Garbanzo (*Cicer arietinum*) **170–171**
Bean, Horticultural (*Phaseolus vulgaris*) **172**
Bean, Lima (*Phaseolus lunatus*) **173**
Bean, Romano (*Phaseolus vulgaris*) 175
Bean, Scarlet Runner (*Phaseolus coccinus*) 23, **175**, 351
  crop rotation 84
Bean, Snap (*Phaseolus vulgaris*) 23, **176**
Bean, Soy (*Glycine max*) 171
Bee (beneficial) 129 *See* Honeybee
Beefsteak Plant. *See* Perilla
Beet (*Beta vulgaris*) 4, 5, 24, 26, 41, 142, 156, 160, **178**
  cercospora leaf spot 156
  leafhopper 160
Beet, Marinated (recipe) *179*
Belgian Endive. *See* Chicory
Belgian fence 325–326
Beneficial insects
  attractive baits 131
  common 128–130
  encouraging 131, 271
  purchasing or importing 132
Benincasa hispida. See Winter Melon
Bergamot Mint. *See* Mint
Bermuda Grass (*Cynodon dactylon*) **112**
Bermuda onion 225
Beta vulgaris. See Beet; Swiss Chard
Bindweed (*Convolvulus arvensis*) **113**
Binomial latin names 361
Bioallethrin 367

Bird netting 151
Birds
  beneficial 130
  pests **150**
Bitter Melon (*Momordica charantia*) **180**
Black Bean. *See* Bean, Dry
Black Bean Tostadas (Recipe) *110*
Black Mustard. *See* Mustard Seed
Blackberry brambles (*Rubus* spp.) **113–114**, 158, **329**
Blackbird 150
Blossom-end rot
  on tomato 259
Blueberry (*Vaccinium* spp.) **329**
Bluejay 150
Boiling onion. *See* Onion, Pearl
Bok Choy (*Brassica rapa*) **180**
Bolivian Sunroot (*Polymnia edulis*) 123, **181**, 351
Borage (*Borago officinalis*) **277**, 307
Borecole. *See* Kale
Bouquet
  creating 315
  garni. *See* Herbs
  with leafy vegetables *315*
  with seed stalks of weeds *315*
Braconid wasp (*Diaeretiella rapae*) 138
Brassica. See Mustard, Wild, Field or California
  chinensis. See Bok Choy
  juncea. See Mustard, Florida Broadleaf; Mustard Greens
  napus. See Kale, Siberian; Rutabaga
  nigra. See Mustard Seed, Black
  oleracea. See Kale; Kohlrabi
  rapa. See Bok Choy; Cabbage, Chinese; Tendergreen; Turnip
Brassicaceae. See Mustard family
Breba (spring fig crop) 330
Bristly Mallow. *See* Mallow, Bristly
Broad Bean. *See* Bean, Fava
Broccoli (*Brassica oleracea*) 4, 5, 17, 26, **182**
  crop rotation 84
  pairing up for greater production 57
Broccoli Raab 223
Brussels Sprout (*Brassica oleracea*) 4, 26, **185**
  when to plant *184*

Buckhorn Plantain. *See* Plantain, Narrow-Leaved
Buckwheat, for green manure 76
Bugs, true (beneficial) 130
Bush bean. *See* Bean, Snap
Buying seeds 39–40
Buying starts and transplants 41–42

C

Cabbage (*Brassica oleracea*) 5, 17, 26, 123, 142, 157, 158, **186**, 350
Cabbage, Chinese (*Brassica rapa*) **200**
Cabbage
  crop rotation 84
  family. *See* Mustard family
Cabbage, Flowering. *See* Kale
Cabbage leaves, stuffed (recipe) 188
Cabbage looper 132, **139**
Cabbage moth 124
Cabbage, Napa. *See* Cabbage, Chinese
Cabbage root maggot 125, **138**
Cabbageworm, imported **139**
Cactus 152
Cactus pads 5. *See also* Nopalitos in Tomato Sauce
Cactus, Prickly Pear (*Opuntia ficus-indica*) **188**
Calamondin (*Citrus reticulata* x *Fortunella mitis*) **330**, 333
Calendula 152, 157, 159
California Burclover (*Medicago hispida*) **104**
California cuisine 343
California Laurel. *See* Bay, California
California Pesto and Pasta (recipe) 275
California Poppy 157, 158
California Rape. *See* Mustard
California Rare Fruit Growers Society 326
Calla lily 92
Camomile, English (*Chamomaelum nobile*) **278**
Camomile, German (*Matricaria recutita*) **278**
Cantaloupe. *See* Melon
Capsella bursa-pastoris. See Shepherds-Purse
Capsicum annuum var. *annuum. See* Pepper, Sweet and Hot

Captan (fungicide) 40, 364
Carbamate 363
Carbaryl 363, 364
Cardoon (*Cynara cardunculus*) **190**
Carnation 159, 307
Carrot (*Daucus carota*) 3, 5, 16, 26, 123, **191**
  crop rotation 84
Cat pests 151
Cat Thyme (*Teucrium marum*) **279**
Catfacing, on tomato 259
Catmint (*Nepeta mussini*) **279**
Catnip (*Nepeta cataria*) 270
Cattley Guava. *See* Strawberry Guava
Cauliflower (*Brassica oleracea*) 23, **193**
Celeriac (*Apium graveolens* var. *rapaceum*) 154, **194**
Celery (*Apium graveolens* var. *dulce*) 5, 123, 146, **197**
  home treating of seed 155
Celery, Chinese (*Apium graveolens* var. *dulce*) 270, **280**
Celery, Cutting or Dinant. *See* Celery, Chinese
Celery late blight 154, **155**
Celery Root. *See* Celeriac
Celtuce (*Latuca sativa* var. *angustata*) **198**
Chamomaelum nobile. *See* Camomile, English
Chanclette (recipe) *201*
Chard, Swiss. *See* Swiss Chard
Chayote squash (*Sechium edule*) 198, 352
Cheeseweed. *See* Mallow (*Malva* spp.)
Chelates 80
Chenopodium
  album. *See* Lambsquarters
  ambrosioides. *See* Epazote
  bonus-henricus. *See* Good King Henry
  gigantium. *See* Magenta Spreen
  murale. *See* Lambsquarters
Cherry (*Prunus* spp.) **330**
  need for winter cold 324
Chervil (*Anthriscus cerefolium*) 221, 271, 273
Chicken, Spicy Szechuan. *See* Spicy Szechuan Chicken
Chicken Stock, Homemade (recipe) 349

Chickweed (*Stellaria media*) 92, 93, **104**
Chicory (*Cichorium intybus*) 208, 221
Chill factor, for fruit trees 324
Chinese
  celery. *See* Celery, Chinese
  leek. *See* Garlic chives
  lettuce. *See* Celtuce
  parsley. *See* Coriander
Chives (*Allium Schoenoprasum*) 152, 271, 272, **281**, 307
Chlorothalonil 364
Chrysanthemum 61, 158, 313, 314
Chrysanthemum, Garland (*Chrysanthemun coronarium*) **210**
  as volunteer 93
Chufa. *See* Nutsedge
Cichorium
  endiva. *See* Endive
  intybus. *See* Chicory
Cilantro 123, 269, 271, 273, 351. *See also* Coriander
Cineraria (*Senecio* × *hybridis*) 101
Citrullus lanatus. *See* Watermelon
Citrus 324, 326
  aurantifolia. *See* Lime
  limon. *See* Lemon
  pruning 325
  reticulata. *See* Calamondin; Mandarin Orange
  sinensis. *See* Orange
  x *paradisi*. *See* Grapefruit
Clay soil, description 71
Claytonia parviflora. *See* Miner's Lettuce
Click Beetle. *See* Wireworm
Climatic limitations 1
  See also Microclimates
Cloches 27
Clover, for green manure 76
Clubroot **155**
Cocannouer, Joseph 92
Cocktail onion. *See* Onion, Pearl
Cold frame 27, 55, 56, 58
Cole crops. *See* Mustard family
Coleslaw (recipe) *187*
Collards (*Brassica oleracea*) **202**
  as volunteer 93
Colorado potato beetle 121
Columbine 5, 157, 159, 313
Comfrey (*Symphytum* x *uplandicum*) 270, **281**

Common Plantain. *See* Plantain, Broadleaf
Common Vetch. *See* Vetch
Community gardens 29
Companion plants 271
Compendium
  of Fruits **327**–342
  of Herbs 274–305
  of Pests 136–160
  of Vegetables 165–268
  of Weeds 104–120
Compost 74
  carbon-nitrogen ratio 87
  cold and slow 88
  controversial ingredients 89
  correcting 87
  earthworm 90
  fast vs. slow 86
  hot and fast 88
  ingredients
    for all piles 89
    for hot piles 89
    what not to add 89
  kitchen scraps 74
  making 86–89
  sheet 88
Condiments 353
Conium maculatum. *See* Poison Hemlock
Conserving household water 69
Convergent lady beetle (*Hippodamia convergens*) 128
Convolvulus (Morning glory)
  cneorum 113
  mauritanicus 113
  tricolor 113
Cool summer crops 3
Copper Sulfate 365
Cordon 325–326
Coriander (*Coriandrum sativum*) 270, **282**
Corn Salad (*Valerianella locusta*) 221, **205**
Corn, Sweet (*Zea mays*) 3, 11, 23, 123, **140**, 153, 202, 344
  Early Sunglow 17
  earworm 204–205
  extra-sweet hybrids 203
  smut 205
Cornflower 3, 313
Coronopus didymus. *See* Swine Cress
Corsican Mint. *See* Mint
Cotula (*Cotula australis*) **104**
Crabgrass (*Digitaria sanguina*) **104**
Crambe maritima. *See* Kale, Sea

Cress, Garden *See* Garden Cress
Crookneck squash. *See* Squash, Summer
Crop rotation 84–86
  and soil amendments 86
  and soilborne disease 84–85
  crop categories 85
  for a small garden 85
  sample plans 84
  with legumes 84
Crops
  heavy feeding 85
  light feeding 85
  soil builders 85
Cross-pollination 41
Crowned sparrow 150
Cryptotaenia japonica. *See* Parsley, Japanese
Cucumber (*Cucumis sativus*) 4, 23, 123, 154, 160, **205**, 350
  crop rotation 84
  pollination 207
Cucumber beetle 121, **140**
Cucumber Raita (recipe) 206
Cucumber Salad, Southeast Asian (recipe) 206
Cucurbita spp. *See also* Gourd; Squash, Winter and Summer; Pumpkin; Bitter melon; Winter melon; Cucumber; Watermelon
Cultivar, defined 361
Curly Dock. *See* Dock
Curly dwarf virus of artichoke **160**
Cut flowers
  chart 316, 317
  making them last 322
Cutting Leaf Celery. *See* Celery, Chinese
Cutworm 132, **140**
Cydonia oblonga. See Quince
Cymbopogon citratus. See Lemongrass
Cynara cardunculus. See Cardoon
Cynodon dactylon. See Bermuda Grass
Cyperus esculentus. See Nutsedge
Cyst nematode 146

D

Daffodil 146
Dahlia 157, 158, 314
Damping-off 54, **156**
Dandelion (*Taraxacum officinale*) 92, **115**, 158, 221

DDT 122
Decay of plants 27–28
Deer pests **151**
Degree days, for fruit ripening 324
Delay of the maximum, (map) 14
Delay of the maximum (temperature) 358
Diaeretiella rapae. See Parasitic wasp (beneficial)
Diazinon™ 127, 363, 365
Digitaria sanguinalis. See Crabgrass
Dill (*Anethum graveolens*) 271, **283**
Diospyros kaki. See Persimmon, Asian
Disease resistant strains 154
Disease tolerant strains 154
Dittany of Crete (*Origanum dictamnus*) **294**
Doan Gwa. *See* Winter Melon
Dock (*Rumex crispus*) 92, 98, **115–116**
Dog pests **152**
Double digging 83
Downy mildew of onion **156**
Drax, ant control 138
Drip irrigation 65

E

Earth almond. *See* Nutsedge
Earthworms 363
  and carbaryl 79
  and fertilizer 79
  benefits of 79
  compost 90
  minimizing damage to colonies 79
Earwig **141**
  beneficial aspect 130
Edible flowers
  safety tips 308
Eggplant (*Solanum melongena*) 158, **208**, 348
Egyptian Onion. *See* Onion, Top
Elephant Garlic. *See* Garlic, Elephant
Elm 158
Endive (*Chicorium endiva*) 123, **208**, 221
English ivy. *See* Ivy, English
English Thyme. *See* Thyme, Common
Epazote (*Chenopodium ambrosioides*) 92, **284**
Equisetum
  arvense. See Horsetail
  hyemale. See Horsetail

Eriobotrya japonica. See Loquat
Escargot 147
Escarole. *See* Endive
Espalier 325–326
Evaporation, rate of 66
Experiments, learning from 9

F

F_1 hybrid, defined 43
Fat Hen. *See* Lambsquarters
Fatty Acids. *See* Potassium Salts
Fava bean. *See* Bean, Fava
Feijoa sellowiana. See Pineapple Guava
Fencing
  color and microclimate 33
  glass 31
Fennel (*Foeniculum vulgare*) 92, **116**
Fennel (*Foeniculum vulgare* var. *dulce*) 221, **285**
Fennel, Bronze (*Foeniculum vulgare* var. *rubrum*) **285**
Fennel, Florence (*Foeniculum vulgare* var. *azoricum* **285**
Fenvalerate 367
Fertilizer
  banding 82
  fish emulsion 82
  formulas, how to apply 82
  kelp, liquid 82
  NPK 81
  organic 81
  types 81–82
  using 80–82
Field Mustard. *See* Mustard,
Fig (*Ficus carica*) 324, 325, **330**
Finocchio. *See* Florence Fennel
Fireblight 159, 325
Fixed copper spray 157
Flea beetles **142**
Flicker **150**
Floating row cover 38, 49–50, 50
Flowering Cabbage. *See* Kale
Flowering Kale. *See* Kale
Flowers
  cut (chart) 316–321
  edible (chart) 310
  from vegetables 315
  poisonous 308
  sun requirements 29
Foeniculum
  vulgare. See Fennel
  vulgare var. *azoricum. See* Florence Fennel

vulgare var. *dulce*. *See* Fennel
vulgare var. *rubrum*. *See* Fennel,
    Bronze
Fog
    and plant size *16*
    drip 68
    gap (geographic) 358
    extent of, map 15
    variation (geographic) 358
    winter 359
Fog pump 357
Foo Gwa. *See* Bitter Melon
Food preservation 28
Forficula auricularia. *See* Earwig
    (beneficial aspect)
Forget-me-not 313
    self-seeding 93
Fortunella
    crassifolia. *See* Kumquat
    margarita. *See* Kumquat
Foxglove 152, 158
Fragaria
    vesca. *See* Strawberry, Alpine
    x *ananassa*. *See* Strawberry
Frame materials 37
Freesia 5, 152, 313
French marigolds (*Tagetes
    patula*) 147
French-intensive, bio-dynamic
    gardening 66
Fried Squash Blossoms. *See* Squash
    Blossoms, Fried
Frisé. *See* Endive
Frosts 4, 27, 323
Fruit Trees
    citrus *333*
    dwarf varieties 325
    high humidity 325
    purchasing 326
    what works 326–327
Fruiting crop production esti-
    mates 23
Fruiting vegetables, sun require-
    ments
    29
Fuchsia 158
Fungal leaf spots **156**
Fungus diseases, listed 154–158

G

Gallium odoratum. *See* Sweet Woo-
    druff
Garden
    ecosystem 124
    how much to plant 23–24

map 8
    rotation plan 85
    planning, with eating in
        mind *348*
    sitter 68,
Garden abundance, dealing with
    350–351
Garden beds
    advantages 35
    dimensions 35
    framed 35–37
Garden Cress (*Lepidium sativum*)
    210, 221
Garlic (*Allium sativum*) 3, 4, 17,
    26, 60, 123, **211**, 270, 350
    and weeds 98
    crop rotation 84
Garlic chives (*Allium tuberosum*)
    26, **286**, 352
Garlic, Elephant (*Allium ampelo-
    prasum*) **212**
Garlic, Top-Setting (*Allium sativum*
    var. *ophioscordon*) **212**
Gaultheria procumbens. *See* Winter-
    green, Teaberry
Genetic resistance to pest attack 126
Geranium 157, 158
    scented 61
Germination, troubleshooting 49
Ginger (*Zingiber officinale*) **286**
Gladiolus 314
Glyphosate 96, 100, 365
Godetias 3
Good King Henry (*Chenopodium
    bonus-henricus*) 105
Gooseberry, Cape. *See* Ground-
    Cherry
Gopher and Mole pests **152**
Gopher spurge (*Euphorbia
    lathyrus*) 152
Gourd (*Cucurbita* sp.) **212**
Gow Choy. *See* Garlic chives
Grafting 61, 326
Granex onion 225
Grape (*Vitis* spp.) 158, **330**, 344
Grape hyacinth 313
Grapefruit (*Citrus* x
    paradisi) **331**, 333
Grasses, Perennial **116**
Greek Oregano. *See* Oregano
Green Amaranth. *See* Pigweed
Green lacewing (*Chrysoperla carnea*)
    132
Green manure 76, 84

Greenhouse effect 360
Greens, Collard. *See* Collards
Ground beetle (beneficial) 128
Ground layering 62
Ground-Cherry (*Physalis peruviana*)
    213
Groundsel, Common (or Senecio)
    (*Senecio vulgaris*) **104–
    105, 158**

H

Hail, occurrence of 5
Hamburg Parsley. *See* Parsley, Root
Hedera
    canariensis. *See* Ivy, Algerian
    helix. *See* Ivy, English
"Heirloom" seed varieties 43
Helianthus
    annuus. *See* Sunflower
    tuberosus. *See* Sunchoke
Herbal extracts, for insect repellent
    271
Herbicides 96
    and vegetables 96
Herbs
    bouquet garni 273
    cooking with 273
    growing 270–271
    harvesting 271–272
    in containers *272*
    ornamentals 269–270
    pests 271
    preserving 273
    pruning 271
    scented 270
    sun requirements 29
Heung Kun. *See* Celery, Chinese
Himalaya Blackberry 92
    cultivation *114*
Hinn Choy. *See* Amaranth
Hon Tsai Tai (*Brassica rapa*) 223
Honeybee 129, 135, 248, 363
Honeydew. *See* Melon
Hop Oregano. *See* Dittany of Crete
Hops (*Humulus lupulus*) 270, **288**
Horse Bean. *See* Bean, Fava
Horseradish (*Armoracia rusticana*)
    158, **213**
Horsetail (*Equisetum hyemale* and *E.
    arvense*) **116**
Horticultural Bean. *See* Bean,
    Horticultural
House finch 150
House sparrow 150

Huckleberry, Evergreen (*Vaccinium ovatum*) **331**
Humulus lupulus. *See* Hops
Hungarian Camomile. *See* Camomile, German
Hungry Gap. *See* Kale, Siberian
Hunting wasp (beneficial) 129
Husk Tomato. *See* Ground-Cherry
Hyacinth 314
Hybrid plants, seed 43–44

I

Ice plant 158
Ichneumonid wasp 129
Indian Fig. *See* Cactus, Prickly Pear
Indoor starts, time limits of 51
Integrated Pest Management (IPM) 124–127
   decision-making process 127
Interpreting seed packets 17
Ipomoea batatas. See Sweet Potato
Irish potato famine 157
Iron deficiency, symptoms of 80
Ivy, Algerian (*Hedera canariensis*) **116–117**
Ivy, English (*Hedera helix*) **116–117**

J

Jerusalem Artichoke. *See* Sunchoke
Jerusalem Oak Pazote. *See* Epazote
Ji Soo. *See* Perilla
Jicama (*Pachyrhizus erosus*) **214**, 352
Jeavons, John 66
Johnnie-jump-up 159, 313
   self-seeding 93
Joy of Cooking 352
Judean Pellitory (*Parietaria judaica* or *P. hespera hespera*) **105**

K

Kale (*Brassica oleracea*) **214**
Kale, Sea (*Crambe maritima*) **243**
Kale, Siberian (*Brassica napus*) **214**
Kennelworth ivy 92
Kidney bean. *See* Bean, Dry
Kintsai. *See* Celery, Chinese
Kiwi Fruit (*Actinidia deliciosa*) **331**
Knotted Marjoram. *See* Marjoram
Kohlrabi (*Brassica oleracea*) 4, 26, 47, **215**
Kumquat (*Fortunella margarita* and *F. crassifolia*) 332, 333

L

Lacewing (beneficial) 128
Lactuca sativa. See Celtuce (*Latuca sativa* var. *angustata*)
Lady beetle (beneficial) 128
Lamb's Lettuce. *See* Corn Salad
Lambsquarters (*Chenopodium album* and *C. murale*) 92, **105–106**
Larvae, defined 137
Late blight of potato and tomato 157
Lauris nobilis. See Bay Laurel
Lavender English (*Lavandula angustifolia*) **290**
Lavender French (*Lavandula dentata*) **290**
Lavender Spanish (*Lavandula stoechas*) **290**
LD50, defined 364
Leafhopper 160
Leafminer 135, **142**
leek
Leek (*Allium ampeloprasum*) 5, 23, 26, 123, 143, **216**, 350
Leek Quiche (recipe) *217*
Legume Family 169
   innoculant for 76
   root nodules on 76
Lemon (*Citrus limon*) 323, **332**, 333
Lemon Balm (*Melissa officinalis*) **290**
Lemon verbena (*Aloysia triphylla*) 61, **290**
Lemongrass (*Cymbopogon citratus*) 60, **290**
Lepidium sativum. *See* Garden Cress
Lesser ashy gray lady beetle 158
Lettuce (*Lactuca sativa*) 4, 5, 26, 41, 123, 142, **150**, **218**, 350
   crop rotation 84
   starts 41
Lettuce, Chinese. *See* Celtuce
Lettuce drop 220
Lettuce, Lamb's. *See* Corn Salad
Lettuce, Wilted (recipe) *220*
Licorice Mint. *See* Anise Hyssop
Lilac 158
Lima bean. *See* Bean, Lima
Lime (*Citrus aurantifolia*) **332**, 333
Lime, Rangpur 333
Lime Sulfur 365
Limiting factors, for fruit trees 323
Lippia citriodora. See Lemon Verbena

Liquid fertilizer 82
Llacon. *See* Bolivian Sunroot
Loam soil, description 71
Loquat (*Eriobotrya japonica*) **332**
Lycopersicon lycopersicum. See Tomato

M

Mache. *See* Corn Salad
Magenta Spreen (*Chenopodium gigantium*) 105
Mail-order seed catalogs 39
Main Dish Risotto (recipe) *297*
Majorana
   hortensis. See Marjoram
   onites. See Pot Marjoram
Malathion 123, 363, 366
Mallow (*Malva* spp.) **106**
Mallow, Bristly (*Modiola caroliniana*) **117**
Malus spp. *See* Apple
Malva spp. *See* Mallow
Mandarin Orange (*Citrus reticulata*) **334**
Maneb 363
Manure (or Compost) Tea 80
Maple 158
Marguerite daisy 158, 313
Marigold 307, 314
Maritime climate 358
Marjoram (*Origanum majorana*) 273, **291**, 348
Matricaria
   chamomilla. See Camomile, German
   recutita. See Camomile, German
Mealybug 160
Medicago hispida. See California Burclover
Mediterranean climate 359
Mediterranean fruit fly 123
Melissa officinalis. *See* Lemon Balm
Melon (*Cucumis melo*) 11, **222**
Melon, winter. *See* Winter Melon
Mentha
   requienii. See Mint: Corsican Mint
   spicata. See Mint: Spearmint
   suaveolens. See Mint: Apple;
   '*Variegata*' *See* Mint: Pineapple Mint
   x *piperita. See* Mint: Peppermint
   var. *citrata. See* Mint: Bergamot Mint
Mesclun (salad mix) *221*
Metaldehyde 366

Metam-sodium or metham   147
Methoxychlor   366
Mexican Tarragon. *See* Tarragon, Winter
Mexican Tea. *See* Epazote
Mexican Vegetables (recipe)   352
Microclimates   11–14
    barrier with an overhang   33
    how to identify   31 33
Microorganism (beneficial)   130
Miner's Lettuce (*Montia perfoliata*)   92, **106–107,** 146
Minestrone (recipe)   174
Minigreenhouse   16, 59
Mint   92, 272, 273
    Apple Mint (*Mentha suaveolens*)   **292**
    Bergamot Mint (*Mentha x piperita* var. *citrata*)   **292**
    Corsican Mint (*Mentha requienii*)   **292**
    family, about   293
    Pineapple Mint (*Mentha suaveolens* 'Variegata')   **292**
    Spearmint (*Mentha spicata*)   26, **292**
Mite   125, 132, **145**
    beneficial. *See* Spiders and mites
Mitsuba. *See* Parsley, Japanese
Mizuna   223
Mockingbird   **150**
Modiola caroliniana. See Mallow, Bristly
Mole. *See* Gopher and Mole pests
Mondo grass   152
Montia perfoliata. See Miner's Lettuce
Morning glory, wild. *See* Bindweed
Mother's milk   134
Mulch, plastic   78–79
Mulching   77–80
    for rain   80
    to warm the soil   79–80
    with aluminum foil   79
Mustard   92
    as volunteer   93
    family, about   183
    rotation of   86
Mustard, Florida broadleaf (*Brassica juncea*)   **293**
Mustard, Greens (*Brassica juncea*)   **222**
Mustard, Noodles and Tofu Saute. *See* Turnips, Noodles, and Tofu Saute
Mustard, Seed (*Brassica nigra*)   **293**

Mustard, Spinach. *See* Tendergreen
Mustard, Wild field or California (*Brassica* spp.)   **107**

N

Nandina   158
Nasturtium   92, 121, 307, 313
    self-seeding   93
Nasturtium Flower Salad Dressing (recipe)   306
Nasturtium officinale. See Watercress
Natural beneficial creatures   127–128
Nectarine. *See* Peach and Nectarine
Nectarine, need for winter cold   324
Neem   362, 365
Nematode   **146**
    predatory   132
Nepeta
    cataria. See Catnip. *See* Catmint
Nettle (*Urtica urens*)   107
New Zealand Spinach   123, 158
Nicotine sulfate   366
Nightshade (*Solanum* spp.)   **107–108**
    about   234
    family   142
Nira. *See* Garlic chives
Nitrogen   80
    symptoms of deficiency or surplus   80
No-till gardening   77–78
Nopalea cochenillifera. See Cactus, Prickly Pear
Nopalitos (Cactus pads) in Tomato Sauce (recipe)   190
Nursery starts, how to buy   41–42
Nutsedge (*Cyperus esculentus*)   **117**
Nymphs, defined   137

O

Ocean temperature, offshore   357
Ocimum
    basilicum. See Basil
    sanctum. See Basil, Holy
Oil, Summer   366
Olive   158
Onion   5
    about bolting   227
    day length   225
    and weeds   98
    maggot   132
    potato   244
    root maggot   121, **143**
    seed, crop rotation   84
    white rot   157

Onion, Bulb (*Allium cepa*)   60, 123, **223,** 270, 307
Onion, Bunching (*Allium fistulosum*)   **229**
Onion, green   4, 350
    how to grow   226
Onion Lily (*Allium triquetrum*)   92, **118**
    as edible weed   93,
Onion, Pearl (*Allium cepa*)   **229**
Onion, Top (*Allium cepa*)   **143, 230**
Open-pollinated plants, seed   43–44
Opossum   **153**
Opuntia ficus-indica. See Cactus
Orach (*Atriplex hortensis*)   105
Orange (*Citrus sinensis*)   333, **334**
Orange Mint. *See* Mint
Oregano (*Origanum heracleoticum*)   26, 269, 271, **294,** 348
Oregano, Italian (*Origanum vulgare*)   **294**
Oregano, Sicilian (*Origanum × majorana*)
Organic matter, types and sources   74–77
Organochlorine   363
Organophosphate   363
Origanum
    hortensis. See Marjoram
    majorana. See Marjoram
    onites. See Pot Marjoram
    vulgare. See Oregano, Italian
    × majorana. See Oregano, Sicilian
Orius. See Bugs, true (beneficial)
Ornamental food plants   34
Oxalis (*Oxalis* spp.)   **118–119**
Oyster Plant. *See* Salsify, Common

P

Pac Choy. *See* Bok Choy
Pachyrhizus erosus. See Jicama
Pacific Northwest storm region   69
Painted-tongue   314
Pansy   159, 307, 314
Parasitic wasp (beneficial)   128–129
Parathion   363
Parietaria
    judaica. See Judean Pellitory
    hespera hespera. See Judean Pellitory
Parsley (*Petroselinum crispum* var. *crispum*)   26, 146, 269, 271, 273, **295,** 348, 350
    as volunteer   93

Parsley, Chinese. *See* Coriander
Parsley, Japanese (*Cryptotaenia japonica*) **296**
Parsley, Root (*Petroselinum crispum var. tuberosum*) **230**
Parsnip (*Pastinaca sativa*) 123, **231**
Passion Fruit (*Passiflora* spp.) **334**
Paths, dimensions of 37
PCNB (Quintozine) 367
Pea (*Pisum sativum*) 4, 5, 16, 17, 26, 41, 122, 123, 157, **231**
    crop rotation 84
Pea, Aparagus. *See* Asparagus Pea (*Lotus tetragonolobus*)
Peach and Nectarine (*Prunus persica and P. persica*) 158, **335**, 344
    need for winter cold 324
Peach leaf curl 325
Pear, Asian (*Pyrus pyrifolia*) **336**
Pear, European (*Pyrus communis*) 159, 326, **335**, 344
    need for winter cold 324
Pepper, Sweet and Hot (*Capsicum annuum var. annuum*) 23, 123, 158, **233**, 348
Peppergrass. *See* Garden Cress
Peppermint. *See* Mint: Peppermint
Perilla (*Perilla frutescens*) **296**
Permethrin 367
Persea americana. See Avocado
Persimmon, Asian (*Diospyros kaki*) 158, 326, **336**
Pest control
    biological 125, 126–127
    cultural 125, 126
    mechanical 125, 126
    timing of 125
Pest-free (or resistant) crops 123
Pesticide
    active ingredient 134. *See also* Appendix III
    dermal toxicity 133
    disposal of 136
    inhalation toxicity 133
    minimizing damage to beneficials 135
    mutagenicity of 133
    oncogenicity of 133
    oral toxicity 133
    reading labels 133–134
    residue 123
    resistance 122
    soap spray 126
    teratogenicity of 133

Pests
    identification 124–125
    night feeders 124
    outbreak, conditions effecting 121–122
    resurgence after pesticides use 122
    vertebrate 150
Petroselinum
    crispum var. crispum. See Parsley
    crispum var. neapolitanum. See Parsley
    crispum var. tuberosum. See Parsley, Root
    hortense var. radicosum. See Parsley, Root
Phaseolus
    coccinus. See Bean, Scarlet Runner
    multiflorus. See Bean, Scarlet Runner
    vulgaris. See Bean, Snap
Pheromones 124
Phosphorus 80
    deficiency symptoms 80
Physalis
    edulis. See Ground-Cherry
    ixocarpa. See Tomatillo
    peruviana. See Ground-Cherry
    pruinosa. See Ground-Cherry
Pickling Onion. *See* Onion, Pearl
Pigeon 150
Pigweed (*Amaranthus retroflexus*) **108**
Pillbug (or Sowbug) **149**
Pineapple Guava (*Feijoa sellowiana*) **337**
Pineapple Mint. *See* Mint
Pineapple weed (*Matricaria matricarioides*) 279
Pinto Bean. *See* Bean, Dry
Pisum sativum. See Pea
Plant
    containers 38
    diseases **154**
    division, cutting and layering 60
    nutrition 80
    spacing 47
    tolerance to soap and detergent in gray water 70
Plantain, Broadleaf (*Plantago major*) **119–120**
Plantain, Narrow-Leaved (*Plantago lanceolata*) **119–120**
Planting depth 47
Plum, European (*Prunus domestica*) 158, 323, 325, **337**, 344
    winter cold requirements 324

Plum, Japanese (*Prunus salicina*) **337**
Point Piedras Blancas 11
Point Reyes, average maximum daily temperature for 11
Poison Hemlock (*Conium maculatum*) **108–109**
Pole bean. *See* Bean, Snap
Polymnia
    edulis. See Bolivian Sunroot
    sonchifolia. See Bolivian Sunroot
Pomegranate (*Punica granatum*) **337**
Poorman's Weatherglass. *See* Scarlet Pimpernel
Portulaca oleracea. See Purslane
Pot Marjoram (*Origanum onites*) **294**
Potassium Salts 367
Potato (*Solanum tuberosum*) 3, 5, 60, 93, 123, 158, **235**, 344
    crop rotation 84
    growing in towers 236
    tolerance to acidity 72
Potato, sweet. *See* Sweet Potato
Powdery mildew **157–158**
Praying Mantis (beneficial) 130
Preparing soil for seeding 46
Prickly pear cactus 123
Privet 158
Prunus
    armeniaca. See Apricots
    domestica. See Plum, European
    dulcis var. dulcis. See Almond
    persica. See Peach and Nectarine
    persica nucipersica. See Peach and Nectarine
    salicina. See Plum, Japanese
Psidium
    catteleianum. See Strawberry Guava
    littorale. See Strawberry Guava
Pumpkin 23, 123, 142, 160, 344. *See also* Squash, Winter and Pumpkin
Punica granatum. See Pomegranate
Pupa, defined 137
Purslane (*Portulaca oleracea*) 92, 98, **109**
    as edible weed 93
Pyrethrum 367
Pyrus
    communis. See Pear, European
    pyrifolia. See Pear, Asian

Q

Quackgrass (*Agropogon repens*) 120
Quince (*Cydonia oblonga*) 159, **338**
Quince, flowering 313

R

Rabbit pests **153**
Raab. *See* Broccoli Raab
Raccoon **153**
    live trapping **154**
Radicchio. *See* Chicory
Radish (*Raphanus sativus*) 5, 142,
    158, **239**
Rainfall average,
    for San Francisco 359
Raised beds. *See* Garden beds
Ranunculus 5, 159, 313, 314
Rape, California. *See* Mustard, Wild
Raphanus sativus. *See* Radish; Wild
    Radish
Raspberry (*Rubus* spp.) 158, **338**
Recipes:
    Backyard Omelet 350
    Beet, Marinated 179
    Black Bean Tostadas 110
    Broiled Tomatoes with Herbs &
        Cheese 254
    Cabbage leaves, stuffed 188
    California Pesto and Pasta 275
    Chicken Stock, Homemade 349
    Chanclette (chayote) 201
    Cheesy Italian Sausage Stew 177
    Coleslaw 187
    Cucumber Raita 206
    Cucumber Salad, Southeast
        Asian
        206
    Curry, Mixed Vegetable. *See* Year-
        round Vegetable Curry
    Fried Green Tomatoes 261
    Fried Squash Blossoms 309
    Himalayan Potato Curry 237
    Homemade Chicken Stock 349
    Leek Quiche 217. *See also* Potato
        Leek Soup
    Main Dish Risotto 297
    Marinated Beets 179
    Marinated Sunchokes 251
    Mexican Vegetables 352
    Minestrone 174
    Nasturtium Flower Salad Dressing
        306
    Nasturtiums with Curried Cream
        Cheese 196
    Nopalitos (cactus pads) in Tomato
        Sauce 190

Potato Leek Soup 196
Pumpkin or Squash Soup 248
Quick Homemade Tomato Sauce
    346
Sautéed Green Beans 242
Scarlet Runner Beans. *See* Cheesy
    Italian Sausage Stew, Sautéed
    Green Beans
Soup, Pumpkin or Squash 248
Southeast Asian Cucumber Salad
    206
Southwest Chile Vegetable Soup
    347
Spicy Szechuan Chicken 287
Stuffed Zucchini 345
Stuffed Cabbage Leaves 188
Thai Fish Soup 283
Turnips, Noodles, and Tofu
    Sauté 262
Wilted Lettuce 220
Year-round Vegetable Curry 195
Zucchini
    Zucchini Fritters 353.
    See also Minestrone, Southwest
    Chile Vegetable Soup, Stuffed
    Zucchini
Reclaiming neglected land 98–100
Record keeping 8
Red clover, for green manure 76
Red Fennel. *See* Fennel, Bronze
Redworms. *See* Earthworms, compost
Regional conditions for gardening
    14–16
Reptiles (beneficial) 130
Rhizoctonia 158
Rhododendron 313
Rhubarb (*Rheum rhabarbarum*) 60,
    240
Risotto. *See* Main Dish Risotto
    (recipe)
Robin **150**
Rocambole. *See* Garlic, Top-Setting
Rock fertilizer 81
Rocket (or Roquette). *See* Arugula
Roman Camomile. *See* Camomile,
    English
Romano bean. *See* Bean, Romano
Rooting hormone 61
Rosemary (*Rosmarinus
    officinalis*) 26,
    61, 270, **298**, 348
Rotation, crop categories 85.
    See also Crop rotation
Rotenone 367
Rototilling 73, 83
Rough Pigweed. *See* Pigweed

Rove beetle (*Ocypus olens*) 128, 149
Rubus
    idaeus. *See* Raspberry
    occidentalis. *See* Raspberry
    strigosus. *See* Raspberry
Rubus spp. *See* Blackberry; Blackberry
    Brambles
Rumex
    acetosa. *See* Sorrel, Garden
    acetosella. *See* Sorrel
    crispus. *See* Dock
    scutatus. *See* Sorrel, French
Russian Comfrey. *See* Comfrey
Russian Kale. *See* Kale, Siberian
Rutabaga (*Brassica napus*) **241**

S

Sage 26, 61, 270, 298, 348
Sage, Clary (*Salvia sclarea*) **298**
Sage, Garden (*Salvia officinalis*) **298**
Sage, Pineapple (*Salvia elegans*) **298**
Sage, Variegated (*Salvia tricolor*) **298**
Salamander, California slender 130
    for pest control 122
Salsify, Black (*Scorzonera hispanica*)
    241
Salsify, Common (*Tragopogon
    porrifolius*) 123, 146, **241**
    as volunteer 93
Salt tolerance, in plants 32
Salvia spp. *See* Sage
San Francisco **4**
    average annual rainfall 359
    solar access laws 29
San Francisco League of Urban
    Gardeners (SLUG) 261
Sandy soil, description 71
Sardinians and fava bean. *See* Bean,
    Fava, possible allergy to
Satureja
    douglasii. *See* Yerba Buena
    hortensis. *See* Summer Savory
    illyrica. *See* Winter Savory
    intricata. *See* Winter Savory
    montana. *See* Winter Savory
Saving seeds 41
Scabiosa 152
Scallop squash. *See* Squash, Summer
Scarlet Pimpernel (*Anagallis
    arvensis*)
    109
Scatter-sowing 46–47
Scientific names of plants
    changes in 361
    use of 42–43, 361

Scolymus hispanicus. *See* Spanish
    Oyster Plant
Scorzonera hispanica. *See* Salsify, Black
Scouring Rush. *See* Horsetail
Sechium edule. *See* Chayote Squash
Seed banks, nonprofit   43
Seed catalogs   368
Seed viability   48
Seeding
    chart   52, 53
    containers   54–55
    direct sowing   45–51
    mix   51–54
        common ingredients   54
        homemade   54
    spacing for   46
Seedlings
    caring for transplants   57–59
    containers, as a source of damping-
        of   55
    enough light for   55
    fertilizer for   54
    handling of   56
    hardening off   56–57
    need to pot up   56
    post-germination care   56
    protection   49–50
    signs of being root bound   56
    thinning   50
    transplants
        and pests   60
        planting into garden   57
        providing warmth for   59
        signs of sunburn   58
Seeds
    best for saving   41
    planting in containers   55–56
    presprouting   47
Self-pollination   41
Senecio
    vulgaris. *See* Groundsel, Common
    × *hybridis*. *See* Cineraria
Serpent Garlic. *See* Garlic, Top-
    Setting
Sevin™   127
Shade from trees, reduction of   29
Shallot (*Allium cepa*)   60, 143, **243**
Sheep Sorrel. *See* Sorrel
Shepherds-Purse (*Capsella bursa-
    pastoris*)   92, **111**
Shiso. *See* Perilla
Shungiku. *See* Chrysanthemum,
    Garland
Sicilian Oregano. *See* Oregano
Silybum marianum. *See* Milk Thistle

Sloping yards   35
Slug. *See* Snail and Slug
Small spaces for gardens   29
Smog, variations in   359
Snail and Slug   **147**
Snake, as pest control   122
Snapdragon   158, 314
Soaker hose   63
Soap, insecticidal   126, 367
Soil
    adding organic matter to   76
    analysis, professional   72
    bio-active, advantages of   78
    compaction   73
    conditions for digging   82–84
    double digging   83
    evaluation of   71–72
    humus-rich, advantages of   74
    improvement
        with green manure   76
        with organic matter   72–75
    lime
        and cole crops   86
        for acidity   86
    local conditions   73
    magnesium in   73
    moisture   46
        checking   65
    no-till method   83
    nutrients
        content of   80
        typical   72
    optimizing the life in   78
    pH   72
        how to change   72
    pollution   75
        cadmium   75
        lead arsenate   75
        lead paint   75
    rocks in, advantage and disadvan-
        tage of   73
    salt in   73
    serpentine, amendments for   73
    solarization   99, 266
    structure   74
    temperature   45
        and mulching   77
    texture   71
    type, determination of   71
Solanum spp. *See* Nightshade
Sonchus asper. *See* Sowthistle, Prickly
Sonchus oleraceus. *See* Sowthistle,
    Common
Sooty mold fungus   137
Sorghum   344
Sorrel (*Rumex acetosella*)   92, **120**

Sorrel, French (*Rumex scutatus*)   **244**
Sorrel, Garden (*Rumex acetosa*)   **244**
Soup
    Chicken Stock, Homemade   349
    Minestrone   174
    Potato Leek   196
    Pumpkin or Squash   248
    Soup Stock, making   349
    Southwest Chile Vegetable   347
    Thai Fish   283
Southern Mustard. *See* Mustard
    Greens
Southwest Chile Vegetable Soup
    (recipe)   347
Sowbug. *See* Pillbug
Sowthistle, Common (*Sonchus
    oleraceus*)   92, **111**
Sowthistle, Prickly (*Sonchus asper*)
    111
Spanish Oyster Plant (*Scolymus
    hispanicus*)   **241**
Spearmint. *See* Mint
Species, defined   361
Sphinx moth. *See* Tomato Hornworm
Spicy Szechuan Chicken
    (recipe)   287
Spiders and mites (beneficial)   122,
    130
Spinach (*Spinacia
    oleracea*)   16, 123,
    142, 156, 158, **245**
Spinach, Malabar (*Basella alba*)   **246**
Spinach, New Zealand (*Tetragonia
    tetragonioides*)   92, **246**
Spittlebug   165
Spring seeding crops (biennials)   28
Squash   123, 154, 348
    and powdery mildew   121
    summer, crop rotation   84
Squash Blossoms, Fried (recipe)   309
Squash, Summer (*Cucurbita
    pepo*)   23, 27, **247**
Squash, Winter and Pumpkin
    (*Cucurbita* spp.)   23, 158, **249**
Starling   150
Stellaria media. *See* Chickweed
Stem and bulb nematode   146
Stem cuttings, softwood cuttings   61
Stew, Cheesy Italian Sausage
    (recipe)
    177
Sticky Traps (for insect monitoring)
    143
Stock   314
Storing and testing seeds   40

Stout, Ruth   77
Strawberry (*Fragaria x ananassa*)   3, 151, 156, 158, **338**
   "Strawberry" pots   340
Strawberry, Alpine (*Fragaria vesca* 'Alpine')   **341**
Strawberry Guava (*Psidium cattel*)   **341**
Strawberry Jicama.   *See* Bolivian Sunroot
Strawflower   158
Sukiyaki Greens.   *See* Chrysanthemum, Garland
Sulfur   367
Sulfur dust   158
Summer savory   271
Summer Savory (*Satureja hortensis*)   **299**
Summer Squash.   *See* Squash
Summer sun angle, formula   30
Summer weather   3
Sun and shade   29–30
Sun requirements of vegetables and herbs   29
Sunchoke (*Helianthus tuberosus*)   4, 123, 313, **251**
Sunchokes, Marinated (recipe)   *251*
Sunflower (*Helianthus annuus*)   142, 158, **252**
Sunscald (tomato)   259
Sunset Western Garden Book   152
Sweet Alyssum   159, 313
Sweet Basil.   *See* Basil
Sweet Bay.   *See* Bay Laurel
Sweet Corn.   *See* Corn, Sweet
Sweet False Camomile.   *See* Camomile, German
Sweet Fennel.   *See* Fennel
Sweet Mace.   *See* Tarragon, Winter
Sweet Marjoram.   *See* Marjoram
Sweet Pea   5, 157, 158, 313
Sweet Potato (*Ipomoea batatas*)   **253**
Sweet Success.   *See* Cucumber
Sweet William   159
Sweet Woodruff (*Gallium odoratum*)   **300**
Swine Cress (*Coronopus didymus*)   **111–112**
Swiss chard
Swiss Chard (*Beta vulgaris*)   4, 5, 26, 41, 123, 156, **253**
Symphytum peregrinum   281

× *uplandicum.   See* Comfrey
Synthetic fertilizer   81
   use of during cold weather   82
Syrphid fly (beneficial)   129, 131

T

Tachinid fly (beneficial)   129
Tagetes lucida.   See Tarragon, Winter
Tah Tsai   181
Tampala.   *See* Amaranth
Tangerine   333.   *See also* Mandarin Orange
Taraxacum officinale.   See Dandelion
Tarragon, French (*Artemesia dracunculus* var. *sativa*)   60, 61, 271, **301**, 348
Tarragon, Russian   271
Tarragon, Winter (*Tagetes lucida*)   270, **301**
Tatsoi.   *See* Tah Tsai
Temperature
   as function of distance from coast   11
   inversion   359
Tendergreen (*Brassica rapa*)   **222**
Tenodeora aridifolia sinensis.   See Praying Mantis
Terracing   35
Tetragonia
   expansa.   See Spinach, New Zealand
   tetragonioides.   See Spinach, New Zealand
Tetragonolobus purpureus.   See Asparagus Pea
Teucrium marum.   See Cat Thyme
Thai Fish Soup (recipe)   283
Thrips   132
Thyme, Caraway (*Thymus herba-barona*)   **302**
Thyme, Common (*Thymus vulgaris*)   26, 61, 269, 271, 273, **302**, 348
Thyme, Lemon (*Thymus* × *citrodorus*)   **302**
Tobacco Hornworm.   *See* Tomato Hornworm
Tobacco mosaic virus   160, 266
Tomatillo (*Physalis ixocarpa*)   **255**
Tomato (*Lycopersicon lycopersicum*)   4, 11, 23, 41, 122, 123, 154, 160, **255**
   and refrigeration   260
   crop rotation   84

days to harvest   256
determinate and indeterminate varieties   260, 261
fusarium   158, 159
hornworm   121
parthenocarpic varieties   260
physiological problems of   259
rotation of   86
russet mite   146, 266
San Francisco variety trial results   263
staking, caging and pruning of   257
suggested varieties (chart)   264–265
types   258
verticillium wilt   261
Tomato Sauce, Quick Homemade (recipe)   346
Tomatoes, Fried Green (recipe)   261
Tomato, Husk.   *See* Ground-Cherry
Topsoil   77
Tragopogon porrifolius.   See Salsify, Common
Transplants
   and weather   41
   best time of day to plant   57
   growing your own   51
   shock   57–59
Trapping for gophers and moles   153
Treated seeds   40–41
Tree onion.   *See* Onion, Top
Tricolor Sage.   *See* Sage
True Laurel.   *See* Bay Laurel
Tulip   152, 314
Tulsi.   *See* Basil, Basil, Holy
Turnip (*Brassica rapa*)   **266**
Turnip-Rooted Celery.   *See* Celeriac
Turnip-Rooted Parsley.   *See* Parsley, Root
Turnips, Noodles, and Tofu Sauté (recipe)   262

U

Umbellularia californica.   See Bay, California
Upland Cress.   *See* Garden Cress
Urtica urens.   See Nettle
Using sunlight above ground level   30

V

Vaccinium
  angustifolium. *See* Blueberry
  ashei. *See* Blueberry
  corymbosum. *See* Blueberry
  ovatum. *See* Huckleberry, Ever-
    green
Valerianella locusta. *See* Corn Salad
Variety, defined 361
Vascular Wilt **158–159**
Vedalia beetle 132
Vegetable Pear. *See* Chayote Squash
Vegetarianism 346
Vegetative propagation
  ground layering 62
  root cuttings 61
  stem cuttings 61
Verticillium wilt 158, 261
  cultural control 159
  symptoms on strawberry 159
  symptoms on tomato 158
Vetch (*Vicia sativa*) 92, **112**
  for green manure 76
Virus 159–160
  curly top 160
  insect vectors 160
  tobacco mosaic 160, 268
Vitis spp. *See* Grape

W

Walking onion. *See* Onion, Top
Wall O' Water™ 59, 256
Warm season crops 3
Watercress (*Nasturtium
  officinale*) **267**
Watering
  best time of day for 67
  conservation during drought 69–
    70
  disadvantages of sprinkling 63
  how to water 64–65
  seedbeds 66
  signs of trouble 67
  through the year 67–68
  to depth in different soils 63
  with an automatic timer 64, 70
  with drip irrigation 63–64
  with gray water 70
  with homemade devices 64

Watermelon (*Citrullus lanatus*) 222
Wax Gourd. *See* Winter Melon
Weeds
  advantages of 92
  annuals and biennials 93
  control tactics
    meeting crop needs 94
    shallow hoeing 94
  control tactics for annuals 95
    hand pulling 95
    planting in row 95
    postponing delicate crops 95
    presprouting 95
  control tactics for perennials
    cutting the tops 97
    digging out 97
    mulching to smother 97–98
    thick planting 94
  defined 91–92
  eradication vs. limited toler-
    ance 93
  help in identifying 100
  in winter 98
  on paths 35
  perennials 93
  pros and cons 92–93
  season of growth 93
  timing of control 94
  uses of 92
Welsh Onion. *See* Onion, Bunching
Western spotted cucumber
    beetles 125
Western toad 130
Wheat 344
Wheelchair gardening 36
Whitefly 125, 135, 144, 160
White Goosefoot. *See* Lambsquarters
Wild Anise. *See* Fennel
Wild Beet. *See* Pigweed
Wild Lettuce. *See* Sowthistle,
    Common
Wild Marjoram. *See* Oregano, Italian
Wild Morning Glory. *See* Bindweed
Wild Mustard. *See* Mustard, Wild
Wild Onion. *See* Onion Lily
Wild Radish (*Raphanus sativus*)
    92, **112**
Wilted Lettuce. *See* Lettuce, Wilted

Wind
  shelter from 30–31
  wind-baffling material for fence-
    tops 31
Winged Pea. *See* Asparagus Pea
Winter gardening 24–28
  crops 26
Winter Melon (*Benincasa
    hispida*) **268**
Winter Savory (*Satureja
    montana*) 26, **299**, 348
Winter squash. *See* Squash, Winter
    and Pumpkin
Winter sun angle, formula 30
Winter Sweet Marjoram. *See* Oregano
Wintergreen, Teaberry (*Gaultheria
    procumbens*) **342**
Wireworm (Click beetles) 132, **145**
Wood products
  and nitrogen 77
  use of 77
Woodruff. *See* Sweet Woodruff
Worm. *See* Earthworm

Y

Yard space for a vegetable garden
    33–35
Yard-Long Bean. *See* Bean, Asparagus
Year-round gardening 1
  advantages of 28
Yellow Nutgrass. *See* Nutsedge
Yerba Buena (*Satureja
    douglasii*) 270,
    302

Z

Zea mays. *See* Corn
Zinc deficiency, symptoms of 80
Zingiber officinale. *See* Ginger
Zinnia 152, 159
Zucchini 3, 158, 160, 352. *See also*
    Squash, Summer
Zucchini Fritters (recipe) 353
Zucchini, Stuffed (recipe) 345
Zucchini yellow mosaic virus
    154, **160**